Office 2007

THE MISSING MANUAL

*The book that
should have been
in the box*®

Office 2007

Chris Grover, Matthew MacDonald,
and E. A. Vander Veer

POGUE PRESS™
O'REILLY®

Beijing · Cambridge · Farnham · Köln · Sebastopol · Taipei · Tokyo

Office 2007: The Missing Manual
by Chris Grover, Matthew MacDonald, and E. A. Vander Veer

Copyright © 2007 O'Reilly Media, Inc. All rights reserved.
Printed in the United States of America.

Published by O'Reilly Media, Inc., 1005 Gravenstein Highway North, Sebastopol, CA 95472.

O'Reilly books may be purchased for educational, business, or sales promotional use. Online editions are also available for most titles (*safari.oreilly.com*). For more information, contact our corporate/institutional sales department: (800) 998-9938 or *corporate@oreilly.com*.

Printing History:

April 2007:   First Edition.

ISBN: 978-0-596-51422-8
[M]

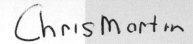

Table of Contents

OFFICE 2007: THE MISSING MANUAL

Part Five: Appendixes

The Missing Credits

About the Authors

 Chris Grover (Word) got his first computer in 1982 when he realized it was easier to write on a computer than an IBM Selectric. He never looked back. Chris has worked as a technical writer, advertising copywriter, and product publicist for more than 25 years. He is the author of *Word 2007: The Missing Manual* and co-author of *Digital Photography: The Missing Manual*. In addition to computer topics, he's written book reviews, software reviews and articles on subjects ranging from home remodeling to video recorder repairs. His latest project is the launching of Bolinas Road Creative (*www.bolinasroad.com*), an agency that helps small businesses promote their products and services. Chris lives in Fairfax, California with his wife and two daughters who have learned to tolerate his computer and gadget obsessions.

 Matthew MacDonald (Excel, Access) is an author and programmer extraordinaire. He's the author of *Excel 2007: The Missing Manual*, *Access 2007: The Missing Manual*, *Creating Web Sites: The Missing Manual*, and over a dozen books about programming with the Microsoft .NET Framework. In a dimly remembered past life, he studied English literature and theoretical physics.

 E. A. Vander Veer (PowerPoint) started out in the software trenches, lexing and yaccing and writing shell scripts with the best of them. She remained busy and happy for years writing C++ programs and wresting data from recalcitrant databases. After a stint as an Object Technology Evangelist, she found a way to unite all of her passions: writing about cool computer stuff in prose any human being can understand. Books followed—over a dozen so far—including *Flash 8: The Missing Manual*, *PowerPoint 2007: The Missing Manual*, *JavaScript for Dummies*, and *XML Blueprints*. Her articles appear in online and print publications including Byte, CNET, Salon.com, WEBTtechniques, and CNN.com. She lives in Texas with her husband and daughter. Email: *emilyamoore@rgv.rr.com*.

About the Creative Team

Dawn Mann (editor, technical reviewer) has been with O'Reilly for over four years and is assistant editor for the Missing Manual series. When not working, she likes rock climbing, playing soccer, and causing trouble. Email: *dawn@oreilly.com*.

Peter Meyers (editor) works as an editor at O'Reilly Media on the Missing Manual series. He lives with his wife and cats in New York City. Email: *peter.meyers@gmail.com*.

Nan Barber (editor) has worked with the Missing Manual series since its inception—long enough to remember booting up her computer from a floppy disk. Email: *nanbarber@oreilly.com*.

Michele Filshie (editor, copy editor) is O'Reilly's coordinating editor in the Dynamic Media Division. Before turning to the world of computer-related books, Michele spent many happy years at Black Sparrow Press. She lives in Sebastopol. Email: *mfilshie@oreilly.com*.

Nellie McKesson (production editor) is a graduate of St. John's College in Santa Fe, NM. She currently lives in Cambridge, MA, where her favorite places to eat are Punjabi Dhaba and Tacos Lupita.

Sohaila Abdulali (copy editor) is a freelance writer and editor. She has published a novel, several children's books, and numerous short stories and articles. She recently finished an ethnography of an aboriginal Indian woman. She lives in New York City with her husband Tom and their small but larger-than-life daughter, Samara. She can be reached through her Web site at *www.sohailaink.com*.

Jill Steinberg (copy editor) is a freelance writer and editor based in Seattle, and has produced content for O'Reilly, Intel, Microsoft, and the University of Washington. Jill was educated at Brandeis University, Williams College, and Stanford University. Email: *saysjill@mac.com*.

Greg Guntle (technical reviewer, Word) is a Windows veteran covering Office, Programming, Networks and Operating Systems. He's been providing technical editing services for the past 20 years.

Rick Jewell (technical reviewer, Word) has been in the technical industry since 1995. He's now a Beta Support Engineer for Microsoft. Since Microsoft acquired Groove in April of 2005, he's been a technical support engineer supporting the Groove product suite, which is part of the Premium edition of Microsoft Office 2007.

Rhea Howard (technical reviewer, Excel) works in the Operations department at O'Reilly Media and is an avid Excel user. She currently splits her time between Sebastopol and San Francisco.

Zack Barresse (technical reviewer, Excel) started teaching himself Excel in 2003 and fast became an addict. In October 2005, he was awarded the Microsoft MVP award for Excel. Along with Jake Hilderbrand, he owns *www.VBAeXpress.com*, a site dedicated to VBA. His full-time gig is as an ambulance EMT. Zack's a family man and a volunteer lieutenant with his local fire department.

Echo Swinford (technical reviewer, PowerPoint) has spent 10 years in the medical presentations and education industry. She's currently finishing her Master's degree in New Media at the Indiana University-Purdue University at Indianapolis School of Informatics. Her first book, *Fixing PowerPoint Annoyances*, was published by O'Reilly Media in February 2006, and she has a string of tech editing credits with other publishers. Echo has been a Microsoft PowerPoint MVP since early 2000. She can be contacted for projects and consuling at *freelance@echosvoice.com*.

Geetesh Bajaj (technical reviewer, PowerPoint) has been designing PowerPoint presentations and templates for over a decade and heads Indezine, a presentation design studio based out of Hyderbad, India. His indezine.com site attracts nearly a million page views each month, and it has hundreds of free PowerPoint templates and other goodies for visitors to download. In addition, Geetesh also issues a biweekly PowerPoint newsletter on indezine.com that has tends of thousands of subscribers.

Juel Bortolussi (technical reviewer, Access) has worked as an Access database developer for inventory and asset management systems in the design, beverage, and publishing industries. She thinks this book would make a great classroom text-book, providing students with database skills. Email: *juel@oreilly.com*.

Michael Schmalz (technical reviewer, Access) works in banking and performs business and technology consulting in a variety of industries. He has done techni-cal editing for O'Reilly on Microsoft Office books. Michael has a degree in finance from Penn State. He lives with his wife and daughter in Pennsylvania.

Acknowledgements

Many thanks to the whole Missing Manuals creative team, especially to Nan Bar-ber, who had her work cut out for her making my prose readable. Peter Meyers helped shape the book and gently kept us all on track. Dawn Mann, Greg Guntle, and Rick Jewell checked and double-checked the technical details. Thanks to Michele Filshie for copy editing, indexing, and working weekends.

As always, thanks to my beautiful wife Joyce, my collaborator in that other project—life. And hugs for Mary and Amy who help me approach everything I do with fresh enthusiasm and a bundle of questions.

—*Chris Grover*

Writing books about programs as sprawling and complex as Excel and Access is a labor of love (love of pain, that is). I'm deeply indebted to a whole host of people, including those who helped me track down all the neat and nifty things you can do with the latest version of Office (including bloggers extraordinaire David Gainer, Jensen Harris, and Erik Rucker), those who kept the books clear, concise, and tech-nically accurate (Peter Meyers, Sarah Milstein, Brian Sawyer, Zack Barresse, Rhea

Howard, Juel Bortolussi, and Michael Schmalz), and those who put up with me while I wrote it (more on that in a moment). I also owe thanks to many people who worked to get this book formatted, indexed, and printed—you can meet many of them on the Missing Credits page.

Completing this book required a few sleepless nights (and many sleep-deprived days). I extend my love and thanks to my daughter Maya, who put up with it without crying most of the time; my dear wife Faria, who mostly did the same; and our moms and dads (Nora, Razia, Paul, and Hamid), who contributed hours of babysitting, tasty meals, and general help around the house that kept this book on track. So thanks everyone—without you half of the book would still be trapped inside my brain!

—*Matthew MacDonald*

It takes a team of dedicated, hardworking professionals to turn any manuscript into a finished book, and the O'Reilly team is one of the best in the business. Extra thanks go out to Nan Barber, whose competence, surefootedness, and directness make her the kind of editor every author dreams of; Echo Swinford and Geetesh Bajaj, whose experience and dead-eye accuracy helped shape this book immeasurably; and Peter Meyers, who made sure the trains ran on time (while still managing to be a genuinely nice guy).

—*E. A. Vander Veer*

The Missing Manual Series

Missing Manuals are witty, superbly written guides to computer products that don't come with printed manuals (which is just about all of them). Each book features a handcrafted index; cross-references to specific pages (not just chapters); and RepKover, a detached-spine binding that lets the book lie perfectly flat without the assistance of weights or cinder blocks.

Recent and upcoming titles include:

Access 2007: The Missing Manual by Matthew MacDonald

AppleScript: The Missing Manual by Adam Goldstein

AppleWorks 6: The Missing Manual by Jim Elferdink and David Reynolds

CSS: The Missing Manual by David Sawyer McFarland

Creating Web Sites: The Missing Manual by Matthew MacDonald

Digital Photography: The Missing Manual by Chris Grover and Barbara Brundage

Dreamweaver 8: The Missing Manual by David Sawyer McFarland

Dreamweaver CS3: The Missing Manual by David Sawyer McFarland *eBay: The Missing Manual* by Nancy Conner

Excel 2003: The Missing Manual by Matthew MacDonald

Excel 2007: The Missing Manual by Matthew MacDonald

FileMaker Pro 8: The Missing Manual by Geoff Coffey and Susan Prosser

Flash 8: The Missing Manual by E.A. Vander Veer

Flash CS3: The Missing Manual by E.A. Vander Veer and Chris Grover

FrontPage 2003: The Missing Manual by Jessica Mantaro

GarageBand 2: The Missing Manual by David Pogue

Google: The Missing Manual, Second Edition by Sarah Milstein, J.D. Biersdorfer, and Matthew MacDonald

Home Networking: The Missing Manual by Scott Lowe

iMovie 6 & iDVD: The Missing Manual by David Pogue

iPhoto 6: The Missing Manual by David Pogue

iPod: The Missing Manual, Fifth Edition by J.D. Biersdorfer

Mac OS X: The Missing Manual, Tiger Edition by David Pogue

Office 2004 for Macintosh: The Missing Manual by Mark H. Walker and Franklin Tessler

PCs: The Missing Manual by Andy Rathbone

Photoshop Elements 5: The Missing Manual by Barbara Brundage

PowerPoint 2007: The Missing Manual by E.A. Vander Veer

QuickBase: The Missing Manual by Nancy Conner

QuickBooks 2006: The Missing Manual by Bonnie Biafore

Switching to the Mac: The Missing Manual, Tiger Edition by David Pogue and Adam Goldstein

The Internet: The Missing Manual by David Pogue and J.D. Biersdorfer

Windows 2000 Pro: The Missing Manual by Sharon Crawford

Windows XP Home Edition: The Missing Manual, Second Edition by David Pogue

Windows Vista: The Missing Manual by David Pogue

Windows XP Pro: The Missing Manual, Second Edition by David Pogue, Craig Zacker, and Linda Zacker

Word 2007: The Missing Manual by Chris Grover

The "For Starters" books contain only the most essential information from their larger counterparts—in larger type, with a more spacious layout, and none of the more advanced sidebars. Recent titles include:

Access 2003 for Starters: The Missing Manual by Kate Chase and Scott Palmer

Access 2007 for Starters: The Missing Manual by Matthew MacDonald

Excel 2003 for Starters: The Missing Manual by Matthew MacDonald

Excel 2007 for Starters: The Missing Manual by Matthew MacDonald

Mac OS X Leopard for Starters: The Missing Manual by David Pogue

PowerPoint 2007 for Starters: The Missing Manual by E. A. Vander Veer

Quicken for Starters: The Missing Manual by Bonnie Biafore

Windows Vista for Starters: The Missing Manual by David Pogue

Windows XP for Starters: The Missing Manual by David Pogue

Word 2007 for Starters: The Missing Manual by Chris Grover

Introduction

Having a computer stocked with Microsoft Office comes close to being a civic duty for today's corporate citizens—not to mention the rest of humanity. That's always been great news for Microsoft, which counts Word, Excel, PowerPoint, and Access as a big reason why its cash hoard is bigger than, say, your country's treasury.

For years, Microsoft has come pretty close to taking this near monopoly for granted, knowing that, lemming-like, office workers everywhere would dutifully upgrade to the latest version of these programs. After all, when it comes to creating documents, spreadsheets, presentations, and databases, no one ever got fired for choosing Microsoft, right?

Now, with the introduction of Office 2007, our friends in Redmond are finally returning the favor. The 2007 versions of these programs have all been given a thorough—and thoroughly user-friendly—makeover. The changes may take some gettting used to, but, hey, that's why you've got this book.

Note: This book is written with Microsoft's latest and greatest release in mind: Office 2007, which is for Windows only. The most recent Mac version of Office is covered in *Office 2004 for Macintosh: The Missing Manual.*

What's New in Office 2007

Ever since Microsoft Office conquered the world (way back in the 1990s), programs like Word, Excel, PowerPoint, and Access haven't changed a lot. Although a genuinely useful new feature appeared once in a while, Microsoft spent most of its time wedging in odd gimmicks like a talking paper clip.

Office 2007 breaks this pattern and introduces some of the most dramatic changes since Office 95. The most obvious difference is the thoroughly revamped *user interface* (the windows, toolbars, menus, and keyboard shortcuts you use to interact with Office applications). After spending far too long trying to simplify the haphazard, toolbar-choked interfaces in most Office programs, Microsoft finally worked up the courage to redesign it all from scratch. The result is a radically redesigned look and feel that actually makes sense. The centerpiece of this redesign is the super-toolbar called the *ribbon*.

The Ribbon

The ribbon is the best thing to hit the Office scene in years. Everything you'll ever want to do in any of the Office programs is packed into the ribbon. The contents of the ribbon depend on which program you're in, but the central premise—a command center for every action you'd want to perform—remains consistent.

Note: Access 2007 doesn't show the ribbon until you create a database.

You can think of the ribbon as a big, fat, nonmovable toolbar. It may look as though it's taking up an enormous amount of room on your screen (see Figure I-1), but it doesn't take up any more space than the old menu bar plus a couple of toolbars. Furthermore, the ribbon always appears in the same place and it never gets any bigger. And because you can't customize the ribbon or reposition it the way you could toolbars in Office 2003, you can't accidentally lose the ribbon.

Tip: Office 2007's new ribbon is one of those features that's easier to understand when you see it in action. You can see a *screencast* (onscreen demonstration) of Word's ribbon on the "Missing CD" page for this book at *www.missingmanuals.com*.

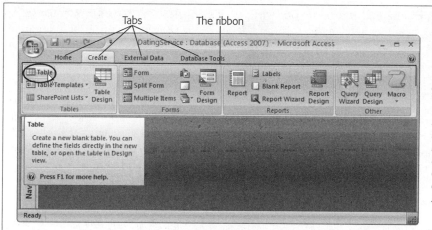

Figure I-1:
The ribbon's full of craftsman-like detail. When you hover over a button, you don't see a paltry two- or three-word description in a yellow box. Instead, you see a friendly pop-up box with a complete mini-description. Here, the mouse is hovering over the Table command in Access 2007.

The ribbon makes it easier to find features and remember where they are, because each tool is grouped into a logically related *tab* (more on tabs in a moment). Even better, once you find the button you need you can often find other, associated commands by looking at the section where the button is placed. In other words, the ribbon isn't just a convenient tool—it's also a great way to explore each program.

Tip: Want to reclaim the screen real estate that the ribbon occupies? Just double-click the current tab, and the ribbon collapses, leaving only the row of tab titles visible. Double-click the tab again to pop the buttons back into sight.

One nice characteristic of the ribbon's tabs is that they never change—in other words, you don't see commands mysteriously moving around or winking out of existence. Microsoft designed the ribbon to be predictable, so commands always remain in the same place. However, commands *will* change their arrangement a bit if you resize the program's window, so that they better use the available space (Figure I-2).

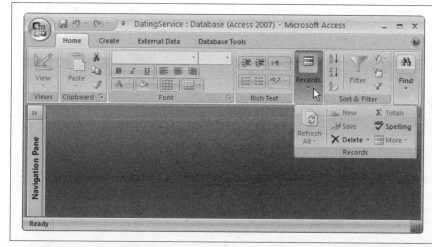

Figure I-2:
In this example, Access doesn't have the room to display the Home tab's Views, Records, or Find sections, so they're all replaced with buttons. If you click any of these buttons, then a panel appears with the content you're looking for.

Depending on the size of your window, it's possible that the button you need to click won't include any text. Instead, it shows up as a small icon. In this situation, you can hover over the mystery button to see its name before deciding whether to click it.

Tabs

To accommodate all these buttons, the ribbon's divided into task-specific *tabs*. When you launch each Office program, you start at the Home tab—the other tabs you see depend on which program you're in. Excel, for example, starts out with seven tabs in the ribbon. When you click one of these tabs, you see a whole new collection of buttons (Figure I-3).

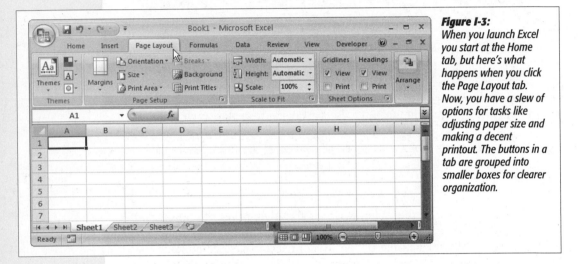

Figure I-3:
When you launch Excel you start at the Home tab, but here's what happens when you click the Page Layout tab. Now, you have a slew of options for tasks like adjusting paper size and making a decent printout. The buttons in a tab are grouped into smaller boxes for clearer organization.

Contextual tabs are tabs that let you work with specialized kinds of objects, such as pictures or charts. They appear above the ribbon, and in this book you'll see them written with a vertical bar after the contextual part of the name: Chart Tools | Format. Contextual tabs appear only when you need them to and automatically disappear when you're finished with them. For example, when you select a chart on your slide, the Chart Tools | Design, Chart Tools | Layout, and Chart Tools | Format tabs appear. Then, when you select a hunk of text, PowerPoint recognizes that you're finished formatting your chart and hides the Chart Tools tabs.

It's worth spending some time getting accustomed to the tab-based ribbon. Try clicking one tab after the other, rifling back and forth through the sections to see what they hold. You'll learn more about all these commands as you make your way through this book.

Tip: If you have a scroll mouse, you can breeze through the tabs even faster by moving the mouse pointer over the ribbon, and then moving the scroll wheel up or down.

Groups

When you launch each Office program, the Home tab is automatically selected, which displays options organized in sections, or *groups*. For example, if you're in PowerPoint, options in the Font group of the Home tab let you bold and underline your text; options in the Paragraph group let you align your text and format it as a bulleted or numbered list.

Command buttons

As you'd expect, to select one of the options on a ribbon, just click the button. For example, to underline a heading in PowerPoint, select the heading text you want to underline, zip to the Font group, and click the Underline button. To change the color of your text, first select it, and then head to the Font group of the Home tab and click the Font Color button.

Dialog box launchers

To give you complete control over every element of your slideshow while sticking to their design philosophy of offering all options on the ribbon, the Office 2007 designers placed a tiny *dialog box launcher* button in the bottom-right corner of many ribbon groups. When you click a dialog box launcher, Office pops up a dialog box related to that group. For example, clicking the Font dialog box launcher in PowerPoint displays the Font dialog box as shown in Figure I-4.

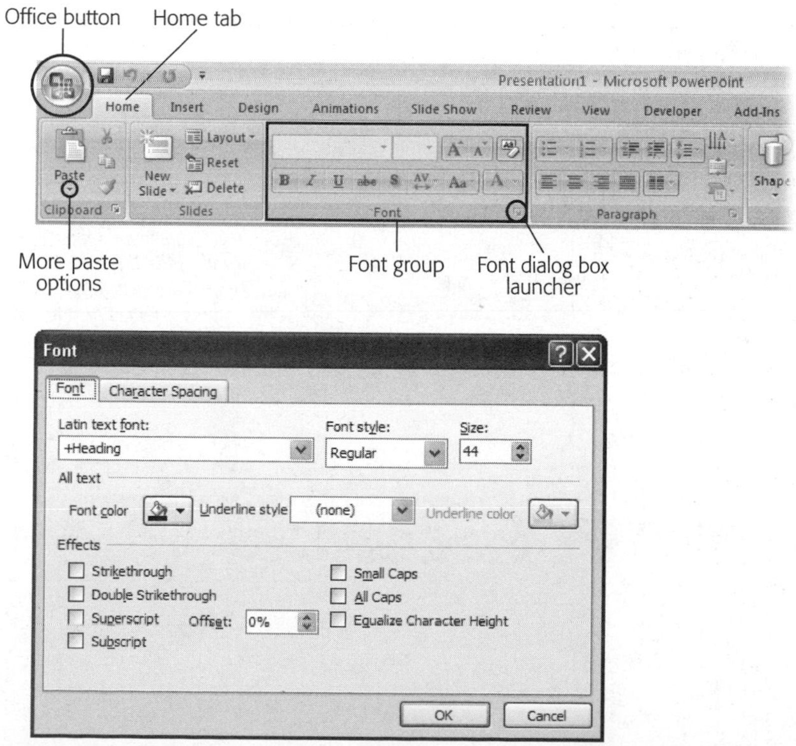

Figure I-4:
If you click the dialog box launcher in the bottom-right corner of the Font group (top, circled), you'll be presented with the font dialog box (bottom).

Using the Ribbon with the Keyboard

If you're an unredeemed keyboard lover, you'll be happy to hear that you can trigger ribbon commands with the keyboard. The trick is using *keyboard accelerators*, a series of keystrokes that starts with the Alt key (the same key you used to use to get to a menu). When using a keyboard accelerator, you *don't* hold down all the keys at the same time. (As you'll soon see, some of these keystrokes contain so many letters that you'd be playing Finger Twister if you tried holding them all down simultaneously.) Instead, you hit the keys one after the other.

The trick to using keyboard accelerators is to understand that once you hit the Alt key, there are two things you do, in this order:

1. **Pick the ribbon tab you want.**

2. **Choose a command in that tab.**

Before you can trigger a specific command, you *must* select the correct tab (even if it's already displayed). Every accelerator requires at least two key presses after you hit the Alt key. You need even more if you need to dig through a submenu.

By now, this whole process probably seems hopelessly impractical. Are you really expected to memorize dozens of different accelerator key combinations?

Fortunately, Office is ready to help you out with a new feature called *keytips*. Here's how it works. Once you press the Alt key, letters magically appear over every tab in the ribbon (Figure I-5). Once you hit a key to pick a tab, letters appear over every button in that tab. You can then press the corresponding key to trigger the command (Figure I-6).

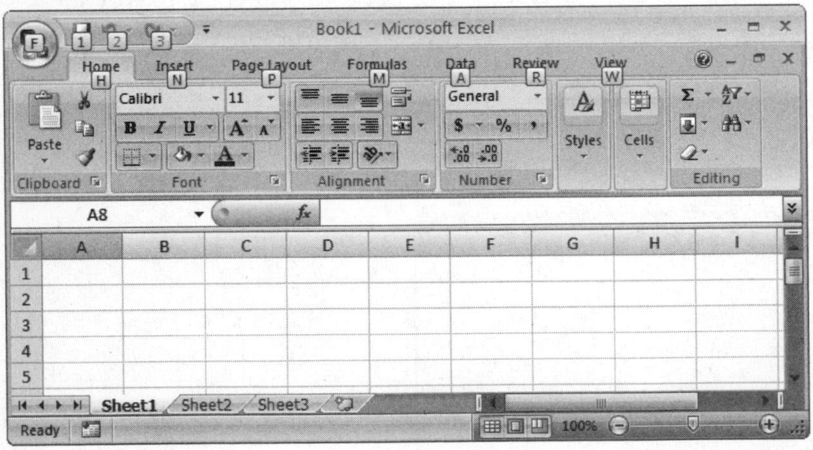

Figure I-5:
When you press Alt, Excel helps you out with keytips next to every tab. If you follow up with M (for the Formulas tab), you'll see letters next to every command in that tab, as shown in Figure I-6.

OFFICE 2007: THE MISSING MANUAL

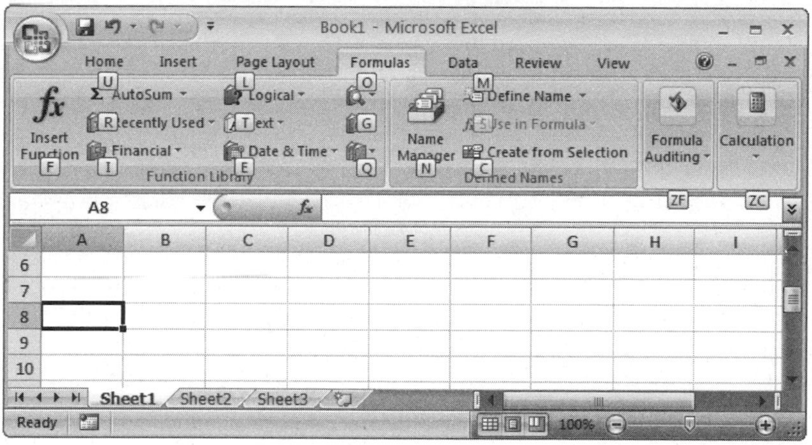

Figure I-6:
You can now follow up with F to trigger the Insert Function button, U to get to the Auto-Sum feature, and so on. Don't bother trying to match letters with tab or button names—there are so many features packed into the ribbon that in many cases the letters don't mean anything at all.

In some cases, a command might have two letters, in which case you need to press both keys, one after the other. (For example, the Find & Select button on the Home tab has the letters FD. To trigger it, press Alt, then H, then F, and then D.)

Some other shortcut keys—notably, the ones most people have been using for years—don't use the ribbon. These key combinations start with the Ctrl key. For instance, Ctrl+C copies highlighted text, and Ctrl+S saves your current work. Usually, you find out about a shortcut key by hovering over a command with the mouse. Hover over the Paste button in the ribbon's Home tab, and you see a tooltip that tells you its timesaving shortcut key is Ctrl+V.

The Office Menu

There's still one small part of the traditional Microsoft menu system left in Office 2007—sort of. The traditional File menu that lets you open, save, and print files has been transformed into the *Office menu*. You get there using the Office button, which is the big round logo in the top-left corner of the window (Figure I-7) of all the Office 2007 programs.

The Office menu is generally used for three things:

• Working with files (creating, opening, closing, and saving them).

• Printing your work.

• Configuring how applications behave. Choose Word Options (the name of the button depends on which program you're using) at the bottom of the menu to get to the Options dialog box, an all-in-one place for configuring each program.

There's one menu quirk that takes a bit of getting used to. Some Office menu commands hide submenus that have more commands. Take the Print command. You can choose Print from the Office menu to fire off a quick printout of your work. But if you click the right-pointing arrow at the edge of the Print command (or if you hover over it for a moment), then you see a submenu with more options, as shown in Figure I-8.

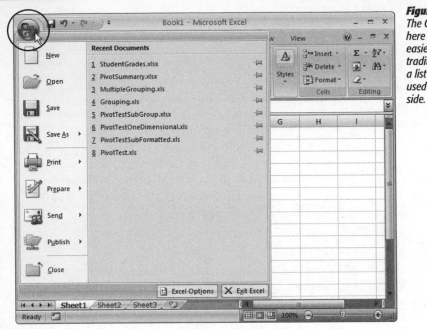

Figure I-7:
The Office menu (shown here in Excel) is bigger and easier to read than a traditional menu. It also has a list of the documents you used recently on the right side.

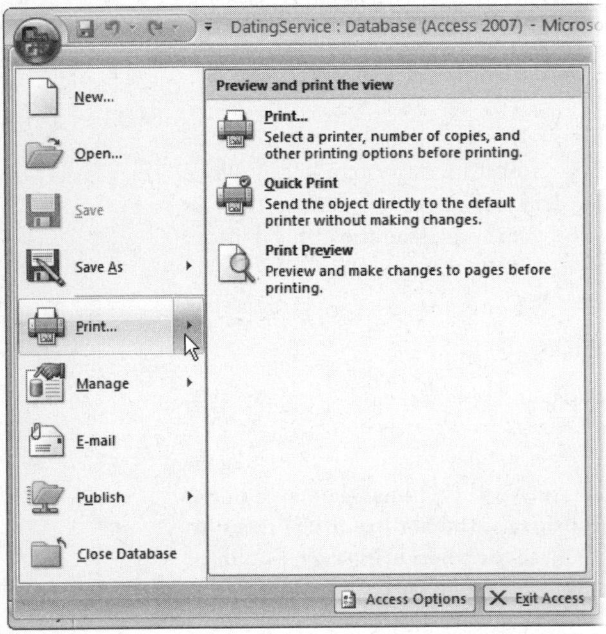

Figure I-8:
Print's both a clickable menu command and a submenu, as you can see in this example from Access. To see the submenu, you need to hover over Print (without clicking), or click the arrow at the right edge (shown here). The ribbon also has a few buttons that work this way.

The Quick Access Toolbar

Keen eyes will have noticed the tiny bit of screen real estate that sits on the right side of the Office button, just above the ribbon (Figure I-9). It holds a series of tiny icons, like the toolbars in older versions of Office. This is the Quick Access toolbar (or QAT to acronym-loving nerds).

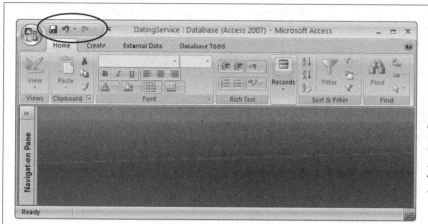

Figure I-9:
The Quick Access toolbar puts the Save, Undo, and Redo command right at your fingertips. These commands are singled out because most people use them more frequently than any other commands. But as you'll learn in Appendix A, you can add anything you want here.

If the Quick Access toolbar was nothing but a specialized shortcut for three commands, it wouldn't be worth the bother. However, the nifty thing about the Quick Access toolbar is that you can customize it. In other words, you can remove commands you don't use and add your own favorites; Appendix A shows you how.

Microsoft has deliberately kept the Quick Access toolbar very small. It's designed to provide a carefully controlled outlet for those customization urges. Even if you go wild stocking the Quick Access toolbar with your own commands, the rest of the ribbon remains unchanged. (And that means a coworker or spouse can still use your computer without suffering a migraine.)

Live Preview

Have you ever paused with your mouse over a command or a formatting option and wondered what it would do to your document? Those days are over. Live Preview is a new feature of Office 2007. In Word, Excel, and PowerPoint 2007, when you hold your mouse over a formatting style or color, you see a preview right within your document, spreadsheet, or slide (Figure I-10). If you like the look, click your mouse button. If you don't, move your mouse away from the button or menu option, and your document snaps back to its previous appearance. And, of course, you can preview some more options.

Live Preview saves time and hassle by letting you instantly see how an effect looks on your document before you commit to it. (In the old days, you had to select an option to see how it looked; then, if you didn't like it, you had to select Undo and start all over again.)

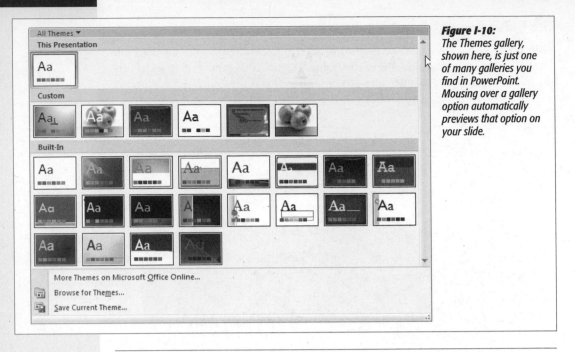

Figure I-10:
The Themes gallery, shown here, is just one of many galleries you find in PowerPoint. Mousing over a gallery option automatically previews that option on your slide.

Note: Live previews aren't for everybody. Some folks don't like the idea of Office changing their document's appearance—even temporarily—unless they tell it to by clicking something. To turn off Live Preview, choose Office button → [Word/Excel/PowerPoint] Options → Popular and then turn off the checkbox next to Enable Live Preview.

Mini-Toolbar

Office 2007 did away with most of the toolbars that appeared in earlier versions of the programs, but not all of them. One that remains is the pop-up mini-toolbar (Figure I-11) which appears in Word, PowerPoint, and Access. The formatting commands on the mini-toolbar are the same as those found on the ribbon, so you don't *need* it to get your work done, but some folks find it handy. If it's driving you nuts, turn off the mini-toolbar by clicking the Office button → [Word/PowerPoint/Access] Options and then, in the Options window that appears, select Popular and turn off the "Show Mini Toolbar on selection" checkbox.

The Very Basics

You'll find very little jargon or techno-geek terminology in this book. You will, however, see a few terms and concepts that you'll encounter frequently in your computing life. If your fingers have ever graced a computer keyboard, you're probably familiar with the following:

- Press the keys on your keyboard, and text appears in your document.

- Hold the Shift key down to type capitals or to enter the various punctuation marks you see above the numbers keys (!@#$*&^).

How the R[   ]nning
and Hand Knitting and Spinning
Changed the Course of Western
Civilization

Figure I-11:
Technically, the mini-toolbar breaks the Office 2007 design team's commitment not to have stuff come out of nowhere and then disappear, but because so many people spend a lot of time formatting text, they decided it was worth keeping. The mini-toolbar appears slightly transparent, and disappears immediately if you ignore it and begin typing.

- Press Caps Lock and your keyboard types only capital letters, but the numbers and other symbols continue to work as usual.

- To correct an error you've just made, you can use the Backspace key. Press it down once, and the cursor moves backward one space, erasing the last character you typed. If you continue to hold it down, it will keep on going, eating up your work like a starving man at a smorgasbord.

- The Delete (or Del) key, usually on or near the numerical keypad, does the same thing but for the character in *front* of the insertion point.

If you've got that under your belt, then you're ready for the rest of *Office 2007: The Missing Manual*. This book assumes you're familiar with just a few other terms and concepts:

- **Clicking.** This book gives you several kinds of instructions that require you to use your computer's mouse or trackpad. To *click* means to point the arrow cursor at something on the screen and then—without moving the cursor at all—to press and release the clicker button on the mouse (or laptop trackpad). To double-click, of course, means to click twice in rapid succession, again without moving the cursor at all. To *drag* means to move the cursor while pressing the button continuously. To *right-click*, click as described above, but press the mouse button on the right.

  When you see an instruction like *Shift-click* or *Ctrl-click*, simply press the specified key as you click.

- **Keyboard shortcuts.** Every time you take your hand off the keyboard to move the mouse, you lose time and potentially disrupt your creative flow. That's why many experienced computer fans use keystroke combinations instead of menu commands wherever possible. When you see a shortcut like Ctrl+S in this book, it's telling you to hold down the Ctrl key, and, while it's down, press the letter S, and then release both keys. Similarly, the finger-tangling shortcut Ctrl+Alt+S means hold down Ctrl, and then press and hold Alt, and then press S (so that all three keys are held down at once).

> **Note:** In some cases, a command may have two letters, and you need to press both keys, one after the other. For example, if you see Alt+H, FD, you need to press Alt, then H, then F, and then D.

- **All roads lead to Rome.** Office 2007 usually gives you several ways to choose the same option—by clicking a ribbon option, by right-clicking an object on a slide and then choosing from the shortcut menu that appears, or by pressing a key combination. Some folks prefer the speed of keyboard shortcuts; others like the satisfaction of a visual command array available in menus or toolbars. This book lists the alternatives so that you experiment to see which you like best.

About This Book

Despite the many improvements in software over the years, one feature hasn't improved a bit: Microsoft's documentation. In fact, with Office 2007, you get no printed user guide at all. To learn about the thousands of features included in this software collection, Microsoft expects you to read the online help.

Occasionally, these help screens are actually helpful, like when you're looking for a quick description explaining a mysterious new function. On the other hand, if you're trying to learn how to, say, create an attractive chart, you'll find nothing better than terse and occasionally cryptic instructions.

This book is the manual that *should* have accompanied Office 2007. In these pages, you'll find step-by-step instructions and tips for using almost every Office feature, including those you haven't (yet) heard of.

About the Outline

This book is divided into five parts, each containing several chapters:

- **Part One: Word 2007** starts with basics like launching Word and starting a new document, and ends with advanced planning techniques like using Word's Ouline feature. In between you'll learn everything else you need to know to master Word.

- **Part Two: Excel 2007** shows you how to create and edit Excel spreadsheets, perform calculations using formulas, and put your data into tables and charts.

- **Part Three: PowerPoint 2007** teaches you how to create everything you need to deliver a professional and visually pleasing presentation: slides, diagrams, handouts, drawings, slide transitions, and more.

- **Part Four: Access 2007** guides you through creating a database, sorting your data, linking tables with relationships, creating queries, and everything else you need to know to keep track of your important data.

• **Part Five: Appendixes.** This book wraps up with two short appendixes. Appendix A is dedicated to modifying Office 2007's new Quick Access Toolbar. Appendix B explains how to find your way around Microsoft's built-in and online help pages, and how to get assistance from a vast online community of Office fans and experts.

About → These → Arrows

Throughout this book, and throughout the Missing Manual series, you'll find sentences like this one: "Click Start → All Programs → Microsoft Office → Microsoft Office Word 2007." That's shorthand for a much longer instruction that directs you to click the Start button to open the Start menu, and then choose All Programs. From there, click the Microsoft Office folder, and then click Word's icon to launch the program.

Similarly, this kind of arrow shorthand helps to simply the business of choosing commands and menus, as shown in Figure I-12.

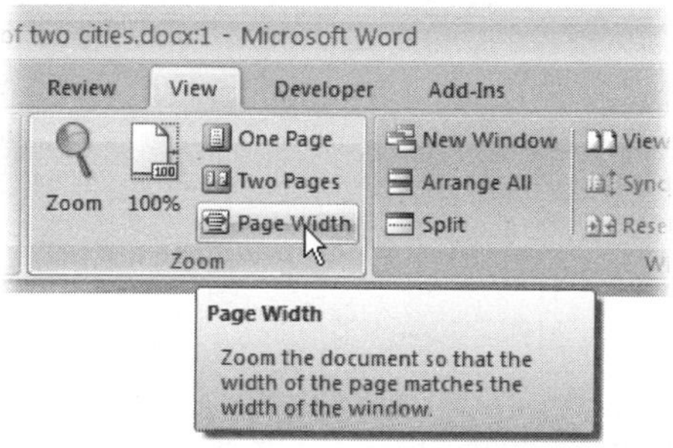

Figure I-12:
Arrow notations help to simplify Office 2007's ribbon structure and commands. For example, "Choose View → Zoom → Page Width" is a more compact way of saying: "Click the View tab, and then go to the Zoom group and click Page Width," as shown here.

Drop-down buttons

From time-to-time you'll encounter buttons in the ribbon that have short menus attached to them. Depending on the button, this menu might appear as soon as you click the button, or it might appear only if you click the button's drop-down arrow, as shown in Figure I-13.

When dealing with this sort of button, the last step of the instructions in this book tells you what to choose from the drop-down menu. For example, say you're directed to "Home → Clipboard → Paste → Paste Special." That tells you to select the Home tab, look for the Clipboard section, click the drop-down part of the Paste button (to reveal the menu with extra options), and then choose Paste Special from the menu.

Tip: Be on the lookout for drop-down arrows in the ribbon—they're tricky at first. You need to click the *arrow* part of the button to see the full list of options. When you click the other part of the button, you don't see the list. Instead, Office fires off the standard command (the one Office thinks is the most common choice) or the command you used most recently.

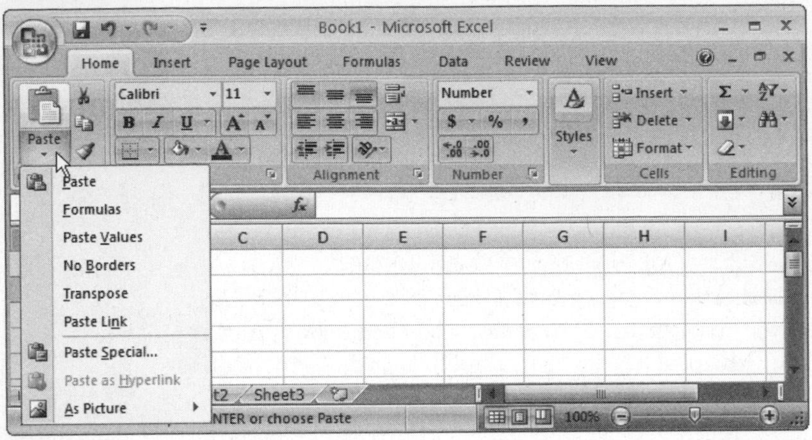

Figure I-13:
Excel gives you several options for pasting text from the clipboard. Click the top part of the Paste button to perform a plain-vanilla paste (with all the standard settings), or click the bottom part to see the menu of choices shown here.

Examples

As you read this book, you'll see a number of examples that demonstrate features of each of the Office programs. Many of these examples are available as files that you can download. Just surf to *www.missingmanuals.com*, click the link for this book, and then click the "Missing CD" link to visit a page where you can download a zip file that includes the examples, organized by chapter.

About MissingManuals.com

At the *missingmanuals.com* Web site, you'll find articles, tips, and updates to this book and all the books in the Missing Manual series. In fact, you're invited and encouraged to submit such corrections and updates yourself. In an effort to keep the book as up-to-date and accurate as possible, each time we print more copies of this book, we'll make any confirmed corrections you've suggested. We'll also note such changes on the Web site, so that you can mark important corrections into your own copy of the book, if you like. (Click the book's name, and then click the Errata link, to see the changes.)

In the meantime, we'd love to hear your own suggestions for new books in the Missing Manual line. There's a place for that on the Web site, too, as well as a place to sign up for free email notification of new titles in the series.

Safari® Enabled

When you see a Safari® Enabled icon on the cover of your favorite technology book, that means the book is available online through the O'Reilly Network Safari Bookshelf.

Safari offers a solution that's better than e-books. It's a virtual library that lets you easily search thousands of top tech books, cut and paste code samples, download chapters, and find quick answers when you need the most accurate, current information. Try it for free at *http://safari.oreilly.com*.

Part One: Word 2007

1

Creating, Opening, and Saving Documents

Word. Microsoft Word has been the world's most popular word processor for so long, it needs only one name—like Oprah or Madonna. Unlike certain celebrities, though, Word has undergone a makeover that goes well beyond cosmetic. Microsoft has redesigned the way you interact with the program and has redefined the underlying document format (don't worry; your old Word documents will still work).

Some things haven't changed: Just like previous versions, Word 2007 still makes it easy to create professional-looking letters, business reports, and novels. But Microsoft has loaded the program with new features to make designing and formatting attractive documents easier than ever. So even if you're well acquainted with its predecessors, you might need a little help getting used to the new Word. For example, some of the commands that are old favorites—like Cut and Paste—are in new places. This chapter gives you an overview of the major changes, and the chapters that follow give you all the details.

Just as in previous version of Word, every project you create in Word 2007 begins and ends the same way: You start by creating a document, and you end by saving your work. Sounds simple, but to manage your Word documents effectively, you need to know these basics and beyond. This chapter shows you all the different ways to create a document in Word 2007—like starting from an existing document or adding text to a predesigned template—and how to choose the best one for your particular project.

You'll also learn how to work faster and smarter by changing your view of your document. If you want, you can use Word's Outline view when you're brainstorming, and then switch to Print view when you're ready for hard copy. This chapter gets you up and running with these fundamental tools so you can focus on the important stuff—your words.

Tip: If you've used Word before, then you're probably familiar with opening and saving documents. Still, you may want to skim this chapter to catch up on the differences between this version of Word and the ghosts of Word past. You'll grasp some of the big changes just by examining the figures. For more detail, check out the gray boxes and the notes and tips—like this one!

What Word Does

You type words, and they appear onscreen, what else? Well, maybe in the first version of Word. But in Word 2007, the program does a whole lot more. Word's designers knew what kinds of documents folks are likely to create, and stocked the program with predesigned templates that have all the important elements in place—headings, signature line, text boxes, and so on. You don't even have to worry about making it look nice: Word comes with attractive, built-in color schemes—called themes—that you can apply with a single click. Here are just some of the things you can create:

- **Letters, lists, notecards, and other personal documents.** You can even print your own greeting cards and invitations.

- **Programs, menus, and booklets.** Some of Word's templates are multipage affairs, letting you create scrapbooks, catalogs, playbills, and more.

- **Brochures, reports, business cards, and other business documents.** Word even has a feature that lets you create tables, so you don't have to use a spreadsheet program like Excel for simple tables. Word's are better looking, too.

To create all these documents, all you have to do is type the words. But even there, Word takes some of the work off your hands. It has tools that help you check your spelling and grammar, and look up facts and definitions. Word's AutoText feature even does some of the typing for you. And if you need an illustration, Word gives you a slew of pictures you can plunk right onto the page—no drawing skills required.

Note: The word portion of this book is based on *Word 2007: The Missing Manual* (O'Reilly). That book is a truly complete reference for Word 2007, covering every feature, including geeky stuff like creating indexes and tables of contents in Word, collaborating with other writers in the same document, and running off form letters by merging Word with a list of names and addresses. If you get really deep into Word and want to learn more, *Word 2007: The Missing Manual* can be your trusted guide.

The New Word

In the past, when Microsoft introduced new versions of Word, it seemed as if the developers had simply tacked new features on top of the old program wherever they'd fit. Sometimes the result was sort of like putting fins on a Volkswagen beetle.

With Word 2007, however, Microsoft listened to the critics who complained about Word's maze of menus and dialog boxes. There were also legitimate complaints about illogically placed commands and important tools that were buried. With Word 2007, all the commands have been reorganized and placed on the ribbon (page 2) according to task and function. Is the new system going to put a smile on everyone's face? No, probably not. Is it an improvement that makes Word easier to use for most people? Yes.

Another concern was security. Microsoft has made major changes in Word's file formats to minimize the chance that you'll open a document containing a virus. It would be naïve to think these steps will eliminate virus threats, but they'll certainly help.

In addition to the new features common to all the Office 2007 applications—see the introduction for a rundown—Word got some upgrades all its own:

- **Building Blocks for better docs.** Word 2007's Building Blocks save time and stress if you consider yourself a writer (or a doctor, or a manager), not a designer. Building Blocks are predesigned, preformatted elements that you can easily drop into your document. Microsoft has thrown in dozens of things like headers, footers, tables of contents, and fax cover pages. Choose a Building Block with the look you want, and then pop it into your document, knowing it will look good and include any of the pertinent details, like page number, document title, even your name.

- **Help! Get me security.** That was the cry of many Word users when they opened a document only to let loose a virus on their poor, unsuspecting computer. Microsoft has tackled security problems from several different directions. For example, Word 2007 has a new file format that makes it easier to ferret out documents that may contain virus-infected programs. (When it comes to Word viruses, the main culprits are Visual Basic for Applications and the tools it creates, called ActiveX controls.) In Word 2007, it's also easier than ever to add digital signatures to documents to make sure files come from a trusted source and haven't been tampered with.

- **File this way, please.** The groans are audible any time an industry standard like Microsoft Word makes major changes to its file format. The file format is the way a program writes information to a computer disc. As mentioned earlier, Microsoft is switching to a new file format for the best of reasons—to make all our computers safer from viruses. The downside of a new file format is that you can't open the new documents with older versions of Word unless you install a compatibility pack for the older programs.

Launching Word

The first time you launch Word after installation, the program asks you to confirm your name and initials. This isn't Microsoft's nefarious plan to pin you down: Word uses this information to identify documents that you create and modify.

Word uses your initials to mark your edits when you review and add comments to Word documents that other people send to you.

You have three popular ways to fire up Word, so use whichever method you find quickest:

- **Start menu.** The Start button in the lower-left corner of your screen gives you access to all programs on your PC—Word included. To start Word, choose Start → All Programs → Microsoft Office → Microsoft Office Word.

- **Quick Launch toolbar.** The Quick Launch toolbar at the bottom of your screen (just to the right of the Start menu) is a great place to start programs you use frequently. Microsoft modestly assumes that you'll be using Word a lot, so it usually installs the Word icon in the Quick Launch toolbar. To start using Word, just click the W icon, and voila!

Tip: When you don't see the Quick Launch toolbar, here's how to display it: On the bar at the bottom of your screen, right-click an empty spot. From the menu that pops up, choose Toolbars → Quick Launch. When you're done, icons for some of your programs appear in the bottom bar. A single click fires up the program.

- **Opening a Word document.** Once you've created some Word documents, this method is fastest of all, since you don't have to start Word as a separate step. Just open an existing Word document, and Word starts itself. Try going to Start → My Recent Documents, and then, from the list of files, choose a Word document. You can also double-click the document's icon on the desktop or wherever it lives on your PC.

Tip: If you need to get familiar with the Start menu, Quick Launch toolbar, and other Windows features, then pick up a copy of *Windows XP: The Missing Manual,* Second Edition or *Windows Vista: The Missing Manual.*

So, what happens once you've got Word's motor running? If you're a newcomer, you're probably just staring with curiosity. If you're familiar with previous versions of Word, though, you may be doing a double take (Figure 1-1). In Word 2007, Microsoft combined all the old menus and toolbars into a new feature called the ribbon. Click one of the tabs above the ribbon, and you see the command buttons change below. The ribbon commands are organized into groups, with the name of each group listed at the bottom.

Creating a New Document

When you start Word without opening an existing document, the program gives you an empty one to work in. If you're eager to put words to page, then type away.

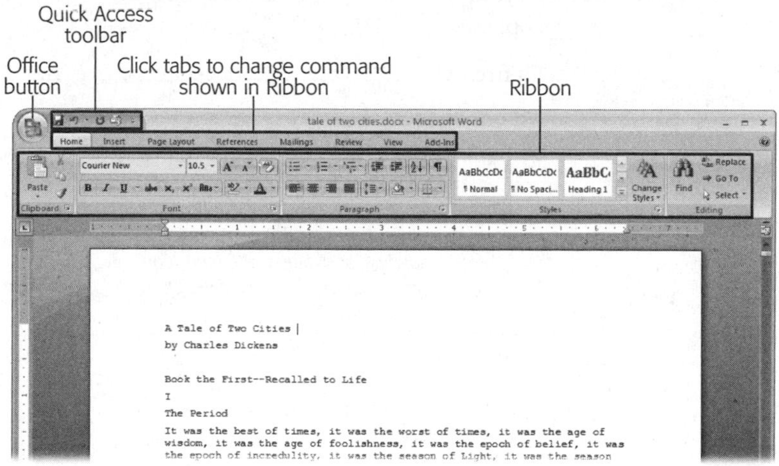

Figure 1-1:
When you start Word 2007 for the first time, it may look a little top-heavy. The ribbon takes up more real estate than the old menus and toolbars. This change may not matter if you have a nice big monitor. But if you want to reclaim some of that space, you can hide the ribbon by double-clicking the active tab. Later, when you need to see the ribbon commands, just click a tab.

Sooner or later, though, you'll want to start *another* new document. Word gives you three ways to do so:

- **Creating a new blank document.** When you're preparing a simple document—like a two-page essay, a note for the babysitter, or a press release—a plain, unadorned page is fine. Or, when you're just brainstorming and you're not sure what you want the final document to look like, you probably want to start with a blank slate or use one of Word's templates (more on that in a moment) to provide structure for your text.

- **Creating a document from an existing document.** For letters, resumes, and other documents that require more formatting, why reinvent the wheel? You can save time by using an existing document as a starting point. When you have a letter format that you like, you can use it over and over by editing the contents.

- **Creating a document from a template** (page 25). Use a template when you need a professional design for a complex document, like a newsletter, a contract, or meeting minutes. Templates are a lot like forms—the margins, formatting, and graphics are already in place. All you do is fill in your text.

Tip: Microsoft provides a mind-boggling number of templates with Word, but they're not the only source. You can find loads more on the Internet, as described on page 26. Your employer may even provide official templates for company documents.

To start your document in any of the above ways, click the Windows logo in the upper-left corner of the screen. That's Office 2007's new *Office button*. Click it, and a drop-down menu opens, revealing commands for creating, opening, and saving documents. Next to these commands, you see a list of your Word documents. This list includes documents that are open, as well as those that you've recently opened.

The Office button is also where you go to print and email your documents (Figure 1-2).

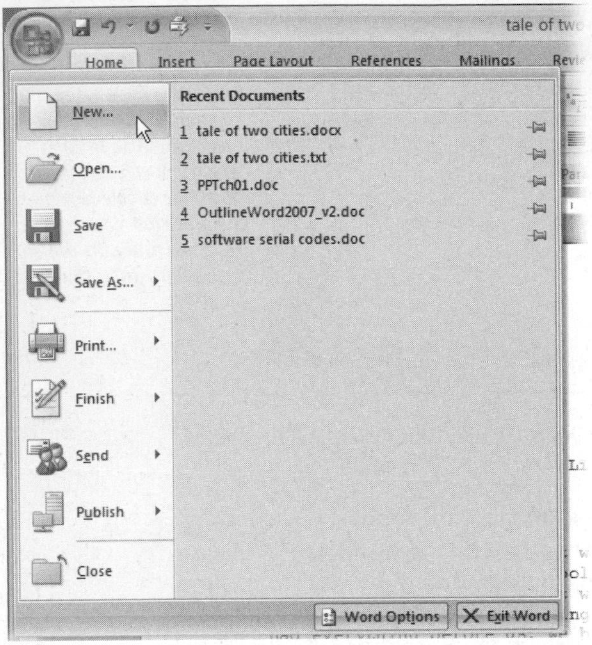

Figure 1-2:
The phrase most frequently uttered by experienced Word fans the first time they start Word 2007 is, "Okay, where's my File menu?" Never fear, the equivalent of the File menu is still there—it's just camouflaged a bit. Clicking the Office button (the one that looks like a Windows logo) reveals the commands you use to create, open, and save Word documents.

Creating a New Blank Document

Say you want a new blank document, just like the one Word shows you when you start the program. No problem—here are the steps:

1. **Choose Office button → New.**

   The New Document dialog box appears.

2. **In the upper-left corner of the large "Create a new Word document" panel, click "Blank document" (Figure 1-3).**

   The New Document box presents a seemingly endless number of options, but don't panic. The "Blank document" option you want is on the left side of the first line.

3. **At the bottom of the New Document dialog box, click Create.**

   The dialog box disappears, and you're gazing at the blank page of a new Word document.

Better get to work.

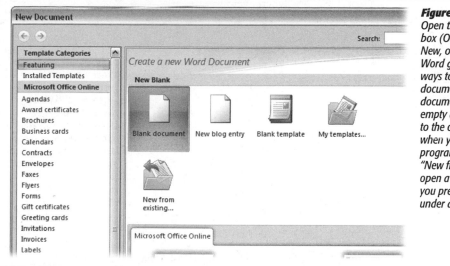

Figure 1-3:
Open the New Document box (Office button → New, or Alt+F, N), and Word gives you several ways to create a new document. Click "Blank document" to open an empty document, similar to the one Word shows when you first start the program. Or you can click "New from existing" to open a document that you previously created under a new name.

Creating a New Document from an Existing Document

A blank Word document is sort of like a shapeless lump of clay. With some work, you can mold it to become just about anything. Often, however, you can save time by opening an existing document that's similar to the one you want to create. Imagine that you write the minutes for the monthly meetings of the Chief Executive Officer's Surfing Association (CEOSA). When it's time to write up the June minutes, it's a lot faster to open the minutes from May. You keep the boilerplate text and all the formatting, but you delete the text that's specific to the previous month. Now all you have to do is enter the text for June and save the document with a new name: JuneMinutes.docx.

Note: The .docx extension on the end of the filename is Word 2007's new version of .doc. The switch from three-letter to four-letter filename extensions indicates a change in the way Word stores documents. (If you need to share documents with folks using earlier versions of Word, choose Office button → Save As → Word 97-2003 document when you save the file. See the box on page 25 for details.)

Word gives you a "New from existing" document-creation option to satisfy your desire to spend more time surfing and less time writing meeting minutes. Here's how to create a new document from an existing document:

1. **Choose Office button → New (Alt+F, N) to open the New Document window. Then click "New from existing…" (it sits directly below the "Blank document" button).**

   The three dots at the end of the button's title tell you that there's another dialog box to come. And sure enough, when you click "New from existing…", it opens another box, appropriately titled "New from Existing Document" (Figure 1-4). This box looks—and works—like a standard Windows Open File box. It lets you navigate to a specific folder and open a file.

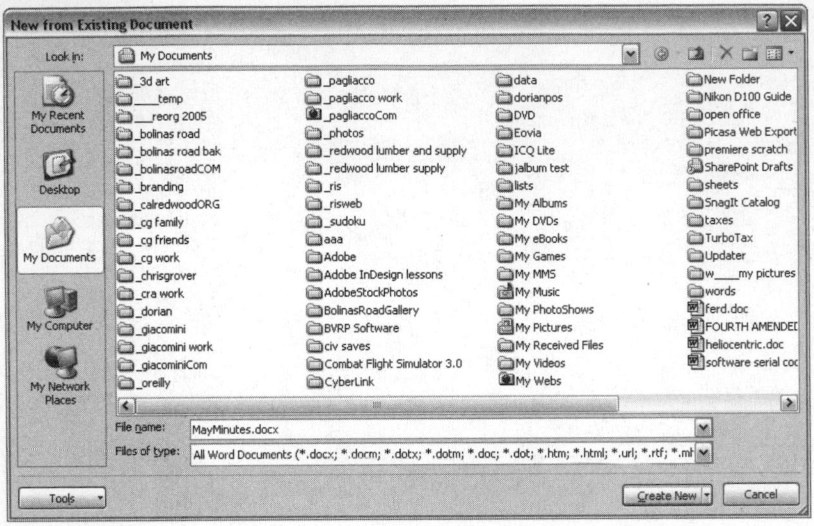

Figure 1-4:
Use the New from Existing Document box to find an existing Word document that you'd like to open as a model for your new document. When you click Create New at bottom-right, Word opens a new copy of the document, leaving the original untouched. You can modify the copy to your heart's content and save it under a different file name.

2. **On your computer, find the existing document you're using for a model.**

   You can use the bar on the left to change the folder view. Word starts you in your My Documents folder, but you can switch to your desktop or your My Computer icon by clicking the icons on the left. Double-click folder icons in the large window to open them and see their contents.

3. **Click to select the file, and then click Create New (in the lower-right corner). (Alternatively, just double-click the file's icon to open it. This trick works in all Open File boxes.)**

   Instead of the usual Open button at the bottom of the box, the button in the New from Existing Document box reads Create New—your clue that this box behaves differently in one important respect: Instead of opening an existing file, you're making a *copy* of an existing file. Once open, the file's name is something like Document2.docx instead of the original name. This way, when you save the file, you don't overwrite the original document. (Still, it's best to save it with a new descriptive name right away.)

Tip: Windows' Open File boxes, like "New from Existing Document", let you do a lot more than just find files. In fact, they let you do just about anything you can do in Windows Explorer. Using keyboard shortcuts, you can cut (Ctrl+X), copy (Ctrl+C), and paste (Ctrl+V) files. A right-click displays a shortcut menu with even more commands, letting you rename files, view Properties dialog boxes, and much more. You can even drag and drop to move files and folders.

Word's New File Formats: .docx and .docm

With Office 2007, Microsoft took the drastic step of changing its file formats in hopes of improving your computer's security. Malicious programmers were using Office's macros to do nasty things to unsuspecting computers. The *.docx* format, the new standard for Word files, doesn't permit macros, making it safe from those threats. The *.docm* format indicates that a document contains macros or other bits of programming code. When opening one of these files, play it safe: If you don't know who created the .docm file, then don't open it.

The downside of the new file formats is that older versions of Word don't know how to open these .docx and .docm documents. To open Word 2007 files with an older version (even Word 2003), you need to install the Microsoft Office Compatibility Pack.

This software fix gives pre-2007 versions of Word the power to open documents in the new formats. Even then, you may not be able to use or edit parts of the file that use new Word features (like themes, equations, and content controls). To download the free compatibility pack, go to *www.office.microsoft.com* and type *office 2007 compatibility* into the search box at the top of the page.

Also, if you're preparing a Word document for someone who's using an older Word version, then you have to save it in a compatible format, as described in the note on page 23. (Fortunately, the compatibility issue doesn't go both ways: Word 2007 can open old .doc docs just fine.)

Creating a New Document from a Template

Say you're creating meeting minutes for the first time. You don't have an existing document to give you a leg up, but you do want to end up with handsome, properly formatted minutes. Word is at your service—with *templates*. Microsoft provides dozens upon dozens of prebuilt templates for everything from newsletters to postcards. Remember all the busy stuff in the New Document box in Figure 1-3? About 90 percent of the items in there are templates.

In the previous example, where you use an existing document to create the meeting minutes for the Chief Executive Officer's Surfing Association (CEOSA), each month you open the minutes from the previous month. You delete the information that pertains to the previous month and enter the current month's minutes. A template works pretty much the same way, except it's a generic document, designed to be adaptable to lots of different situations. You just open it and add your text. The structure, formatting, graphics, colors, and other doodads are already in place.

Note: The subject of Word templates is a lengthy one, especially when it comes to creating your own, so there's a whole chapter devoted to that topic in *Word 2007: The Missing Manual*.

Here's how to get some help from one of Microsoft's templates for meeting minutes:

1. **Choose Office button → New (Alt+F, N) to open the New Document window.**

   On the left of the New Document box is a Template Categories list. The top entry on this list is Installed Templates—the ones Word has installed on your computer.

You could use any of these, but you also have a world of choice waiting for you online. On its Web site Microsoft offers hundreds of templates for all sorts of documents, and you can access them right from the New Document box. If you have a fast Internet connection, then it's just as quick and easy to use an online template as it is using the ones stored on your computer. In fact, you'll use an online template for this example.

Note: If you can't connect to the Internet right now, then simply choose one of the installed templates instead. Click Create, and then skip to step 4.

---

2. **Scroll down the Template Categories list to the Microsoft Office Online heading. Under this heading, select Minutes.**

   In the center pane, you'll see all different types of minutes templates, from PTA minutes to Annual shareholder's meeting minutes (Figure 1-5). When you click a template's icon, a preview appears in the pane on the right.

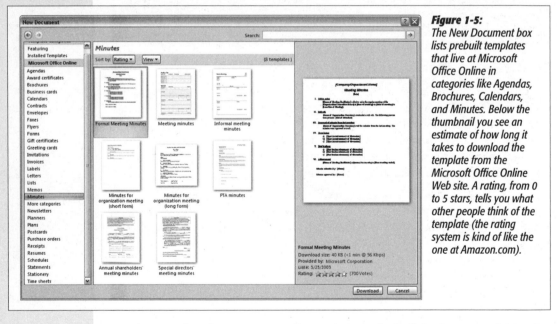

Figure 1-5:
The New Document box lists prebuilt templates that live at Microsoft Office Online in categories like Agendas, Brochures, Calendars, and Minutes. Below the thumbnail you see an estimate of how long it takes to download the template from the Microsoft Office Online Web site. A rating, from 0 to 5 stars, tells you what other people think of the template (the rating system is kind of like the one at Amazon.com).

3. **When you're done perusing the various styles, click the Formal Meeting Minutes icon. (After all, CEOSA is a very formal organization.) Then click Download.**

   Word downloads and opens the document.

4. **Start writing up the minutes for the CEO Surfers.**

   To follow the template's structure, replace all the words in square brackets ([ ]) with text relevant to CEOSA.

Tip: If you'd rather not download the Formal Meeting Minutes template every time you use it, then you can save the file on your computer as a Word template. The steps for saving files are just around the corner on page 38.

Opening an Existing Document

If you've mastered creating a document from an existing document and creating a document from a template, you'll find that opening an existing document is a snap. The steps are nearly identical.

1. **Choose Office button → Open (Alt+F, O). In the Open window (Figure 1-6), navigate to the folder and file you want to open.**

   The Open window starts out showing your My Documents folder, since that's where Word suggests you save your files. When your document's in a more exotic location, click the My Computer icon, and then navigate to the proper folder from there.

Tip: When you open a document you've used recently, you may see its name right on the Office button → Recent Documents menu. If so, simply click to open it without a trip to the Open dialog box.

2. **With the file selected, click Open in the lower-right corner.**

   The Open box goes away and your document opens in Word. You're all set to get to work. Just remember, when you save this document (Alt+F, S or Ctrl+S), you write over the previous file. Essentially, you create a new, improved, and only copy of the file you just opened. If you don't want to write over the existing document, use the Save As command (Alt+F, A), and then type a new name in the File Name text box.

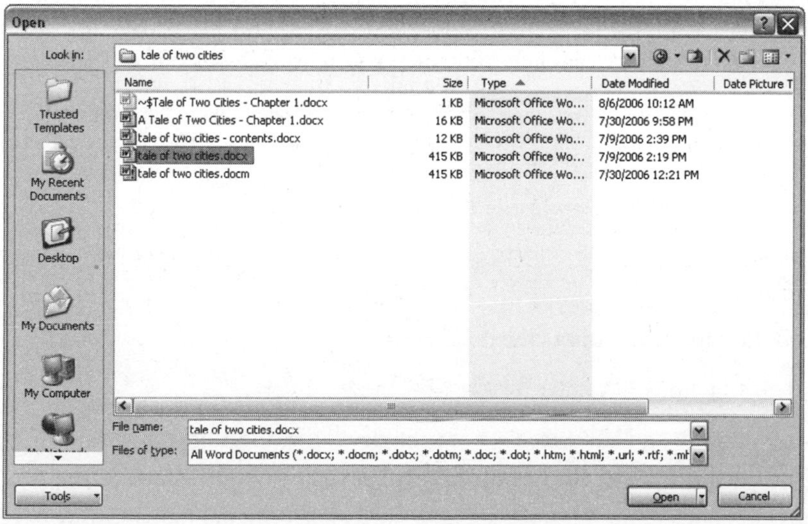

Figure 1-6:
This Open dialog box shows the contents of the tale of two cities folder, according to the "Look in" box at the top. As you can see in the "File name box" at the bottom of the window, the file tale of two cities.docx is selected. By clicking Open, Mr. Dickens is ready to go to work.

Tip: Opening a file in Word doesn't mean you're limited to documents *created* in Word. You can choose documents created in other programs from the Files of Type drop-down menu at the bottom of the Open dialog box. Word then shows you that type of document in the main part of the window. You can open Outlook messages (.msg), Web pages (.htm or .html), or files from other word processors (.rtf, .mcw, .wps).

Your Different Document Views

Now that you know a handful of ways to create and open Word documents, it's time to take a look around the establishment. You may think a document's a document—just look at it straight on and get your work done. It's surprising, though, how changing your view of the page can help you work faster and smarter. When you're working with a very long document, you can change to Outline view and peruse just your document's headlines without the paragraph text. In Outline view, you get a better feeling for the manuscript as a whole. Likewise, when you're working on a document that's headed for the Web, it makes sense to view the page as it will appear in a browser. Other times, you may want to have two documents open on your screen at once (or on each of your two monitors, you lucky dog), to make it easy to cut and paste text from one to the other.

The key to working with Word's different view options is to match the view to the job at hand. Once you get used to switching views, you'll find lots of reasons to change your point of view. Find the tools you need on the View tab (Figure 1-7). To get there, click the View tab (Alt+W) on the ribbon (near the top of Word's window). The tab divides the view commands into four groups:

- **Document Views.** These commands change the big picture. For the most part, use these when you want to view a document in a dramatically different way: two pages side by side, Outline view, Web layout view, and so on.

- **Show/Hide.** The Show/Hide commands display and conceal Word tools like rulers and gridlines. These tools don't show when you print your document; they're just visual aids that help you when you're working in Word.

- **Zoom.** As you can guess, the Zoom tools let you choose between a close-up and a long shot of your document. Getting in close makes your words easier to read and helps prevent eyestrain. But zooming out makes scrolling faster and helps you keep your eye on the big picture.

Tip: In addition to the Zoom tools on the ribbon, handy Zoom tools are available in the window's lower-right corner. Check out the + (Zoom In) and – (Zoom Out) buttons and the slider in between them. See page 32 for the details on using them.

- **Window.** In the Window group, you'll find creative ways to organize document windows on your screen—like split views of a single document or side-by-side views of two different documents.

All the commands in the View tab's four groups are covered in the following pages.

Note: As you can see in this section, Word gives you a wealth of different ways to look at a document. If you'd like to adjust how you view your Word documents even further, there's a whole chapter devoted to customizing Word in *Word 2007: The Missing Manual*.

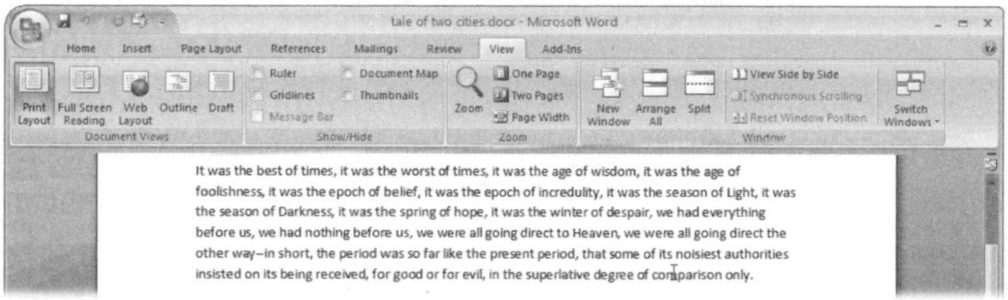

Figure 1-7:
The View tab is your document-viewing control center. Look closely, and you see it's divided into four groups with names at the bottom of the ribbon: Document Views, Show/Hide, Zoom, and Window. To apply a view command, just click the button or label.

Document Views: Five Ways to Look at Your Manuscript

Word gives you five basic document views. To select a view, go to the View tab (Alt+W) and choose one of the Document Views on the left side of the ribbon (Figure 1-8). You have another great option for switching from one view to another that's always available in the lower-right corner of Word's window. Click one of the five small buttons to the left of the slider to jump between Print Layout, Full Screen Reading, Web Layout, Outline, and Draft views. Each view has a special purpose, and you can modify them even more using the other commands on the View tab.

Figure 1-8:
On the left side of the View tab, you find the five basic document views: Print Layout, Full Screen Reading, Web Layout, Outline, and Draft. You can edit your document in any of the views, although they come with different tools for different purposes. Outline view provides a menu that lets you show or hide headings at different outline levels.

Note: Changing your view in no way affects the document itself—you're just looking at the same document from a different perspective.

- **Print Layout (Alt+W, P).** The most frequently used view in Word, Print Layout is the one you see when you first start the program or create a new blank document. In this view, the page you see on your computer screen looks much as it does when you print it. This view's handy for letters, reports, and most documents headed for the printer.

• **Full Screen Reading (Alt+W, F).** If you'd like to get rid of the clutter of menus, ribbons, and all the rest of the word-processing gadgetry, then use Full Screen Reading view. As the name implies, this view's designed primarily for reading documents. It includes options you don't find in the other views, like a command that temporarily decreases or increases the text size. In the upper-right corner you see some document-proofing tools (like a text highlighter and an insert comment command), but when you want to change or edit your document, you must first use the View Options → Allow Typing command.

• **Web Layout (Alt+W, L).** This view shows your document as if it were a single Web page loaded in a browser. You don't see any page breaks in this view. Along with your text, you see any photos or videos that you've placed in the document—just like a Web page.

• **Outline (Alt+W, U).** For lots of writers, an outline is the first step in creating a manuscript. Once they've created a framework of chapters and headings, they dive in and fill out the document with text. If you like to work this way, then you'll love Outline view. It's easy to jump back and forth between Outline view and Print Layout view or Draft view, so you can bounce back and forth between a macro and a micro view of your epic. (For more details on using Word's Outline view, see page 187.)

• **Draft (Alt+W, E).** Here's the no-nonsense, roll-up-your-sleeves view of your work (Figure 1-9). You see most formatting as it appears on the printed page, except for headers and footers. Page breaks are indicated by a thin dotted line. In this view, it's as if your document is on one single roll of paper that scrolls through your computer screen. This view's a good choice for longer documents and those moments when you want to focus on the words without being distracted by page breaks and other formatting niceties.

Show and Hide Window Tools

Word gives you some visual aids that make it easier to work with your documents. Tools like rulers and gridlines don't show up when you print your document, but they help you line up the elements on the page. Use the ruler to set page margins and to create tabs for your documents. Checkboxes on the View tab let you show or hide tools, but some tools aren't available in all the views, so they're grayed out. You can't, for example, display page rulers in Outline or Full Screen Reading views.

Use the checkboxes in the Show/Hide group of the View tab (Figure 1-10) to turn these tools on and off:

• **Ruler.** Use the ruler to adjust margins, set tabs, and position items on your page. For more detail on formatting text and paragraphs, see page 71.

• **Gridlines.** When you click the Gridlines box, it looks like you created your document on a piece of graph paper. This effect isn't too helpful for an all-text document, but it sure comes in handy if you're trying to line up photos on a page.

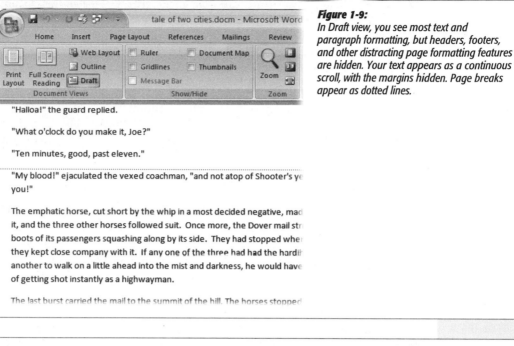

Figure 1-9:
In Draft view, you see most text and paragraph formatting, but headers, footers, and other distracting page formatting features are hidden. Your text appears as a continuous scroll, with the margins hidden. Page breaks appear as dotted lines.

Figure 1-10:
Use the Show/Hide group on the View tab to display or conceal Word tools. The Ruler gives you a quick and easy way to set tabs and margins. The Document Map is particularly helpful when you work with longer documents because it displays headings in the bar on the left of the screen. In the left pane, you can see that Mr. Dickens wrote more than his fair share of chapters.

• **Message Bar.** The Message Bar resides directly under the ribbon, and it's where you see alerts about a document's behavior. For example, when a document is trying to run a macro and your Word settings prohibit macros, an alert appears in the Message Bar. Click the checkbox to show or hide the Message Bar.

- **Document Map.** If you work with long documents, you'll like the Document Map. This useful tool appears to the left of your text (you can see it in Figure 1-10), showing the document's headings at various levels. Click the little + and – buttons next to a heading to expand or collapse the outline. Click a heading, and you jump to that location in your document.

- **Thumbnails.** Select the Thumbnails option, and you see little icons of your document's pages in the bar on the left. Click a thumbnail to go to that page. In general, thumbnails are more useful for shorter documents and for pages that are visually distinctive. For longer documents, you'll find the Document Map easier to use for navigation.

Zooming Your View In and Out

When you're working, do you ever find that you sometimes hold pages at arm's length to get a complete view, and then, at other times, you stick your nose close to the page to examine the details? Word's Zoom options (Figure 1-11) let you do the same thing with your screen—but without looking nearly as silly.

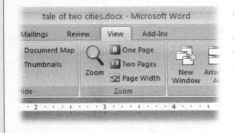

Figure 1-11:
The Zoom group of options lets you view your document close up or at a distance. The big magnifying glass opens the Zoom dialog box with more controls for fine-tuning your zoom level. For quick changes, click one of the three buttons on the right: One Page, Two Pages, or Page Width.

Note: Even though the text appears to get bigger and smaller when you zoom, you're not actually changing the document in any way. Zoom is similar to bringing a page closer so you can read the fine print. If you want to actually change the font size, then use the formatting options on the Home tab (Alt+H, FS).

On the View tab, click the big magnifying glass to open the Zoom dialog box (Figure 1-12). Depending on your current Document View (see page 29), you can adjust your view by percentage or relative to the page and text (more on that in a moment). The options change slightly depending on which Document View you're using. The Page options don't really apply to Web layouts, so they're grayed out and inactive if you're in the Web Layout view.

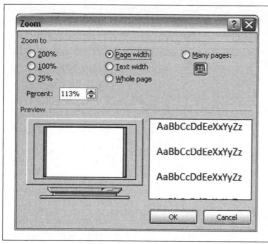

Figure 1-12:
The Zoom dialog box lets you choose from a variety of views. Just click one of the option buttons, and then click OK. The monitor and text sample at the bottom of the Zoom box provide visual clues as you change the settings.

Zooming by percentage

In the box's upper-left corner, you find controls to zoom in and out of your document by percentage. The view varies depending on your computer screen and settings, but in general, 100% is a respectable, middle-of-the-road view of your document. The higher the percentage, the more zoomed in you are, and the bigger everything looks—vice versa with a lower percentage.

The three radio buttons (200%, 100%, and 75%) give you quick access to some standard settings. For in-between percentages (like 145%), type a number in the box below the buttons, or use the up-down arrows to change the value. For a quick way to zoom in and out without opening a dialog box, use the Zoom slider (Figure 1-13) in the lower-right corner of your window. Drag the slider to the right to zoom in on your document, and drag it to the left to zoom out. The percentage changes as you drag.

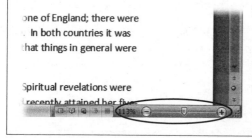

Figure 1-13:
The Zoom slider at the bottom of the document window gives you a quick and easy way to change your perspective. Drag the slider to the right to zoom in on your document, and drag it to the left to zoom out. To the left of the slider are five View buttons: Print Layout, Full Screen Reading, Web Layout, Outline, and Draft (page 29).

Zooming relative to page or text

Not everyone's a number person. (That's especially true of writers.) So you may prefer to zoom without worrying about percentage figures. The Zoom dialog box (on the View tab, click the magnifying-glass icon) gives you four radio buttons with plain-English zoom settings:

Page width. Click this button, and the page resizes to fill the screen from one side to the other. It's the fastest way to zoom to a text size that most people find comfortable to read. (You may have to scroll, though, to read the page from top to bottom.)

Text width. This button zooms in even farther, because it ignores the margins of your page. Use this one if you have a high-resolution monitor (or you've misplaced your reading glasses).

Whole page. When you want to see an entire page from top to bottom and left to right, click this button. It's great for getting an overview of how your headings and paragraphs look on the page.

Many pages. This view is the equivalent of spreading your document out on the floor, and then viewing it from the top of a ladder. You can use it to see how close you are to finishing that five-page paper, or to inspect the layout of a multi-page newsletter.

Warning: When you're zoomed out to Whole or "Many pages" view, watch those fingers on the keyboard. You can still make changes to your text in these views, even though you can't see what you're doing.

Changing page view from the ribbon

The ribbon offers radio buttons for three popular page views. (You can see them back in Figure 1-11, to the Zoom tool's right.) They're a quick and dirty way to change the number of pages you see onscreen without fiddling with zoom controls.

- **One Page.** This view shows the entire page in Word's document window. If your screen is large enough, you can read and edit text in this view.

- **Two Pages.** In this view, you see two pages side by side. This view's handy when you're working with documents that have two-page spreads, like booklets.

- **Page Width.** This button does the exact same thing as the Page Width button in the Zoom dialog box (page 32). It's more readable than the One Page and Two Page options, because the page fills the screen from edge to edge, making the text appear larger.

The Window Group: Doing the Splits

Back when dinosaurs roamed the earth and people used typewriters (or very early word processors), you could work on only one document at a time—the one right in front of you. Although Word 2007 has more options for viewing multiple documents and multiple windows than ever, some folks forget to use them. Big mistake. If you ever find yourself comparing two documents or borrowing extensively from some other text, then having two or more documents visible on your screen can double or triple your work speed.

The commands for managing multiple documents, views, and windows are in the View tab's Window group (Figure 1-14).

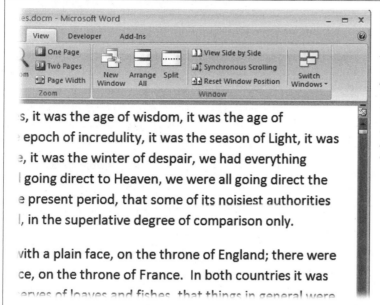

Figure 1-14:
In the Window group, the three commands—New Window, Arrange All, and Split—let you open and view your work from multiple vantage points. The commands View Side by Side, Synchronous Scrolling, and Reset Window Position are helpful when reviewing and comparing documents. The big Switch Windows button lets you hop from one document to another.

- **New Window (Alt+W, N).** When you're working on a long document, sometimes you want to see two different parts of the document at the same time, as if they were two separate documents. You may want to keep referring to what you said in the Introduction while you're working on Chapter 5. Or perhaps you want to keep an Outline view open while editing in Draft view. That's where the New Window command comes in. When you click this button (or hit this keystroke), you've got your document open in two windows that you can scroll independently. Make a change to one window, and it immediately appears in the other.

- **Arrange All (Alt+W, A).** Great—now you've got documents open in two or more windows, but it takes a heck of a lot of mousing around and window resizing to get them lined up on your screen at the same time. Click Arrange All and, like magic, your open Word document windows are sharing the screen, making it easy to work on one and then the other. Word takes an egalitarian approach to screen real estate, giving all windows an equal amount of property (Figure 1-15).

- **Split (Alt+W, S).** The Split button divides a single window so you can see two different parts of the same document—particularly handy if you're copying text from one part of a document to another. The other advantage of the Split command is that it gives you more room to work than using Arrange All for multiple windows because it doesn't duplicate the ribbon, ruler, and other Word tools (Figure 1-16).

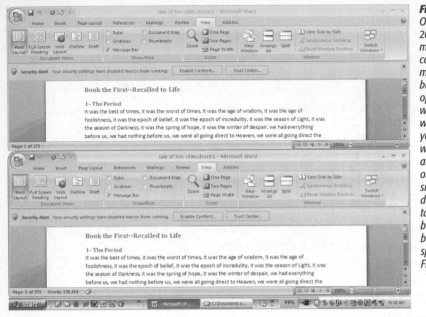

Figure 1-15:
One downside of Office 2007's ribbon: It takes up more space on your computer's screen than menus or even the older button bars. When you open a couple of windows, you're not left with much space to do your work, especially when you're working on an ultra-portable laptop or a computer with a small screen. You can double-click the active tab to hide the ribbon, but in most cases, you're better off working with a split screen, as shown in Figure 1-16.

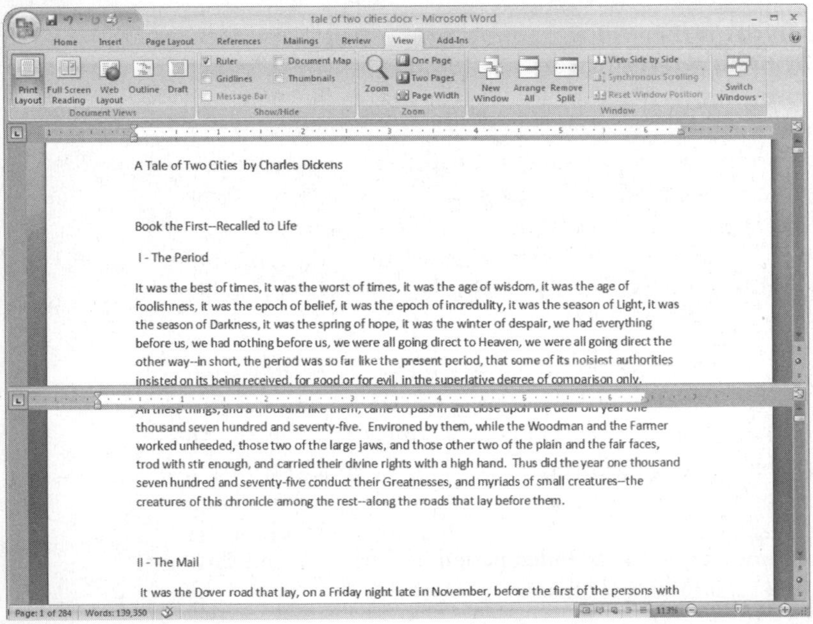

Figure 1-16:
When you're viewing two different parts of a single document, use the Split command; it leaves you more room to work than two separate windows, as shown in Figure 1-15. Each section of the split window has a scroll bar, so you can independently control different parts of your document. If you want to fine-tune your split, just drag the middle bar exactly where you want it. When you're done, click Remove Split to return to a single screen view.

Viewing multiple windows

One common reason for wanting to see two documents or more on your screen at once is so you can make line-by-line comparisons. Imagine you have two Word documents that are almost identical, but you have to find the spots where there are differences. A great way to make those differences jump out is to put both versions on your screen side by side and scroll through them. As you scroll, you can see differences in the paragraph lengths and the line lengths. Here are the commands to help you with the process:

- **View Side by Side (Alt+W, B).** Click the View Side by Side command and Word arranges two windows vertically side by side. As you work with side-by-side documents, you can rearrange windows on your screen by dragging the very top of the Window frame. You can resize the windows by pointing to any edge of the frame. When you see a double arrow, just drag to resize the window. Synchronous Scrolling (described next) is automatically turned on.

- **Synchronous Scrolling (Alt+W, Y).** The Synchronous Scrolling feature keeps multiple document windows in lock step. When you scroll one window, the other windows automatically scroll too. Using the same button or keystroke, you can toggle Synchronous Scrolling on and off as you work with your documents.

- **Reset Windows Position (Alt+W, T).** If you've moved or resized your document windows as described earlier under View Side by Side, then you can click this button to reset your view so the windows share the screen equally.

Saving and Closing Documents

From the earliest days of personal computing, the watchword has been "save early, save often." There's nothing more frustrating than working half the day and then having the Great American Novel evaporate into the digital ether because your power goes out. So, here are some tips to protect your work from disasters human-made and natural:

- Name and save your document shortly after you first create it. You'll see the steps to do so later in this section.

- Get in the habit of doing a quick save with Alt+F, S (think *File Save*) when you pause to think or get up to go to the kitchen for a snack. (Note for old-timers: Ctrl+S still works for a quick save too.)

- If you're leaving your computer for an extended period of time, save and close your document with Alt+F, C (think *File Close*).

FREQUENTLY ASKED QUESTION

Where Are My Keyboard Shortcuts?

Ribbons, buttons, and menus are all well and good when you're doing something new or complicated. But when you know where you're going, a good keyboard shortcut can save time. Word 2007 has dozens of keyboard shortcuts. If you don't have your favorites memorized, use the Alt key to reveal them.

Press the Alt key, and you see small badges with letters and numbers pop up next to menus and buttons. These are your shortcuts. If you're looking for the keyboard shortcut to close your document, follow these steps:

1. **Press and release the Alt key to show the keyboard shortcut badges.**

   When you do this, the badges appear over menu items and ribbon buttons. (The Alt key acts as a toggle. If you change your mind and don't want to use a shortcut, then press the Alt key again and you're back in normal typing mode.)

2. **Press F to open the Office menu.**

   Pressing F (which used to stand for File menu) does the same thing as clicking the button with your mouse, except that now it sports little keyboard shortcut badges.

3. **Press C to close your document.**

   Looking at the bottom of the Office menu, you see the Close command. A small C badge indicates that pressing C closes your document.

As you can guess, most keyboard shortcuts are based on the initial letter of the actual command words. This doesn't always work out for popular letters. As a result, you have cases like the References tab, which has the keyboard shortcut S.

Even if you don't deliberately work to memorize the keyboard shortcuts, you'll find that you begin to learn your favorites as you use them. Before long, your fingers will tap them out automatically.

If a substantial portion of your brain is occupied by keyboard shortcuts from previous versions of Word, never fear. Most of those old commands still work—including Ctrl+B for Bold, Ctrl+N for new document, and F7 for spell checking.

The Many Ways to Save Documents

It's the Microsoft Way to give you multiple ways to do most everything. Whether that's because the company's programmers believe in giving you lots of choices, or because they can't make up their minds about the best way to do something is a question best left to the philosophers. But the point is, you do have a choice. You don't have to memorize every keystroke, button, and command. Especially with saving, the important thing is to find a way you like and stick with it. The next section gives some ways you can save the document you're working on.

Saving by keyboard shortcut

- **Ctrl+S.** If you're an old hand at Word, this keyboard shortcut may already be burned in your brain. It still works with Word and other Office programs. This command quickly saves the document and lets you get back to work.

- **Alt+F, S.** This keyboard shortcut does the exact same thing as Ctrl+S. Unlike Ctrl+S, though, you get visual reminders of which keys to press when you press the Alt key. See the box above.

Saving by menu command

- **Office button → Save.** If you don't want to use keyboard shortcuts, you can mouse your way to the same place using menus. Like the options above, this command saves your file with its current name.

- **Office button → Save As.** The Save As option lets you save your file with a new name (Figure 1-17). When you use this command, you create a new document with a new name that includes any changes you've made. (The individual steps are described in the next section.)

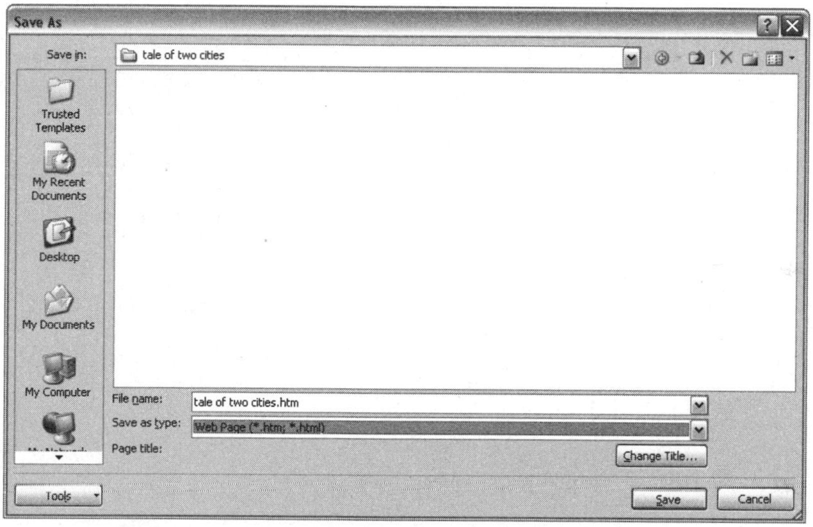

Figure 1-17:
Use Office button → Save As to save your file with a new name or in a different file format. In this example, the Word file tale of two cities is being saved as an HTML type file—a format used for Web pages.

- **Office button → Close.** When you close a document, Word checks to see if you made any changes to the file. When you've made changes, Word always asks whether you'd like to save the document (Figure 1-18).

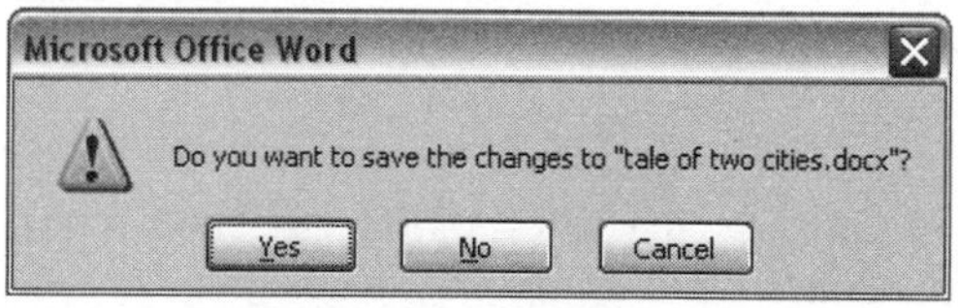

Figure 1-18:
When you see this message box, you have three choices: Yes saves your document before closing it; No closes your document without saving it; Cancel leaves your document open without saving it.

Saving with a new name

When you save a new document or save a document with a new name (Save As), you've got three things to consider: a filename, a file location, and a file format.

WORD TO THE WISE

Preventing and Recovering from Disaster

Lightning strikes. Children trip over power cords. Computers crash. Saving your work frequently and keeping backup copies of your documents are important safeguards. You can have Word save backup copies every time you save a document, so you always have the last two versions of your work stored on your computer. Word doesn't automatically save backup copies of your files, but it's easy enough to change this setting. Click the Office button, and then click Word Options at the bottom of the box.

After the Word Options dialog box opens, scroll down to the Save group, and turn on the "Always create backup copy" checkbox. Choose Office button → Open to find and open your backup file (Figure 1-19).

When disaster strikes in spite of your meticulous preventive measures, Word can help too. Word's new file formats have been designed to be easier to recover and repair. In many cases, if a picture or a table is corrupted in the file, you can still retrieve everything else (Figure 1-20).

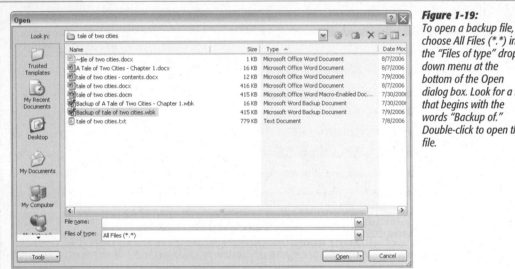

Figure 1-19:
To open a backup file, choose All Files (.*) in the "Files of type" drop-down menu at the bottom of the Open dialog box. Look for a file that begins with the words "Backup of." Double-click to open the file.*

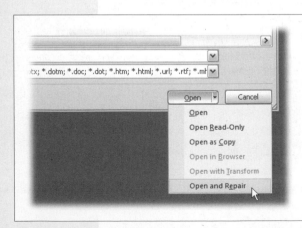

Figure 1-20:
When you can't open a file with a normal Open command, click the arrow to the right of the Open button, and choose Open and Repair from the drop-down menu. Some parts of your file may still be damaged, but you can usually recover most of your work.

Here are the steps for saving a file, complete with a new name:

1. **Choose Office button → Save As to open the Save As box.**

   You use the Save As command when you're saving a file with a new name. Word also displays the Save As box the first time you save a new document.

2. **Use the "Save in" drop-down list or double-click to open folders in the window to find a location to store your file.**

   The buttons in the upper-right corner can also help you navigate. See the details in Figure 1-21. Word doesn't care where you save your files, so you can choose your desktop or any folder on your computer.

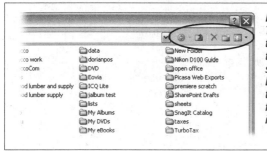

Figure 1-21:
The Save As dialog box has all the controls you need to navigate to any location on your computer—including five nifty buttons in the upper-right corner. From left to right: The left arrow button steps you backward through your past locations (just like the back button in a Web browser). The up arrow takes you out to the folder enclosing the one you're in now. The X button deletes folders and files—be careful with it. Click the folder with the star in the corner to create a new folder.

Tip: The more files you save on your computer, the more helpful it is to have a logical folder and file system. If you keep hundreds of Word documents, you may want to have different folders named: letters, memos, reports, and newsletters.

---

3. **At the bottom of the Save As dialog box, type a name in the File name box.**

   Word accepts long names, so you don't need to skimp. Use a descriptive name that will help you identify the file two weeks or two years from now. A good name saves you time in the long run.

4. **Use the "Save as type" box to choose a file type.**

   In most cases you don't need to change the file type. Word automatically selects either *.docx* or *.docm* depending on the contents of your file, but Word can save files in over a dozen different formats. If you're sharing the file with someone who's using an older version of Word, then choose Word 97-2003 Document to save the document in .doc format. If you're sharing with someone who uses a Mac or Linux computer, then you may want to use the more universal Rich Text Format (.rtf).

Tip: If you want to use your document as a template in the future, then choose Word Template (dotx).

Unless you're sharing your file with someone using an older version of Word or a different operating system or making a template, stick with the new standard Word file types .docx (for normal Word files) and .docm (for files that run macros). See the box on page 25 for a complete rundown.

5. **Click Save.**

Word does the rest. All you need to do is remember where you saved your work.

Understanding Word File Types

When you save your first file in Word 2007, you'll find a bewildering array of file types. Don't sweat it—you'll use some new file types on the list frequently, but you'll probably ignore a lot of types. The two you'll use most often are .docx and .docm.

- **.docx.** New format for most Word documents. Pre-2007 versions of Word can't open these documents without the help of the Office Compatibility Pack, as described in the box on page 25.

- **.docm.** New format for Word documents containing macros. (Microsoft is making an effort to increase computer security by reining in Office macros.)

- **.dotx.** New format for templates (page 25).

- **.dotm.** New format for templates containing macros.

- **.doc.** Format for all the previous versions of Word including: Word 6.0, Word 95, and Word 97-2003.

- **.dot.** The template format for previous versions of Word.

- **.xps.** XML Paper specification. This format is Microsoft's answer to PDF for creating documents that anyone can open on any computer.

- **.pdf.** Adobe Reader (also known as Acrobat) files. PDF stands for Portable Document Format.

- **.mhtm, .mhtml.** Single file Web page. In other words, all the files that make up a Web page (including images) are contained in one single file. (There's no difference between .mhtm and .mhtml files; they're just 4-letter and 5-letter versions of the same filename extension.)

- **.htm, .html.** Standard Web page format. This format is for the Web pages you see on the Internet. When the page includes photos or other files, links on the page point to those external files. (There's no difference between .htm and .html; both mean the same thing.)

- **.rtf.** Rich Text Format, a file format used to exchange files with other word processors and other types of computers like Macs and Linux computers.

- **.txt.** This plain text format doesn't have a lot of the formatting you can do in Word. It makes for a nice, small file size, and you can open it on any computer, but it's not pretty.

- **.xml.** eXtensible Markup Language is a standard language for describing many different types of data.

- **.wps.** This format indicates a document created in Office's little sibling, Microsoft Works.

CHAPTER 2

Entering and Editing Text

Despite advanced features like grammar checking, indexing, and image editing, Word is still, at heart, a word processor. You probably spend most of your time entering text and massaging it into shape. Amidst all the slick graphics and gee-whiz automation, Word 2007 makes it faster and easier than ever for you to enter and edit your text. A quick read through this chapter will reveal timesaving techniques that'll help you spend less time hunting, pecking, and clicking, so you can move on to the important stuff—polishing your prose and sharing it with the world.

This chapter starts with a quick review of the basics—putting words on the page and moving around your document. You'll also learn how to cut, copy, paste, and generally put text exactly where you want it. To top it off, you'll explore the Find and Replace features and learn how to save keystrokes using Word's Quick Parts.

Typing in Word

Whenever you're entering text into Word, the *insertion point* is where all the action takes place (Figure 2-1). It's that vertical, blinking bar that's a little taller than a capital letter. When you press a key, a letter appears at the insertion point, and the blinking bar moves a space to the right. To type in a different spot, just click somewhere in your text, and the insertion point moves to that location.

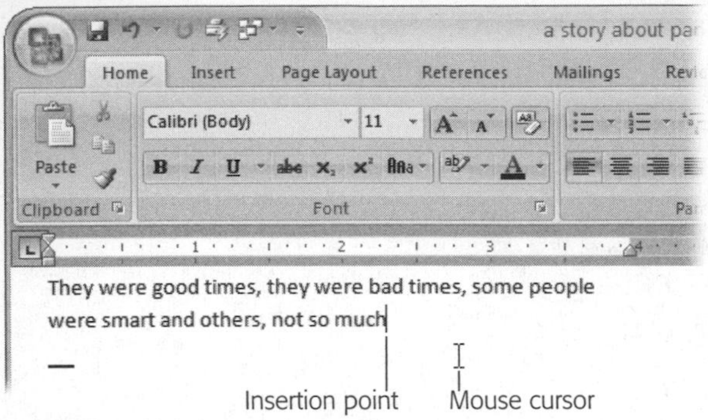

Figure 2-1:
As you type, the characters appear at the insertion point. Sometimes people call the insertion point the "cursor," but the insertion point and the mouse cursor are actually two different things. You use the mouse cursor to choose commands from the ribbon, select text, and place the insertion point in your document. The cursor can roam all over the Word window, but the insertion point remains hard at work, blinking patiently, waiting for you to enter the next character.

They were good times, they were bad times, some people were smart and others, not so much

Insertion point   Mouse cursor

Press Shift to type capitals or to enter the various punctuation marks you see above the numbers keys (!@#$*&^). When you want to type several words in uppercase letters, press the Caps Lock key. You don't have to keep holding it down. It works like a toggle. Press it once and you're in caps mode. Press it again and you're back to lowercase.

The Backspace key and the Delete key both erase characters, but there's a difference: The Backspace erases the characters behind the insertion point, while the Delete key eliminates characters in front.

WORD TO THE WISE

Choosing Between Insert and Overtype Mode

Most of the time, you type in *insert mode*. Put your cursor in the middle of a sentence, start typing, and Word inserts the letters you type at that point. Existing text scoots along to the right to make room.

In the other mode—*overtype mode*—every time you type a character, it *writes over* and erases the next one. Before Word 2007, most people stumbled upon overtype mode by accident. They'd click in the middle of a sentence and start typing—and the letters to the right of the cursor started to disappear! In those earlier versions of Word, pressing the Insert key threw you right into overtype mode. It was an easy mistake to make, since Insert is just above the much-used Delete key (on most keyboards).

Microsoft made overtype mode harder to get to, so people would not accidentally type over all their hard work. Now the Insert key doesn't do anything unless you make a few tweaks to Word's settings.

If you miss that old overtype mode and want to toggle back and forth with the Insert key, follow these steps:

1. Go to Office button → Word Options to open the Word Options dialog box.

2. In the left bar, select Advanced.

3. In the first group of options, called Editing Options, turn on the "Use the Insert Key to control overtype mode" checkbox.

If you want to use overtype mode as your regular text entry mode, turn on the "Use overtype mode" checkbox.

Note: Word's cursor changes its appearance like a chameleon, hinting at what will happen when you click the mouse button. When you move the cursor over the ribbon, it turns into an arrow, indicating that you can point and click a command. Hold it over your text, and it looks like an I-beam, giving you a precise tool for placing the insertion point between characters.

But if all you do with Word is type, you're missing out on 95 percent of its potential. What makes Word a 21st-century tool is the ease with which you can edit text, as described next.

Click and Type for Quick Formatting

Word's *Click and Type* feature makes it easy to position and align text on a blank spot on the page. It's great for those jobs where you want to position a block of text in an unusual place. Imagine you're putting together a title page for a report and you want the title about a third of the way down on the right side of the page with text aligned to the right. All you have to do is position your mouse cursor where you want the text. Notice, as you move the cursor around the page, sometimes four small lines appear near the I-beam. When the cursor's on the right side of the page, the lines trail off to the left (Figure 2-2).

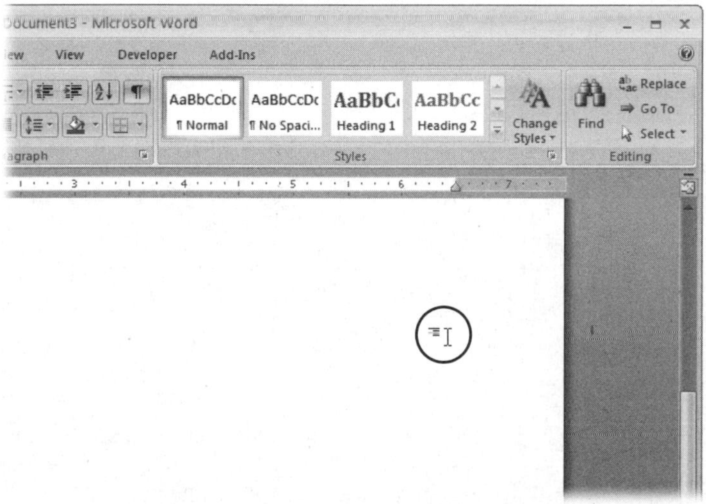

Figure 2-2:
The Click and Type cursor changes (circled) depending on where it's located on the page. Here the cursor indicates that text will be aligned to the right.

When the cursor's in the center of the page, the lines are centered at the bottom of the I-beam. As usual, the cursor is giving a hint about what will happen next.

If you double-click when the cursor's on the right side of the page (with the lines trailing off to the left), then several things happen. Most noticeable, your insertion point is exactly where you clicked. Behind the scenes, Word makes several other adjustments. If necessary, Word positions the insertion point vertically and horizontally on the page by adding paragraph marks and tabs as needed. Word changes the paragraph alignment setting to Align Right—it's just as if you clicked the button on the ribbon. Fortunately, you don't need to worry about these details; all you have to do is type the text (Figure 2-3).

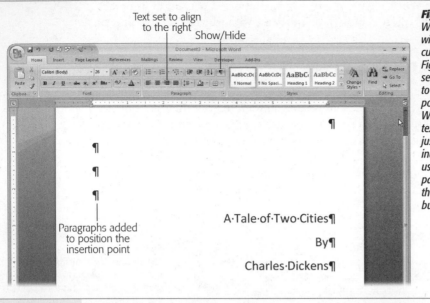

Figure 2-3:
When you double-click with the Click and Type cursor shown in Figure 2-2, Word adds several paragraph marks to position the insertion point down the page. When you type some text, it's right-aligned—just as the cursor indicated. (To see these usually hidden paragraph marks, click the paragraph mark button on the Home tab.)

Text set to align to the right
Show/Hide

Paragraphs added to position the insertion point

A·Tale·of·Two·Cities¶

By¶

Charles·Dickens¶

POWER USERS' CLINIC

Entering Special Characters

Letters, numbers, and punctuation are the common currency of most documents. Still, you may want to use a bunch of other fairly common characters, like © and ®, that don't show up on your keyboard. And where are all those foreign characters, math symbols, and fractions?

They're waiting for you on the Insert tab. Choose Insert → Symbols → Symbol (Figure 2-4). If the character you need is on the menu, then click to insert it into your text. If you don't see it, click "More symbols" to see a more comprehensive list of characters. The first group—Symbols—gives you access to every character Word can put on the page.

Use the Font box on the left to select your typeface. If you want to use the typeface you're currently using in your document, as is often the case, then leave this set to "(normal text)." Use the Subset drop-down menu to choose a language (like Greek, Cyrillic, or Latin), or choose from other groupings (accented letters, math symbols, and so on). You can also use the scroll bar on the right to visually search for a symbol. Symbols that you've used recently are lined up near the bottom of the dialog box, so you can grab them quickly.

Selecting Text

Even among the best writers, the first draft needs a lot of editing before it's ready for public viewing. You'll need to change words, delete boring parts, and move sentences (or even whole paragraphs) to reorganize your text.

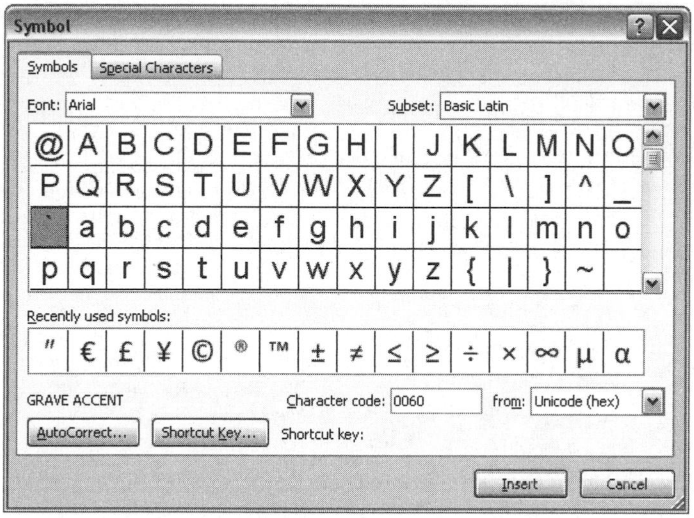

Figure 2-4:
To insert a character in your text, either double-click the character or single-click it, and then click Insert. The right-hand tab—Special Characters—contains a list of specialized punctuation marks like dashes and nonbreaking hyphens.

In Word, as in most programs, you have to *select* something before you can do anything to it. Say you want to change the word "good" to "awesome": Select "good," and then type your new, improved adjective in its place. To delete or move a block of text, first select it, and then use the mouse, keyboard, or ribbon commands to do the deed. Since selection is such a fundamental editing skill, Word gives you many different and new ways to do it, including the mini-toolbar (see Figure 2-5). If you've been dragging your mouse around for the past 20 years, you're lagging behind. This section shows you some timesaving selection techniques—with and without the mouse.

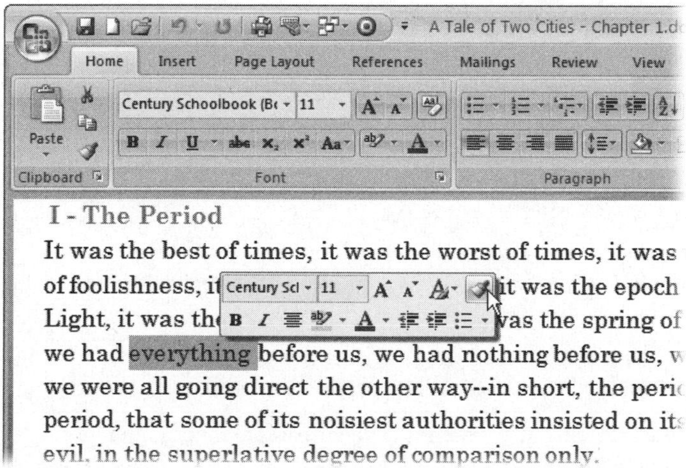

Figure 2-5:
As you make selections, you'll notice the mini-toolbar pops up occasionally. It's faint at first, but when you move the mouse toward the toolbar, it comes into focus, giving you easy access to the most often used formatting commands, including the format painter.

Selecting with the Mouse

The mouse is an easy, visual, intuitive way to make selections. It's the first way most people learn, and besides, it's right there on your desktop. Here's how to select various document parts using your mouse:

- **Select individual characters.** Click to place the insertion point at the beginning of the text you want to select. Press and hold the left mouse button and drag over the characters. As you drag, the characters you select are highlighted to indicate they're part of the selection (Figure 2-6).

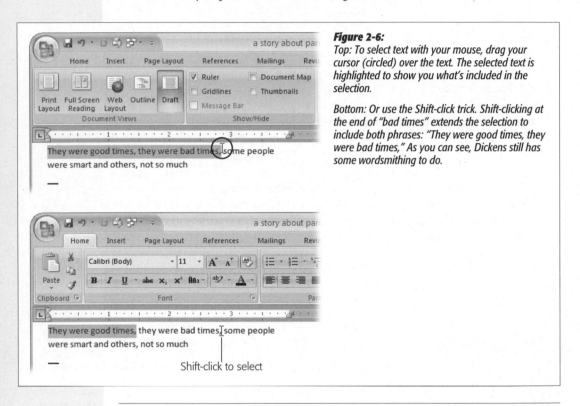

Figure 2-6:
Top: To select text with your mouse, drag your cursor (circled) over the text. The selected text is highlighted to show you what's included in the selection.

Bottom: Or use the Shift-click trick. Shift-clicking at the end of "bad times" extends the selection to include both phrases: "They were good times, they were bad times," As you can see, Dickens still has some wordsmithing to do.

Shift-click to select

Tip: Word doesn't care if you move forward or backward as you select text. It simply uses the point where you click as either the beginning or the ending point of the selection. These examples describe how to select text moving forward, but most of the techniques, including the keyboard techniques, work going backward too. Don't be afraid to experiment. Before you know it, you'll be proficient selecting text with both the mouse and the keyboard.

- **Select a word.** Double-click the word. The entire word's highlighted.

- **Select a sentence.** Ctrl-click the sentence. The entire sentence is highlighted.

- **Select a line of text.** Move the cursor into the left margin. The cursor changes to an arrow. Click right next to the line you want to select. The line's highlighted, showing that it's selected.

- **Select a whole paragraph.** Move the cursor into the left margin. When it changes into an arrow, double-click next to the paragraph. The entire paragraph is highlighted. To add more paragraphs, keep your finger on the mouse button and drag until the cursor points at another paragraph, and another…

- **Select a block of text.** Click to place the insertion point at the beginning of the block you want to select. (No need to keep pressing the mouse button.) Hold the Shift key down, and then click at the other end of the selection. The block of text is highlighted, and your wrist is happy. Everybody wins.

- **Select an entire document.** Move the cursor into the left margin, so that it changes into an arrow. Click the left mouse button three times. Your entire document's highlighted. (In other words, do the same thing as for selecting a paragraph, except you triple-click instead of double-click.)

Tip: This section focuses on selecting text, but the same techniques apply to tables and pictures, which Word handles as parts of your text.

Selecting with the Keyboard

When it comes to selecting fine details, like a single letter, the mouse can make you feel like you're trying to thread a needle with mittens on. And if you're a fast typist, taking your hands away from the keyboard to grasp the mouse causes a needless loss of time. Word nerds, in fact, do as much as possible from the keyboard, even selecting.

If you've never selected text using the keyboard before, prepare to be amazed:

- **Select individual characters.** Tap the arrow keys to place the insertion point on one end of the selection. Press the Shift key as you use the left or right arrow keys to highlight the characters you want to select.

- **Select a word.** Start with the insertion point at the beginning or end of the word. Press Ctrl+Shift+right arrow to select the word to the right or Ctrl+Shift+left arrow to select the word to the left. To select more words, just keep hitting the arrow key.

- **Select a sentence.** Put the insertion point at the beginning of the sentence. Press Shift+right arrow repeatedly until you reach the end of the sentence. (OK, so this method is a workaround. Word doesn't have a single keyboard command to select an entire sentence.)

- **Select to end of line.** Press Shift+End. Word highlights all the text from the insertion point to the end of line.

- **Select to beginning of line.** Press Shift+Home to select text from the insertion point to the beginning of the line.

- **Select a paragraph.** Place the insertion point at the beginning of the paragraph and press Ctrl+Shift+down arrow.

- **Select a block of text.** Click to place the insertion point at the beginning of your selection. Hold the Shift key down and use any of the arrow keys (up, down, left, and right) or navigation keys (Home, End, Page Up, and Page Down) to mark your selection.

- **Select an entire document.** Press Ctrl+A. (Think select All). Word highlights the entire document. You can also select the entire document by pressing the F8 key repeatedly. See the box on below.

Extending a Selection

What if you've selected some text and then realize you'd like to add a little bit more to your selection? You have a couple of options. The most common method: Extend your selection by Shift-clicking in your text, as shown previously in Figure 2-6. Word highlights the text between the previous selection and your Shift-click and includes it in the new selection.

A similar, but even more elegant way to extend a selection is with the F8 key. Pressing F8 sets one end of your selection at the insertion point. Click either forward or backward in your document, and everything in between the insertion point and your click is instantly highlighted and selected. F8 has several other surprising selection powers. See the box below for all the details.

POWER USERS' CLINIC

F8—The Selection Superhero

For an unassuming function key sitting there almost unused at the top of your keyboard, the F8 key has surprisingly powerful text selection skills. Pressing it helps you select much more than you can with any other single keystroke or mouse click.

- **Sticky selection end point.** Pressing F8 at the beginning of your intended selection makes any selection method you use stay "on" without your having to press any keys. Here's how it works: Put your insertion point at the beginning of where you want to start a selection. Press F8 once (don't hold it down), and then use the mouse or arrow keys to complete the selection. Look ma, no hands! Word makes the selection just as if you were pressing the Shift key while navigating to a new point.

- **Select a word.** Press F8 twice to select a whole word. Used this way, F8 works just like double-clicking the word.

- **Select a sentence.** Press F8 three times to select a sentence.

- **Select a paragraph.** Press F8 four times to select all the text in a paragraph.

- **Select an entire document.** Press F8 five times. Voila! The whole document is selected.

The F8 key with its sticky behavior keeps selecting text left and right until you turn it off. Press the Esc key to deactivate the F8 key's selection proclivities. Then you can once again move the insertion point without selecting text.

Selecting Multiple Chunks of Text in Different Places

If you're into efficiency and multitasking, Word's multiple selection feature was made for you. Multiple selections save you time by applying formatting to similar, but disconnected elements. Say you have several paragraphs of text and you decide you'd like to make the first sentence in each paragraph bold (Figure 2-7) for emphasis. After you select the sentences, you can format them all at once. You can also collect items from several locations and then copy and paste them into a new spot. See page 57 for more on cutting and pasting.

To make a multiple selection, simply make your first selection and then press the Ctrl key while you make another. The areas you select don't need to be connected.

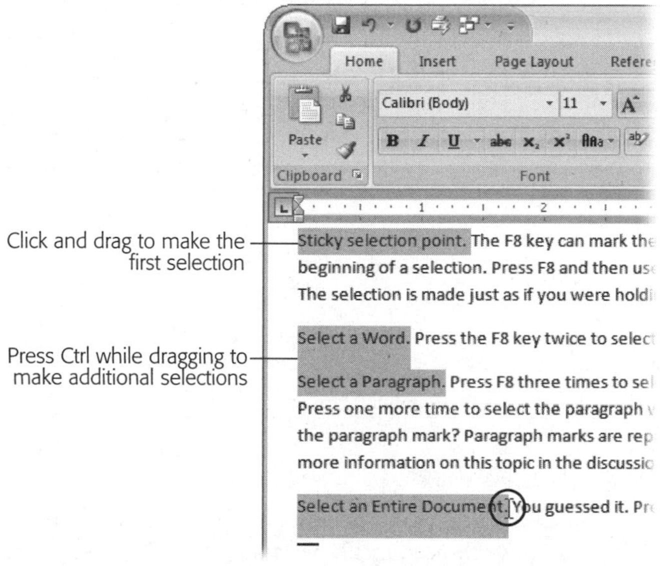

Click and drag to make the first selection

Press Ctrl while dragging to make additional selections

Figure 2-7:
By making multiple selections with the Ctrl key, you can do cool things like apply the same formatting to several disconnected words at once. For example, you can Ctrl-drag to select the first sentence in each paragraph, as shown here. The mouse cursor (circled) shows where the last drag ended. You can then make the sentences bold (Ctrl+B) for emphasis. (Find more on typeface formatting in Chapter 3.)

Tip: You can also use just about any of the selection techniques mentioned earlier in this section to add to the multiple selection. For example, when you want to add an entire paragraph to your selection, press Ctrl while you double-click in the left margin next to the paragraph.

So, here are the steps to follow for the example in Figure 2-7:

1. **Drag to select the first sentence in the first paragraph.**

   Word highlights the sentence to indicate it's selected.

2. **Press Ctrl, and keep holding it as you drag to select the first sentence in the *next* paragraph.**

   Word highlights each sentence you select but nothing in between. Repeat this step for each sentence you want to select.

3. **Press Ctrl+B.**

Word makes the selected sentences bold and leaves them highlighted. You can enter another command if you want—bold italics, anyone?

Moving Around Your Document

Using that nice blue scrollbar on the right side of your document is the most obvious way to navigate your document. And if your mouse has a wheel on it, then using it to scroll is pretty speedy too. But when your document's more than a few pages long, trying to scroll to the exact point you're looking for is just plain inefficient.

Word's most powerful ways of boogieing around your document don't involve scrolling at all. You can use the keyboard to hop from place to place. For really long documents, as with long journeys, the best way to get around is by using landmarks. For example, you can check all the graphics in a document by jumping directly from one to the next. Or you can go directly to a specific heading in a 400-page business report by telling Word to find it for you. You can even create your own landmarks using Word's bookmarking feature. Word's got the tools, and this section tells you how to use 'em.

Tip: If you're working with a large document, then Word has some other great ways to find your way around. You can use Outline view (View → Documents View → Outline) to easily navigate between chapter and section headings. The Document Map (View → Documents View → Document Map) shows a similar view in the bar along the left side of your document. If your pages include distinctive graphics, then the Thumbnail View (View → Show/Hide → Thumbnails) can help you find the spot you want by eye.

Keyboarding Around Your Document

You've heard it before: You lose time every time you take your hands off the keyboard to fumble for the mouse. For short jaunts especially, get in the habit of using these keyboard commands to move the insertion point:

- **Move left or right.** Left/right arrow keys.

- **Move to the beginning or the end of a line.** Home/End. (On most keyboards, these keys are just above the arrow keys. On most laptops, the Home and End keys are either along the right side or in the top-right corner.)

- **Move up or down a line.** Up/down arrow keys.

- **Move up or down a paragraph.** Ctrl+up/down arrow.

- **Move up or down one screenful of text.** Page up/down.

- **Move to the beginning or the end of a document.** Ctrl+Home/End.

Using the Scroll Bars

If you've used Word or any of the other Microsoft Office programs in the past, that skinny bar down the right side of your document should look familiar. In the center of the bar is a box that you drag to move up or down your document. The bar also has some arrow buttons at top and bottom for finer control (shown in Figure 2-8). Click the buttons to scroll just a line or two at a time. To cover big distances, click in the bar above or below the box, and the document scrolls one screen at a time.

Easier still, you can scroll without using the scroll bar at all; see Figures 2-9 and 2-10 for instructions.

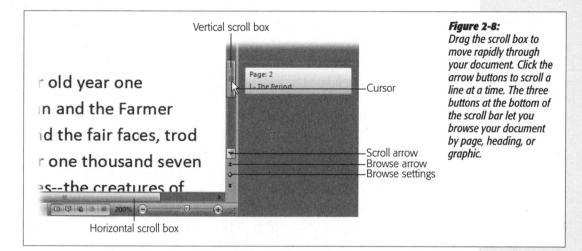

Vertical scroll box

r old year one

n and the Farmer

d the fair faces, trod

r one thousand seven

s--the creatures of

Horizontal scroll box

Page: 2
1 - The Period

Cursor

Scroll arrow
Browse arrow
Browse settings

Figure 2-8:
Drag the scroll box to move rapidly through your document. Click the arrow buttons to scroll a line at a time. The three buttons at the bottom of the scroll bar let you browse your document by page, heading, or graphic.

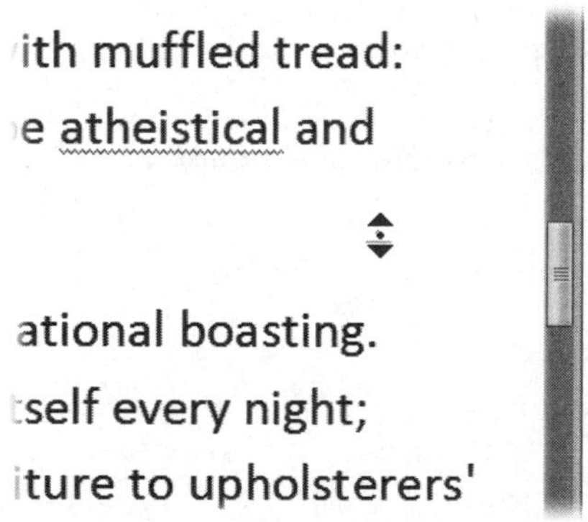

ith muffled tread:

e atheistical and

ational boasting.

self every night;

ture to upholsterers'

Figure 2-9:
Click the mouse wheel, and you see the scroll symbol shown here. When this symbol is present, you can scroll your document by moving the mouse cursor away from the symbol. Move your cursor down to start to scroll down. The further you move the cursor down the screen, the faster the document scrolls. Click the wheel button to stop the auto-scrolling.

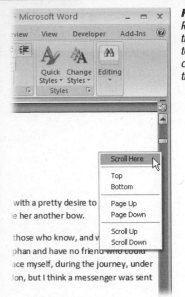

Figure 2-10:
Right-click the scroll bar, and you see a pop-up menu with navigation shortcuts. At the top of the list is Scroll Here, which is the equivalent of dragging the scroll box to the location you clicked on the scroll bar. (In previous versions of Word, you could Shift-click for the same result.) Other shortcuts take you to the beginning or the end of your document and scroll a line or a screenful at a time.

Browsing by Headings and Other Objects

For longer documents, the most interesting controls are at the bottom of the scroll bar: two double arrows separated by a round button. What makes these *Browse buttons* so handy is the fact that you can customize their behavior to match your needs. The round button puts you in control. Click it, and you see the Select Browse Settings menu (Figure 2-11).

Figure 2-11:
The Browse Settings menu lets you set the behavior of the Browse buttons and perform other useful navigation tasks. For example, you can set the buttons to browse by headings, pages, or even graphics within your document. These settings make the Browse buttons an extremely powerful navigation feature. It's a shame they're overlooked and underused.

At first, the icons in the "Browse by" toolbar may seem a little cryptic, but never fear, you can get help. Hold the cursor over the icons, and their function is explained in the text box at the top. The "Open the Go To box" and "Open the Find box" options open the dialog box where you can search for specific text and jump to a certain location in your document, as described later in this chapter (page 64). The rest of the options determine what happens when you click the double-arrow Browse buttons. For example, when you click Browse by Headings, clicking the Browse arrows then takes you forward (or back) through your document, jumping from one heading to the next and skipping everything in between.

As you learn to use more advanced features like end notes and comments, described later in this book, you'll find it very convenient to use them as your landmarks, as well.

Browsing by Bookmark

The bookmarks that slip between the pages of books are elegant in their simplicity, even decorative, but they're kind of primitive. They only do one thing—mark a point between two adjacent pages—and if they fall out, well then they don't do anything at all. Word's electronic bookmarks let you get much more specific. You can use them to mark the exact *word* where you left off. And since there's no limit on how many you can put in a document, you can use them to help organize a long document as you work your way through it. Bookmarks don't show up when you print the document; they're just reference points that let you jump instantly to places you want to return to most often.

Creating bookmarks

You can create as many bookmarks as you want in a document with just a few mouse clicks. Bookmarks are invisible in your documents, but that's just Word's factory setting. You can change your Word Options to show bookmarks in your text. (Maybe Microsoft turns them off because the bookmarks are sort of unattractive—they appear as brackets around the bookmarked text.)

To see bookmarks in your text, choose Office button → Word Options → Advanced. (The Word Options button is at the bottom of the Office menu, near the Exit button.) Scroll down to the options under "Show document content," and then turn on the "Show bookmarks" checkbox.

Here's how to insert a bookmark in your Word document:

1. **Select the text you want to bookmark.**

   The selected text is the location of the bookmark. If the text moves as you edit, the bookmark stays with the text.

   You can also create a bookmark without selecting text: Word simply places the bookmark at the insertion point. However, it's a little easier to keep track of your bookmarks if you select text.

2. **Go to Insert → Links → Bookmark.**

   The Bookmark dialog box opens (Figure 2-12).

3. **In the "Bookmark name" box, type a name for the bookmark.**

   Use a descriptive name, one that describes the location in the text, or perhaps the work you need to do at that spot. For example, if you're marking a place to come back and add something about guillotines, name it LaGuillotine.

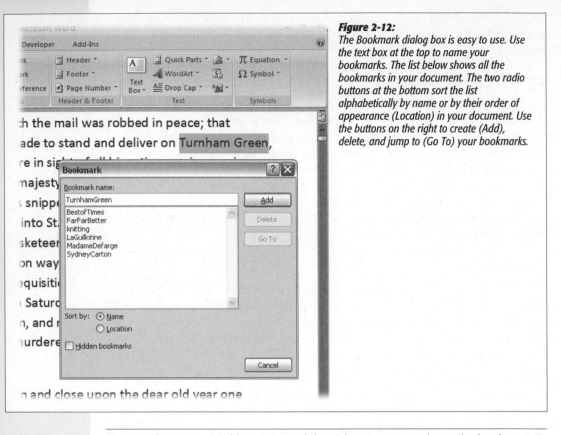

Note: For its own computerish reasons, Word doesn't let you use spaces in your bookmark name. To separate words, you can use dashes or underscores instead.

4. **Click Add.**

   When you click Add, the dialog box disappears, and your bookmark is set and ready for use.

Jumping to bookmarks

Using bookmarks is even easier than creating them. The quickest way to use a bookmark is to hit F5 key to bring up the Go To dialog box (Figure 2-13). From the "Go to what" list, select Bookmark. When you've done that, the drop-down list at right shows all the bookmarks in your document. Select one, and then click the Go To button. Your document scrolls to put the highlighted, bookmarked text at the top of your screen. Click Close to hide the dialog box. After you've searched for a bookmark, you can use the Browse buttons below the scroll bar to jump to other bookmarks.

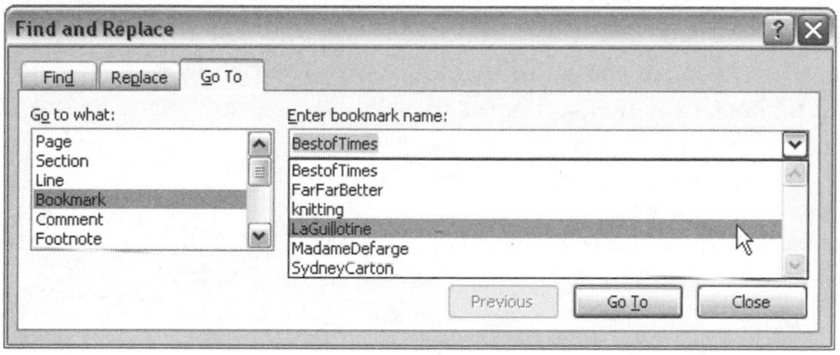

Figure 2-13:
Bookmarks are useful if you need to jump back and forth between different locations. To move to a bookmark, open the Go To dialog box (F5), and then select Bookmark from the list at left. The drop-down list at right lists all the bookmarks in your document. Simply choose one from the list.

Tip: The Find, Replace, and Go To dialog boxes have memory. While you're working in a document, it remembers the tab and list items you last used. So, if earlier you found a particular bookmark, then the next time you click Go To (or press F5), Word finds that same bookmark.

Deleting bookmarks

About the only reason you'd want to delete a bookmark is if your list's getting cluttered and it's hard to find the bookmark you want. In any case, it's easy to delete bookmarks using the same dialog box you use to create them (Figure 2-12). Just pick the soon-to-be-terminated bookmark from the list and click Delete. It's a goner.

Cutting, Copying, and Pasting

When it comes time to edit your text and shape it into a masterpiece of communication, the job is all about cutting, copying, and pasting. Compared to actually using scissors and paste (which is what writers and editors did in the pre-PC era), Word makes manipulating text almost effortless. You're free to experiment, moving words, sentences, and paragraphs around until you've got everything just right.

UP TO SPEED

The Many Paths to Go To

The Go To, Find, and Replace dialog boxes are actually three different tabs in the same window. You either open the dialog box directly to one of the tabs, or, if it's already open, then just click a tab at the top of the box. As usual, Microsoft provides many ways to open this particular box:

• **Home→Editing→Find.** Opens the Find tab.

• **Home→Editing→Replace.** Opens the Replace tab.

• **Home→Editing→Go To.** Opens the Go To tab.

• **Browse Settings button.** Click Browse Settings (the tiny circle in the window's lower-right corner, as shown in Figure 2-8), and then click the Go To (arrow) or Find (binoculars).

• **Ctrl+F.** Opens the Find tab.

• **Ctrl+H.** Opens the Replace tab.

• **Ctrl+G or F5.** Opens the Go To tab.

• **Double-click Status bar.** Double-clicking the status bar in the lower-left corner also opens the Go To tab.

By now, you've probably figured that most Word functions can be done in at least two ways—by keyboard and by mouse. That's certainly the case when it comes to the basic editing functions, as shown in the table. If you're typing away and don't want to take your hands off the keyboard, then you'll probably want to use the keyboard shortcuts, which can all be performed with a flick of your left hand.

Command	Ribbon Command	Ribbon Icon	Keyboard Shortcut
Cut	Home → Clipboard → Cut	Scissors	Ctrl+X
Copy	Home → Clipboard → Copy	2 pages	Ctrl+C
Paste	Home → Clipboard → Paste	Clipboard	Ctrl+V

Editing with the Ribbon

- Word's new ribbon is where all the commands live, and it's hardly a surprise that cut, copy, and paste are the first commands on the first tab (Home) in the first group (Clipboard). As you can see in Figure 2-14, these commands are conveniently located right near another place you frequently mouse over to, the Office button.

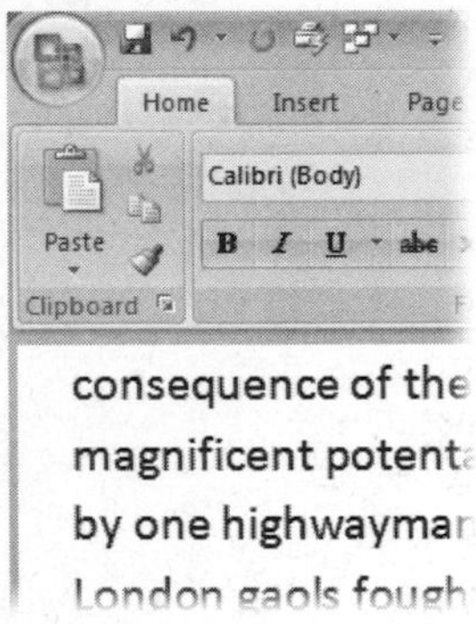

Figure 2-14:
The basic editing commands Cut, Copy, and Paste are easy to find. Go to Home → Clipboard, and there they are. As always, the first step is to select the text that you want to cut (scissors) or copy (two pages). Then, position the insertion point at the location where you want to paste (clipboard) the text.

Once you've found the commands, here's how to use 'em:

- **Cut (Home → Clipboard → Cut).** Just as described on page 46, you need to select text (or an object, like a picture or a table) before you can cut it from your document. When you invoke the Cut command, your selected item disappears, but Cut is very different from a Delete or a Clear command. The Cut command actually stores the cut item on the Office Clipboard, where you can bring it back later using the Paste command. You can actually open this Clipboard and see recently cut and copied items. The Office Clipboard works across all Microsoft Office programs, so you can cut a paragraph from your novel and paste it into an Outlook email or PowerPoint slide.

- **Copy** (**Home** → **Clipboard** → **Copy**). As you may expect, Copy makes a duplicate of the selected text or object and stores it on the Clipboard. It leaves the selection in place in its original location.

- **Paste** (**Home** → **Clipboard** → **Paste**). Before you use the Paste command, you must first cut or copy some text (or a picture or other object). Then, put the insertion point exactly where you want to place the item, and then paste away.

Note: See page 62 for more about working with Word's Clipboard.

Editing with Keyboard Shortcuts

The keyboard shortcuts are the quickest and easiest editing commands to use as you're typing along, because you don't need to take your hands off the keyboard. You can use the Cut, Copy, and Paste commands with only a couple fingers of the left hand. These shortcuts use the Ctrl key in combination with nearby keys on the bottom row—X, C, and V. As an added bonus, the adjacent Z key is used for the Undo command—another oft-used editor's tool. These keys perform the exact same functions as the ones run when you use the ribbon commands using Word's ribbon:

- **Cut.** Ctrl+X.

- **Copy.** Ctrl+C.

- **Paste.** Ctrl+V.

- **Undo.** Ctrl+Z.

Editing with the Mouse

After Cut, Copy, and Paste, the next great leap forward for writers and editors was the *graphical user interface* (GUI) and the ability to use a mouse to drag and drop text. After all, most of editing is deleting unneeded words and pushing the others around into the most effective positions. With a mouse, you can really see what you're doing: Take *this* and drag it over *there*.

But some people are never satisfied. And lo and behold, Microsoft added a right mouse button. When you right-click, you get a pop-up menu that includes Cut, Copy, Paste, and other commands, right where you need them (Figure 2-15). The pop-up menu contains only the most common commands, to save you a trip all the way up to that ribbon. To get to more advanced commands (like line spacing or alphabetic sorting), you do have to use the ribbon.

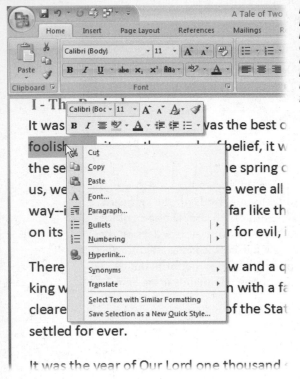

Figure 2-15:
Right-click in your text to display the Edit shortcut menu. If you've selected text, you can use the Cut and Copy commands. Word 2007 adds a slew of additional commands, including language translation, hyperlink creation, and formatting options. As an added bonus, you see the mini-toolbar with formatting commands above the edit commands.

It's easy to drag and drop text to a new location using just your mouse. Take your hands off the keyboard, lean back in your chair, grab the mouse, and follow these steps:

1. **Click (the left mouse button) and drag to select the text that you want to relocate.**

   Word highlights the text to show you what you've selected. Let go of the mouse button when you're done.

2. **Click the selected text and, holding down the mouse button, drag the mouse to the new location for the text.**

   As shown in Figure 2-16 (top), a little rectangle below the cursor means you're dragging something. As you move the mouse, the insertion point follows, marking where the moved text will appear.

3. **Release the mouse button.**

   Releasing the mouse button finishes the job, placing the moved text at the insertion point, as shown in Figure 2-16 (bottom).

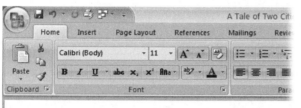

Figure 2-16:
Gutenberg would be amazed at how easy it is to reset type with Word.

Top: Select the text you want to move, and then point to it and click. Continue to hold the left mouse button while you drag the text to a new location.

Bottom: When you release the mouse button, Word plops the text into the new location.

Moving Text Between Two Documents

Moving text from one document to another isn't much different from moving it from place to place within a document. You can use keyboard or ribbon commands to cut and paste, or you can drag and drop between documents (Figure 2-17). In fact, it's just as easy to move text between documents created by different programs. For example, you can cut or copy text in Word and paste it into documents created in Outlook, PowerPoint, Access, Excel, and many non-Microsoft programs, too. Even the same keyboard shortcuts do the trick: Ctrl+X (Cut), Ctrl+C (Copy), and Ctrl+V (Paste). Of course, you can also use menu commands if you insist.

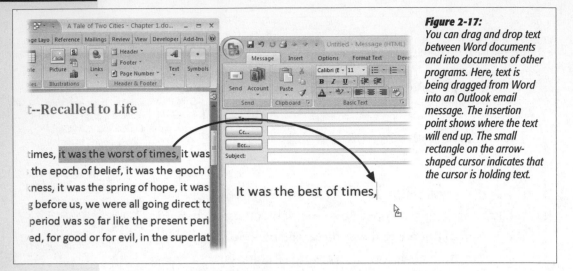

Figure 2-17:
You can drag and drop text between Word documents and into documents of other programs. Here, text is being dragged from Word into an Outlook email message. The insertion point shows where the text will end up. The small rectangle on the arrow-shaped cursor indicates that the cursor is holding text.

Viewing and Pasting Clippings

More often than not, when you cut or copy text, a picture, or an object, you want to paste it into a new location right away. But what if you wanted to copy several items and paste them into the same location? Or, what if you want to again paste an item that you copied several edits ago? Enter the Office Clipboard. The Clipboard's nothing new to Microsoft Office programs, but the 2007 version gives this familiar tool a new look (Figure 2-18). As you cut and copy text, graphics, and other objects, Word (or whatever Office program you're in) stashes them here for reuse. The Clipboard lets you view the stored items and lets you paste them into other documents with just a click or two.

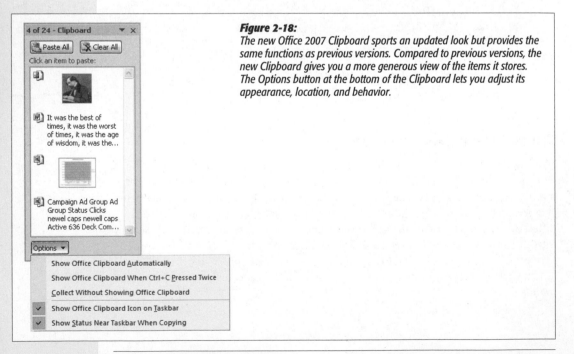

Figure 2-18:
The new Office 2007 Clipboard sports an updated look but provides the same functions as previous versions. Compared to previous versions, the new Clipboard gives you a more generous view of the items it stores. The Options button at the bottom of the Clipboard lets you adjust its appearance, location, and behavior.

Your most recent cut items or copied items appear at the top of the Clipboard and move down as you add more. When you use the Paste command (Ctrl+V), Word is simply pasting the item at the top of the Clipboard at the insertion point. That's what happens whether the Clipboard is open or closed. To paste a different item instead of the most recent, just place the insertion point where you want it, and then click that item on the Clipboard, as shown in Figure 2-19.

Figure 2-19:
Use the Office Clipboard to paste text, graphics, and other objects into your documents. Unlike the Cut and Paste commands, the Clipboard isn't limited to the last item you cut or copied. You can choose from an appetizing menu of words and images that you recently edited. Deleting removes the item from the Clipboard.

Working with the Clipboard Task Pane

Open the Clipboard task pane by clicking the launcher in the lower-right corner of the Clipboard group (Home → Clipboard). (You find it in exactly the same spot in Access, Excel, and PowerPoint.) With the Clipboard task pane open, you see all the items you recently cut or copied. Click an item to paste it into your Word document at the insertion point. Or, if you want, you can switch to another program (Alt+Tab) and paste it there. Point to an item on the Clipboard, and you see a drop-down menu with two options: Paste and Delete. It's easier to simply click to paste an item, but Delete gives you a handy way to clean up the Clipboard contents before you use the Paste All command. The Paste All and Clear All buttons are at the top of the Clipboard task pane.

The Options menu (at bottom) is where you fine-tune the Clipboard's behavior:

- **Show Office Clipboard Automatically.** Turn on this option to have the Clipboard appear whenever you copy an item.

- **Show Office Clipboard when Ctrl+C Pressed Twice.** This option works easily as you're typing. Press Ctrl+C once to copy selected text; press Ctrl+C a second time, and you see the Clipboard.

- **Show Office Clipboard Icon on Taskbar.** With this option selected, the Office Clipboard appears in the Taskbar in the lower-right corner of your screen.

- **Show Status Near Taskbar when Copying.** Each time you cut or copy an item, a screen tip appears near the Taskbar detailing how many items are on the Clipboard.

But wait—the Clipboard's coolness is just getting warmed up. Not only can you see multiple pasteable items, you can paste them in bunches too. The Clipboard acts as a collection palette. For example, suppose you've created a dinner menu for your restaurant in Word, and you want to create a new lunch menu that includes just a few of the items from the dinner menu. Follow these steps to collect and paste those tasty morsels into a new document:

1. **With the source document open in front of you (in this case, the dinner menu), go to Home → Clipboard, and then click the small square next to the Clipboard group label.**

   This square, with an arrow in the lower-right corner, is called the Clipboard *launcher*, and its job is to open and close the Clipboard. Initially, the Clipboard opens in a panel on the left side of the window, but you can drag it from that location and use it like a freestanding palette.

2. **At the top of the Clipboard, click Clear All to remove any previously copied items.**

   If you've been working on other projects, there may be items already on your Clipboard, including those from other Office programs. Since you probably don't want all that stuff on your lunch menu, clear the decks with the Clear All button.

Note: Clippings stay on the Office Clipboard until you clear them—or until you exit all Microsoft Office programs (Word, Outlook, Excel, and PowerPoint).

---

3. **Copy (Ctrl+C) the entrees, side dishes, and beverages you want to put on the lunch menu.**

   Use any of the methods described in this chapter to find, select, and copy the items. As you copy each item, Word adds it to the clipboard.

4. **Open a new document (Office button → New → Blank) to use as your lunch menu.**

   A new Word window opens, but notice that you still have access to the Clipboard with all your copied menu entries.

5. **Click Paste All.**

   When you click Paste All, the Clipboard's entire contents appear in your new document. (Now all you need to do is figure out the lunch prices.)

Finding and Replacing Text

Scanning every word of your 400-page novel to find the exact spot where you first mentioned Madame DeFarge is drudgery with a capital D. Fortunately, Word performs this task quickly and without whining or demanding overtime pay. What's more, it's just as easy to find and then replace text. Suppose you decide to change the name of the character from Madame DeFarge to Madame de Stael.

Simple—here's how to do a Find and Replace:

1. **Open the Find and Replace dialog box (Figure 2-20). For example, press Ctrl+H.**

   You have many ways to open the Find and Replace dialog box, as explained in the box on page 57. If your hands are on the keyboard, then Ctrl+H is the fastest.

   When the dialog box opens, you see tabs at the top for each of the panels: Find, Replace, and Go To. The controls and options under the Find and Replace tabs are nearly identical. The main difference is that the Replace tab includes *two* text boxes—"Replace with" as well as "Find what."

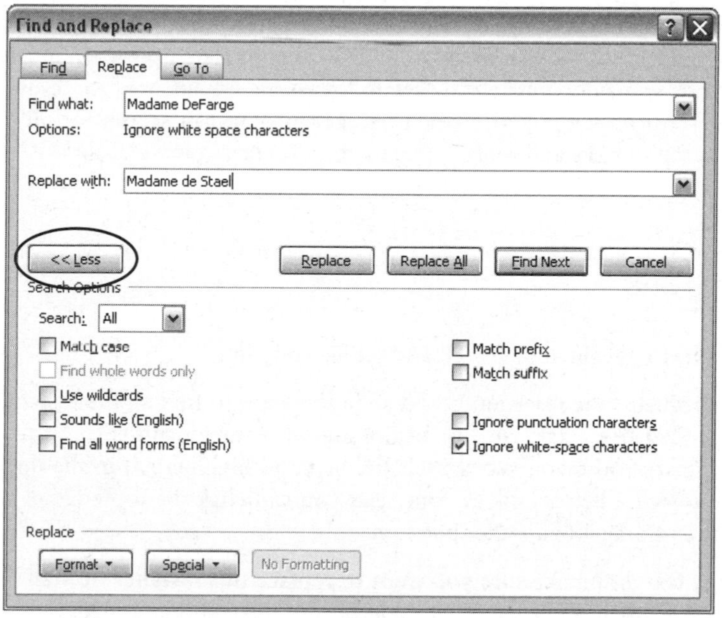

Figure 2-20:
Initially, the Replace box is pretty simple, but when you click More, you see a number of options for fine-tuning your search. (And the More button turns into a Less button, as shown here.) The box on page 67 explains all the Search options in detail.

2. **In the "Find what" box, type the text you want to find, and, in the "Replace with" box, type the replacement text.**

   For example, type *Madame DeFarge* in "Find what" and *Madame de Stael* in "Replace with."

Note: The "Find what" is a drop-down box that remembers your past searches. So the next time you go to this box, Madame DeFarge will be there waiting for you.

---

3. **If you wish, click More to reveal additional Find options.**

When you click More, the box expands, and you see a number of additional controls that can fine-tune your search. For example, if you're searching for "Madame DeFarge" but you don't know how it's capitalized, then make sure the Match Case checkbox is turned off. That way, Word finds every occurrence even if you didn't capitalize it the same way throughout. For an explanation of all the Search options, see the box on page 67.

The Format button at the bottom of the screen lets you refine your search by including formatting details. For instance, you can limit your search to a specific paragraph style such as Heading 1.

The Special button at the bottom of the box helps you find characters that aren't easy to enter with your keyboard, like paragraph marks, column breaks, and em dashes. These sound like odd things to search for, but they're enormously helpful when you're reformatting a document. For example, imagine someone sends you a document and they followed the odious practice of using two carriage returns at the end of each paragraph. You can search for all the double paragraph marks and replace them with a single paragraph mark. Problem solved.

Tip: A better way to leave extra space between paragraphs is to include it in the paragraph formatting itself. See page 81 for details.

---

4. **Click Find Next to begin your search and replace mission.**

The search begins at the insertion point, so if you want to find all the instances of Madame DeFarge, start at the beginning of your document. A quick Ctrl+Home takes you there. Word finds the text and highlights it in the document. If you need a better look at your text, you can click the top edge of the Replace box and drag it to another position.

5. **Examine the text and make sure you want to replace this instance of Madame DeFarge with Madame de Stael. Click Replace, and the text is swapped.**

Word automatically finds the next instance of your search text.

6. **If you're certain that you want to replace every instance of Madame DeFarge, click Replace All.**

Word makes all the changes and reports back with the number of replacements it made.

Search Options Explained

Computers are dumb. They don't know that, if you type *bird* in the Find dialog box, you're looking for flying things, not some Mr. Birdley. So Microsoft gives you the Find and Replace dialog boxes with some options to help you make them smarter. Here's what the options do when you turn on their checkboxes:

- **Match case.** Find shows you only words that exactly match the uppercase and lowercase letters of your search entry. So, *DeFarge* finds "DeFarge" but not "defarge."

- **Find whole words only.** Find only shows you complete words that match your entry. For example, if you enter *some*, the search shows you the word "some" but not the word "somewhere."

- **Use wildcards.** Wild cards let you expand your search. For example, ^? is the wildcard that matches any character. A search for ^?*ill* returns the words "will," "bill," "kill," "dill," and so forth.

- **Sounds like.** Finds words that sound like your entry. (Consider this help for the spelling-impaired.) If, say, you enter *inglund*, then Word finds "England."

- **Find all word forms.** Type *is*, and Word finds "was," "were," and "being."

- **Match prefix.** Finds characters at the beginning of a word, so *re* finds "reason" but not "are." (In this option and the next, Word doesn't consider prefix and suffix in a grammatical sense; it's just looking for the beginning and the ending of words.)

- **Match suffix.** Use this option to find characters at the end of a word. For example, *ed* finds "mashed" but not "eddy."

- **Ignore punctuation characters.** Word doesn't include periods, commas, hyphens, apostrophes, and other punctuation marks when it makes a match. For example, *coachlamps* finds coach-lamps.

- **Ignore white-space characters.** Word leaves paragraph marks, spaces, tabs, and other nonprinting, "space" characters out of the search. In this case, *coachlamps* finds "coach lamps."

Saving Keystrokes with Quick Parts

Suppose your company has an extremely long name and an even longer address (complete with nine-digit Zip code). Now say you type in the name and address about three times an hour. Wouldn't it be great to just type *address* and have Word fill in the whole shebang? That's exactly the kind of magic you can do with Word 2007's Quick Parts feature. You can have Word memorize whole chunks of text, and then spit them back out when you type an abbreviation word followed by the F3 key.

Quick Parts evolved from the AutoText feature found in earlier versions of Word. AutoText was one of the program's most overlooked and underused features. Quick Parts work like this: You store text, graphics, or anything else you've created in Word in a Quick Part and give it a name, preferably something short and memorable. When you want to retrieve the Quick Part, simply type that name, and then press F3. Word replaces the name with the entire contents of the Quick Part. Few keystrokes, mucho text.

Here are step-by-step instructions for creating a new Quick Part:

1. **Select the text you want to save as a Quick Part.**

   Your selection can include text, pictures, and other objects that Office recognizes. There's virtually no size limit. You can even use an entire document as a Quick Part (like a rejection letter that you send out every day).

2. **Use Alt+F3 to open the Create New Building Block dialog box (Figure 2-21).**

   The Alt+F3 keyboard shortcut's the quickest route to creating a new Quick Part Building Block. (And, after all, speed's the name of the Quick Part game.) You see six boxes in the Create New Building Block dialog box, but the first one, Name, is the most important.

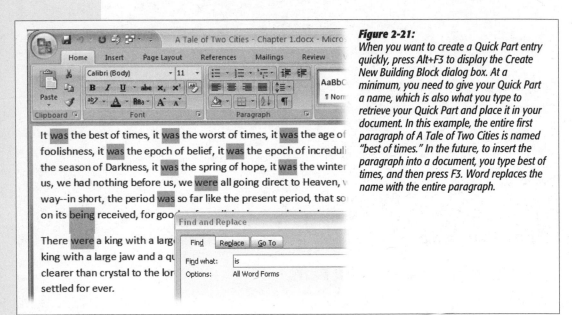

Figure 2-21:
When you want to create a Quick Part entry quickly, press Alt+F3 to display the Create New Building Block dialog box. At a minimum, you need to give your Quick Part a name, which is also what you type to retrieve your Quick Part and place it in your document. In this example, the entire first paragraph of A Tale of Two Cities is named "best of times." In the future, to insert the paragraph into a document, you type best of times, and then press F3. Word replaces the name with the entire paragraph.

3. **Give your Quick Part a Name.**

   Think carefully when you type a name for your Quick Part, because the name is the key you use to retrieve the Quick Part. The name can be as short or as long as you want. For speed's sake, shorter is better, but you don't want to make it so cryptic you can't remember it.

4. **Type a Description and, if you wish, choose a Category for your Quick Part.**

   A description is optional, but it's helpful for other people who use Word, or even for you, a couple of years down the road. And if you create a lot of Quick Parts, then you may find it helpful to store them in different categories as a way to organize them. For example, you can create a Help Desk category with answers to frequently asked questions and a Contracts category with a legal boilerplate.

Tip: You can use the Gallery drop-down menu to store your entry as something other than a Quick Part. For example, you could store it as a Cover Page or as a Bibliography.

---

5. **Leave the "Save in" drop-down menu set to Building Blocks.dotx.**

   The Quick Part is saved in Building Blocks.dotx, a Word template that's available to any document. You can find more information about using templates on page 137.

6. **From the Options menu, choose how you want the text to appear every time you press F3.**

   The first option, "Insert content only," is a good one to use if you plan to use the Quick Part within paragraphs. The second option, "Insert content in its own paragraph," works well for address blocks or entire paragraphs, such as the answers to frequently asked questions. The last option, "Insert content in its own page," is a logical choice for a memo or other text that rightfully belongs on its own.

CHAPTER 3

Formatting Text, Paragraphs, and Headings

Formatting is the fine art of making your documents effective and attractive. Good formatting distinguishes different parts of your text and helps your readers take in your message. You can apply formatting to just about every element of your document, from a single character to entire paragraphs. Body text needs to be readable and easy on the eyes. Headings should be big and bold, and they should also be consistent throughout your document. Important words need to resonate with emphasis. Quotes and references should be set off from the other text.

This chapter starts with the basics: how to format individual characters and words—selecting fonts and making characters bold, italicized, underlined, or capitalized. You learn how to format paragraphs with indents and spacing, and how to control the way Word breaks up the words in a line and the lines in a paragraph. Finally, you find out how to copy and reuse formatting with tools like the Format Painter and style sets.

Formatting Basics

Word deals with formatting on three levels encompassing small and specific on up to big and broad—through characters, paragraphs, and sections. You apply different types of formatting to each of these parts. Character formatting includes selecting a font, a font size, bold or italics, and so on. At the paragraph level, you apply indents, bullets, and line spacing. For each section of your document (even if there's only one), you set the page size, orientation, and margins, as described in the previous chapter. Sometimes it helps to think of the parts of a document as Russian nesting dolls: Characters go inside paragraphs, which go inside sections, which fit inside your document.

Each type of formatting has its own dialog box, giving you access to all possible settings. You can also apply most types of formatting via the ribbon, the mini-toolbar, or the keyboard shortcut.

- **Characters.** Use the Font dialog box (Alt+H, FN) to format characters. Letters, numbers, and punctuation marks are all printable characters and, as such, you can format them. Once you select a character or a group of characters, you can apply any of the formatting commands on the Home tab's Font group (Alt+H). You can choose a font and a size for any character in your document. You can make characters bold, underlined, superscript, or change them to just about any color of the rainbow.

Note: Prior to the use of computers, groups of letters, numbers, and punctuation of a certain style, such as Helvetica or Bodoni, were called *typefaces*. The term *font* was more specific, referring to variations within a typeface such as bold, narrow, or italic. Today, the terms are interchangeable. Word uses the term *font*, probably because it's shorter and therefore easier to fit into a dialog box.

- **Paragraphs.** Use the Paragraph dialog box (Alt+H, PG) to format paragraphs. You can set formatting for text alignment, indents, line spacing, line breaks, and paragraph breaks. You don't have to select a paragraph to format it; just click to place the insertion point within a paragraph. Because characters are part of paragraphs (remember those Russian nesting dolls), every paragraph includes a basic font description. When you select characters within a paragraph and change the font settings, you override the basic font description in the paragraph's style.

- **Sections.** Use the Page Setup dialog box (Alt+P, SP) to format sections. When you change margins, page orientation, page size, and the number of columns per page (all described in Chapter 4), you're formatting the section. Many documents have only one section, so when you make formatting changes to a section, you're actually formatting the entire document.

Formatting Characters

Every character in your document is formatted. The formatting describes the typeface, the size of the character, the color, and whether or not the character is underlined, bold, or capitalized. It's easy to change the formatting, and Word gives you quite a few different ways to do it. The easiest and most visual way is with the ribbon (Home → Font). You can further fine-tune the font formatting using the Font dialog box (Alt+H, FN).

For quick formatting, you may not need to go any further than the mini-toolbar that pops up when you select text for formatting. And when you get really good, you can do most of your formatting with keyboard shortcuts, never even slowing down long enough to reach for the mouse.

Whichever method you use, formatting is a two-step process. First, tell Word which text you want to format by selecting it. Then format away. Or, you can set up your formatting options first, and then begin to type. Your letters and words will be beautifully formatted from the get-go.

Formatting with the Ribbon or the Font Dialog Box

Since character formatting is one of the most often used Word features, Microsoft put the most popular settings right on the Home tab. If you don't see what you're looking for there, then you must open the Font dialog box. The good thing about the dialog box is that it puts all your character formatting options in one place so you can quickly make multiple changes. It's one-stop shopping if you want to change the typeface and the size, and add that pink double-underline.

Here are the steps:

1. **Select a group of characters, as shown in Figure 3-1.**

   You can use any of the selection methods described in Chapter 2. You can drag to select a single character. You can double-click to select a word. Or you can move the mouse cursor to the left side of a paragraph, and then double-click to select the whole paragraph.

   Of course, if you haven't typed anything yet, you can always go right to the ribbon and make your formatting choices first. Then type away.

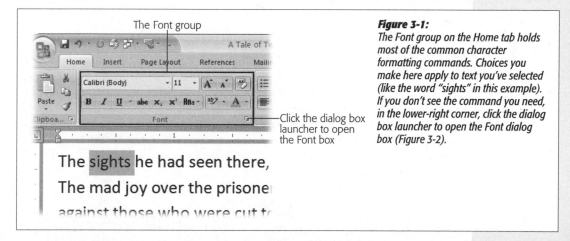

The Font group

Click the dialog box launcher to open the Font box

Figure 3-1:
The Font group on the Home tab holds most of the common character formatting commands. Choices you make here apply to text you've selected (like the word "sights" in this example). If you don't see the command you need, in the lower-right corner, click the dialog box launcher to open the Font dialog box (Figure 3-2).

2. **Go to Home → Font or the Font dialog box (click the little launcher button shown in Figure 3-1 or press Alt+H, FN) and make your formatting choices.**

   Many of the buttons in the Font group act like toggles. So, when you select text and click the underline button, Word underlines all the characters in the selection. When you click the underline button again, the underline goes away.

If you can't find the command you want on the ribbon, or if you want to make several character formatting changes at once, open the Font box (Figure 3-2).

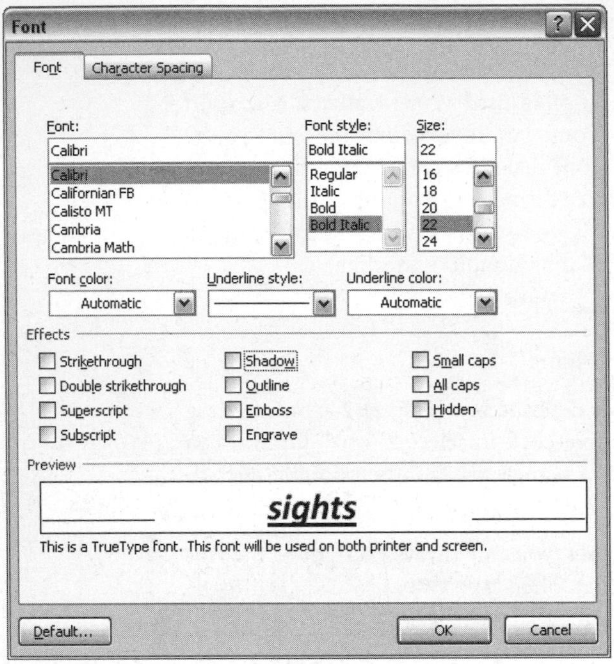

Figure 3-2:
Open the Font box (Alt+H+FN) to change the typeface, style, size, color, and other effects. Like many dialog boxes, the Font box gives you access to more commands than you find on the ribbon.

Formatting with the Mini-Toolbar

Word's mini-toolbar isn't quite as much fun as your hotel room's mini-bar, but there are times when you'll be glad it's there. A new feature in Word 2007, the mini-toolbar pops up after you've selected text (Figure 3-3). It's faint at first, but if you move your mouse toward it, the mini-toolbar comes into focus showing commands, most of which are character formatting commands. Just click one of the buttons to format your selection (or move your mouse away from the toolbar if you want it to go away).

Formatting with Keyboard Shortcuts

When you're typing away and the muses are moving you, it's a lot easier to hit Ctrl+I to italicize a word than it is to take your hands off the keyboard and grab a mouse. Because most formatting commands work like toggles, formatting options like bold, underline, and italics become second nature. For example, to italicize a word, just press Ctrl+I at the beginning, type the word, and then press Ctrl+I at the end. Table 3-1 is your cheat sheet to every character formatting shortcut known to Word.

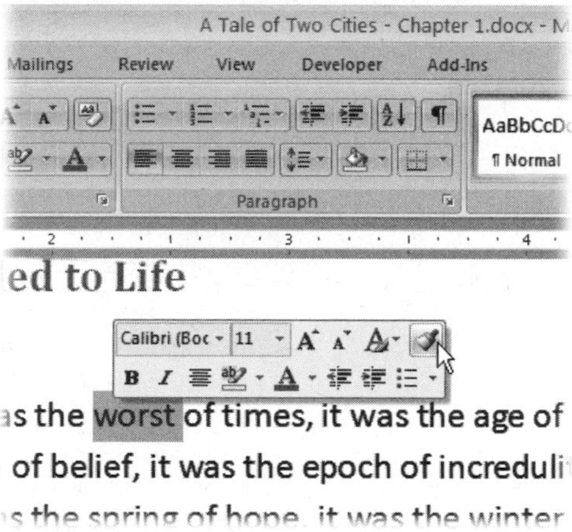

Figure 3-3:
The mini-toolbar gives you access to the most commonly used commands. It just so happens that most of these commands are character formatting commands.

Table 3-1. As a result of Word's evolution, most formatting commands have more than one keyboard shortcut. A new set of keyboard shortcuts is part of the reorganization that came up with Word 2007's new ribbon feature. But if commands like Ctrl+B for bold and Ctrl+U for underline are permanently burned into your brain, don't worry: Those commands from previous versions still work just fine.

Command	Keyboard Shortcut	Old Keyboard Shortcut	Description
Font	Alt+H, FF, arrow keys, Enter	Ctrl+D, arrow keys, Enter	Alt+H, FF selects the font drop-down menu; use the arrow keys to highlight the font; press Enter to finish the selection.
Font Size	Alt+H, FS, arrow keys, Enter	Ctrl+Shift+P, arrow keys, Enter	Alt+H, FS selects the font size drop-down menu; use the arrow keys to highlight the size; press Enter to finish the selection.
Increase Font Size	Alt+H, FG	Ctrl+>	Increases font size.
Decrease Font Size	Alt+H, FK	Ctrl+<	Decreases font size.
Bold	Alt+H,1	Ctrl+B	Toggles bold on and off.
Italic	Alt+H,2	Ctrl+I	Toggles italics on and off.
Underline	Alt+H, 3, Enter	Ctrl+U	Toggles underline on and off.
Double underline	Alt+H, 3, down arrow, Enter	Ctrl+Shift+D	Toggles double underline on and off.
Underline style	Alt+H, 3, arrow keys		Alt+H, 3 selects the underline style drop-down menu; use the arrow keys to highlight the style; press Enter to finish the selection.

Command	Keyboard Shortcut	Old Keyboard Shortcut	Description
Strikethrough	Alt+H, 4		Toggles strikethrough on and off.
Subscript	Alt+H, 5	Ctrl+=	Toggles subscript on and off.
Superscript	Alt+H, 6	Ctrl++	Toggles superscript on and off.
Change Case	Alt+H, 7, arrow keys	Shift+F3	Toggles through five case options: sentence case, lowercase, uppercase, capitalize each word, toggle case.
Color	Alt+H, FC, arrow keys, Enter		Alt+H, FS FC selects the font color drop-down menu; use the arrow keys to highlight the color; press Enter to finish the selection.
Highlight Text	Alt+H, I, Enter		Alt+H, I selects the highlight drop-down menu; Enter highlights the selection.
Clear formatting	Alt+H, E	Ctrl+Spacebar	Removes text formatting from the selection.

NOSTALGIA CORNER

Where's the Animated Type?

In what may be an unprecedented move, Microsoft actually *reduced* the number of text formatting options in Word 2007. Fortunately, the defunct feature is something most folks won't miss—animated type. In Word 2003, Alt+O, FX opened the Effects panel on the Font dialog box. There you found such animated effects as Blinking Background, Las Vegas Lights, Marching Black Ants, Marching Red Ants, Shimmer, and Sparkle. (Microsoft intended these effects for use on Web sites, of course, not on printed documents.)

Presumably, the general public had good enough taste to shun these annoying type effects, and Microsoft dropped them due to disuse.

In any case, if you absolutely must have red marching ants dancing around the perimeter of your letters, the only way to enlist them is to cut and paste preformatted text from an older version of Word.

Changing Capitalization

Any letter can be uppercase or lowercase, but when you get to words and sentences, you find some variations on the theme. It's not unusual to have a heading or a company name where all the letters are capitalized. Sentences start with an initial cap on the first word only, and titles usually have the major words capped. In an effort to automate anything that can possibly be automated, Microsoft provides the Change Case menu (Alt+H, 7) on the ribbon (Figure 3-4).

The Change Case command defies the usual rules about selecting before you apply character formatting. If you don't select anything, Word assumes you want to

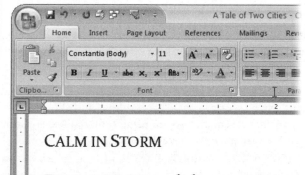

apply the Change Case command to an entire word, so the program selects the word at the insertion point. If you've selected text, the command works, as you'd expect, only on the selection.

Small caps for headers

Small caps (Figure 3-5) are another variation on the capitalization theme. You won't find this option on the Change Case button; for small caps you have to use the Font dialog box, which you find on the right side under Effects (where underline or strikethrough are). Small caps are great for headings and letterhead (especially if you're a lawyer or an accountant), but you wouldn't want to use them for body text. It's difficult to read all capitalized text for an entire paragraph.

Figure 3-5:
Small caps are a great way to distinguish a heading or subheading from body text, like the words "Calm in Storm." Initial letters get full-sized capitals while the letters that would normally be lowercase get small capitals.

Formatting Paragraphs

Formatting a paragraph usually entails changing its shape. You may be squeezing it in with indents or stretching it out with additional line spacing. Other kinds of formatting change a paragraph's very nature, like adding a border or making it part of a numbered or bulleted list. The Paragraph formatting group (Home → Paragraph) is right next door to the Font group (Figure 3-6). You don't need to *select* text to format a paragraph; just make sure the insertion point is in the paragraph you want to format. However, if you want to format several paragraphs at once, select them all before you apply a command.

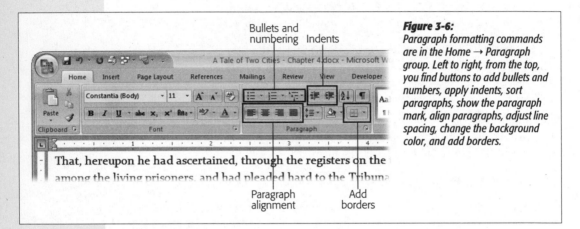

Figure 3-6:
Paragraph formatting commands are in the Home → Paragraph group. Left to right, from the top, you find buttons to add bullets and numbers, apply indents, sort paragraphs, show the paragraph mark, align paragraphs, adjust line spacing, change the background color, and add borders.

Aligning Text

It's easy to apply alignment to text. With your insertion point in the paragraph you want to change, click one of the alignment buttons in the Paragraph group on the Home Tab. For example, Home → Paragraph → Left sets the current paragraph's alignment. As shown in Figure 3-7, you have four choices when it comes to aligning your paragraphs:

- **Left (Alt+H, AL).** Aligns the lines in the paragraph flush on the left side and ragged on the right. Left alignment is standard for letters, reports, and many business documents.

- **Centered (Alt+H, AC).** Centers each line in the paragraph, leaving both left and right margins ragged. This setting is appropriate for headings and short chunks of text, as in invitations and advertisements. Avoid using centered text for long paragraphs, since it's hard for readers' eyes to track from the end of one line to the beginning of the next when the left margin is uneven.

- **Right (Alt+H, AR).** Aligns the lines in the paragraph flush on the right side and ragged on the left. This unusual alignment is most often used for setting captions or quotations apart from the main text.

- **Justified (Alt+H, AJ).** Adds space between letters and words so that both the left and right sides of the paragraph are straight and flush with the margins. Justified margins give text a more formal look suitable for textbooks or scholarly documents. If your justified text looks odd because big gaps appear between the letters or words, try using a long line—that is, putting more characters per line. You can do this by extending the margins (Alt+P, M) or by changing the size of your font (Alt+H, FS).

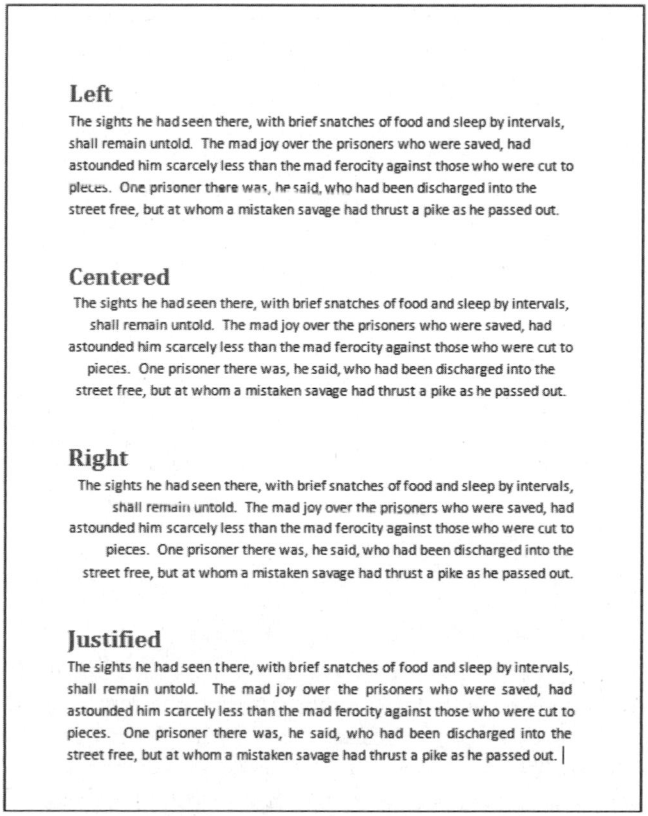

Left

The sights he had seen there, with brief snatches of food and sleep by intervals, shall remain untold. The mad joy over the prisoners who were saved, had astounded him scarcely less than the mad ferocity against those who were cut to pieces. One prisoner there was, he said, who had been discharged into the street free, but at whom a mistaken savage had thrust a pike as he passed out.

Centered

The sights he had seen there, with brief snatches of food and sleep by intervals, shall remain untold. The mad joy over the prisoners who were saved, had astounded him scarcely less than the mad ferocity against those who were cut to pieces. One prisoner there was, he said, who had been discharged into the street free, but at whom a mistaken savage had thrust a pike as he passed out.

Right

The sights he had seen there, with brief snatches of food and sleep by intervals, shall remain untold. The mad joy over the prisoners who were saved, had astounded him scarcely less than the mad ferocity against those who were cut to pieces. One prisoner there was, he said, who had been discharged into the street free, but at whom a mistaken savage had thrust a pike as he passed out.

Justified

The sights he had seen there, with brief snatches of food and sleep by intervals, shall remain untold. The mad joy over the prisoners who were saved, had astounded him scarcely less than the mad ferocity against those who were cut to pieces. One prisoner there was, he said, who had been discharged into the street free, but at whom a mistaken savage had thrust a pike as he passed out.

Figure 3-7:
Set the alignment of your paragraphs using the buttons on the ribbon. Four settings are available: Left, Centered, Right, and Justified.

Indenting Paragraphs

One of the most common reasons for indenting a paragraph is to set off quoted text from the rest of the document. Usually, you move the paragraph's left edge in about a half inch from the left margin. Word makes it easy to indent text in this way. Just use the Increase Indent button on the ribbon (shown back in Figure 3-6) or the shortcut Alt+H, AI. If you change your mind and want to remove the indent, use the companion command Decrease Indent (Alt+H, AO).

The ribbon buttons handle most everyday indentation chores, but what if you need to customize your indents? To do that, open the Paragraph dialog box to the Indents and Spacing tab (Alt+H, PG), and you see the Indentation tools in the middle of the tab (Figure 3-8).

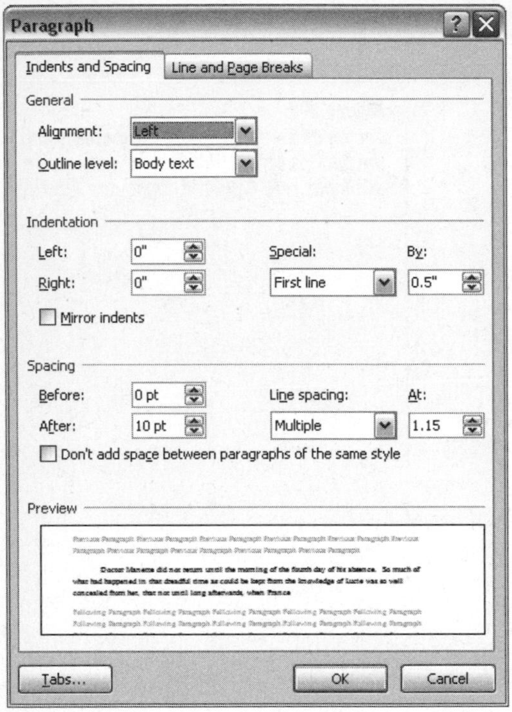

Figure 3-8:
The Paragraph box is divided into four sections. From the top you see: General, Indentation, Spacing, and Preview. As you adjust your paragraph formatting using tools from the first three groups, you see the changes take place in an example paragraph in the Preview window.

The indentation tools in the Paragraph box let you set indents with much more precision than the simple Increase and Decrease buttons. For one thing, you can indent your paragraph from both margins using the Left and Right text boxes. Type a number in the box or use the arrow buttons to make an adjustment. Look in the Preview window at bottom to get a sense of the changes you're making.

Novels, short stories, and other manuscripts often indent the first line of each paragraph. To set up this format, click the Special drop-down menu, and then choose "First line." Type a number, in inches, in the By box on the right. A quarter inch (.25") is usually an attractive first-line indent.

Tip: By the way, don't hit Tab to create a first-line indent. For one thing, it creates an amateurish, typewriter-like half-inch indent. And you lose all the benefits of paragraph formatting. For example, when you press Enter to start a new paragraph, Word automatically carries your settings forward, with a perfect first-line indent just like the paragraph above. If you use the Tab key, you have to remember to hit it at the beginning of every paragraph, and there's the danger of messing up your indents if you change the tab settings (page 87).

For the reverse of the "First line" indent, choose the hanging indent where the first line extends to the left margin, while the rest of the paragraph is indented the amount shown in the By box. This kind of indentation makes great looking glossaries, bibliographies, and such.

Spacing Between Paragraphs

For documents like business letters or reports that use block-style paragraphs, there's usually a little space between each. You can adjust this spacing between paragraphs to set off some blocks of text from the rest.

Use the Paragraph dialog box (Figure 3-8) to adjust the distance between paragraphs. On the left, you can enter numbers to set the space before the paragraph and the space after. With body text paragraphs, it's good to set the same, relatively small distance before and after—say, three points. For headers, you may want to put a little extra space before the header to distance it from the preceding text. That space makes it clear that the header is related to the text beneath it. Generally speaking, the more significant the header, the larger the type and the greater the spacing around it.

Spacing Between Lines

In the Paragraph box, to the right of the paragraph spacing controls, you find the "Line spacing" tools. Use these controls to set the distance between lines *within* paragraphs. You have three presets and three custom settings:

- **Single** keeps the lines close together, with a minimum amount of space between. Single spacing is usually easy to read, and it sure saves paper.

- **1.5 lines** gives your text a little more breathing room, and still offers a nice professional look.

- **Double** is the option preferred by teachers and editors, so there's plenty of room for their helpful comments.

- **At least** is a good option if you have a mix of font sizes or include inline graphics with your text. This option ensures that everything fits, as Figure 3-9 illustrates.

- **Exactly** puts you in control. Type a number in the At box, and Word won't mess with that setting.

- **Multiple** is the oddball of the bunch. Think of Multiple as a percentage of a single line space: 1=100 Percent; .8=80 percent; 1.2=120 Percent; and so on.

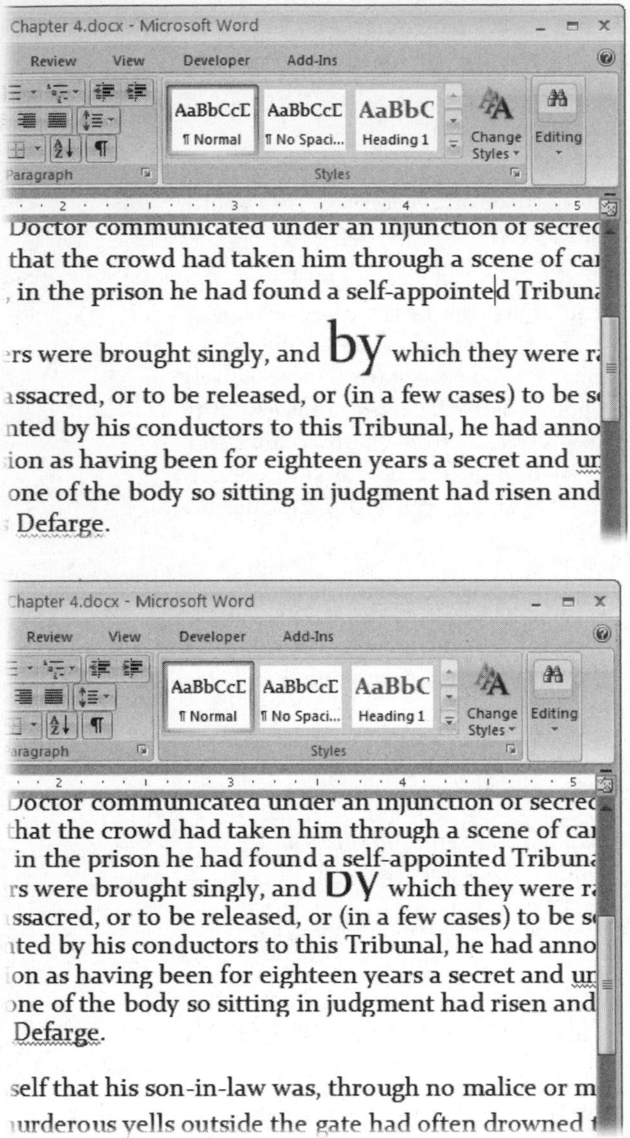

Figure 3-9:
Line spacing controls the space between lines within a paragraph. These examples show the same paragraph, with two different settings. All the type is set to 11 points except for the word "by," which is 24-point type.

Top: Using the "At least" option with 12 points entered in the At box (see Figure 3-8), this setting adjusts so that the oversized word fits.

Bottom: Selecting Exactly from the "Line spacing" drop-down menu with 12 points in the At box, the b and y get clipped off.

Inserting Page Breaks and Line Breaks

Some things just look wrong, such as a heading at the bottom of a page with no text beneath it. That heading should be at the top of the next page. Sure, you could force it over there with a page break (Ctrl+Enter), but that can cause trouble if you edit your text and things move around. You could end up with a page break in some weird spot. The solution is to adjust your Line and Page Break settings so that headings and paragraphs behave the way you want them to.

On the Paragraph box's Line and Page Breaks tab (Figure 3-10), you can adjust how paragraphs handle these breaks. The behavior becomes part of the paragraph's formatting and travels with the text no matter where you move the text or breaks. The keyboard shortcut to get there is Alt+H, PG, Alt+P. You can use four settings:

- **Widow/Orphan control.** Single lines abandoned at the top (widows) or bottom (orphans) of the page look out of place. Turn on this checkbox, and Word keeps the whole family, er, *paragraph* together.

- **Keep with next.** Certain paragraphs, like headings, need to stay attached to the paragraph that comes immediately after them. Choose the "Keep with next" option for your headings, and they always appear above following paragraph.

- **Keep lines together.** Sometimes you have a paragraph that shouldn't be split between two pages, like a one-paragraph quote or disclaimer. Use this option to keep the paragraph as one unit.

- **Page break before.** Use this command with major headings to make sure new sections of your document start on a new page.

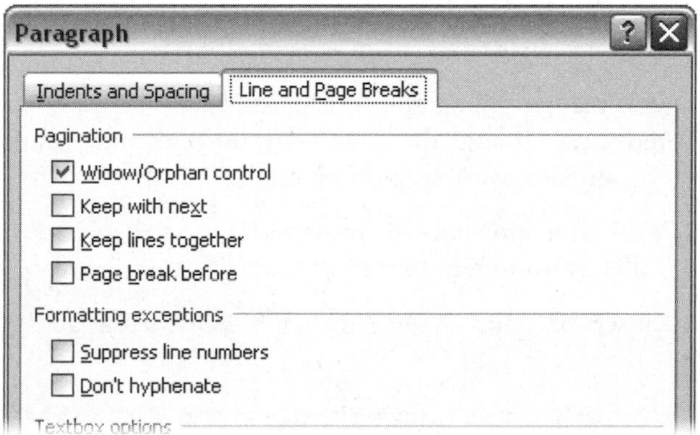

Figure 3-10:
Use the Line and Page Break settings to control the appearance of your text and to avoid awkward transitions between pages.

Creating Bulleted and Numbered Lists

Bullets and numbers add impact and help organize information. The bullets in the previous section call attention to the Line and Page Breaks commands and show that the commands are related to each other. Numbered paragraphs send a different signal, implying that the items listed are sequential or have a hierarchy. This book uses numbered paragraphs for step-by-step instructions. Meeting minutes are usually numbered, both as a point of reference and to indicate the order of the meeting's events.

Like the other paragraph formatting options, you don't have to select a paragraph to format it. It's enough just to have the insertion point in the paragraph. When using bullets or numbers, you usually want to format more than one paragraph. To do that, make a selection, and then click the bullet or number button.

Bulleted paragraphs

It's easy to turn an ordinary paragraph into a bulleted paragraph—Word does all the heavy lifting for you. You may spend more time choosing a bullet style than applying it.

Here's how to create a bulleted list:

1. **Go to Home → Paragraph, and then click the triangle next to the Bullet button to open the Bullets menu (or press Alt+H, U).**

   At the top of the menu (Figure 3-11), you see bullet styles that you used recently. In the middle, you see your Bullet Library. The bottom section shows bullet styles that have already been used in the document. At the very bottom are two commands for customizing bullets.

2. **On the Bullets menu, click to choose a bullet style.**

   When you click a bullet to apply that style to the paragraph, a couple of things happen. Word adds the bullet and automatically formats the paragraph with a hanging indent (page 81), so that the first line of the paragraph extends farther to the left than the other lines. The bullet appears in this overhang, calling attention to the bullet and setting off the paragraph from the other body text.

3. **Type some text, and then press Enter to start a new paragraph.**

   When you hit Enter to create a new paragraph, Word assumes that you're continuing with your bulleted list, so it adds the same bullet and indent automatically. You don't have to do anything; just keep on writing.

4. **When you're through with your bulleted list, press Enter, and then click the Home → Paragraph → Bullet button again to turn off bullet formatting.**

   The paragraph with the insertion point changes from a bulleted paragraph to a normal paragraph.

If you have a few paragraphs that you've already written, and you want to change them to bulleted paragraphs, just select all the paragraphs, and then click the Bullet button.

Customizing bullets

You don't have to settle for the bullets shown on the menu—Word has more choices tucked away. You can even use your own graphics for bullets, like a miniaturized version of your company logo. To explore the Bullet options available to you, open the Bullet menu (Alt+H, U), and then, at the bottom of the menu, click Define New Bullet. The Define New Bullet Box opens, showing you three buttons at the top: Symbol, Picture, and Font. Use the Symbol to browse through additional bullet options that are built into Word's type libraries. Use the Font button to apply character styles to your choice such as font size, shadow, or bold formatting.

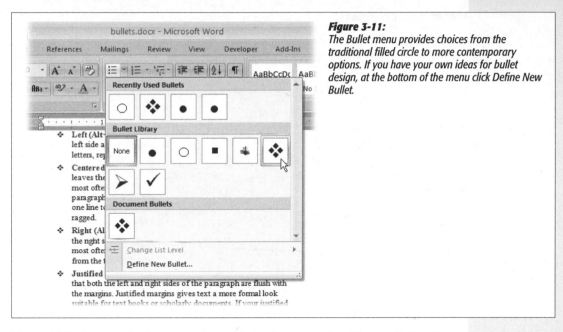

Figure 3-11:
The Bullet menu provides choices from the traditional filled circle to more contemporary options. If you have your own ideas for bullet design, at the bottom of the menu click Define New Bullet.

The middle button is the most interesting—it opens the Picture Bullet box (Figure 3-12) where you see a whole slew of bullets based on picture files.

These files are the same sort used for drawings and photographs, with filename extensions like .jpg, .gif, .pct, and .emf. In addition to these dozens of bullet options, you can use your own picture or graphic files as bullets. Just click the Import button at the bottom-left corner to open the Add Clips to Organizer box. Use this Windows file box to select any picture on your computer and add it to your bullet library.

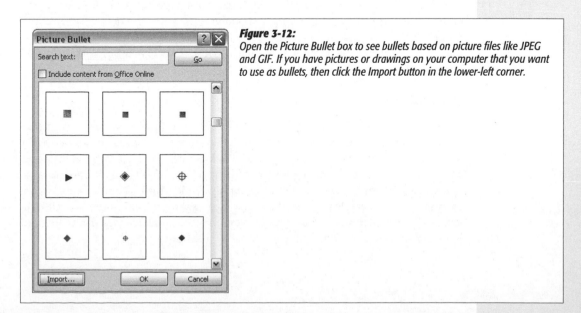

Figure 3-12:
Open the Picture Bullet box to see bullets based on picture files like JPEG and GIF. If you have pictures or drawings on your computer that you want to use as bullets, then click the Import button in the lower-left corner.

Numbered paragraphs

In most cases, numbered paragraphs work just like bulleted paragraphs. You can follow the step-by-step instructions in the previous section for making bulleted paragraphs to make numbered paragraphs. Just click the Numbering button, and then choose a number style (Figure 3-13).

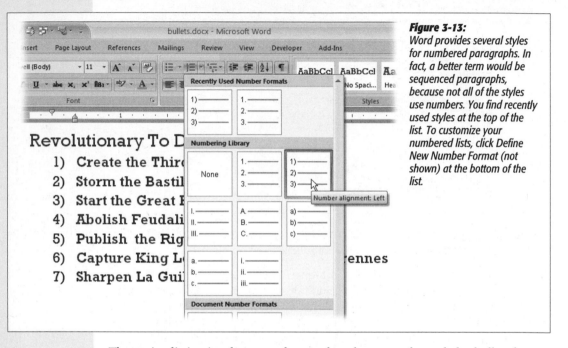

Figure 3-13:
Word provides several styles for numbered paragraphs. In fact, a better term would be sequenced paragraphs, because not all of the styles use numbers. You find recently used styles at the top of the list. To customize your numbered lists, click Define New Number Format (not shown) at the bottom of the list.

The main distinction between the numbered paragraphs and the bulleted paragraphs is in the options. For numbered paragraphs, you can choose from Arabic numbers, Roman numerals, numbers set off by parentheses, and alphabetic sequences. You can even use words such as One, Two, Three, or First, Second, Third.

Multilevel lists

Multilevel lists are a more advanced numbering format. They help you create project and document outlines, as well as legal documents divided into articles and sections. In a multilevel list, each new level is indented (nudged to the right), and usually each new level has a new number format (Figure 3-14). In addition to outline and legal numbering, multilevel lists can use bullets instead of numbers. So for example, you can create a bulleted list that uses squares for level one, triangles for level two, and circles for level three. If you choose a bulleted multilevel list, the lines within the levels aren't sequenced; they're just bulleted.

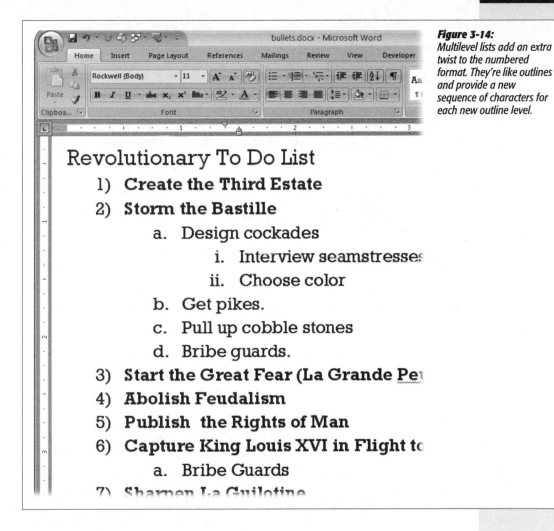

Figure 3-14:
Multilevel lists add an extra twist to the numbered format. They're like outlines and provide a new sequence of characters for each new outline level.

Setting Tabs

The lowly Tab key contains more power than you may think. Sure, you can use the Tab key to scoot the insertion point across the page in half-inch increments. But Word's tab tool is capable of much loftier feats: You can use it to design a dinner menu, create a playbill, or develop a series of consistently formatted reports.

Tab stops are all about precision alignment, giving you control over the way you present text and numbers to your readers. For example, on your dinner menu you can use *tab leaders* (dotted lines like the ones in this book's table of contents) so that your reader's eye tracks from Wild Salmon to the exceptionally reasonable price you're asking. Once you have settings you like, you can save and reuse them. (How's that for efficiency?)

Before you start working with tabs, you need to know a few basic terms:

- **Tabs.** Technically considered *tab characters*, tabs are hidden formatting characters, similar to space characters. Tabs are embedded in your document's text.

- **Tab stops.** These paragraph settings define the position and characteristics of tabs in your document. Think of tab stops as definitions, describing your tabs. To define them, you use Word tools, like the Ruler or the Tabs dialog box.

- **Tab key.** The key on your computer keyboard that inserts tabs into your text.

Press the Tab key, and Word inserts a tab in the text at that point. The tab character makes the insertion point jump left to right and stop at the first tab stop it reaches. If you haven't set any new tab stops, Word uses the built-in set of tab stops—one every half inch across the width—that every new, blank document starts out with.

How Tab Stops Work

Tab stop settings apply to paragraphs. If a paragraph has several lines, the tab stops are the same for all the lines within that paragraph. If you haven't deliberately set tab stops, Word provides built-in tab stops at half-inch intervals. These stops are left tab stops, meaning the text aligns on the left side. You can see all tab stops on the horizontal ruler—they show as small vertical tick marks in the gray area below the number scale (Figure 3-15).

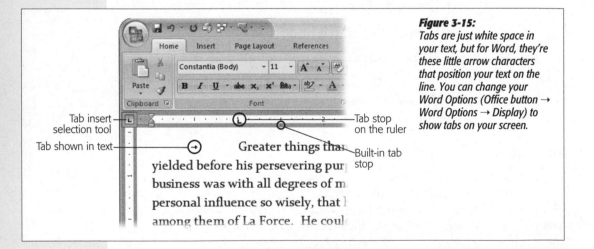

Figure 3-15:
Tabs are just white space in your text, but for Word, they're these little arrow characters that position your text on the line. You can change your Word Options (Office button → Word Options → Display) to show tabs on your screen.

Tab insert selection tool
Tab shown in text
Tab stop on the ruler
Built-in tab stop

Tip: If you don't see tab stops in the ruler, click within a paragraph. Remember, tab stops are paragraph settings, so your insertion point must be in a paragraph to see them.

Viewing Tab Marks in Your Text

Tabs are invisible on the printed page, like spaces or paragraph marks. Sometimes, when your document behaves unexpectedly, it helps to reveal the hidden characters so you can see if tabs are the culprit. After all, when they're hidden, all you see is white space on the page. However, spaces, tabs, and indents each behave quite differently.

To view tabs within your text:

1. **Choose Office button → Word Options to open the Word Options dialog box (Figure 3-16).**

   The Word Options button is at the bottom of the Office menu.

2. **On the left side of the Word Options box, choose the Display option.**

   The panel on the right is divided into three parts. The top section shows page display options, the middle section shows formatting marks, and the bottom section holds printing options.

3. **In the middle group, turn on the "Tab characters" checkbox to make your tabs visible.**

   An icon next to this checkbox shows you the symbol for tab characters. This mark shows up on your computer screen but not in printed text.

4. **Click OK to save the settings and close the dialog box.**

   The box closes and you see the tabs as small arrows in your text.

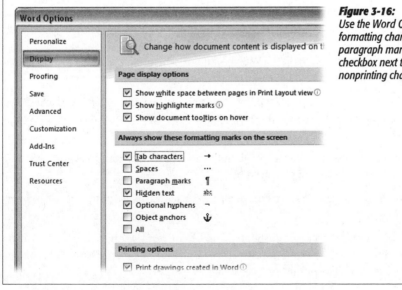

Figure 3-16:
Use the Word Options box to reveal formatting characters like tabs, spaces, and paragraph marks. When you turn on the checkbox next to the mark, you see these nonprinting characters on your screen.

Deleting and Editing Tabs

Because tabs are characters within your document, you can delete, copy, and paste them, just as you would any other character or text fragment. Maybe you want to delete a tab; just click immediately after a tab character, and then press the Backspace key. You can also use the Tabs box (Figure 3-17) to control tabs.

With tabs, you can use almost any editing trick that you'd use on other characters. You can select and drag a tab to a different place in your text. You can use shortcut keys, such as Ctrl+X to cut a tab and Ctrl+V to paste it someplace else. (All of these activities are much, much easier when you've set your Word Options to view tab marks as described previously.)

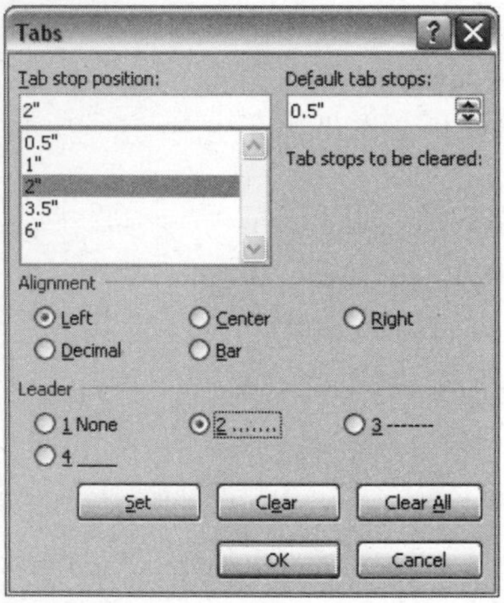

Figure 3-17:
The Tabs box puts you in complete control of all things tabular. When you select a specific tab in the upper-left box, you can customize its alignment and leader characters.

Types of Tabs

Five types of tabs are available in Word—one of which isn't a true tab but works well with the others:

- **Left tab.** The most common type of tab, it aligns text at the left side; text flows from the tab stop to the right. When you start a new, blank document, Word provides left tabs every half inch.

- **Center tab.** Keeps text centered at the tab stop. Text extends evenly left and right with the tab stop in the middle.

- **Right tab.** Aligns text to the right. Text flows backwards from the tab stop, from right to left.

- **Decimal tab.** Used to align numbers, whether or not they have decimals. Numbers align with the decimal point centered on the tab stop. Numbers without decimal points align similar to a right tab.

- **Bar tab.** The Bar tab is the oddball of the group and, no, it has nothing to do with your local watering hole. It also has nothing to do with aligning text. It inserts a vertical bar in your text as a divider. The bar appears in every line in the paragraph. This tab stop ignores tabs inserted in your text and behaves in the same manner whether or not tab characters are present.

Note: There may be a certain Microsoftian logic in grouping the Bar tab with the tab feature, but Word provides other ways to place vertical lines on your pages that you may find more intuitive. You can use Insert → Insert Shapes → More and choose the line for free-form lines. Or you can use borders for paragraphs or tables.

Tab Leaders

Tab leaders help readers connect the dots by providing a trail from one tabbed item to the next. They're ideal for creating professional-looking menus, playbills, and more. As visual aids, leaders are quite helpful, and they work equally well for text and numbers.

Here are some examples:

```
Hamlet, Prince of Denmark..........Sir Laurence Olivier
Ophelia, daughter to Polonius.......Roseanne Barr
```

Four Leader options can be used with each type of tab stop except the bar tab:

```
None No leader here
Dotted........................... You've seen this before
Dashed_ _ _ _ _ _ _ _ _ _ _ _ _ _ For a different, intermittent look
Underline_____ When only a solid line will do
```

Using Word's Rulers

If you're visually oriented, you may prefer the ruler for futzing with tab stops, page margins, and indents. Two rulers are available—horizontal and vertical. The horizontal ruler appears at the top of the page, giving you quick access to your tab, indent, and margin settings. To make the rulers visible, press Alt+W, R, or click the View Ruler button at the top of the right-hand scroll bar (Figure 3-18).

Tip: The ruler marks off your page in the measuring units of your choice. The factory setting uses inches, but if you want to make changes, you can do that in Word Options. Go to Office button → Word Options → Advanced. Scroll down to the group under Display, and then change the drop-down menu labeled "Show measurements in units of" to your preferred units of measurement.

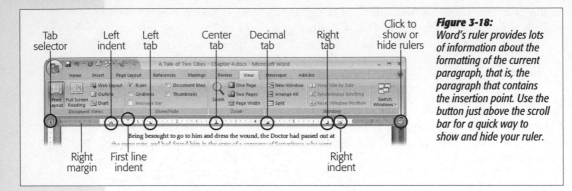

Figure 3-18:
Word's ruler provides lots of information about the formatting of the current paragraph, that is, the paragraph that contains the insertion point. Use the button just above the scroll bar for a quick way to show and hide your ruler.

Managing Tab Settings with the Ruler

In Figure 3-18, the ruler measures the page in inches. The grayed areas at both ends of the ruler indicate the page margins. The numbers on the ruler mark the distance from the left margin in both directions, left and right. Note the number 1, at the left edge of the page in Figure 3-18.

Setting tab stops

Word's every-half-inch tab stops can work for many of your documents, but sooner or later, you may need to put a tab stop in a different place or change its style. No problem—it's easy enough to do with the ruler.

Setting a new tab stop is a two-step process:

1. **Using the selection box to the left of the ruler, choose the type of tab you want.**

   The icon in this box shows what kind of tab you're about to apply—Left, Center, Right, Decimal, or Bar. When you hold your cursor over the box for a second or two, a little screen tip appears describing the formatting option. Click the box to cycle through the tab stop and indent options.

2. **Once you've selected the tab type you want, click the ruler to position the tab.**

   Click the point on the ruler where you want to place the tab stop. An icon appears on the ruler showing the position and the type of tab stop.

Tip: If you find the tab icons a little confusing, here's some help: Think of the vertical line as the tab stop and the horizontal line at the bottom as the direction your text flows. For example, the Left tab icon is L shaped, indicating that text flows to the right, away from the tab stop. The Center tab icon has the vertical line in the middle.

You can add an almost limitless number of tab stops—one for every tick mark on the ruler. If you need greater precision, use the Tab dialog box described on page 90. Setting a tab stop removes all the built-in tab stops to its left, but the ones to the right remain.

Adjusting and removing tab stops with the ruler

If a tab stop isn't exactly where you want it, you don't have to delete it—just drag it to a new position on the ruler. If you wish to remove a tab stop, drag it up or down off the ruler, and it disappears. When you make these changes, your document shows the consequences. Any tabs in your text shift over to the next readily available tab stop, which can be a built-in tab stop or one that you've set.

Setting Margins with the Ruler

You can always use the Page Layout tools (Page Layout → Page Setup → Margins or Alt+P, M) to set your margins with a click of the mouse, but for visual control, nothing beats the ruler (Figure 3-19). The lighter part of the ruler shows the text area, and the darker part shows your margins. Making adjustments is simply a matter of clicking and dragging the margin to a new location. Keep in mind that changing your margin affects the entire document section; more often than not, that means it affects the entire document because many documents are a single section. (For more details on working with sections, see page 125.)

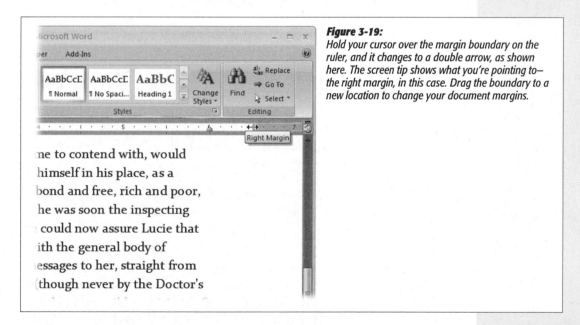

Figure 3-19:
Hold your cursor over the margin boundary on the ruler, and it changes to a double arrow, as shown here. The screen tip shows what you're pointing to—the right margin, in this case. Drag the boundary to a new location to change your document margins.

Tip: To avoid confusion, remember that indents are used to change the width of a single paragraph, while margins are used to change the paragraph width for an entire section or document.

Adjusting Paragraph Indents with the Ruler

Using the ruler to adjust indentation is similar to changing margins. It's just a matter of clicking and dragging. Indents are bit more complicated because you have a few more options, and that means more tools and widgets (Figure 3-20).

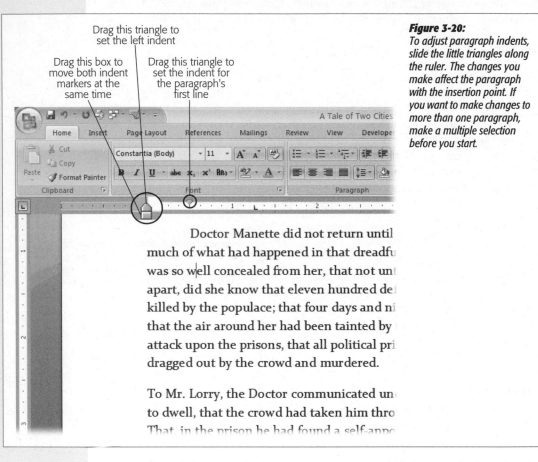

Figure 3-20:
To adjust paragraph indents, slide the little triangles along the ruler. The changes you make affect the paragraph with the insertion point. If you want to make changes to more than one paragraph, make a multiple selection before you start.

It can take awhile to get used to adjusting paragraph indents with the ruler. For one thing, you need a steady hand and accurate clicking to zero in on those little triangle buttons. The top triangle sets the first line indent and moves independently. The bottom triangle creates a hanging indent, and you can move it independently too, as long as you grab only that triangle. That little box below the triangle is your left indent, and if you drag it, both it and the top (first line) indent marker move together.

Fast Formatting with Format Painter

Whether it's a special heading or a paragraph of text, formatting a paragraph just the way you want it is a lot of work. Once you have the margins, indents, and tabs in place, and you've got the font style and size set, you've invested a chunk of time in the project.

Fortunately, you can capitalize on that investment. The Format Painter works like magic. You can use it to copy the formatting of a word, heading, or paragraph onto something else. You don't have to worry about any of the formatting details. You don't even need to *know* how something is formatted, so long as you like the way it looks.

Here's how it works:

1. **Select the character or paragraph with the formatting that you want to copy.**

   You can copy and paint either the character or the paragraph formatting. If you want to copy just text formatting (font, size, text color, and so on), select a few letters or a word with that formatting, not the whole paragraph. Selecting an entire paragraph, complete with the paragraph mark at the end, copies both the character formatting and the paragraph formatting. If you don't select anything, the Format Painter uses the formatting from the current paragraph, so to copy paragraph formatting alone (for example, tabs and indents), just click anywhere in the paragraph.

2. **Go to Home → Clipboard and click the Format Painter button, or just press Alt+H, FP.**

   Your cursor acquires a tiny paintbrush icon. If you have only one quick change to make, just click the Format Painter once. However, if you want to copy the same formatting to several different locations, double-click the Format Painter. When you double-click, the button stays locked down, indicating that it will stay on and let you paint multiple times until you're ready to stop.

3. **Drag the Format Painter over the text or paragraph that you want to change.**

   Here's the fun part. Like magic, your selection takes on all the formatting that you copied. If you double-clicked for multiple format painting, you can keep on dragging over text or clicking paragraphs. When you're through, hit Esc. The Format Painter button pops back up, and your cursor changes back to its normal I-beam appearance.

Formatting with Styles

Like the Format Painter, Word's styles are great time-savers because they let you apply a whole bunch of formatting commands in one fell swoop. Unlike Format Painter, Word's styles are permanent repositories of formatting information that you can always apply with one click. So, if you've discovered or created the perfect style (formatting) for a heading, you can apply that same style to headings today, tomorrow, or a week from tomorrow.

Microsoft provides sets of predesigned Quick Styles. These sets include a Normal style for body text and a number of Heading styles. You can also find a variety of styles for lists, quotes, references, and for paragraphs or text that deserve special emphasis. With a click of your mouse, you can apply any one of these styles and make dramatic changes to your document (Figure 3-21).

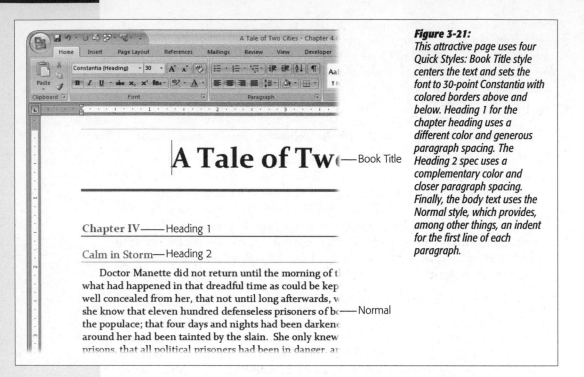

Figure 3-21:
This attractive page uses four Quick Styles: Book Title style centers the text and sets the font to 30-point Constantia with colored borders above and below. Heading 1 for the chapter heading uses a different color and generous paragraph spacing. The Heading 2 spec uses a complementary color and closer paragraph spacing. Finally, the body text uses the Normal style, which provides, among other things, an indent for the first line of each paragraph.

Some styles define character formatting, such as font, font size, font style, and special effects such as underlining or strikethrough. Other styles define both character formatting and paragraph formatting. Paragraph formatting includes things like paragraph alignment, line spacing, bullets, numbering, indents, and tab settings.

Applying Quick Styles

It's easy to preview and apply a style to your text. The action takes place in the Styles group on the Home tab. Follow these steps:

1. **Select the text or paragraph that you want to format.**

   When you want to apply a style to an entire paragraph, just click to put the insertion point in that paragraph. When you want to apply a style to text, you need to select the text first.

2. **Go to Home → Styles and hold your cursor over a style to see a live preview in your document.**

   The Styles group shows a few styles right on the ribbon. To see more styles, use the arrows on the right to scroll through the list, or click the double down-arrow button at bottom to open the entire menu (Figure 3-22).

   When you hold the mouse cursor over a style, the text in your document changes, showing you the effect of applying that style.

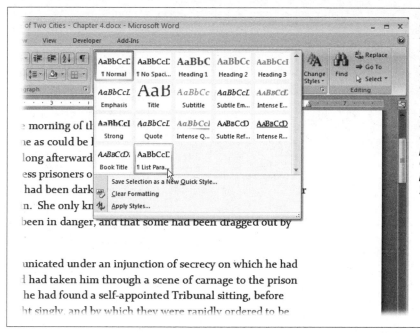

3. Click to apply the style.

   When you click a style on the ribbon or in the menu, Word applies that style to your paragraph or text selection.

Modifying Styles

When you apply a style to a paragraph of text, you do more than just change its formatting. In essence, you've attached that style to the paragraph. If you make changes to that style later, the paragraph reflects those changes. Imagine that you have a style called Heading 1 that centers the headings on the page. You've used this style repeatedly throughout your 400-page novel about the French Revolution. Say, you decide your novel would look better with that heading aligned on the left margin rather than centered. Instead of making the change to each individual heading, you edit the Heading 1 style. When you change the style definition, all your headings that are based on the Heading 1 style change to match.

Here are the steps to modifying a style. In this example, you give the Heading 1 style left alignment:

1. **Go to Home → Styles and click the Styles dialog box launcher (Figure 3-23).**

   In the Styles box, you can click to apply any one of the styles to your current selection or paragraph. Even when the Styles box is open, you can click within your text to move the insertion point to a different paragraph. And you can use the scroll bar, the PageUP and PageDN keys, or any other method to navigate through your document.

When you hold your cursor over a style, a screen tip pops up showing you details. Turn on the Show Preview checkbox at bottom to see a more visual representation of each of the styles.

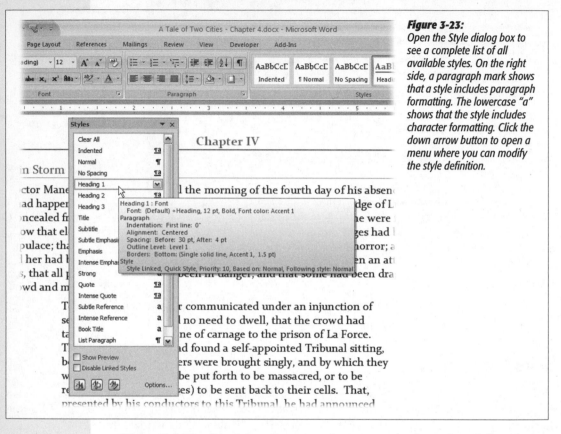

Figure 3-23:
Open the Style dialog box to see a complete list of all available styles. On the right side, a paragraph mark shows that a style includes paragraph formatting. The lowercase "a" shows that the style includes character formatting. Click the down arrow button to open a menu where you can modify the style definition.

2. **Right-click Heading 1 (or whatever style you want to change), and then choose Modify from the shortcut menu.**

   The Modify Style dialog box opens (Figure 3-24). Here you can get under the hood and tinker with all the formatting options.

Tip: *When you right-click anywhere on the style name, or click the V button in the Styles dialog box, a context menu shows you several choices for changing and working with the selected style. At the top of the list is "Update Heading 1 to Match Selection." This option changes all the formatting in the selected style so that it's identical to the current paragraph or selection.*

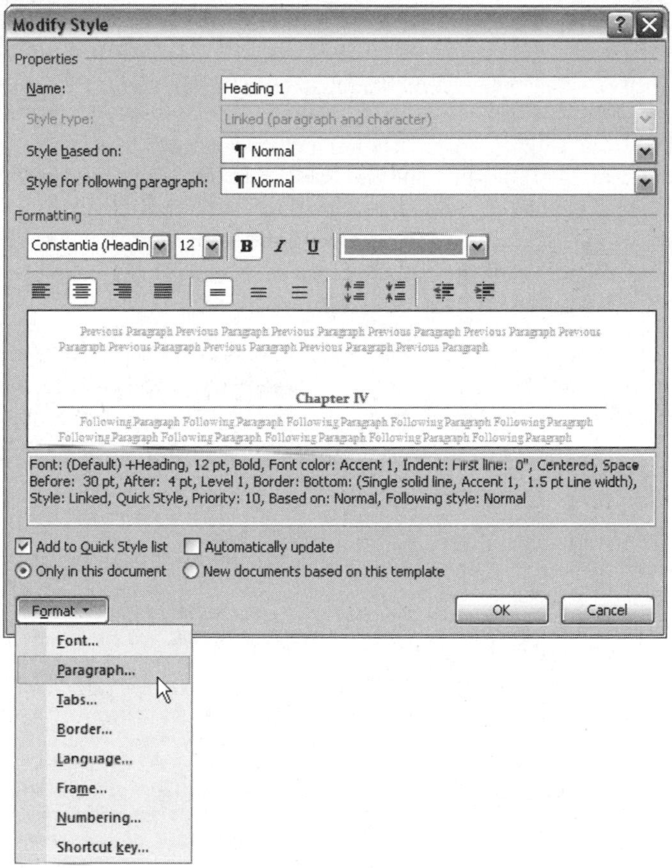

Figure 3-24:
The Modify Style box is command central for tinkering with your style definitions. The properties at the top determine the behavior of the styles when you're working with text. The preview window in the center shows an example of the style in action. Use the Format button in the lower-left corner to open dialog boxes to make changes in the character and paragraph formatting.

3. **In the lower-left corner of the Modify Style box, click the Format button, and then choose Paragraph.**

   The Paragraph dialog box opens. Yep, it's exactly the same box you open when you click the Paragraph dialog box launcher on the ribbon or press Alt+H, PG (see Figure 3-8). In fact, the Format button leads you to many familiar dialog boxes, from Fonts to Borders to Tabs. The difference, of course, is that you're now changing a style format, not just a few paragraphs.

4. **At the top of the Paragraph box, in the General group, click the Alignment drop-down menu, and then choose Left.**

   In this example, you're just making a single change, but you can also make changes to any of the other formatting options in this box.

5. **Close the Paragraph box, the Modify Style box, and the Styles box.**

   Everything's done except the cleanup. Close each of the boxes you've opened to go back to your text and continue editing.

Managing Style Sets

A *style set* is a collection of styles. Microsoft includes several predesigned style sets with Word, with names like Classic, Distinctive, Elegant, Formal, and Modern. Go to Home → Styles → Change Styles (or press Alt+H, FQ) to see them listed under the Change Styles button (Figure 3-25). Each of Word's predesigned style sets includes a Normal style, several heading styles (Heading 1, Heading 2, and so on), and other paragraph and character styles (like Title, Subtitle, Intense, Strong, and Reference). Even though a style has the same name in different sets—like Heading 1—the formatting is likely to be quite different. So when you change your document's style set, you can get a radically different look.

The style set that's in use has a checkmark next to the name. If you move your cursor over the name of a different style set, Live Preview shows you your text formatted with that new style set. To make the change permanent, just click the name. The menu closes, and your text has a whole new look.

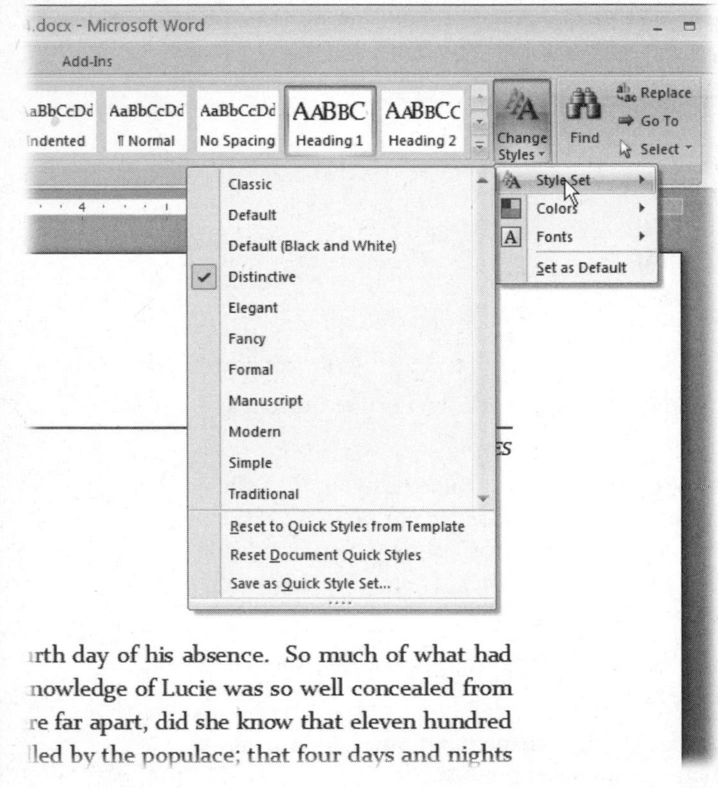

Figure 3-25:
Click the Change Styles button, and then click Style Set to see the different style sets available. Using the Colors and Fonts options, you can make quick changes to the look of your document. Second thoughts? Click "Reset to Quick Styles from Template" to undo any changes made in haste. At the very bottom, you can use the "Save as Quick Style Set" command to immortalize your current styles as a brand-new style set.

Creating Your Own Style Set

The best way to create your own style set is to start with one of Microsoft's predesigned sets, and then modify it. Here's a basic procedure for customize an existing style set to meet your needs.

1. **Use Live Preview to browse the existing style sets and choose one that's a reasonably close match to what you have in mind.**

   For example, open a document to a place where you can see a few different types of styles, like body text, some headings, and maybe a numbered or bulleted list.

2. **Go to Home → Styles → Change Styles → Style Set (Alt+H, GY). Work your way down the list of style sets, and click one that has a look that's similar to the one you want.**

   The Style Sets submenu lists the style sets available. Hold your mouse cursor over the name of a style set, and Live Preview shows you how that style set changes your document. In the next steps, you'll modify the style set to be exactly what you want.

3. **If necessary, modify the colors and fonts using the options on the Change Styles menu.**

   The first and most obvious changes you can make are to the colors and fonts. The commands to make those changes are right there on the Change Styles menu (Home → Styles → Change Styles). The previewing procedure is the same: Just hold your mouse cursor over a Font or Color style, and you see your document change. Click to choose a color or font style.

   Start with the Normal paragraph style. Consider the font, font size, color, and any other character formatting that you may want to change. (But don't get crazy; after all, this is the *Normal* paragraph style.) After the Normal paragraph style, move on to the Heading styles. The font size and color you choose for your headings set the tone for your entire document.

4. **Examine the existing paragraph styles, and if necessary, make changes.**

   Consider the line spacing and indents for normal paragraph. Do you want more or less space around them on the page? Choose the paragraph spacing for each heading style. Think about borders—perhaps you'd like a nice line above or below a heading. Work your way through any of the existing paragraph or character styles that you know you'll use.

5. **Consider the paragraph styles you need, and add new ones if they're missing.**

   After you've modified the existing styles, think about styles that you'd like to have but aren't part of the set. Maybe you need a numbered list, or a special sidebar paragraph with a border running all the way around it. Create whatever styles you need, and then add them to your style set.

Don't worry if you can't think of everything just now. You can always add new styles later when you're using the style set.

6. **When you're done customizing your style set, go to Home → Styles → More → Save Selection as Quick Style Set (or Atl+H, L), and then save it with a new name.**

The Save command is at the very bottom of the submenu. As a last step, save your style with a name, and it becomes one of the available style sets (Figure 3-26). A standard Windows Save dialog box opens. Type a name for your style set in the "File name" text box, and then click Save. After you've saved it, your customized style shows on the Change Styles menu with all the rest.

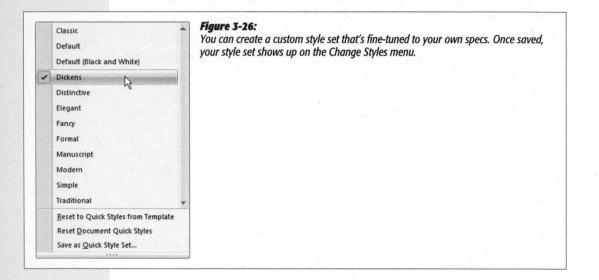

Figure 3-26:
You can create a custom style set that's fine-tuned to your own specs. Once saved, your style set shows up on the Change Styles menu.

Setting Up the Document

Your document makes a first impression before anyone reads a word. The paper size, color, and borders give the reader an overall sense of the document's theme and quality. Margins, the text layout, and perhaps a watermark send further visual clues. Making the right choices about your document setup helps you send the right message to your readers. Say you're working on an invitation; using a smaller, elegant paper size and adding a subtle border lets your recipients know right away that they're in for a sophisticated event.

In this chapter, you'll learn how to set and change all the page layout features that people notice first, starting with paper size, orientation, and margins. You'll also learn how to adjust margins and make changes to the headers and footers. Finally, you'll learn how to work with multiple columns and how to control Word's hyphenation inclinations.

Choosing Paper Size and Layout

When you edit a document in Word, what you see on your computer screen looks almost exactly like the final printed page. To get that correct preview, Word needs to know some details about the paper you're using, like the page size and orientation. You have two different ways to change the page settings: using the Page Layout tab (Figure 4-1) or the Page Setup dialog box (Figure 4-2). When you click the Page Layout tab, the ribbon's buttons and icons change to show you options related to designing your page as a whole. Your options are organized in five groups: Themes, Page Setup, Page Background, Paragraph, and Arrange.

Of Menus and Boxes

Word gives you two ways to set options: through ribbon menus and dialog boxes. In general, the ribbon's drop-down menus give you access to quick, predesigned solutions, while dialog boxes give you greater control over more details. Menu options usually focus on one or two settings, while dialog boxes are much more complex affairs, letting you change several settings at once.

The Page Layout → Page Setup → Size menu, shown in Figure 4-1, lets you choose a standard paper size with one click. But what if you're not using one of the standard paper sizes on the Size menu? In that case, click More Paper Sizes (at the bottom of the Size menu).

The Page Setup dialog box opens to the Paper tab (Figure 4-2). Here, you can customize the page size—by entering numbers in the Width and Height text boxes—and tweak other paper-related settings. These other settings, such as the Paper Source settings (which let you tell your printer which tray to take the paper from), are typical of the fine-tuning controls you find in dialog boxes.

On the Margins and Layout tabs, you can control your document's margins, orientation, headers, and footers. You'll learn more about all of these settings later in this chapter.

Changing Paper Size

If you want to quickly change the page size to a standard paper size like letter, legal, or tabloid, the Page Layout → Page Setup → Size menu is the way to go (Figure 4-1). With one quick click, you change your document's size. If there's text in your document, Word reshapes it to fit the page. Say you change a ten-page document from letter size to the longer legal-size page. Word spreads out your text over the extra space, and you'll have fewer pages overall.

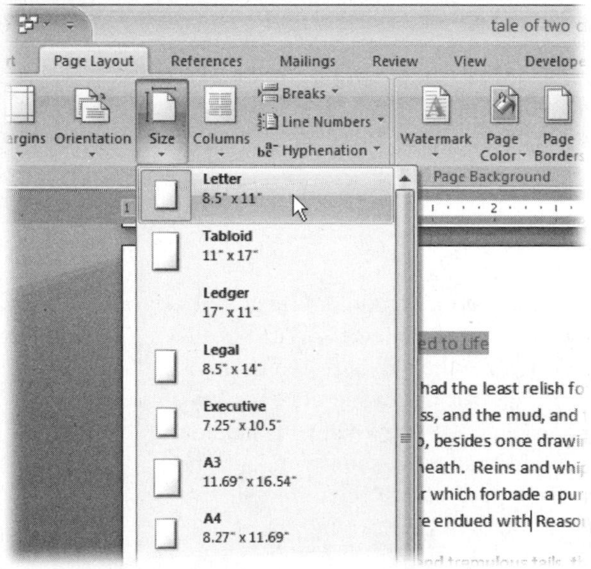

Figure 4-1:
The Size menu, like many Word 2007 menus, uses icons as well as text to give you quick visual cues. Your choices include Letter (8.5"x 11"), Tabloid (11" x 17"), and more. If you're using standard-size paper (including standard international sizes like A3 and A4), you can click one of these choices, and you're done.

Customizing paper size and source

If you can't find the paper size you need on the Size menu, then you need to customize your paper size, which you do in the Page Setup dialog box's Paper tab. Here are the steps:

1. **Choose Page Layout → Page Setup → Size. At the bottom of the Size menu, click More Paper Sizes.**

   The Page Setup dialog box appears, with the Paper tab showing (Figure 4-2). Why the Paper tab? Because you opened the box using the More Paper Sizes button.

2. **In the Width and Height boxes, enter the size of your custom paper.**

   The quickest way to change the Width and Height settings is to select the numbers in the boxes and type your new page dimensions. Your new numbers replace the previous settings. You can also click the up and down arrows to the right of the text boxes, but it's slow going as the sizes change in tenths of an inch. Notice that as you change the dimensions, the Preview image at the bottom of the Page Setup box changes to match.

3. **Click OK at the bottom, to close the dialog box and make the changes.**

   The Page Setup box closes, and your custom-sized document shows in Word.

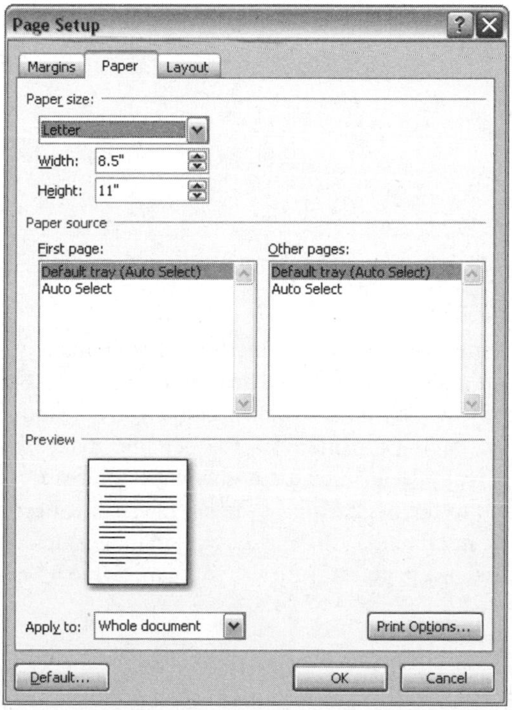

Figure 4-2:
Using the Paper tab of the Page Setup box, you can choose from standard paper sizes or set your own custom paper size. Dialog boxes are great for making several changes at once. On this tab you can also choose a paper source (if you're lucky enough to have a printer with more than one paper tray). You can read more about printing in Chapter 7.

Note: At the bottom of the Page Setup dialog box is an "Apply to" option with two choices: "Whole document" and "This point forward." If you choose "Whole document," Word applies these paper size and other page layout settings to your entire document. If you choose "This point forward," Word creates a page break at the insertion point, and starts using the new settings only after the break.

Setting Paper Orientation

Most business documents, school papers, and letters use a *portrait* page orientation, meaning the page is taller than it is wide. But sometimes you want a short, wide page—*landscape* page orientation—to accommodate a table, chart, or photo, or just for artistic effect. Whatever the reason, using the Orientation menu (Page Layout → Page Setup → Orientation) is the easiest way to make the change (Figure 4-3). Just click one of the two options: Portrait or Landscape.

If you've already got the Page Setup box open, you'll find the Orientation options on the Margins tab (Page Layout → Page Setup → Margins → Custom Margins).

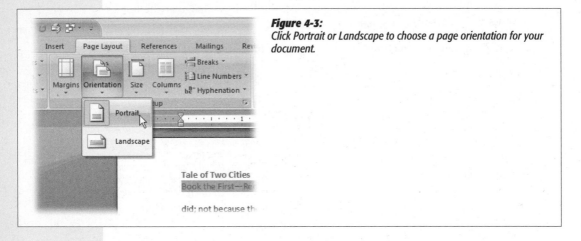

Figure 4-3:
Click Portrait or Landscape to choose a page orientation for your document.

Setting Document Margins

Page margins are more than just empty space. The right page margins make your document more readable. Generous page margins make text look inviting and give reviewers room for notes and comments. With narrower margins, you can squeeze more words on the page; however, having too many words per line makes your document difficult to read. With really long lines it's a challenge for readers to track from the end of one line back to the beginning of the next. Margins become even more important for complex documents, such as books or magazines with facing pages. With Word's margins and page setup tools, you can tackle a whole range of projects.

Selecting Preset Margins

Word's Margins menu (Page Layout → Page Setup → Margins) gives you a way to quickly apply standard margins to your pages. The preset margins are a mixed bag of settings from a half inch to one and a quarter inches. For most documents, you can choose one of these preset margins and never look back (Figure 4-4).

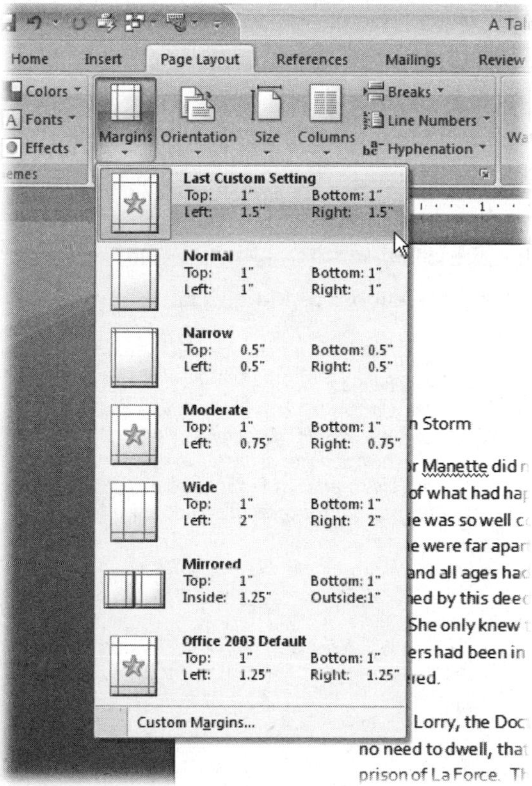

Figure 4-4:
The Margins menu provides some standard settings such as the ever popular one inch all the way around. Word calls this favorite of businesses and schools the Normal margin. If you've customized your margins, your most recent settings appear at the top of the menu.

For each of the preset margin options you see dimensions and an icon that hints at the look of the page:

- **Normal** gives you one inch on all sides of the page.

- **Narrow** margins work well with multicolumn documents, giving you a little more room for each column.

- **Moderate** margins with three-quarter inches left and right let you squeeze a few more words in each line.

- The **Wide** preset gives you more room for marginal notes when you're proofing a manuscript.

To select one of the preset margins, go to Page Layout → Page Setup → Margins, and then click one of the options. You can also use the shortcut key Alt+P, M, and then use your up and down arrow keys to highlight one of the margins. Press Enter to use the highlighted margin.

> **Note:** Word measures margins from the edge of the page to the edge of the body text. Any headers and footers that you add (page 112) appear *in* the margin areas.

Setting Custom Margins

What if none of the preset margins on the menu suits your needs? Say your company's style guide insists on one-and-a-half-inch margins for all press releases. Here's how to customize your margins:

1. **Go to Page Layout → Page Setup → Margins → Custom Margins to open the Page Setup box to the Margins tab (Figure 4-5).**

   The Page Setup box has three tabs at the top. The Margins tab is on the left.

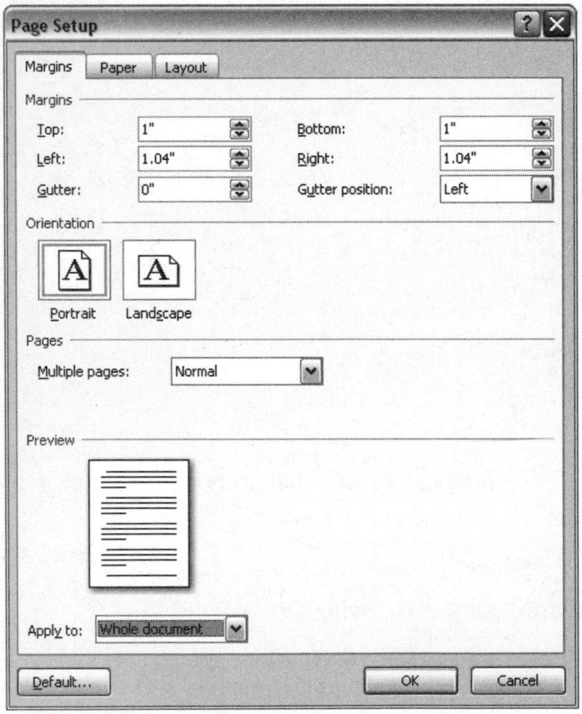

Figure 4-5:
The Margins tab is divided into four groups of controls: Margins, Orientation, Pages, and Preview. Use the text boxes at the top to set your top, bottom, and side margins. Use the gutter settings to specify the part of the page that's hidden by a binding.

2. **At the top of the box, enter dimensions for top, bottom, left, and right margins.**

The boxes in the Margins section already contain your document's current settings. To change the Top margin to one and a half inches, select the current setting, and then type *1.5*, or you can click the arrows on the right side of the box to change the margin number. Make the same change in the Bottom, Left, and Right margin text boxes.

Tip: While you're here in the Page Setup box, double-check the page Orientation setting. Margins and page orientation have a combined effect. In other words, if you want a quarter-inch top margin, make sure the orientation is set correctly depending on whether you want the "top" of the page to be on the long side or the short side of the paper.

---

3. **Click OK to apply the changes to your document.**

   The Page Setup box closes and your document takes shape with the new margins. If the changes are substantially different from the previous settings, you may find that you have a different number of pages in your document.

Setting Margins for Booklets

The vast majority of the documents spewing forth from our collective printers are printed on a single side of the page. If they're bound at all, it's likely to be with a staple or a paper clip in the upper-left corner. Documents like this don't need fancy margins or page setups. But, if you're putting together a booklet, corporate report, or newsletter, you need more sophisticated tools.

Open the Page Setup box to the Margins tab (Page Layout → Page Setup → Margins → Custom Margins or Alt+P, MA). In the Pages group, click the "Multiple pages" drop-down menu to see the options.

- **Normal** is the setting you use for most single-sided documents.

- **Mirror margins** are great for documents with facing pages, like bound reports or newsletters. This setting makes outside and inside margins identical. Outside margins are the left margin on the left page and the right margin on the right page. Inside margins are in between the two facing pages. Documents with facing pages may also have a gutter, which is a part of the page that is hidden when the document is bound.

- **2 pages per sheet** prints two pages on a single side of the paper. If you've defined headers and footers, they'll show up on both pages. Usually you cut these pages after printing to create separate pages.

- **Book fold** is similar to the option above and prints two pages on one side of the paper. The difference is that the book fold layout is designed so you can fold the paper down the middle to create a booklet with facing pages.

When you make a selection from the "Multiple pages" menu, some of the other options in the Margins box change too. For example, if you choose "Mirror margins," the labels above for the Right and Left margins change to Inside and Outside.

Applying Page Borders

A tasteful, properly applied border can add a certain flair to your document. However, an inappropriate border can make your document look cheesy (Figure 4-6). Enough said?

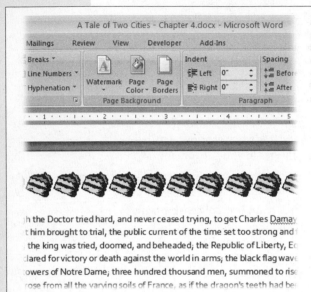

Figure 4-6:
The Page Layout → Page Background → Page Borders menu lets you add a simple line border around a paragraph, picture, or page. You can also add an art border, but don't get carried away. This cake border is a bad choice for Marie Antoinette and most other adults.

Okay, now that you've been warned, here's how to add page borders:

1. **Choose Page Layout → Page Background → Page Borders to open the Borders and Shading box.**

   The Borders and Shading box has three tabs. Make sure you're using the Page Border tab. (The first Borders tab puts borders around paragraphs, pictures, and other objects on the page.)

2. **On the left, choose a setting to define the border.**

   Start with the five settings on the left, to define the border in broad strokes ranging from no border to drop shadows. You can select only one of these settings.

3. **Choose a line style, color, and width, or choose an art border.**

   If you're going with a line border, choose a line type from the Style drop-down menu. You can choose from more than two dozen lines, including solid, dotted, double, and wavy. Then use the drop-down menus to choose a Color and Width (Figure 4-7).

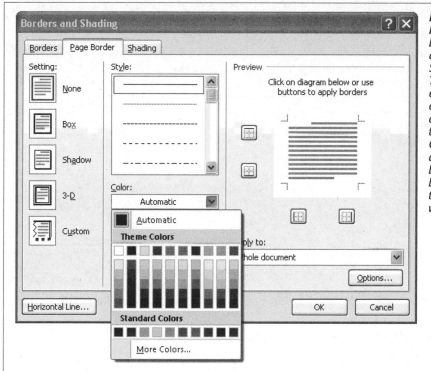

Figure 4-7:
If you choose a line border, you can choose a color as well as a style. Selecting from the Theme Colors palette ensures that your color coordinates with the document's current theme. The Standard Colors palette gives you access to several basic, bright colors. Preview the border, and then select the sides of the page that will have borders.

If you want an art border—trees, hearts, pieces of cake, and so on—select your design from the Art menu (just below the Width menu). Note that some of the art styles use different patterns for different sides of the page and for the corner design.

Note: Whether you choose lines or art for your border, you can adjust the width. You can increase line widths to a thick 6 points and art widths to 31 points.

The Preview on the right side of the Borders and Shading box shows what sides of your page will have borders. Click the borders to toggle them on or off. Using this technique, you can choose to show a border on a single side of the page or on any combination of sides.

4. **In the lower-right corner of the box, use the "Apply to" control to set the pages that will have borders.**

Maybe you want your first page to have a different border from the rest of the document. If the first page of your document uses letterhead, you may want a first page with no border at all, so select "This section - all except first page." Or, to put a border around the cover page but no other pages, choose the "This section - first page only" setting. As with paper size and other page layout settings, Word lets you apply borders differently in different sections of your document. See page 125 for more on sections.

5. **Click OK to accept the settings and to close the Borders and Shading box.**

A Colorful Background

The Page Color option lets you fill in the entire background of a page. Avoid the temptation to use this feature to create a pretty background. Nothing screams "Amateur designer!" more than loud background colors and patterns that fight with the text on the page.

Printing a colored background also drinks up gallons of expensive printer ink, so if you just want a colored background, print your document on colored paper instead. In truth, Microsoft intended the Page Color feature more for those rare birds who use Word to create Web pages, rather than for printed documents.

However, you may occasionally use a background color (with heavy stock) to create postcards, colored covers, business cards, and so on.

If you use a dark text color, make sure you use a light page color and vice versa. Avoid extremely busy background patterns, textures, and images that make it hard to read your text.

Choose Page Layout → Page Background → Page Color, and you'll see a drop-down menu of options as shown previously in Figure 4-7. If you move your mouse over a color (without clicking), then you see the page change color, immediately giving you a preview. In fact, if you're previewing a very dark page color, Word's smart enough to change the text from black to white. That doesn't mean it's impossible to come up with some garish page color options. When you settle on a color, click to choose it.

Adding Headers and Footers

Headers and footers are where Word puts the bits of information that appear at the top or bottom of every page of most multipage documents (Figure 4-8). They remind you of the page number, chapter title, and so on, as you read along. For business memos and reports, headers are a great place to repeat the document's subject and publication date. (If you're the author of the report and want your boss to know, consider adding your name under the title.)

Note: Word's *fields* are bits of text automated with the help of some behind-the-scenes computer code. You can insert fields into your document to show information that's likely to change, like today's date or a page number. Because it's a field, this text updates itself automatically, as discussed in the box on page 116.

Introducing the Header and Footer Tools

Unlike some of the other features in this chapter, the header and footer tools are on the Insert tab (not the Page Layout tab). As you can see in Figure 4-9, three menus appear in the Header & Footer group—Header, Footer, and Page Number. Each of the menus provides predesigned page elements, known in Word-speak as *Building Blocks*. So, for example, if you select a header Building Block, it may add text and several graphic elements to the top of your page.

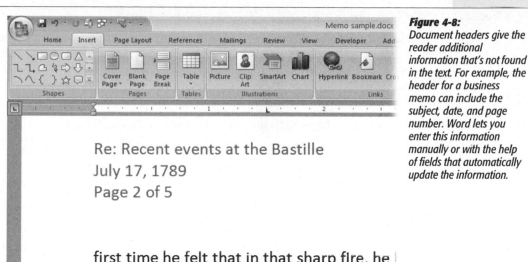

Figure 4-8:
Document headers give the reader additional information that's not found in the text. For example, the header for a business memo can include the subject, date, and page number. Word lets you enter this information manually or with the help of fields that automatically update the information.

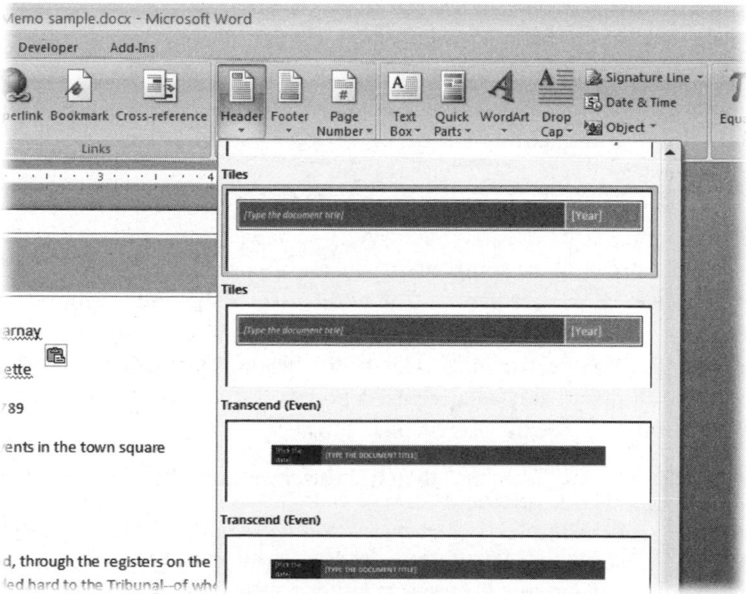

Figure 4-9:
The Header, Footer, and Page Number menus help you insert predesigned page elements, known as Building Blocks, into your document. You can see what each one looks like right on the menu. At the bottom of the menu, you find options to create (or remove) custom headers, footers, and page numbers.

Inserting and Modifying a Header Building Block

Go to Insert → Header & Footer → Header, and you see more than a dozen prede-signed header options. You can keep these canned headers as they are, or use them as a starting point for your own imagination. The following steps show you how to use a Building Block to add a header to your document and then tweak it a bit by inserting an additional field.

1. **Go to Insert → Header & Footer → Header to open the Header menu.**

   If you've used earlier versions of the program, you'll notice that the drop-down menus in Word 2007 are larger and much more visual. The Header menu is a good example, as it gives you a clear representation of the available predesigned headers.

2. **Use the scroll bar on the right to find the Tiles header.**

   You can drag the box in the scroll bar to move quickly through the menu, or use the arrow buttons to browse through the examples.

3. **Click the Tiles header to insert it into your document.**

   When you select the Tiles header, you're adding more than text to your document: A Building Block comes with all its own accessories. The Tiles header includes a box with a rule around it and two tiles of color. Inside the tiles are bracketed words.

   When you insert a header, a couple of other things happen too. The Header menu closes and a new Design tab appears on your ribbon, with a Header & Footer Tools tab above. Along with that, a whole slew of new buttons and tools appear on the ribbon (left to right): Header & Footer, Insert, Navigation, Options, Position, and the Close Header and Footer button.

4. **Click the bracketed words "Type the document title," and then type a title of your choice.**

   The bracketed words are a prompt that you're supposed to enter new text in that spot. A single click anywhere on the words selects the entire group. Type your title, say, *A Tale of Two Cities*. When you type, the other words and the brackets disappear. When you add a title to the header, Word uses this text to update the title shown in the Document Properties (Office button → Prepare → Properties). For details, see the box on page 116.

5. **Click the bracketed word Year, and then use the calendar control to update the header's Year field.**

   This standard Word tool lets you enter a date by selecting it. At the top, you see the month and year. Click the buttons on either side to move backward or for-ward through the months. Click a date on the calendar below to select a spe-cific date. Word uses the year from the date you selected to update the Year text in the header. Or you can enter a year simply by typing it.

You can modify Building Blocks after you add them to your document by typing your own text, which you'll do next.

6. **Click the header to the right of your title. If the title is highlighted, use the right arrow key to deselect the title, and then type a hyphen (-) followed by a space.**

You can also add automatically updating text by inserting a field, which is how Word creates those ever-changing dates and page numbers. Word has fields for lots of other stuff too. You can't create (or edit) a field by typing directly in your document, though. You must use the Field dialog box.

7. **Choose Insert → Quick Parts → Field.**

The Field dialog box opens showing an alphabetical list of field names on the left side, as shown in Figure 4-10. Fields store information about your document and keep track of other information that you can use in your documents.

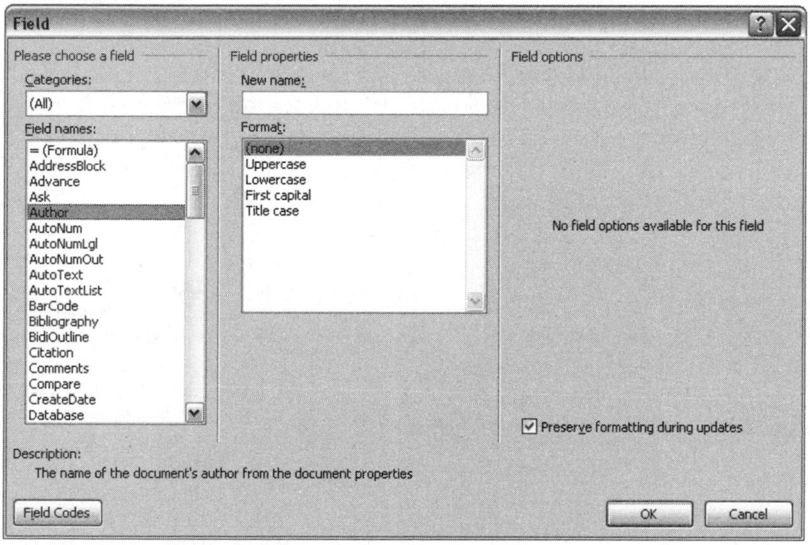

Figure 4-10:
Using fields, you can add automatically updating page numbers, dates, and names. The Field dialog box shows a whole list of fields (left) and provides ways to format them (right) so that they work just right.

8. **Double-click the Author field name to insert it into the header.**

The author's name appears next to the title in the header. (If you're working on your own computer, it's probably your name.) This text is grayed out to show that it's a field and that you can't edit it directly.

9. **Double-click anywhere on the document's body text to close the Header & Footer Tools contextual tab.**

You have two options for closing the header and going back to editing your document. You can double-click anywhere outside the header, or, on the right side of the ribbon, you can click the Close Header and Footer button. Either way, the header fades out and the text of your document sharpens up. Your insertion point appears back in the body text, and you're ready to work.

Adding a Matching Footer Building Block

Most of the header Building Blocks have complementary footers. For example, the Tiles header used in the step-by-step example provides title and date information, while the Tiles footer provides company and page information (Figure 4-11). The steps for inserting the Tiles footer are nearly identical to the header steps. Just start with the Footer menu: Choose Insert → Header & Footer → Footer or press Alt+N, O.

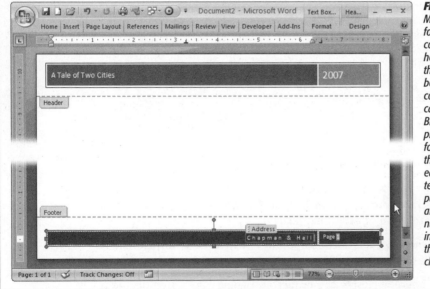

Figure 4-11:
Most of the header and footer Building Blocks come in pairs. By using a header and footer with the same name, you can be sure of having a consistent design. You can modify Building Blocks—like this predesigned header and footer—after you insert them in your text. Just edit as you would any text. It's best to leave the page numbers as they are, though. This page number is grayed out to indicate that it's a field that automatically changes for each page.

Creating Custom Headers and Footers

Microsoft provides a lot of competently designed headers and footers with Word, but you're free to create your own. After all, Microsoft's Building Blocks may not be to your taste, or maybe you have to follow company guidelines for your documents. It's not difficult to create your own headers in Word. Here's how to create a custom footer with a company name on the left and page numbers on the right:

1. **Go to Insert → Header & Footer → Footer → Edit Footer.**

   The insertion point moves from the body of your document to the footer space at the bottom.

2. **Type your company name, press Enter, and then type your city and country.**

   Pressing Enter puts the city and country on a new line below the company name. Text that you type directly into the footer appears on every page unless you make changes to the header and footer options.

3. **Press Tab twice to move the insertion point to the right side of the footer.**

   The first time you press Tab, the insertion point moves to the center of the page. If you enter text at that point, Word centers the text in the footer. The second time you press Tab, the insertion point moves to the right margin. Text that you enter there is aligned on the right margin.

4. **Type *Page*, and then press the Space bar.**

   As you type, the insertion point remains on the right margin and your text flows to the left.

5. **Choose Header & Footer Tools | Design → Insert → Quick Parts → Field (or press Alt+JH, Q, F) to open the Field dialog box.**

   The Quick Parts menu shows several different options: Document Property, Field, and Building Blocks Organizer.

6. **In the list of Field Names, double-click Page to insert the Page field in the footer.**

   Remember, if you simply type a number into the footer, you'll end up with the same number on every page. Instead, you place the Page field in your footer to tell Word to insert the correct number on each page. The page number appears in the footer next to the word "Page." The number is grayed out, indicating that it's a field and you can't edit the number.

7. **Type *of* and then a space. Press Alt+JH, Q, F to open the Field box again, and then double-click the NumPages field to insert it in your footer after the space.**

   The NumPages field keeps track of the number of pages in your document. When you're done, your footer looks like the one in Figure 4-12.

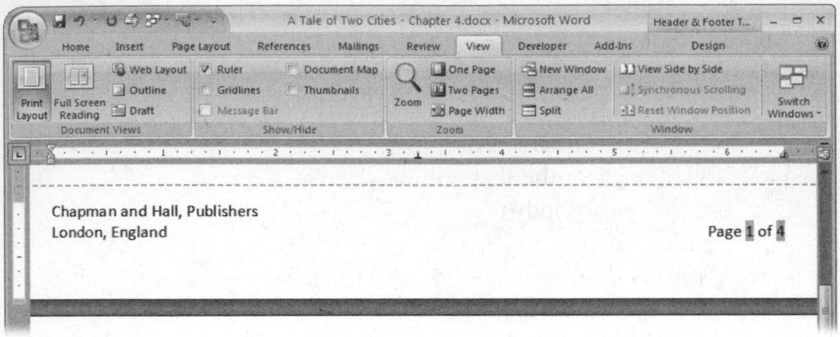

Figure 4-12:
This custom footer may not be as flashy as Microsoft's Building Blocks, but what Chapman and Hall wants, Chapman and Hall gets. The company name and city are plain typed-in text, while the page number and number of pages are fields that update automatically.

Removing Headers, Footers, and Page Numbers

It's easy to remove any headers, footers, or page numbers that you've added to your document. You'll find a command at the bottom of each of the respective menus to do just that. If you want to remove a header, follow these steps:

1. **Go to Insert → Header & Footer → Header to open the Header menu.**

   You see the same menu that you used to insert the header Building Block into your document. At the bottom of the menu, below all the Header examples, you see the Remove Header command.

2. **Click Remove Header.**

   The Header menu closes, and the entire header disappears from your document—text, graphics, and all.

The steps for removing a footer or a page number Building Block are nearly identical. Just start with the Footer menu (Insert → Header & Footer → Footer) or the Page Number menu (Insert → Header & Footer → Page Number).

Working with Multiple Columns

Word makes it easy to work with multiple newspaper-style columns. Instead of your having to use tabs or spaces to separate the column one line at a time, Word lets you set up the column guidelines and then type away. When you type text in a multicolumn layout, your words appear in the left column first. After you reach the end or bottom of the column, the insertion point jumps to the top of the next column and you begin to fill it, from top to bottom.

To use multiple columns, go to Page Layout → Page Setup → Columns, and then click one of the following options:

- **One.** Whether you know it or not, every page in Word has a column layout. The standard layout is one big column stretching from margin to margin.

- **Two.** With two columns, your document begins to look like a pamphlet or a school textbook.

- **Three.** Three columns are about as much as a standard 8.5×11-inch page can handle, unless you switch to Landscape orientation. In fact, you may want to reduce the body text size to about 9 or 10 points and turn on hyphenation. Otherwise, you can't fit very many words on a line.

- **Left.** This layout has two columns, with the narrower column on the left. The narrow column is a great place to introduce the text with a long heading and subheading or a quote pulled from the larger body text.

- **Right.** The mirror image of the Left layout, this option uses two columns with a narrow column at right.

- **More Columns.** Use the More Columns option to open the Columns dialog box (Figure 4-13) where you can create a customized column layout.

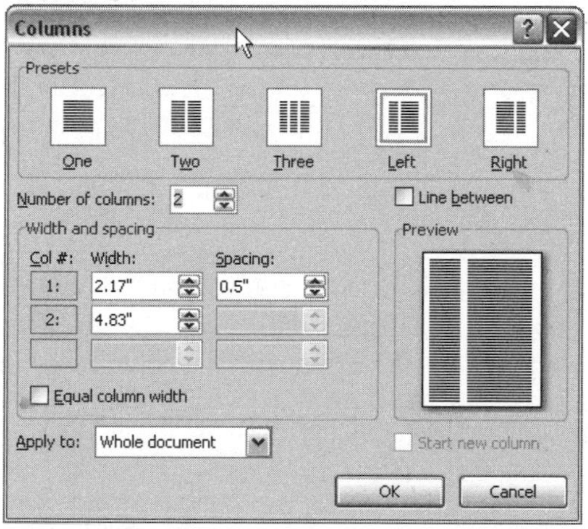

Figure 4-13:
At the top of the Columns dialog box, you see the same presets as on the Columns menu. Below them, controls let you create your own multicolumn layouts. The preview icon on the right changes as you adjust the settings.

Tip: If you want to use keyboard shortcuts to select column options, press Alt+P, J and then use the up and down arrow keys to highlight one of the options. With your choice highlighted, hit Enter.

When you get to the bottom of a column, Word automatically flows your text to the top of the next one, but you can also force Word to end the column and jump to the next one. There are two ways to create a *column break*. The quickest way while you're typing is to use the keyboard shortcut Ctrl+Shift+Enter (or Alt+P, BC). Or, if you forget the shortcut, you can use the ribbon: Page Layout → Page Setup → Breaks → Column.

Customizing Columns

Go to Page Layout → Page Setup → Columns → More Columns to open the Columns box (Figure 4-13) where you can create custom page layouts with multiple columns. By entering a number in the "Number of columns" text box, you can create more than three columns per page.

Choosing Between Columns and Tables

Word gives you two tools to divide your text into strips—columns and tables. Even though they may look the same on paper, they work and act differently. If you're writing a newsletter or a pamphlet, you probably want newspaper-style columns, so you can just type (or paste in) your text and let Word distribute it smoothly from one column to the next. But if you're listing the names of volunteers who joined the PTA each semester, you're better off using a table to create the columns, so you can keep each name on its own line.

As a rule of thumb, use newspaper-style columns (Page Layout → Page Setup → Columns) when you need a consistent number of evenly spaced columns on each page and when you expect the reader to read from the top to the bottom of a column before moving to the next column. Use tables to organize information in rows and columns, like a spreadsheet. Readers are just as likely to read tables left to right as they are from top to bottom. There's more information on tables in *Word 2007: The Missing Manual*.

If you turn on the "Equal column width" checkbox, Word automatically sets all the columns to the same width, so you don't have to do the math (Figure 4-14). Turn off this checkbox, and you can get creative by entering a different width and spacing for each column. Use the scroll bar on the right if you can't see all of the columns. Turn on the "Line between" box to place a line (also known as a *rule*) between your columns for a crisp professional look.

Near the bottom of the Columns box is a drop-down menu labeled "Apply to." If you want to use your column settings for your entire document, leave this set to "Whole document." If you want to create a new section with the column settings, select "This point forward" from the menu.

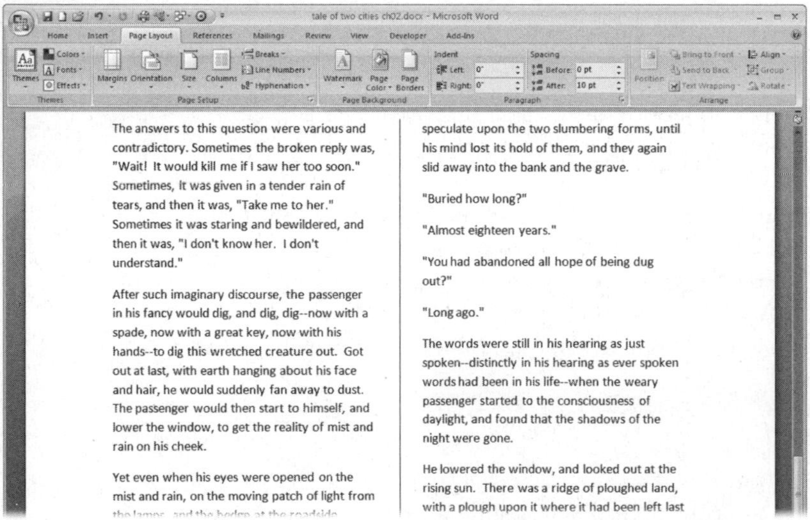

Figure 4-14:
You can fine-tune your columns options to create just the right effect. This example uses the "Equal column width" and the "Line between" options.

Hyphenation

Without hyphenation, if a word is too long to fit on the line, Word moves it down to the beginning of the next line. If a word is particularly long, it can leave some pretty big gaps at the end of the line. Justified text is aligned on both the left and right margins, like most of the text in this book. If you have justified text and no hyphenation, you often get large, distracting gaps between words, where Word is trying to spread out the text along the line. When used properly, hyphenation helps make text more attractive on the page and easier to read. In most cases, you can relax and let Word handle the hyphenating.

You just have to choose one of three basic hyphenation styles from the Page Layout → Page Setup → Hyphenation menu (Alt+P, H), as shown in Figure 4-15:

- **None.** No hyphenation at all. For informal letters, first drafts, and many reports, you may choose not to use hyphenation. It's a good-looking choice for documents that have fairly long lines (60 to 80 characters) and left-aligned text.

- **Automatic.** Word makes hyphenation decisions based on some simple rules that you provide. Consider using automatic hyphenation for documents that have line lengths of about 50 characters or less, including documents that use newspaper-style columns.

- **Manual.** In this scheme, Word asks you about each word it wants to hyphenate, giving you the final decision. Use manual hyphenation when you need to be particularly scrupulous about your grammar and when you need to be certain that you don't hyphenate a company name, a person's name, or some other equally important word.

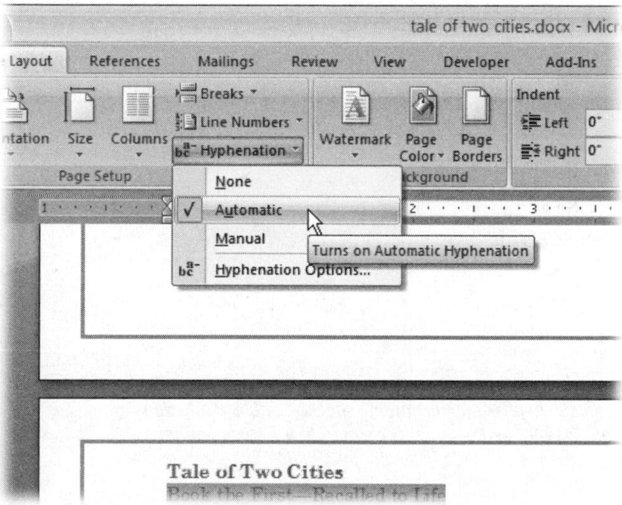

Figure 4-15:
Choose Automatic from the hyphenation menu, and Word takes care of all hyphenation decisions. Word's hyphenation feature works quite well and usually needs no help from you.

Hyphenation Rules of Thumb

Hyphenation rules are notoriously complicated, and, to make matters worse, they change by language and country. For example, Americans and British hyphenate differently. Still, you should follow these basic rules of thumb:

- **Use hyphenation with documents that have shorter lines.** A document that uses two or three columns on the page needs hyphenation to avoid large gaps in the text.

- **Use hyphenation with justified text.** Justified text, which is aligned on both the left and right margins, makes documents look formal and tidy—but not if big gaps appear between letters and words. Avoid those gaps by letting Word hyphenate your justified text.

- **Avoid hyphenating company names and proper names.** Most people don't like to have their name messed with, and your boss feels the same way about the company name. Use manual hyphenation to prevent Word from dividing certain words.

- **Avoid hyphenating more than two lines in a row.** According to many standard style guides, it's wrong to use hyphenation on more than two consecutive lines. Use manual hyphenation to remove a hyphen if you see too many in a row.

- **Avoid overusing hyphens.** Excessive hyphenation, even if not on consecutive lines, distracts the eye and makes a document more difficult to read.

Automatic Hyphenation

It's easy to turn on automatic hyphenation. Just choose Page Layout → Page Setup → Hyphenation (or press Alt+P, H). Still, you may want to assert some control over how and when Word uses hyphenation. To do that, open the Hyphenation box (Figure 4-16) by choosing Page Layout → Page Setup → Hyphenation → Hyphenation Options (Alt+P, HH). This box has two important options that let you control hyphenation:

- **Hyphenation zone.** This zone is the maximum space that Word allows between the end of a word and the right margin. If the space is larger than this, Word hyphenates a word to close the gap. For most documents, .25" (a quarter of an inch) is a reasonable choice. A larger distance may give you fewer hyphens but a more ragged look to your right margin.

- **Limit consecutive hyphens to.** A "ladder" of three or more hyphens makes text difficult to read. Enter *2* in this box, and Word won't hyphenate more than two lines in a row.

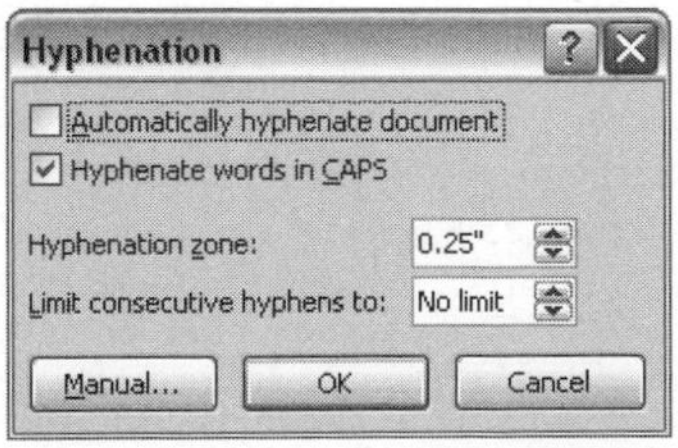

Figure 4-16:
Use the Hyphenation box to set the ground rules for hyphenation. Turn on the "Automatically hyphenate document" checkbox at top to have Word automatically hyphenate words according to the rules you set.

Manual Hyphenation

The term *manual hyphenation* sounds like more work than it actually is. *Computer-assisted hyphenation* would be a better term. When you turn on manual hyphenation (Alt+P, HM), Word automatically finds and shows you words that fall within the hyphenation zone, using the hyphenation rules you set in the Hyphenation box (Figure 4-17).

Word then shows you the word in a box and suggests where to place the hyphen. If you agree, click Yes. If you'd rather hyphenate the word in a different spot, click to put the insertion point where you want the hyphen, and then click Yes.

You many not always agree with Word when it comes to hyphen placement. For example, as shown here, Word wants to put the hyphen in the wrong spot in the word "mischance." To manually set the hyphen, click to put the insertion point between the "s" and the "c," and then click Yes.

It's best to run the Manual Hyphenation command (Page Layout → Page Setup → Hyphenation → Manual or Alt+P, HM) immediately before you print or save the final draft of your document. If last-minute edits change the line lengths and line breaks, you need to run manual hyphenation again.

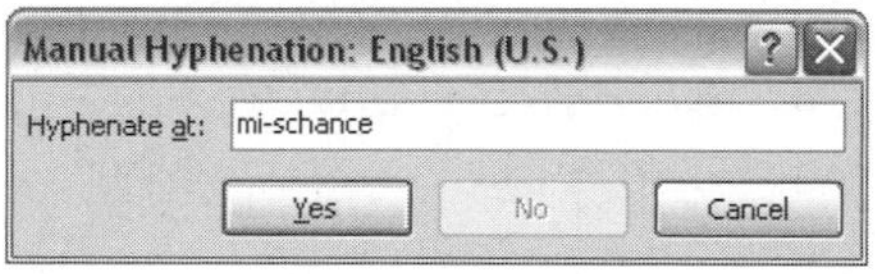

Figure 4-17:
You may not always agree with Word when it comes to hyphen placement. In this case, the hypen is in the wrong spot in the word "mischance." To manually set the hyphen, click to put the insertion point between the "s" and the "c," and then click Yes.

Removing Hyphenation from Your Document

It's easier to remove hyphenation from your document if you've used automatic rather than manual hyphenation. In the case of automatic hyphenation, you simply turn it off: Choose Page Layout → Page Setup → Hyphenation → None, or use the keyboard shortcut Alt+P, HN. All the automatic hyphens in your document disappear and the words rearrange themselves accordingly.

But when you use manual hyphenation, Word inserts optional hyphens in your document that don't go away even if you turn hyphenation off. If you set Hyphenation to None (Alt+P, HN), then Word continues to split words at the end of lines using the optional hyphens. The only way to find and delete the optional hyphens is with Word's Find and Replace dialog box.

Here are the steps to remove optional hyphens from your document:

1. **Choose Home → Replace (or press Ctrl+H) to open the Find and Replace dialog box to the Replace tab.**

   If you don't see a Special button at the bottom, click the More button on the left to expand the box. (If the box is expanded, the More button is labeled "Less" and clicking it shrinks the box.)

2. **Click in the "Find what" box to put the insertion point in the box.**

   Normally, you'd just type in the text that you're searching for, but the optional hyphen is a special character that you won't find on your keyboard. Searching for optional hyphens requires a couple of extra steps.

3. **Click the Special button to reveal the list of special characters.**

   The Find and Replace tool can search for a number of special characters. Some of them, like the optional hyphen and the paragraph mark, are nonprinting characters. Others, like the em dash need more than a single keystroke to produce.

4. **From the menu of special characters, choose Optional Hyphen.**

   The Special menu closes when you make a choice from the list. In the "Find what" box, you see ^-, the code Word uses to indicate an optional hyphen. Leave the "Replace with" box empty, because you want to replace the optional hyphens with nothing, which effectively removes them.

5. **Click Replace All to remove all optional hyphens from your text.**

   Word quickly removes the optional hyphens and displays a message telling you how many changes were made. Click Close to dismiss the alert box, and then, in the Find and Replace box (Figure 4-18), click Close. Mission accomplished.

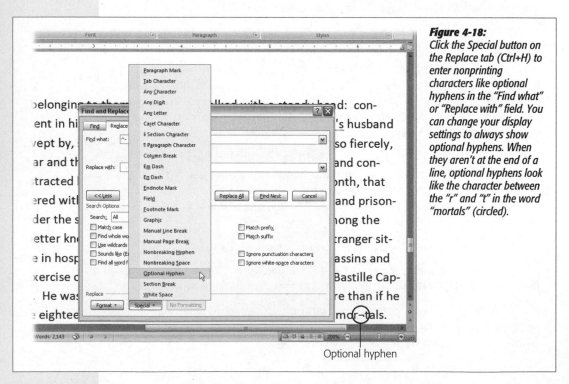

Figure 4-18:
Click the Special button on the Replace tab (Ctrl+H) to enter nonprinting characters like optional hyphens in the "Find what" or "Replace with" field. You can change your display settings to always show optional hyphens. When they aren't at the end of a line, optional hyphens look like the character between the "r" and "t" in the word "mortals" (circled).

Optional hyphen

Dividing Your Document into Sections

The longer and more complex your document is, the more likely it is to contain different *sections*. Word's sections don't have anything to do with how you've divided your document with headings and subheadings. They're electronic divisions you create by adding *section breaks* to your document. Section breaks are a close cousin to page breaks, except that a section can contain any number of pages. More important, each section in a Word document can have its own page formatting.

Many people work with Word for years without ever really understanding Word's sections. But breaking your document into different sections gives you a lot more flexibility within the same document. For example:

- **To change the page orientation.** If you want to have some pages in portrait orientation and others in landscape orientation (charts or graphs, for example), you need to insert a section break where the format changes (Figure 4-19).

- **To use different sizes of paper in a single document.** If you want to insert some tabloid-size pages in the middle of a document that's the standard 8.5×11 inches, you need to use page breaks where the format changes.

- **To change the number of columns on the page.** Perhaps you want to change from a single-column format to a double-column format; you need to insert a section break where the format changes. You can even put the break right smack in the middle of a page.

- **To change page margins in a single document.** When you want to change page margins, not just adjust a paragraph's indentation, you need to create a section break where the margins change.

Inserting Section Breaks

As you can see from the previous list, sections are all about page formatting, so it's not surprising that the section break commands are found under the Page Layout tab (Page Layout → Page Setup → Breaks or Alt+P, B). When you click the Breaks button in the Page Setup group, the menu is divided into two parts: Page Breaks and Section Breaks.

Note: When you use the Breaks menu (Figure 4-19), remember that the breaks shown at the top aren't section breaks. They're just text formatting breaks like page breaks and column breaks. The commands on the bottom are section breaks, as advertised.

Section breaks have two major distinctions. There are Next Page breaks, which create a new page for the new section, and there are Continuous breaks, which place a divider mark in the text with no visible interruption. Everything below that mark is in a new section. You use a Next Page break when you're changing the paper size or orientation. Or you can use a Next Page break if you want each chapter to start

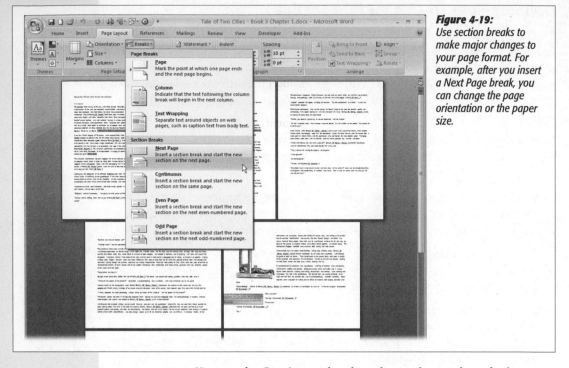

Figure 4-19:
Use section breaks to make major changes to your page format. For example, after you insert a Next Page break, you can change the page orientation or the paper size.

on a new page. You use the Continuous break to change the number of columns or the margins in your document in the middle of a page.

The other two options—Even Page and Odd Page—are just variations on Next Page. They create section breaks and start the new section on the next even or odd page. For example, you use this option to make sure that all your chapters begin on a right-hand page (like the ones in this book).

Here's how to insert a section break and change the paper orientation for the new section from Portrait to Landscape.

1. **Click within your text to place the insertion point where you want the section break.**

   You're going to insert a Next Page break, so click after the end of a sentence or paragraph. Also, make sure you're in Print Layout view, so you can see the results of the break.

2. **Choose Page Layout → Page Setup → Breaks, and then select Next Page from the drop-down menu.**

   If you're at the end of your document, Word creates a new empty page, and your insertion point is on the new page, ready to go. If you're in the middle of a document, Word creates a page break and moves your insertion point and all the remaining text to the new section.

3. With the insertion point in the new section, click the Orientation button (Page Layout → Page Setup → Orientation), and then choose Landscape.

    When you make Page Setup changes in your new section, they affect only the new section. So when you change the page orientation to landscape, you see pages before the break in portrait orientation and pages after the break in landscape orientation.

In Print Layout view, you see how your document looks with section breaks inserted. In Draft view, section breaks appear in your document as dotted lines. The line doesn't print, but it's visible on your computer screen (Figure 4-20).

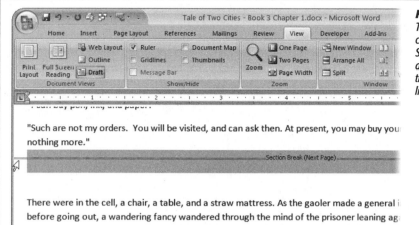

Figure 4-20:
To delete a section break, change to Draft view. Section breaks show as dotted, double lines. Select the break by clicking the line, and then press Delete.

CHAPTER 5

Themes and Templates

Formatting your text, headings, lists, and other page elements individually—as described in the previous couple of chapters—takes time that you may not have. And with so many choices in fonts, colors, and graphic ornaments, putting together a good-looking document can be overwhelming. No wonder so many people stick with Times New Roman body text and Arial headings! Fortunately, graphic designers at Microsoft have created *themes*, a new Word 2007 feature that lets you apply a complete, coordinated package of fonts, colors, heading styles, and more with a single click.

While themes are all about style and appearance, *templates* are about content. Part of Word for more than a decade, templates provide boilerplate text and blank spaces for you to fill with your own information. Templates also set you up with snappy graphics and consistent margins, indents, and paragraph formatting. A good template even provides cues to tell you what information you need to fill in the blanks.

Word's themes and templates help you make your documents look like they came from a Fortune 500 company's publications division. Even if you don't know a font from a fondue, you can crank out professional looking business proposals, resumés, and more.

Choosing a Theme

When you're on deadline putting together, say, a business proposal, you don't want to waste precious minutes worrying about fonts, heading colors, and the design of tables, charts, and graphs. Instead, simply choose a theme with a click of your mouse (Figure 5-1), and you've got a professional looking document.

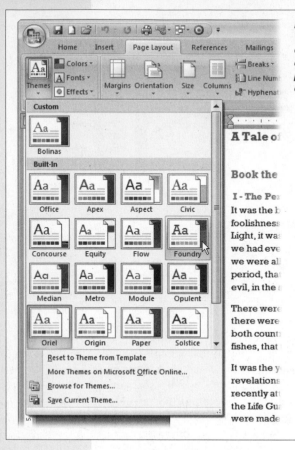

Figure 5-1:
Word 2007's themes are prepackaged collections of colors, fonts, and effects that work together to create attractive pages. Hold your mouse cursor over a theme to preview its effect on your document. Applying a theme is as simple as clicking the design you like best.

Themes are made up of three parts:

- **Colors.** Each theme contains 12 colors, each of which is assigned to a specific document part. One color (usually black) is used for body text. Another color (dark blue, say) is used for Heading 1 paragraphs. Lesser headings—like Heading 2 and Heading 3—may use a lighter shade of the same color. Other complementary colors are used for accent and hyperlinks (links to the Internet).

- **Fonts.** Each theme specifies one or two fonts—one for the body text and one for headings. Also known as typefaces, fonts define the actual shape of the letters on the screen and on the page. They have a subtle but significant effect on the appearance and feeling of a document. Some typefaces don't always play well with others, but fortunately, you don't have to worry about that when you choose themes, since their typeface combinations are always compatible.

- **Effects.** Each theme uses one of Word's 20 built-in graphic effects. These effects include design touches like shadows, line styles, 3-D, and so on. Most of these effects have more of an impact in PowerPoint presentations than in Word documents, but they come with the theme's package.

When you choose a theme, you're applying color, font, and effect formatting to the elements in your document (Figure 5-2).

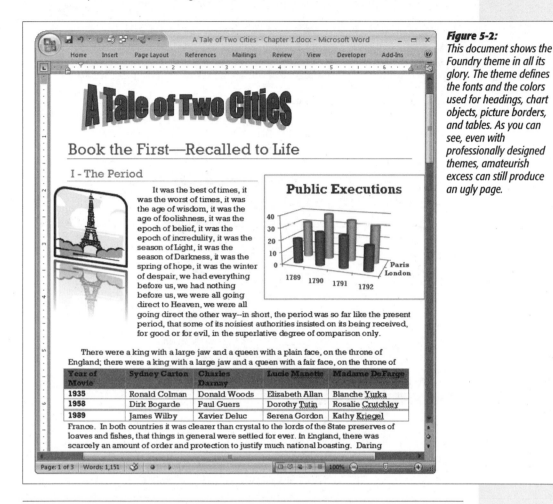

Figure 5-2:
This document shows the Foundry theme in all its glory. The theme defines the fonts and the colors used for headings, chart objects, picture borders, and tables. As you can see, even with professionally designed themes, amateurish excess can still produce an ugly page.

Tip: If you use Excel or PowerPoint as well as Word, you'll be glad to know that all Microsoft Office programs use the same themes. That makes it very easy to keep a consistent, professional look across all documents you create for a specific job or project. Figure 5-3 shows you an example.

Here are examples of the parts of your document that take their formatting cues from the selected theme:

- **Body text.** Font, size, style, and color.
- **Headings.** Font, size, style, and color.
- **Tables.** Font specs (same as above), border and line styles, and colors.
- **Charts.** Font specs, borders, lines, chart graphic styles, and colors.

- **Picture.** Border colors.

- **SmartArt.** Font specs, graphic colors.

- **Clip art.** Major outline and border colors.

- **Drop caps.** Font specs and color.

- **WordArt.** Font colors change, but the actual typestyle remains the same.

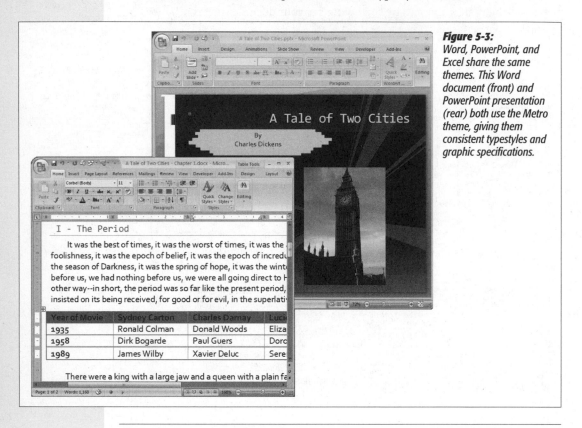

Figure 5-3:
Word, PowerPoint, and Excel share the same themes. This Word document (front) and PowerPoint presentation (rear) both use the Metro theme, giving them consistent typestyles and graphic specifications.

Note: For more on themes and Word's various art options (SmartArt, clip art, WordArt, and more), grab a copy of *Word 2007: The Missing Manual*.

Here's how to choose a theme for your document:

1. **Go to Page Layout → Themes (or press Alt+P, TH).**

   The Themes menu is on the far left of the Page Layout tab (Figure 5-1). It's like an artist's palette where you see sample colors and typefaces. Themes are divided into two categories with Custom themes at the top and Built-In themes below.

Note: You see Custom Themes only if you've created your own custom document themes.

---

2. **If the themes aren't all visible, drag the scroll bar on the right to get a better view.**

   In the lower-right corner, the three dots indicate that you can click that spot to drag the corner and resize the menu. If you'd rather have the menu stretch across the top of your window so you can see your document beneath, then just drag the corner.

3. **With your mouse, point to a theme (but don't click) to see a Live Preview.**

   The Themes menu uses Microsoft's new Live Preview feature—all you have to do is point to a theme, and your document changes to show you how it will look using that theme. You can quickly view and compare the available choices. (See, computer games aren't the only programs that use all of your computer's graphics power.)

4. **Once you decide on a theme, click to select it.**

   One click chooses a theme and applies formatting changes throughout your document. Headings, borders, and lines change color. Body text, headings, and title fonts also change (Figure 5-4).

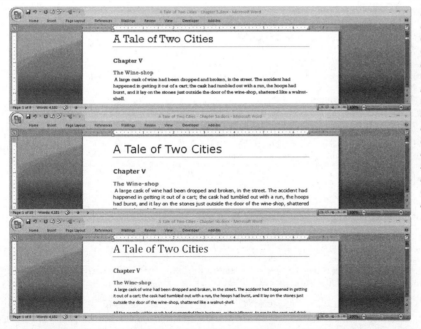

Figure 5-4:
Here's the same document with three different themes. On top is the Foundry theme with a font that looks a little like something that would come out of a typewriter. In the middle is the Aspect theme featuring Verdana—a modern looking sans-serif type. On the bottom is the Office theme, ensconced in hues of Microsoft.

Finding More Themes

Word comes with 20 built-in themes, but you may still find yourself looking for more. Perhaps you work in an office on a computer that was set up by your employer, and someone has created official company themes that you need to use. If that's the case, then you need to know where to look for those themes on your computer, especially if you (or someone you love) have inadvertently moved them. You can also look beyond your computer: Creative types are constantly coming up with new, exciting themes and sharing them on the Web.

Browsing for themes on your computer

Open the Themes menu (Page Layout → Themes → Themes or Alt+P, TH), and you find custom themes at the top of the list (Figure 5-5). Custom themes are ones that you or someone else created, and they're stored in the Document Themes folder inside your Template folder (*C:\Documents and Settings\[Your Name]\ Templates\Document Themes*).

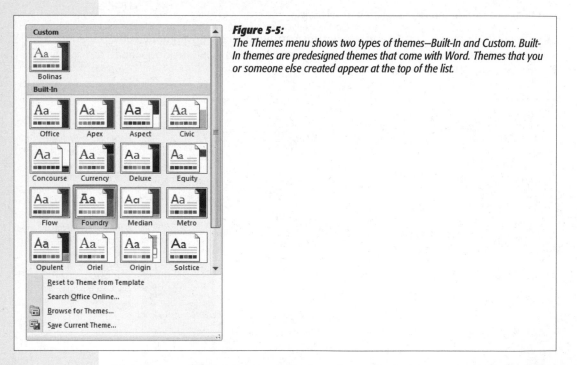

Figure 5-5:
The Themes menu shows two types of themes—Built-In and Custom. Built-In themes are predesigned themes that come with Word. Themes that you or someone else created appear at the top of the list.

If themes are stored (or moved) somewhere else on your computer, then they won't show up on the Themes menu, but Word can help you look for them. To search for themes, click the Browse for Themes button near the bottom of the Themes menu. The Choose Theme or Themed Document box opens. As shown in

Figure 5-6, this standard Windows file box is set up to show you *.thmx, *.docx, *xlsx, and other file types that contain Office themes. The "Files of type" menu is set to Office Themes and Themed Documents, which acts as a filter, so the main window shows you only files that match these types (and folders that contain them).

POWER USERS' CLINIC

Moving Themes to Your Themes Folder

If you frequently browse to use a custom theme, then you'll save time copying the theme to your Document Themes folder. That way, the theme always shows up in the Custom group on the Themes menu, and you'll never have to search for it again. Here's how to move a theme from your My Documents folder to your Document Themes folder:

1. Choose Page Layout → Themes → Themes → Browse for Themes to open the Choose Theme or Themed Document box (Figure 5-6).

2. Use the buttons on the left and the drop-down menu at the top to hunt down a folder with Office themes. (Theme files end in .thmx.)

3. When you find the file you want to copy, right-click it, and then choose Copy from the File shortcut menu.

4. Navigate to your Document Themes folder. If you sign on to your computer with the name *Christopher*, then start in your My Computer window, and go to *C:\Documents and Settings\Christopher\Templates\Document Themes* (Figure 5-7).

5. Right-click an empty spot in the Document Themes folder, and then choose Paste.

You see your Themes document added to the Document Themes folder. Open your Themes menu, and it's there at the top of the list.

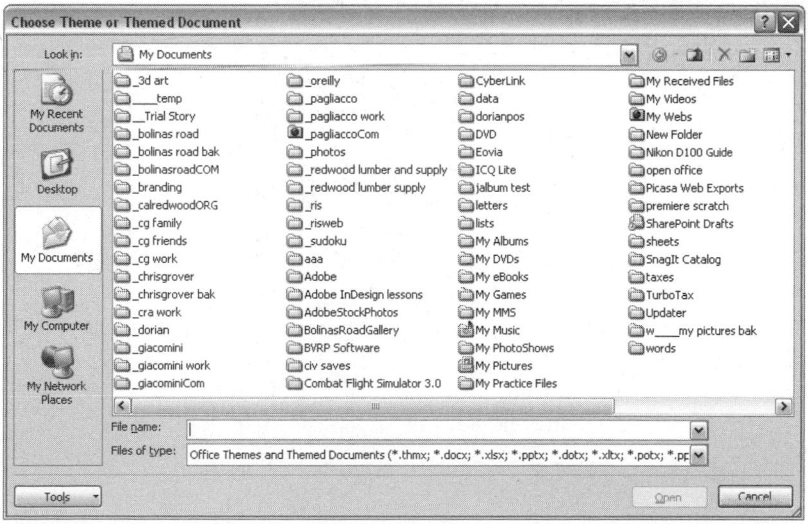

Figure 5-6:
If you click Browse for Themes, then you get a standard Windows file box. You can use this box to navigate through your system to seek out files that end in ".thmx." And if you can't find themes this way, see the box on page 137 for another way to search.

Figure 5-7:
Word stores themes in a folder inside your Templates folder. Microsoft likes to hide this folder so you won't find it with your other files in your My Documents folder. Instead, you must look in the Documents and Settings folder on your hard drive. On most computers that's Local Disk (C:).

Searching for themes online

You can look for themes on the Internet, too. A good place to start is Microsoft Office Online (*www.microsoft.com/office*), shown in Figure 5-8. As time goes on, it's likely that more themes, fonts, and colors will be available. And don't forget to do a Google search. Type *Office 2007 themes* in Google's search box, and you'll see at least a half million entries.

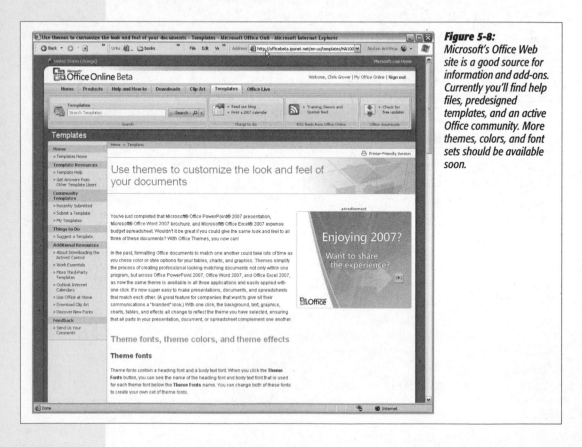

Figure 5-8:
Microsoft's Office Web site is a good source for information and add-ons. Currently you'll find help files, predesigned templates, and an active Office community. More themes, colors, and font sets should be available soon.

Searching for Themes on Your Computer

If you think themes may be hiding on your computer that aren't in your My Documents folder, then you can search them out using Windows Explorer.

1. **Go to Start › My Documents**.

   Windows Explorer opens and you see the contents of a folder in the large box on the right. The panel on the left changes as you click buttons and menu commands.

2. **Near the top of the window, click Search (or press Ctrl+F) to open the Search task pane.**

   At the pane's left, click the "All files and folders" button (since you want to search your entire computer).

3. **In the "All or part of the file name" box, type *.thmx.**

   (The asterisk (*) character is a wild card that matches any file name with any number of character

So when you enter **.thmx* you're telling your computer to look for all files that end with ".*thmx*.")

4. **In the "Look in" drop-down menu at the bottom, choose My Computer to tell Windows Explorer to search all the files and folders on your computer. (Those theme files can't hide from you!)**

5. **Click Search. Before long, you see files ending in .thmx start to pop up in the window on the right.**

Ignore themes that show up in expected places, like *\Program Files\Microsoft Office\Document Themes 12* and *\Templates\Document Themes*, because all these themes already show up in Word's Theme menu. You're looking for themes in other locations. When you find likely candidates, copy and paste them into your *C:\Documents and Settings\Christopher\Templates\Document Themes* folder.

Choosing a Template

When you use a template, you're taking advantage of the work and wisdom of those who have gone before you. As the saying goes, "Why reinvent the wheel?" Microsoft must adhere to this philosophy because, in Word 2007, they've made templates an even more integral part of the program. Just look at the New Document dialog box (Alt+F, N). Your computer screen fills up with templates (Figure 5-9). You'll find templates for resumés, newsletters, calendars, and greeting cards. The business category alone contains hundreds of templates. When you're working on deadline or you need a professionally designed document, finding the right template to do the job will save time in the long run.

Here's a partial sampling of the types of templates you'll find. In the New Document dialog box, they appear alphabetically in the left panel:

- **Planning.** Agendas, calendars, lists, planners, schedules.

- **Stationery and mailing.** Business cards, greeting cards, envelopes, faxes, invitations, labels, letters, postcards.

- **General business.** Contracts, forms, invoices, memos, minutes, purchase orders, receipts, reports, resumés, statements, time sheets.

- **Marketing.** Award certificates, brochures, gift certificates, flyers, newsletters.

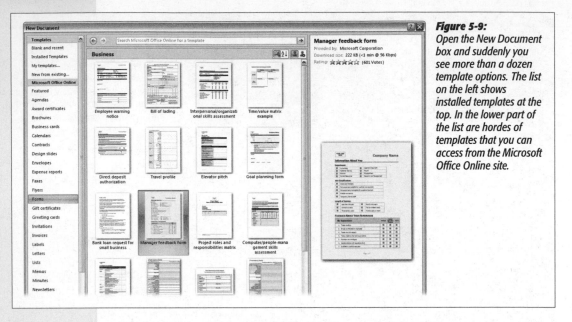

Figure 5-9:
Open the New Document box and suddenly you see more than a dozen template options. The list on the left shows installed templates at the top. In the lower part of the list are hordes of templates that you can access from the Microsoft Office Online site.

If that's not enough, in typical Microsoftian overkill there's even a category called More Categories, where, believe it or not, you find 50 more categories, which run the gamut from Address Books, Games, and Paper Folding projects to Quizzes and Scorecards.

When you use a template, you're not opening a template file, you're opening a copy of it, sort of like pulling the top sheet off a pad of forms. The original template file remains untouched. Here are some of the goodies you'll find in a new document you've opened from a template:

- **Graphics.** Templates for brochures, business cards, greeting cards, and newsletters almost always include drawing, clip art, lines, and borders. Frequently you'll find templates that include photos (Figure 5-10).

- **Formatting.** Setting up the page formats, indents, and line spacing, and positioning every single bit of text on the page can be a big job. For projects like forms, purchase orders, and invoices, you may end up tearing your hair out. Fortunately, using a template is a lot easier on your scalp.

- **Boilerplate text.** Often in templates the text is just there for position. You replace the text with your own words. However, some templates include boilerplate text that you want to leave in place. Contracts, fax cover pages, forms, and even resumés may include body text or headings that you want to keep.

- **AutoText entries.** Sophisticated templates sometimes add automated features like AutoText entries. A template designed to handle a common complaint may include a lengthy AutoText entry that begins, "We are so very sorry that the widget didn't live up to your expectations." To insert the diatribe, all you have to do is type *sorry*, and then press the F3 key.

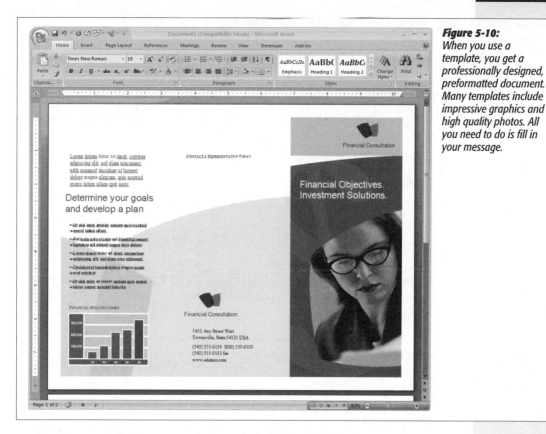

Figure 5-10:
When you use a template, you get a professionally designed, preformatted document. Many templates include impressive graphics and high quality photos. All you need to do is fill in your message.

- **Content controls.** Some templates include widgets, like text boxes and drop-down menus, that let you create electronic forms in Word, just like the forms you fill out on Web sites.

- **Macros.** Templates that include a lot of automatic features probably use macros—mini-programs that run inside Word documents—to create their magic. Macros let you run several commands with the click of a button or a keyboard shortcut.

Templates Behind the Scenes

Every Word document has at least one template attached to it, whether you know it or not. Even when you start a blank document, the Normal template is what provides a basic page layout and serves up your preferred font and AutoText entries. The tools and formats in the Normal template are always available to all your documents, so it's called a *global template*.

Document templates are different from global ones. They often provide extensive formatting, boilerplate text, and in some cases macros and other tools to help you get the job done. The settings and tools in document templates are available only to documents that are based on that template. So you won't find AutoText from your invoice template in a document you created using a greeting card template.

Starting a Document from a Template

The New Document dialog box lets you access the hundreds of Office templates that are available online—many more than Word installs on your computer. If you have a computer with a cable or DSL Internet connection, then using an online template is almost as fast as using an installed one.

Here's how to download a business card template and use it to create your own cards:

1. **Go to Office button → New (or press Alt+F, N).**

   The New Document box opens, offering several ways to create a new document (Figure 5-9). To find a business card template, look to the Templates categories list on the left.

2. **In the left panel, under the Microsoft Office Online heading, click "Business cards."**

   Each category contains dozens of templates. When you select "Business cards," you see cards for just about every industry on earth—except English Novelist (Figure 5-11).

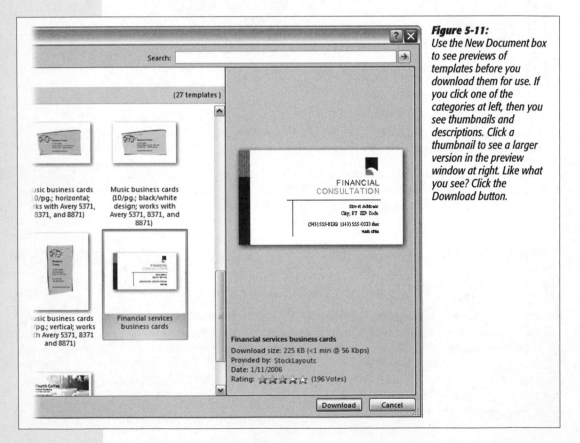

Figure 5-11:
Use the New Document box to see previews of templates before you download them for use. If you click one of the categories at left, then you see thumbnails and descriptions. Click a thumbnail to see a larger version in the preview window at right. Like what you see? Click the Download button.

3. **Scroll down the middle panel, and then click the "Financial services business cards" template to preview it in the rightmost panel.**

The preview shows how your document will look. It creates 10 cards per page when you print on a full-sized sheet. You'll find some additional details about the card below the preview panel. Note the file size is 225 KB. Even a 56 Kpbs (slow dial-up Internet access) takes less than a minute to download this template.

At bottom is a rating showing that this particular design has received four out of five stars, according to votes from 196 people like you. The rating system is a way for you to learn if a certain template has been helpful to others. You can vote on this template, too, as described in Figure 5-12.

Figure 5-12:
In the New Document box, select a template, and then click Help to view details about that template in a window like this one. Add your vote to the rating by clicking one of the stars under the Feedback heading.

4. **In the middle panel, double-click the template to start the download.**

If all goes well, then you see an alert box telling you that the download is taking place (Figure 5-13). When the download is complete, Word opens a new document based on the template.

Note: The Microsoft Genuine Advantage box may rear its head during the download process. When you see this message box, Microsoft is checking whether you have legal and licensed versions of their programs. If you don't, then you won't be able to download the template.

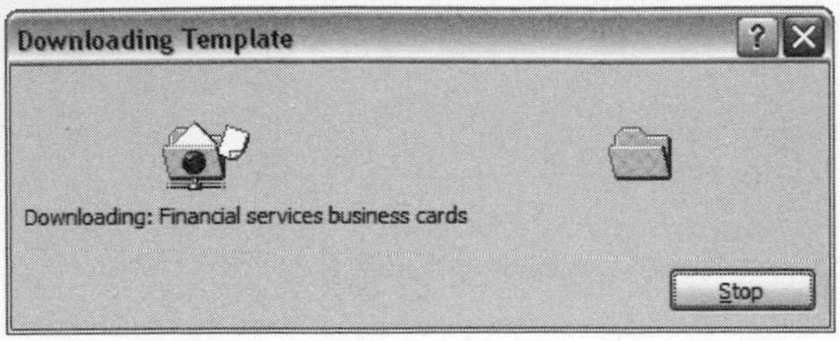

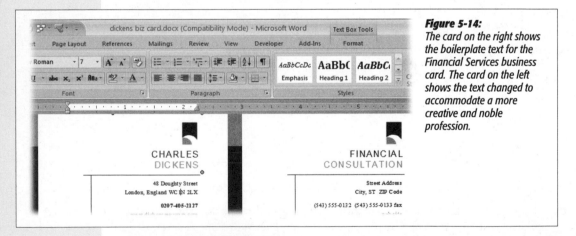

Figure 5-13:
The download alert box appears when the download begins. If you change your mind, click Stop. Otherwise, the box automatically goes away when the download is complete.

5. **Replace the boilerplate text with your own text.**

   As with any template, you need to replace the boilerplate text with your own information. Figure 5-14 compares the newly inserted text next to the original template. In the case of the business cards, you need to copy (Ctrl+C) and paste (Ctrl+V) your text in each of the cards on the page.

6. **Save the file with a new name.**

   When you're happy with the changes, save your document in a folder where you can find it later.

7. **Print the document.**

   When you're ready, run the presses. You probably don't want to print business cards on regular flimsy paper. Instead, you can find sturdier card stock at an office supply store. Avery, one company that makes labels and other forms, has several products for business cards including some with micro-perforated edges that give you a clean, professional result.

Figure 5-14:
The card on the right shows the boilerplate text for the Financial Services business card. The card on the left shows the text changed to accommodate a more creative and noble profession.

Using Installed Templates

Using a template that's already on your computer isn't much different than using one of the templates from Microsoft Office Online (Figure 5-15). After you open the New Document box (Alt+F, N), click Installed Templates at the top of the left panel. The middle panel shows you thumbnails of all templates on your computer. (You won't find as much variety here as you get online.)

You can preview the installed templates just like you did the online counterparts. Click a template thumbnail to preview it in the right panel. Using an installed template works exactly the same as using one from Microsoft Office Online, as described in the previous section, except that you skip the download process. Just double-click the template to open a new document from it, and then get to work as described starting in step 5 on page 142.

After you've used a template, the next time you start a new document, you'll see the template's name in the Recently Used Templates list (Figure 5-16). The templates that you use most frequently end up as permanent members of this list—how's that for handy?

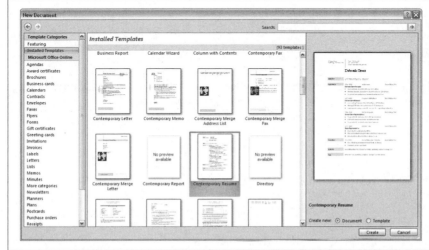

Figure 5-15:
If you're lucky enough to have a fast Internet connection, then you'll hardly notice whether your templates are online or installed on your computer. The process of selecting, previewing, and using a template is almost exactly the same.

Figure 5-16:
Templates that you used recently appear on the right side of the New Document dialog box. To create a new document using a template, just double-click the name, or select it, and then click Create in the lower-right corner (not shown).

CHAPTER 6

Spelling, Grammar, and Reference Tools

When you've worked for hours on a resumé or a report, the last thing you want to do is send it out with goofs. Word's spelling and grammar tools help you avoid that kind of embarrassment. In this chapter, you'll learn how to use these tools. You'll also get a clear understanding of when and how Word makes automatic changes to your text. Even more important, you'll learn how to set up these tools to work the way you like to work.

If you really want to sound smart, Word can help you with some extra research, giving you access to a comprehensive Web-based reference library, including dictionary, encyclopedia, thesaurus, Web search, and language translation tools (Figure 6-1).

Turning on Spelling and Grammar Checking

Spelling errors make any document look unprofessional, so ignoring Word's spell checker is just plain silly. And while grammar and style are largely subjective, the grammar-checking tool can help you spot glaring errors (like mixing up "it's" and "its"). When Microsoft first added these tools to Word, some people resented the intrusion, as discussed in the box on page 149. The fact is, you're in control. You can choose whether you want Word to check your work as you type, flagging misspelled words and questionable grammar (Figure 6-2), or whether you prefer to get the words on the page first, and then review the spelling and grammar at the end.

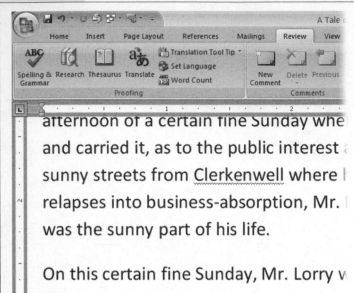

Figure 6-1:
Access to Word's Spelling and Grammar checker is on the Review → Proofing group, along with the thesaurus, the translation tool, and a slew of Web-based research tools.

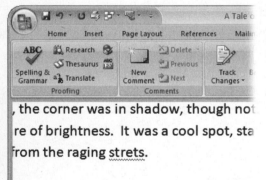

Figure 6-2:
When you use the "Check spelling as you type" option, Word places wavy red lines under possibly misspelled words. Some people consider this a distraction from their writing and choose to do a manual spell check when they've finished writing.

Follow these steps to set up Word's spelling and grammar-checking tools to work the way you like to work:

1. **Click the Office button (Alt+F) and in the lower-right corner of the menu, click Word Options.**

   The list on the left gives you several buttons that divide the Options into different groups. The options for the spelling and grammar tools are in Proofing.

2. **Click the Proofing category (Figure 6-3).**

   The panel on the right changes to show checkboxes and buttons grouped into four categories: "AutoCorrect options," "When correcting spelling in Office programs," "When correcting spelling in Word," "When correcting grammar in Word," and "Exceptions for."

3. **Turn on the options in "When correcting spelling for Office programs" for the types of errors you want Word *not* to worry about.**

   For example, Internet addresses and filenames often set off the spell checker, resulting in a distracting sea of red waves. You can also tell Word to ignore words in uppercase and words that include numbers, which are often company names or special terms that Word doesn't know how to spell. Use the check-boxes to have the spell checker ignore these types of words.

Tip: You can "teach" Word how to spell these unfamiliar words and include them in spell checks by adding them to Word's spelling dictionary (page 150).

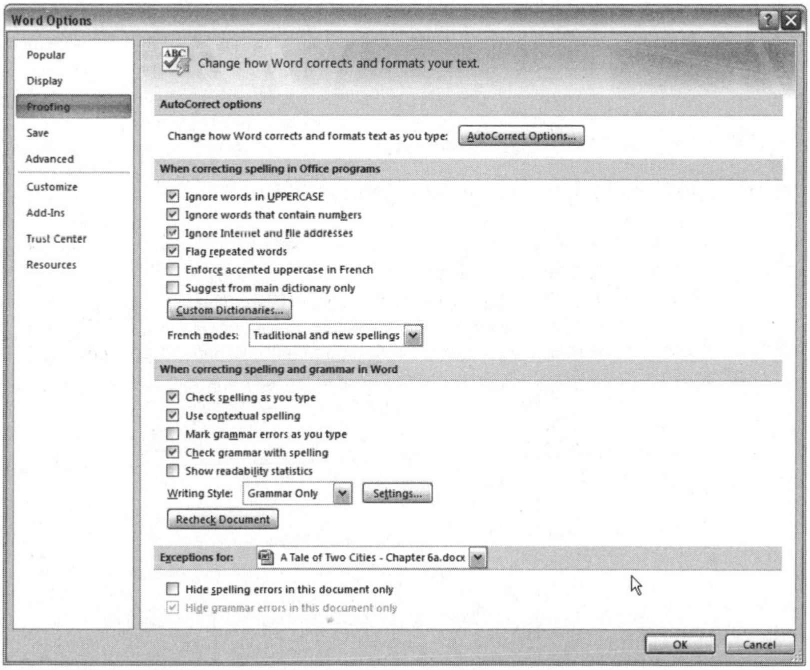

Figure 6-3:
Not only can you choose whether Word checks your spelling and grammar as you type, but Word also gives you a bunch of ways to fine-tune the program's level of persnicketyness. (By the way, this chapter was originally written in Word, and that last word was flagged with a red underline.)

4. **Word starts out with background spell checking turned on; if it annoys you, turn off the "Check spelling as you type" checkbox.**

   This unassuming checkbox is the most important option. Turning it on turns on the wavy red lines under misspelled words.

   Sometimes the word you type is spelled correctly, but it's the wrong word in the context. For example, "I'll see you in too weeks" is a contextual error. Word checks for this type of mistake if you turn on the "Use contextual spelling" checkbox.

5. **If you're interested in some grammar help from Word, turn on the "Check grammar with spelling" checkbox.**

   This setting makes Word flag questionable construction as you work, with a wavy *green* underline. Or you can leave it turned off and check grammar when you're through writing, as described on page 154.

   If you don't want Word checking your grammar at all, turn off the "Check grammar with spelling" checkbox.

Tip: To fine-tune your grammar options, click the Settings button to open the Grammar Settings box (Figure 6-4). In this box, you can control whether the grammar checker flags capitalization, run on sentences, and so on.

---

6. **Click OK to close the Word Options box.**

   Your new spelling and grammar settings go into effect.

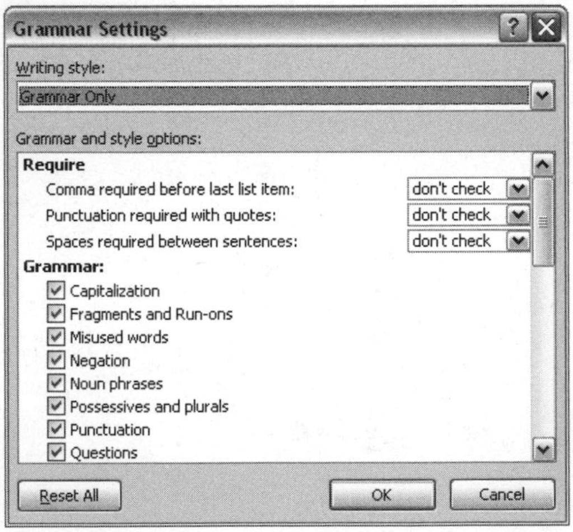

Figure 6-4:
You encounter even more debate and personal opinion when it comes to setting rules about grammar and style. Word gives you more options for controlling the program's tendency to flag your immortal prose.

NOSTALGIA CORNER

The Wavy Line Debate

When Microsoft first introduced background spell checking and the wavy red line, it was roundly pooh-poohed by a large portion of the Word-using population. Some people didn't like the distraction of the red snakes popping up all over. These lines interfered with their concentration on their work. Other people noticed that background spell checking slowed down already slow computers. And, of course there were the folks who considered it unnecessary. "I always check my spelling when I'm *finished* writing." Microsoft continued to ship Word with background spell checking turned on. After all, people who didn't like it had the option to turn it off.

Over the years, the wavy lines have won some converts. Folks who once found background spell checking distracting began to leave it on as they upgraded Word.

Those people who were new to Word probably didn't know they could turn it off. Computers continued to increase in horsepower, so speed was no longer a big issue. If your computer can edit video, it probably won't be stressed by handling spell checking in the background, even for a very long document. The Automatic spell checking isn't going away and the solution is the same as always. Pick your path to pristine prose and set up Word accordingly.

By the way, if you *don't* want Word to check spelling in the background, you can make it stop. Open Word Options (Alt+F, I), and then click the Proofing option on the left. The third group of options is named "When correcting spelling and grammar in Word." Turn off the "Check spelling as you type" checkbox, and you've turned off background spell checking.

Checking Spelling

Word's spell checker reads every word in your document and looks it up in its behind-the-scenes dictionary file. If the word isn't in the dictionary, the spell checker flags it as a possibly misspelled word. Spell checker handles misspelled words in three ways:

- **AutoCorrect.** The spell checker looks to see if the word is in its list of words to correct automatically. Words like "hte" for "the" or "shwo" for "show," for example, are in the AutoCorrect list. (You can add and remove words from the AutoCorrect list, and if you prefer, you can turn off AutoCorrect entirely. To see how, flip ahead to page 156.)

- **Check spelling as you type.** If you've set up Word to check spelling errors as you type, the spell checker puts a wavy red line under the word in question (Figure 6-2).

- **Check spelling manually.** Check spelling in one pass. The spell checker asks you about each questionable word when you run a manual spell check.

Checking Spelling As You Type

Unless you've turned this option off, as described in the previous steps, Word checks the spelling of each word you type, comparing it to its spelling dictionary. When a word is not in the dictionary, the spell checker brings it to your attention—not with a whack across the knuckles with a ruler, but with a wavy red underline (Figure 6-2).

To correct a word flagged with a wavy red line, right-click it. A shortcut menu shows suggested spellings for the word you flubbed (Figure 6-5). To choose a word from the list, just click it, and the correctly spelled word replaces the misspelled word.

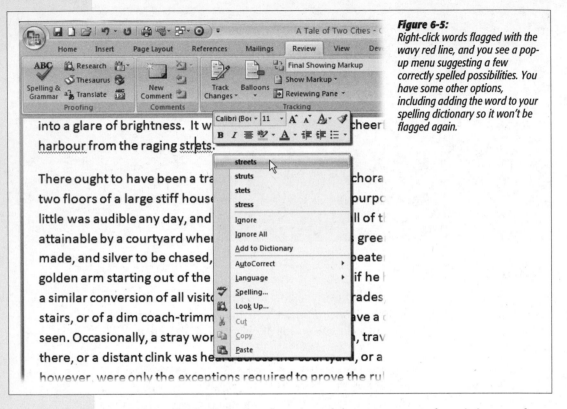

Figure 6-5:
Right-click words flagged with the wavy red line, and you see a pop-up menu suggesting a few correctly spelled possibilities. You have some other options, including adding the word to your spelling dictionary so it won't be flagged again.

Sometimes the spell checker flags a word, but you want to keep it in your document just the way it is (and make Word stop underlining it, for heaven's sake). For these words, the shortcut menu gives you three courses of action (Figure 6-6):

- **Ignore.** Click Ignore, and the spell checker ignores this instance of the word (in this document only) and removes the underline.

- **Ignore All.** When you choose this option, the spell checker doesn't flag any occurrence of the word in this document. No more wavy red lines for that baby.

- **Add to Dictionary.** When you add a word to the dictionary, you'll never see a wavy line under the word again, in this document or any other. Word adds the word to a file named CUSTOM.DIC. Over time, your custom dictionary collects all the special words that you don't want flagged in a spell check.

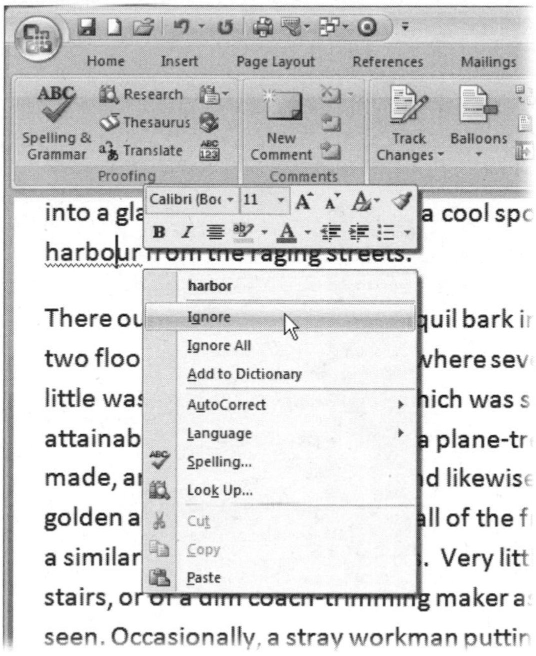

Figure 6-6:
In addition to a spelling suggestion, Word gives you three other options. You can ignore the word just this once, you can ignore all occurrences of the word in the document, or you can add the word to your dictionary, so that Word won't flag it as misspelled in any document.

Checking Spelling Manually

When you opt for manual spelling and grammar checking, you can do these tasks in one pass, at your leisure, like after you've finished writing. To start a spelling and grammar check, choose Review → Proofing → Spelling and Grammar or press Alt+R, S. (F7, that old favorite spelling key, still works too.) You see a dialog box like the one in Figure 6-7.

Often, you're checking the spelling and the grammar at the same time, so in the upper-left corner, the Spelling and Grammar box tells you about the problem. In the case of a misspelled word, you see "Not in Dictionary" over a text box that shows the entire sentence with the word highlighted. The box below offers suggestions. On the right side of the dialog box, you see several buttons. Use one of the top three buttons—Ignore Once, Ignore All, and Add to Dictionary—when you want to keep the word spelled as it is. These options do the same thing as the shortcut menu options described earlier.

The bottom three buttons let you make changes to the misspelled words. When you select a word from the Suggestions list, and then click Change, Word replaces the highlighted word with the suggestion. When you click Change All, Word looks through your whole document, and corrects any other occurrences of the misspelled words at the same time. Clicking the AutoCorrect button tells Word to make the correction automatically, as you type, every time you misspell the word.

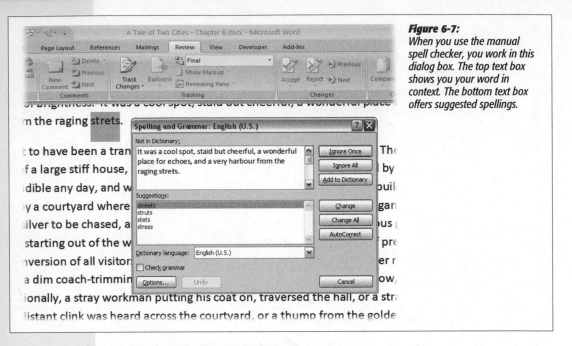

Figure 6-7:
When you use the manual spell checker, you work in this dialog box. The top text box shows you your word in context. The bottom text box offers suggested spellings.

Managing Custom Dictionaries

Word has a standard spelling dictionary, which is just one huge list of common words in their correct spellings. When you tell Word to add a word to the dictionary, it doesn't actually add the word to its standard dictionary. It adds it to a new file that's all yours. This file, CUSTOM.DIC, contains your personal preferred spellings. Over time, your CUSTOM.DIC file collects the oddly spelled names of your friends and family, slang terms you frequently use, and a host of other words.

Tip: You can transfer your custom dictionary to another computer by simply copying your CUSTOM.DIC file to the new machine. (Your CUSTOM.DIC file lives in a folder named *C:\Documents and Settings\User Name\Microsoft\Application Data\Proof.*)

Removing a word from your custom dictionary

Oops! You've added a misspelled word to your custom dictionary. Now Word won't ever flag "dosn't" again. All is not lost. You can edit your custom dictionary right within Word. Here are the steps:

1. **Go to Office button → Word Options (Alt+F, I). In the list on the left, click Proofing.**

   Access to the custom dictionary is with the Spelling and Grammar tools.

2. **Roughly in the middle of the window, among the Spelling settings, click the Custom Dictionaries button.**

   The Custom Dictionaries box opens (Figure 6-8).

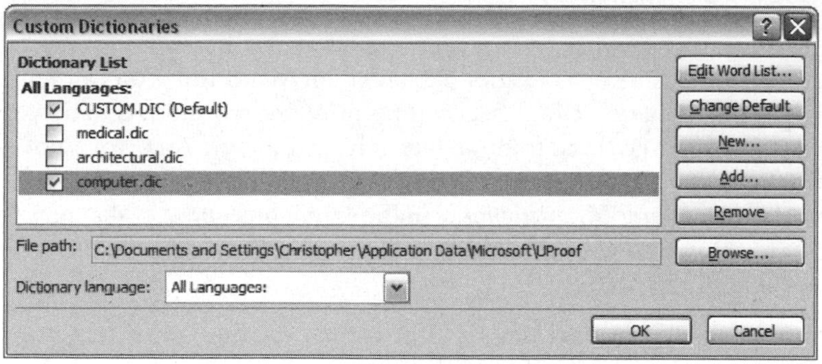

Figure 6-8:
Use the Custom Dictionaries box to manage your personal dictionary and add professional dictionaries to Word. Here's where you choose the dictionaries in use, add new dictionaries, and open your custom dictionaries for editing.

3. **In the list on the left, choose CUSTOM.DIC.**

   When you add words to your dictionary while checking spelling, Word stores them in the CUSTOM.DIC file. If you've created any additional custom dictionaries, you'll see them in this list too.

4. **Click Edit Word List to open the dictionary.**

   Yet another dialog box opens with CUSTOM.DIC in the title bar (Figure 6-9). Your custom words are in the list labeled Dictionary.

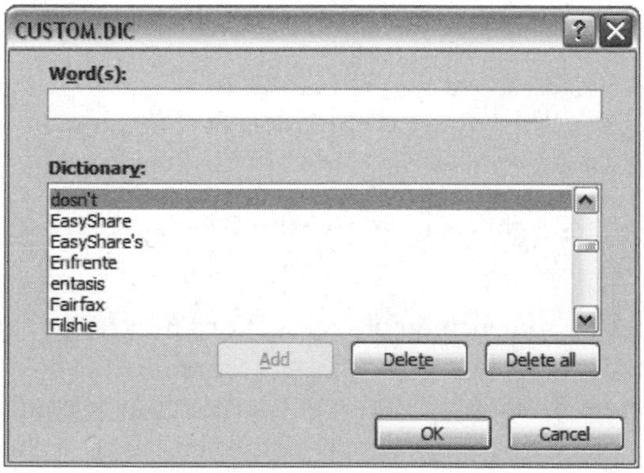

Figure 6-9:
You can add and delete words from your custom dictionary CUSTOM.DIC. To add a word, type it in the box at the top, and then click Add. Remove words from the list by selecting the word in the Dictionary button, and then clicking Delete. Be careful with that Delete All button—it really does delete all the words in your custom dictionary.

5. **Select the misspelled word, and then click Delete.**

   The list is alphabetized, so you can use the scroll bars on the right to find your misspelled word. As a shortcut, you can click the first word in the list, and then type the first letter of the word you want. Say you're looking for "dosn't"; press D, and the list jumps to words starting with D.

   Once you find the word, click it, and then click Delete at bottom.

6. **Close the windows by clicking OK.**

   You've opened three dialog boxes to get to edit your dictionary. Clean things up by clicking OK in each. Now the non-word "dosn't" officially earns a wavy line.

Adding professional dictionaries to Word

It seems that every profession, business, and industry has its own language, and often that means it has its own custom dictionary for Word too. You can find all sorts of custom dictionaries, either free or for a price. Search the Web, and you'll find dictionaries for everything from architecture to zoology. And if it's not out there, you can always create your own. Google is a good place to start the search. Just type *"Microsoft Word" .dic dictionaries* in the search box and see what pops up. If you want to zero in on a specific business like construction or computers, then add that word to your search.

Once you find a dictionary and download or copy it to your computer, you can add it to Word's dictionary list. Here are the steps:

1. **Open the Custom Dictionaries box (Figure 6-8), as described in steps 1–2 on page 152.**

2. **Click the Add button on the right to open one of Windows' standard file boxes.**

   A box labeled Add Custom Dictionary appears. You see the standard tools for navigating through your computer folders and hunting down files. Use the tools on the left and the drop-down menu on top to navigate to the folder containing your new dictionary.

3. **Double-click your dictionary file, or select it, and then, at the bottom of the window, click Open.**

   The Add Custom Dictionary box closes, and you're back at the Custom Dictionaries box. Your new dictionary is listed along with CUSTOM.DIC and all the rest.

4. **If you plan on using the dictionary right away, make sure there's a checkmark in the box next to its name.**

   Using the checkboxes, you can choose which dictionaries Word uses for its spell check. To minimize misspellings, use only the dictionaries relevant to your current document. A slip of the typing fingers could end up matching a medical term. Also, for each dictionary you add, it can take Word a little longer to check spelling, though you probably won't notice the difference.

Checking Grammar and Style

Word's grammar and style tools work almost exactly like the spelling tools. You have the same choice between background checking and manual checking. If you check grammar and style in the background while you type, word puts a wavy green line under suspect sentences and phrases. If you check grammar manually, you view problem sentences in the Spelling and Grammar dialog box (Figure 6-10).

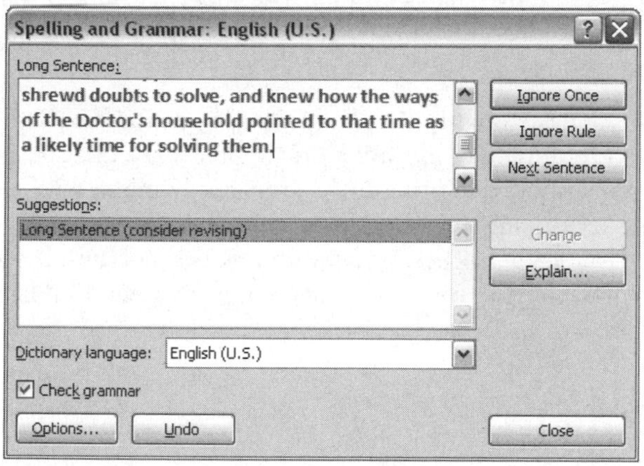

Figure 6-10:
In the Spelling and Grammar dialog box, text in the upper-left corner describes the error, and suggestions appear at bottom. For a more detailed description of the problem, click Explain.

You may feel that Word's grammar police are a little too strict for your personal style of writing. If that's the case, you can tinker with the settings (Office button → Word Options → Proofing). Here are some of the options you toggle on or off in the Grammar Settings box (Figure 6-4):

- **Capitalization.** Finds words that should be capitalized, (like *madame* DeFarge).

- **Fragments and run-ons.** Checks for complete sentences and flags overly long meandering sentences that seem to just go on and on and you can't wait for them to stop but they never do.

- **Misused words.** Looks for the incorrect use of adjectives and adverbs.

- **Negation.** Flags double negatives.

- **Noun phrases.** Checks for proper usage of "a" and "an" and finds phrases where the number doesn't agree with the noun. For example, it wouldn't like "A Tale of Two City."

- **Possessives and plurals.** Leave this option checked if you have a problem forgetting apostrophes in phrases like "the ships hold."

- **Punctuation.** Checks your usage of quotation marks, commas, colons, and all those other little marks.

- **Questions.** Checks for question marks, and flags questions with non-standard structure.

- **Relative clauses.** Finds errors in relative clauses, such as the use of "which" instead of "who" in a clause referring to people.

- **Subject-verb agreement.** Flags sentences where the verbs don't match the nouns, as in "All of the nobles has gone to the guillotine."

- **Verb phrases.** Finds errors in verb usages such as incorrect tense.

Style checking is even more subjective than grammar checking. If you feel there ain't no reason Microsoft should meddle when you say you're real mad at the congressman, you can turn this feature off.

You can tweak the Style checking settings in the Word Options dialog box (Office button → Word Options → Proofing). For example, the "When correcting spelling and grammar in Word" section has a Writing Style drop-down menu with two options: Grammar & Style or Grammar Only. If you choose Grammar & Style, Word hunts down problems such as clichés, passive sentences, and run-on sentences. It's always your choice though; turn on the suggestions that you find helpful and that match your own personal style.

Controlling AutoCorrect

The AutoCorrect feature packs more punch than you may expect, and it works across several of the Office programs, including Word, Publisher, and Outlook. With AutoCorrect, if you accidentally type *hte*, Word changes it to "the." The program doesn't ask you for permission (it comes with AutoCorrect turned on). You may not even notice when Word makes the change. Obviously, AutoCorrect is not a feature for control freaks. On the other hand, there's some surprising power in the concept. Have you ever tried to figure out how to type the © symbol? If you have AutoCorrect on, and you type (c), it magically turns into the copyright symbol. That's just the beginning. AutoCorrect lets you enter a lot of other symbols right from the keyboard, from math symbols to arrows to smiley faces. And just imagine, if you work for the *American Gastroenterological Association*, wouldn't it be great to type in *aga* and let AutoCorrect type in all those words, especially that middle one?

How AutoCorrect Works

AutoCorrect changes words immediately after you type them, so you see the change when it happens right behind your insertion point. If you don't like what AutoCorrect did, press Ctrl+Z to undo it. The text goes back to the characters you typed, and AutoCorrect won't mess with it again.

Fine-tuning AutoCorrect Options

Given that AutoCorrect's reason for being is to change the words that you write, it's important to know how to bring it under control. To adjust AutoCorrect settings, open the AutoCorrect dialog box (Office button → Word Options → Proofing → AutoCorrect Options). You can also jump to the AutoCorrect dialog box from any word in your text with a wavy red spelling line. Right-click the word, and then choose AutoCorrect → AutoCorrect Options from the shortcut menu. The AutoCorrect dialog box gives you access to a lot of settings, so it may take a few moments to sort out how all the options work. At the very top, the "Show Auto-Correct Options buttons" checkbox controls whether or not the little lightning-bolt menu buttons (Figure 6-11) show up in your text.

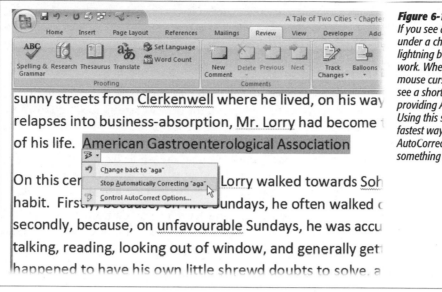

Figure 6-11:
If you see a hollow blue line under a character or you see a lightning bolt, AutoCorrect is at work. When you move your mouse cursor to the spot, you see a shortcut menu like this providing AutoCorrect options. Using this shortcut menu is the fastest way to make AutoCorrect stop autocorrecting something you don't want it to!

The checkboxes at the top of the AutoCorrect dialog box all deal with common typos and finger flubs (Figure 6-12).

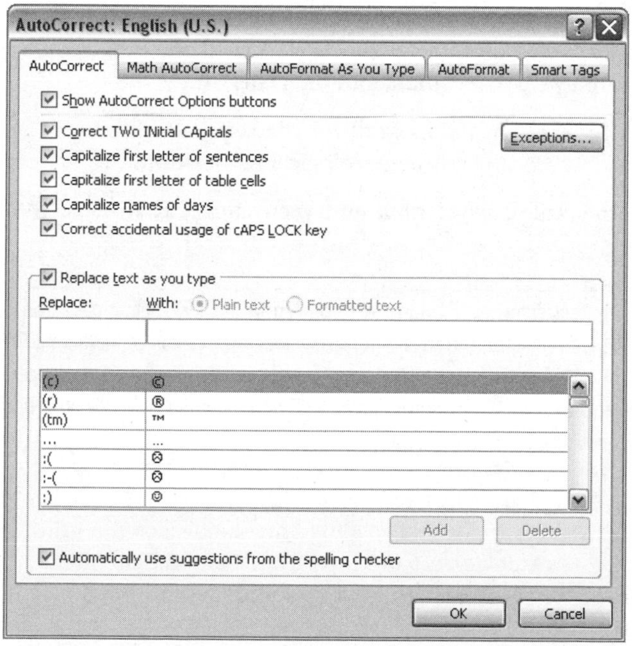

Figure 6-12:
AutoCorrect likes to mess with your words as you type them. Fortunately, you can rein it in using this box. Use the checkboxes at the top to turn on (or off) AutoCorrect's fixes for some common typos. The box at bottom lists the changes AutoCorrect makes. By adding your own replacement pairs to this list, you can even use AutoCorrect as if it were AutoText.

Tip: As shown in this example, you can use the AutoCorrect feature as if it were AutoText. The difference is AutoCorrect automatically turns *aga* into American Gastroenterological Association. When you use Auto-Text, you need to press the F3 key after you type *aga*. So, it's your choice: AutoCorrect for fewer keystrokes, or AutoText for manual control.

The most important checkbox is smack in the middle of the box: "Replace text as you type." When this box is turned on, AutoCorrect corrects spelling errors and makes other replacements as you type. The list box below shows the text that AutoCorrect looks for (on the left) and the text that it uses as a replacement (on the right). Use the scroll bar to browse through the whole list. If you turn on the checkbox at the bottom, AutoCorrect also automatically corrects misspelled words using the same dictionary as for spell checks. No wavy underline. Just fixed spelling.

In addition to controlling how AutoCorrect works, you even get to decide what errors it corrects—by editing the Replace and With lists in this dialog box. Here's how to add your own entry to the list of replacements AutoCorrect makes:

1. **Choose Office button → Word Options → Proofing. At the top of the Proofing panel, click the AutoCorrect Options button.**

   The AutoCorrect dialog box opens.

2. **Make sure the "Replace text as you type" checkbox is turned on.**

   This checkbox is AutoCorrect's master on/off switch.

3. **In the Replace text box, type *aga*, and then press Tab. In the With box, type *American Gastroenterological Association*, and then click Add.**

   You've just told Word to be on the lookout for the sequence of letters "aga," and to replace it with "American Gastroenterological Association."

4. **Click OK to close the AutoCorrect box, and then click OK to close Word Options.**

Note: If AutoCorrect is making replacements you don't like, you can fix this by deleting pairs from this list. Suppose every time you type *are*, AutoCorrect tries to replace it with "Association of Restaurant Entrepreneurs." To remove this annoyance, select the pair "are" and "Association of Restaurant Entrepreneurs," and then click Delete. If you choose "Stop Automatically Correcting" from the AutoCorrect Options button menu (Figure 6-11), Word deletes that entry from the list.

Autocorrecting Math, Formatting, and Smart Tags

AutoCorrect is more than a spelling correction tool. A better term may be *AutoReplace*, since it can apply automatic formatting fixes to mathematical symbols and special text characters like quotation marks and dashes. The AutoCorrect feature also governs Smart Tags—those little "i" buttons that pop up and save you time by performing actions that you'd normally have to open other programs to do. (See the box on page 160 for more detail on Smart Tags.)

As on the AutoCorrect tab, the Math AutoCorrect, AutoFormat, and Smart Tag tabs let you turn certain kinds of fixes on or off. The Math tab also has Replace and With lists that let you type fancy math symbols by hitting a few letters on the keyboard.

- **Math.** Go to Office button → Word Options → Proofing → AutoCorrect Options and click the Math AutoCorrect tab to see how AutoCorrect gives you quick access to math symbols. Sure, you could hunt down some of these symbols with Word's symbol tool (Insert → Symbols → Symbol), but if you use the same math symbols frequently, AutoCorrect provides quicker, easier access. You can customize Math AutoCorrect by typing characters in the Replace and With boxes. It works just like the AutoCorrect tool for words.

- **Formatting.** Go to Office button → Word Options → Proofing → AutoCorrect Options, AutoFormat As You Type tab or AutoFormat tab. Have you ever wondered how Word's smart quotes feature works? You enter straight quotes ("), actually the symbol for inches, on both sides of a quote, yet Word automatically provides curly quotes, curled in the proper direction on both ends of the quote. That's AutoCorrect working behind the scenes. AutoCorrect can jump into action when you start making a numbered list or a bulleted list. It can provide a respectable em dash (—), every time you type two hyphens. The Auto-Format options are presented as checkboxes. Just turn on the ones you want to use.

- **Smart Tags.** Go to Office button → Word Options → Proofing → AutoCorrect Options, Smart Tags tab. Word's Smart Tags work behind the scenes as you type, looking for connections between your words and other resources. Type a name, and Smart Tags checks to see if that person is in your Outlook address book. If the person is, a dotted purple line appears under the name. Move your mouse over the word, and you see the Smart Tag "i" for information button. Click this button, and you can shoot an email off to your pal. Smart Tags perform a number of other tasks, like converting measurements and adding dates to your calendar. You can adjust the settings in the Smart Tags tab of the Auto-Correct box: Click the "Label text with smart tags" box to turn Smart Tags on, and then use the other checkboxes to choose the type of words you want tagged.

POWER USERS' CLINIC

Smart Tags

As you're typing in Word, any number of little helpers pop up from time to time. There's the mini-toolbar, the AutoCorrect Options button, those wavy red lines that the spell checker lays down. And then there are Smart Tags (Figure 6-13). Microsoft's underlying idea is a perfectly good one—to let you share information and features among Office programs with fewer mouse clicks. For example, when you type the name of an Outlook Contact in a Word document, the Smart Tag appears in your document, with a dotted purple line and a little "i" for information button that reveals a shortcut menu when you click it.

You can choose from the menu and send an email, schedule a meeting, or insert an address without the extra steps of launching Outlook and tracking down the contact's name all over again. When you're typing somebody's name, Word figures that you may be thinking of that person and puts a few typical options at your fingertips.

If you're one of those "shut up and let me type" types, you can turn off Smart Tags in the AutoCorrect dialog box. Just click the Smart Tags tab, and then turn off the "Show Smart Tag Actions buttons" checkbox.

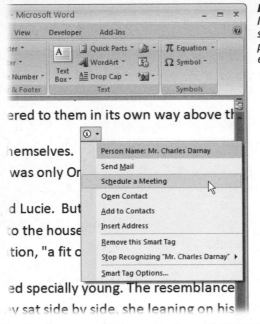

Figure 6-13:
If you let them, Smart Tags appear in your document as little shortcut menus that link to information in other Microsoft programs. Choose from the menu to perform tasks like sending email or scheduling meetings.

Exploring Word's Research Tools

Word's Research panel provides links to a library shelf of Internet research tools that you can use from within Word. To open the panel, go to Review → Proofing → Research. The Research task pane opens at the screen's right (Figure 6-14).

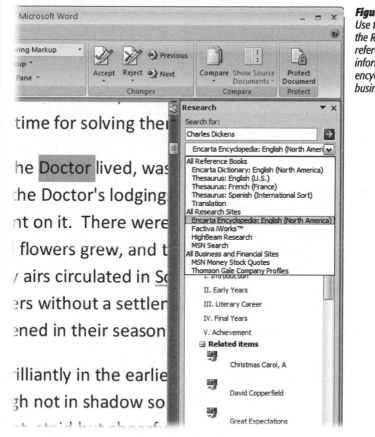

Figure 6-14:
*Use the drop-down menu at the top of
the Research task pane to choose
references when you're searching for
information. Word provides dictionaries,
encyclopedias, Internet search tools, and
business reference resources.*

Here's a list of the tools tucked away in the Research panel:

- **Encarta Dictionary.** Like any dictionary, Microsoft's version provides definitions, parts of speech, and pronunciation.

- **Thesaurus.** Provides synonyms and alternate word choices.

- **Encarta Encyclopedia.** Finds links to articles in the MSN Encarta Encyclopedia.

Note: Encarta started life as a CD-ROM product before everyone was connected to the Internet. Originally, Microsoft purchased the rights to contents of the Funk and Wagnall's encyclopedia and merged that content with other sources.

- **Factiva iWorks.** A service of Dow Jones & Reuters, Factiva provides business and news information.

- **HighBeam Research.** Finds references in newspapers, magazines, journals, books, photos, maps, encyclopedia articles, dictionaries, thesauruses, and almanacs.

• **MSN Search.** Microsoft's Internet search tool.

• **MSN Money Stock Quotes.** Microsoft's financial information service.

• **Thomson Gale Company Profiles.** Provides business and financial details of companies.

Note: If you're not connected to the Internet, obviously you can't use these online tools. Furthermore, their responsiveness depends on the speed of your connection. Some of the Proofing tools, such as the spell checker, thesaurus, and some of the translation tools, still work even if you're not connected. Encarta, Factiva, and the business research sites don't.

Finding Information with the Research Task Pane

For the most part, anyone with an Internet connection and a browser can use all of Word's research tools. You use the same panel and the same quick and easy search process whether you're looking for company information in Thomson Gale, researching a topic for a school paper in HighBeam Research, or looking up the pronunciation of a word in the Encarta Dictionary. You don't have to go hunting all over the Web, and then learn how to use the tools on different sites.

Here's how to research a topic:

1. **Go to Review → Proofing → Research (Alt+R, R).**

   The Research task pane opens to the right of your document. If you want, you can click the top bar and drag the Research task pane out of the Word window so that it floats independently like a palette.

2. **At the top of the Research task pane, type your search terms in the "Search for" text box.**

   If your search words appear in your document, there's a shortcut: Select the words in your document, and then choose Review → Proofing → Research. The search words appear automatically in the "Search for" box, and Word immediately begins to search for references using your last selected reference source.

3. **Use the All Reference Books drop-down menu to select your reference source.**

   Say you're looking for information on Bulldog Brewing Company but don't need the dictionary definition of an English canine. Choose Thomson Gale Company Profiles. The search begins as soon as you make a selection.

   Or, if you leave the menu set to All Reference Books, click the green Start Search button with the arrow. In this case, Word searches in all the reference books and lists the results in the Research pane.

   Be patient. This is, after all, an Internet search. Sooner or later you'll see the results in a large text box (Figure 6-15).

4. If necessary, use a link to follow up in your Web browser.

Often the results include links to Web sites. If you want to continue your research, click the links, and your browser opens to the Web site, such as MSN Money or HighBeam Research.

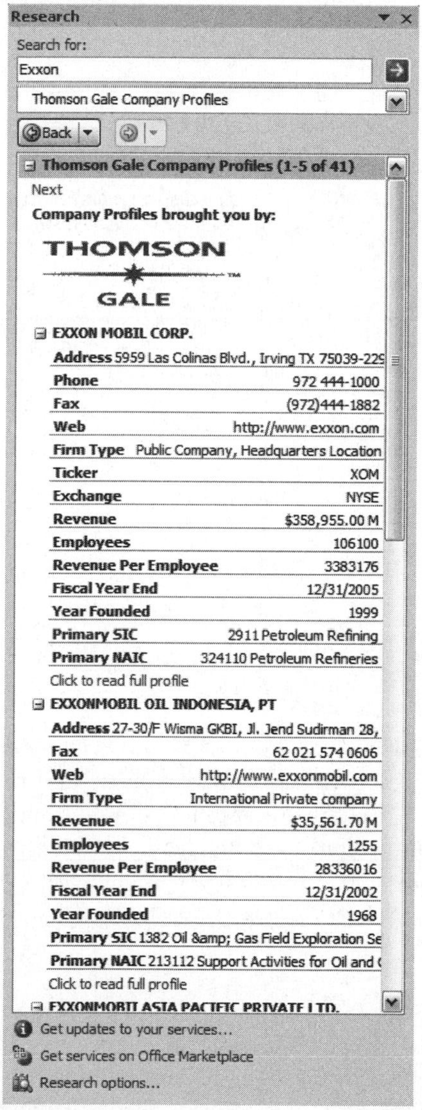

Figure 6-15:
Use Word's Research task pane to get access to Word's thesaurus, Encarta dictionary, encyclopedia, and translation tools. Clicking the arrow next to the Back button opens a menu where you can return to the results of your last few searches.

Accessing Word's Thesaurus

A well-thumbed thesaurus sits on many writers' bookshelves, somewhere between Strunk and White's *The Elements of Style* and Bartlett's *Familiar Quotations*. By providing synonyms and antonyms to common words, a thesaurus helps writers find what Flaubert called *le mot juste*—"the perfect word." Word's thesaurus (Figure 6-16) makes it so easy to look up a synonym that your hard-copy thesaurus may start gathering dust.

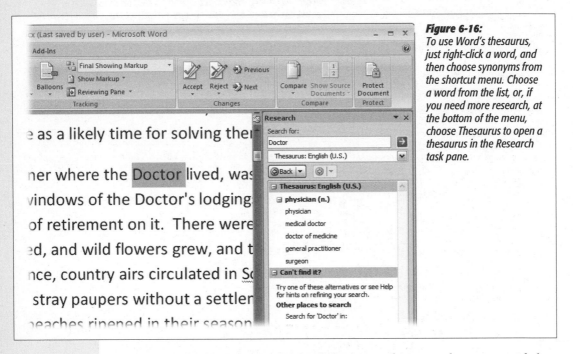

Figure 6-16:
To use Word's thesaurus, just right-click a word, and then choose synonyms from the shortcut menu. Choose a word from the list, or, if you need more research, at the bottom of the menu, choose Thesaurus to open a thesaurus in the Research task pane.

To use Word's thesaurus, just right-click any word in your document, and then point to Synonyms in the pop-up menu. A submenu appears with appropriate synonyms. If that's not enough for you, at the bottom of the menu, click the Thesaurus option to open the Research task pane, with your word entered in the "Search for" box (Figure 6-16). Click the green arrow to look up the reference.

Translating Text

Word's research tools include language translation. When you select a word in your text and click the Translate button on the ribbon (Review → Proofing → Translate or Alt+R, L), Word begins to look up the word using the last language selection for the translation (Figure 6-17). (Word speaks Arabic, Chinese, Dutch, English, French, German, Greek, Italian, Japanese, Portuguese, Russian, Spanish, and Swedish.)

Accurate translation is more of an art than a science. As a result, computer automation goes only part of the journey. Along with the translation of words and phrases, you get an offer to professionally translate your entire document for a fee (Figure 6-18). (Or, you can ask a friend who speaks the language for help.)

Translation ScreenTips

Translation screen tips are another pop-up helper you can turn on. Go to Review → Proofing → Translation ScreenTip, and choose a language from the drop-down menu. Screen tips are available in English, French, Spanish, and other languages. Once you choose your language, all you have to do to see a translation and definitions for the word is to pause your mouse cursor over the word for a couple of seconds (Figure 6-19). The multilanguage details are surprisingly complete.

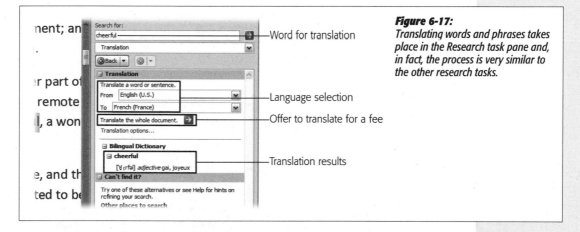

Figure 6-17:
Translating words and phrases takes place in the Research task pane and, in fact, the process is very similar to the other research tasks.

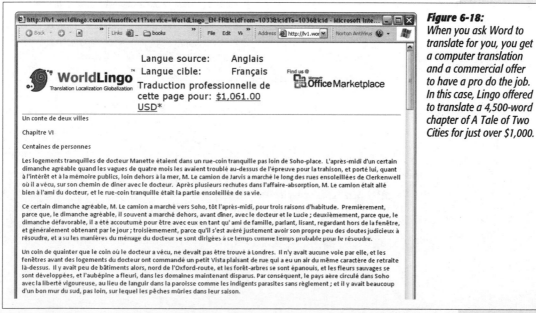

Figure 6-18:
When you ask Word to translate for you, you get a computer translation and a commercial offer to have a pro do the job. In this case, Lingo offered to translate a 4,500-word chapter of A Tale of Two Cities for just over $1,000.

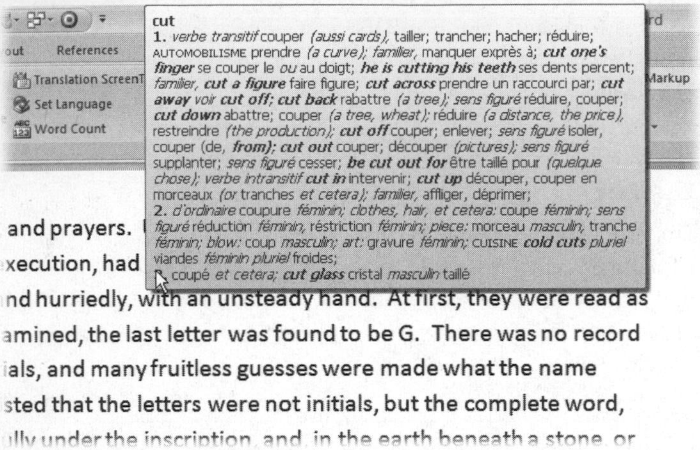

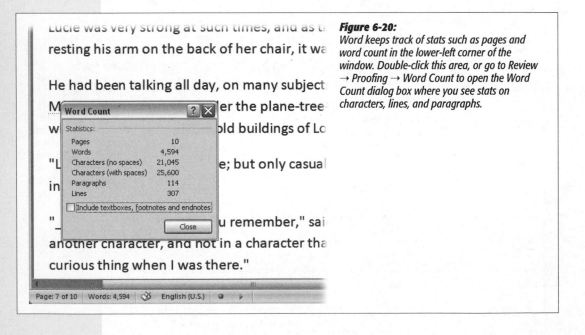

Figure 6-19:
Word's translation screen tips are great if you're in the process of learning a language or you're working in a language that isn't your first. Pause your cursor over a word, and you see a complete dictionary entry in two languages. Entries include parts of speech and idiomatic phrases.

Checking Your Word Count

It's often necessary to count your document's words, lines, paragraphs, and pages. Word keeps a running tab of pages and words in the status bar at the document window's lower-right corner (Figure 6-20). To see more details, double-click the status bar to bring up the Word Count box. Addressing gripes from earlier versions of Word, Microsoft has added checkboxes that let you include or exclude text boxes, footnotes, and endnotes from the count.

Figure 6-20:
Word keeps track of stats such as pages and word count in the lower-left corner of the window. Double-click this area, or go to Review → Proofing → Word Count to open the Word Count dialog box where you see stats on characters, lines, and paragraphs.

Printing Word Documents

At some point in their lives, most Word documents are headed for the printer. Even when you email a document or create an Adobe Acrobat (PDF) file, your recipient may want to print it. In fact, some people like to proofread a hard copy before sending off any document, believing they're more likely to catch mistakes that way.

Word puts a lot of printing power at your fingertips. This chapter shows you how to do things that would make Gutenberg drop his type, starting with the quickest and easiest ways to print your entire document. You'll learn how to choose and use the best printer for the job (say, your color inkjet for photos), a laser or fax for documents, and a PDF file for good measure. And if you're sending that document via snail mail, then you'll need to print an envelope or a label. Word's got you covered there too.

Quick and Easy Printing

When you first install Word, the shortest route to the printer is the Quick Print button. With a document open in Word, go to Office button → Print → Quick Print. With a couple clicks your complete document begins to spew forth from your printer.

Tip: To print with even fewer clicks, add the Quick Print button to the Quick Access toolbar, as described in Figure 7-1.

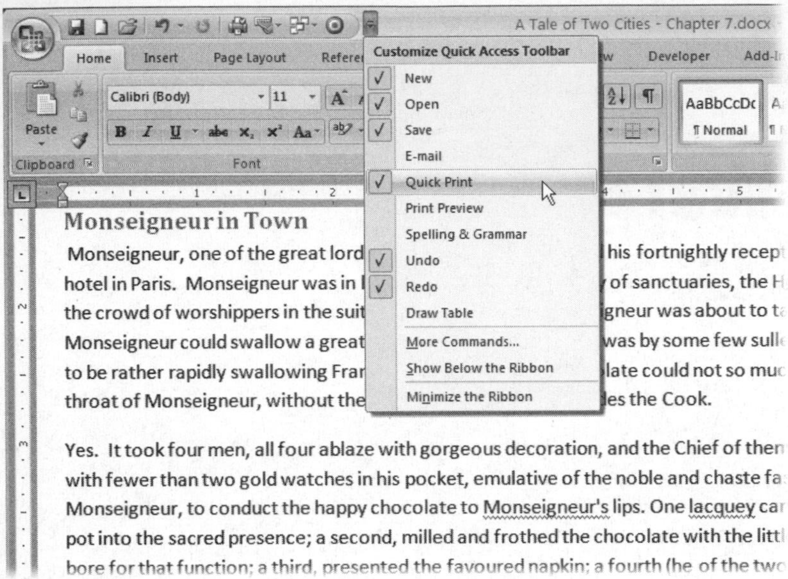

Figure 7-1:
You can customize the Quick Access toolbar to hold any command button. For the convenience of one-click printing, add the Quick Print button. On the right side of the toolbar, click the Customize Quick Access toolbar button, and then turn on the Quick Print option.

The Quick Print process does have its limitations; it prints one copy of the entire document, single sided, every time. If you want to print just a few pages, print multiple or collated copies, or print on both sides of the paper, you must take a couple extra steps. Perhaps the biggest limitation of one-click printing is that your printer must be set up properly. It needs to be turned on, it needs to have paper, and it needs to be connected to your computer and set to run. Otherwise, the Quick Print button does nothing except give you an error message once it's given up.

You can use another quick and easy printing shortcut—printing a document directly from Windows Explorer. Select a file in Explorer, and then choose File → Print from Explorer's menu (Figure 7-2). Yet another Explorer option is to right-click the file, and then choose Print from the shortcut menu. Windows opens the file in Word (launching Word first, if necessary), and Word then prints the document. (If Word wasn't already running when you gave the Print command, then it closes down when printing's done. If Word was already running, just the document closes.) Like the one-click print button, you can't specify any particulars when you print from Windows in this way, but it's a quick and easy way to spit out one copy of your document.

Print Preview

Old movies have that great image of the writer ripping paper out of the typewriter, wadding it up in a ball, and throwing it on the floor. If you're not interested in that much drama (or wasted paper) when you work, then get to know Print Preview. You find Print Preview with a couple of other print commands on the Office menu. To see them, go to Office button → Print (Figure 7-3).

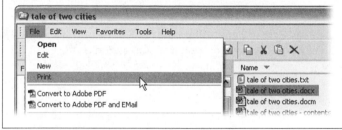

Figure 7-2:
You can print Word files directly from Windows Explorer by selecting your document in Explorer, and then choosing File → Print. Windows' Print command works for just about any printable document, including those created in Word. Windows finds and runs the program needed to print the file.

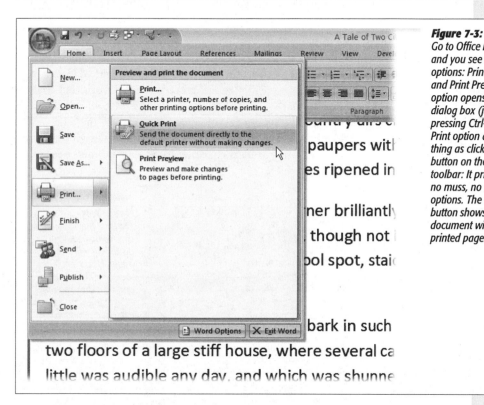

Figure 7-3:
Go to Office button → Print, and you see three print options: Print, Quick Print, and Print Preview. The Print option opens the Print dialog box (just like pressing Ctrl+P). The Quick Print option does the same thing as clicking the Print button on the Quick Access toolbar: It prints one copy—no muss, no fuss, no options. The Print Preview button shows you how your document will look on the printed page.

When you click Print Preview, your Word window changes quite a bit. You can't edit text in this view; it's just for reviewing your work before you print. Up at the top, a single tab appears on the ribbon: Print Preview. On the left, you find two buttons with printer icons—Print and Options. Some familiar-looking tools occupy the Page Setup group. The launcher in the lower-right corner of that group indicates that, with a click, you can bring up the Page Setup dialog box. The tools in the Zoom and Preview groups help you view the page before you go to press. Click the big magnifying glass, and you bring up the Zoom box. The buttons give you a single-page view and a two-page view, so you can get a feeling for facing page layouts. In the Preview group, you can toggle the page rulers on and off. The Magnifier checkbox appears. It works like a toggle and turns your mouse cursor into a Zoom tool. One click and you zoom in; click again and you zoom out.

In Print Preview, you can use the Next Page and Previous Page buttons to look through your document, but it's just as easy to use the scroll bar on the right side of the window. The most curious and confusing button in the group is the Shrink One Page button. You may think this button performs some kind of Alice in Wonderland trick on one of your pages, but no, it makes an attempt to reduce the overall number of pages in the document. This button performs this magic by slightly reducing the type size and reducing the letter spacing. For example, if you preview your document and find it's 11 pages long, but page 11 has just a few lines at the top, then you can click Shrink One Page, and Word squeezes the material into a nice even 10 pages.

The whole purpose of Print Preview is to show you your document exactly the way it will look on the printed page. Word's Print Layout does a pretty good job of that when you're writing and editing, but Print Preview is more accurate. Headers and footers are positioned precisely, and they're not grayed out. Non-printing characters like tabs and paragraph marks don't show up in Print Preview. And if you're using facing pages, Print Preview gives you a good feel for the end result (Figure 7-4). Print Preview's a great place to check to see if your margins are wide enough and to catch widows and orphans (Chapter 3) and abandoned headers at the bottom of the page (Chapter 4).

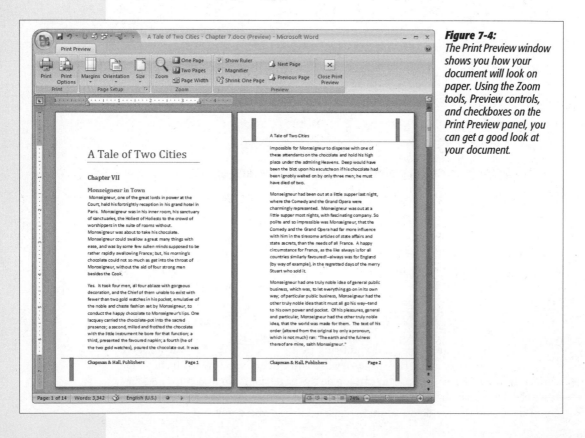

Figure 7-4:
The Print Preview window shows you how your document will look on paper. Using the Zoom tools, Preview controls, and checkboxes on the Print Preview panel, you can get a good look at your document.

What's more, if you find something wrong, Print Preview puts all the tools you need for a quick fix right there on the ribbon (Figure 7-5). You can resolve a lot of last-minute problems with the Page Setup tools on the ribbon. You can also use the regular Page Setup dialog box; press Alt+P, PS to open it. You can adjust margins, change the page layout, and choose the paper source in your printer.

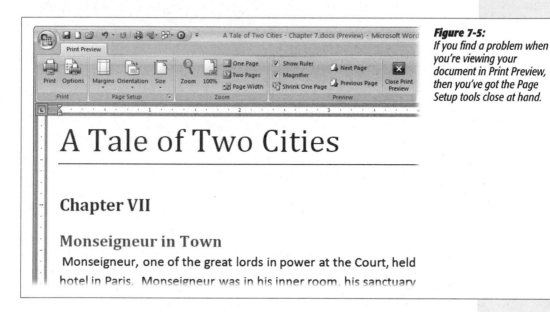

Figure 7-5:
If you find a problem when you're viewing your document in Print Preview, then you've got the Page Setup tools close at hand.

Choosing a Printer

These days, it's not unusual to have a couple of printers and printer-type options. For example, you may have a black and white laser printer for quickly and cheaply printing basic text documents. You may also have a color ink-jet printer for printing photos and the occasional color chart or graph. On top of that, perhaps you have a fax modem connected to your computer. (Windows thinks of fax machines as printers. When you think about it, they are sort of long-distance printers.) If you have the full-blown Adobe Acrobat program on your computer, Adobe PDF shows up everywhere you see your computer's printers listed. (Word considers creating PDFs, too, to be a type of printing.)

Having several printer options doesn't confuse Word one bit. You just need to let Word know which printer you want to use. To do that, open the Print dialog box, which in typical Microsoft fashion you can do at least three different ways. The quickest and easiest to remember is to press Ctrl+P. If you like to mouse up to the ribbon, then choose Office button → Print. For good measure, you can also use the new keyboard shortcut Alt+F, P. However you arrive at the Print dialog box, it looks like Figure 7-6.

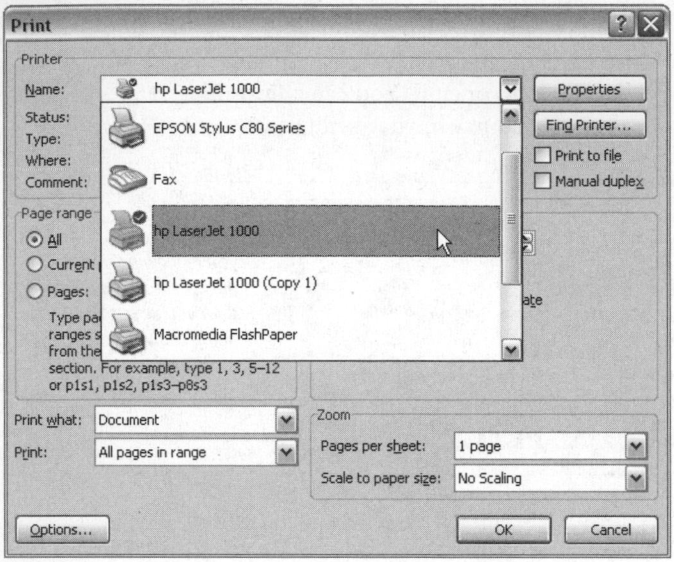

Figure 7-6:
The Print dialog box has a bunch of buttons and menus that you can use to make your printer do exactly what you want. In the upper-left corner, use the drop-down menu to choose your printer. Details about your printer appear below the menu.

At the top of the Print box you find a group of controls labeled Printer. Use the drop-down menu at the top to choose the printer you want to use for this print job. Under this menu you see some details about your printer—its type and how it's connected to your computer. On the right, you see two buttons. The top Properties button opens a dialog with details specific to your printer. If you're on a network and share printers, the Find Printer button can help you locate a printer.

Setting Your Default Printer

If you don't specifically choose a printer, Windows always uses one particular printer—known as the *default* printer. You'll see a checkmark next to its printer icon in the list (Figure 7-6).

You can promote any of your printers to this exalted position, but you can't do it within Word. You need to use the Windows system for this job. Here are the steps:

1. **In your screen's lower-left corner, go to Start → Printers and Faxes.**

   "Printers and Faxes" is in the Start menu's lower-right corner. When you click it, the Start menu goes away, and the "Printer and Faxes" box opens in a window that looks remarkably like Windows Explorer—because that's exactly what it is (Figure 7-7). You're in a special location in Explorer that's devoted to printers.

2. **In the Printers and Faxes box, right-click the printer you want to use most of the time, and from the shortcut menu, choose "Set as Default Printer."**

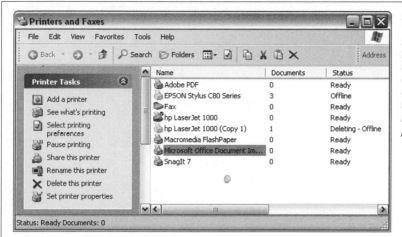

Figure 7-7:
Your Printers and Faxes dialog box probably looks different from this one, because it lists the printers and devices connected to your own computer. The Task Pane on the left gives you the tools you need to add and remove a printer from your computer.

Exploring Printer-Specific Properties

Different printers have different talents. Choose from color printers and black-and-white printers, printers that can print on both sides of the paper, printers that can use huge pieces of paper, and even computer thingys that behave like printers but aren't really printers. Adobe Acrobat and fax machines fall into this category. You need some way to get at the controls for these printers and, obviously, the controls are different for each one. You use the Printer Properties boxes to fine-tune the behavior of your printers and printing devices. For example, Figure 7-8 shows the properties for a black and white laser printer. Figure 7-9 shows the Properties box for a color inkjet printer. Figure 7-10 is the Properties box for the professional version of Adobe Acrobat. It's not really a printer at all; it just thinks it is.

Printing to an Adobe PDF File

Say you want to create an attachment that you can email or put up on a Web site that anyone, on any computer, can open and print. First, read the box on page 176 and install the Adobe PDF add-in. Once you've installed the add-in, creating a PDF file is as easy as saving a file.

Go to Office button → Save As → PDF or XPS. The "Publish as PDF or XPS" dialog box opens. It looks just like a Save As dialog box. It has all the standard navigation tools, so you can choose a folder to hold the file. In the "Save as type" drop-down menu near the bottom, choose PDF, and then click the Publish button in the lower-right corner (where you'd normally see a Save button). When you're done, you've created a PDF file that you or anyone else can read and print with Adobe Reader.

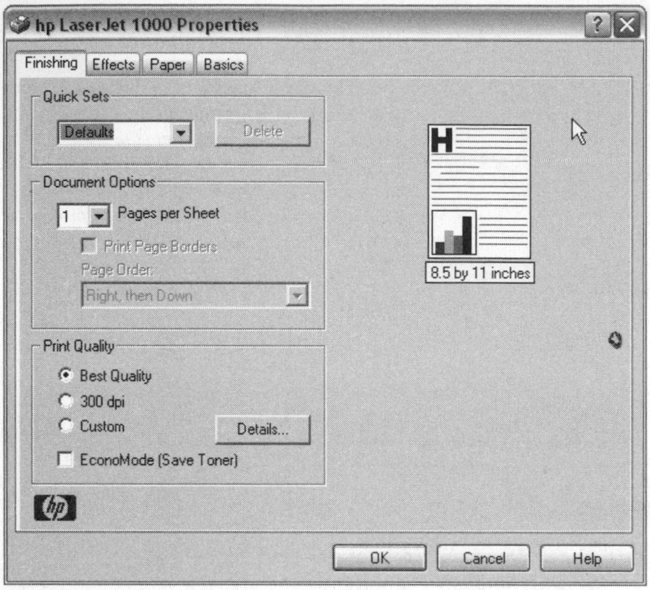

Figure 7-8:
This Properties box for a Hewlett-Packard LaserJet is simple and utilitarian. It gives you a little bit of control over the quality of the print, and under the Effects tab, you can scale your document to print at a larger or smaller size.

Figure 7-9:
The Properties for this Epson color printer give you lots of options that are helpful for printing photos. For example, you can adjust the printer for different types of photo paper, to make sure you get the best possible prints. Because it's an inkjet printer, the Utility tab provides tools to clean the print head and nozzles.

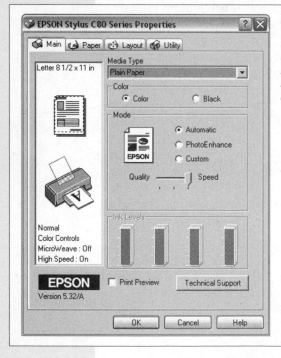

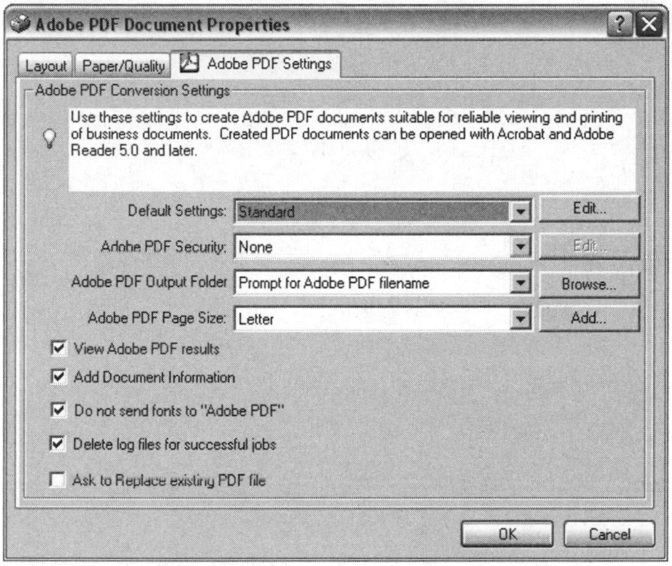

Figure 7-10:
Adobe Acrobat isn't really a printer, but when you install Acrobat Pro (the commercial program used to create Adobe PDF files), it creates a "printer" for PDF files. When you "print" your document, you're actually writing a PDF file. The Properties box lets you choose options for file security and paper size.

Faxing with Word

Think of faxing a document as a form of long-distance printing. You tell Word to print a document, and it sends the pages over the phone lines and prints it out on your friend's fax machine. You need to have a fax modem in your computer, and the person on the other end needs a fax machine (see the box on page 180). Other than that, it's a lot like printing. Here are the steps:

1. **With your document open in Word, press Ctrl+P or choose Office button → Print.**

   The Print box, as shown in Figure 7-6, opens.

2. **Use the drop-down menu at the top of the Print box to select your fax modem as the printer, and then click OK to start the Send Fax Wizard.**

   The Print box closes and the Send Fax Wizard opens (Figure 7-12). The Send Fax Wizard consists of several dialog boxes. The first box is stunningly useless. It does nothing but welcome you to the Send Fax Wizard and make you click the Next button an extra time. The next screen is more functional. You use it to tell your computer where to send the fax.

Adobe Acrobatics

The dawn of the personal computer revolution generated talk about the paperless office. Of course, that never happened. If anything, personal computers and printers brought about a quantum leap in paper consumption. Still, if any computer tool came close to realizing an alternative to paper, it's Adobe Acrobat or PDF (Portable Document Format). The idea was to create a computer file format that can perfectly capture what's printed on the page—text, graphics, the whole kit and caboodle. The files need to be compact so they can be sent over the Internet. And anyone should be able to read and print these files without paying for additional software.

Adobe created Acrobat to meet all these needs, and before too long, everyone was using this new Portable Document Format to distribute reports and booklets over the Internet. Folks started calling them PDF files, because the filenames end in .pdf (Figure 7-11). Now you'll find PDFs online for just about everything. You can probably download the manual for your TV, your cell phone, and your refrigerator from the manufacturers' Web sites as PDF files. The Census Bureau and many other government agencies provide the information they collect as PDFs.

Businesses are using PDFs more and more as a way to distribute reports, spreadsheets, and other documents. Unlike an Excel spreadsheet, you don't need Excel to open a PDF, since the Adobe Reader program comes on all computers (and if not, it's only a free download away). Furthermore, with a PDF, no one can inadvertently erase or change your information once your document is open.

Adobe's format was so successful that it spawned some imitators. It doesn't make much sense to imitate a standard by creating an incompatible format, but that's what happened. Microsoft launched it's own format called XPS, which stands for XML Paper Specification. And an open source format has similar properties and aspirations—the Open Document format. After some wrangling, Microsoft decided to provide support for *all three* of these formats in Word 2007. The XPS format is included with Word. To add either Adobe PDF or Open Document support, you need to download an add-in program to make it part of Word. To find the add-in that installs both PDF and XPS capabilities to your computer, go to *http://www.microsoft.com/office* and enter *pdf xps* in the search box at the top of the page.

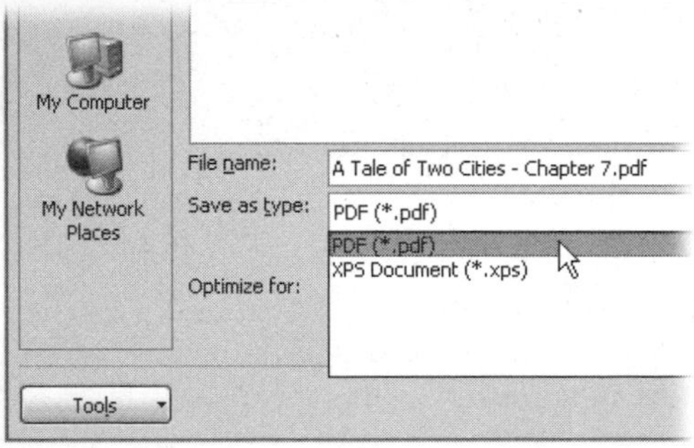

Figure 7-11:
Use PDF files (also known as Acrobat) to distribute copies of your documents via email or over the Web. People who receive your files can view and print them using Adobe's free Adobe Reader available at www.adobe.com/products/acrobat/ readstep2.html.

3. **Enter names (optional) and fax numbers into the Send Fax Wizard.**

   You can click the Address Book button to choose a name and fax number from your Outlook address book, or you can type into the "To" and "Fax number" text boxes. Click Add to add recipients to the list at the bottom. When your list is complete, click Next.

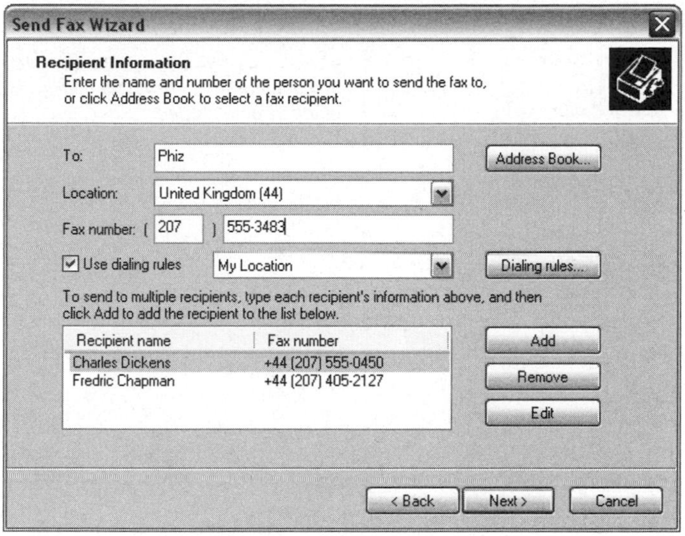

Figure 7-12:
The Send Fax Wizard walks you through the process of addressing and sending your fax. You start by entering names and fax numbers or choosing recipients from your Windows address book.

4. **Choose whether to include a cover page.**

   If you turn on the cover page checkbox, the wizard prompts you for a subject and a note. The wizard automatically fills in details that Word collected when you installed the program, such as your name and contact info. If you need to, you can review and change those details by clicking the Sender Information button at right. When you're done with the details about the cover page, click Next.

5. **Use the next wizard screen to schedule your fax.**

   You have three options for scheduling. You can send it now, or you can choose to send it when discount rates apply. Last but not least, you can enter a specific hour and minute. When you've scheduled your fax delivery, click Next.

6. **Check the details and preview the fax, and then click the Finish button to send it.**

   The last box of the Send Fax Wizard gives you one last chance to review your fax recipients and to preview the fax by clicking the Preview Fax button (Figure 7-13). A viewer pops up where you can inspect your fax page by page before you send it. When you're certain that everything is okay, click Finish to send your fax on its way.

Changing Print Settings

Sometimes clicking Quick Print doesn't do the trick. Perhaps you want to make several copies of your document, or maybe you want to print only certain pages. To tackle those chores and others, you need to give Word and your printer more specific instructions. To do that, open the Print box (Figure 7-14) by choosing Office button → Print → Print (or pressing Ctrl+P).

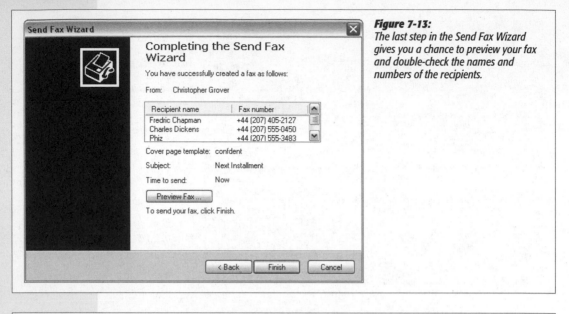

Figure 7-13:
The last step in the Send Fax Wizard gives you a chance to preview your fax and double-check the names and numbers of the recipients.

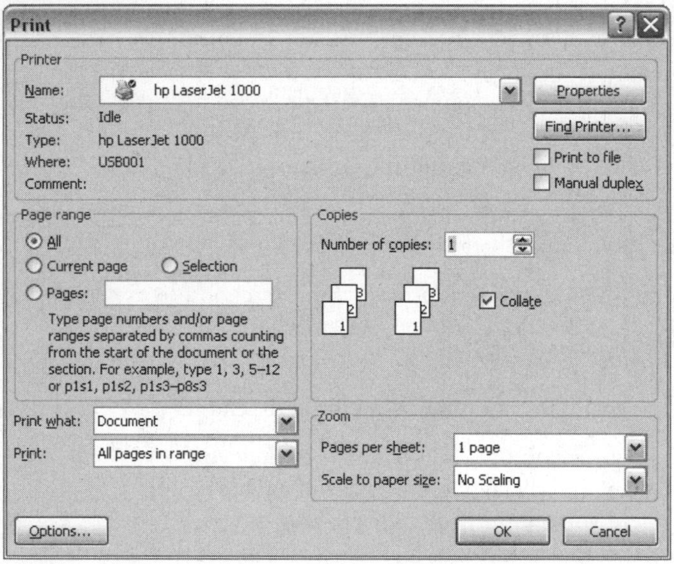

Figure 7-14:
When your print job gets more complicated, you need to use the Print box. In addition to letting you choose a specific printer, the Print box lets you print multiple copies or print just a portion of your opus. You can also get at specific settings for your printer via the Properties box.

Printing Part of Your Document

Word is pretty flexible when it comes to printing bits and pieces of your document. You can choose to print specific pages, or you can select a part of your document, and then tell Word to print only what you've selected. You make your choices using radio buttons in the Print dialog box's "Page range" section, described next.

- **All.** This option prints your entire document using the Print dialog box's current settings. You can choose to print and collate multiple copies of your entire document, if you want.

- **Current page.** This option is ideal for printing a test page. Word prints the page that's currently showing in the window (not the page with the insertion point).

- **Pages.** You can select consecutive pages, random pages, or a combination of the two. For example, if you type *7, 9, 12-15* in the Pages text box, then Word prints exactly those pages (Figure 7-15).

- **Selection.** Select the text you want to print before opening the Print box (Ctrl+P), and then click the Selection button. Word prints only the text that you've selected. This method helps you proofread a specific chunk of your text or print an individual element like a chart or a picture.

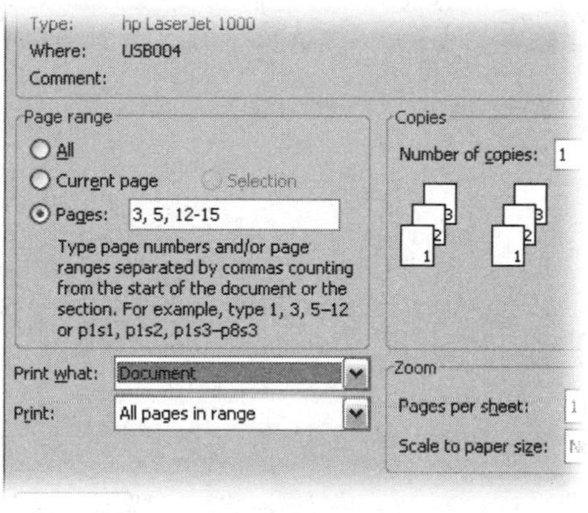

Figure 7-15:
In the "Page range" section of the Print box, you can choose to print your entire document or just a part of it. Using the Print drop-down menu, you can print either your document alone, or the document with its properties, paragraph styles, and other technical details.

Printing and Collating Multiple Copies

Open the Print dialog box (Ctrl+P) to tell Word you want to print multiple copies and provide details about how you'd like them served up (Figure 7-16). The Copies section of the Print box is on the right side. Type a number in the "Number of copies" box, and then turn on the Collate checkbox if you'd like each copy ordered in sequence. If you don't turn on Collate, your printer will spit out all the page 1s, then all the page 2s, and so forth.

Printing on Both Sides of the Page

Printing on both sides of the paper produces attractive, professional newsletters, reports, and brochures. Your subject matter can benefit from nice big two-page spreads. Or maybe you'd just like to cut down on the amount of paper you're using. Whatever the reason, you can print on both sides (also known as *duplex* printing).

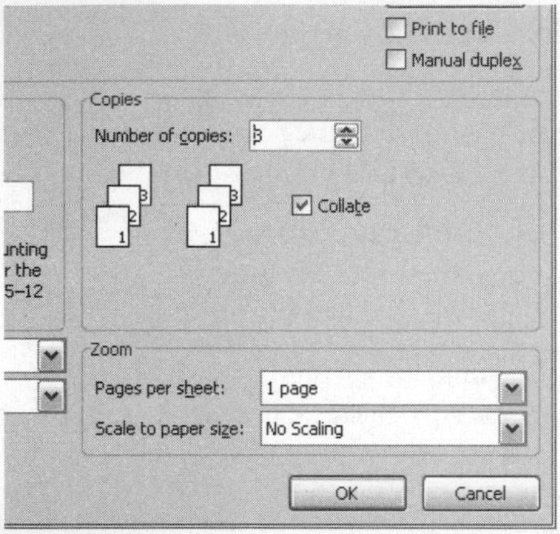

Figure 7-16:
On the right side of the Print box, you can tell Word how many copies to print and whether or not you'd like them collated. In the Zoom section at bottom, you can choose to print more than one page per sheet of paper; Word automatically shrinks everything to fit. The "Scale to paper size" drop-down menu shrinks or enlarges your document to fit a different size of paper.

Fax Modem vs. Fax Machine

In the days before everyone used email, fax machines took the world by storm. At first, people asked if you had a fax, and then they just asked for your fax number. If you don't have a fax machine, a computer with a fax modem is a pretty good substitute. Any document that you can print, you can send as a fax. Today, most modems also include the smarts to send a fax, and you can get one for only $50 or so.

To see whether your computer has a fax modem, go to Start → Control Panel → Printers and Faxes. When the control panel opens, you'll see Fax listed, but that doesn't necessarily mean you have a fax modem installed. In the list, right-click the word Fax, and then choose Properties from the shortcut menu to open the Fax Properties box.

Last, but not least, click the Devices tab. If your computer can send a fax, you'll see the name of the fax modem listed in the Devices panel.

You can receive faxes with a fax modem too, but if you plan on receiving a lot of faxes, you may want to get a phone line specifically for fax traffic—otherwise your friends are likely to be greeted with a fax screech when they call. If you want the complete capabilities of a fax machine, then you need to add a scanner to your setup. Then you can scan newspaper articles, comic strips, and other important documents and fax them to colleagues.

Word gives you two ways to print both sides of the page—the easy way and the hard way. Unfortunately, the easy way is more expensive. It requires you to have a duplex printer that knows how to print both sides. Duplex printers vary, so you may need to explore your printer's Properties (Ctrl+P, Alt+P) to make sure it's ready for printing on both sides. If so, you'll also see some extra options in the Print dialog box to turn two-sided printing on.

If you don't have a duplex printer (most people don't), you can get the same result if you're willing to do a little paper juggling:

1. **Go to Office button → Print to open the Print dialog box. Turn on the "Manual duplex" checkbox.**

   The Manual duplex checkbox is on the right side, below the Properties button, as shown in Figure 7-17.

2. **Click OK to start printing.**

   Word prints all the odd-numbered pages on one side of the paper, and then it prompts you to remove the printed pages and place them back in the printer tray.

3. **Take the printed pages out of the tray, flip them over, and then click OK.**

   Word prints the even-numbered pages on the backs.

   You may want to experiment on five or six pages to get the routine down. The process is different for different printers. You need to watch for a couple of things with the second print run. First, you need to learn whether to place the pages face up or face down. You may also need to reorder the pages so they print properly. Hint: On the second run, page 2 prints first, so you want page 1 at the top of the pile.

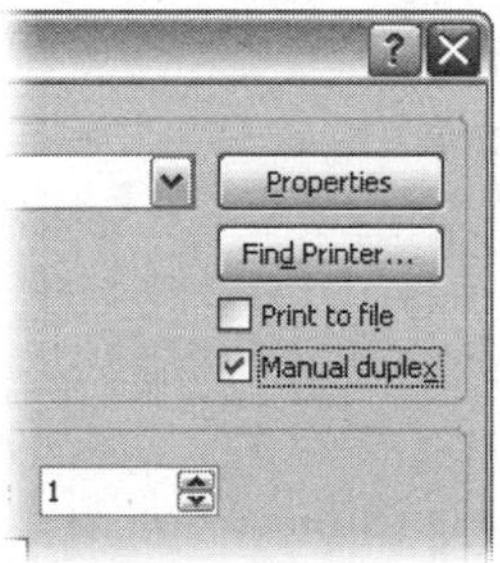

Figure 7-17:
Even if you don't have a fancy duplex printer for printing both sides of the paper, Word will help you out. Turn on "Manual duplex," and Word first prints the odd pages, and then prompts you when it's time to reload.

Printing Envelopes

Computers have always been great for printing documents on standard-size paper, but envelopes present a little bit more of a challenge. Envelopes are oddly shaped and kind of thick. And on some machines, the text needs to print sideways. Fortunately, Word 2007 and most modern printers have overcome the hurdles presented by printing on envelopes.

The first step for successful envelope printing is to make sure that your return address info is stored in Word.

1. **Go to Office button → Word Options and click Advanced.**

   The buttons on the left side of the Word Options box show you different panels of Word.

2. **Scroll down to the General group.**

   Oddly, the General group is almost at the bottom of the Advanced options.

3. **Enter your information in the "Mailing address" box. Click OK when you're done.**

With your vital details stored in Word, you're ready to print an envelope. Here are the steps:

1. **On the ribbon, go to Mailings → Create → Envelopes (Alt+M, E).**

   Most of the tools on the Mailings tab are for mail merge and mass mailings. The Create group, with two buttons—Envelopes and Labels—is on the left side. Clicking Envelopes opens the "Envelopes and Labels" dialog box to the Envelopes tab, as shown in Figure 7-18.

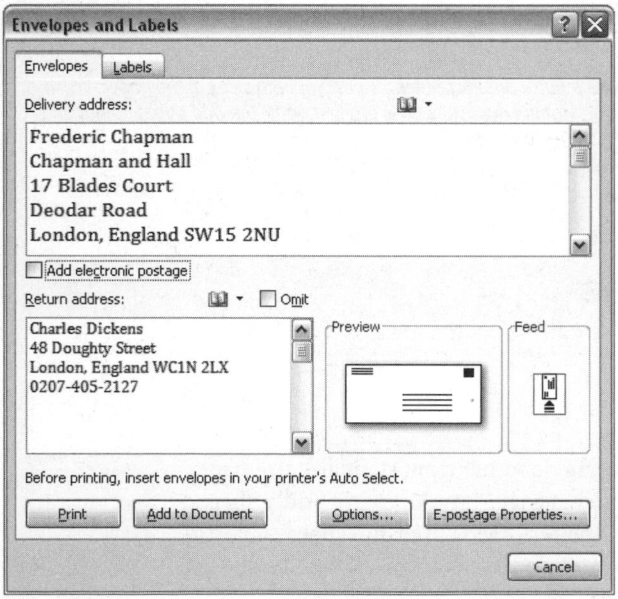

Figure 7-18:
The Envelopes tab in the Envelopes and Labels dialog box provides a place to enter both a delivery and return address. The Preview and Feed icons in the lower-right corner show you how the envelope will look and the way to place your envelope in the printer.

2. **At the top of the Envelopes tab, in the "Delivery address" text box, type a name and address.**

   Just type in the information on different lines as you'd put it on an envelope.

   The little book icon above and to the right of the Delivery address text box opens your Outlook address book. Click it to select an existing contact. (Look, Ma—no retyping!)

Note: The first time you click the Address Book icon, the Choose Profile box opens. There you can select a source for addresses, including your Outlook address book.

---

3. **In the bottom text box, inspect your return address and edit if necessary.**

   If you provided an address in your Word Options, as described in the previous steps, that information appears in the Return address box. If you want, you can change the details now. Just delete the existing address and type the new information. (If your envelopes have a preprinted return address, turn on the Omit checkbox to prevent your stored return address from printing on the envelope.)

4. **Check the preview window and take notice of the feed direction for your envelope.**

   The Preview panel shows you how the envelope will look with the addresses printed on it. The Feed panel gives you guidance for placing envelopes in your printer.

Tip: The Options button leads to another dialog box where you can choose a different envelope size (assuming your printer can handle it). You can also change the font and font size.

Printing Labels

Word comes ready and wiling to work with standard address labels. If you just want to print a single label, or if you want to print a bunch of the same label, then follow the steps in this section.

Word is prepared to handle labels from Avery and many other manufacturers. Take note of the maker and model number of the labels you've bought, and follow the manufacturer's instructions for loading them into your printer. Then follow these steps to print one or more of the same label:

1. **Go to Mailings → Create → Labels.**

   The "Envelope and Labels" dialog box opens to the Labels tab.

2. **In the Address box at top, type the address you want to put on the label.**

   If you want to print a batch of your own return address labels, click the box in the upper-right corner labeled "Use return address."

3. **Click the Label section. (It's not just a preview—it's a button!)**

The Label Options dialog box opens, as shown in Figure 7-19. Choose your label manufacturer, and then choose your label's model number. This information tells Word how many labels are on a sheet and how they're spaced. Click OK when you're done.

4. **In the Print section, select "Full page of the same label" or "Single label."**

If you want to print the same label a bunch of times on a sheet of labels, choose the first radio button, "Full page of the same label."

You can print a single label from a sheet of labels, saving the rest of the sheet for another project. Click the "Single label" radio button, and then identify the row and column for Word, so it knows which label to print on.

5. **Click Print when you're ready to go.**

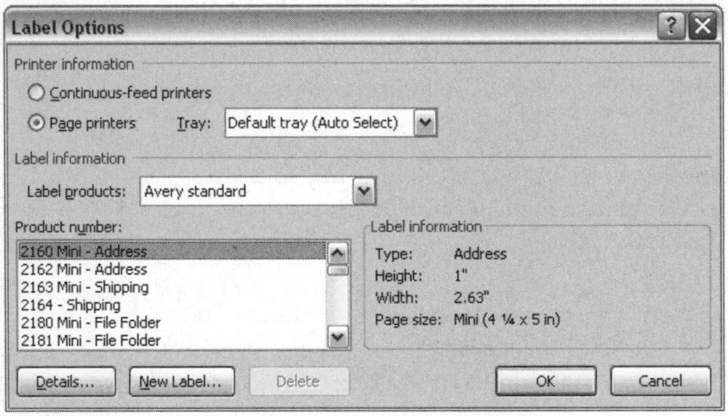

Figure 7-19:
Word's label printing tool is all set to work with a mind-boggling variety of label types. It also gives you some ways to make the most of your label resources. For example, using the "Single label" button (not shown), you can print one label on a sheet and save the rest for another project.

Setting Print Options

The Word Options window is where you tweak Word to make it behave the way you want. Some print settings worth knowing about are, somewhat oddly, tucked away on the Display panel. Go to Office button → Word Options → Display. The printing settings are at the bottom. A checkmark indicates the option is turned on. Here's what you find:

- **Print drawings created in Word.** The factory setting is to have this option turned on. Turn it off if you ever want to print a document without any graphics or floating text boxes.

- **Print background colors and images.** Page color and background images work better for Web pages than they do for printed documents. When you install Word, this option is turned off, but you can always toggle it back on.

- **Print document properties.** Turn this option on, and Word prints your document, and then prints the document properties—author, title, and so on—on a separate page at the end. (If you've never checked out your document properties, take a look by choosing Office button → Prepare → Properties.)

- **Print hidden text.** You can hide text in your document using a font style command (Alt+H, FN, Alt+H). With this box turned on, that text doesn't stay hidden when you print.

- **Update fields before printing.** Word fields include things like the date in a header (see the box on page 116) or a contact from your Outlook address book. It's usually a good idea to leave this box turned on because it makes sure you have the most up-to-date information before you print.

- **Update linked data before printing.** Like the fields option above, this option is turned on when you install Word, and it's good to leave it that way. If you link a table or chart from an Excel spreadsheet, this option makes sure it's using the most recent info.

CHAPTER 8

Planning with Outlines

If your teachers kept hammering you about how important outlining is and made you do elaborate outlines before you tackled writing assignments, forgive them. They were right. Nothing beats an outline for the planning stages of a document. When you're facing writer's block, you can start listing your main topics in a Word document, and then break your topics into smaller pieces with some subtopics underneath. Before your know it, you're filling out your ideas with some essential bits of body text. You've broken through the block.

Word's Outline view is a fabulous outlining tool. It lets you move large blocks of headings and text from one part of your document to another, and rank headings and their accompanied text higher or lower in relative importance. In Outline view, you can even show or hide different parts of your document, to focus your attention on what's important at the moment. Best of all, Outline view is just another document view, so you don't have to outline in a separate document.

Switching to Outline View

Outline view is another way of looking at your document, like Draft view or Print Layout view. In other words, in Outline view, you're just looking at your document in outline form. When you switch into Outline view, your heading text (Heading 1, Heading 2, Heading 3, and so on) simply appears as different outline levels (Figure 8-1). Similarly, you can start a document as an outline—even do all your writing in outline form—and then switch to Print Layout view and have a perfectly normal looking document.

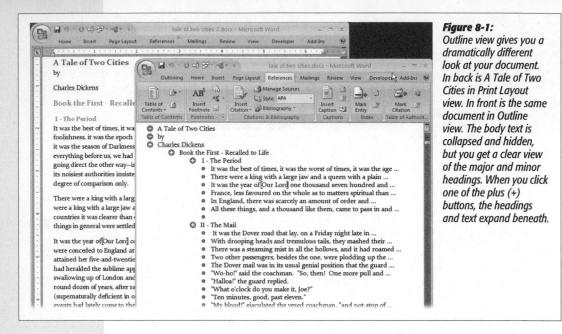

Figure 8-1:
Outline view gives you a
dramatically different
look at your document.
In back is A Tale of Two
Cities in Print Layout
view. In front is the same
document in Outline
view. The body text is
collapsed and hidden,
but you get a clear view
of the major and minor
headings. When you click
one of the plus (+)
buttons, the headings
and text expand beneath.

Tip: Jumping back and forth between Outline view and the other views can be very conducive to brainstorming. If you're working with your document in Print Layout view or Draft view and need to get a feeling for the way one topic flows into another, then pop into Outline view, collapse the body text, and examine your headings.

To switch views in Word, go to View → Document Views and click the button you want, or use the keyboard shortcuts in the following list:

- Use **Outline view** (Alt+W, U) to develop headings, establish a sequence for presenting topics, establish a hierarchy between topics, and jump from one section to another in long documents.

- Use **Draft view** (Alt+W, E) for writing rapidly when you don't want to worry about anything except getting ideas down on the page. In Draft view you aren't hindered by too many formatting niceties.

- Use **Print Layout view** (Alt+W, P) when you're putting the finishing touches on your document. In this view, you get a feel for the way your document looks to your readers.

When you switch to Outline view, a new Outlining tab appears on the ribbon. The Outlining Tools group at left has two parts, separated by a vertical bar. You use the controls to move paragraphs around and change their outline levels for (more on that shortly). The tools on the right side don't actually affect the outline—they just control the way it looks.

When it comes to outlining, Word divides your document into two distinctly different elements:

- **Headings or topics.** You can tell headings are the most important element in outlines by the big + or − button at their left. With headings, it's all about rank. Every heading has a level, from 1 to 9. More important headings have lower-level numbers and are positioned closer to the left margin. Level 1 starts at far left, Level 2 comes below it and is indented slightly to the right, followed by Level 3, 4, and so on.

  Each heading is called a *subhead* of the one that came before. For example, Level 2 is a subhead of Level 1, Level 3 is a subhead of Level 2, and so on.

- **Body text.** For outlining, body text takes the back seat. It just gets that little dot, and if it's in the way, you can hide it entirely, or you can view only the first line—just enough to give you a hint of what's beneath. Body text doesn't really get assigned to a level; it stays glued to the heading above it.

Promoting and Demoting Headings

Planning a document is a little bit like putting a puzzle together. You try a piece here and then over there. A topic you thought was minor suddenly looms larger in importance. When you're brainstorming and plotting, it's important to keep an open mind. Word's helpful because it's so easy to try things out, and you can Ctrl+Z to undo whenever you need to.

When you *promote* a topic, you move it toward the left margin. At the same time, it moves up a rank in the headings hierarchy; so, a Level 3 header becomes a Level 2 header, and so forth. For most documents that means the formatting changes too. Higher-level headers typically have larger or bolder type—something that distinguishes them from their less impressive brethren. To *demote* a heading is the opposite; you move a heading toward the right, usually making it a subordinate of another topic.

For you, these promotions and demotions are easy. In fact, you encounter a lot less complaining here than you'd find in promoting and demoting employees in your company. The easiest way to promote and demote is to click a header and move it to the left or to the right. When you move it a little bit, a vertical line appears, providing a marker to show you the change in rank, as shown in Figure 8-2.

Note: When you promote or demote a heading, the body text goes with it, but you have a choice whether or not the subheads move below it (page 191).

When you're brainstorming and pushing ideas around in your document, you don't want to get distracted by the mechanics. When it comes to outlines, you may be grateful that Word provides so many different ways to do the same thing. You get to choose the method that works best for you, and keep your focus on shaping your document.

Word gives you three ways to manipulate the pieces of your outline:

- **Dragging.** For outlining, nothing's more intuitive and fun than clicking and dragging. You can put some words in a heading, and then just drag them to another location. As you drag topics and text, Word provides great visual clues to let you know the end result (Figure 8-2).

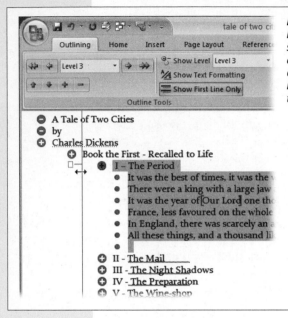

Figure 8-2:
Dragging works well when you're brainstorming. It's satisfying to push, pull, and drag your document into shape as if it were clay and you're the sculptor. As you drag, your cursor changes to a double arrow. The long vertical line indicates the outline level you're currently dragging through.

- **Ribbon.** The buttons on the Outlining → Outline Tools group give you quick, visual access to the commands for promoting and demoting headings and for showing and hiding the bits and pieces of your document. It's a bit more mechanical than just clicking and dragging the pieces where you want them (Figure 8-3).

One potentially confusing thing about the Outlining tab are those two drop-down menus showing levels. They look almost identical and both give you a choice among the nine topic levels that Outline has to offer. Here's the key: The menu on the left promotes or demotes the current item, while the menu on the right shows or hides levels.

- **Keyboard shortcuts.** Keyboard shortcuts are ideal when your hands are already on the keys and you're typing away. During the planning stages, speed isn't as much of an issue, but if you took your teachers' advice to heart and do lots of outlining, keyboard shortcuts can really streamline your work. Just remember that all these commands use Alt+Shift plus another key, as shown in the following table.

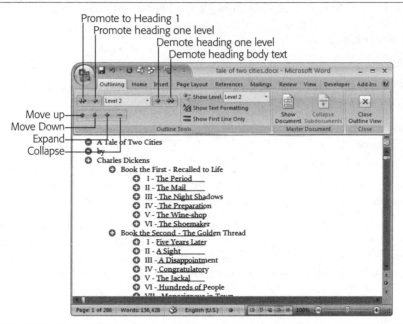

Promote to Heading 1
Promote heading one level
Demote heading one level
Demote heading body text

Move up
Move Down
Expand
Collapse

Figure 8-3:
The buttons on the Outlining tab provide a command central for promoting and demoting topics and showing just the right part of your document. The up and down buttons move topics forward and backward in the document, providing a great way to move big chunks of text.

Action	Keyboard Shortcut
Promote Heading Up a Level	Alt+Shift+Right arrow, or Tab
Demote Heading Down a Level	Alt+Shift+Left arrow, or Shift+Tab
Demote Heading to Body Text	Alt+Shift+5 (number pad), or Ctrl+Shift+N
Expand Outline Item	Alt+Shift++
Collapse Outline Item	Alt+Shift+_
Expand or Collapse Outline Item	Alt+Shift+A, * key (number pad)
Show *n* Level Heading	Alt+Shift+*n*, n=number key (top row, not the number pad)
Show Only First Line of Text	Alt+Shift+L

Tip: Another keyboard shortcut helps with outlining: the / key on the number pad. That one little key conceals any fancy character formatting you've applied so you can focus on your outline. See page 195 for more on the Show/Hide Text Formatting command.

Controlling Subheads During Promotion or Demotion

When you promote or demote an outline item, any subheads and subtopics below it move with that item, but only if you collapse the items below, so that they're hidden. In other words, when you move the header above, the subheads keep their relationships even though you can't see them. When you drag topics, the subheads go along, because when you select a topic, you automatically select the subtopics, too.

Word gives you a number of ways to move the header but leave everything else where it is. Here's a step-by-step description of the ways you can promote or demote a heading all by its lonesome:

1. **Click anywhere in the text of the header.**

   Don't select the entire header; just place the insertion point somewhere in the text.

2. **Change the header level using one of the ribbon buttons or by pressing a keyboard shortcut.**

   Use the shortcut keys Alt+Shift+Left arrow or Alt+Shift+Right arrow to promote or demote the header. As long as the subtopics below aren't highlighted, they won't move when you do the header promoting or demoting.

   You can use any of the ribbon controls that promote and demote headers in the same way. As long as the subtopics aren't selected, they won't change (Figure 8-4). The buttons that you can use include: Promote to Heading 1, Promote, Outline Level (drop-down menu), Demote to Body Text.

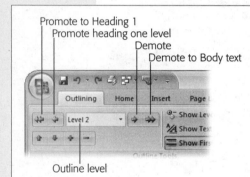

Promote to Heading 1
Promote heading one level
Demote
Demote to Body text

Outline level

Figure 8-4:
Use the various promotion and demotion buttons and the Level drop-down menu on the Outlining tab to organize your outline. If subheads are collapsed under a topic or they're selected, they maintain their relationships when you demote or promote the header. Otherwise, if only the header is selected, it moves and the subtopics stay put.

Note: Working with outlines is actually a lot simpler to do than it sounds. Want to test drive Word's outline features? To check out the screencast—an online, animated tutorial—of the examples in this chapter, head over to the "Missing CD" page at *www.missingmanuals.com*.

Moving Outline Items

Part of organizing your thoughts means moving them to an earlier or later position in the document, without changing their outline level. Say you decide a section you've typed in the middle of your document would make a great introduction. You can move it to the beginning of the document, without promoting or demoting it. Moving topics and items up and down in your document is very similar to moving them left and right. (Figure 8-5). If you want to take subtopics along with an item when you move it, make sure that they're selected (or collapsed) under the item that you're moving.

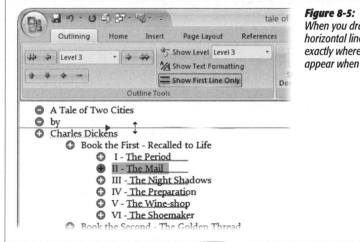

Figure 8-5:
When you drag a header up and down, you see a horizontal line that acts as a marker to show you exactly where the heading (and connected text) will appear when you let go of the mouse button.

In addition to dragging, Word gives you two other ways to move topics up and down in your outline. Select the heading you want to move, and then click the Move Up or Move Down buttons on the Outlining tab (Figure 8-6). You can also use the shortcut keys Alt+Shift+up arrow or Alt+Shift+down arrow.

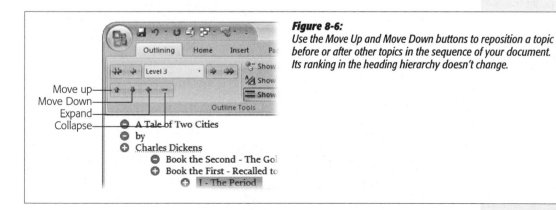

Figure 8-6:
Use the Move Up and Move Down buttons to reposition a topic before or after other topics in the sequence of your document. Its ranking in the heading hierarchy doesn't change.

Showing Parts of Your Outline

Outline view doesn't just let you see and organize the structure of your prose; it also helps you zero in on what's important while you make decisions about the shape and flow of your work. If you want, you can show your headings only so you can focus on their wording with all the other text out of the way. When you want to read inside a certain section, you can expand it while leaving everything else collapsed. (Or, if you're having trouble with a passage, you can collapse it so you don't have to look at it for a while.)

Expanding and Collapsing Levels

You know that old saying about not being able to see the forest for the trees. On the Outlining tab, the Expand and Collapse buttons help you put things in perspective (Figure 8-6). Collapse a topic, and you can read through the major headers and get a feel for the way your document flows from one topic to another. When you need to explore the detail within a topic to make sure you've covered all the bases, expand the topic and dig in.

When you're mousing around, the easiest way to expand or collapse a topic is to double-click the + sign next to the words. It works as a toggle—a double-click expands it, and another double-click closes it. The topics with a minus sign next to them have no subtopics, so you can't expand or collapse them.

If you're interested in making grander, more global kinds of changes, turn to the Outlining → Outline Tools → Show Level menu; it's the drop-down menu on the right (Figure 8-7). Just choose a level, and your outline expands or collapses accordingly.

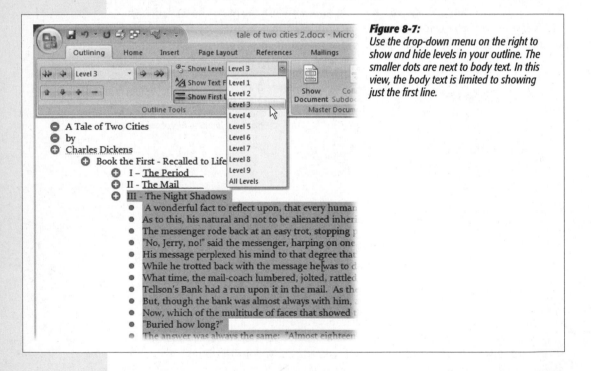

Figure 8-7:
Use the drop-down menu on the right to show and hide levels in your outline. The smaller dots are next to body text. In this view, the body text is limited to showing just the first line.

Showing and Hiding Text

Text takes a subordinate position when it comes to outlining and planning, so it's not surprising that Word provides a couple different ways for you to hide the body text (Figure 8-8). You can double-click the headings above the body text to expand and collapse the topic, just as you would with subheads. The + and − buttons on the Outlining tab work the same way. You can also use the keyboard shortcuts Alt++ to expand and Alt+_ to collapse body text under a heading.

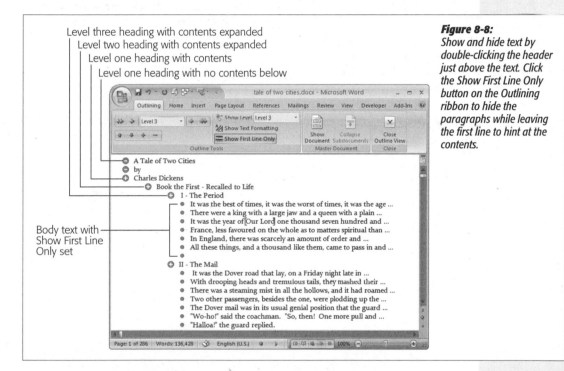

Figure 8-8:
Show and hide text by double-clicking the header just above the text. Click the Show First Line Only button on the Outlining ribbon to hide the paragraphs while leaving the first line to hint at the contents.

Showing Only the First Line

Because each paragraph of body text is like a sub-subtopic, Word's outline view lets you work with them as such. Click the Show First Line Only button, and all you see is the first line of each paragraph. That should be enough to get a sense of the topic that's covered. It's just another way that Outline lets you drill down into your document while you're in a planning and plotting phase.

Showing Text Formatting

Your document's character formatting—different fonts, font colors, and sizes that may bear no relation to the Level 1, Level 2 hierarchy—can be distracting in Outline view.

The easiest thing is to turn the formatting off. You can click the Show Formatting button on the Outlining ribbon (Figure 8-9) to toggle formatting on or off, or you can use the shortcut key, which is the / (forward slash) on the number pad.

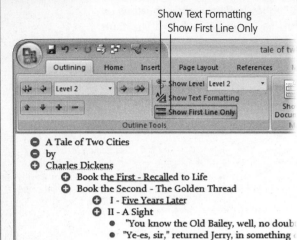

Show Text Formatting
Show First Line Only

Figure 8-9:
Use the Show Text Formatting checkbox (or the / key on the number pad) to hide text formatting, as shown here. This image also shows the result of clicking the Show First Line Only button or pressing Alt+Shift+L to show and hide all the paragraph text except the first line.

Part Two:
Excel 2007

2

Creating and Navigating Worksheets

Most people don't need much convincing to use Excel, Microsoft's premier spreadsheet software. The program comes preinstalled on a lot of computers, making it the obvious choice for millions of number crunchers. Despite its wide use, however, few people know where to find Excel's most impressive features or why they'd want to use them in the first place.

The Excel portion of this book fills that void, explaining everything from basic Excel concepts to time- and frustration-saving shortcuts. You'll learn how Excel 2007 works, when to steer clear of obscure options that aren't worth the trouble to learn, and how to home in on the hidden gems that'll win you the undying adoration of your coworkers, family, and friends—or at least your accountant.

Of course, every Excel grandmaster needs to start somewhere. In this chapter, you'll create a spreadsheet and learn how to move around in it, enter basic information, and save it for posterity. Along the way, you'll take a quick tour of the Excel window, and stop to meet the different tabs in the ribbon, the status bar, and the formula bar.

Note: The Excel portion of this book is written with Microsoft's latest and greatest release in mind: Excel 2007. This section won't help you if you're using an earlier version of Excel, because Microsoft has dramatically changed Excel's user interface (the "look and feel" of the program). However, if you're an unredeemed Excel 2003 or Excel 2002 fanatic, you can get help from another O'Reilly book, which is simply named *Excel 2003: The Missing Manual*. The Mac version of Excel is covered in *Office 2004 for Macintosh: The Missing Manual*.

What You Can Do with Excel

Excel and Word are the two powerhouses of the Microsoft Office family. While Word lets you create and edit documents, Excel specializes in letting you create, edit, and analyze *data* that's organized into lists or tables. This grid-like arrangement of information is called a *spreadsheet*. Figure 9-1 shows an example.

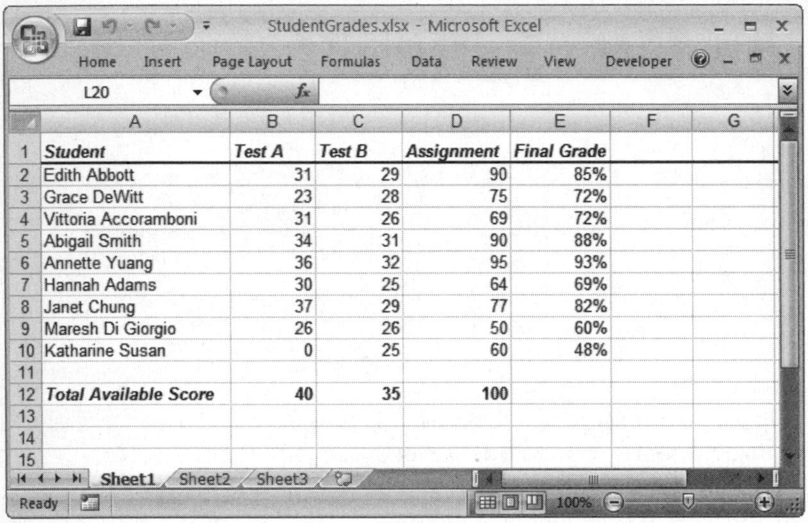

Figure 9-1:
This spreadsheet lists nine students, each of whom has two test scores and an assignment grade. Using Excel formulas, it's easy to calculate the final grade for each student.

	A	B	C	D	E	F	G
1	*Student*	*Test A*	*Test B*	*Assignment*	*Final Grade*		
2	Edith Abbott	31	29	90	85%		
3	Grace DeWitt	23	28	75	72%		
4	Vittoria Accoramboni	31	26	69	72%		
5	Abigail Smith	34	31	90	88%		
6	Annette Yuang	36	32	95	93%		
7	Hannah Adams	30	25	64	69%		
8	Janet Chung	37	29	77	82%		
9	Maresh Di Giorgio	26	26	50	60%		
10	Katharine Susan	0	25	60	48%		
11							
12	*Total Available Score*	40	35	100			
13							
14							
15							

Tip: Excel shines when it comes to *numerical* data, but the program doesn't limit you to calculations. While it has the computing muscle to analyze stacks of numbers, it's equally useful for keeping track of the DVDs in your personal movie collection.

Some common spreadsheets include:

- **Business documents** like financial statements, invoices, expense reports, and earnings statements.

- **Personal documents** like weekly budgets, catalogs of your *Star Wars* action figures, exercise logs, and shopping lists.

- **Scientific data** like experimental observations, models, and medical charts.

These examples just scratch the surface. Resourceful spreadsheet gurus use Excel to build everything from cross-country trip itineraries to logs of every Kevin Bacon movie they've ever seen.

Note: Keen eyes will notice that Figure 9-1 doesn't include the omnipresent Excel ribbon, which usually sits atop the window, stacked with buttons. That's because it's been collapsed neatly out of the way to let you focus on the spreadsheet. You'll learn how to use this trick yourself on page 212.

Excel's not just a math wizard. If you want to add a little life to your data, you can inject color, apply exotic fonts, and even check your spelling. And if you're bleary-eyed from staring at rows and rows of spreadsheet numbers, you can use Excel's many chart-making tools to build everything from 3-D pie charts to more exotic scatter graphs. Excel can be as simple or as sophisticated as you want it to be.

NOSTALGIA CORNER

Excel 2003 Menu Shortcuts

If you've worked with a previous version of Excel, you might have trained yourself to use menu shortcuts—key combinations that open a menu and pick out the command you want. For example, if you press Alt+E in Excel 2003, the Edit menu pops open. You can then press the S key to choose the Paste Special command.

At first glance, it doesn't look like these keyboard shortcuts will amount to much in Excel 2007. After all, Excel 2007 doesn't even have a corresponding series of menus! Fortunately, Microsoft went to a little extra trouble to make life easier for longtime Excel aficionados. The result is that you can still use your menu shortcuts, but they work in a slightly different way.

When you hit Alt+E in Excel 2007, you see a tooltip appear over the top of the ribbon (Figure 9-2) that lets you know you've started to enter an Excel 2003 menu shortcut. If you go on to press S, you wind up at the familiar Paste Special dialog box, because Excel knows what you're trying to do. It's almost as though Excel has an invisible menu at work behind the scenes.

Of course, this feature can't help you out all the time. It doesn't work if you're trying to use one of the few commands that doesn't exist any longer. And if you need to see the menu to remember what key to press next, you're out of luck. All Excel gives you is the tooltip.

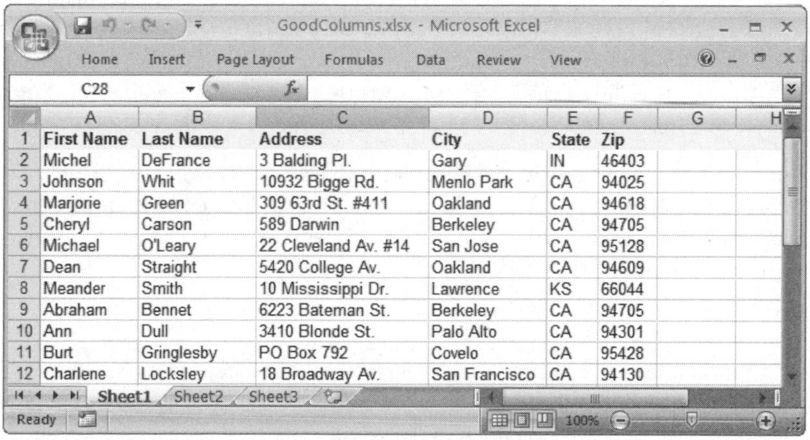

Figure 9-2:
By pressing Alt+E, you've triggered the "imaginary" Edit menu from Excel 2003, and earlier versions. You can't actually see it (because in Excel 2007 this menu doesn't exist). However, the tooltip lets you know that Excel is paying attention. You can now complete your action by pressing the next key for the menu command you're nostalgic for.

Excel's New Features

The slick new ribbon (page 2) is Excel's most dramatic change, but it's not the only new feature in Excel 2007. Other hot additions include:

- **Fewer limits.** Excel worksheets can now be bigger, formulas can be more complex, and cells can hold way more text. Although 99.87 percent of Excel fans never ran into any of these limits in previous versions, it's nice to know that the Excel engine continues to get more powerful.

- **Faster speeds.** One of the newest pieces of computing hardware is a *dual core CPU*. (The CPU is the brain of any computer.) A dual core CPU can perform two tasks at once, but it performs best with software that knows how to take advantage of the way it works. Excel 2007 knows all about dual core CPUs, which means intense calculations are even faster on these computers.

- **Better-looking charts.** Excel charts have always been intelligent, but they've never made good eye candy. Excel 2007 shakes things up with a whole new graphics engine that lets you add fantastic looking charts to your spreadsheets.

- **Formula AutoComplete.** The latest in a whole bunch of auto-do-something features, formula AutoComplete just might be the most helpful innovation yet. It prompts you with possible values when you type in complex formulas.

- **Tables.** When Microsoft created Excel 2003, they added a wildly popular *list* feature that helped people manage lists of information. In Excel 2007, lists morph into *tables* and get even more powerful.

- **Save-as-PDF.** A PDF file is Adobe's popular electronic document format that lets you share your work with other people, without losing any of your formatting (and without letting them change any of your numbers). Due to legal headaches, this feature didn't quite make it into the Excel 2007 installation, but it's available as a free download from Microsoft. Chapter 1 has the details.

Of course, this list is by no means complete. Excel 2007 is chock-full of refinements, tweaks, and tune-ups that make it easier to use than any previous version. You'll learn all the best tricks throughout this book. And if you've used a previous version of Excel, look for the "Nostalgia Corner" boxes, which tell how things have changed.

Note: The material in this part of the book is based on *Excel 2007: The Missing Manual* (O'Reilly). That book is a truly complete reference for Excel 2007, covering every feature, including geeky stuff like XML, VBA, ERROR.TYPE( ) functions, and other things you'll probably never encounter—or even want to. But if you get really deep into Excel and want to learn more, *Excel 2007: The Missing Manual* can be your trusted guide.

Creating a Basic Worksheet

When you first launch Excel, it starts you off with a new, blank *worksheet*, as shown in Figure 9-3. A worksheet is the grid of cells where you type your information and formulas; it takes up most of the window. This grid is the most important part of the Excel window. It's where you'll perform all your work, such as entering data, writing formulas, and reviewing the results.

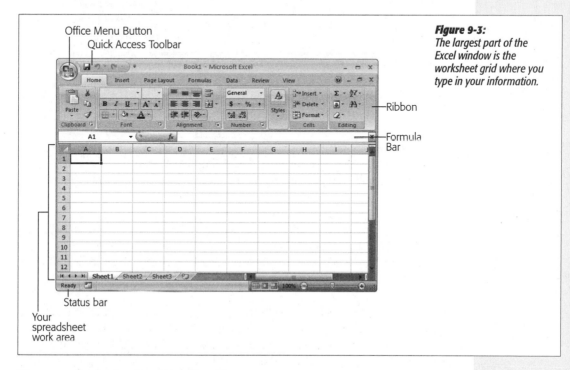

Office Menu Button
Quick Access Toolbar
Ribbon
Formula Bar
Your spreadsheet work area
Status bar

Figure 9-3:
The largest part of the Excel window is the worksheet grid where you type in your information.

Here are a few basics about Excel's grid:

- **The grid divides your worksheet into rows and columns.** Columns are identified with letters (A, B, C …), while rows are identified with numbers (1, 2, 3…).

- **The smallest unit in your worksheet is the *cell*.** Cells are identified by column and row. For example, C6 is the address of a cell in column C (the third column), and row 6 (the sixth row). Figure 9-4 shows this cell, which looks like a rectangular box. Incidentally, an Excel cell can hold up to 32,000 characters.

- **A worksheet can span an eye-popping 16,000 columns and 1 million rows.** In the unlikely case that you want to go beyond those limits—say you're tracking blades of grass on the White House lawn—you'll need to create a new worksheet. Every spreadsheet file can hold a virtually unlimited number of worksheets, as you'll learn in Chapter 12.

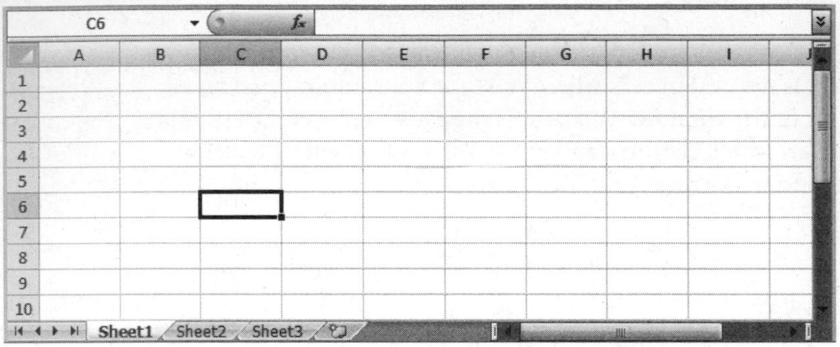

Figure 9-4:
Here, the current cell is C6. You can recognize the current (or active) cell based on its heavy black border. You'll also notice that the corresponding column letter (C) and row number (6) are highlighted at the edges of the worksheet. Just above the worksheet, on the left side of the window, the formula bar tells you the active cell address.

- **When you enter information, you enter it one cell at a time.** However, you don't have to follow any set order. For example, you can start by typing information into cell A40 without worrying about filling any data in the cells that appear in the earlier rows.

Note: Obviously, once you go beyond 26 columns, you run out of letters. Excel handles this by doubling up (and then tripling up) letters. For example, column Z is followed by column AA, then AB, then AC, all the way to AZ and then BA, BB, BC—you get the picture. And if you create a ridiculously large worksheet, you'll find that column ZZ is followed by AAA, AAB, AAC, and so on.

The best way to get a feel for Excel is to dive right in and start putting together a worksheet. The following sections cover each step that goes into assembling a simple worksheet. This one tracks household expenses, but you can use the same approach to create any basic worksheet.

Starting a New Workbook

When you fire up Excel, it opens a fresh workbook file. If you've already got Excel open and you want to create *another* workbook, just select Office button → New. This step pops up the New Workbook window that's shown in Figure 9-5.

Note: A *workbook* is a collection of one or more *worksheets*. That distinction isn't terribly important now because you're using only a single worksheet in each workbook you create. But in Chapter 12, you'll learn how to use several worksheets in the same workbook to track related collections of data.

For now, all you need to know is that the worksheet is the grid of cells where you place your data, and the workbook is the spreadsheet file that you save on your computer.

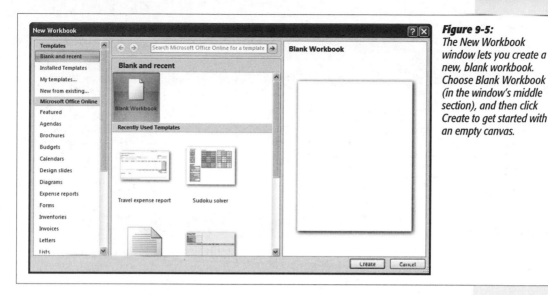

Figure 9-5:
The New Workbook window lets you create a new, blank workbook. Choose Blank Workbook (in the window's middle section), and then click Create to get started with an empty canvas.

You don't need to pick the file name for your workbook when you first create it. Instead, that decision happens later, when you *save* your workbook (page 218). For now, you start with a blank canvas that's ready to receive your numerical insights.

Note: Creating new workbooks doesn't disturb what you've already done. Whatever workbook you were using remains open in another window. You can use the Windows taskbar to move from one workbook to the other. Page 227 shows the taskbar close up.

Adding the Column Titles

The most straightforward way to create a worksheet is to design it as a table with headings for each column. It's important to remember that even for the simplest worksheet, the decisions you make about what's going to go in each column can have a big effect on how easy it is to manipulate your information.

For example, in a worksheet that stores a mailing list, you *could* have two columns: one for names and another for addresses. But if you create more than two columns, your life will probably be easier since you can separate first names from street addresses from Zip codes, and so on. Figure 9-6 shows the difference.

You can, of course, always add or remove columns later. But you can avoid getting gray hairs by starting a worksheet with all the columns you think you'll need.

The first step in creating your worksheet is to add your headings in the row of cells at the top of the worksheet (row 1). Technically, you don't need to start right in the first row, but unless you want to add more information before your table—like a title for the chart or today's date—there's no point in wasting the space. Adding information is easy—just click the cell you want and start typing. When you're finished, hit Tab to complete your entry and move to the next cell to the right (or Enter to head to the cell just underneath).

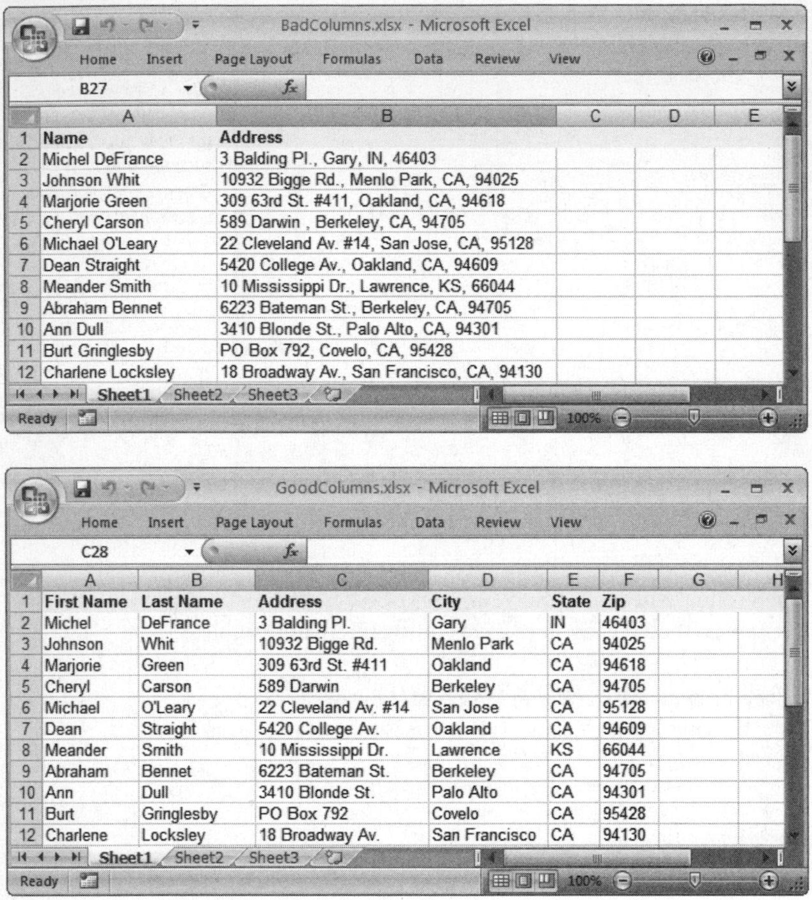

	A	B
1	Name	Address
2	Michel DeFrance	3 Balding Pl., Gary, IN, 46403
3	Johnson Whit	10932 Bigge Rd., Menlo Park, CA, 94025
4	Marjorie Green	309 63rd St. #411, Oakland, CA, 94618
5	Cheryl Carson	589 Darwin , Berkeley, CA, 94705
6	Michael O'Leary	22 Cleveland Av. #14, San Jose, CA, 95128
7	Dean Straight	5420 College Av., Oakland, CA, 94609
8	Meander Smith	10 Mississippi Dr., Lawrence, KS, 66044
9	Abraham Bennet	6223 Bateman St., Berkeley, CA, 94705
10	Ann Dull	3410 Blonde St., Palo Alto, CA, 94301
11	Burt Gringlesby	PO Box 792, Covelo, CA, 95428
12	Charlene Locksley	18 Broadway Av., San Francisco, CA, 94130

	A	B	C	D	E	F
1	First Name	Last Name	Address	City	State	Zip
2	Michel	DeFrance	3 Balding Pl.	Gary	IN	46403
3	Johnson	Whit	10932 Bigge Rd.	Menlo Park	CA	94025
4	Marjorie	Green	309 63rd St. #411	Oakland	CA	94618
5	Cheryl	Carson	589 Darwin	Berkeley	CA	94705
6	Michael	O'Leary	22 Cleveland Av. #14	San Jose	CA	95128
7	Dean	Straight	5420 College Av.	Oakland	CA	94609
8	Meander	Smith	10 Mississippi Dr.	Lawrence	KS	66044
9	Abraham	Bennet	6223 Bateman St.	Berkeley	CA	94705
10	Ann	Dull	3410 Blonde St.	Palo Alto	CA	94301
11	Burt	Gringlesby	PO Box 792	Covelo	CA	95428
12	Charlene	Locksley	18 Broadway Av.	San Francisco	CA	94130

Figure 9-6: *Top: If you enter the first and last names together in one column, Excel can sort only by the first names. And if you clump the addresses and Zip codes together, you give Excel no way to count how many people live in a certain town or neighborhood because Excel can't extract the Zip codes.*

Bottom: The benefit of a six-column table is significant: it lets you sort (reorganize) your list according to people's last names or where they live.

Note: The information you put in an Excel worksheet doesn't need to be in neat, ordered columns. Nothing stops you from scattering numbers and text in random cells. However, most Excel worksheets resemble some sort of table, because that's the easiest and most effective way to deal with large amounts of structured information.

For a simple expense worksheet designed to keep a record of your most prudent and extravagant purchases, try the following three headings:

- **Date Purchased** stores the date when you spent the money.
- **Item** stores the name of the product that you bought.
- **Price** records how much it cost.

Right away, you face your first glitch: awkwardly crowded text. Figure 9-7 shows how you can adjust column width for proper breathing room.

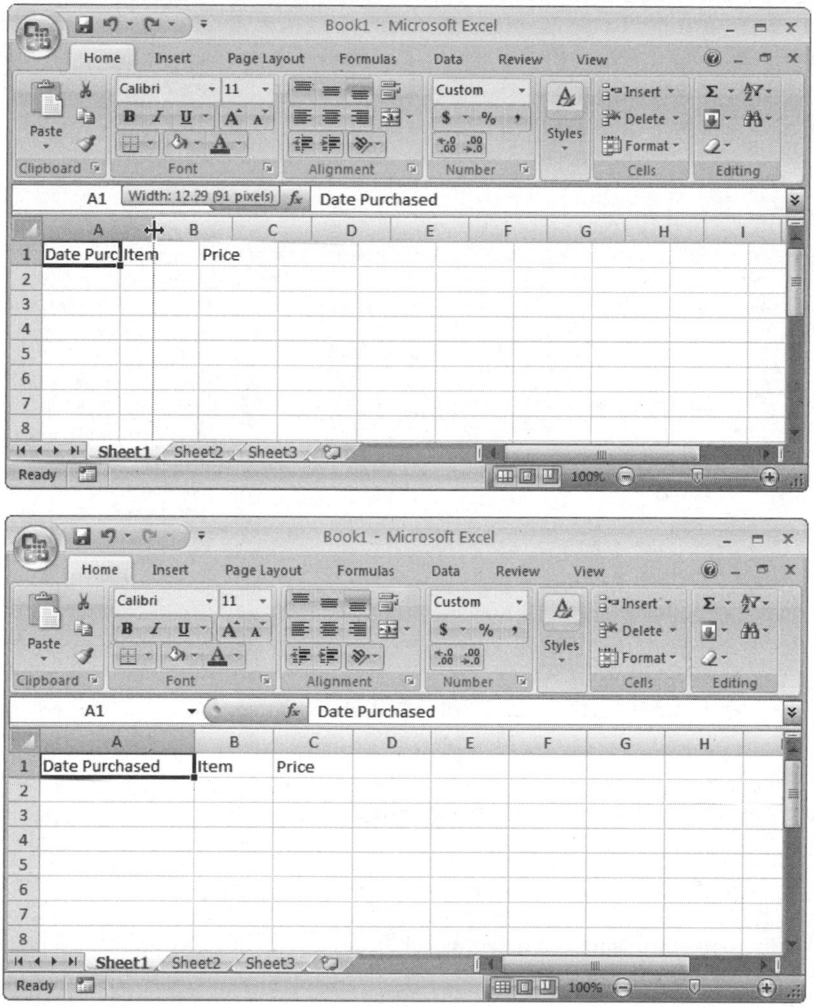

Figure 9-7:
Top: The standard width of an Excel column is 8.43 characters, which hardly allows you to get a word in edgewise. To solve this problem, position your mouse on the right border of the column header you want to expand so that the mouse pointer changes to the resize icon (it looks like a double-headed arrow). Now drag the column border to the right as far as you want.

Bottom: When you release the mouse, the entire column of cells is resized to the new size.

Adding Data

You can now begin adding your data: simply fill in the rows under the column titles. Each row in the expense worksheet represents a separate purchase that you've made. (If you're familiar with databases, you can think of each row as a separate record.)

As Figure 9-8 shows, the first column is for dates, the second column is for text, and the third column holds numbers. Keep in mind that Excel doesn't impose any rules on what you type, so you're free to put text in the Price column. But if you don't keep a consistent kind of data in each column, you won't be able to easily analyze (or understand) your information later.

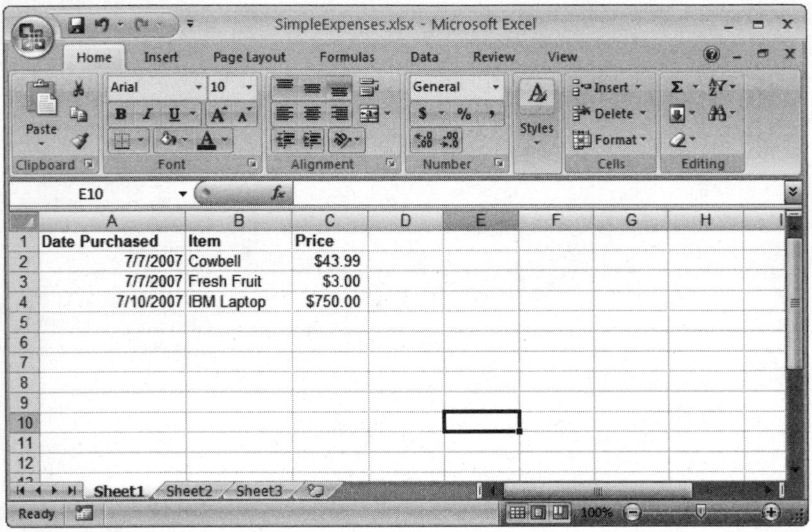

Figure 9-8:
This rudimentary expense list has three items (in rows 2, 3, and 4). The alignment of each column reflects the data type (by default, numbers and dates are right-aligned, while text is left-aligned), indicating that Excel understands your date and price information.

That's it. You've created a living, breathing worksheet. The next two sections explain how to edit data and move around the grid.

Editing Data

Every time you start typing in a cell, Excel erases any existing content in that cell. (You can also quickly remove the contents of a cell by just moving to it and pressing Delete.)

If you want to edit cell data instead of replacing it, you need to put the cell in *edit mode*, like this:

1. **Move to the cell you want to edit.**

   Use the mouse or the arrow keys to get to the correct cell.

2. **Put the cell in edit mode by pressing F2.**

   Edit mode looks almost the same as ordinary text entry mode. The only difference is that you can use the arrow keys to move through the text you're typing and make changes. (When you aren't in edit mode, pressing these keys just moves you to another cell.)

   If you don't want to use F2, you can also get a cell into edit mode by double-clicking it.

3. **Complete your edit.**

Once you've modified the cell content, press Enter to commit your change or Esc to cancel your edit and leave the old value in the cell. Alternatively, you can turn off edit mode (press F2 again), and then move to a new cell. As long as you stay in edit mode, Excel won't let you move to another cell.

Tip: If you start typing new information into a cell and you decide you want to move to an earlier position in your entry (to make an alteration, for instance), just press F2. The cell box still looks the same, but you're now in edit mode, which means that you can use the arrow keys to move within the cell (instead of moving from cell to cell). You can press F2 again to return to the normal data entry mode.

As you enter data, you may discover the Bigtime Excel Display Problem: cells in adjacent columns can overlap one another. Figure 9-9 shows the problem. One way to fix this problem is to manually resize the column, as shown in Figure 9-7. Another option is to use *wrapping* to fit multiple lines of text in a single cell, as described on page 299.

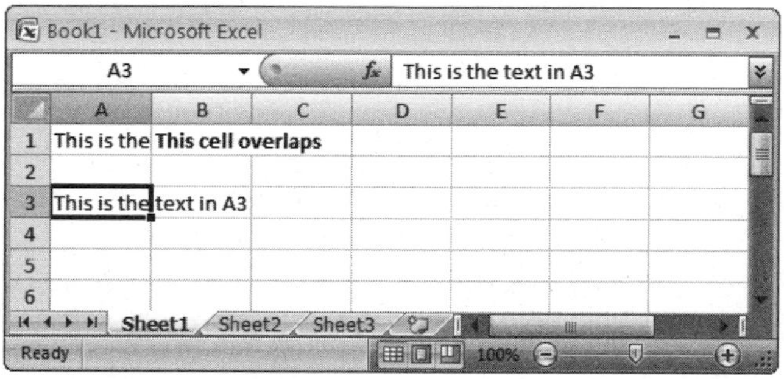

Figure 9-9:
Overlapping cells can create big headaches. For example, if you type a large amount of text into A1, and then you type some text into B1, you see only part of the data in A1 on your worksheet (as shown here). The rest is hidden from view. But if, say, A3 contains a large amount of text and B3 is empty, the content in A3 is displayed over both columns, and you don't have a problem.

Navigating in Excel

Learning how to move around the Excel grid quickly and confidently is an indispensable skill. To move from cell to cell, you have two basic choices:

- **Use the arrow keys on the keyboard.** Keystrokes move you one cell at a time in any direction.

- **Click the cell with the mouse.** A mouse click jumps you directly to the cell you've clicked.

As you move from cell to cell, you see the black focus box move to highlight the currently active cell. In some cases, you might want to cover ground a little quicker. You can use any of the shortcut keys listed in Table 9-1. The most useful shortcut keys include the Home key combinations, which bring you back to the beginning of a row or the top of your worksheet.

Table 9-1. *Shortcut Keys for Moving Around a Worksheet*

Key Combination	Result
→ (or Tab)	Moves one cell to the right.
← (or Shift+Tab)	Moves one cell to the left.
↑	Moves one cell up.
↓ (or Enter)	Moves one cell down.
Page Up	Moves up one screen. Thus, if the grid shows 10 cells at a time, this key moves to a cell in the same column, 10 rows up (unless you are already at the top of the worksheet).
Page Down	Moves down one screen. Thus, if the grid shows 10 cells at a time, this key moves to a cell in the same column, 10 rows down.
Home	Moves to the first cell (column A) of the current row.
Ctrl+Home	Moves to the first cell in the top row, which is A1.
Ctrl+End (or End, Home)	Moves to the last column of the last occupied row. This cell is at the bottom-right edge of your data.

Note: Shortcut key combinations that use the + sign must be entered together. For example, "Ctrl+Home" means you hold down Ctrl and press Home at the same time. Key combinations with a comma work in sequence. For example, the key combination "End, Home" means press End first, release it, and then press Home.

Excel also lets you cross great distances in a single bound using a *Ctrl+arrow key* combination. These key combinations jump to the *edges* of your data. Edge cells include cells that are next to other blank cells. For example, if you press Ctrl+→ while you're inside a group of cells with information in them, you'll skip to the right, over all filled cells, and stop just before the next blank cell. If you press Ctrl+ → again, you'll skip over all the nearby blank cells and land in the next cell to the right that has information in it. If there aren't any more cells with data on the right, you'll wind up on the very edge of your worksheet.

The *Ctrl+arrow key* combinations are useful if you have more than one table of data in the same worksheet. For example, imagine you have two tables of data, one at the top of a worksheet and one at the bottom. If you are at the top of the first table, you can use Ctrl+↓ to jump to the bottom of the first table, skipping all the rows in between. Press Ctrl+↓ again, and you leap over all the blank rows, winding up at the beginning of the second table.

Tip: You can also scroll off into the uncharted regions of the spreadsheet with the help of the scrollbars at the bottom and on the right side of the worksheet.

Finding your way around a worksheet is a fundamental part of mastering Excel. Knowing your way around the larger program window is no less important. The next few sections help you get oriented, pointing out the important stuff and letting you know what you can ignore altogether.

The Tabs of the Ribbon

In the introduction you learned about the ribbon, the super-toolbar that offers one-stop shopping for all of Excel's features. All the most important Office applications—including Word, Access, PowerPoint, and Excel—use the new ribbon. However, each program has a different set of tabs and buttons.

GEM IN THE ROUGH

Getting Somewhere in a Hurry

If you're fortunate enough to know exactly where you need to go, you can use the Go To feature to make the jump. Go To moves to the cell address you specify. It comes in useful in extremely large spreadsheets, where just scrolling through the worksheet takes half a day.

To bring up the Go To dialog box (shown in Figure 9-10), choose Home → Editing → Find & Select → Go To. Or you can do yourself a favor and just press Ctrl+G. Enter the cell address (such as C32), and then click OK.

The Go To feature becomes more useful the more you use it. That's because the Go To window maintains a list of the most recent cell addresses that you've entered. In addition, every time you open the Go To window, Excel automatically

adds the current cell to the list. This feature makes it easy to jump to a far-off cell and quickly return to your starting location by selecting the last entry in the list.

The Go To window isn't your only option for leaping through a worksheet in a single bound. If you look at the Home → Editing → Find & Select menu, you'll find more specialized commands that let you jump straight to cells that contains formulas, comments, conditional formatting, and other advanced Excel ingredients that you haven't learned about yet. And if you want to hunt down cells that have specific text, you need the popular Find command (Home → Editing → Find & Select → Find), which is covered on page 270.

Figure 9-10:
You'll notice that in the Go To list, cell addresses are written a little differently than the format you use when you type them in. Namely, dollar signs are added before the row number and column letter. Thus, C32 becomes $C$32, which is simply the convention that Excel uses for fixed cell references. (You'll learn much more about the different types of cell references in Chapter 15.)

Throughout this book, you'll dig through the different tabs of the ribbon to find important features. But before you start your journey, it's nice to get a quick overview of what each tab provides. Here's the lowdown:

- **Home** includes some of the most commonly used buttons, like those for cutting and pasting information, formatting your data, and hunting down important bits of information with search tools.

- **Insert** lets you add special ingredients like tables, graphics, charts, and hyperlinks.

- **Page Layout** is all about getting your worksheet ready for the printer. You can tweak margins, paper orientation, and other page settings.

- **Formulas** are mathematical instructions that you use to perform calculations. This tab helps you build super-smart formulas and resolve mind-bending errors.

- **Data** lets you get information from an outside data source (like a heavy-duty database) so you can analyze it in Excel. It also includes tools for dealing with large amounts of information, like sorting, filtering, and subgrouping.

- **Review** includes the familiar Office proofing tools (like the spell checker). It also has buttons that let you add comments to a worksheet and manage revisions.

- **View** lets you switch on and off a variety of viewing options. It also lets you pull off a few fancy tricks if you want to view several separate Excel spreadsheet files at the same time.

GEM IN THE ROUGH

Collapsing the Ribbon

Most people are happy to have the ribbon sit at the top of the Excel window, with all its buttons on hand. However, serious number crunchers demand maximum space for their data. They'd rather look at another row of numbers than a pumped-up toolbar. If this describes you, then you'll be happy to find out you can *collapse* the ribbon, which shrinks it down to a single row of tab titles, as shown in Figure 9-11. To collapse it, just double-click any tab title.

Even when the ribbon's collapsed, you can still use all its features. All you need to do is click a tab. For example, if you click Home, the Home tab pops up over your worksheet. As soon as you click the button you want in the Home tab (or click a cell in your worksheet), the ribbon collapses itself again. The same trick works if you trigger a command in the ribbon using the keyboard, as described on page 6.

If you use the ribbon only occasionally, or if you prefer to use keyboard shortcuts, it makes sense to collapse the ribbon. Even when collapsed, the ribbon commands are available—it just takes an extra click to open the tab. On the other hand, if you make frequent trips to the ribbon, or you're learning about Excel and you like to browse the ribbon to see what features are available, don't bother collapsing it. The two or three rows that you'll lose are well worth keeping.

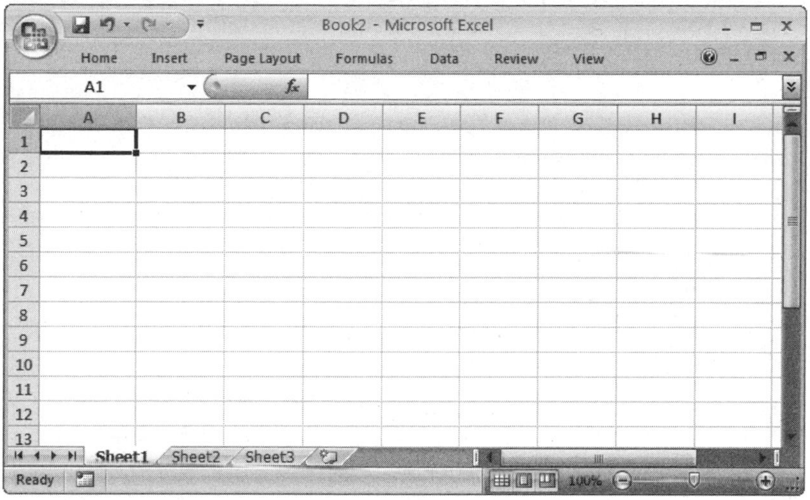

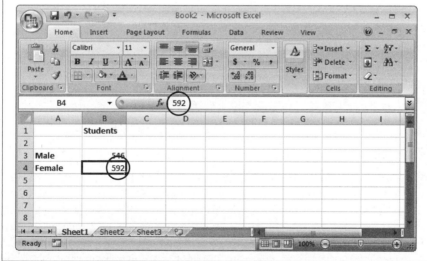

Figure 9-11:
Do you want to use every square inch of screen space for your cells? You can collapse the ribbon (as shown here) by double-clicking any tab. Click a tab to pop it open temporarily, or double-click a tab to bring the ribbon back for good. And if you want to perform the same trick without raising your fingers from the keyboard, you can use the shortcut key Ctrl+F1.

The Formula Bar

The *formula bar* appears above the worksheet grid but below the ribbon (Figure 9-12). It displays the address of the active cell (like A1) on the left edge, and it also shows you the current cell's contents.

Figure 9-12:
The formula bar (just above the grid) shows information about the active cell. In this example, the formula bar shows that the current cell is B4 and that it contains the number 592. Instead of editing this value in the worksheet, you can click anywhere in the formula bar and make your changes there.

You can use the formula bar to enter and edit data, instead of editing directly in your worksheet. This approach is particularly useful when a cell contains a formula or a large amount of information. That's because the formula bar gives you more work room than a typical cell. Just as with in-cell edits, you press Enter to confirm your changes or Esc to cancel them. Or you can use the mouse: When you start typing in the formula bar, a checkmark and an "X" icon appear just to the left of the box where you're typing. Click the checkmark to confirm your entry, or "X" to roll it back.

Note: You can hide (or show) the formula bar by choosing View → Show/Hide → Formula Bar. But the formula bar's such a basic part of Excel that you'd be unwise to get rid of it. Instead, keep it around until Chapter 15, when you'll learn how to build formulas.

Ordinarily, the formula bar is a single line. If you have a *really* long entry in a cell (like a paragraph's worth of text), you need to scroll from one side to the other. However, there's another option—you can resize the formula bar so it fits more information, as shown in Figure 9-13.

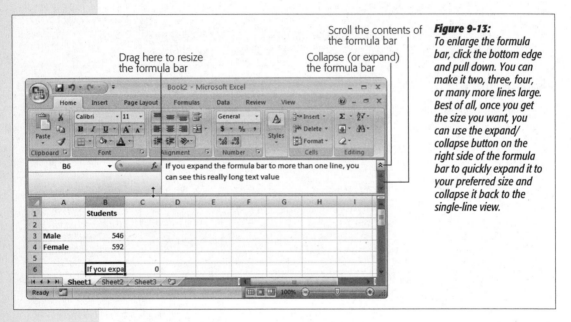

Scroll the contents of the formula bar

Drag here to resize the formula bar

Collapse (or expand) the formula bar

Figure 9-13:
To enlarge the formula bar, click the bottom edge and pull down. You can make it two, three, four, or many more lines large. Best of all, once you get the size you want, you can use the expand/collapse button on the right side of the formula bar to quickly expand it to your preferred size and collapse it back to the single-line view.

The Status Bar

Though people often overlook it, the status bar (Figure 9-14) is a good way to keep on top of Excel's current state. For example, if you save or print a document, the status bar shows the progress of the printing process. If you're performing a quick action, the progress indicator may disappear before you have a chance to even notice it. But if you're performing a time-consuming operation—say, printing out an 87-page table of the airline silverware you happen to own—you can look to the status bar to see how things are coming along.

Tip: To hide or show the status bar, choose View → Show/Hide → Status Bar.

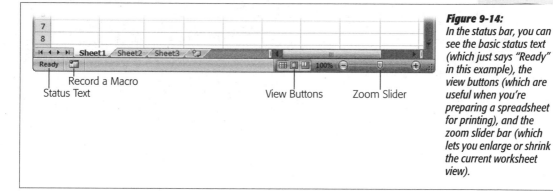

Figure 9-14:
In the status bar, you can see the basic status text (which just says "Ready" in this example), the view buttons (which are useful when you're preparing a spreadsheet for printing), and the zoom slider bar (which lets you enlarge or shrink the current worksheet view).

The status bar combines several different types of information. The leftmost part of the status bar shows the Cell Mode, which displays one of three indicators.

• The word "Ready" means that Excel isn't doing anything much at the moment, other than waiting for you to take some action.

• The word "Enter" appears when you start typing a new value into a cell.

• The word "Edit" means the cell is currently in edit mode, and pressing the left and right arrow keys moves through the cell data, instead of moving from cell to cell. As discussed earlier, you can place a cell in edit mode or take it out of edit mode by pressing F2.

Farther to the right on the status bar are the view buttons, which let you switch to Page Layout View or Page Break Preview. These different views help you see what your worksheet will look like when you print it. They're covered in Chapter 14.

The zoom slider is next to the view buttons, at the far right edge of the status bar. You can slide it to the left to zoom out (which fits more information into your Excel window at once) or slide it to the right to zoom in (and take a closer look at fewer cells). You can learn more about zooming on page 312.

In addition, the status bar displays other miscellaneous indicators. For example, if you press the Scroll Lock key, a Scroll Lock indicator appears on the status bar (next to the "Ready" text). This indicator tells you that you're in *scroll mode*. In scroll mode, the arrow keys don't move you from one cell to another; instead, they scroll the entire worksheet up, down, or to the side. Scroll mode is a great way to check out another part of your spreadsheet without leaving your current position.

You can control what indicators appear in the status bar by configuring it. To see a full list of possibilities, right-click the status bar. A huge list of options appears, as shown in Figure 9-15. Table 9-2 describes the most useful status bar options.

Note: The Caps Lock indicator doesn't determine whether or not you can use the Caps Lock key—that feature always works. The Caps Lock indicator just lets you know when Caps Lock mode is on. That way you won't be surprised by an accidental keystroke that turns your next data entry INTO ALL CAPITALS.

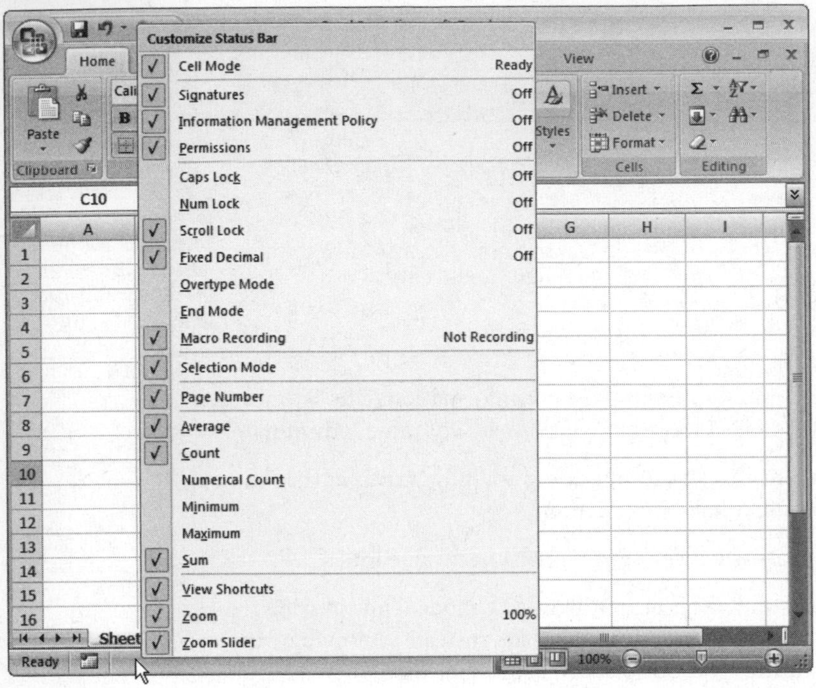

Figure 9-15:
Every item that has a checkmark appears in the status bar when you need it. For example, if you choose Caps Lock, the text "Caps Lock" appears in the status bar whenever you hit the Caps Lock key to switch to all-capital typing.

Table 9-2. *Status Bar Indicators*

Indicator	Meaning
Cell Mode	Shows Ready, Edit, or Enter depending on the state of the current cell, as described on page 215.
Caps Lock	Indicates whether Caps Lock mode is on. When Caps Lock is on, every letter you type is automatically capitalized. To turn Caps Lock mode on or off, hit Caps Lock.
Num Lock	Indicates whether Num Lock mode is on. When this mode is on, you can use the numeric keypad (typically at the right side of your keyboard) to type in numbers more quickly. When this sign's off, the numeric keypad controls cell navigation instead. To turn Num Lock on or off, press Num Lock.
Scroll Lock	Indicates whether Scroll Lock mode is on. When it's on, you can use the arrow keys to scroll the worksheet without changing the active cell. (In other words, you can control your scrollbars by just using your keyboard.) This feature lets you look at all the information you have in your worksheet without losing track of the cell you're currently in. You can turn Scroll Lock mode on or off by pressing Scroll Lock.
Overtype Mode	Indicates when Overwrite mode is turned on. Overwrite mode changes how cell edits work. When you edit a cell and Overwrite mode is on, the new characters that you type overwrite existing characters (rather than displacing them). You can turn Overwrite mode on or off by pressing Insert.

Table 9-2. *Status Bar Indicators (continued)*

Indicator	Meaning
End Mode	Indicates that you've pressed End, which is the first key in many two-key combinations; the next key determines what happens. For example, hit End and then Home to move to the bottom-right cell in your worksheet. See Table 9-1 for a list of key combinations, some of which use End.
Selection Mode	Indicates the current Selection mode. You have two options: normal mode and *extended selection*. When you press the arrows keys and extended selection is on, Excel automatically selects all the rows and columns you cross. Extended selection is a useful keyboard alternative to dragging your mouse to select swaths of the grid. To turn extended selection on or off, press F8. You'll learn more about selecting cells and moving them around in Chapter 11.
Page Number	Shows the current page and the total number of pages (as in "Page 1 of 4"). This indicator appears only in Page Layout view (as described on page 325).
Average, Count, Numerical Count, Minimum, Maximum, Sum	Show the result of a calculation on the selected cells. For example, the Sum indicator shows the total of all the numeric cells that are currently selected. You'll take a closer look at this handy trick on page 348.
View Shortcuts	Shows the three view buttons that let you switch between Normal view, Page Layout View, and Page Break Preview (as described on page 337).
Zoom	Shows the current zoom percentage (like 100 percent for a normal-sized spreadsheet, and 200 percent for a spreadsheet that's blown up to twice the magnification).
Zoom Slider	Shows a slider that lets you zoom in closer (by sliding it to the right) or out to see more information at once (by sliding it to the left).

Excel Options

You might have already seen the Excel Options window, which provides a central hub where you can adjust how Excel looks, behaves, and calculates (see Figure 9-16). To get to this window, click the Office button, and then choose Excel Options on the bottom-right edge.

The top five sections in the Excel Options window let you tweak a wide variety of different details. Some of these details are truly handy, like the options for opening and saving files (which are described at the end of this chapter). Others are seldom-used holdovers from the past, like the option that lets Excel act like Lotus—an ancient piece of spreadsheet software—when you hit the "/" key.

Tip: Some important options have a small i-in-a-circle icon next to them, which stands for "information." Hover over this icon and you see a tooltip that gives you a brief description about that setting.

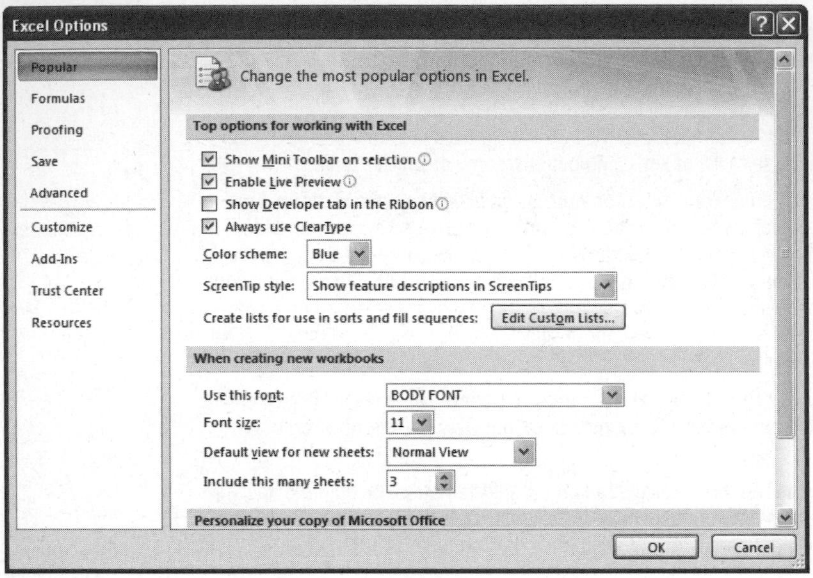

Figure 9-16:
The Excel Options window is divided into nine sections. To pick which section to look at, choose an entry from the list on the left. In this example, you're looking at the Popular settings group. In each section, the settings are further subdivided into titled groups. You may need to scroll down to find the setting you want.

Beneath the top five sections are four more specialized sections:

- **Customize** lets you put your favorite commands on the Quick Access toolbar, a maneuver you can learn more about in Appendix A.

- **Add-Ins** lets you configure other utilities (mini-programs) that work with Excel and enhance its powers.

- **Trust Center** lets you tweak Excel's security settings that safeguard against dangerous actions (think: viruses).

- **Resources** provides a few buttons that let you get extra diagnostic information, activate your copy of Office (which you've no doubt done already), and get freebies and updates on the Web.

While you're getting to know Excel, you can comfortably ignore most of what's in the Excel Options window. But you'll return here many times throughout this book to adjust settings and fine-tune the way Excel works.

Saving Files

As everyone who's been alive for at least three days knows, you should save your work early and often. Excel is no exception. You have two choices for saving a spreadsheet file:

- **Save As.** This choice allows you to save your spreadsheet file with a new name. You can use Save As the first time you save a new spreadsheet, or you can use it to save a copy of your current spreadsheet with a new name, in a new folder, or as a different file type. (Alternate file formats are discussed on page 220.)

To use Save As, select Office button → Save As, or press F12. Figure 9-17 shows you the Save As dialog box as it appears on a Windows XP computer. (The Windows Vista version of the Save As dialog box has all the same features, but way more style.)

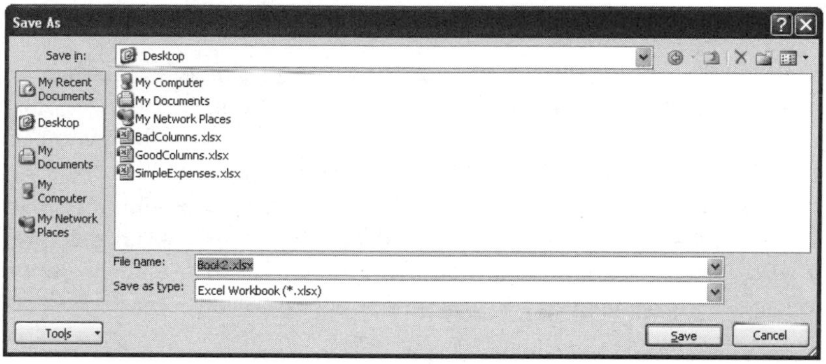

Figure 9-17:
The Save As dialog box lets you jump to common folders using the big buttons on the left, or you can browse a folder tree using the drop-down "Save in" menu. Once you've found the folder you want, type the file name at the bottom of the window, and then pick the file type. Finally, click Save to finish the job.

- **Save.** This option updates the spreadsheet file with your most recent changes. If you use Save on a new file that hasn't been saved before, it has the same effect as Save As: Excel prompts you to choose a folder and file name. To use Save, select Office button → Save, or press Ctrl+S. Or, look up at the top of the Excel window in the Quick Access toolbar for the tiny Save button, which looks like an old-style diskette.

Tip: Resaving a spreadsheet is an almost instantaneous operation, and you should get used to doing it all the time. After you've made any significant change, just hit Ctrl+S to make sure you've stored the latest version of your data.

The Excel 2007 File Format

Since time immemorial, Excel fans have been saving their lovingly crafted spreadsheets in *.xls* files (as in AirlineSilverware.xls). Excel 2007 changes all that. In fact, it introduces a completely new file format, with the extension *.xlsx* (as in Airline-Silverware.xlsx).

At first glance, this seems a tad over the top. But the new file format has some real advantages:

- **It's compact.** The new Excel file format uses Zip file compression, so spreadsheet files are smaller—way smaller (as much as 75 percent smaller than their original sizes). And even though the average hard drive is already large enough to swallow thousands of old-fashioned Excel files, the new compact format is easier to email around.

- **It's less error-prone.** The new file format carefully separates ordinary content, pictures, and macro code into separate sections. (Macros are automated routines that perform a specific task in a spreadsheet.) Microsoft claims that this change makes for tougher files. Now, if a part of your Excel file is damaged (for example, due to a faulty hard drive), there's a much better chance that you can still retrieve the rest of the information. (You'll learn about Excel disaster recovery on page 223.)

- **It's extensible.** The new file format uses XML (the eXtensible Markup Language), which is a standardized way to store information. XML storage doesn't benefit the average person, but it's sure to earn a lot of love from companies that plan to build custom software that uses Excel documents. As long as Excel documents are stored in XML, these companies can create automated programs that pull the information they need straight out of a spreadsheet, without going through Excel. These programs can also generate made-to-measure Excel documents all on their own.

For all these reasons, .xlsx is the format of choice for Excel 2007. However, Microsoft prefers to give people all the choices they could ever need (rather than make life really simple), and Excel file formats are no exception. Along with the standard .xlsx, there's the closely related *.xlsm* cousin, which adds the ability to store macro code. If you've added any macros to your spreadsheet, Excel prompts you to use this file type when you save your spreadsheet.

Saving Your Spreadsheet in Older Formats

Most of the time, you don't need to think about Excel's file format—you can just create your spreadsheets, save them, and let Excel take care of the rest. The only time you need to stop and think twice is when you need to share your work with other, less fortunate people who have older versions of Excel.

When you find yourself in this situation, you have two choices:

- **Save your spreadsheet in the old format.** You can save a copy of your spreadsheet in the traditional .xls Excel standard that's been supported since Excel 97. To do so, choose Office button → Save As → Excel 97-2003 Format.

- **Use a free add-in for older versions of Excel.** People who are stuck with Excel 2000, Excel 2002, or Excel 2003 *can* read your Excel 2007 files—they just need a free add-in that's provided by Microsoft. This is a good solution because it's doesn't require any work on your part. People with past-its-prime versions of Excel can find the add-in they need by surfing to *www.microsoft.com/downloads* and searching for "compatibility pack file formats" (or use the secret shortcut URL *http://tinyurl.com/y5w78r*).

Often, the best thing you can do is keep your spreadsheet in the newer format and save a *copy* in the older format (using Office button → Save As → Excel 97-2003 Format). You can then hand that copy out to your backward friends.

Some eccentric individuals have even older or stranger spreadsheet software on their computers. If you want to save a copy of your spreadsheet in a more exotic file type, you can choose Office button → Save As, and then find the desired format in the "Save as type" drop-down list (Figure 9-18). Excel lets you save your spreadsheet using a variety of different formats, including the classic Excel 95 format from a decade ago. If you're looking to view your spreadsheet using a mystery program, use the CSV file type, which produces a comma-delimited text file that almost all spreadsheet applications on any operating system can read (comma-delimited means the information has commas separating each cell).

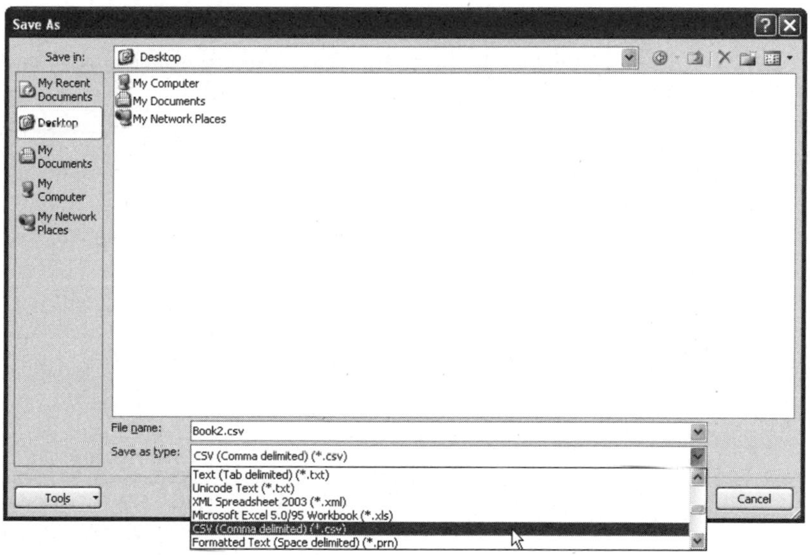

Figure 9-18:
Excel offers a few useful file type options in the "Save as type" list. CSV format is the best choice for compatibility with truly old software (or when nothing else seems to work). If you're a longtime Excel fan, you'll notice that the list has been slimmed down a bit—for example, there's no option to use the old dBase and Lotus formats from the DOS world.

Tip: When you save your Excel spreadsheet in another format, make sure you keep a copy in the standard .xlsx format. Why bother? Because other formats aren't guaranteed to retain all your information, particularly if you choose a format that doesn't support some of Excel's newer features.

Saving Your Spreadsheet As a PDF

Sometimes you want to save a copy of your spreadsheet so that people can read it even if they don't have Excel (and even if they're running a different operating system, like Linux or Apple's OS X). In this situation, you have several choices:

- **Use the Excel Viewer.** Even if you don't have Excel, you can install a separate tool called the Excel Viewer, which is available from Microsoft's Web site (search for "Excel Viewer" at *www.microsoft.com/downloads*). However, few people have the viewer, and even though it's free, few want to bother installing it. And it doesn't work on non-Windows computers.

- **Save your workbook as an HTML Web page.** That way, all you need to view the workbook is a Web browser (and who doesn't have one of those?). The only disadvantage is that you could lose complex formatting. Some worksheets may make the transition to HTML gracefully, while others don't look very good when they're squashed into a browser window. And if you're planning to let other people print the exported worksheet, the results might be unsatisfactory.

- **Save your workbook as a PDF file.** This gets you the best of both worlds—you keep all the rich formatting (so your workbook can be printed), and you let people who don't have Excel (and possibly don't even have Windows) view your workbook. The only disadvantage is that this feature isn't included in the basic Excel package. Instead, you need to install a free add-in to get it.

To get the Save As PDF add-in, surf to *www.microsoft.com/downloads* and search for "PDF." The links lead you to a page where you can download the add-in and install it with just a couple of clicks.

Once you install the Save As PDF add-in, all your Office applications have the ability to save their documents in PDF format. In Excel, you work this magic by choosing Office button → Save As → PDF, which brings up the "Publish as PDF" dialog box (Figure 9-19).

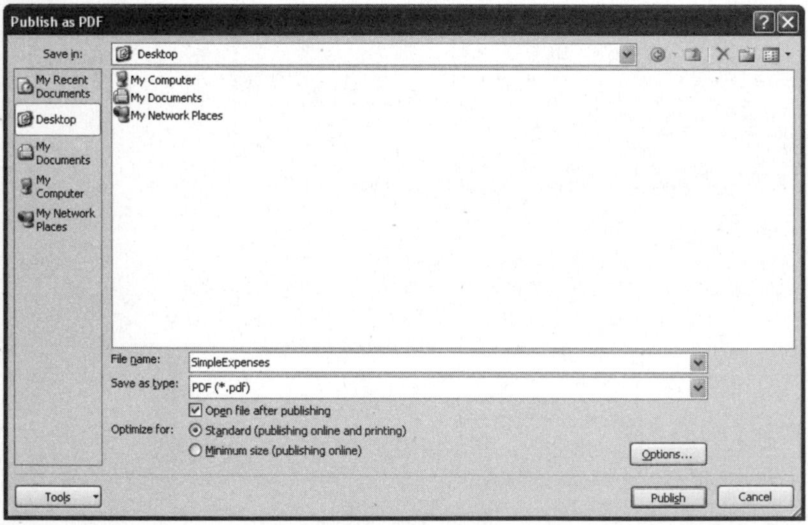

Figure 9-19:
The "Publish as PDF" dialog box looks a lot like the Save As dialog box, except it has a Publish button instead of a Save button. You can switch on the "Open file after publishing" setting to tell Excel to open the PDF file in Adobe Reader (assuming you have it installed) after the publishing process is complete, so you can check the result.

When you save a PDF file, you get a few extra options in the Save As dialog box. PDF files can be saved with different resolution and quality settings (which mostly affect any graphical objects that you've placed in your workbook, like pictures and charts). Normally, you use higher quality settings if you're planning to print your PDF file, because printers use higher resolutions than computer monitors.

The "Publish as PDF" dialog box gives you some control over the quality settings with the "Optimize for" options. If you're just saving a PDF copy so other people can *view* the information in your workbook, choose "Minimum size (publishing online)" to save some space. On the other hand, if there's a possibility that the people reading your PDF might want to print it out, choose "Standard (publishing online and printing)" to save a slightly larger PDF that makes for a better printout.

Finally, if you want to publish only a portion of your spreadsheet as a PDF file, click the Options button to open a dialog box with even more settings. You can choose to publish just a fixed number of pages, just the selected cells, and so on. These options mirror the choices you get when sending a spreadsheet to the printer. You also see a few more cryptic options, most of which you can safely ignore. (They're intended for PDF nerds.) One exception is the "Document properties" option—turn this off if you don't want the PDF to keep track of certain information that identifies you, like your name.

Tip: Getting the Save As PDF add-in is a bit of a hassle, but it's well worth the effort. In previous versions of Excel, people who wanted to create PDFs file had to get another add-in or buy the expensive full version of the Adobe Acrobat software. The Save As PDF feature was originally slated for inclusion in Excel (with no add-in required), but anti-trust concerns caused ultra-cautious Microsoft to leave it out.

Disaster Recovery

The corollary to the edict "Save your data early and often" is the truism "Sometimes things fall apart quickly...before you've even had a chance to back up." Fortunately, Excel includes an invaluable safety net called AutoRecover.

AutoRecover periodically saves backup copies of your spreadsheet while you work. If you suffer a system crash, you can retrieve the last AutoRecover backup even if you never managed to save the file yourself. Of course, even the AutoRecover backup won't necessarily have *all* the information you entered in your spreadsheet before the problem occurred. But if AutoRecover saves a backup every 10 minutes (the standard), at most you'll lose 10 minutes of work.

AutoRecover comes switched on when you install Excel, but you can tweak its settings. Select Office → Excel Options, and then choose the Save section. Under the "Save workbooks" section, make sure that "Save AutoRecover information" is turned on. You can also make a few other changes to AutoRecover settings:

- You can also adjust the backup frequency in minutes. Figure 9-20 has some tips on timing.

- You can choose the folder where you'd like Excel to save backup files. (The standard folder works fine for most people, but feel free to pick some other place.) Unfortunately, there's no handy Browse button to help you find the folder, so you need to find the folder you want in advance (using a tool like Windows Explorer), write it down somewhere, and then copy the full folder path into this dialog box.

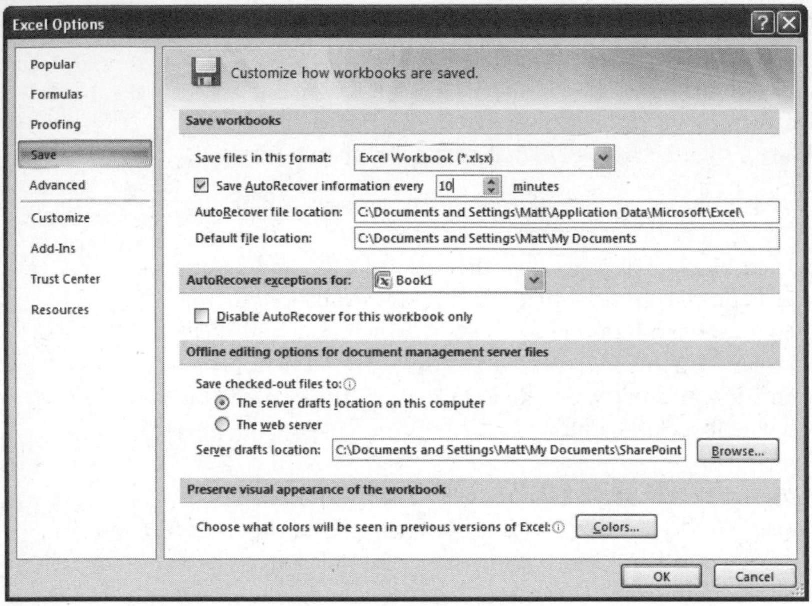

Figure 9-20:
You can configure how often AutoRecover saves backups. There's really no danger in being too frequent. Unless you work with extremely complex or large spreadsheets—which might suck up a lot of computing power and take a long time to save—you can set Excel to save the document every five minutes with no appreciable slowdown.

- Under the "AutoRecover exceptions" heading, you can tell Excel not to bother saving a backup of a specific spreadsheet. Pick the spreadsheet name from the list (which shows all the currently open spreadsheet files), and then turn on the "Disable AutoRecover for this workbook only" setting. This setting is exceedingly uncommon, but you might use it if you have a gargantuan spreadsheet full of data that doesn't need to be backed up.

If your computer does crash, when you get it running again, you can easily retrieve your last AutoRecover backup. In fact, the next time you launch Excel, it automatically checks the backup folder, and, if it finds a backup, it opens a Document Recovery panel on the left of the Excel window.

If your computer crashes in mid-edit, the next time you open Excel you'll probably see the same file listed twice in the Document Recovery window, as shown in Figure 9-21. The difference is the status. The status [AutoSaved] indicates the most recent backup created by Excel. The status [Original] indicates the last version of the file that *you* saved (which is safely stored on your hard drive, right where you expect it).

To open a file that's in the Document Recovery window, just click it. You can also use a drop-down menu with additional options (Figure 9-21). Make sure you save the file before you leave Excel. After all, it's just a temporary backup.

If you attempt to open a backup file that's somehow been scrambled (technically known as *corrupted*), Excel automatically attempts to repair it. You can choose Show Repairs to display a list of any changes Excel had to make to recover the file.

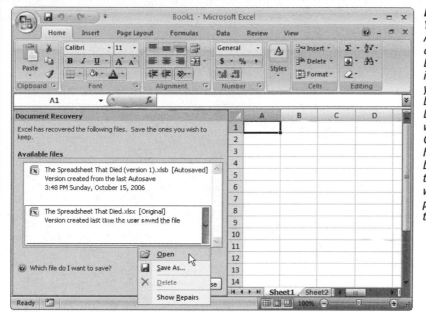

Figure 9-21:
You can save or open an AutoRecover backup just as you would an ordinary Excel file; simply click the item in the list. Once you've dealt with all the backup files, close the Document Recovery window by clicking the Close button. If you haven't saved your backup, Excel asks you at this point whether you want to save it permanently or delete the backup.

Opening Files

Opening existing files in Excel works much the same as it does in any Windows program. To get to the standard Open dialog box, choose Office button → Open. Using the Open dialog box, you can browse to find the spreadsheet file you want, and then click Open to load it into Excel.

Excel can open many file types other than its native .xlsx format. To learn the other formats it supports, launch the Open dialog box, and, at the bottom, open the "Files of type" menu, which shows you the whole list. If you want to open a file but you don't know what format it's in, try using the first option on the menu, "All Files." Once you choose a file, Excel scans the beginning of the file and informs you about the type of conversion it will attempt to perform (based on what type of file Excel thinks it is).

Note: Depending on your computer settings, Windows might hide file extensions. That means that instead of seeing the Excel spreadsheet file MyCoalMiningFortune.xlsx, you'll just see the name MyCoal-MiningFortune (without the .xlsx part on the end). In this case, you can still tell what the file type is by looking at the icon. If you see a small Excel icon next to the file name, that means Windows recognizes that the file is an Excel spreadsheet. If you see something else (like a tiny paint palette, for example), you need to make a logical guess about what type of file it is.

Plan to take another crack at a recent spreadsheet? You can find the most recently opened documents in Excel's Recent Documents list. To see this list, just open the Office button—it appears as a separate column on the right. The best part about the Recent Documents list is the way you can *pin* a document there so it stays forever, as shown in Figure 9-22.

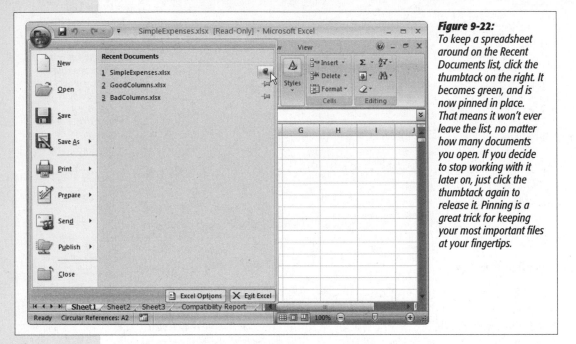

Figure 9-22:
To keep a spreadsheet around on the Recent Documents list, click the thumbtack on the right. It becomes green, and is now pinned in place. That means it won't ever leave the list, no matter how many documents you open. If you decide to stop working with it later on, just click the thumbtack again to release it. Pinning is a great trick for keeping your most important files at your fingertips.

Opening Multiple Spreadsheets at Once

As you open multiple spreadsheets, Excel creates a new window for each one. You can easily jump from one spreadsheet to another by clicking the appropriate spreadsheet button in the Windows taskbar at the bottom of your screen.

If you have *taskbar grouping* switched on, you'll find that your computer has an odd habit of spontaneously bunching together taskbar buttons. For example, shortly after you open four Excel files, you might find them in one taskbar button (see Figure 9-23). Taskbar grouping does save screen space, but it also makes it a little more awkward to get to the Excel spreadsheet you want. You now need two mouse clicks instead of one—the first to click the taskbar button, and the second to choose the window you want from the group.

Tip: If the taskbar grouping seems like more trouble than it's worth, you can switch off this behavior. Just right-click an empty space in the taskbar and choose Properties. In the Taskbar and Start Menu Properties dialog box that appears, clear the checkmark next to the "Group similar taskbar buttons" option.

Figure 9-23:
Similar taskbar buttons sometimes get bunched into groups. You can tell that a button contains a group of files when a drop-down arrow appears on the right side of the button, and a number appears on the left side. The number indicates how many buttons Windows has grouped together.

The taskbar, though convenient, isn't perfect. One problem is that long file names don't fit on the taskbar buttons, which can make it hard to spot the files you need. And the struggle to find an open file becomes dire if your taskbar is also cluttered with other applications and *their* multiple windows.

Fortunately, Excel provides a couple of shortcuts that are indispensable when dealing with several spreadsheets at a time:

- To jump from one spreadsheet to another, find the window in the View → Window → Switch Windows list, which includes the file name of all the currently open spreadsheets (Figure 9-24).

- To move to the next spreadsheet, use the keyboard shortcut Ctrl+Tab or Ctrl+F6.

Figure 9-24:
When you have multiple spreadsheets open at the same time, you can easily move from one to the other using the Switch Windows list.

- To move to the previous spreadsheet, use the shortcut key Ctrl+Shift+Tab or Ctrl+Shift+F6.

When you have multiple spreadsheets open at the same time, you need to take a little more care when closing a window so you don't accidentally close the entire Excel application—unless you want to. Here are your choices:

- **You can close all the spreadsheets at once.** To do so, you need to close the Excel window. Select Office button → Exit Excel from any active spreadsheet, or just click the close icon (the infamous X button) in the top-righthand corner.

- **You can close a single spreadsheet.** To do so, right-click the spreadsheet on the taskbar, and click Close. Or, switch to the spreadsheet you want to close (by clicking the matching taskbar button) and then choose Office button → Close.

Note: One of the weirdest limitations in Excel occurs if you try to open more than one file with the same name. No matter what steps you take, you can't coax Excel to open both of them at once. It doesn't matter if the files have different content or if they're in different folders or even different drives. When you try to open a file that has the same name as a file that's already open, Excel displays an error message and refuses to go any further. Sadly, the only solution is to open the files one at a time, or rename one of them.

CHAPTER 10

Adding Information to Worksheets

Now that you've created a basic worksheet, and you're acquainted with Excel and its spiffy new interface, it's time to get down and dirty adding data. Whether you want to plan your household budget, build a sales invoice, or graph your soaring (or plunging) net worth, you first need to understand how Excel interprets the information you put in your worksheet.

Depending on what kind of data you type into a cell, Excel classifies it as a date, a number, or a piece of text. In this chapter, you'll learn how Excel makes up its mind, and how you can make sure it makes the right decision. You'll also learn how to use Excel's best timesavers, including the indispensable Undo feature.

Adding Different Types of Data

One of Excel's most important features is its ability to distinguish between different types of information. A typical worksheet contains both text and numbers. There isn't a lot you can do in Excel with ordinary text (other than alphabetize a list, perform a simple spell check, and apply some basic formatting). On the other hand, Excel gives you a wide range of options for numeric data. For example, you can string your numbers together into complex calculations and formulas, or you can graph them on a chart. Programs that don't try to separate text and numbers—like Microsoft Word, for example—can't provide these features.

Most of the time, when you enter information in Excel, you don't explicitly indicate the type of data. Instead, Excel examines the information you've typed in, and, based on your formatting and other clues, classifies it automatically.

Excel distinguishes between four core data types:

- **Ordinary text.** Column headings, descriptions, and any content that Excel can't identify as one of the other data types.

- **Numbers.** Prices, integers, fractions, percentages, and every other type of numeric data. Numbers are the basic ingredient of most Excel worksheets.

- **Dates and times.** Dates (like Oct 3, 2007), times (like 4:30 p.m.), and combined date and time information (like Oct 3, 2007, 4:30 p.m.). You can enter date and time information in a variety of formats.

- **True or false values.** This data type (known in geekdom as a *Boolean* value) can contain one of two things: TRUE or FALSE (displayed in all capitals). You don't need Boolean data types in most worksheets, but they're useful for programmer types and power users who want to create complex formulas.

One useful way to tell how Excel is interpreting your data is to look at cell alignment, as explained in Figure 10-1.

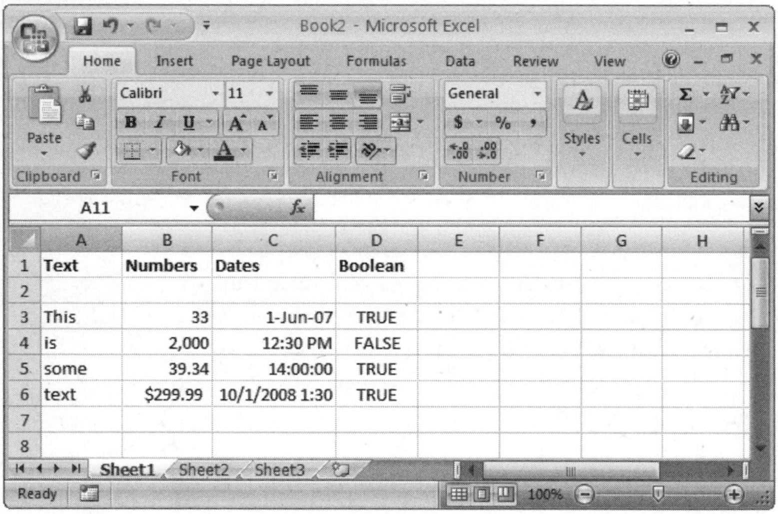

Figure 10-1:
Unless you explicitly change the alignment, Excel always left-aligns text (that is, it lines it up against the left edge of a cell), as in column A. On the other hand, it always right-aligns numbers and dates, as in columns B and C. And it centers Boolean values, as in column D.

Note: The standard alignment of text and numbers doesn't just represent the whims of Excel—it also matches the behavior you want most of the time. For example, when you type in text, you usually want to start at the left edge so that subsequent entries in a column line up. But when entering numbers, you usually want them to line up on the *decimal point* so that it's easier to scan a list of numbers and quickly spot small and large values. Of course, if you don't like Excel's standard formatting, you're free to change it, as you'll see in Chapter 13.

As Figure 10-1 shows, Excel can display numbers and dates in several different ways. For example, some of the numbers include decimal places, one uses a comma, and one has a currency symbol. Similarly, one of the time values uses the 12-hour clock while another uses the 24-hour clock. Other entries include only date information or both date and time information. You might assume that when you type in a number, it will appear in the cell exactly the way you typed it. For example, when you type 3-comma-0-0-0 you expect to see 3,000. However, that doesn't always happen. To see the problem in action, try typing *3,000* in a cell. It shows up exactly the way you entered it. Then, type over that value with *2000*. The new number appears as 2,000. Excel remembers your first entry, and assumes that you want to use thousand separators in this cell *all the time*.

These differences may seem like a spreadsheet free-for-all, but don't despair—you can easily set the formatting of numbers and dates. (In fact, that's the subject of Chapter 13.) At this point, all you need to know is that the values Excel *stores* in each cell don't need to match exactly the values that it *displays* in each cell. For example, the number 4300 could be formatted as plain old 4300 or as the dollar amount $4,300. Excel lets you format your numbers so you have exactly the representation you want. At the same time, Excel treats all numbers equivalently, no matter how they're formatted, which lets you combine them together in calculations. Figure 10-2 shows you how to find the underlying stored value of a cell.

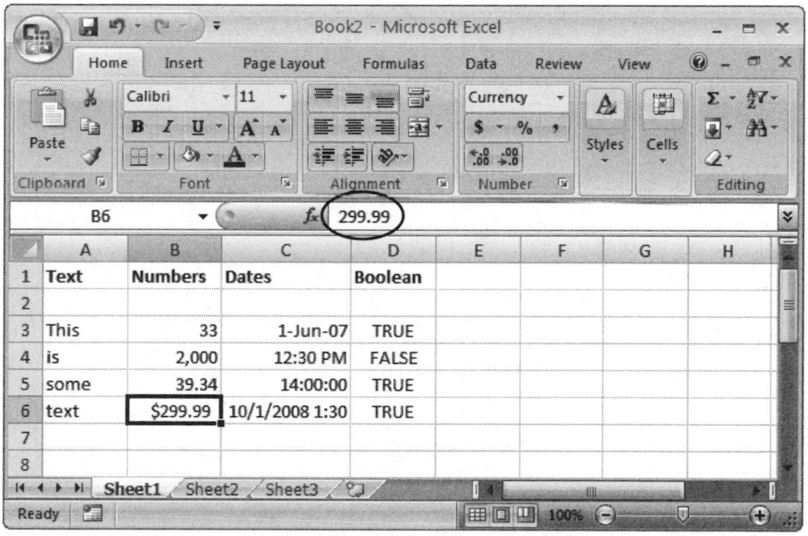

Figure 10-2:
You can see the underlying value that Excel is storing for a cell by selecting the cell and then glancing at the formula bar. In this sheet, you can see that the value $299.99 is actually stored without the dollar currency symbol, which Excel applied only as part of the display format. Similarly, Excel stores the number 2,000 without the comma; it stores the date 1-Jun-07 as 6/1/2007; the time 12:30 p.m. as 12:30:00 PM, and the time 14:00:00 as 2:00:00 PM.

Note: Excel assigns data types to each cell in your worksheet, and you can't mix more than one data type in the same cell. For example, when you type in *44 fat cats*, Excel interprets the whole thing as text because it contains letters. If you want to treat 44 as a number (so that you can perform calculations with it, say), then you need to split this content into two cells—one that contains the number 44 and one that contains the remaining text.

Controlling Your Data Types

By looking at cell alignment, you can easily tell how Excel is interpreting your data. That's helpful. But what happens when Excel's interpretation is at odds with your wishes? For example, what if you type in something you consider a *number* but Excel freakishly treats it as *text*, or vice versa? The first step to solving this problem is grasping the logic behind Excel's automatic decision-making process.

How Excel decides your data is text

If your cell meets any of the following criteria, Excel automatically treats the content as ordinary *text*:

- **It contains any letters.** Thus, C123 is text, not a number.

- **It contains any punctuation that Excel can't interpret numerically.** Punctuation allowed in numbers and dates includes the comma (,), the decimal point (.), and the forward slash (/) or dash (-) for dates. When you type in any other punctuation, Excel treats the cell as text. Thus, 14! is text, not a number.

Occasionally, Excel reads your data the wrong way. For example, you may have a value—like a social security number or a credit card number—that's made up entirely of numeric characters but that you want to treat like text because you don't ever want to perform calculations with it. But Excel doesn't know what you're up to, and so it automatically treats the value as a number. You can also run into problems when you precede text with the equal sign (which tells Excel that you have a formula in progress), or when you use a series of numbers and dashes that you don't intend to be part of a date (for example, you want to enter 1-2-3 but you don't want Excel to read it as January 2, 2003—which is what it wants to do).

In all these cases, the solution's simple. Before you type the cell value, start by typing an apostrophe ('). The apostrophe tells Excel to treat the cell content as text. Figure 10-3 shows you how it works.

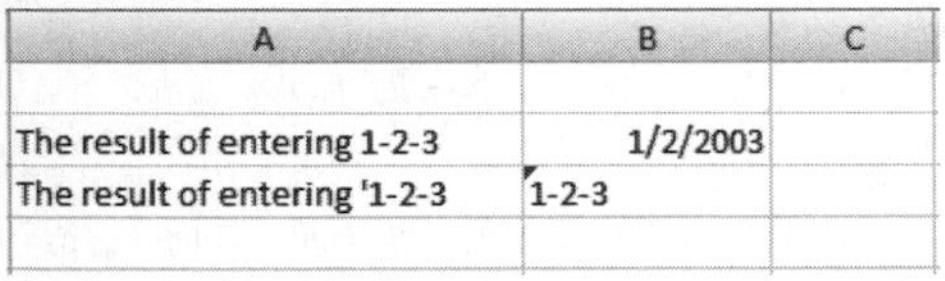

A	B	C
The result of entering 1-2-3	1/2/2003	
The result of entering '1-2-3	1-2-3	

Figure 10-3:
To have Excel treat any number, date, or time as text, just precede the value with an apostrophe (you can see the apostrophe in the formula bar, but not in the cell). This worksheet shows the result of typing 1-2-3, both with and without the initial apostrophe.

When you precede a numeric value with an apostrophe, Excel checks out the cell to see what's going on. When Excel determines that it can represent the content as a number, it places a green triangle in the top left corner of the cell and gives you a few options for dealing with the cell, as shown in Figure 10-4.

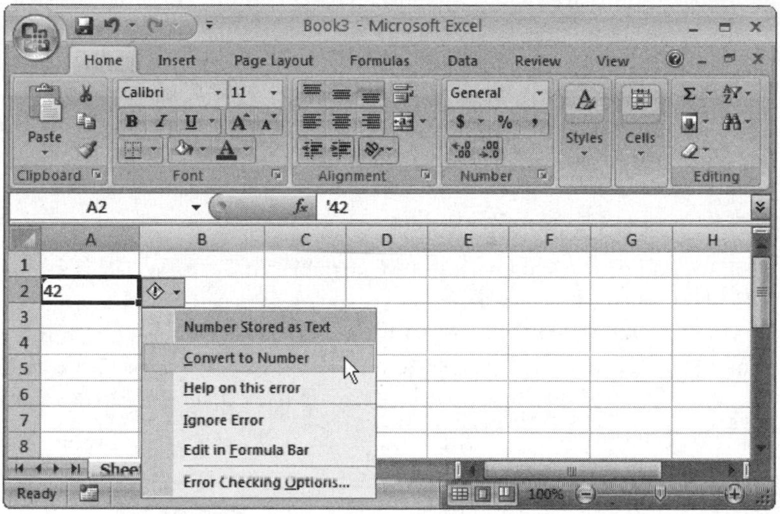

Figure 10-4:
*In this worksheet, the
number 42 is stored as text,
thanks to the apostrophe
that precedes it. Excel notices
the apostrophe, wonders if
it's an unintentional error,
and flags the cell by putting
a tiny green triangle in the
top-left corner. If you move
to the cell, an exclamation
mark icon appears, and, if
you click that, a menu
appears, letting you choose
to convert the number or
ignore the issue for this cell.*

Note: When you type in either *false* or *true* (using any capitalization you like), Excel automatically recognizes the data type as Boolean value instead of text, converts it to the uppercase word FALSE or TRUE, and centers it in the cell. If you want to make a cell that contains *false* or *true* as text and *not* as Boolean data, start by typing an apostrophe (') at the beginning of the cell.

How Excel decides your data is numeric

Excel automatically interprets any cell that contains only numeric characters as a number. In addition, you can add the following non-numeric characters to a number without causing a problem:

- One decimal point (but not two). For example, 42.1 is a number, but 42.1.1 is text.

- One or more commas, provided you use them to separate groups of three numbers (like thousands, millions, and so on). Thus 1,200,200 is a valid number, but 1,200,20 is text.

- A currency sign ($ for U.S. dollars), provided it's at the beginning of the number.

- A percent symbol at the beginning or end of the number (but not both).

- A plus (+) or minus (–) sign before the number. You can also create a negative number by putting it in parentheses. In other words, entering (33) is the same as entering –33.

- An equal sign at the start of the cell.

The most important thing to understand about entering numbers is that when you choose to add other details like commas or the dollar sign, you're actually doing two things at once: you're entering a value for the cell *and* you're setting the format for the cell, which affects how Excel displays the cell. Chapter 13 provides more information about number styles and shows how you can completely control cell formatting.

How Excel decides your data is a date or time

When typing in a date, you have a choice of formats. You can type in a full date (like *July 4, 2007*) or you can type in an abbreviated date using dashes or slashes (like *7-4-2007* or *7/4/2007*), which is generally easier. If you enter some numbers formatted as a date, but the date you entered doesn't exist (like the 30th day in February or the 13th month), then Excel interprets it as text. Figure 10-5 shows you the options.

Figure 10-5:
Whichever way you type in the date in a cell, it always appears the same on the formula bar (the specific formula bar display depends on the regional settings on your computer, explained next).

Because you can represent dates a few different ways, working with them can be tricky, and you're likely to encounter some unexpected behavior from Excel. Here are some tips for using dates, trouble-free:

- **Instead of using a number for the month, you can use a three-letter month abbreviation, but you must put the month in the middle.** In other words, you can use *7/4/2007* and *4/Jul/2007* interchangeably.

- **When you use a two-digit year as part of a date, Excel tries to guess whether the first two digits of the year should be 20 or 19.** When the two-digit year is from 00 to 29, Excel assumes it belongs to the 21st century. If the year is from 30 to 99, Excel plants it in the 1900s. In other words, Excel translates 7/4/29 into 7/4/2029, while 7/4/30 becomes 7/4/1930.

Tip: If you're a mere mortal and you forget where the cutoff point is, enter the year as a four-digit number, which prevents any confusion.

- **If you don't type in any year at all, Excel automatically assumes you mean the current year.** For example, when you enter 7/4, Excel inserts the date 7/4/2007 (assuming it's currently 2007 on your computer's internal clock). When you enter a date this way, the year component doesn't show up in the cell, but it's still stored in the worksheet (and visible on the formula bar).

- **Excel understands and displays dates differently depending on the regional settings on your computer.** Windows has a setting that determines how your computer interprets dates (see the box on page 236). On the U.S. system, Month-Day-Year is the standard progression. But on the UK system, Day-Month-Year is the deal. For example, in the U.S., either 11-7-08 or 11/7/08 is shorthand for November 7, 2008. In the UK, the same notations refer to July 11, 2008.

  Thus, if your computer has U.S. regional settings turned on, and you type in *11/7/08*, then Excel understands it as November 7, 2008, and the formula bar displays 11/7/08.

Note: The way Excel *recognizes* and *displays* dates varies according to the regional settings on your computer, but the way Excel *stores* dates does not. This feature comes in handy when you save a worksheet on one computer and then open it on another computer with different regional settings. Because Excel stores every date the same way, the date information remains accurate on the new computer, and Excel can display it according to the new regional settings.

Typing in times is more straightforward than typing in dates. You simply use numbers, separated by a colon (:). You need to include an hour and minute component at minimum (as in 7:30), but you can also add seconds, milliseconds, and more (as in 7:30:10.10). You can use values from 1 to 24 for the hour part, though if your system is set to use a 12-hour clock, Excel converts the time accordingly (in other words, 19:30 becomes 7:30 PM). If you want to use the 12-hour clock when you type in a time, follow your time with a space and the letters P or PM (or A or AM).

Finally, you can create cells that have both date and time information. To do so, just type the date portion first, followed by a space, and then the time portion. For example, Excel happily accepts this combo: 7/4/2008 1:30 PM.

Behind the scenes, Excel stores dates as *serial numbers*. It considers the date January 1, 1900 to be day 1. January 2, 1900 is day 2, and so on, up through the year 9999. This system is quite nifty because if you use Excel to subtract one date from another, then you actually end up calculating the difference in days, which is exactly what you want. On the other hand, it means you can't enter a date in Excel that's earlier than January 1, 1900 (if you do, Excel treats your date like text).

Similarly, Excel stores times as fractional numbers from 0 to 1. The number 0 represents 12:00 a.m. (the start of the day) and 0.999 represents 11:59:59 p.m. (the end of the day). As with dates, this system allows you to subtract one time value from another.

Regional Dating

Windows has regional settings for your computer, which affect the way Microsoft programs understand things like dates and currency. You can change the settings, and they don't have to correspond to where you live—you can set them for your company headquarters on another continent, for instance. But keep in mind that these affect all the programs on your computer.

To make a switch, go to the Start menu in Windows and choose Settings → Control Panel, and then double-click Regional and Language Options, which brings up a dialog box. The Regional Options tab has the settings you want. The most important setting is in the first box, which has a drop-down list you can use to pick the region you want, like English (United States) or Swedish (Finland).

You can fine-tune the settings in your region, too. This makes sense only if you have particular preferences about how dates should be formatted that don't match the standard options. Click the Customize button next to the region box to bring up a new dialog box, and then click the Date tab (shown in Figure 10-6).

No matter what the regional settings are, you can always use the international date standard, which is Year/Month/Day, though you must supply a four-digit year (as in 2008/7/4). When you use a two-digit year, Excel assumes you're trying to use the Month-Day-Year or Day-Month-Year pattern.

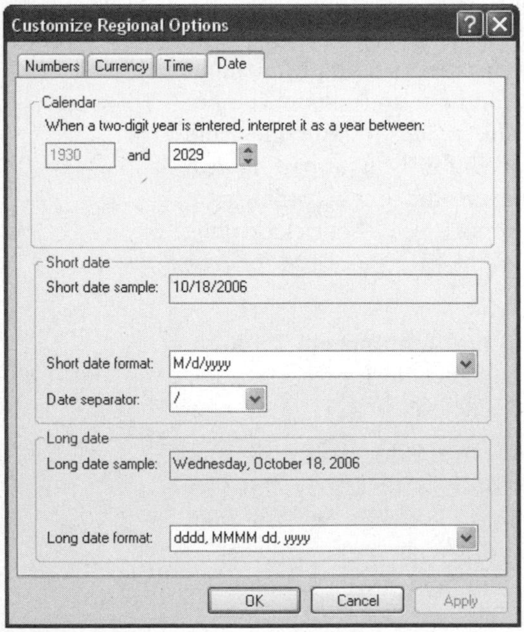

Figure 10-6:
Tweaking the regional settings on your computer gives you complete control over how Excel recognizes dates. Use the pull-down menus to specify the date separator, order of month, day, and year components in a date, and how Excel should interpret two-digit years.

Quick Ways to Add Data

Some of Excel's timesaving frills can make your life easier when you're entering data in a worksheet. This section covers four such features: AutoComplete, Auto-Correct, AutoFill, and AutoFit, along with Excel's top candidates for the Lifetime Most Useful Achievement award: Undo and Redo.

> **Note:** Excel really has two types of automatic features. First off, there are features that do things to your spreadsheets *automatically*, namely AutoComplete and AutoCorrect. Sometimes that's cool and convenient, but other times it can send you running for the old manual typewriter. Fortunately, you can turn off both. Excel also has "auto" features that really aren't that automatic. These include AutoFill and AutoFit, which never run on their own.

AutoComplete

Some worksheets require that you type in the same information row after row. For example, if you're creating a table to track the value of all your *Sesame Street* collectibles, you can type in *Kermit* only so many times before you start turning green. Excel tries to help you out with its AutoComplete feature, which examines what you type, compares it against previous entries in the same column, and, if it recognizes the beginning of an existing word, fills it in.

For instance, in your *Sesame Street* worksheet, if you already have Kermit in the Characters column, when you start typing a new entry in that column beginning with the letter K, Excel automatically fills in the whole word Kermit. Excel then selects the letters that it's added (in this case, *ermit*). You now have two options:

- **If you want to accept the AutoComplete text, move to another cell.** For example, when you hit the right arrow key or press Enter to move down, Excel leaves the word Kermit behind.

- **If you want to blow off Excel's suggestion, just keep typing.** Because Excel automatically selects the AutoComplete portion of the word (*ermit*), your next keystrokes overtype that text. Or, if you find the AutoComplete text is distracting, then press Delete to remove it right away.

> **Tip:** When you want to use the AutoComplete text but change it slightly, turn on edit mode for the cell by pressing F2. Once you enter edit mode, you can use the arrow keys to move through the cell and make modifications. Press Enter or F2 to switch out of edit mode when you're finished.

AutoComplete has a few limitations. It works only with text entries, ignoring numbers and dates. It also doesn't pay any attention to the entries you've placed in other columns. And finally, it takes a stab at providing you with a suggestion only if the text you've typed in matches another column entry *unambiguously*.

This means that when your column contains two words that start with K, like Kermit and kerplop, Excel doesn't make any suggestion when you type *K* into a new cell, because it can't tell which option is the most similar. But when you type *Kerm*, Excel realizes that kerplop isn't a candidate, and it supplies the AutoComplete suggestion Kermit.

If you find AutoComplete annoying, you can get it out of your face with a mere click of the mouse. Just select Office button → Excel Options, choose the Advanced section, and look under the "Editing options" heading for the "Enable Auto-Complete for cell values" setting. Turn this setting off to banish AutoComplete from your spreadsheet.

AutoCorrect

As you type text in a cell, AutoCorrect cleans up behind you—correcting things like wrongly capitalized letters and common misspellings. AutoCorrect is subtle enough that you may not even realize it's monitoring your every move. To get a taste of its magic, look for behaviors like these:

- If you type *HEllo*, AutoCorrect changes it to *Hello*.

- If you type *friday*, AutoCorrect changes it to *Friday*.

- If you start a sentence with a lowercase letter, AutoCorrect uppercases it.

- If you scramble the letters of a common word (for example, typing *thsi* instead of *this*, or *teh* instead of *the*), AutoCorrect replaces the word with the proper spelling.

- If you accidentally hit Caps Lock key, and then type *jOHN sMITH* when you really wanted to type *John Smith*, Excel not only fixes the mistake, it also switches off the Caps Lock key.

Note: AutoCorrect doesn't correct most misspelled words, just common typos. To correct other mistakes, use the spell checker described on page 278.

For the most part, AutoCorrect is harmless and even occasionally useful, as it can spare you from delivering minor typos in a major report. But if you need to type irregularly capitalized words, or if you have a garden-variety desire to rebel against standard English, then you can turn off some or all of the AutoCorrect actions.

To reach the AutoCorrect settings, select Office button → Excel Options. Choose the Proofing section, and then click the AutoCorrect Options button. (All Auto-Correct options are language specific, and the title of the dialog box that opens indicates the language you're currently using.) Most of the actions are self-explanatory, and you can turn them off by turning off their checkboxes. Figure 10-7 explains the "Replace text as you type" option, which isn't just for errors.

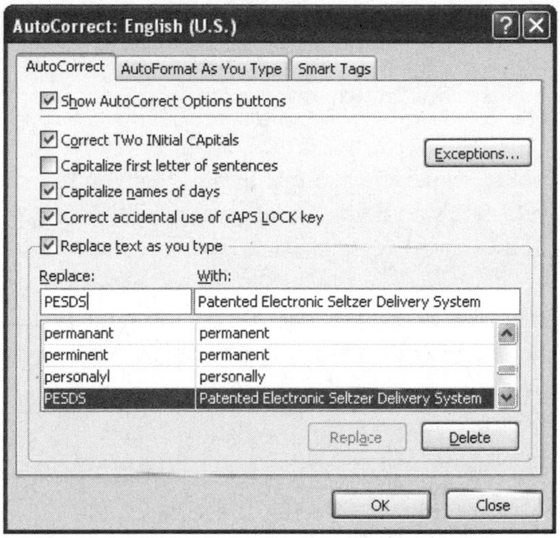

Figure 10-7:
Under "Replace text as you type" is a long list of symbols and commonly misspelled words (the column on the left) that Excel automatically replaces with something else (the column on the right). But what if you want the copyright symbol to appear as a C in parentheses? You can remove individual corrections (select one, and then click Delete); or you can change the replacement text. And you can add your own rules. For example, you might want to be able to type PESDS and have Excel insert Patented Electronic Seltzer Delivery System. Simply type in the "Replace" and "With" text, as shown here, and then click OK.

Tip: For really advanced AutoCorrect settings, you can use the Exceptions button to define cases where Excel *won't* use AutoCorrect. When you click this button, the AutoCorrect Exceptions dialog box appears with a list of exceptions. For example, this list includes abbreviations that include the period but shouldn't be capitalized (like pp.) and words where mixed capitalization is allowed (like WordPerfect).

AutoFill

AutoFill is a quirky yet useful feature that lets you create a whole column or row of values based on just one or two cells that Excel can extrapolate into a series. Put another way, AutoFill looks at the cells you've already filled in a column or row, and then makes a reasonable guess about the additional cells you'll want to add. People commonly use AutoFill for sequential numbers, months, or days.

Here are a few examples of lists that AutoFill can and can't work with:

- The series 1, 2, 3, 4 is easy for Excel to interpret—it's a list of steadily increasing numbers. The series 5, 10, 15 (numbers increasing by five) is just as easy. Both of these are great AutoFill candidates.

- The series of part numbers CMP-40-0001, CMP-40-0002, CMP-40-0003 may seem more complicated because it mingles text and numbers. But clever Excel can spot the pattern easily.

- Excel readily recognizes series of months (*January, February, March*) and days (*Sun, Mon, Tue*), either written out or abbreviated.

• A list of numbers like 47, 345, 6 doesn't seem to follow a regular pattern. But by doing some analysis, Excel can guess at a relationship and generate more numbers that fit the pattern. There's a good chance, however, that these won't be the numbers you want, so take a close look at whatever Excel adds in cases like these.

Bottom line: AutoFill is a great tool for generating simple lists. When you're working with a complex sequence of values, it's no help—unless you're willing to create a custom list (page 379) that spells it out for Excel.

Tip: AutoFill doubles as a quick way to *copy* a cell value multiple times. For example, if you select a cell in which you've typed *Cookie Monster*, you can use the AutoFill technique described below to fill every cell in that row or column with the same text.

To use AutoFill, follow these steps:

1. **Fill in a couple of cells in a row or column to start off the series.**

   Technically, you can use AutoFill if you fill in only one cell, although this approach gives Excel more room to make a mistake if you're trying to generate a series. Of course, when you want to copy only a single cell several times, one cell is a sufficient start.

2. **Select the cells you've entered so far. Then click (and hold) the small black square at the bottom-right corner of the selected box.**

   You can tell that your mouse is in the correct place when the mouse pointer changes to a plus symbol (+).

3. **Drag the border down (if you're filling a column of items) or to the right (if you're filling a row of items).**

   As you drag, a tooltip appears, showing the text that Excel is generating for each cell.

   While you're dragging, you can hold down Ctrl to affect the way that Excel fills a list. When you've already filled in at least *two* cells, Ctrl tells Excel to just copy the list multiple times, rather than look for a pattern. When you want to expand a range based on just *one* cell, Ctrl does the opposite: It tells Excel to try to predict a pattern, rather than just copy it.

   When you release the mouse, Excel automatically fills in the additional cells, and a special AutoFill icon appears next to the last cell in the series, as shown in Figure 10-8.

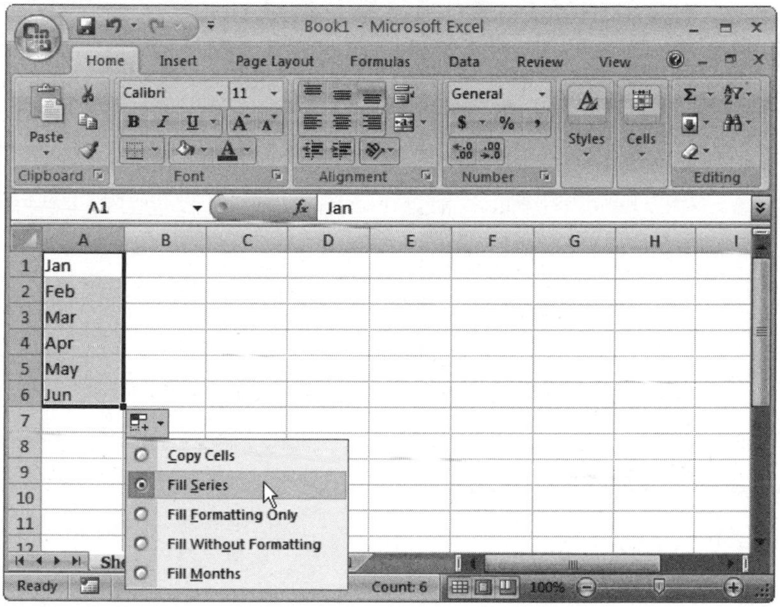

Figure 10-8:
After AutoFill does its magic, Excel displays a menu that lets you fill the series without copying the formatting, or copy the formatting without filling the series. You can also choose to copy values instead of generating a list. For example, if you choose to copy values—or Copy Cells, as Excel calls it—then in the two-item series Jan, Feb, you end up with Jan, Feb, Jan, Feb, rather than Jan, Feb, Mar, Apr.

Custom AutoFill lists

Excel stores a collection of AutoFill lists that it refers to every time you use the feature. You can add your own lists to the collection, which extends the series Auto-Fill recognizes. For example, Excel doesn't come set to understand Kermit, Cookie Monster, Grover, Big Bird, Oscar, and Snuffleupagus as a series, but you can add it to the mix.

But why bother to add custom lists to Excel's collection? After all, if you need to type in the whole list before you use it, is AutoFill really saving you any work? The benefit occurs when you need to create the same list in *multiple* worksheets, in which case you can type it in just once and then use AutoFill to recreate it as often as you'd like.

To create a custom list, follow these steps:

1. **Choose Office button → Excel Options.**

   The familiar Excel Options window appears.

2. **Choose the Popular section, and then click Edit Custom Lists.**

   Here, you can take a gander at Excel's predefined lists, and add your own (Figure 10-9).

3. **In the "Custom lists" box on the left side of the dialog box, select NEW LIST.**

   This action tells Excel that you're ready to create a new list.

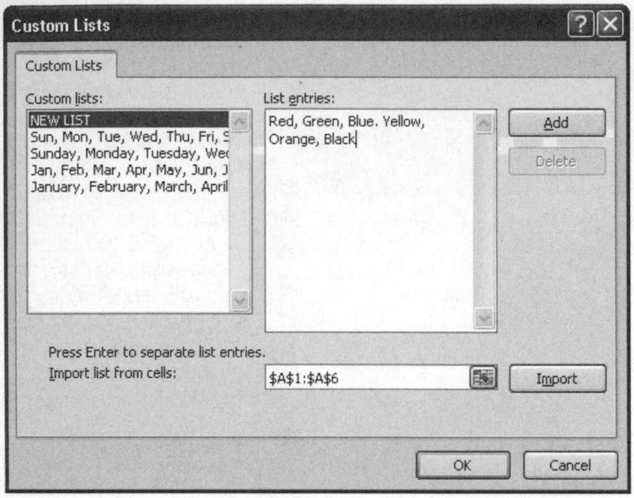

Figure 10-9:
Here, a new custom list of colors is being added.

4. **In the "List entries" box on the right side of the dialog box, type in your list.**

   Separate each item with a comma or by pressing Enter. The list in Figure 10-9 shows a series of color names separated by commas.

   If you've already typed your list into your worksheet, you can save some work. Instead of retyping the list, click inside the text box labeled "Import list from cells." Then, click the worksheet and drag to select the cells that contain the list. (Each item in the list must be in a separate cell, and the whole list should be in a series of adjacent cells in a single column or a single row.) When you're finished, click Import, and Excel copies the cell entries into the new list you're creating.

5. **Click Add to store your list.**

   At any later point in time, you can return to this dialog box, select the saved list, and modify it in the window on the right. Just click Add to commit your changes after making a change, or click Delete to remove the list entirely.

6. **Click OK to close the Custom Lists dialog box, and OK again to close the Excel Options window.**

   You can now start using the list with the current worksheet or in a new worksheet. Just type the first item in your list and then follow the AutoFill steps outlined in the previous section.

AutoFit

Page 207 (Figure 9-7) explained how you can drag the edge of a column to resize it. For greater convenience, Excel also provides an AutoFit feature that automatically enlarges columns to fit overflowing contents perfectly (unfortunately, it doesn't include a shrink-to-fit option).

A Few More Ways to Adjust Column Width

Excel gives you the ability to precisely control column widths. To change the width of a column, right-click the column header at the top of the column, and then choose Column Width. The standard unadjusted column size is a compact 8.43 characters, but you can change that to any number of characters. (Because different fonts use different size letters, the number of characters you specify here may not correspond directly to the number of characters in your column.)

You can also adjust multiple column widths at the same time.

Just select multiple columns (click the first column header, and then drag to the left or to the right to select more columns). Now, when you apply a new width, Excel uses it for all the selected columns.

Finally, you can customize the standard width for columns, which is the width that Excel assigns to columns in every new worksheet that you create. To set the standard width, choose Home → Cells → Format → Default Width from the menu, and then change the number.

The AutoFit feature springs into action in three situations:

- When you type a number or date that's too wide to fit into a cell, Excel automatically widens the column to accommodate the new content. (Excel doesn't automatically expand columns when you type in text, however.)

- If you double-click the right edge of a column header, Excel automatically expands the column to fit the widest entry it contains. This trick works for all types of data, including dates, numbers, and text.

- If you select Home → Cells → Format → AutoFit Selection, Excel automatically expands the column to fit the content in the active cell. This feature is helpful if you have a column that's made up of relatively narrow entries, but which also has a long column title. In this situation, you may not want to expand the column to the full width of the title. Instead, you may wish to size the column to fit a typical entry and allow the title to spill over to the next column.

Note: When a column is already large enough for its content, AutoFit has no effect.

While AutoFit automatically widens columns when you type in a number or date in a cell, you can still shrink a column after you've entered your information.

Keep in mind, however, that when your columns are too narrow, Excel displays the cell data differently, depending on the type of information. When your cells contain *text*, it's entirely possible for one cell to overlap (and thereby obscure) another, a problem first described in Chapter 9. However, if Excel allowed truncated *numbers*, it could be deceiving. For example, if you squash a cell with the price of espresso makers so that they appear to cost $2 (instead of $200), you might wind up ordering a costly gift for all your coworkers. To prevent this problem, Excel never truncates a number or date. Instead, if you've shrunk a cell's width so that the number can't fit, then you'll see a series of number signs (like #####) filling in the whole cell. This warning is just Excel's way of telling you that you're out of space. Once you enlarge the column by hand (or by using AutoFit), the original number reappears. (Until then, you can still see the number stored in the cell by moving to the cell and looking in the formula bar.)

Undo and Redo

While editing a worksheet, an Excel guru can make as many (or more) mistakes as a novice. These mistakes include copying cells to the wrong place, deleting something important, or just making a mess of the cell formatting. Excel masters can recover much more quickly, however, because they rely on Undo and Redo. Get in the habit of calling on these features, and you'll be well on your way to Excel gurudom.

How do they work? As you create your worksheet, Excel records every change you make. Because the modern computer has vast resources of extra memory and computing power (that is, when it's not running the latest three-dimensional real-time action game), Excel can keep this log without slowing your computer down one bit.

If you make a change to your worksheet that you don't like (say you inadvertently delete your company's entire payroll plan), you can use Excel's Undo history to reverse the change. In the Quick Access toolbar, simply click the Undo button (Figure 10-10), or press the super-useful keyboard shortcut Ctrl+Z. Excel immediately restores your worksheet to its state just before the last change. If you change your mind again, you can revert to the changed state (known to experts as "undoing your undo") by choosing Edit → Redo, or pressing Ctrl+Y.

Things get interesting when you want to go farther back than just one previous change, because Excel doesn't just store one change in memory. Instead, it tracks the last *100* actions you made. And it tracks just about anything you do to a worksheet, including cell edits, cell formatting, cut and paste operations, and much more. As a result, if you make a series of changes you don't like, or if you discover a mistake a little later down the road, then you can step back through the entire series of changes, one at a time. Every time you press Ctrl+Z, you go back one change in the history. This ability to reverse multiple changes makes Undo one of the most valuable features ever added to any software package.

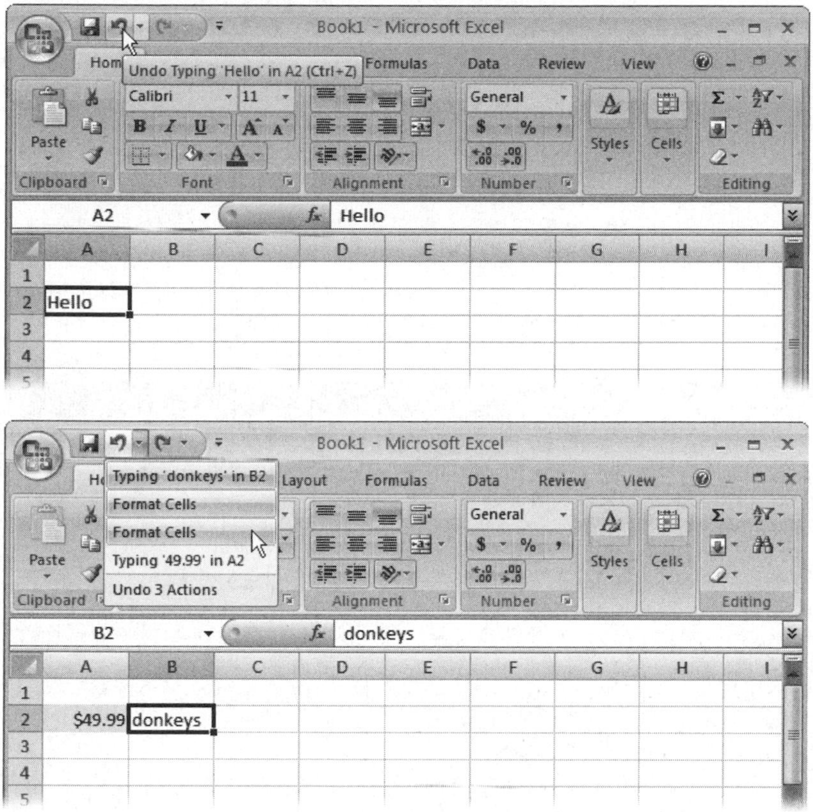

Figure 10-10:
Top: When you hover over the Undo button, you see a text description for the most recent action, which is what you'll undo if you click away. Here, the text Hello has just been typed into a cell, as Excel explains.

Bottom: Click the down-pointing arrow on the edge of the Undo button to see a history of all your recent actions, from most recent (top) to oldest (bottom). If you click an item that's down the list, you'll perform a mega-undo operation that undoes all the selected actions. In this example, three actions are about to be rolled back—the text entry in cell B2, and two format operations (which changed the number format and the background fill of cell A2).

Tip: The Undo feature means you don't need to be afraid of performing a change that may not be what you want. Excel experts often try out new actions, and then simply reverse them if the actions don't have the desired effect.

The Undo feature raises an interesting dilemma. When you can go back 100 levels into the history of your document, how do you know exactly what changes you're reversing? Most people don't remember the previous 100 changes they made to a worksheet, which makes it all too easy to reverse a change you actually *want* to keep. Excel provides the solution by not only keeping track of old worksheet versions, but also by keeping a simple description of each change. You don't see this description if you use the Ctrl+Z and Ctrl+Y shortcuts. However, when you hover over the button in the Quick Access toolbar, you'll see the action you're undoing listed there.

For example, if you type *hello* into cell A1, and then delete it, when you hover over the Undo button in the Quick Access toolbar, it says "Undo Clear (Ctrl+Z)". When you choose this option, the word *hello* returns. And if you hover over the Undo button again, it now says, "Undo Typing 'hello' in A2 (Ctrl+Z)", as shown in Figure 10-10, top.

Note: Occasionally, when you perform an advanced analysis task with an extremely complex worksheet, Excel may decide it can't afford to keep an old version of your worksheet in memory. When Excel hits this point, it warns you before you make the change, and gives you the chance to either cancel the edit or continue (without the possibility of undoing the change). In this rare situation, you may want to cancel the change, save your worksheet as a backup, and then continue.

GEM IN THE ROUGH

Using Redo to Automate Repetitive Tasks

Redo is commonly used to reverse an Undo. In other words, if you cancel an action and then change your mind, you can use Redo to quickly reapply the change. But Redo also has a much more interesting ability: it lets you repeat any action multiple times. The neat thing is that you can repeat this action *on other cells*.

For example, imagine you hit Ctrl+B to change a cell to bold. When you open the Edit menu, you'll see that the Redo item now says Repeat Font. If you move to another cell and hit Ctrl+Y, Excel applies the bold formatting to the new cell. In this case, you're not saving much effort, because it's just as easy to use Ctrl+B or Ctrl+Y. However, imagine you finish an operation that applies a set of sophisticated formatting changes to a cell. For example, say you increase the font size, bold the text, and apply a border around the cell (Chapter 13 tells you how to do these things).

When you press Ctrl+Y, Excel applies all the changes at once—which is much easier than calling up the Formatting dialog box and then selecting the same options.

The trick when using Redo is to make sure you don't perform another action until you've finished repeating your changes. For example, if you make some formatting changes and then stop to delete an incorrect cell value, then you can no longer use Redo to apply your formatting because Excel applies the last change that you made—in this case, clearing the cell. (Of course, when you mistakenly apply Redo, you can always call on Undo to get out of the mess.)

If you're ever in doubt about what'll happen when you use Redo, just hover over the Redo button in the Quick Access toolbar. You'll see a text description, like Repeat Font or Repeat Column Width.

CHAPTER 11

Moving Data Around a Worksheet

Simple spreadsheets are a good way to get a handle on Excel. But in the real world, you often need a spreadsheet that's more sophisticated—one that can grow and change as you start to track more information. For example, on the expenses worksheet you created in Chapter 9, perhaps you'd like to add information about which stores you've been shopping in. Or maybe you'd like to swap the order in which your columns appear. To make changes like these, you need to add a few more skills to your Excel repertoire.

This chapter covers the basics of spreadsheet modification, including how to select cells, how to move data from one place to another, and how to change the structure of your worksheet. What you learn here will make you a master of spreadsheet manipulation.

Selecting Cells

First things first: before you can make any changes to an existing worksheet, you need to select the cells you want to modify. Happily, selecting cells in Excel—try saying that five times fast—is easy. You can do it many different ways, and it's worth learning them all. Different selection techniques come in handy in different situations, and if you master all of them in conjunction with the formatting features described in Chapter 13, you'll be able to transform the look of any worksheet in seconds.

Making Continuous Range Selections

Simplest of all is selecting a *continuous range* of cells. A continuous range is a block of cells that has the shape of a rectangle (high school math reminder: a square is a kind of rectangle), as shown in Figure 11-1. The easiest way to select a continuous range is to click the top-left cell you want to select. Then drag to the right (to select more columns) or down (to select more rows). As you go, Excel highlights the selected cells in blue. Once you've highlighted all the cells you want, release the mouse button. Now you can perform an action, like copying the cells' contents, formatting the cells, or pasting new values into the selected cells.

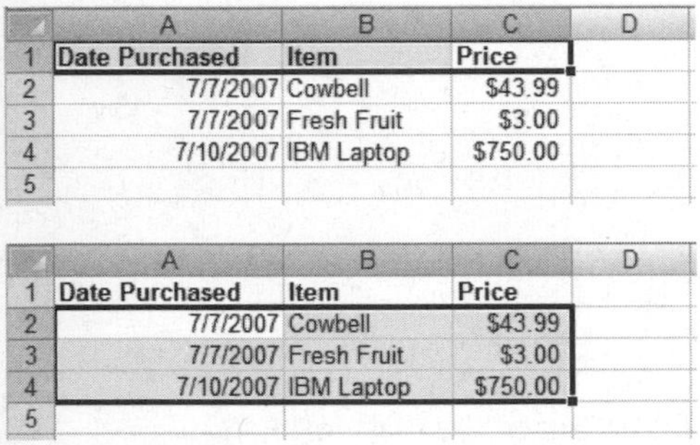

Figure 11-1:
Top: The three selected cells (A1, B1, and C1) cover the column titles.

Bottom: This selection covers the nine cells that make up the rest of the worksheet. Notice that Excel doesn't highlight the first cell you select.

In the simple expense worksheet from Chapter 9, for example, you could first select the cells in the top row and then apply bold formatting to make the column titles stand out. (Once you've selected the top three cells, press Ctrl+B, or chose Home → Font → Bold.)

Note: When you select some cells and then press an arrow key or click into another cell *before* you perform any action, Excel clears your selection.

Excel gives you a few useful shortcuts for making continuous range selections (some of these are illustrated in Figure 11-2):

- Instead of clicking and dragging to select a range, you can use a two-step technique. First, click the top-left cell. Then hold down Shift and click the cell at the bottom-right corner of the area you want to select. Excel highlights all the cells in between automatically. This technique works even if both cells aren't visible at the same time; just scroll to the second cell using the scroll bars, and make sure you don't click any other cell on your way there.

- If you want to select an entire column, click the header at the top of the column. For example, if you want to select the second column, then click the gray "B" box above the column. Excel selects all the cells in this column, right down to row 1,048,576.

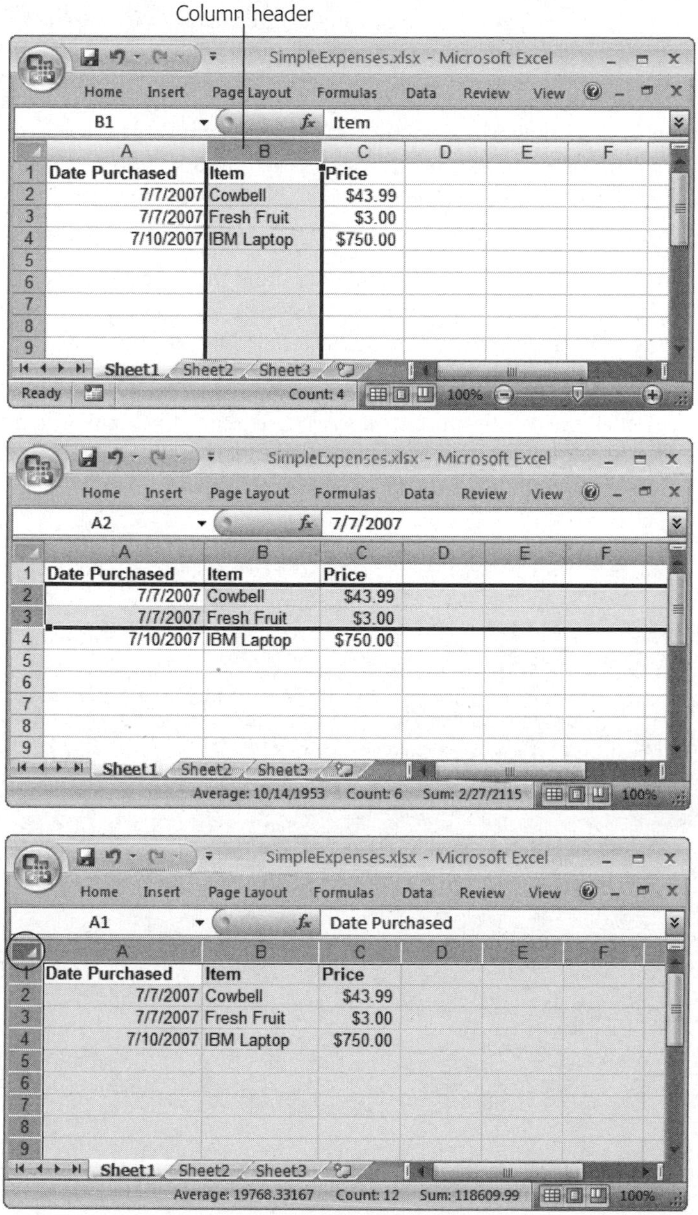

Column header

Figure 11-2:
Top: Click a column header to select that entire column.

Middle: Click a row number to select that entire row.

Bottom: To select every cell in the worksheet, click the empty gray square just outside the top-left corner of the worksheet (circled).

- If you want to select an entire row, click the numbered row header on the left edge of the row. For example, you can select the second row by clicking the gray "2" box to the left of the row. All the columns in this row will be selected.

- If you want to select multiple adjacent columns, click the leftmost column header, and then drag to the right until all the columns you want are selected. As you drag, a tooltip appears indicating how many columns you've selected. For example, if you've selected three columns, you'll see a tooltip with the text 3C (C stands for "column").

- If you want to select multiple adjacent rows, click the topmost row header and then drag down until all the rows you want are selected. As you drag, a tooltip appears indicating how many rows you've selected. For example, if you've selected two rows, you'll see a tooltip with the text 2R (R stands for "row").

- If you want to select all the cells in the entire worksheet, click the blank gray box that's just outside the top-left corner of the worksheet. This box is immediately to the left of the column headers and just above the row headers.

TIME-SAVING TIP

A Truly Great Calculation Trick

Excel provides a seriously nifty calculation tool in the status bar. Just select two or more cells, and look down to the status bar where you'll see the number of cells you've selected (the count), along with their sum and their average (shown in Figure 11-3).

To choose what calculations appear in the status bar, right-click anywhere on the status bar, and then, in the menu that appears, choose one of the following options:

- **Average.** The average of all the selected numbers or dates.

- **Count.** The number of selected cells (including any cells with text in them).

- **Numerical Count.** The number of selected cells that contain numbers or dates.

- **Minimum.** The selected number or date with the smallest value (for dates this means the earliest date).

- **Maximum.** The selected number or date with the largest value (for dates this means the latest date).

- **Sum.** The sum of all selected numbers. Although you can use Sum with date values, because of the way Excel stores date values, adding dates together generates meaningless results.

Tip: When you're selecting multiple rows or columns, make sure you click *between* the column header's left and right edges, not on either edge. When you click the edge of the column header, you end up resizing the column instead of making a selection.

Making Non-Contiguous Selections

In some cases, you may want to select cells that are *non-contiguous* (also known as nonadjacent), which means they don't form a neat rectangle. For example, you might want to select columns A and C, but not column B. Or, you might want to select a handful of cells scattered throughout the worksheet.

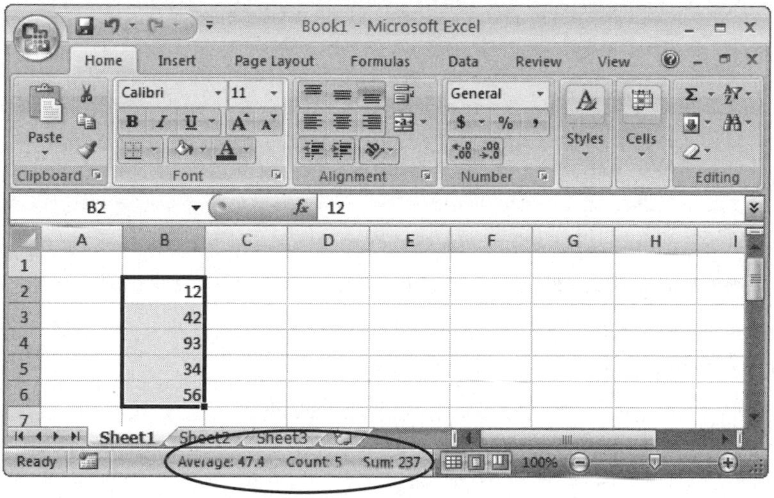

Figure 11-3:
The nicest detail about the status bar's quick calculations is that you can mix-and-match several at a time. Here, you see the count, average, and sum of the selected cells.

The trick to non-contiguous cell selection is using the Ctrl key. All you need to do is select the cells you want while holding down Ctrl. You can select individual cells by Ctrl-clicking them, or you can select multiple blocks of cells on different parts of the sheet by clicking and dragging in several different places while holding down Ctrl. You can also combine the Ctrl key with any of the shortcuts discussed earlier to select entire columns or rows as a part of your selection. Excel highlights in blue the cells you select (except for the last cell selected, which, as shown in Figure 11-4, isn't highlighted because it becomes the active cell).

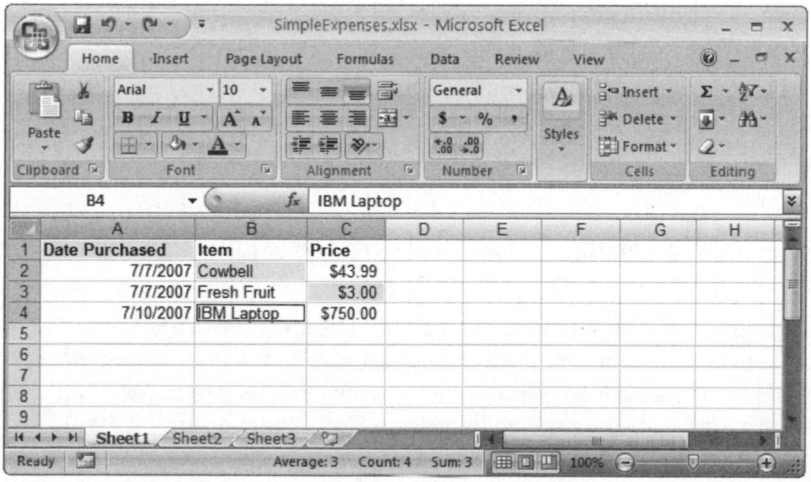

Figure 11-4:
This figure shows a non-contiguous selection that includes four cells (A1, B2, C3, and B4). The last selected cell (B4) isn't highlighted because it's the active cell. This behavior is a little bit different from a continuous selection, in which the first selected cell is always the active cell. With a non-contiguous selection, the last selected cell becomes the active cell.

Note: Excel restricts what you can do with non-contiguous selections. For example, you can format the cells in a non-contiguous selection, but you can't cut or copy the selection.

Automatically Selecting Your Data

Excel provides a nifty shortcut that can help you select a series of cells without dragging or Shift-clicking anything. It's called AutoSelect, and its special power is to select all the data values in a given row or column until it encounters an empty cell.

To use AutoSelect, follow these steps:

1. **Move to the first cell that you want to select.**

   Before continuing, decide which direction you want to extend the selection.

2. **Hold down Shift. Now, double-click whichever edge of the active cell corresponds to the direction you want to AutoSelect.**

   For example, if you want to select the cells below the active cell, then double-click its bottom edge. (You'll know you're in the right place when the mouse pointer changes to a four-way arrow.)

3. **Excel completes your selection automatically.**

   AutoSelection selects every cell in the direction you choose until it reaches the first blank cell. The blank cell (and any cells beyond it) won't be selected.

Making Selections with the Keyboard

The mouse can be an intuitive way to navigate around a worksheet and select cells. It can also be a tremendous time-suck, especially for nimble-fingered typists who've grown fond of the keyboard shortcuts that let them speed through actions in other programs.

Fortunately, Excel is ready to let you use the keyboard to select cells in a worksheet. Just follow these steps:

1. **Start by moving to the first cell you want to select.**

   Whichever cell you begin on becomes the anchor point from which your selected area grows. Think of this cell as the corner of a rectangle you're about to draw.

2. **Now, hold down Shift, and move to the right or left (to select columns) and down or up (to select more rows), using the arrow keys.**

   As you move, the selection grows. Instead of holding down Shift, you can also just press F8 once, which turns on extend mode. When extend mode is on, you'll see the text Extend Selection in the status bar. As you move, Excel selects cells just as though you were holding down Shift. You can turn off extend mode by pressing F8 once you've finished marking your range.

Making a non-contiguous selection is almost as easy. The trick is you need to switch between extend mode and another mode called add mode. Just follow these steps:

1. **Move to the first cell you want to select.**

   You can add cells to a non-contiguous range one at a time, or by adding multiple continuous ranges. Either way, you start with the first cell you want to select.

2. **Press F8.**

   This key turns on extend mode. You'll see the text Extend Selection appear in the Status bar to let you know extend mode is turned on.

3. **If you want to select more than one cell, use the arrow keys to extend your selection.**

   If you just want to select the currently active cell, do nothing; you're ready to go onto the next step. When you want to add a whole block of cells, you can mark out your selection now. Remember, at this point you're still selecting a continuous range. In the steps that follow you can add several distinct continuous ranges to make a non-contiguous selection.

4. **Press Shift+F8 to add the highlighted cells to your non-contiguous range.**

   When you hit Shift+F8, you switch to add mode, and you see the text "Add to Selection" appear in the status bar.

5. **You now have two choices: You can repeat steps 1 to 4 to add more cells to your selection; or, you can perform an action with the current selection, like applying new formatting.**

   You can repeat steps 1 to 4 as many times as you need to add more groups of cells to your non-contiguous range. These new cells (either individuals or groups) don't need to be near each other or in any way connected to the other cells you've selected. If you change your mind, and decide you don't want to do anything with your selection after all, press F8 twice—once to move back into extend mode, and then again to return to normal mode. Now, the next time you press an arrow key, Excel releases the current selection.

Tip: You can also use the keyboard to activate AutoSelect. Just hold down the Shift key, and use one of the shortcut key combinations that automatically jumps over a range of cells. For example, when you hold down Shift and then press Ctrl+→, you'll automatically jump to the last occupied cell in the current row with all the cells in between selected. For more information about the shortcut keys, see Table 9-1 on page 210.

Selecting Cells with the Go To Feature

In Chapter 9, you learned how you could use the Go To feature to jump from one position in a cell to another. A little known Excel secret also lets you use the Go To feature to select a range of cells.

It works like this: Start off at the top-left cell of the range you want to select. Then, open the Go To window by selecting Home → Editing → Find & Select → Go To, or by pressing Ctrl+G. Type in the address of the bottom-right cell in the

selection you want to highlight. Now, here's the secret: Hold down Shift when you click the OK button. This action tells Excel to select the range of cells as it moves to the new cell.

For example, if you start in cell A1, and use the Go To window to jump to B3, then you'll select a block of six cells: A1, A2, A3, B1, B2, and B3.

Moving Cells Around

One of the most common reasons to select groups of cells on a worksheet is to copy or move them from one place to another. Excel is a champion of the basic cut-and-paste feature, and it also gives you worthwhile enhancements that let you do things like drag-and-drop blocks of cells and copy multiple selections to the clipboard at the same time.

Before you get started shuffling data from one place to another, here are a few points to keep in mind:

- Excel lets you cut or copy a single cell or a continuous range of cells. When you cut or copy a cell, *everything* goes with it, including the data and the current formatting.

- When you paste cells onto your worksheet, you have two basic choices. You can paste the cells into a new, blank area of the worksheet, or, you can paste the cells in a place that already contains data. In this second case, Excel overwrites the existing cells with the new pasted data.

- Cutting and copying cells works almost exactly the same way. The only difference you'll see is that when you perform a cut-and-paste operation (as opposed to a copy-and-paste operation), Excel erases the source data once the operation's complete. However, Excel doesn't remove the source cells from the worksheet. Instead, it just leaves them empty. (The next section shows you what to do if you do want to remove or insert cells, not just the data they contain.)

A Simple Cut-and-Paste or Copy-and-Paste

Here's the basic procedure for any cut-and-paste or copy-and-paste operation.

1. **Select the cells you want to cut or copy.**

   You can use any of the tricks you learned in the previous section to highlight a continuous range of cells. (You can't cut and paste non-contiguous selections.)

When you want to cut or copy only a single cell, just move to the cell—you don't actually need to select it.

2. **If you want to cut your selection, choose Home → Clipboard → Cut (or Ctrl+X). When you want to copy your selection, choose Home → Clipboard → Copy (or Ctrl+C).**

Excel highlights your selection with a *marquee border* (Figure 11-5), so-called because the border blinks like the twinkling lights around an old-style movie theater marquee.

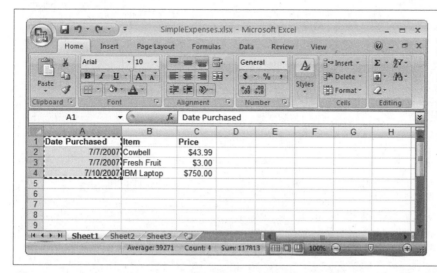

Figure 11-5:
In this example, cells A1 to A4 have been copied. The next step is to move to the place where you want to paste the cells, and then press Enter to complete the operation.

3. **Move to the new location in the spreadsheet where you want to paste the cells.**

If you selected one cell, move to the new cell where you want to place the data. If you selected multiple cells, then move to the top-left corner of the area where you want to paste your selection. If you have existing data below or to the right of this cell, Excel overwrites it with the new content you're pasting.

It's valid to paste over part of the data you're copying. For example, you could make a selection that consists of columns A, B, and C, and paste that selection starting at column B. In this case, the pasted data appears in columns B, C, and D, and Excel overwrites the original content in these columns (although the original content remains in column A).

4. **Paste the data by selecting Home → Clipboard → Paste (or press Ctrl+V or Enter on the keyboard).**

This action completes your cut-and-paste or copy-and-paste operation. When you're performing a cut-and-paste, Excel removes the original data from the spreadsheet just before pasting it in the new location.

Tip: Instead of cutting or copying a block of cells, you can also move the entire column or row that contains the cells. Begin by highlighting one or more columns or rows (by selecting the column or row headers). For example, you could select column A by clicking the column header, and then cut it. You could then right-click the column B header, and choose Paste to move the column A values into column B. When you copy entire columns, Excel automatically adjusts the column widths as part of the copy operation, so the destination column winds up the same width as the source column.

FREQUENTLY ASKED QUESTION

The Mysterious Number Signs

What does it mean when I see ####### in a cell?

A series of number (or pound) signs is Excel's way of telling you that a column isn't wide enough to display the number or date that it contains (see Figure 11-6). Sometimes these signs appear when you're copying a big number into a smaller cell.

Excel doesn't use the number signs with text cells—if those cells aren't large enough to hold their data, the words simply spill over to the adjacent cell (if it's blank), or become truncated (if the adjacent cell has some content). This behavior wouldn't be acceptable with numbers because if Excel cut off a portion of a number, it would appear to be a completely different number.

Fortunately, it's easy to solve this problem—just position the mouse pointer at the right edge of the cell header, and then drag it to the right to enlarge the column. Provided you've made the column large enough, the missing number reappears. For a quicker solution, double-click the right edge of the column to automatically make it large enough.

This error doesn't usually occur while you're entering information for the first time because Excel automatically resizes columns to accommodate any numbers you type in. The problem is more likely to crop up if you shrink a column afterward, or if you cut some numeric cells from a wide column and paste them into a much narrower column. To verify the source of your problem, just move to the offending cell, and then check the formula bar to see your complete number or date.

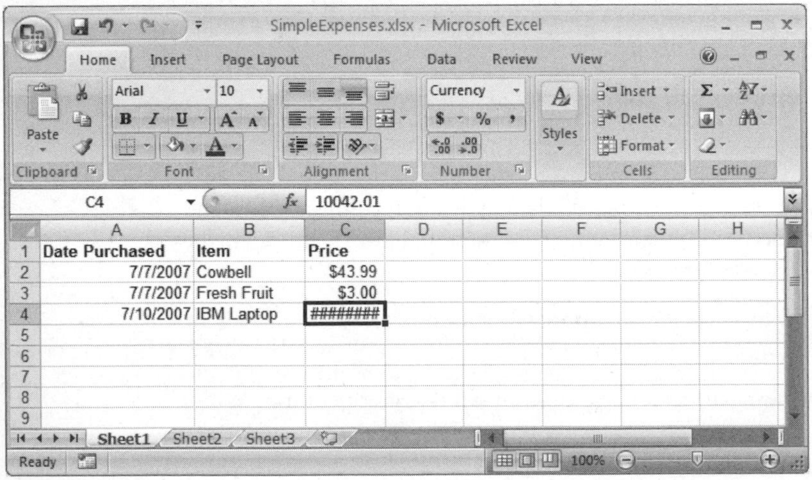

Figure 11-6:
Cell C4 has a wide number in an overly narrow column. You can see the mystery number only if you move to the cell and check out the formula bar (it's 10,042.01), or expand the column to a more reasonable width.

A Fancy Cut-and-Paste or Copy-and-Paste

If you want a really quick way to cut and paste data, you can use Excel's drag-and-drop feature. It works like this:

1. **Select the cells you want to move.**

   Just drag your pointer over the block of cells you want to select.

2. **Click the border of the selection box, and don't release the mouse button.**

   You'll know that you're in the right place when the mouse pointer changes to a four-way arrow. You can click any edge, but *don't* click in the corner.

3. **Drag the selection box to its new location. If you want to copy (rather than simply move) the text, hold down the Ctrl key while you drag.**

   As you drag, a light gray box shows you where Excel will paste the cells.

4. **Release the mouse button to move the cells.**

   If you drop the cells into a region that overlaps with other data, Excel prompts you to make sure that you want to overwrite the existing cells. This convenience isn't provided with ordinary cut-and-paste operations. (Excel uses it for drag-and-drop operations because it's all too easy to inadvertently drop your cells in the wrong place, especially while you're still getting used to this feature.)

The Clipboard

In Windows' early days, you could copy only a single piece of information at a time. If you copied two pieces of data, only the most recent item you copied would remain in the clipboard, a necessary way of life in the memory-starved computing days of yore. But nowadays, Excel boasts the ability to hold 24 separate cell selections in the Office clipboard. This information remains available as long as you have at least one Office application open.

Note: Even though the Office clipboard holds 24 pieces of information, you won't be able to access all this information in Windows applications that aren't part of the Office suite. If you want to paste Excel data into a non-Office application, you'll be able to paste only the data that was added to the clipboard most recently.

When you use the Home → Clipboard → Paste command (or Ctrl+V), you're using the ordinary Windows clipboard. That means you always paste the item most recently added to the clipboard. But if you fire up the Office clipboard, you can hold a lot more. Go to the Home → Clipboard section of the ribbon, and then click the dialog box launcher (the small arrow-in-a-square icon in the bottom-right corner) to open the Clipboard panel. Now Excel adds all the information you copy to *both* the Windows clipboard and the more capacious Office clipboard. Each item that you copy appears in the Clipboard panel (Figure 11-7).

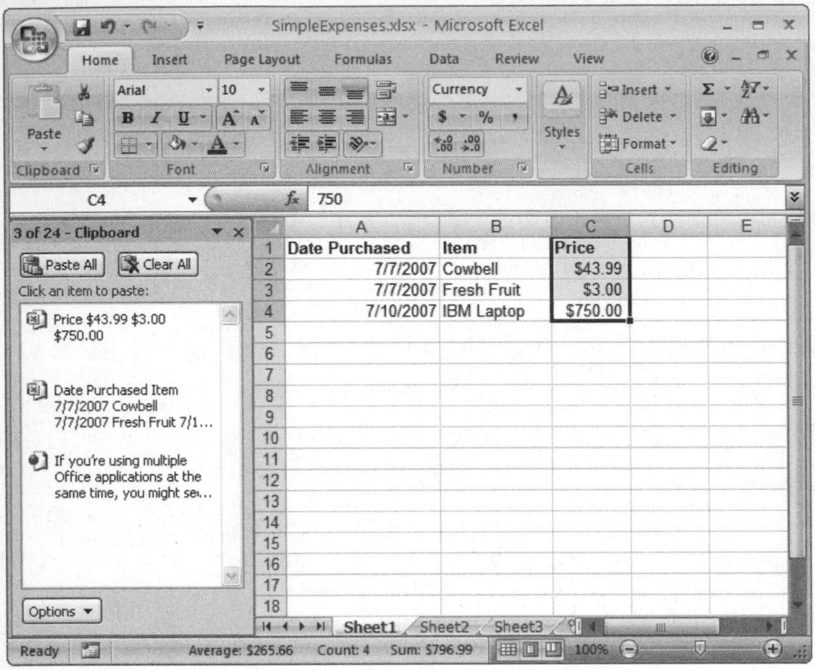

Figure 11-7:
The Clipboard panel shows a list of all the items you've copied to it since you opened it (up to a limit of 24 items). Each item shows the combined content for all the cells in the selection. For example, the first item in this list includes four cells: the Price column title followed by the three prices. If you're using multiple Office applications at the same time, you may see scraps of Word documents, PowerPoint presentations, or pictures in the clipboard along with your Excel data. The icon next to the item always tells you which program the information came from.

Using the Clipboard panel, you can perform the following actions:

- Click Paste All to paste all the selections into your worksheet. Excel pastes the first selection into the current cell, and then begins pasting the next selection starting in the first row underneath that, and so on. As with all paste operations, the pasted cells overwrite any existing content in your worksheet.

- Click Delete All to remove all the selections from the clipboard. This is a useful approach if you want to add more data to the Clipboard, and you don't want to confuse this information with whatever selection you previously copied.

- Click a selection in the list to paste it into the current location in the worksheet.

- Click the drop-down arrow at the right of a selection item to show a menu that allows you to paste that item or remove it from the clipboard.

Depending on your settings, the Clipboard panel may automatically spring into action. To configure this behavior, click the Options button at the bottom of the Clipboard panel to display a menu of options. These include:

- **Show Office Clipboard Automatically.** If you turn on this option, the Clipboard panel automatically appears if you copy more than one piece of information to the clipboard. (Remember, without the Clipboard panel, you can access only the last piece of information you've copied.)

- **Show Office Clipboard When Ctrl+C Pressed Twice.** If you turn on this option, the Clipboard panel appears if you press the Ctrl+C shortcut twice in a row, without doing anything else in between.

- **Collect Without Showing Office Clipboard.** If you turn on this option, it overrides the previous two settings, ensuring that the Clipboard panel never appears automatically. You can still call up the Clipboard panel manually, of course.

- **Show Office Clipboard Icon on Taskbar.** If you turn on this option, a clipboard icon appears in the system tray at the right of the taskbar. You can double-click this icon to show the Clipboard panel while working in any Office application. You can also right-click this icon to change clipboard settings or to tell the Office clipboard to stop collecting data.

- **Show Status Near Taskbar When Copying.** If you turn on this option, you'll see a tooltip near the Windows system tray whenever you copy data. (The *system tray* is the set of notification icons at the bottom-right corner of your screen, in the Windows taskbar.) The icon for the Office clipboard shows a clipboard icon, and it displays a message like "4 of 24 - Item Collected" (which indicates you have just copied a fourth item to the clipboard).

UP TO SPEED

Cutting or Copying Part of a Cell

Excel's cut-and-paste and copy-and-paste features let you move data in one or more cells. But what if you simply want to take a snippet of text from a cell, and transfer it to another cell or even another application? Excel makes this operation possible, but you need to work a little differently.

First, move to the cell that contains the content you want to cut or copy, and then place it in edit mode by double-clicking it with the mouse or pressing F2. You can now scroll through the cell content using the arrow keys. Move to the position where you want to start chopping or copying, hold down Shift, and then arrow over to the right. Keep moving

until you've selected all the text you want to cut or copy. Then, hit Ctrl+C to copy the text, or Ctrl+X to cut it. (When you cut text, it disappears immediately, just like in other Windows applications.) Hit F2 or Enter to exit edit mode once you're finished.

The final step is to paste your text somewhere else. You can move to another cell that has data in it already, press F2 to enter edit mode again, move to the correct position in that cell, and then press Ctrl+V. However, you can also paste the text directly into a cell by just moving to the cell and pressing Ctrl+V without placing it into edit mode. In this case, the data you paste overwrites the current content in the cell.

Special Pasting

When you copy cells, *everything* comes along for the ride, including text, numbers, and formatting. For example, if you copy a column that has one cell filled with bold text and several other cells filled with dollar amounts (including the dollar sign), when you paste this column into its new location, the numbers will still have the dollar sign and the text will still have bold formatting. If you want to change this behavior, you can use the Paste Special command.

It works like this. First, copy your cells in the normal way. (Don't cut them, or the Paste Special feature won't work.) Then, move to where you want to paste the information, and choose Home → Clipboard → Paste → Paste Special (instead of Home → Clipboard → Paste). A new dialog box appears with a slew of options (Figure 11-8).

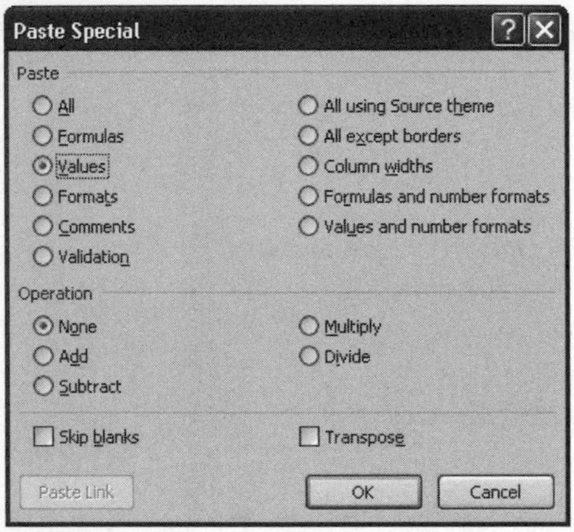

Figure 11-8:
The Paste Special window allows you to choose exactly what Excel will paste, and it also lets you apply a few other settings. Here, Excel will paste the cell values but not the formatting.

These options are divided into two main groups: Paste and Operation. The Paste settings determine what content Excel pastes. This is the most useful part of the window. These settings include:

- **All.** This option is the same as a normal paste operation, and it pastes both formatting and numbers.

- **Formulas.** This option pastes only cell content—numbers, dates, and text—without any formatting. If your source range includes any formulas, Excel also copies the formulas.

- **Values.** This option pastes only cell content—numbers, dates, and text—without any formatting. If your source range includes any formulas, Excel pastes the *result* of that formula (the calculated number) but not the actual formula.

- **Formats.** This option applies the formatting from the source selection, but it doesn't actually copy any data.

- **Comments.** This option copies only the comments that you've added to cells.

- **Validation.** This option copies only cells that use validation (an advanced tool for checking data before it's entered into a cell).

- **All Except Borders.** This option is the same as All, except it ignores any borders that you've applied to the cell. Border formatting is described on page 305.

- **Column Widths.** This option is the same as All, and it also adjusts the columns in the paste region so that they have the same widths as the source columns.

- **Formulas and Number Formats.** This option doesn't paste any data. Here, Excel pastes only formulas and any settings used for formatting how numbers appear. (In other words, you'll lose format settings that control the font, cell fill color, and borders.)

- **Values and Number Formats.** This option pastes everything without any formatting, except for the formatting used to configure how numbers appear. (In other words, you'll lose format settings that control the font, cell fill color, and borders.)

The Operation settings are a little wacky—they allow you to combine the cells you're pasting with the contents of the cells you're pasting into, either by adding, subtracting, multiplying, or dividing the two sets of numbers. It's an intriguing idea, but few people use these settings because they're not intuitive.

Further down the Paste Special dialog box, the "Skip blanks" checkbox tells Excel not to overwrite a cell if the cell you're pasting from is empty. The Transpose checkbox inverts your information before it pastes it, so that all the columns become rows and the rows become columns. Figure 11-9 shows an example.

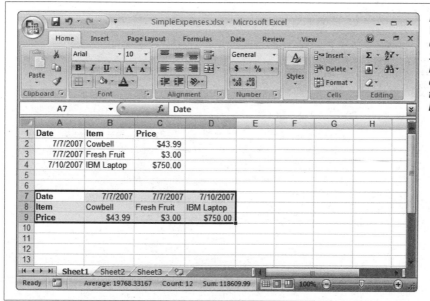

Figure 11-9:
With the Transpose option (from the Paste Special dialog box), Excel's pasted the table at the top and transposed it on the bottom.

Finally, you can use the Paste Link button to paste a link that refers to the original data instead of a duplicate copy of the content. That means that if you modify the source cells, Excel automatically modifies the copies. In fact, if you take a closer look at the copied cells in the formula bar, you'll find that they don't contain the actual data. Instead, they contain a formula that points to the source cell. For example, if you paste cell A2 as a link into cell B4, the cell B4 contains the reference =A2. You'll learn more about cell references and formulas in Chapter 15.

Tip: Once you know your way around the different pasting options, you can often find a quicker way to get the same result. Instead of choosing Home → Clipboard → Paste → Paste Special, you can choose one of the options in the Home → Clipboard → Paste menu. You won't find all the options that are in the Paste Special dialog box, but you do find commonly used options like Paste Values and Transpose.

Even if you don't use the Paste Special command, you can still control some basic paste settings. After you paste any data in Excel, a paste icon appears near the bottom-right corner of the pasted region. (Excel nerds know this icon as a *smart tag*.) If you click this icon, you'll see a drop-down menu that includes the most important options from the Paste Special dialog box, as shown in Figure 11-10.

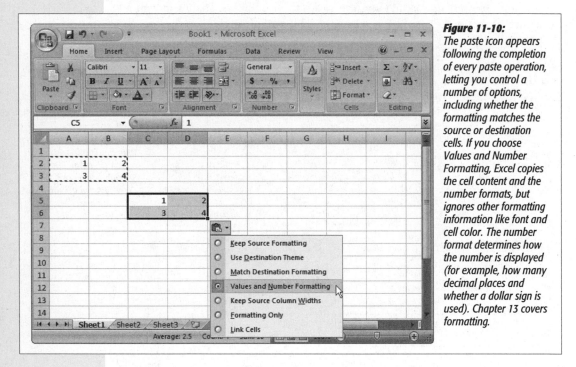

Figure 11-10:
The paste icon appears following the completion of every paste operation, letting you control a number of options, including whether the formatting matches the source or destination cells. If you choose Values and Number Formatting, Excel copies the cell content and the number formats, but ignores other formatting information like font and cell color. The number format determines how the number is displayed (for example, how many decimal places and whether a dollar sign is used). Chapter 13 covers formatting.

Note: The paste icon appears only after a copy-and-paste operation, not a cut-and-paste operation. If you paste cells from the Clipboard panel, the paste icon still appears, but it provides just two options: keeping the source formatting or pasting the data only.

Adding and Moving Columns or Rows

The cut-and-paste and copy-and-paste operations let you move data from one cell (or group of cells) to another. But what happens if you want to make some *major* changes to your worksheet itself? For example, imagine you have a spreadsheet with 10 filled columns (A to J) and you decide you want to add a new column between columns C and D. You could cut all the columns from D to J, and then paste them starting at E. That would solve the problem, and leave the C column free for your new data. But the actual task of selecting these columns can be a little awkward, and it only becomes more difficult as your spreadsheet grows in size.

A much easier option is to use two dedicated Excel commands designed for inserting new columns and rows into an existing spreadsheet. If you use these features, you won't need to disturb your existing cells at all.

Inserting Columns

To insert a new column, follow these steps:

1. **Select the column immediately to the *right* of where you want to place the new column.**

   That means that if you want to insert a new, blank column between columns A and B, start by selecting the existing column B. Remember, you select a column by clicking the column header.

2. **Choose Home → Cells → Insert → Insert Sheet Columns.**

   Excel inserts a new column, and automatically moves all the columns to the right of column A (so column B becomes column C, column C becomes column D, and so on).

Inserting Rows

Inserting rows is just as easy as inserting new columns. Just follow these steps:

1. **Select the row that's immediately *below* where you want to place the new row.**

   That means that if you want to insert a new, blank row between rows 6 and 7, start by selecting the existing row 7. Remember, you select a row by clicking the row number header.

2. **Choose Home → Cells → Insert → Insert Sheet Rows.**

   Excel inserts a new row, and all the rows beneath it are automatically moved down one row.

Note: In the unlikely event that you have data at the extreme right edge of the spreadsheet, in column XFD, Excel doesn't let you insert a new column anywhere in the spreadsheet because the data would be pushed off into the region Beyond The Spreadsheet's Edges. Similarly, if you have data in the very last row (row 1,048,576), Excel doesn't let you insert more rows. If you do have data in either of these spots and try to insert a new column or row, Excel displays a warning message.

Inserting Copied or Cut Cells

Usually, inserting entirely new rows and columns is the most straightforward way to change the structure of your spreadsheet. You can then cut and paste new information into the blank rows or columns. However, in some cases, you may simply want to insert cells into an *existing* row or column.

To do so, begin by copying or cutting a cell or group of cells, and then select the spot you want to paste into. Next, choose Home → Cells → Insert → Insert Copied Cells from the menu (or Home → Cells → Insert → Insert Cut Cells if you're performing a cut instead of a copy operation). Unlike the cut-and-paste feature, when you insert cells, you won't overwrite the existing data. Instead, Excel asks you whether the existing cells should be shifted down or to the right to make way for the new cells (as shown in Figure 11-11).

Figure 11-11:
When you insert copied cells, Excel asks whether it should move the existing cells down or to the right.

You need to be careful when you use the Insert Copied Cells feature. Because you're shifting only certain parts of your worksheet, it's possible to mangle your data, splitting the information that should be in one row or one column into multiple rows or columns! Fortunately, you can always back out of a tight spot using Undo.

Deleting Columns and Rows

In Chapter 9, you learned that you can quickly remove cell values by moving to the cell and hitting the Delete key. You can also delete an entire range of values by selecting multiple cells, and then hitting the Delete key. Using this technique, you can quickly wipe out an entire row or column.

However, using delete simply clears the cell content. It doesn't remove the cells or change the structure of your worksheet. If you want to simultaneously clear cell values and adjust the rest of your spreadsheet to fill in the gap, you need to use the Home → Cell → Delete command.

For example, if you select a column by clicking the column header, you can either clear all the cells (by pressing the Delete key), or remove the column by choosing Home → Cells → Delete. Deleting a column in this way is the reverse of inserting a column. All the columns to the right are automatically moved one column to the left to fill in the gap left by the column you removed. Thus, if you delete column B, column C becomes the new column B, column D becomes column C, and so on. If you take out row 3, row 4 moves up to fill the void, row 5 becomes row 4, and so on.

Usually, you'll use Home → Cells → Delete to remove entire rows or columns. However, you can also use it just to remove specific cells in a column or row. In this case, Excel prompts you with a dialog box asking whether you want to fill in the gap by moving cells in the current column up, or by moving cells in the current row to the left. This feature is the reverse of the Insert Copied Cells feature, and you'll need to take special care to make sure you don't scramble the structure of your spreadsheet when you use this approach.

CHAPTER 12

Managing Worksheets and Workbooks

So far, you've learned how to create a basic worksheet with a table of data. That's great for getting started, but as power users, professional accountants, and other Excel jockeys quickly learn, some of the most compelling reasons to use Excel involve *multiple* tables that share information and interact with each other.

For example, say you want to track the performance of your company: you create one table summarizing your firm's yearly sales, another listing expenses, and a third analyzing profitability and making predictions for the coming year. If you create these tables in different spreadsheet files, you have to copy shared information from one location to another, all without misplacing a number or making a mistake. And what's worse, with data scattered in multiple places, you're missing the chance to use some of Excel's niftiest charting and analytical tools. Similarly, if you try cramming a bunch of tables onto the same worksheet page, you can quickly create formatting and cell management problems.

Fortunately, a better solution exists. Excel lets you create spreadsheets with multiple pages of data, each of which can conveniently exchange information with other pages. Each page is called a *worksheet*, and a collection of one or more worksheets is called a *workbook* (which is also sometimes called a *spreadsheet file*). In this chapter, you'll learn how to manage the worksheets in a workbook. You'll also take a look at two more all-purpose Excel features: Find and Replace (a tool for digging through worksheets in search of specific data) and the spell checker.

Worksheets and Workbooks

Many workbooks contain more than one table of information. For example, you might have a list of the items you've purchased over two consecutive years. You might find it a bit challenging to arrange these different tables. You could stack them (Figure 12-1) or place them side by side (Figure 12-2), but neither solution is perfect.

	A	B	C	D
1	2007 Purchases			
2	Date	Item	Price	
3	7/7/2007	Cowbell	$43.99	
4	7/7/2007	Fresh Fruit	$3.00	
5	7/10/2007	IBM Laptop	$750.00	
6				
7	2006 Purchases			
8	Date	Item	Price	
9	1/8/2006	Gorilla Suit	$140.25	
10	5/30/2006	Crayons	$2.99	
11	8/30/2006	Sofa	$599.00	
12				

Figure 12-1:
Stacking tables on top of each other is usually a bad idea. If you need to add more data to the first table, then you have to move the second table. You'll also have trouble properly resizing or formatting columns because each column contains data from two different tables.

	A	B	C	D	E	F	G
1	2007 Purchases				2006 Purchases		
2	Date	Item	Price		Date	Item	Price
3	7/7/2007	Cowbell	$43.99		1/8/2006	Gorilla Suit	$140.25
4	7/7/2007	Fresh Fruit	$3.00		5/30/2006	Crayons	$2.99
5	7/10/2007	IBM Laptop	$750.00		8/30/2006	Sofa	$599.00
6							

Figure 12-2:
You're somewhat better off putting tables side by side, separated by a blank column, than you are stacking them, but this method can create problems if you need to add more columns to the first table. It also makes for a lot of side-to-side scrolling.

Most Excel masters agree that the best way to arrange separate tables of information is to use separate worksheets for each table. When you create a new workbook, Excel automatically fills it with three blank worksheets named Sheet1, Sheet2, and Sheet3. Often, you'll work exclusively with the first worksheet (Sheet1), and not even realize that you have two more blank worksheets to play with—not to mention the ability to add plenty more.

To move from one worksheet to another, you have a few choices:

- Click the worksheet tabs at the bottom of Excel's grid window (just above the status bar), as shown in Figure 12-3.
- Press Ctrl+Page Down to move to the next worksheet. For example, if you're currently in Sheet1, this key sequence jumps you to Sheet2.
- Press Ctrl+Page Up to move to the previous worksheet. For example, if you're currently in Sheet2, this key sequence takes you back to Sheet1.

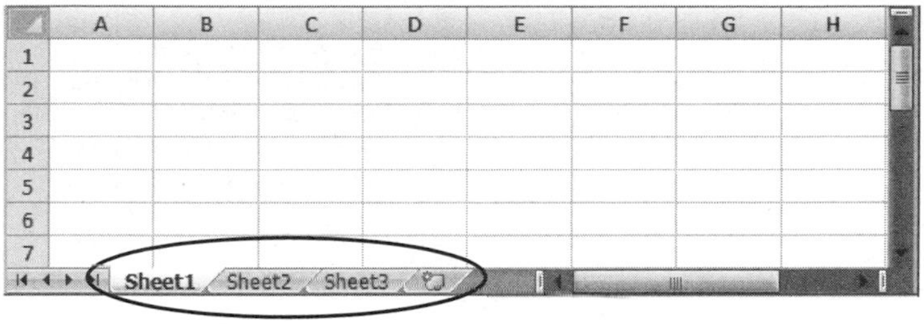

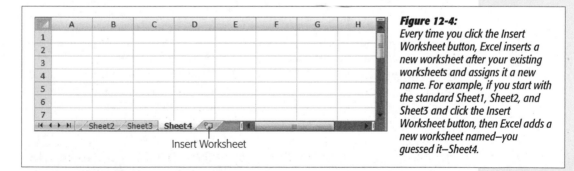

Figure 12-3:
Worksheets provide a good way to organize multiple tables of data. To move from one worksheet to another, click the appropriate Worksheet tab at the bottom of the grid. Each worksheet contains a fresh grid of cells.

Excel keeps track of the active cell in each worksheet. That means if you're in cell B9 in Sheet1, and then move to Sheet2, when you jump back to Sheet1 you'll automatically return to cell B9.

Tip: Excel includes some interesting viewing features that let you look at two different worksheets at the same time, even if these worksheets are in the same workbook. You'll learn more about custom views in Chapter 14.

Adding, Removing, and Hiding Worksheets

When you open a fresh workbook in Excel, you automatically get three blank worksheets in it. You can easily add more worksheets. Just click the Insert Worksheet button, which appears immediately to the right of your last worksheet tab (Figure 12-4). You can also use the Home → Cells → Insert → Insert Sheet command, which works the same way but inserts a new worksheet immediately to the *left* of the current worksheet. (Don't panic; page 269 shows how you can rearrange worksheets after the fact.)

Figure 12-4:
Every time you click the Insert Worksheet button, Excel inserts a new worksheet after your existing worksheets and assigns it a new name. For example, if you start with the standard Sheet1, Sheet2, and Sheet3 and click the Insert Worksheet button, then Excel adds a new worksheet named—you guessed it—Sheet4.

Insert Worksheet

If you continue adding worksheets, you'll eventually find that all the worksheet tabs won't fit at the bottom of your workbook window. If you run out of space, you need to use the scroll buttons (which are immediately to the left of the worksheet tabs) to scroll through the list of worksheets. Figure 12-5 shows the scroll buttons.

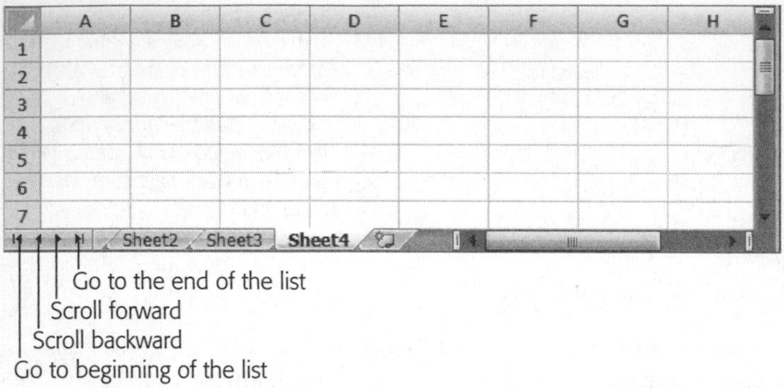

Figure 12-5:
Using the scroll buttons, you can move between worksheets one at a time or jump straight to the first or last tab. These scroll buttons control only which tabs you see—you still need to click the appropriate tab to move to the worksheet you want to work on.

Go to the end of the list
Scroll forward
Scroll backward
Go to beginning of the list

Tip: If you have a huge number of worksheets and they don't all fit in the strip of worksheet tabs, there's an easier way to jump around. Right-click the scroll buttons to pop up a list with all your worksheets. You can then move to the worksheet you want by clicking it in the list.

Removing a worksheet is just as easy as adding one. Simply move to the worksheet you want to get rid of, and then choose Home → Cells → Delete → Delete Sheet (you can also right-click a worksheet tab and choose Delete). Excel won't complain if you ask it to remove a blank worksheet, but if you try to remove a sheet that contains any data, it presents a warning message asking for your confirmation. Also, if you're down to one last worksheet, Excel won't let you remove it. Doing so would create a tough existential dilemma for Excel—a workbook that holds no worksheets—so the program prevents you from taking this step.

Warning: Be careful when deleting worksheets, as you can't use Undo (Ctrl+Z) to reverse this change! Undo also doesn't work to reverse a newly inserted sheet.

Excel starts you off with three worksheets for each workbook, but changing this setting's easy. You can configure Excel to start with fewer worksheets (as few as one), or many more (up to 255). Select Office button → Excel Options, and then choose the Popular section. Under the heading "When creating new workbooks" change the number in the "Include this many sheets" box, and then click OK. This setting takes effect the next time you create a new workbook.

Note: Although you're limited to 255 sheets in a new workbook, Excel doesn't limit how many worksheets you can add *after* you've created a workbook. The only factor that ultimately limits the number of worksheets your workbook can hold is your computer's memory. However, modern day PCs can easily handle even the most ridiculously large, worksheet-stuffed workbook.

Deleting worksheets isn't the only way to tidy up a workbook or get rid of information you don't want. You can also choose to *hide* a worksheet temporarily. When you hide a worksheet, its tab disappears but the worksheet itself remains part of your spreadsheet file, available whenever you choose to unhide it. Hidden worksheets also don't appear on printouts. To hide a worksheet, right-click the worksheet tab and choose Hide. (Or, for a more long-winded approach, choose Home → Cells → Format → Hide & Unhide → Hide Sheet.)

To redisplay a hidden worksheet, right-click any worksheet tab and choose Unhide. The Unhide dialog box appears along with a list of all hidden sheets, as shown in Figure 12-6. You can then select a sheet from the list and click OK to unhide it. (Once again, the ribbon can get you the same window—just point yourself to Home → Cells → Format → Hide & Unhide → Unhide Sheet.)

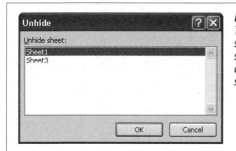

Figure 12-6:
This workbook contains two hidden worksheets. To restore one, just select it from the list, and then click OK. Unfortunately, if you want to show multiple hidden sheets, you have to use the Unhide Sheet command multiple times. Excel has no shortcut for unhiding multiple sheets at once.

Naming and Rearranging Worksheets

The standard names Excel assigns to new worksheets—Sheet1, Sheet2, Sheet3, and so on—aren't very helpful for identifying what they contain. And they become even less helpful if you start adding new worksheets, since the new sheet numbers don't necessarily indicate the position of the sheets, just the order in which you created them.

For example, if you're on Sheet 3 and you add a new worksheet (by choosing Home → Cells → Insert → Insert Sheet), then the worksheet tabs read: Sheet1, Sheet2, Sheet4, Sheet3. (That's because the Insert Sheet command inserts the new sheet just before your current sheet.) Excel doesn't expect you to stick with these auto-generated names. Instead, you can rename them by right-clicking the worksheet tab and selecting Rename, or just double-click the sheet name. Either way, Excel highlights the worksheet tab, and you can type a new name directly onto the tab. Figure 12-7 shows worksheet tabs with better names.

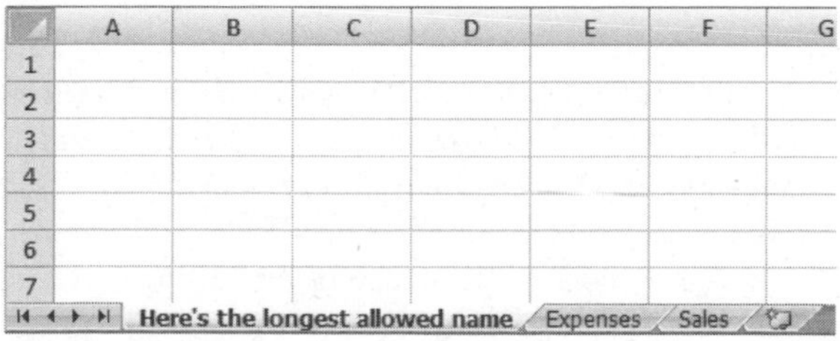

	A	B	C	D	E	F	G
1							
2							
3							
4							
5							
6							
7							

Here's the longest allowed name / Expenses / Sales /

Figure 12-7:
Worksheet names can be up to 31 characters long and can include letters, numbers, some symbols, and spaces.

Note: Excel has a small set of reserved names that you can never use. To witness this problem, try to create a worksheet named History. Excel doesn't let you because it uses the History worksheet as part of its change tracking features. Use this Excel oddity to impress your friends.

Sometimes Excel refuses to insert new worksheets exactly where you'd like them. Fortunately, you can easily rearrange any of your worksheets just by dragging their tabs from one place to another, as shown in Figure 12-8.

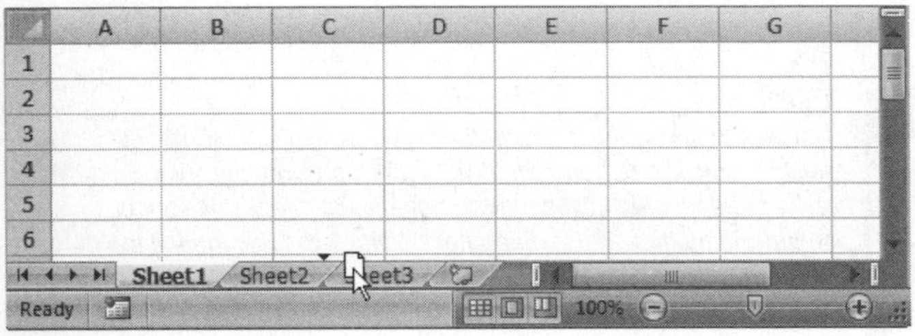

Figure 12-8:
When you drag a worksheet tab, a tiny page appears beneath the arrow cursor. As you move the cursor around, you'll see a black triangle appear, indicating where the worksheet will land when you release the mouse button.

Tip: You can use a similar technique to create *copies* of a worksheet. Click the worksheet tab and begin dragging, just as you would to move the worksheet. However, before releasing the mouse button, press the Ctrl key (you'll see a plus sign [+] appear). When you let go, Excel creates a copy of the worksheet in the new location. The original worksheet remains in its original location. Excel gives the new worksheet a name with a number in parentheses. For example, a copy of Sheet1 is named Sheet1 (2). As with any other worksheet tab, you can change this name.

GEM IN THE ROUGH

Colorful Worksheet Tabs

Names aren't the only thing you can change when it comes to newly added worksheets. Excel also lets you modify a worksheet tab's background color. This minor convenience has no effect on your data or your printout, but it can help you quickly find an important worksheet if it has lots of neighbors.

To change the background color of a worksheet tab, right-click the tab, and then select Tab Color (or move to the appropriate worksheet and Home → Cells → Format → Tab Color). A list of color choices appears; make your selection by clicking the color you want.

Find and Replace

When you're dealing with great mounds of information, you may have a tough time ferreting out the nuggets of data you need. Fortunately, Excel's find feature is great for helping you locate numbers or text, even when they're buried within massive workbooks holding dozens of worksheets. And if you need to make changes to a bunch of identical items, the find-and-replace option can be a real timesaver.

The "Find and Replace" feature includes both simple and advanced options. In its basic version, you're only a quick keystroke combo away from a word or number you *know* is lurking somewhere in your data pile. With the advanced options turned on, you can do things like search for cells that have certain formatting characteristics and apply changes automatically. The next few sections dissect these features.

The Basic Find

Excel's find feature is a little like the Go To tool described in Chapter 9, which lets you move across a large expanse of cells in a single bound. The difference is that Go To moves to a *known* location, using the cell address you specify. The find feature, on the other hand, searches every cell until it finds the content you've asked Excel to look for. Excel's search works similarly to the search feature in Microsoft Word, but it's worth keeping in mind a few additional details:

- Excel searches by comparing the content you enter with the content in each cell. For example, if you searched for the word *Date*, Excel identifies as a match a cell containing the phrase *Date Purchased*.

- When searching cells that contain numeric or date information, Excel always searches the *display text*. For example, say a cell displays dates using the day-month-year format, like *2-Dec-05*. You can find this particular cell by searching for any part of the displayed date (using search strings like *Dec* or *2-Dec-05*). But if you use the search string *12/2/2005,* you won't find a match because the search string and the display text are different. A similar behavior occurs with numbers. For example, the search strings *$3* and *3.00* match the currency value *$3.00*. However, the search string *3.000* won't turn up anything because Excel won't be able to make a full text match.

- Excel searches one cell at a time, from left to right. When it reaches the end of a row, it moves to the first column of the next row.

To perform a find operation, follow these steps:

1. **Move to the cell where you want the search to begin.**

   If you start off halfway down the worksheet, for example, the search covers the cells from there to the end of the worksheet, and then "loops over" and starts at cell A1. If you select a group of cells, Excel restricts the search to just those cells. You can search across a set of columns, rows, or even a non-contiguous group of cells.

2. **Choose Home → Editing → Find & Select → Find, or press Ctrl+F.**

   The "Find and Replace" window appears, with the Find tab selected.

Note: To assist frequent searches, Excel lets you keep the "Find and Replace" window hanging around (rather than forcing you to use it or close it, as is the case with many other dialog boxes). You can continue to move from cell to cell and edit your worksheet data even while the "Find and Replace" window remains visible.

3. **In the "Find what" combo box, enter the word, phrase, or number you're looking for.**

   If you've performed other searches recently, you can reuse these search terms. Just choose the appropriate search text from the "Find what" drop-down list.

4. **Click Find Next.**

   Excel jumps to the next matching cell, which becomes the active cell. However, Excel doesn't highlight the matched text or in any way indicate *why* it decided the cell was a match. (That's a bummer if you've got, say, 200 words crammed into a cell.) If it doesn't find a matching cell, Excel displays a message box telling you it couldn't find the requested content.

   If the first match isn't what you're looking for, you can keep looking by clicking Find Next again to move to the next match. Keep clicking Find Next to move through the worksheet. When you reach the end, Excel resumes the search at the beginning of your worksheet, potentially bringing you back to a match you've already seen. When you're finished with the search, click Close to get rid of the "Find and Replace" window.

Find All

One of the problems with searching in Excel is that you're never quite sure how many matches there are in a worksheet. Sure, clicking Find Next gets you from one cell to the next, but wouldn't it be easier for Excel to let you know right away how many matches it found?

Enter the Find All feature. With Find All, Excel searches the entire worksheet in one go, and compiles a list of matches, as shown in Figure 12-9.

The Find All button doesn't lead you through the worksheet like the find feature. It's up to you to select one of the results in the list, at which point Excel automatically moves you to the matching cell.

The Find All list won't automatically refresh itself: After you've run a Find All search, if you *add* new data to your worksheet, you need to run a new search to find any newly added terms. However, Excel does keep the text and numbers in your found-items list synchronized with any changes you make in the worksheet. For example, if you change cell D5 to Total Price, the change appears in the Value column in the found-items list *automatically*. This tool is great for editing a worksheet because you can keep track of multiple changes at a single glance.

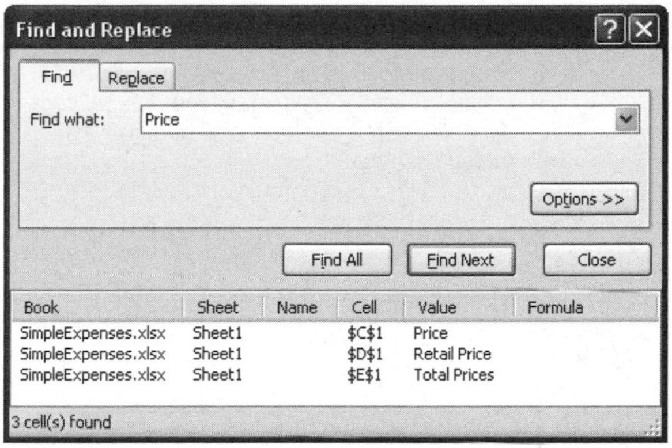

Figure 12-9:
In the example shown here, the search for Price matched three cells in the worksheet. The list shows you the complete text in the matching cell and the cell reference (for example, $C$1, which is a reference to cell C1).

Finally, the Find All feature is the heart of another great Excel guru trick: it gives you another way to change multiple cells at once. After you've performed the Find All search, select all the entries you want to change from the list by clicking them while you hold down Ctrl (this trick allows you to select several at once). Click in the formula bar, and then start typing the new value. When you're finished, hit Ctrl+Enter to apply your changes to every selected cell. Voilà—it's like "Find and Replace", but you're in control!

More Advanced Searches

Basic searches are fine if all you need to find is a glaringly unique phrase or number (*Pet Snail Names* or *10,987,654,321*). But Excel's advanced search feature gives you lots of ways to fine-tune your searches or even search more than one worksheet. To conduct an advanced search, begin by clicking the "Find and Replace" window's Options button, as shown in Figure 12-10.

You can set any or all of the following options:

• If you want your search to span multiple worksheets, go to the Within box, and then choose Workbook. The standard option, Sheet, searches all the cells in the currently active worksheet. If you want to continue the search in the other worksheets in your workbook, choose Workbook. Excel examines the worksheets from left to right. When it finishes searching the last worksheet, it loops back and starts examining the first worksheet.

• The Search pop-up menu lets you choose the direction you want to search. The standard option, By Rows, completely searches each row before moving on to the next one. That means that if you start in cell B2, Excel searches C2, D2, E2, and so on. Once it's moved through every column in the second row, it moves onto the third row and searches from left to right.

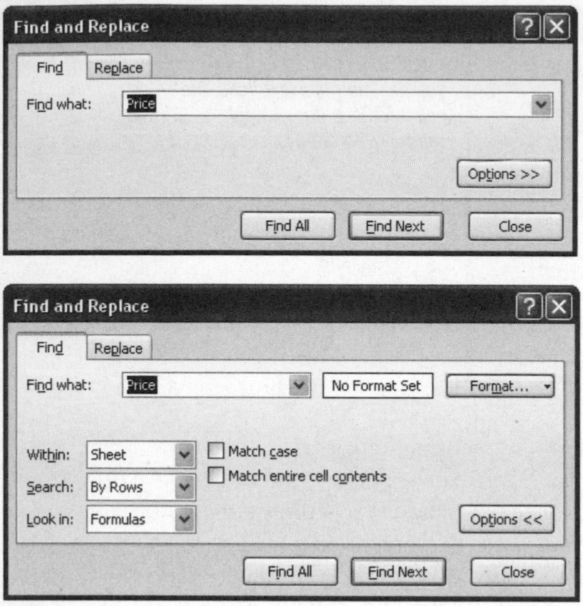

Figure 12-10:
In the standard "Find and Replace" window (top), when you click Options, Excel gives you a slew of additional settings (bottom) so you can configure things like search direction, case sensitivity, and format matching.

On the other hand, if you choose By Columns, Excel searches all the rows in the current column before moving to the next column. That means that if you start in cell B2, Excel searches B3, B4, and so on until it reaches the bottom of the column and then starts at the top of the next column (column C).

Note: The search direction determines which path Excel follows when it's searching. However, the search will still ultimately traverse every cell in your worksheet (or the current selection).

• The "Match case" option lets you specify whether capitalization is important. If you select "Match case", Excel finds only words or phrases whose capitalization matches. Thus, searching for *Date* matches the cell value *Date*, but not *date*.

• The "Match entire cell contents" option lets you restrict your searches to the entire contents of a cell. Excel ordinarily looks to see if your search term is contained *anywhere* inside a cell. So, if you specify the word *Price*, Excel finds cells containing text like *Current Price* and even *Repriced Items*. Similarly, numbers like *32* match cell values like *3253*, *10032*, and *1.321*. Turning on the "Match entire cell contents" option forces Excel to be precise.

Note: Remember, Excel searches for numbers as they're *displayed* (as opposed to looking at the underlying values that Excel uses to store numbers internally). That means that if you're searching for a number formatted using the dollar Currency format ($32.00, for example), and you've turned on the "Match entire cell contents" checkbox, you'll need to enter the number exactly as it appears on the worksheet. Thus, *$32.00* would work, but *32* alone won't help you.

Using Wildcards

Sometimes you sorta, kinda know what you're looking for—for example, a cell with some version of the word "date" in it (as in "date" or "dated" or "dating"). What you really need is a search tool that's flexible enough to keep its eyes open for results that are *similar* but not exactly alike. Power searchers will be happy to know that Excel lets you use *wildcards* in your searches. Wildcards are search symbols that let you search for variations on a word.

The asterisk (*) wildcard represents a group of one or more characters. A search for *s*nd* finds any word that begins with the letter *s* and ends with the letters *nd*; for example, it would find words like *sand*, *sound*, *send*, or even the bizarre series of characters *sgrthdnd*.

The question mark *?* wildcard represents any single character. For example, a search for *f?nd* turns up *find* or *fund*, but not *friend*.

Wildcards are particularly useful when you're using the "Match entire cell contents" option. For example, if you turn on the "Match entire cell contents" option and enter the search term *date** you'll find any cell that *starts* with the word *date*. In contrast, if you performed the same search without turning the "Match entire cell contents" option on, you'd find any cell *containing* the word *date*.

If you happen to want to search for special characters like the asterisk or the question mark, you'll need to use the tilde (~) before the wildcard. For example, the search string *~ ** searches for cells that contain the asterisk symbol.

Finding Formatted Cells

Excel's "Find and Replace" is an equal opportunity search tool: It doesn't care what the contents of a cell look like. But what if you know, for example, that the data you're looking for is formatted in bold, or that it's a number that uses the Currency format? You can use these formatting details to help Excel find the data you want and ignore cells that aren't relevant.

To use formatting details as part of your search criteria, follow these steps:

1. **Launch the Find tool.**

   Choose Home → Editing → Find & Select → Find, or press Ctrl+F. Make sure that the "Find and Replace" window is showing the advanced options (by clicking the Options button).

2. **Click the Format button next to the "Find what" search box.**

   The Find Format dialog box appears (Figure 12-11). It contains the same options as the Format Cell dialog box discussed on page 287.

3. **Specify the format settings you want to look for.**

   Using the Find Format dialog box, you can specify any combination of number format, alignment, font, fill pattern, borders, and formatting. Chapter 5 explains all these formatting settings in detail.

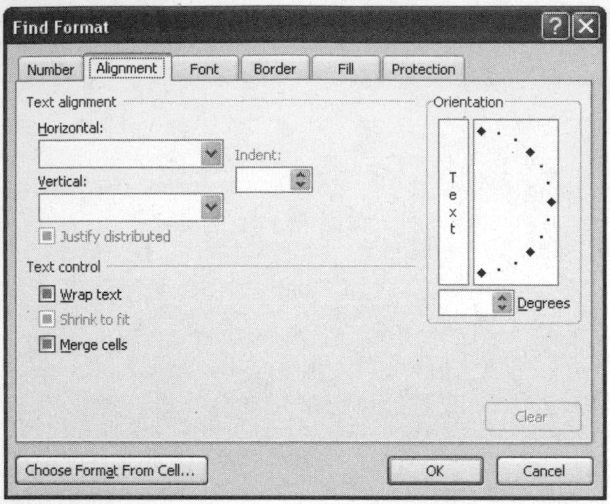

Figure 12-11:
In the Find Format dialog box, Excel won't use any formatting option that's blank or grayed out as part of it's search criteria. For example, here, Excel won't search based on alignment. Checkboxes are a little trickier. In some versions of Windows, it looks like the checkbox is filled with a solid square (as with the "Merge cells" setting in this example). In other versions of Windows, it looks like the checkbox is dimmed and checked at the same time. Either way, this visual cue indicates that Excel won't use the setting as part of its search.

4. **When you're finished, click OK to return to the "Find and Replace" window.**

   Next to the "Find what" search box, a preview appears indicating the formatting of the cell that you'll be searching for, as shown in Figure 12-12.

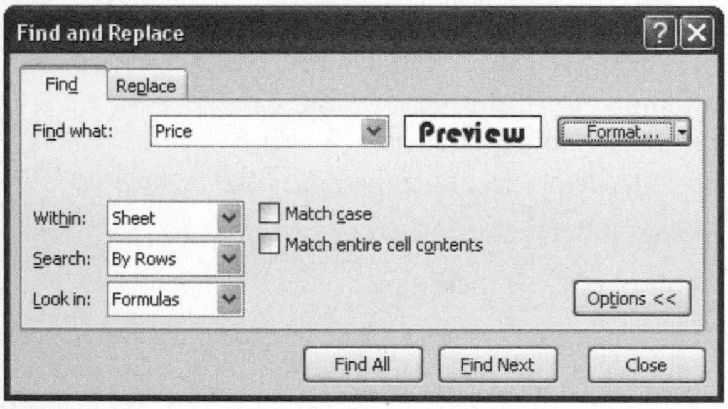

Figure 12-12:
The Find Format dialog box shows a basic preview of your formatting choices. In this example, the search will find cells containing the word Price that also use white lettering, a black background, and the Bauhaus font.

To remove these formatting restrictions, click the pop-up menu to the right of the Format button and then choose Clear Find.

Tip: Rather than specifying all the format settings manually, you can copy them from another cell. Just click the Choose Format From Cell button at the bottom of the Find Format dialog box. The pointer changes to a plus symbol with an eyedropper next to it. Next, click any cell that has the formatting you want to match. Keep in mind that when you use this approach, you copy *all* the format settings.

Finding and Replacing Values

You can use Excel's search muscles to find not only the information you're interested in, but also to modify cells quickly and easily. Excel lets you make two types of changes using its *replace* tool:

- **You can automatically change cell content.** For example, you can replace the word *Colour* with *Color* or the number *$400* with *$40*.

- **You can automatically change cell formatting.** For example, you can search for every cell that contains the word *Price* or the number *$400* and change the fill color. Or, you can search for every cell that uses a specific font, and modify these cells so they use a new font.

POWER USERS' CLINIC

Mastering the Art of Replacement

You can use the "Find and Replace" feature in many imaginative ways. Here are just a few examples:

- **You can automatically delete a specific piece of text.** Just enter the appropriate "Find what" text, and leave the "Replace with" box blank.

- **You can change the formatting used in specific cells.** Just type the same text in both the "Find what" and "Replace with" text, and then click the Format button next to the "Replace with" combo box to set some formatting attributes. (You don't need to specify any formatting settings for your "Find what" search criteria.)

- **You can change the formatting used in a series of cells.** For example, imagine you have a worksheet that has several cells bolded. Say you want to adjust the formatting of these cells to use a new font. To perform this operation, leave both the "Find what" and "Replace with" boxes blank. Then, set the formatting search criteria to look for the bold font attribute, and set the replacement formatting to use the new font. Click Replace All, and all the cells that currently have bold formatting acquire the new font. You might find mastering this technique tricky, but it's one of the most powerful formatting tricks around.

Here's how to perform a replace operation. The box below gives some super-handy tricks you can do with this process.

1. **Move to the cell where the search should begin.**

   Remember, if you don't want to search the entire spreadsheet, just select the range of cells you want to search.

2. **Choose Home → Editing → Find & Select → Replace, or press Ctrl+H.**

   The "Find and Replace" window appears, with the Replace tab selected, as shown in Figure 12-13.

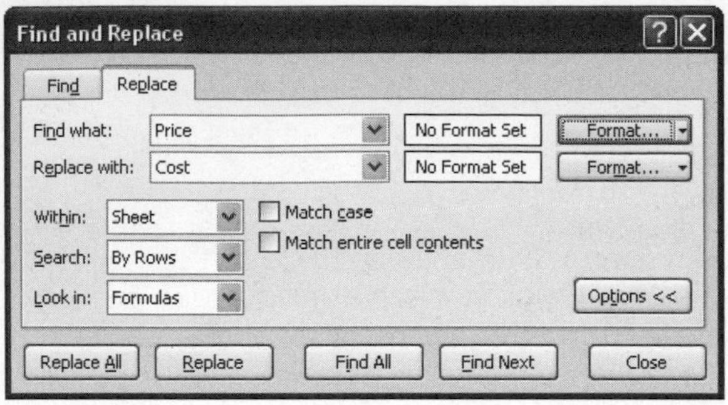

Figure 12-13:
The Replace tab looks pretty similar to the Find tab. Even the advanced options are the same. The only difference is that you also need to specify the text you want to use as a replacement for the search terms you find.

3. **In the "Find what" box, enter your search term. In the "Replace with" box, enter the replacement text.**

   Type the replacement text exactly as you want it to appear. If you want to set any advanced options, click the Options button (see the earlier sections "More Advanced Searches" and "Finding Formatted Cells" for more on your choices).

4. **Perform the search.**

   You've got four different options here. *Replace All* immediately changes all the matches your search identifies. *Replace* changes only the first matched item (you can then click Replace again to move on to subsequent matches or to select any of the other three options). *Find All* works just like the same feature described in the box on page 277. *Find Next* moves to the next match, where you can click Replace to apply your specified change, or click any of the other three buttons. The replace options are good if you're confident you want to make a change; the find options work well if you first want to see what changes you're about to make (although you can reverse either option using Ctrl+Z to fire off the Undo command).

Note: It's possible for a single cell to contain more than one match. In this case, clicking Replace replaces every occurrence of that text in the entire cell.

Spell Check

A spell checker in Excel? Is that supposed to be for people who can't spell 138 correctly? The fact is that more and more people are cramming text—column headers, boxes of commentary, lists of favorite cereal combinations—into their spreadsheets. And Excel's designers have graciously responded by providing the very same spell checker that you've probably used with Microsoft Word. As you might expect, Excel's spell checker examines only text as it sniffs its way through a spreadsheet.

Note: The same spell checker works in almost every Office application, including Word, PowerPoint, and Outlook.

To start the spell checker, follow these simple steps:

1. **Move to where you want to start the spell check.**

   If you want to check the entire worksheet from start to finish, move to the first cell. Otherwise, move to the location where you want to start checking. Or, if you want to check a portion of the worksheet, select the cells you want to check.

   Unlike the "Find and Replace" feature, Excel's spell check can check only one worksheet at a time.

2. **Choose Review → Proofing → Spelling, or press F7.**

   The Excel spell checker starts working immediately, starting with the current cell and moving to the right, going from column to column. After it finishes the last column of the current row, checking continues with the first column of the next row.

   If you don't start at the first cell (A1) in your worksheet, Excel asks you when it reaches the end of the worksheet whether it should continue checking from the beginning of the sheet. If you say yes, it checks the remaining cells and stops when it reaches your starting point (having made a complete pass through all of your cells).

When the spell check finishes, a dialog box informs you that all cells have been checked. If your cells pass the spell check, this dialog box is the only feedback you receive. On the other hand, if Excel discovers any potential spelling errors during its check, it displays a Spelling window, as shown in Figure 12-14, showing the offending word and a list of suggestions.

The Spelling window offers a wide range of choices. If you want to use the list of suggestions to perform a correction, you have three options:

- Click one of the words in the list of suggestions, and then click Change to replace your text with the proper spelling. Double-clicking the word has the same effect.

- Click one of the words in the list of suggestions, and click Change All to replace your text with the proper spelling. If Excel finds the same mistake elsewhere in your worksheet, it repeats the change automatically.

- Click one of the words in the list of suggestions, and click AutoCorrect. Excel makes the change for this cell, and for any other similarly misspelled words. In addition, Excel adds the correction to its AutoCorrect list (described on page 238). That means if you type the same unrecognized word into another cell (or even another workbook), Excel automatically corrects your entry. This option is useful if you've discovered a mistake that you frequently make.

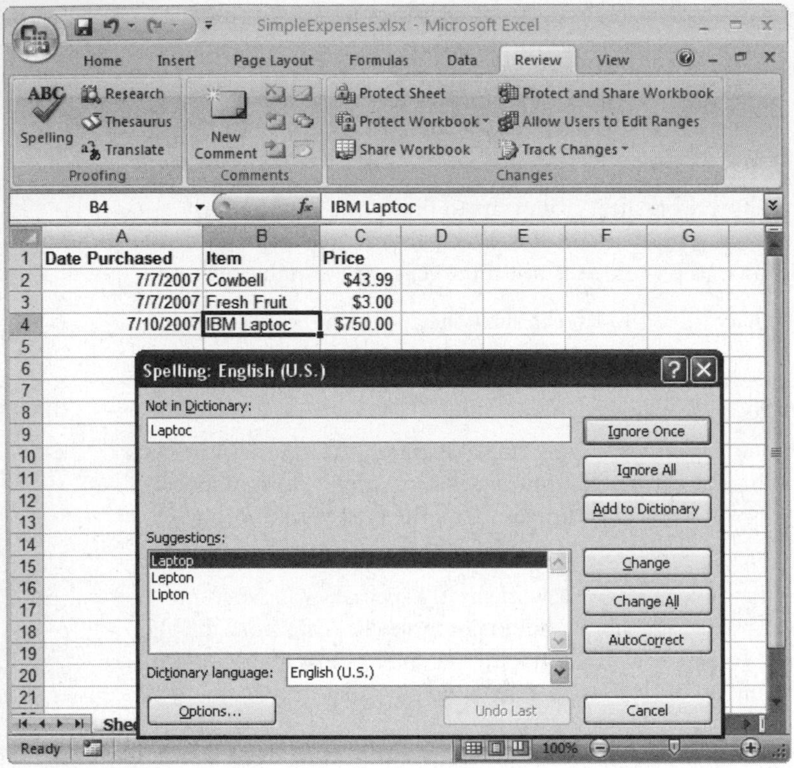

Figure 12-14:
When Excel encounters a word it thinks is misspelled, it displays the Spelling window. The cell containing the word—but not the actual word itself—gets highlighted with a black border. Excel doesn't let you edit your file while the Spelling window is active. You either have to click one of the options on the Spelling window or cancel the spell check.

Tip: If Excel spots an error but it doesn't give you the correct spelling in its list of suggestions, just type the correction into the "Not in Dictionary" box and hit Enter. Excel inserts your correction into the corresponding cell.

On the other hand, if Excel is warning you about a word that doesn't represent a mistake (like your company name or some specialized term), you can click one of the following buttons:

- **Ignore Once** skips the word and continues the spell check. If the same word appears elsewhere in your spreadsheet, Excel prompts you again to make a correction.

- **Ignore All** skips the current word and all other instances of that word throughout your spreadsheet. You might use Ignore All to force Excel to disregard something you don't want to correct, like a person's name. The nice thing about Ignore All is that Excel doesn't prompt you again if it finds the same name, but it does prompt you again if it finds a different spelling (for example, if you misspelled the name).

- **Add to Dictionary** adds the word to Excel's custom dictionary. Adding a word is great if you plan to keep using a word that's not in Excel's dictionary. (For example, a company name makes a good addition to the custom dictionary.) Not only does Excel ignore any occurrences of this word, but if it finds a similar but slightly different variation of that word, it provides the custom word in its list of suggestions. Even better, Excel uses the custom dictionary in every workbook you spell check.

- **Cancel** stops the operation altogether. You can then correct the cell manually (or do nothing) and resume the spell check later.

GEM IN THE ROUGH

Other Proofing Tools

Spreadsheet spell checking is a useful proofing tool. But Excel doesn't stop there. It piles in a few more questionable extras to help you enhance your workbooks. You'll find them all in the Review → Proofing section of the ribbon.

Along with the spellchecker, Excel offers these goodies:

- **Research.** Click this button to open a Research window, which appears on the right side of the Excel window, and lets you retrieve all kinds of information from the Web. The Research window provides a small set of Internet-driven services, including the ability to search a dictionary for a detailed definition, look in the Encarta encyclopedia, or get a delayed stock market quote from MSN Money.

- **Thesaurus.** Itching to promulgate your prodigious prolixity? (Translation: wanna use big words?) The thesaurus can help you take ordinary language and transform it into clear-as-mud jargon. Or, it can help you track down a synonym that's on the edge of your tongue. Either way, use this tool with care.

- **Translate.** Click this button to translate words or short phrases from one language to another. This feature isn't included in the standard Office installation, so you may need to have the Office DVD handy the first time you click this button.

Spell Checking Options

Excel lets you tweak how the spell checker works by letting you change a few basic options that control things like the language used and which, if any, custom dictionaries Excel examines. To set these options (or just to take a look at them), choose Office button → Excel Options, and then select the Proofing section (Figure 12-15). You can also reach these options by clicking the Spelling window's Options button while a spell check is underway.

The most important spell check setting is the language (at the bottom of the window), which determines what dictionary Excel uses. Depending on the version of Excel that you're using and the choices you made while installing the software, you might be using one or more languages during a spell check operation.

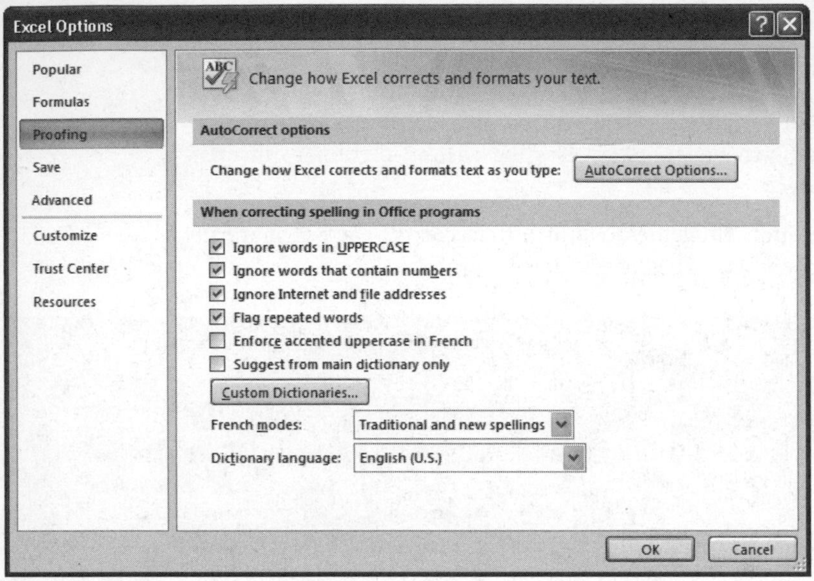

Figure 12-15:
The spell checker options allow you to specify the language and a few other miscellaneous settings. This figure shows the standard settings that Excel uses when you first install it.

Some of the other spelling options you can set include:

- **Ignore words in UPPERCASE.** If you choose this option, Excel won't bother checking any word written in all capitals (which is helpful when your text contains lots of acronyms).

- **Ignore words that contain numbers.** If you choose this option, Excel won't check words that contain numeric characters, like *Sales43* or *H3ll0*. If you don't choose this option, Excel flags these entries as errors unless you've specifically added them to the custom dictionary.

- **Ignore Internet and file addresses.** If you choose this option, Excel ignores words that appear to be file paths (like *C:\Documents and Settings*) or Web site addresses (like *http://FreeSweatSocks.com*).

- **Flag repeated words.** If you choose this option, Excel treats words that appear consecutively ("the the") as an error.

- **Suggest from main dictionary only.** If you choose this option, the spell checker doesn't suggest words from the custom dictionary. However, it still *accepts* a word that matches one of the custom dictionary entries.

You can also choose the file Excel uses to store custom words—the unrecognized words that you add to the dictionary while a spell check is underway. Excel automatically creates a file named custom.dic for you to use, but you might want to use another file if you're sharing someone else's custom dictionary. (You can use more than one custom dictionary at a time. If you do, Excel combines them all to get one list of custom words.) Or, you might want to edit the list of words if you've mistakenly added something that shouldn't be there.

To perform any of these tasks, click the Custom Dictionaries button, which opens the Custom Dictionaries dialog box (Figure 12-16). From this dialog box, you can remove your custom dictionary, change it, or add a new one.

Note: All custom dictionaries are ordinary text files with the extension .dic. Unless you tell it otherwise, Excel assumes that custom dictionaries are located in the *Application Data\Microsoft\UProof* folder in the folder Windows uses for user-specific settings. For example, if you're logged in under the user account Brad_Pitt, you'd find the custom dictionary in the *C:\Documents and Settings\Brad_Pitt\Application Data\ Microsoft\UProof* folder.

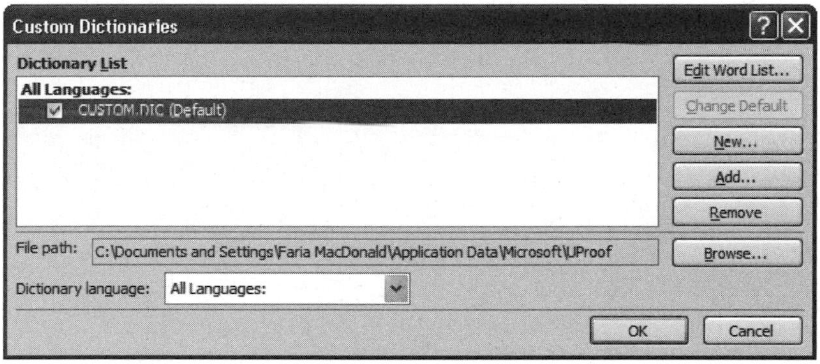

Figure 12-16:
Excel starts you off with a custom dictionary named custom.dic (shown here). To add an existing custom dictionary, click Add and browse to the file. Or, click New to create a new, blank custom dictionary. You can also edit the list of words a dictionary contains (select it and click Edit Word List). Figure 12-17 shows an example of dictionary editing.

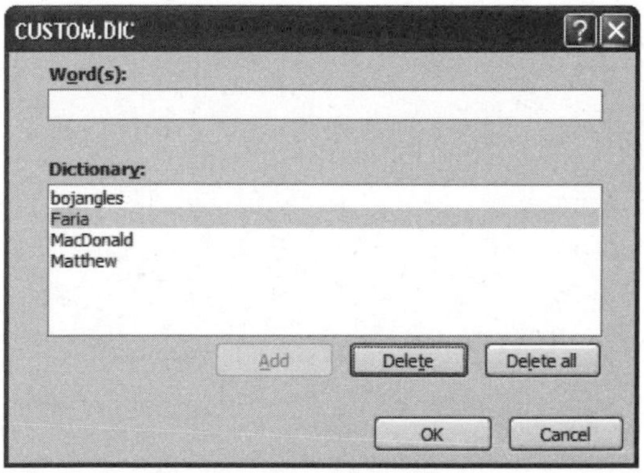

Figure 12-17:
This custom dictionary is fairly modest. It contains three names and an unusual word. Excel lists the words in alphabetical order. You can add a new word directly from this window (type in the text and click Add), remove one (select it and click Delete), or go nuclear and remove them all (click Delete All).

CHAPTER 13

Formatting Cells

When you create a basic workbook, you've taken only the first step toward mastering Excel. If you plan to print your data, email it to colleagues, or show it off to friends, you need to think about whether you've formatted your worksheets in a viewer-friendly way. The careful use of color, shading, borders, and fonts can make the difference between a messy glob of data and a worksheet that's easy to work with and understand.

But formatting isn't just about deciding, say, where and how to make your text bold. Excel also lets you control the way numerical values are formatted. In fact, there are really two fundamental aspects of formatting in any worksheet:

- **Cell appearance.** Cell appearance includes cosmetic details like color, typeface, alignment, and borders. When most people think of formatting, they think of cell appearance first.

- **Cell values.** Cell value formatting controls the way Excel displays numbers, dates, and times. For numbers, this includes details like whether to use scientific notation, the number of decimal places displayed, and the use of currency symbols, percent signs, and commas. With dates, cell value formatting determines what parts of the date are shown in the cell, and in what order.

In many ways, cell value formatting is more significant than cell appearance because it can change the meaning of your data. For example, even though 45%, $0.45, and .450 are all the same number, your spreadsheet readers will see a failing test score, a cheap price for chewing gum, and a world-class batting average.

Note: Keep in mind that regardless of how you *format* your cell values, Excel maintains an unalterable *value* for every number entered. For more on how Excel internally stores numbers, see the box on page 291.

In this chapter, you'll learn about cell value formatting, and then unleash your inner artist with cell appearance formatting. You'll also learn the most helpful ways to use formatting to improve a worksheet's readability. For information about timesaving features like the Format Painter, styles, and themes, check out *Excel 2007: The Missing Manual*.

Formatting Cell Values

Cell value formatting is one aspect of worksheet design you don't want to ignore, because the values Excel stores can differ from the numbers that it displays in the worksheet, as shown in Figure 13-1. In many cases, it makes sense to have the numbers that appear in your worksheet differ from Excel's *underlying* values, since a worksheet that's displaying numbers to, say, 13 decimal places, can look pretty cluttered.

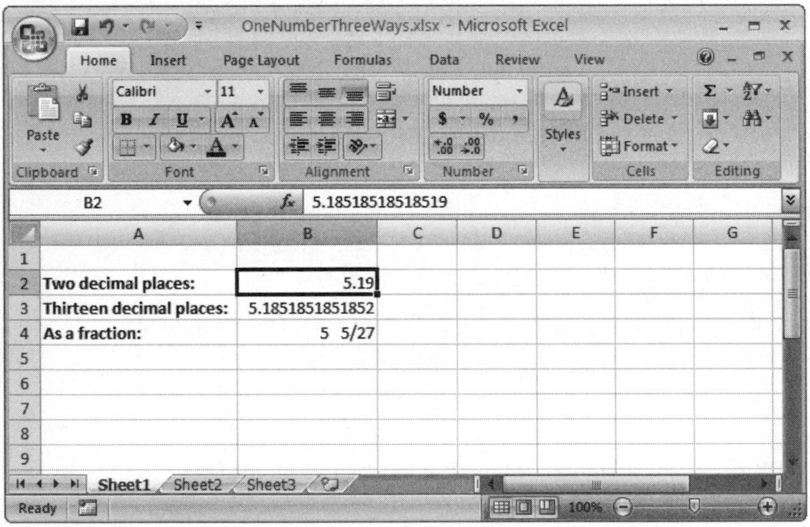

Figure 13-1:
This worksheet shows how different formatting can affect the appearance of the same data. Each of the cells B2, B3, and B4 contains the exact same number: 5.18518518518519. In the formula bar, Excel always displays the exact number it's storing, as you see here with cell B2. However, in the worksheet itself, each cell's appearance differs depending on how you've formatted the cell.

To format a cell's value, follow these steps:

1. **Select the cells you want to format.**

   You can apply formatting to individual cells or a collection of cells. Usually, you'll want to format an entire column at once because all the values in a column typically contain the same type of data. Remember, to select a column, you simply need to click the column header (the gray box at the top with the column letter).

Note: Technically, a column contains *two* types of data: the values you're storing within the actual cells and the column title in the topmost cell (where the text is). However, you don't need to worry about unintentionally formatting the column title because Excel applies number formats only to numeric cells (cells that contain dates, times, or numbers). Excel doesn't use the number format for the column title cell because it contains text.

2. **Select Home → Cells → Format → Format Cells, or just right-click the selection, and then choose Format Cells.**

   In either case, the Format Cells dialog box appears, as shown in Figure 13-2.

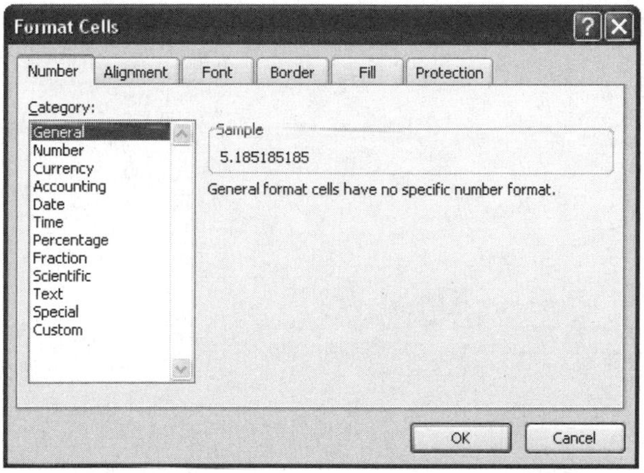

Figure 13-2:
The Format Cells dialog box provides one-stop shopping for cell value and cell appearance formatting. The first tab, Number, lets you configure how numeric values are formatted. You can use the Alignment, Font, Border, and Fill tabs to control the cell's appearance.

3. **Set the format options.**

   The Number tab's options let you choose how Excel translates the cell value into a display value. For example, you can change the number of decimal places that Excel uses to show the number. (Number formatting choices are covered in much more detail in the next section, "Formatting Numbers.")

   Most of the Format Cells dialog box's other tabs are for cell appearance formatting, which is covered later in this chapter.

Note: Once you apply formatting to a cell, it retains that formatting even if you clear the cell's contents (by selecting it and pressing Delete). In addition, formatting comes along for the ride if you copy a cell, so if you copy the content from cell A1 to cell A2, the formatting comes with it. Formatting includes both cell value formatting *and* cell appearance.

The only way to remove formatting is to highlight the cell and select Home → Editing → Clear → Clear Formats. This command removes the formatting, restoring the cell to its original, General number format (which you'll learn more about next), but it doesn't remove any of the cell's content.

4. **Click OK.**

   Excel applies your formatting changes and changes the appearance of the selected cells accordingly.

You'll spend a lot of time in this chapter at the Format Cells dialog box. As you've already seen, the most obvious way to get there is to choose Home → Format → Cells → Format Cells. However, your mouse finger's sure to tire out with that method. Fortunately, there's a quicker route—you can use one of three *dialog box launchers.* Figure 13-3 shows the way.

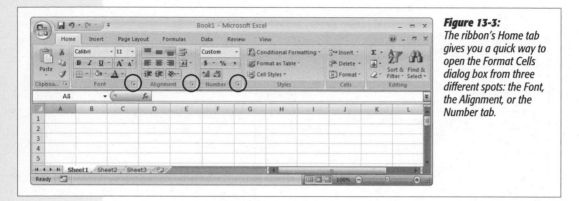

Figure 13-3:
The ribbon's Home tab gives you a quick way to open the Format Cells dialog box from three different spots: the Font, the Alignment, or the Number tab.

Formatting Numbers

In the Format Cells dialog box, the Number tab lets you control how Excel displays numeric data in a cell. Excel gives you a lengthy list of predefined formats (as shown in Figure 13-4). Remember, Excel uses number formats when the cell contains only numeric information. Otherwise, Excel simply ignores the number format. For example, if you enter *Half past 12* in a column full of times, Excel considers it plain ol' text—although, under the hood, the cell's numerical formatting stays put, and Excel uses it if you change the cell content to a time.

When you create a new spreadsheet, every cell starts out with the same number format: General. This format comes with a couple of basic rules:

• If a number has any decimal places, Excel displays them, provided they fit in the column. If the number's got more decimal places than Excel can display, then it leaves out the ones that don't fit. (It rounds up the last displayed digit, when appropriate). If you change a column width, then Excel automatically adjusts the amount of digits it displays.

• Excel removes leading and trailing zeros. Thus, 004.00 becomes 4. The only exception to this rule occurs with numbers between –1 and 1, which retain the 0 before the decimal point. For example, Excel displays the number .42 as 0.42.

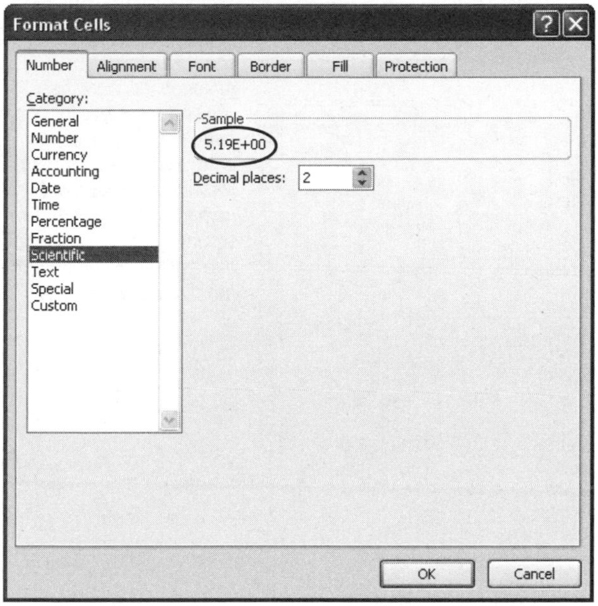

Figure 13-4:
You can learn about the different number formats by selecting a cell that already has a number in it, and then choosing a new number format from the Category list (Home → Cells → Format → Format Cells). When you do so, Excel uses the Format Cells dialog box to show how it'll display the number if you apply that format. In this example, you see that the cell value, 5.18518518518519, will appear as 5.19E+00, which is scientific notation with two decimal places.

As you saw in Chapter 10, the way you type in a number can change a cell's formatting. For example, if you enter a number with a currency symbol, the number format of the cell changes automatically to Currency. Similarly, if you enter three numbers separated by dashes (-) or backward slashes (/), Excel assumes you're entering a date, and adjusts the number format to Date.

However, rather than rely on this automatic process, it's far better just to enter ordinary numbers and set the formatting explicitly for the whole column. This approach prevents you from having different formatting in different cells (which can confuse even the sharpest spreadsheet reader), and it makes sure you get exactly the formatting and precision you want. You can apply formatting to the column before or after you enter the numbers. And it doesn't matter if a cell is currently empty; Excel still keeps track of the number format you've applied.

Different number formats provide different options. For example, if you choose the Currency format, then you can choose from dozens of currency symbols. When you use the Number format, you can choose to add commas (to separate groups of three digits) or parentheses (to indicate negative numbers). Most number formats let you set the number of decimal places.

The following sections give a quick tour of the predefined number formats available in the Format Cells dialog box's Number tab. Figure 13-5 gives you an overview of how different number formats affect similar numbers.

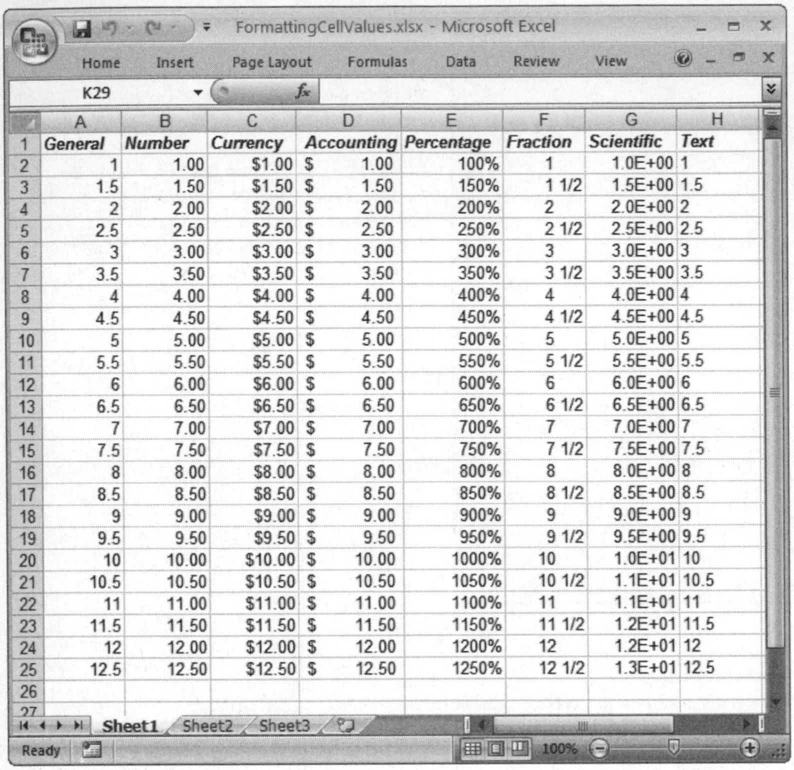

	A	B	C	D	E	F	G	H
1	General	Number	Currency	Accounting	Percentage	Fraction	Scientific	Text
2	1	1.00	$1.00	$ 1.00	100%	1	1.0E+00	1
3	1.5	1.50	$1.50	$ 1.50	150%	1 1/2	1.5E+00	1.5
4	2	2.00	$2.00	$ 2.00	200%	2	2.0E+00	2
5	2.5	2.50	$2.50	$ 2.50	250%	2 1/2	2.5E+00	2.5
6	3	3.00	$3.00	$ 3.00	300%	3	3.0E+00	3
7	3.5	3.50	$3.50	$ 3.50	350%	3 1/2	3.5E+00	3.5
8	4	4.00	$4.00	$ 4.00	400%	4	4.0E+00	4
9	4.5	4.50	$4.50	$ 4.50	450%	4 1/2	4.5E+00	4.5
10	5	5.00	$5.00	$ 5.00	500%	5	5.0E+00	5
11	5.5	5.50	$5.50	$ 5.50	550%	5 1/2	5.5E+00	5.5
12	6	6.00	$6.00	$ 6.00	600%	6	6.0E+00	6
13	6.5	6.50	$6.50	$ 6.50	650%	6 1/2	6.5E+00	6.5
14	7	7.00	$7.00	$ 7.00	700%	7	7.0E+00	7
15	7.5	7.50	$7.50	$ 7.50	750%	7 1/2	7.5E+00	7.5
16	8	8.00	$8.00	$ 8.00	800%	8	8.0E+00	8
17	8.5	8.50	$8.50	$ 8.50	850%	8 1/2	8.5E+00	8.5
18	9	9.00	$9.00	$ 9.00	900%	9	9.0E+00	9
19	9.5	9.50	$9.50	$ 9.50	950%	9 1/2	9.5E+00	9.5
20	10	10.00	$10.00	$ 10.00	1000%	10	1.0E+01	10
21	10.5	10.50	$10.50	$ 10.50	1050%	10 1/2	1.1E+01	10.5
22	11	11.00	$11.00	$ 11.00	1100%	11	1.1E+01	11
23	11.5	11.50	$11.50	$ 11.50	1150%	11 1/2	1.2E+01	11.5
24	12	12.00	$12.00	$ 12.00	1200%	12	1.2E+01	12
25	12.5	12.50	$12.50	$ 12.50	1250%	12 1/2	1.3E+01	12.5
26								

Figure 13-5: *Each column contains the same list of numbers. Although this worksheet shows an example for each number format (except dates and times), it doesn't show all your options. Each number format has its own settings (like the number of decimal places) that affect how Excel displays data.*

General

The General format is Excel's standard number format; it applies no special formatting other than the basic rules described in the box on page 291. General is the only number format (other than Text) that doesn't limit your data to a fixed number of decimal places. That means if you want to display numbers that differ wildly in precision (like 0.5, 12.334, and 0.120986398), it makes sense to use General format. On the other hand, if your numbers have a similar degree of precision (for example, if you're logging the number of miles you run each day), the Number format makes more sense.

Number

The Number format is like the General format but with three refinements. First, it uses a fixed number of decimal places (which you set). That means that the decimal point always lines up (assuming you've formatted an entire column). The Number format also allows you to use commas as a separator between groups of three digits, which is handy if you're working with really long numbers. Finally, you can choose to have negative numbers displayed with the negative sign, in parentheses, or in red lettering.

The Relationship Between Formatting and Values

The format that you choose for a number doesn't affect Excel's internal storage of that number. For example, if a cell contains the fraction 1/3, then Excel stores this value as 0.333333333333333. (The exact number of decimal places varies, depending on the number you've entered, due to the slight approximations computers need to make when converting fractional numbers into 0s and 1s.) When deciding how to format a cell, you may choose to show only two decimal places, in which case the number appears in your worksheet as 0.33. Or, maybe you choose just one decimal place, in which case the number is simply 0.3. In both cases, Excel still keeps the full 15 or so decimal places on hand. To tell the difference between the displayed number and the real number that Excel stores behind the scenes, just move to the cell. Then look at the formula bar, which always shows you the real deal.

Because of this difference between the stored value and the displayed number, there may be some situations in which it looks like Excel's making a mistake. For example, imagine you have three cells, and each stores 0.333333333333333 but displays only 0.3. When you add these three cell values

together, you won't end up with 0.3 + 0.3 + 0.3 = 0.9. Instead, you'll add the more precise stored values and end up with a number that's infinitesimally close to, but not quite, 1. Excel rounds this number up to 1.

This is almost always the way you want Excel to work because you know full well that if you add up 1/3 three times you end up with 1. But, if you need to, you can change this behavior.

To change what Excel does, select Office button → Excel Options, chose the Advanced section, and then scroll down to the "When calculating this workbook" group of settings. A "Set precision as displayed" checkbox appears. When you turn on this checkbox, Excel adjusts all the values in your current spreadsheet so that the stored value matches the displayed value. Unfortunately, with this choice, you'll get less precise data. For example, if you use this option with the 1/3 example, Excel stores the display value 0.3 instead of 0.333333333333333. Because you can't reverse this change, Excel warns you and asks for a final confirmation when you try to apply the "Precision as displayed" setting.

Currency

The Currency format closely matches the Number format, with two differences. First, you can choose a currency symbol (like the dollar sign, pound symbol, Euro symbol, and so on) from an extensive list; Excel displays the currency symbol before the number. Second, the Currency format always includes commas. The Currency format also supports a fixed number of decimal places (chosen by you), and it allows you to customize how negative numbers are displayed.

Accounting

The Accounting format is modeled on the Currency format. It also allows you to choose a currency symbol, uses commas, and has a fixed number of decimal places. The difference is that the Accounting format uses a slightly different alignment. The currency symbol is always at the far left of the cell (away from the number), and there's always an extra space that pads the right side of the cell. Also, the Accounting format always shows negative numbers in parentheses, which is an accounting standard. Finally, the number 0 is never shown when using the

Accounting format. Instead, a dash (-) is displayed in its place. There's really no reason to prefer the Currency or the Accounting format. Think of it as a personal decision, and choose whichever looks nicest on your worksheet. The only exception is if you happen to *be* an accountant, in which case you really have no choice in the matter—stick with your namesake.

Percentage

The Percentage format displays fractional numbers as percentages. For example, if you enter 0.5, that translates to 50%. You can choose the number of decimal places to display.

There's one trick to watch out for with the Percentage format. If you forget to start your number with a decimal, then Excel quietly "corrects" your numbers. For example, if you type 4 into a cell that uses the Percentage format, Excel interprets this as 4%. As a result, it actually stores the value 0.04. A side effect of this quirkiness is that if you want to enter percentages larger than 100%, you can't enter them as decimals. For example, to enter 200%, you need to type in 200 (not 2.00).

Fraction

The Fraction format displays your number as a fraction instead of a number with decimal places. The Fraction format doesn't mean you have to enter the number as a fraction (although you can if you want by using the forward slash, like 3/4). Instead it means that Excel converts any number you enter and display it as a fraction. Thus, to have 1/4 appear you can either enter .25 or 1/4.

Note: If you try to enter 1/4 and you *haven't* formatted the cell to use the Fraction number format, then you won't get the result you want. Excel assumes you're trying to enter a date (in this case, January 4th of the current year). To avoid this misunderstanding, change the number format *before* you type in your fraction. Or, enter it as *0 1/4* (zero and one quarter).

People often use the Fraction format for stock market quotes, but it's also handy for certain types of measurements (like weights and temperatures). When using the Fraction format, Excel does its best to calculate the closest fraction, which depends on a few factors including whether an exact match exists (entering .5 always gets you 1/2, for example) and what type of precision level you've picked when selecting the Fraction formatting.

You can choose to have fractions with three digits (for example, 100/200), two digits (10/20), or just one digit (1/2), using the top three choices in the Type list. For example, if you enter the number 0.51, Excel shows it as 1/2 in one-digit mode, and the more precise 51/100 in three-digit mode. In some cases, you may want all numbers to use the same denominator (the bottom number in the fraction) so that it's easy to compare different numbers. (Don't you wish Excel had been around when you were in grammar school?) In this case, you can choose to show all fractions as halves (with a denominator of 2), quarters (a denominator of 4), eighths (8), sixteenths (16), tenths (10), and hundredths (100). For example, the number 0.51 would be shown as 2/4 if you chose quarters.

Tip: Entering a fraction in Excel can be awkward because Excel may attempt to convert it to a date. To prevent this confusion, always start by entering 0 and then a space. For example, instead of typing 2/3 enter 0 2/3 (which means zero and two-thirds). If you have a whole number and a fraction, like 1 2/3, you'll also be able to duck the date confusion.

Scientific

The Scientific format displays numbers using scientific notation, which is ideal when you need to handle numbers that range widely in size (like 0.0003 and 300) *in the same column*. Scientific notation displays the first non-zero digit of a number, followed by a fixed number of digits, and then indicates what power of 10 that number needs to be multiplied by to generate the original number. For example, 0.0003 becomes 3.00×10^{-4} (displayed in Excel as 3.00E-04). The number 300, on the other hand, becomes 3.00×10^{2} (displayed in Excel as 3.00E02). Scientists—surprise, surprise—like the Scientific format for doing things like recording experimental data or creating mathematical models to predict when an incoming meteor will graze the Earth.

Text

Few people use the Text format for numbers, but it's certainly possible to do so. The Text format simply displays a number as though it were text, although you can still perform calculations with it. Excel shows the number exactly as it's stored internally, positioning it against the left edge of the column. You can get the same effect by placing an apostrophe before the number (although that approach won't allow you to use the number in calculations).

Formatting Dates and Times

Excel gives you lots of options here. You can use everything from compact styles like 3/13/07 to longer formats that include the day of the week, like Sunday, March 13, 2007. Time formats give you a similar range of options, including the ability to use a 12-hour or 24-hour clock, show seconds, show fractional seconds, and include the date information.

To format dates and times, first open the Format Cells dialog box shown in Figure 13-7 (Home → Cells → Format → Format Cells). Choose Date or Time from the column on the left and then choose the format from the list on the right. Date and Time both provide a slew of options.

Shortcuts in the Ribbon

You don't need to waste hours jumping between your worksheet and the Format Cells dialog box. The ribbon gets you to some of the most commonly used number formats in the Home → Number section.

The Home → Number section's most prominent part is the drop-down list of number formats (Figure 13-6). Just underneath are buttons that let you apply one of the three most common formats: Accounting, Percent, or Number. Just to the right are two buttons that let you increase or decrease the number of decimal places that you see at once.

One of the neatest features is the list of currency options for the Accounting button. If you click the drop-down arrow on the Accounting button (which looks like a dollar sign), then you see a list with different currency symbols you can choose (like Pounds, Euros, Chinese Yuan, and so on). But if you click the other portion of the Accounting button (not the arrow), then you get the currency symbol that's appropriate based on your computer's regional settings.

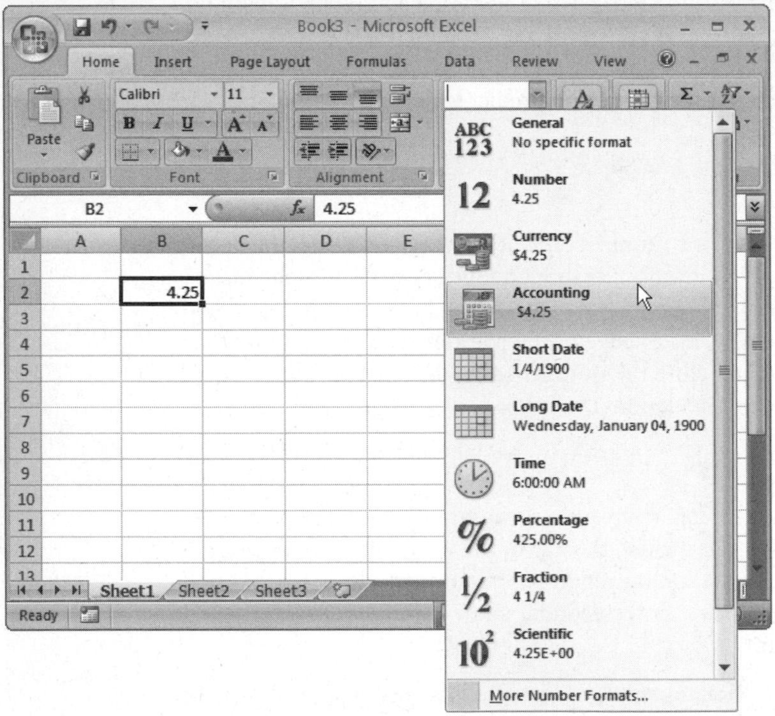

Figure 13-6:
The all-around quickest way to apply a number format is to select some cells, and then, from the number format list, choose an option. Best of all, you see a small preview of what the value in the first selected cell will look like if you apply the format.

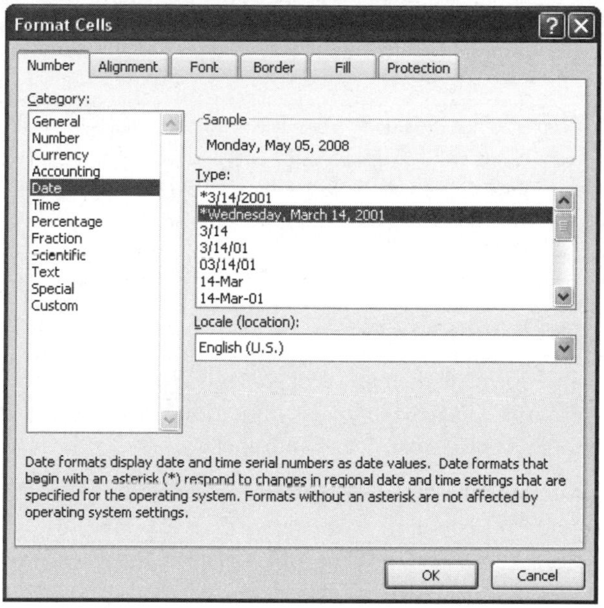

Figure 13-7:
Excel gives you dozens of different ways to format dates and times. You can choose between formats that modify the date's appearance depending on the regional settings of the computer viewing the Excel file, or you can choose a fixed date format. When using a fixed date format, you don't have to stick to the U.S. standard. Instead, choose the appropriate region from the Locale list box. Each locale provides its own set of customized date formats.

Excel has essentially two types of date and time formats:

- **Formats that take the regional settings of the spreadsheet viewer's computer into account.** With these formats, dates display differently depending on the computer that's running Excel. This choice is a good one because it lets everyone see dates in just the way they want to, which means no time-consuming arguments about month-day-year or day-month-year ordering.

- **Formats that *ignore* the regional settings of individual computers.** These formats define a fixed pattern for month, day, year, and time components, and display date-related information in exactly the same way on all computers. If you need to absolutely make sure a date is in a certain format, use this choice.

The first group (the formats that rely on a computer's regional settings) is the smallest. It includes two date formats (a compact, number-only format and a long, more descriptive format) and one time format. In the Type list, these formats are at the top and have an asterisk next to them.

The second group (the formats that are independent of a computer's regional settings) is much more extensive. In order to choose one of these formats, you first select a region from the Locale list, and then you select the appropriate date or time format. Some examples of locales include "English (United States)" and "English (United Kingdom)."

If you enter a date without specifically formatting the cell, Excel usually uses the short region-specific date format. That means that the order of the month and year vary depending on the regional settings of the current computer. If you incorporate the month name (for example, January 1, 2007), instead of the month number (for example, 1/1/2007), Excel uses a medium date format that includes a month abbreviation, like 1-Jan-2007.

Note: You may remember from Chapter 10 that Excel stores a date internally as the cumulative number of days that have elapsed since a certain long-ago date that varies by operating system. You can take a peek at this internal number using the Format Cells dialog box. First, enter your date. Then, format the cell using one of the number formats (like General or Number). The underlying date number appears in your worksheet where the date used to be.

Special Formats for Special Numbers

You wouldn't ever want to perform mathematical operations with some types of numeric information. For example, it's hard to image a situation where you'd want to add or multiply phone numbers or Social Security numbers.

When entering these types of numbers, therefore, you may choose to format them as plain old text. For example, you could enter the text (555) 123-4567 to represent a phone number. Because of the parentheses and the dash (-), Excel won't interpret this information as a number. Alternatively, you could just precede your value with an apostrophe (') to explicitly tell Excel that it should be treated as text (you might do this if you don't use parentheses or dashes in a phone number).

But whichever solution you choose, you're potentially creating more work for yourself because you have to enter the parentheses and the dash for each phone number you enter (or the apostrophe). You also increase the likelihood of creating inconsistently formatted numbers, especially if you're entering a long list of them. For example, some phone numbers may end up entered in slightly similar but somewhat different formats, like 555-123-4567 and (555)1234567.

To avoid these problems, apply Excel's Special number format (shown in Figure 13-8), which converts numbers into common patterns. And lucky you: In the Special number format, one of the Type options is Phone Number (other formats are for Zip codes and Social Security numbers).

Formatting Cell Appearance

Formatting cell values is important because it helps maintain consistency among your numbers. But to really make your spreadsheet readable, you're probably going to want to enlist some of Excel's tools for controlling things like alignment, color, and borders and shading.

To format a cell's appearance, first select the single cell or group of cells that you want to work with, and then choose Home → Cells → Format → Format Cells, or just right-click the selection, and then choose Format Cells. The Format Cells dialog box that appears is the place where you adjust your settings.

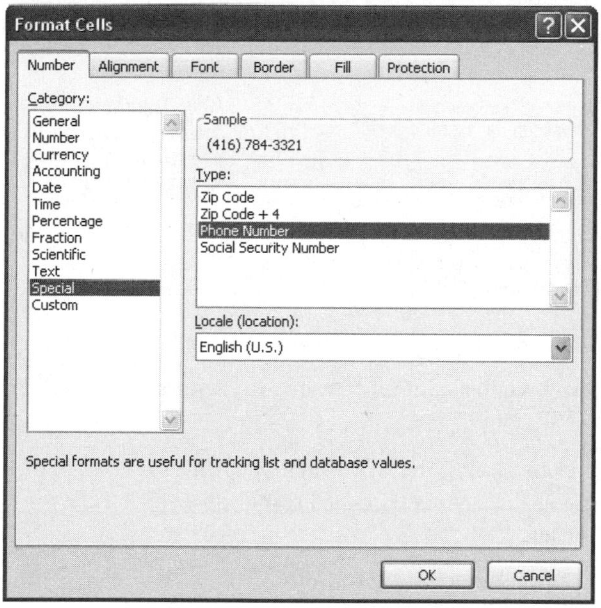

Figure 13-8:
Special number formats are ideal for formatting sequences of digits into a common pattern. For example, in the Type list, if you choose Phone Number, then Excel converts the sequence of digits 5551234567 into the proper phone number style—(555) 123-4567—with no extra work required on your part.

Tip: Even a small amount of formatting can make a worksheet easier to interpret by drawing the viewer's eye to important information. Of course, as with formatting a Word document or designing a Web page, a little goes a long way. Don't feel the need to bury your worksheet in exotic colors and styles just because you can.

Alignment and Orientation

As you learned in the previous chapter, Excel automatically aligns cells according to the type of information you've entered. But what if this default alignment isn't what you want? Fortunately, in the Format Cells dialog box, the Alignment tab lets you easily change alignment as well as control some other interesting settings, like the ability to rotate text.

Excel lets you control the position of content between a cell's left and right borders, which is known as the *horizontal alignment*. Excel offers the following choices for horizontal alignment, some of which are shown in Figure 13-9:

- **General** is the standard type of alignment; it aligns cells to the right if they hold numbers or dates and to the left if they hold text. You learned about this type of alignment in Chapter 10.

- **Left (Indent)** tells Excel to always line up content with the left edge of the cell. You can also choose an indent value to add some extra space between the content and the left border.

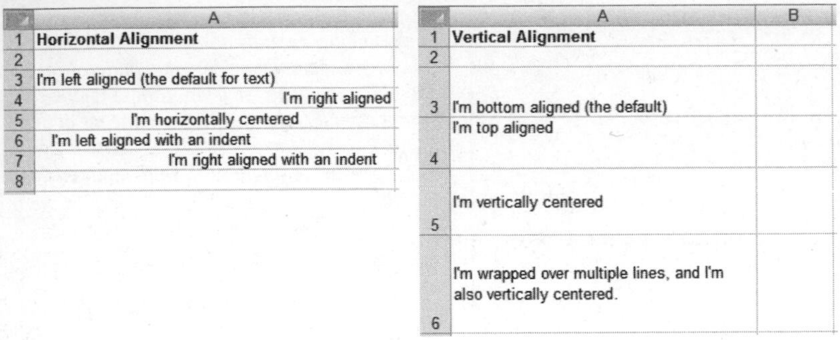

Figure 13-9:

Left: Horizontal alignment options in action.

Right: This sheet shows how vertical alignment and cell wrapping work with cell content.

- **Center** tells Excel to always center content between the left and right edges of the cell.

- **Right (Indent)** tells Excel to always line up content with the right edge of the cell. You can also choose an indent value to add some extra space between the content and the right border.

- **Fill** copies content multiple times across the width of the cell, which is almost never what you want.

- **Justify** is the same as Left if the cell content fits on a single line. When you insert text that spans more than one line, Excel *justifies* every line except the last one, which means Excel adjusts the space between words to try and ensure that both the right and left edges line up.

- **Center Across Selection** is a bit of an oddity. When you apply this option to a single cell, it has the same effect as Center. If you select more than one adjacent cell in a row (for example, cell A1, A2, A3), this option centers the value in the first cell so that it appears to be centered over the full width of all cells. However, this happens only as long as the other cells are blank. This setting may confuse you a bit at first because it can lead to cell values being displayed over cells in which they aren't stored. Another approach to centering large text titles and headings is to use cell merging (as described in the box on page 300).

- **Distributed (Indent)** is the same as Center—if the cell contains a numeric value or a single word. If you add more than one word, then Excel enlarges the spaces between words so that the text content fills the cell perfectly (from the left edge to the right edge).

Vertical alignment controls the position of content between a cell's top and bottom border. Vertical alignment becomes important only if you enlarge a row's height so that it becomes taller than the contents it contains. To change the height of a row, click the bottom edge of the row header (the numbered cell on the left side of the worksheet), and drag it up or down. As you resize the row, the content stays fixed at the bottom. The vertical alignment setting lets you adjust the cell content's positioning.

Excel gives you the following vertical alignment choices, some of which are shown in Figure 13-9:

- **Top** tells Excel that the first line of text should start at the top of the cell.

- **Center** tells Excel that the block of text should be centered between the top and bottom border of the cell.

- **Bottom** tells Excel that the last line of text should end at the bottom of the cell. If the text doesn't fill the cell exactly, then Excel adds some padding to the top.

- **Justify** is the same as Top for a single line of text. When you have more than one line of text, Excel increases the spaces between each line so that the text fills the cell completely from the top edge to the bottom edge.

- **Distributed** is the same as Justify for multiple lines of text. If you have a single line of text, this is the same as Center.

If you have a cell containing a large amount of text, you may want to increase the row's height so you can display multiple lines. Unfortunately, you'll notice that enlarging a cell doesn't automatically cause the text to flow into multiple lines and fill the newly available space. But there's a simple solution: just turn on the "Wrap text" checkbox (on the Alignment tab of the Format Cells dialog box). Now, long passages of text flow across multiple lines. You can use this option in conjunction with the vertical alignment setting to control whether Excel centers a block of text, or lines it up at the bottom or top of the cell. Another option is to explicitly split your text into lines. Whenever you want to insert a line break, just press Alt+Enter, and start typing the new line.

Tip: After you've expanded a row, you can shrink it back by double-clicking the bottom edge of the row header. When you haven't turned on text wrapping, this action shrinks the row back to its standard single-line height.

Finally, the Alignment tab allows you to rotate content in a cell up to 180 degrees, as shown in Figure 13-10. You can set the number of degrees in the Orientation box on the right of the Alignment tab. Rotating cell content automatically changes the size of the cell. Usually, you'll see it become narrower and taller to accommodate the rotated content.

Tip: You can use the Home → Alignment section of the ribbon to quickly change alignment, indenting, rotation, and wrapping, without opening the Format Cells dialog box.

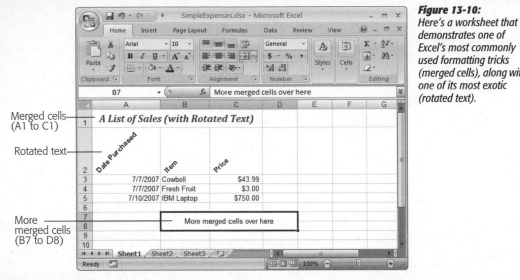

Figure 13-10:
Here's a worksheet that demonstrates one of Excel's most commonly used formatting tricks (merged cells), along with one of its most exotic (rotated text).

Merged cells (A1 to C1)

Rotated text

More merged cells (B7 to D8)

FREQUENTLY ASKED QUESTION

Shrinking Text and Merging Cells So You Can Fit More Text into a Cell

I'm frequently writing out big chunks of text that I'd love to scrunch into a single cell. Do I have any options other than text wrapping?

You betcha. When you need to store a large amount of text in one cell, text wrapping is a good choice. But it's not your only option. You can also shrink the size of the text or merge multiple cells, both from the Format Cells dialog box's Alignment tab.

To shrink a cell's contents, select the "Shrink to fit" checkbox. Be warned, however, that if you have a small column that doesn't use wrapping, this option can quickly reduce your text to vanishingly small proportions.

Joining multiple cells together removes the cells' shared borders and creates one mega-sized cell. Usually, you'll do this to accommodate a large amount of content

that can't fit in a single cell (like a long title that you want to display over every column). For example, if you merge cells A1, B1, and C1, you end up with a single cell named A1 that stretches over the full width of the A, B, and C columns, as shown in Figure 13-10.

To merge cells, select the cells you want to join, choose Home → Cells → Format → Format Cells, and then, on the Alignment tab, turn on the "Merge cells" checkbox. There's no limit to how many cells you can merge. (In fact, you can actually convert your entire worksheet into a single cell if you want to go crazy.) And if you change your mind, don't worry—you simply need to select the single merged cell, choose Home → Cells → Format → Format Cells again, and then turn off the "Merge cells" checkbox to redraw the original cells.

Fonts and Color

As in almost any Windows program, you can customize the text in Excel, applying a dazzling assortment of colors and fancy typefaces. You can do everything from enlarging headings to colorizing big numbers. Here are the individual font details you can change:

• **The font style.** (For example, Arial, Times New Roman, or something a little more shocking, like Futura Extra Bold.) Arial is the standard font for new worksheets.

• **The font size, in points.** The default point size is 10, but you can choose anything from a minuscule 1-point to a monstrous 409-point. Excel automatically enlarges the row height to accommodate the font.

• **Various font attributes, like italics, underlining, and bold.** Some fonts have complimentary italic and bold typefaces, while others don't (in which case Windows uses its own algorithm to make the font bold or italicize it).

• **The font color.** This option controls the color of the text. (Page 306 covers how to change the color of the entire cell.)

To change font settings, first highlight the cells you want to format, choose Home → Cells → Format → Format Cells, and then click the Font tab (Figure 13-11).

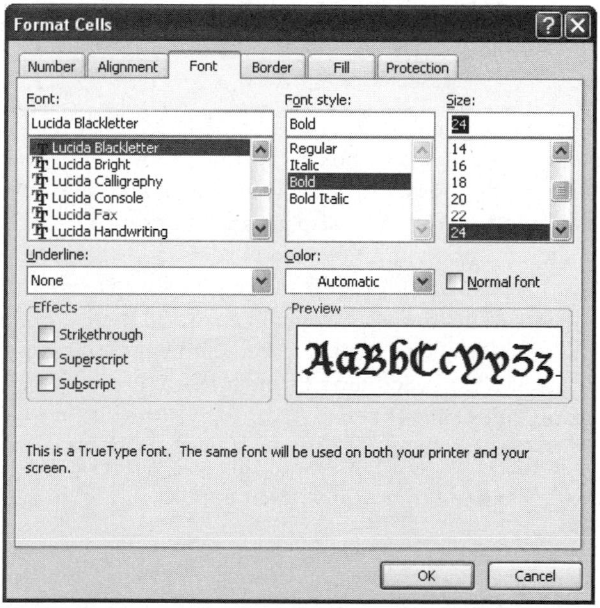

Figure 13-11:
Here's an example of how to apply an exotic font through the Format Cells dialog box. Keep in mind that when displaying data, and especially numbers, sans-serif fonts are usually clearer and look more professional than serif fonts. (Serif fonts have little embellishments, like tiny curls, on the ends of the letters; sans-serif fonts don't.) Arial, the default spreadsheet font, is a sans-serif font.

Tip: Thanks to Excel's handy Redo feature, you can repeatedly apply a series of formatting changes to different cells. After you make your changes in the Format Cells dialog box, simply select the new cell you want to format in the same way, and then hit Ctrl+Y to repeat the last action.

POWER USERS' CLINIC

Formatting Individual Characters

The ribbon lets you perform one task that you can't with the Format Cells dialog box: applying formatting to just a part of a cell. For example, if a cell contains the text "New low price", you could apply a new color or bold format to the word "low."

To apply formatting to a portion of a cell, follow these steps:

1. **Move to the appropriate cell, and then put it into edit mode by pressing F2.**

   You can also put a cell into edit mode by double-clicking it, or by moving to it and clicking inside the formula bar's text.

2. **Select the text you want to format.**

   You can select the text by highlighting it with the mouse, or by holding down Shift while using the arrow keys to mark your selection.

3. **Choose a font option from the ribbon's Home › Font section.**

   You can also change the size, the color, or the bold, italic, or underline settings. And if you don't want to waste time choosing the Home tab if you're currently somewhere else in the ribbon, then you can simply right-click the selected text to show a pop-up toolbar with font options.

   Applying multiple types of text formatting to the same cell can get tricky. The formula bar doesn't show the difference, and, when you edit the cell, you may not end up entering text in the font you want. Also, be careful that you don't apply new font formatting to the cell later; if you do, you'll wipe out all the font information you've added to the cell.

Rather than heading to the Format Cells dialog box every time you want to tweak a font, you can use the ribbon's handy shortcuts. The Home → Font section displays buttons for changing the font and font size. You also get a load of tiny buttons for applying basics like bold, italic, and underline, applying borders, and changing the text and background colors. (Truth be told, the formatting toolbar is way more convenient for setting fonts because its drop-down menu shows a long list of font names, whereas the font list in the Format Cells dialog box is limited to showing an impossibly restrictive six fonts at a time. Scrolling through that cramped space is like reading the phone book on index cards.)

Without a doubt, the most useful ribbon formatting feature is *Live Preview*, a frill that shows you the result of a change *before* you've even applied it. Figure 13-12 shows Live Preview in action.

Note: No matter what font you apply, Excel, thankfully, always displays the cell contents in the formula bar in easy-to-read Calibri font. That makes things easier if you're working with cells that've been formatted using difficult-to-decipher script fonts, or really large or small text sizes.

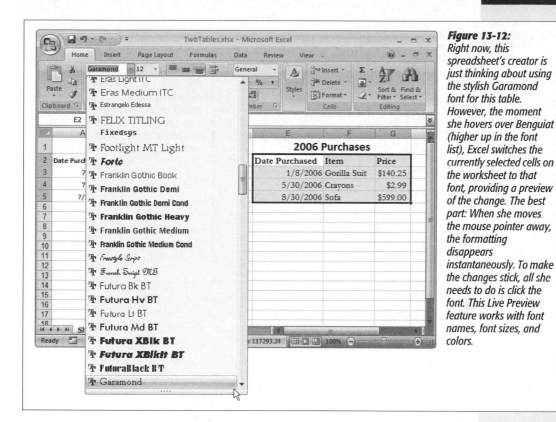

Figure 13-12:
Right now, this spreadsheet's creator is just thinking about using the stylish Garamond font for this table. However, the moment she hovers over Benguiat (higher up in the font list), Excel switches the currently selected cells on the worksheet to that font, providing a preview of the change. The best part: When she moves the mouse pointer away, the formatting disappears instantaneously. To make the changes stick, all she needs to do is click the font. This Live Preview feature works with font names, font sizes, and colors.

Special characters

Most fonts contain not only digits and the common letters of the alphabet, but also some special symbols that you can type directly on your keyboard. One example is the copyright symbol ©, which you can insert into a cell by entering the text *(C)*, and letting AutoCorrect do its work. Other symbols, however, aren't as readily available. One example is the special arrow character →. To use this symbol, you'll need the help of Excel's symbols. Simply follow these steps:

1. **Choose Insert → Text → Symbol.**

    The Symbol dialog box opens, as shown in Figure 13-13. Now it's time to hunt for the symbol you need.

2. **Choose the font and subset (the group of symbols you want to explore).**

    If you're looking for a fairly common symbol (like a mathematical sign, an arrow, an accented letter, or a fraction), you probably don't need to change the font. In the Font box, keep the default selection of "(normal text)", and then, from the Subset box at the right, choose the type of symbol. For example, choose the Arrows subset to see arrow symbols that point in different directions.

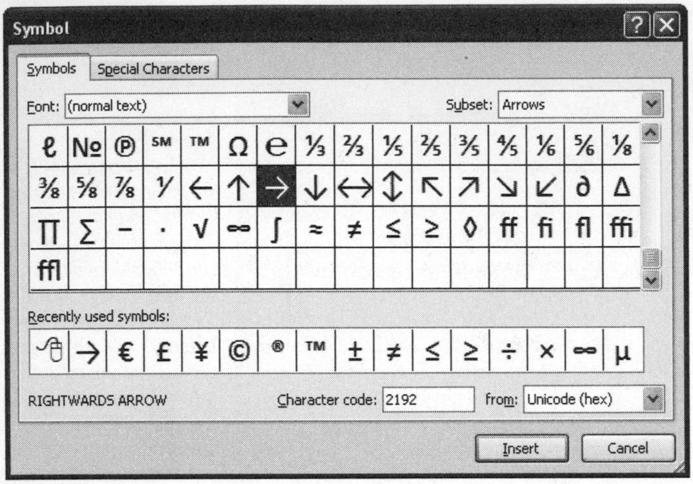

Figure 13-13:
The Symbol dialog box lets you insert one or more special characters. You can choose extended characters that are supported by most fonts (like currency symbols, non-English letters, arrows, and so on). Alternatively, you can use a font that's all about fancy characters, like the Wingdings font that's chock full of tiny graphical icons.

If you want funkier alternatives, choose a fancy font from the Font box on the left. You should be able to find at least one version of the Wingdings font in the list. Wingdings has the most interesting symbols to use. It's also the most likely to be on other people's computers, which makes a difference if you're planning to email your worksheet to other people. If you get your symbols from a really bizarre font that other people don't have, they won't be able to see your symbols.

Note: Wingdings is a special font included with Windows that's made up entirely of symbols like happy faces and stars, none of which you find in standard fonts. You can try and apply the Wingdings font on your own (by picking it from the font list), but you won't know which character to press on your keyboard to get the symbol you want. You're better off using Excel's Symbol dialog box.

3. **Select the character, and then click Insert.**

   Alternatively, if you need to insert multiple special characters, just double-click each one; doing so inserts each symbol right next to each other in the same cell without having to close the window.

Tip: If you're looking for an extremely common special character (like the copyright symbol), you can shorten this whole process. Instead of using the Symbols tab, just click over to the Special Characters tab. Then, look through the small list of commonly used symbols. If you find what you want, just select it, and then click Insert.

There's one idiosyncrasy that you should be aware of if you choose to insert symbols from another font. For example, if you insert a symbol from the Wingdings font into a cell that already has text, then you actually end up with a cell that has two fonts—one for the symbol character and one that's used for the rest of your text.

This system works perfectly well, but it can cause some confusion. For example, if you apply a new font to the cell after inserting a special character, Excel adjusts the entire contents of the cell to use the new font, and your symbol changes into the corresponding character in the new font (which usually isn't what you want). These problems can crop up any time you deal with a cell that has more than one font.

On the other hand, if you kept the font selection on "(normal text)" when you picked your symbol, you won't see this behavior. That's because you picked a more commonplace symbol that's included in the font you're already using for the cell. In this case, Excel doesn't need to use two fonts at once.

Note: When you look at the cell contents in the formula bar, you always see the cell data in the standard Calibri font. This consistency means, for example, that a Wingdings symbol doesn't appear as the icon that shows up in your worksheet. Instead, you see an ordinary letter or some type of extended non-English character, like æ.

Borders and Fills

The best way to call attention to important information isn't to change fonts or alignment. Instead, place borders around key cells or groups of cells and use shading to highlight important columns and rows. Excel provides dozens of different ways to outline and highlight any selection of cells.

Once again, the trusty Format Cells dialog box is your control center. Just follow these steps:

1. **Select the cells you want to fill or outline.**

   Your selected cells appear highlighted.

2. **Select Home → Cells → Format → Format Cells, or just right-click the selection, and then choose Format Cells.**

   The Format Cells dialog box appears.

3. **Head directly to the Border tab. (If you don't want to apply any borders, skip straight to step 4.)**

   Applying a border is a multistep process (see Figure 13-14). Begin by choosing the line style you want (dotted, dashed, thick, double, and so on), followed by the color. (Automatic picks black.) Both these options are on the left side of the tab. Next, choose where your border lines are going to appear. The Border box (where the word "Text" appears four times) functions as a nifty interactive test canvas that shows you where your lines will appear. Make your selection either by clicking one of the eight Border buttons (which contain a single bold horizontal, vertical, or diagonal line), or click directly inside the Border box. If you change your mind, clicking a border line makes it disappear.

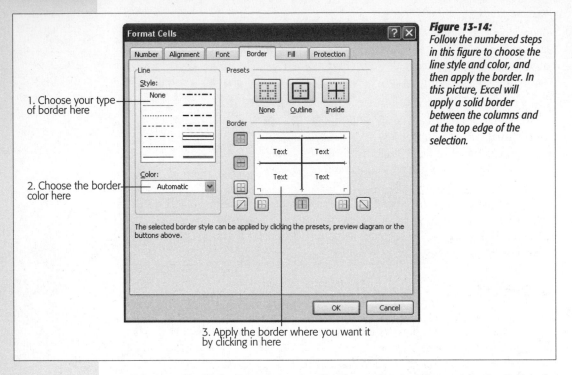

Figure 13-14:
Follow the numbered steps in this figure to choose the line style and color, and then apply the border. In this picture, Excel will apply a solid border between the columns and at the top edge of the selection.

1. Choose your type of border here

2. Choose the border color here

3. Apply the border where you want it by clicking in here

For example, if you want to apply a border to the top of your selection, click the top of the Border box. If you want to apply a line between columns inside the selection, click between the cell columns in the Border box. The line appears indicating your choice.

Tip: The Border tab also provides two shortcuts in the tab's Presets section. If you want to apply a border style around your entire selection, select Outline after choosing your border style and color. Choose Inside to apply the border between the rows and columns of your selection. Choosing None removes all border lines.

4. **Click the Fill tab.**

Here you can select the background color, pattern color, and pattern style to apply shading to the cells in the selection (see Figure 13-15). Click the No Color box to clear any current color or pattern in the selected cells.

Note: When picking a pattern color, you may notice that certain colors are described as *theme colors*. *Themes* are combinations of coordinated fonts, colors, and effects. For more on themes, check out *Excel 2007: The Missing Manual*.

To get a really fancy fill, you can use a *gradient*, which is a blend of two colors. For example, with gradients you can create a fill that starts out white on one side of a cell and gradually darkens to blue on the other. To use a gradient fill, click the Fill Effects button, and then follow the instructions in Figure 13-16.

2. Choose the pattern color here

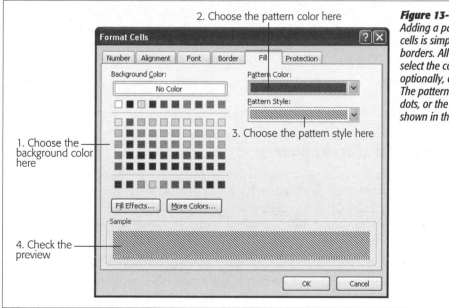

Figure 13-15:
Adding a pattern to selected cells is simpler than choosing borders. All you need to do is select the colors you want and, optionally, choose a pattern. The pattern can include a grid, dots, or the diagonal lines shown in this figure.

1. Choose the background color here

3. Choose the pattern style here

4. Check the preview

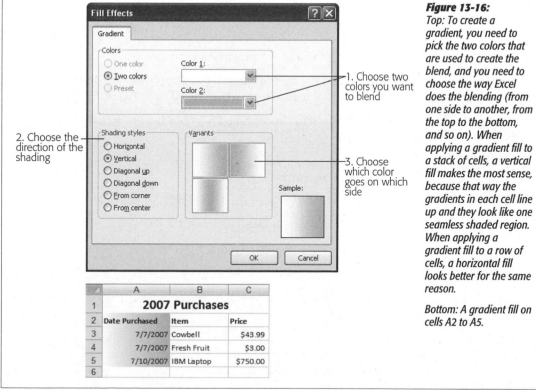

2. Choose the direction of the shading

1. Choose two colors you want to blend

3. Choose which color goes on which side

Figure 13-16:
Top: To create a gradient, you need to pick the two colors that are used to create the blend, and you need to choose the way Excel does the blending (from one side to another, from the top to the bottom, and so on). When applying a gradient fill to a stack of cells, a vertical fill makes the most sense, because that way the gradients in each cell line up and they look like one seamless shaded region. When applying a gradient fill to a row of cells, a horizontal fill looks better for the same reason.

Bottom: A gradient fill on cells A2 to A5.

5. **Click OK to apply your changes.**

   If you don't like the modifications you've just applied, you can roll back time by pressing Ctrl+Z to trigger the indispensable Undo command.

Tip: You can remove a worksheet's gridlines, which is handy when you want to more easily see any custom borders you've added. To remove gridlines, select View → Show/Hide → Gridlines. (This action affects only the current file, and won't apply to new spreadsheets.)

Drawing Borders by Hand

If you need to add a border around a cell or group of cells, the Format Cells dialog box's Border tab does the trick (see Figure 13-14). However, you could have a hard time getting the result you want, particularly if you want to add a combination of different borders around different cells. In this situation, you have a major project on your hand that requires several trips back to the Format Cells dialog box.

Fortunately, there's a little-known secret that lets you avoid the hassle: Excel's Draw Border feature. The Draw Border feature lets you draw border lines directly on your worksheet. This process is a little like working with a painting program. You pick the border style, color, and thickness, and then you drag to draw the line between the appropriate cells. When you draw, Excel applies the formatting settings to each affected cell, just as if you'd used the Borders tab.

Here's how it works:

1. **Look in the ribbon's Home → Font section for the border button.**

   The name of the border button changes to reflect whatever you used it for last. You can most easily find it by its position, as shown in Figure 13-17.

2. **Click the border button, choose Line Style, and then pick the type of line you want.**

   You can use dashed and solid lines of different thicknesses, just as you can in the Format Cells dialog box's Borders tab.

3. **Click the border button, choose Line Color, and then pick the color you want.**

   Now you're ready to start drawing.

4. **Click the border button, and then choose Draw Border.**

   When you choose Draw Border, your mouse pointer changes into a pencil icon.

5. **Using the border pencil, click a gridline where you want to place your border (Figure 13-18).**

   You can also drag side to side or up and down to draw a longer horizontal or vertical line. And if you drag your pointer down *and* to the side, you create an outside border around a whole block of cells.

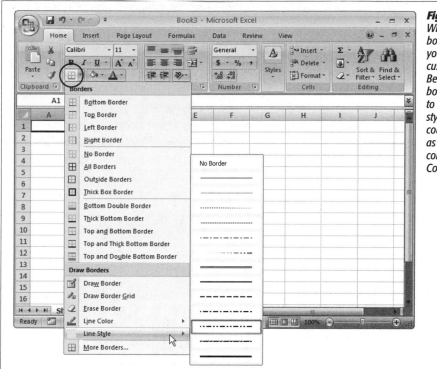

Figure 13-17:
When you click the border button (circled), you see a list of border-customizing commands. Before you draw any borders, it makes sense to customize the border style. For example, you could choose Line Style, as shown here, and for color, you'd choose Line Color.

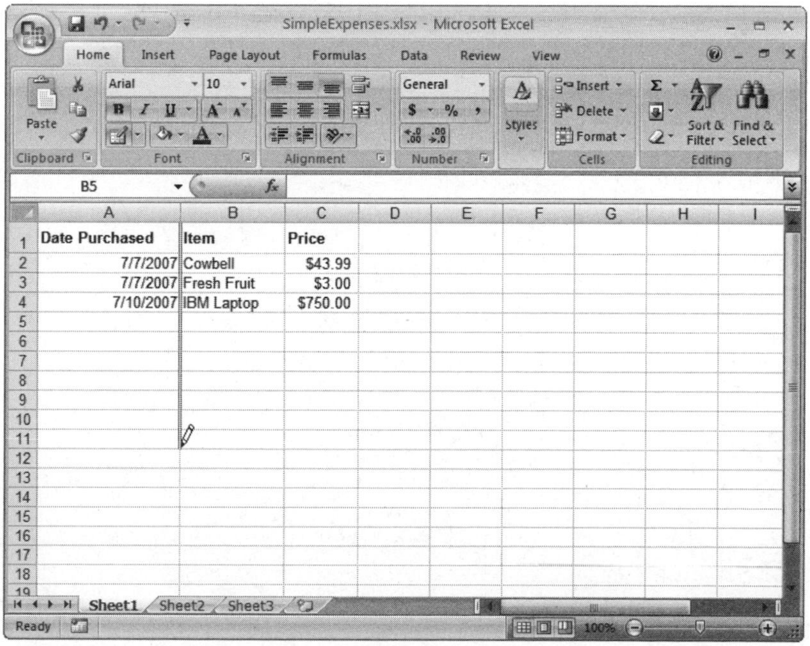

Figure 13-18:
Here, a double-line border is being drawn between column A and column B.

6. **To stop drawing, head back to the border menu, and then choose Draw Border again.**

   If you make a mistake, you can even use an eraser to tidy it all up. Just click the border button, and then choose Erase Border. The mouse pointer changes to an eraser. Now you can click the border you want to remove.

Tip: If you don't want to use the Draw Border feature, you can still make good use of the border button. Just pick a line style and line color, select some cells, and then choose an option from the border menu. For example, if you pick Bottom Border, Excel applies a border with the color and style you chose to the bottom of the current cell selection.

CHAPTER 14

Viewing and Printing Worksheets

The previous chapters have given you all the tools you need to create nicely formatted worksheets. While this is all well and good, these features can quickly bury you in an avalanche of data. If you want to see more than one part of your workbook at once, or if you want an overview of the entire worksheet, then you have to seize control of Excel's viewing features.

These features include zooming (which lets you magnify cells or just fit more information into your Excel window), panes (which let you see more than one part of a worksheet at once), and freezing (which lets you keep certain cells visible at all times). This chapter teaches you how to use all these tools, and how to store a custom view so your spreadsheet looks just the way you want it.

No matter what your worksheets look like on a screen, sometimes the best way to review them is in print. The second half of this chapter tackles printing your worksheets. You'll learn Excel's basic printing options and a few tricks that can help you preview page breaks and make sure large amounts of data get divided the way you want.

Controlling Your View

So far, most of the worksheets in this book have included only a small amount of data. But as you cram your worksheets with dozens of columns, and hundreds or even thousands of rows, editing becomes much trickier. The most challenging problems are keeping track of where you are in an ocean of information and making sure the data you want stays visible. Double that if you have multiple large worksheets in one workbook.

The following sections introduce the basic tools you can use to view your data, along with a few tips for managing large worksheets.

Zooming

Excel's zoom feature lets you control how much data you'll see in the window. When you *reduce* the zoom percentage—say from 100 percent to 10 percent— Excel shrinks your individual cells, letting you see more of them at once, which also makes it harder to read the data. Very small zoom percentages are ideal for looking at the overall layout of a worksheet. When you *increase* the zoom percentage—say from 100 percent to 200 percent—Excel magnifies your cells, letting you see more detail but fewer cells. Larger zoom percentages are good for editing.

Note: Excel lets you zoom in to 400 percent and out all the way to 10 percent.

You can most easily adjust the zoom percent by using the zoom slider in the bottom-right part of the status bar. The zoom slide also displays the current zoom percentage. But if you want to specify the exact zoom percentage by hand (say, 142 percent), then you can choose View → Zoom → Zoom. A Zoom dialog box appears (Figure 14-1).

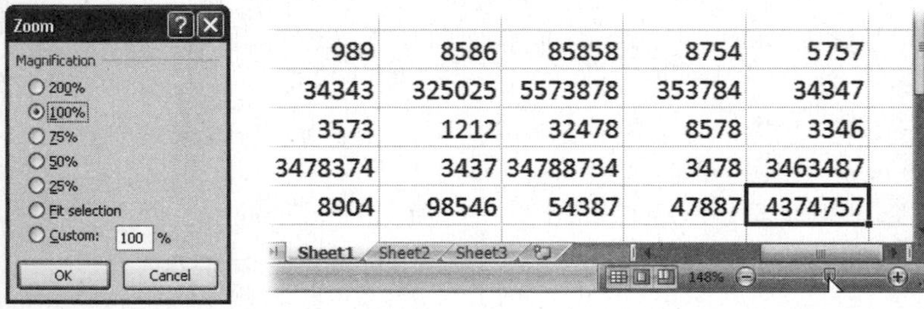

Figure 14-1:
Left: Using the Zoom dialog box, you can select a preset zoom percentage or, in the Custom box, type in your own percentage.

Right: But using the Zoom slider is almost always faster than making frequent trips to the Zoom dialog box.

The standard zoom setting is 100 percent, although other factors like the size of the font you're using and the size and resolution of your computer screen help determine how many cells fit into Excel's window. As a rule of thumb, every time you double the zoom, Excel cuts in half the number of rows you can see. Thus, if you can see 20 rows at 100 percent, then you'll see 10 rows at 200 percent.

Note: Changing the zoom affects how your data appears in the Excel window, but it won't have any effect on how your data is printed or calculated.

You can also zoom in on a range of cells. When your data extends beyond the edges of your monitor, this handy option lets you shrink a portion to fit your screen. Conversely, if you've zoomed out to get a bird's eye view of all your data, and you want to swoop in on a particular section, Excel lets you expand a portion to fit your screen. To zoom in on a group of cells, first select some cells (Figure 14-2), and then choose View → Zoom → Zoom to Selection (Figure 14-3). (You can perform this same trick by highlighting some cells, opening the Zoom dialog box, and then choosing "Fit selection.") Make sure you select a large section of the worksheet—if you select a small group, you'll end up with a truly jumbo-sized zoom.

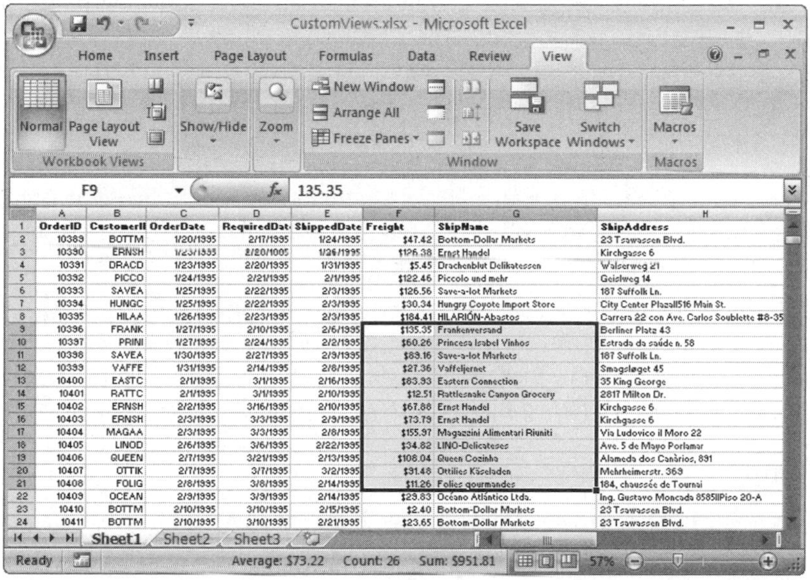

Figure 14-2:
To magnify a range of cells, select them, as shown here, and then choose View → Zoom → Zoom to Selection to have Excel expand the range to fill the entire window, as shown in Figure 14-3.

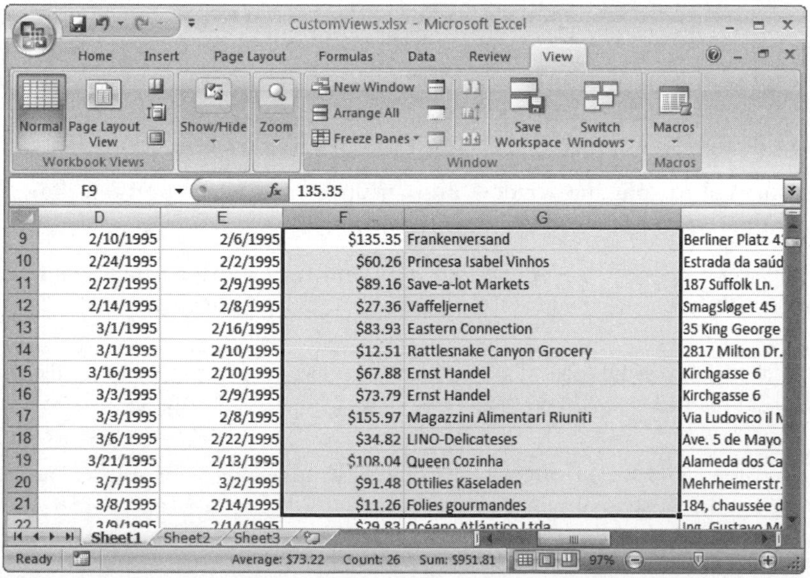

Figure 14-3:
The zoom slider (lower-right corner) shows that Excel automatically zoomed your data from 57 percent (to 97 percent in this figure).

Tip: If you're using a mouse with a scroll wheel, you can zoom with the wheel. Just hold down the Ctrl key, and roll the scroll wheel up (to zoom in) or down (to zoom out).

Viewing Distant Parts of a Spreadsheet at Once

Zooming is an excellent way to survey a large expanse of data or focus on just the important cells, but it won't help if you want to simultaneously view cells that aren't near each other. For example, if you want to focus on both row 1 and row 138 at the same time, then zooming won't help. Instead, try splitting your Excel window into multiple *panes*—separate frames that each provide a different view of the same worksheet. You can split a worksheet into two or four panes, depending on how many different parts you want to see at once. When you split a worksheet, each pane contains an identical replica of the entire worksheet. When you make a change to the worksheet in one pane, Excel automatically applies the same change in the other panes. The beauty of panes is that you can look at different parts of the same worksheet at once.

You can split a window horizontally or vertically (or both). When you want to compare different *rows* in the same worksheet, use a horizontal split. To compare different *columns* in the same worksheet, use a vertical split. And if you want to be completely crazy and see four different parts of your worksheet at once, then you can use a horizontal and a vertical split—but that's usually too confusing to be much help.

Excel gives you two ways to split the windows. Here's the easy way:

1. **Find the splitter controls on the right side of the screen.**

   Figure 14-4 shows you where to find them.

2. **Drag either control to split the window into two panes. As you drag, Excel displays a gray bar showing where it'll divide the window. Release the splitter control when you're happy with the layout. (At this point, you don't need to worry about whether you can actually view the data you want to compare; you're simply splitting up the window.)**

   If you want to split the window into an upper and lower portion, drag the horizontal control down to the location where you want to split the window.

   If you want to split the window into a left and right portion, drag the vertical control leftwards—to the location where you want to split the window.

Note: If for any reason you *do* want to split the window into four panes, use both controls. The order you follow isn't important.

If you don't like the layout you've created, simply move the splitter bars by dragging them just as you did before.

Figure 14-4:
Every Excel window
contains both horizontal
and vertical splitter
controls.

3. **Within each pane, scroll to the cells you want to see.**

   For example, if you have a 100-row table that you split horizontally in order to compare the top five rows and the bottom five, scroll to the top of the upper pane, and then scroll to the bottom of the lower pane. (Again, the two panes are replicas of each other; Excel is just showing you different parts of the same worksheet.)

Using the scroll bars in panes can take some getting used to. When the window is split in two panes, Excel synchronizes scrolling between both panes in *one direction*. For example, if you split the window into top and bottom halves, Excel gives you just one *horizontal* scroll bar (at the bottom of the screen), which controls both panes (Figure 14-5). Thus, when you scroll to the left or right, Excel moves both panes horizontally. On the other hand, Excel gives you separate *vertical* scroll bars for each pane, letting you independently move up and down within each pane.

Tip: If you want the data in one pane—for example, column titles—to remain in place, you can freeze that pane. The next section tells you how.

The reverse is true with a vertical split; in this case, you get one vertical scroll bar and two horizontal bars, and Excel synchronizes both panes when you move up or down. With four panes, life gets a little more complicated. In this case, when you scroll left or right, the frame that's just above or just below the current frame moves, too. When you scroll up or down, the frame that's to the left or to the right moves with you. Try it out.

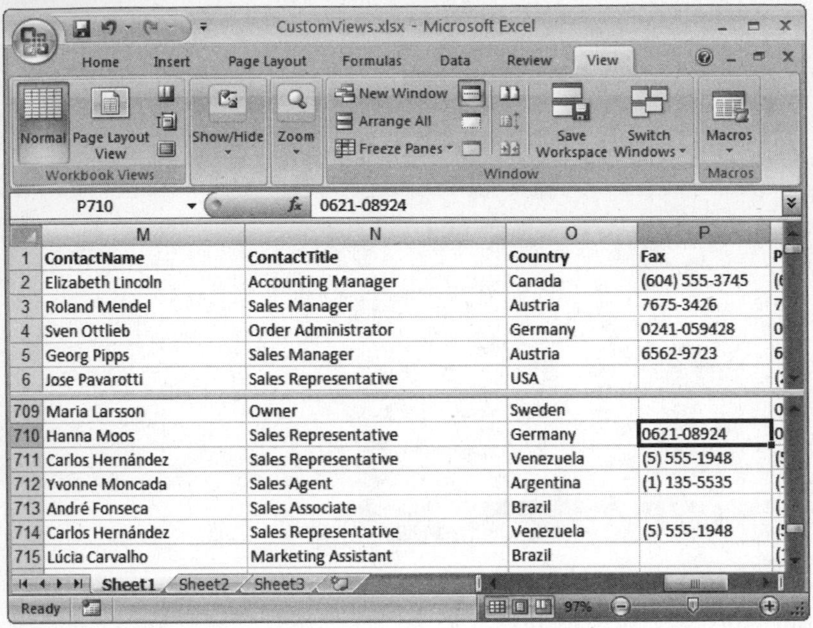

Figure 14-5:
Here you can see the data in rows 1 through 6 and rows 709 through 715 at the same time. As you move from column to column, both panes move in sync, letting you see, for instance, the phone number information in both panes at once. (You can scroll up or down separately in each pane.)

Note: If you want to remove your panes, then just drag the splitter bars back to the edges of the window, or double-click it.

You can also create panes by using the ribbon command View → Window → Split. When you do, Excel carves the window into four equal panes. You can change the pane sizes as described above, or use View → Window → Split again to return to normal.

Note: If you use Excel's worksheet navigation tools—like the Go To and Find commands—*all* your panes move to the newly found spot. For example, if you use the Find command in one pane to scroll to a new cell, the other panes display the same cell.

Freezing Columns or Rows

Excel has another neat trick up its sleeve to help you manage large worksheets: *freezing*. Freezing is a simpler way to make sure a specific set of rows or columns remains visible at all times. When you freeze data, it remains fixed in place in the Excel window, even as you move to another location in the worksheet in a different pane. For example, say you want to keep visible the first row that contains column titles. When you freeze that row, you can always tell what's in each column—even when you've scrolled down several screenfuls. Similarly, if your first column holds identifying labels, you may want to freeze it so that when you scroll off to the right, you don't lose track of what you're looking at.

OFFICE 2007: THE MISSING MANUAL

GEM IN THE ROUGH

Filling the Screen with Cells

If you really want to see the maximum number of cells at once, Excel provides a little-known feature that strips away the ribbon, the formula bar, and all other extraneous screen elements, making more room for cells. To make the switch, choose View → Workbook View → Full Screen. To return things to the way they were, right-click anywhere on the worksheet grid, and then choose Close Full Screen.

Most people find that Full Screen mode is just a little too drastic. Another good option is to collapse the ribbon, which reclaims a significant portion of screen real estate. To do so, in the ribbon, double-click any tab title. Excel hides the ribbon surface, but leaves just the tab titles above your worksheet. Even when the ribbon is collapsed, you can still use it—just click a tab title (which pops that tab back into view), and then click the command you want. The ribbon disappears again as soon as you're done. If you're an unredeemed keyboard lover, then you can use the ribbon in the same way whether it's collapsed or expanded. Just press Alt, and then follow the keytips (page 6). And if you get tired of the collapsed ribbon, you can double-click any tab title or press Ctrl+F1 to show the full ribbon once again.

Tip: Excel lets you print out worksheets with a particular row or column fixed in place. Page 333 tells you how.

You can freeze rows at the top of your worksheet, or columns at the left of your worksheet, but Excel does limit your freezing options in a few ways:

- **You can freeze rows or columns only in groups.** That means you can't freeze column A and C without freezing column B. (You can, of course, freeze just one row or column.)

- **Freezing always starts at column A (if you're freezing columns) or row 1 (if you're freezing rows).** That means that if you freeze row 13, Excel also freezes all the rows above it (1 through 12) at the top of your worksheet.

- **If a row or column isn't visible and you freeze it, you can't see it until you unfreeze it.** For example, if you scroll down so that row 100 appears at the top of the worksheet grid, and then freeze the top 100 rows, you can't see rows 1 to 99 anymore. This may be the effect you want, or it may be a major annoyance.

Note: As far as Excel is concerned, frozen rows and columns are a variation on panes (described earlier). When you freeze data, Excel creates a vertical pane for columns or a horizontal pane for rows. It then fixes that pane so you can't scroll through it.

To freeze a row or set of rows at the top of your worksheet, just follow these steps:

1. **Make sure the row or rows you want to freeze are visible and at the top of your worksheet.**

   For example, if you want to freeze rows 2 and 3 in place, make sure they're visible at the top of your worksheet. Remember, rows are frozen starting at row 1. That means that if you scroll down so that row 1 isn't visible, and you freeze row 2 and row 3 at the top of your worksheet, then Excel also freezes row 1— and keeps it hidden so you can't scroll up to see it.

---

2. **Move to the first row you want** *unfrozen*, **and then move left to column A.**

   At this point, you're getting into position so that Excel knows where to create the freeze.

3. **Select View → Freeze Panes → Freeze Panes.**

   Excel splits the worksheet, but instead of displaying a gray bar (as it does when you create panes), it uses a solid black line to divide the frozen rows from the rest of the worksheet. As you scroll down the worksheet, the frozen rows remain in place.

   To unfreeze the rows, just select View → Freeze Panes → Unfreeze Panes.

Freezing columns works the same way:

1. **Make sure the column or columns you want to freeze are visible and at the left of your worksheet.**

   For example, if you want to freeze columns B and C in place, make sure they're visible at the edge of your worksheet. Remember, columns are frozen starting at column A. That means that if you scroll over so that column A isn't visible, and you freeze columns B and C on the left side of your worksheet, Excel also freezes column A—and keeps it hidden so you can't scroll over to see it.

2. **Move to the first column you want** *unfrozen*, **and then move up to row 1.**

   At this point, you're getting into position so that Excel knows where to create the freeze.

3. **Select View → Freeze Panes → Freeze Panes.**

   Excel splits the worksheet, but instead of displaying a gray bar (as it does when you create panes), Excel uses a solid black line to divide the frozen columns from the rest of the worksheet. As you scroll across the worksheet, the frozen columns remain in place.

   To unfreeze the columns, select View → Freeze Panes → Unfreeze Panes.

Tip: If you're freezing just the first row or the leftmost column, then there's no need to go through this whole process. Instead, you can use the handy View → Freeze Panes → Freeze Top Row or View → Freeze Panes → Freeze First Column.

You can also freeze columns and rows *at the same time,* which is useful when you have identifying information that you need to keep visible both on the left and the top of your worksheet. Figure 14-6 shows an example.

Tip: You can also create a horizontal or vertical pane by using one of the splitter bars, and then freezing that pane. Just drag the splitter bar to the appropriate position, and select View → Freeze Panes → Freeze Panes.

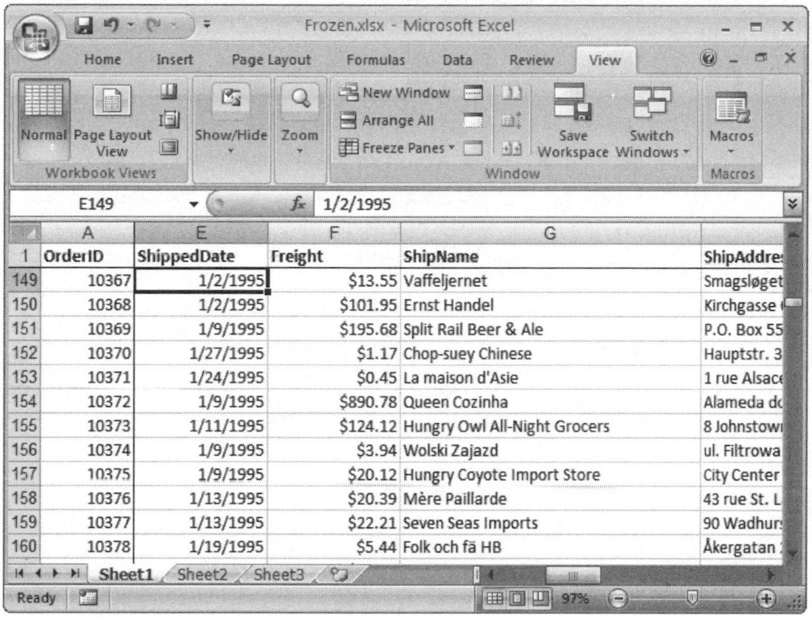

Figure 14-6:
Here, both column A and row 1 are frozen, and thus always remain visible. The easiest way to create these frozen regions is to scroll to the top of the worksheet, position the active cell at B2, and choose View → Freeze Panes → Freeze Panes. Excel then automatically freezes the rows above and the columns to the left in separate panes.

Hiding Data

In some cases your problem isn't that you need to keep data visible, but that you need to *hide* it. For example, say you have a column of numbers that you need only for a calculation but don't want to see when you edit or print the sheet. Excel provides the perfect solution: *hiding* rows and columns. Hiding doesn't delete information, it just temporarily tucks it out of view. You can restore hidden information any time you need it.

Technically, hiding a row or column is just a special type of resizing. When you instruct Excel to hide a column, it simply shrinks the column down to a width of 0. Similarly, when you hide a row, Excel compresses the row height.

You can hide data a few ways:

- To hide a column, right-click the column header (the letter button on the top of the column), and then choose Hide. Or, put your cursor in any row in that column, and then select Home → Cells → Format → Hide & Unhide → Hide Columns.

- To hide a row, right-click the row header (the number button at the left of the row), and then choose Hide. Or, put your cursor in any column in that row, and then select Home → Cells → Format → Hide & Unhide → Hide Rows.

- To hide multiple rows or columns, just select all the ones you want to disappear before choosing Hide.

To unhide a column or row, select the *range* that includes the hidden cells. For example, if you hid column B, select columns A and C by dragging over the numeric row headers. Then choose Home → Cells → Format → Hide & Unhide → Unhide Columns (or Unhide Rows). Or just right-click the selection, and then choose Unhide. Either way, Excel makes the missing columns or rows visible and then highlights them so you can see which information you've restored.

Tip: To unhide all columns (or rows) in a worksheet, select the entire worksheet (by clicking the square in the top-left corner of the grid), and then select Home → Cells → Format → Hide & Unhide → Unhide Columns (or Unhide Rows).

Forgetting that you've hidden data is as easy as forgetting where you put your keys. While Excel doesn't include a hand-clapper to help you locate your cells, it does indicate that some of your row numbers or column letters are missing, as shown in Figure 14-7.

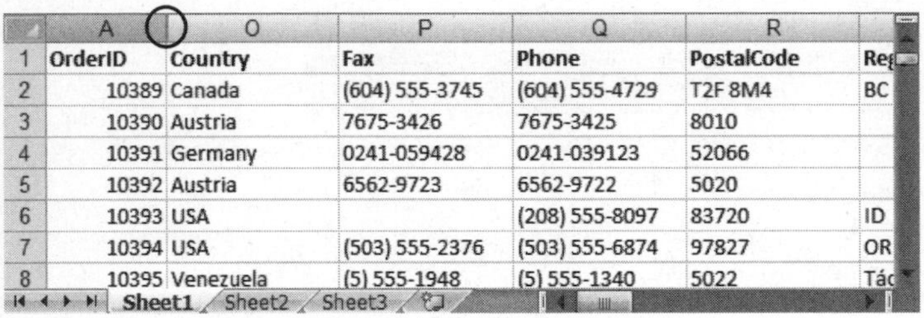

	A	O	P	Q	R	
1	OrderID	Country	Fax	Phone	PostalCode	Reg
2	10389	Canada	(604) 555-3745	(604) 555-4729	T2F 8M4	BC
3	10390	Austria	7675-3426	7675-3425	8010	
4	10391	Germany	0241-059428	0241-039123	52066	
5	10392	Austria	6562-9723	6562-9722	5020	
6	10393	USA		(208) 555-8097	83720	ID
7	10394	USA	(503) 555-2376	(503) 555-6874	97827	OR
8	10395	Venezuela	(5) 555-1948	(5) 555-1340	5022	Tác

Figure 14-7: *This worksheet jumps directly from column A to column O, which tells you that B through N are hidden.*

Saving View Settings

If you regularly tweak things like the zoom, visible columns, and the number of panes, you can easily spend more time adjusting your worksheet than editing it. Fortunately, Excel lets you save your view settings with *custom views*. Custom views let you save a combination of view settings in a workbook. You can store as many custom views as you want. When you want to use a particular view you've created, simply select it from a list and Excel applies your settings.

Custom views are particularly useful when you frequently switch views for different tasks, like editing and printing. For example, if you like to *edit* with several panes open and all your data visible, but you like to *print* your data in one pane with some columns hidden, custom views let you quickly switch between the two layouts.

Note: You can't save a custom view for one worksheet and apply it to another.

Custom views can save the following settings:

- The location of the active cell. (In other words, your position in the worksheet. For example, if you've scrolled to the bottom of a 65,000-row spreadsheet, then the custom view returns you to the active cell in a hurry.)

- The currently selected cell (or cells).

- Column widths and row heights, including hidden columns and rows.

- Frozen panes (page 316).

- View settings, like the zoom percentage, which you set using the ribbon's View tab.

- Print settings, like the page margins.

- Filter settings, which affect what information Excel shows in a data list (see Chapter 16).

To create a custom view, follow these steps:

1. **Adjust an open worksheet for your viewing pleasure.**

   Set the zoom, hide or freeze columns and rows, and move to the place in the worksheet where you want to edit.

2. **Choose View → Workbook Views → Custom View.**

   The Custom Views dialog box appears, showing you a list of all the views defined for this workbook. If you haven't created any yet, this list is empty.

3. **Click the Add button.**

   The Add View dialog box appears.

4. **Type in a name for your custom view.**

   You can use any name, but consider something that'll remind you of your view settings (like "50 percent Zoom"), or the task that this view is designed for (like "All Data at a Glance"). A poor choice is one that won't mean anything to you later ("View One" or "Zoom with a View").

   The Add View dialog box also gives you the chance to specify print settings or hidden rows and columns that Excel *shouldn't* save as part of the view. Turn off the appropriate checkboxes if you don't want to retain this information. Say you hide column A, but you clear the "Hidden rows, columns, and filter settings" checkbox because you don't want to save this as part of the view. The next time you restore the view, Excel won't make any changes to the visibility of column A. If it's hidden, it stays hidden; if it's visible, it stays visible. On the other hand, if you want column A to always be hidden when you apply your new custom view, then keep the "Hidden rows, columns, and filter settings" checkbox turned on when you save it.

After you've typed your view name and dealt with the inclusion settings, click OK to create your new view. Excel adds your view to the list.

5. **Click Close.**

   You're now ready to use your shiny new view or add another (readjust your settings and follow this procedure again).

Applying your views is a snap. Simply select View → Workbook Views → Custom Views to return to the Custom Views dialog box (Figure 14-8), and then select your view from the list and click Show. Because Excel stores views with the workbook, they'll always be available when you open the file, even if you take that file to another computer.

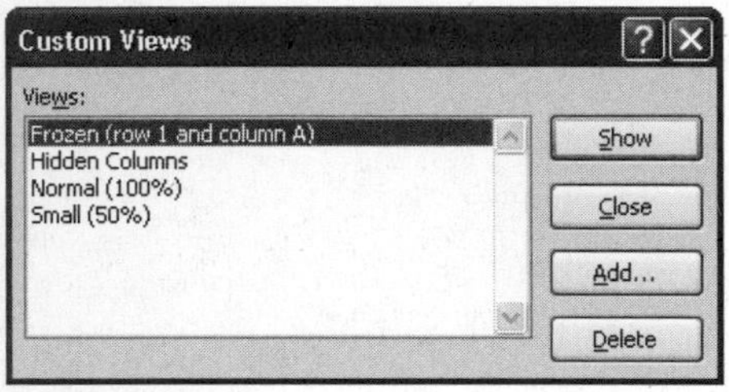

Figure 14-8:
You can use this dialog box to show or delete existing views or to create new ones (click Add, and then follow the procedure from step 4, above).

Tip: For some examples of custom views in action, visit this book's "Missing CD" page at *www. missingmanuals.com* and download CustomViews.xls, a sample spreadsheet with an array of custom views already set up.

Printing

Printing in Excel is pretty straightforward—as long as your spreadsheet fits on a normal 8.5 × 11-inch piece of paper. If you're one of the millions of spreadsheet owners who don't belong to that club, welcome to the world of Multiple Page Disorder: the phenomenon in which pages and pages of apparently unrelated and noncontiguous columns start spewing from your printer. Fortunately, Excel comes with a slew of print-tweaking tools designed to help you control what you're printing. First off, though, it helps to understand the default settings Excel uses when you click the print button.

Note: You can change most of the settings listed; this is just a list of what happens if you *don't* adjust any settings before printing a spreadsheet.

- In the printout, Excel uses all the formatting characteristics you've applied to the cells, including fonts, fills, and borders. However, Excel's gridlines, row headers, and column headers *don't* appear in the printout.

• If your data is too long (all the rows won't fit on one page) or too wide (all the columns won't fit), Excel prints the data on multiple pages. If your data is both too long *and* too wide, Excel prints in the following order: all the rows for the first set of columns that fit on a printed page, then all the rows for the next set of columns that fit, and so on (this is known as "down, then over"). When printing on multiple pages, Excel never prints *part* of an individual column or row.

• Excel prints your file in color if you use colors and you've got a color printer.

• Excel sets margins to 0.75 inches at the top and bottom of the page, and 0.7 inches on the left and right sides of the page. Ordinarily, Excel doesn't include headers and footers (so you don't see any page numbers).

• Excel doesn't include hidden rows and columns in the printout.

How to Print an Excel File

Printing a worksheet is similar to printing in any other Windows application. Follow these steps:

1. **Choose Office button → Print.**

   The Print dialog box appears, as shown in Figure 14-9.

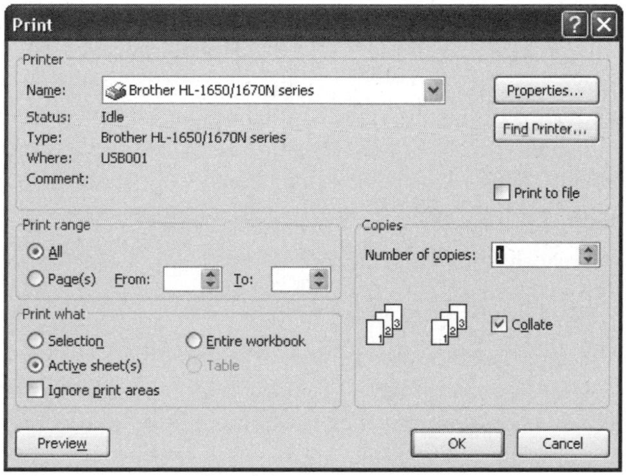

Figure 14-9:
The Excel Print dialog box looks more or less like the Print dialog box in other Windows applications. The key difference is the "Print what" box, which lets you choose to print the current worksheet, all worksheets, or a selected range of cells.

2. **Select a printer from the drop-down list.**

   When the Print dialog box first appears, Excel automatically selects your default printer. If you have more than one printer installed, and you want to use a different printer, then you need to select this printer from the Name pull-down menu. You can also adjust printer settings by clicking the Properties button. Every printer has its own set of options here, but common Properties settings include print quality and paper handling (like double-sided printing for those lucky enough to have a printer that supports it).

3. **Choose what you want to print from the "Print what" box.**

   The standard option, "Active sheet(s)," prints the current worksheet. If you select "Entire workbook," Excel prints all the worksheets in your file. Finally, to print out just a portion of a worksheet, select a range of cells, columns, or rows, and then choose Selection.

   If you've set a print area on your worksheet (see the box on page 325), you can choose "Ignore print areas" to print the full worksheet, not just the print area.

4. **Use the "Print range" box to limit the number of pages that Excel prints.**

   If you choose All in the "Print range" box, Excel prints as many pages as it needs to output all the data you've chosen in the "Print what" box. Alternately, you can choose a range of pages using the Page(s) option. For example, you can choose to print only the first three pages by printing pages from 1 to 3. You can also print just the fourth page by printing from 4 to 4.

Note: In order to use the "Print range" box effectively, you need to know how many pages you need to print your worksheet and what data will appear on each page. Excel's Page Layout view (page 325), is just the ticket.

---

5. **Use the "Number of copies" box to print multiple copies of your data.**

   If you want to print more than one identical copy of your data, change the "Number of copies" text box accordingly. The Collate option determines whether Excel duplicates each page separately. For example, if you print 10 pages and Collate isn't turned on, Excel prints 10 copies of page 1, 10 copies of page 2, and so on. If Collate *is* turned on, Excel prints the entire 10-page document, and then prints out another copy, and so on. You'll still end up with 10 copies of each page, plus, for added convenience, they'll be grouped together.

6. **Click OK to send the spreadsheet to the printer.**

   Excel prints your document using the settings you've selected.

If you're printing a very large worksheet, Excel shows a Printing dialog box for a few seconds as it sends the pages to the printer. If you decide to cancel the printing process—and you're quick enough—you can click the Cancel button in this Printing dialog box to stop the operation. If you don't possess the cat-like reflexes you once did, you can also open your printer queue to cancel the process. Look for your printer icon in the notification area at the bottom-right of your screen, and double-click that icon to open a print window. Then, select the offending print job in the list, and then press Delete (or choose Document → Cancel from the print window's menu). Some printers also provide their own cancel button that lets you stop a print job even after it's left your computer.

Printing Parts of a Spreadsheet

When working with large worksheets, you'll often want to print only a small portion of your total data. Excel gives you several ways to limit your printout. You can hide the rows or columns you aren't interested in, or you can select the cells you want to print, and, in the Print dialog box's "Print what" box, choose Selection. But if you frequently need to print the same area, you're better off defining and using a *print area*.

A print area designates a portion of your worksheet as the only region that Excel will print. (The one exception is if you choose Selection from the "Print what" box, in which case Excel prints the selected cells, not the print area.) Once you define a print area, Excel retains it until you remove it.

That means you can make changes, save, close, and open your spreadsheet, and the same print area remains in place.

To set a print area, select the rows, columns, or group of cells, and then choose Page Layout → Page Setup → Print Area → Set Print Area. The portion of the worksheet that you've highlighted now has a thin dashed outline, indicating that this is the only region Excel will print. You can only have one print area at a time, and setting a new one always clears the previous one. To remove your print area so that you can print the entire worksheet, choose Page Layout → Page Setup → Print Area → Clear Print Area.

Quick Printing

If you know that the currently selected printer is the one you want to use, and you don't want to change any other print settings, you can skip the Print dialog box altogether using the popular (but slightly dangerous) Quick Print feature. Just choose Office button → Print → Quick Print to create an instant printout, with no questions asked.

The Quick Print feature's so commonly used that many Excel experts add it to the Quick Access toolbar so it's always on hand. If you want to do this, hover over the Office button → Print → Quick Print command, right-click it, and then choose Add To Quick Access Toolbar. (Appendix A has more about customizing the Quick Access toolbar.)

Previewing Your Printout

When you're preparing to print that 142-page company budget monstrosity, there's no reason to go in blind. Instead, prudent Excel fans use Page Layout view to check out what their printouts look like *before* they appear on paper. The tool is especially helpful if you've run rampant with formatting, or you want to tweak a variety of page layout settings, and you want to see what the effects will be before clicking Print.

To see the Page Layout view for a worksheet, choose View → Workbook Views → Page Layout View. Or, for an even quicker alternative, use the tiny Page Layout View button in the status bar, which appears immediately to the left of the zoom slider. Either way, you see a nicely formatted preview (Figure 14-10).

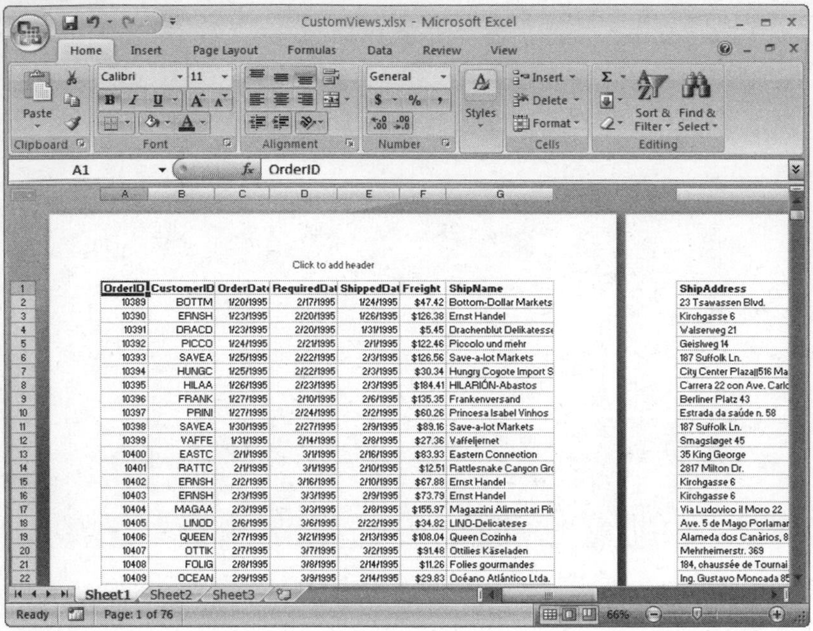

Figure 14-10:
The Page Layout view shows the first (and part of the second) page of this worksheet's 76 printed pages. This worksheet has 19 columns, but since they're wider than the width of a single printed page, the first page includes only the leftmost seven columns, as shown here. You can scroll to the right to see the additional columns that'll turn up on other pages, or scroll down to see more rows.

How does Page Layout view differ from Normal view? You'll see several differences, including:

- Page Layout view paginates your data. You see exactly what fits on each page, and how many pages your printout requires.

- Page Layout view reveals any headers and footers you've set as part of the page setup. These details don't appear in the Normal worksheet view.

- Page Layout view shows the margins that Excel will use for your pages.

- Page Layout view doesn't show anything that Excel won't print (like the letters at the top of each column). The only exception is the cell gridlines, which are shown to help you move around your worksheet.

- Page Layout view includes a bit of text in the Status bar that tells you where you are, page-wise, in a large spreadsheet. For example, you might see the text "Page: 5 of 26."

Note: Don't confuse Page Layout view with an ordinary print preview. A print preview provides a fixed "snapshot" of your printout. You can look, but you can't touch. Page Layout view is vastly better because it shows what your printout will look like *and* it lets you edit data, change margins, set headers and footers, create charts, draw pictures—you get the idea. In fact, you can do everything you do in Normal view mode in Page Layout view. The only difference is you can't squeeze quite as much data into the view at once.

If you aren't particularly concerned with your margin settings, you can hide your margins in Page Layout view so you can fit more information into the Excel window. Figure 14-11 shows you how.

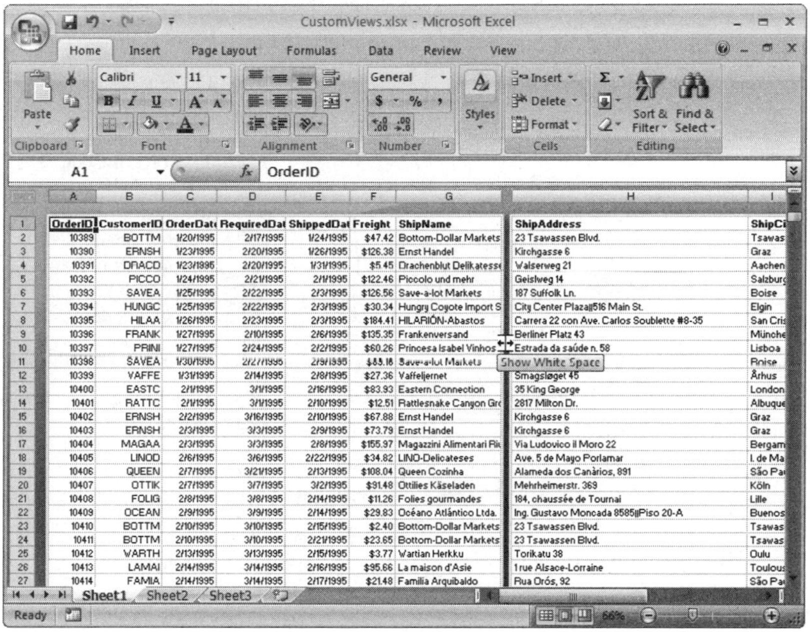

Figure 14-11:
Move your mouse between the pages and your mouse pointer changes into this strange two-arrow beast. You can then click to hide the margins in between pages (as shown here), and click again to show them (as shown in Figure 14-10). Either way, you see an exact replica of your printout. The only difference is whether you see the empty margin space.

Here are some of the tasks you may want to perform in Page Layout view:

- If the print preview meets with your approval, choose Office button → Print to send the document to the printer.

- To tweak print settings and see the effect, choose the Page Layout tab in the ribbon and start experimenting. You'll learn more about these settings on page 201.

- To move from page to page, you can use the scroll bar at the side of the window, or you can use the keyboard (like Page Up, Page Down, and the arrow keys). When you reach the edge of your data, you see shaded pages with the text "Click to add data" superimposed. If you want to add information further down the worksheet, just click one of these pages and start typing.

- To adjust the page margins, first make sure the ruler is visible by turning on the View → Show/Hide → Ruler checkbox. Then, drag one of the margin lines on the ruler, as shown in Figure 14-12. If you want to set page margins by typing in the exact margin width, use the Page Layout tab of the ribbon instead (page 330).

- When you're ready to return to the Normal worksheet view, choose View → Workbook Views → Normal (or just click the Status bar's tiny Normal View button).

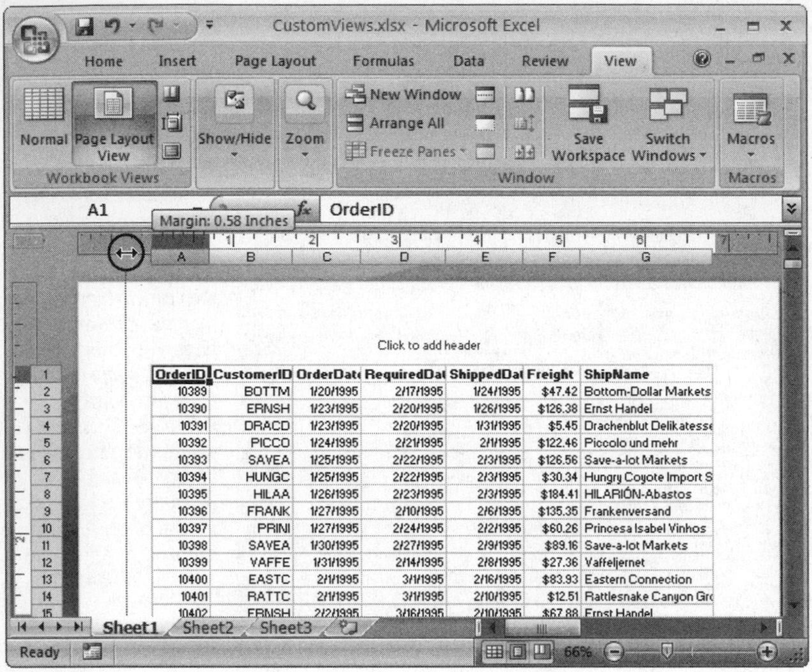

Figure 14-12:
The Page Layout view lets you set margins by dragging the margin edge with your mouse. Here, the left margin (circled) is about to be narrowed down to 0.58 inches. If you're also using a header or footer (below), make sure you don't drag the page margin above the header or below the footer. If you do, then your header or footer will overlap your worksheet's data.

Creating Headers and Footers

A *header* is a bit of text that's printed at the top of every page in your printout. A *footer* is a bit of text that's printed at the bottom of every page. You can use one, both, or neither in a printout.

Ordinarily, every new workbook starts out without a header or footer. However, Page Layout view gives you an easy way to add either one (or both). Just scroll up to the top of any page to create a header (or the bottom to create a footer), and then look for the box with the text "Click to add header" or "Click to add footer". Click inside this box, and you can type the header or footer text you want.

Note: You won't see the header or footer boxes if you've drastically compressed your margins. That's because the header and footer don't fit. To get them back, resize the margins so that they're larger. When you're finished adding the header or footer, you can try adjusting the margins again to see just how small you can get them.

Of course, a good header or footer isn't just an ordinary piece of text. Instead, it contains information that changes dynamically, like the file name, current page, or the date you printed it. You can get these pieces of information using specialized header and footer *codes*, which are distinguished by their use of square brackets.

For example, if you enter the code *[Page]* into a footer, then Excel replaces it with the current page number. If you use the code *[Date]*, then Excel substitutes the current date (when you fire off your printout). Of course, no one wants to memorize a long list of cryptic header and footer codes. To help you get these important details right, Excel adds a new tab to the ribbon named Header & Footer Tools | Design (Figure 14-13) when you edit a header or footer.

The quickest way to get a header or footer is to go to the Header & Footer Tools | Design → Header & Footer section (shown in Figure 14-13), and then choose one of the Header or Footer list's ready-made options. Some of the options you can use for a header or footer include:

• Page numbering (for example, Page 1 or Page 1 of 10)

• Worksheet name (for example, Sheet 1)

• File name (for example, myfile.xlsx or C:\MyDocuments\myfile.xlsx)

• The person who created the document, and the date it was created

• A combination of the above information

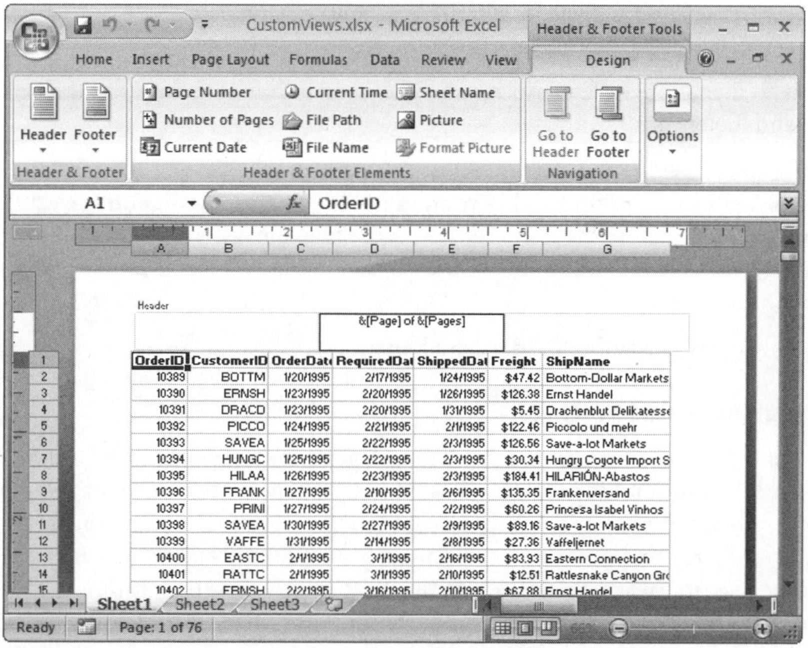

Figure 14-13:
The Header & Footer Tools | Design tab is chock-full of useful ingredients you can add to a header or footer. Click a button in the Header & Footer Elements section to insert a special Excel code that represents a dynamic value, like the current page.

Oddly enough, the header and footer options are the same. It's up to you to decide whether you want page numbering at the bottom and a title at the top, or vice versa.

If none of the standard options matches what you need, you can edit the automatic header or footer, or you can create your own from scratch. Start typing in the header or footer box, and use the buttons in the Header & Footer Elements section to paste in the code you need for a dynamic value. And if you want to get more creative, switch to the Home tab of the ribbon, and then use the formatting buttons to change the font, size, alignment, and color of your header or footer.

Finally, Excel gives you a few high-powered options in the Header & Footer Tools | Design → Options section. These include:

- **Different First Page.** This option lets you create one header and footer for the first page, and use a different pair for all subsequent pages. Once you've checked this option, fill in the first page header and footer on the first page, and then head to the second page to create a new header and footer that Excel can use for all subsequent pages.

- **Different Odd & Even pages.** This option lets you create two different headers (and footers)—one for all even-numbered pages and one for all odd-numbered pages. (If you're printing a bunch of double-sided pages, you can use this option to make sure the page number appears in the correct corner.) Use the first page to fill in the odd-numbered header and footer, and then use the second page to fill in the even-numbered header and footer.

- **Scale with Document.** If you select this option, then when you change the print scale to fit in more or less information on your printout, Excel adjusts the headers and footers proportionately.

- **Align with Page Margins.** If you select this option, Excel moves the header and footer so that they're centered in relation to the margins. If you don't select this option, Excel centers them in relation to the whole page. The only time you'll notice a difference is if your left and right margins are significantly different sizes.

All these settings affect both headers and footers.

Customizing Print Settings

Excel's standard print settings are fine if you've got a really small amount of data in your worksheet. But most times, you'll want to tweak these settings so that you can easily read what you print. The Page Layout tab of the ribbon is your control center (Figure 14-14). It lets you do everything from adding headers and footers to shrinking the size of your data so you can cram more information onto a single printed page.

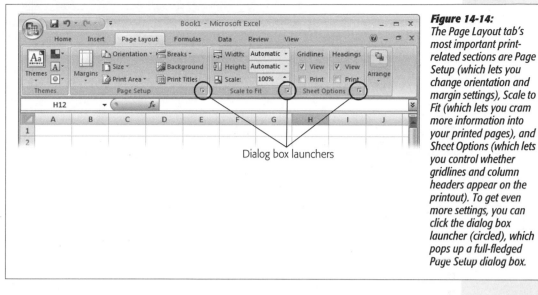

Dialog box launchers

Figure 14-14:
The Page Layout tab's most important print-related sections are Page Setup (which lets you change orientation and margin settings), Scale to Fit (which lets you cram more information into your printed pages), and Sheet Options (which lets you control whether gridlines and column headers appear on the printout). To get even more settings, you can click the dialog box launcher (circled), which pops up a full-fledged Page Setup dialog box.

Margins

The Page Layout → Page Setup → Margins list (Figure 14-15) lets you adjust the size of your printed page's *margins* (the space between your worksheet data and the edge of the page). All you need to do is pick one of the preset options. The margin numbers indicate the distance between the item indicated (for example, the top of the page, or the footer on the bottom) and the edge of the paper.

Note: The units Excel uses for margins depend on the regional settings on your computer (which you can adjust through the Control Panel's Regional and Language Options icon). Unfortunately, Excel doesn't indicate the type of units in the Page Setup dialog box, and it doesn't give you any choice to override your regional settings and use different units.

Logically enough, when you reduce the size of your margins, you can accommodate more information. However, you can't *completely* eliminate your margins. Most printers require at least a little space (usually no less than .25 inches) to grip onto the page, and you won't be able to print on this part (the very edge of the page). If you try to make the margins too small, Excel won't inform you of the problem; instead, it'll just stick with the smallest margin your current printer allows. This behavior is different from that of other Microsoft Office applications (like Word). To see this in action, try setting your margins to 0, and then look at the result in the print preview window. You'll see there's still a small margin left between your data and the page borders.

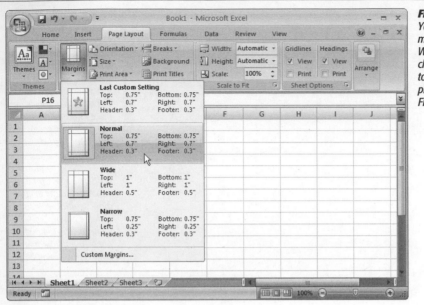

Figure 14-15:
You can choose a helpful margin preset (Normal, Wide, or Narrow), or choose Custom Margins to fine-tune your margins precisely, as shown in Figure 14-16.

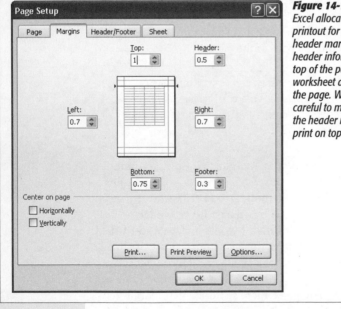

Figure 14-16:
Excel allocates space at the top and bottom of your printout for a header or footer. In this example, the header margin is set to 0.5, which means that any header information will appear half an inch below the top of the page. The top margin's set to 1, meaning the worksheet data will appear one inch below the top of the page. When adjusting either of these settings, be careful to make sure the top margin's always larger than the header margin; otherwise, your worksheet's data will print on top of your header.

Tip: A good rule of thumb is to adjust margins symmetrically (printouts tend to look nicest that way). Thus, if you shrink the left margin to 0.5, make the same change to the right margin. Generally, if you want to fit more data and you don't need any header or footer space, then you can safely reduce all your margins to 0.5. If you really want to cram in the maximum amount of data you can try 0.25, but that's the minimum margin that most printers allow.

When you have only a few rows or columns of information, you may want to use one of the "Center on page" options at the bottom of the tab. Select Horizontally to center your columns between the left and right margins. Select Vertically to center your data between the top and bottom of the page.

Paper size and orientation

Orientation is the all-time most useful print setting. This setting lets you control whether you're printing on pages that are upright (in portrait mode) or turned horizontally on their sides (in landscape mode). If Excel is splitting your rows across multiple pages when you print your worksheet, it makes good sense to switch to landscape orientation. That way, Excel prints your columns across a page's long edge, which accommodates more columns (but fewer rows per page).

If you're fed up with trying to fit all your data on an ordinary sheet no matter which way you turn it, you may be tempted to try using a longer sheet of paper. You can then tell Excel what paper you've decided to use by choosing it from the Paper Size menu. (Of course, the paper needs to fit into your printer.) Letter is the standard 8.5×11-inch sheet size, while Legal is another common choice—it's just as wide but comes in a bit longer at 8.5×14 inches.

Note: When using different types of paper, remember to place the paper in your printer *before* you start the print job.

Sheet settings

Margins and orientation are the most commonly adjusted print settings. However, Excel has a small family of additional settings hidden on the Page Setup dialog box's Sheet tab. To see these, go to the Page Layout → Page Setup section of the ribbon, and click the dialog box launcher (the tiny square-with-an-arrow icon in the bottom-right corner). The Page Setup dialog box appears, as shown in Figure 14-17.

The Sheet tab includes the following settings:

- **Print area** lets you specify the range of cells you want to print. While this tool definitely gets the job done, it's easier to use the Print Area tool (described in the box on page 325). Some people find the Print dialog box's Selection setting (page 324) also a more efficient method.

- **Print titles** lets you print specific rows at the top of every page, or specific columns on the left side of every page. For example, you could use this setting to print column titles on the top of every page.

- **Gridlines** prints the grid of lines separating columns and rows that you see on your worksheet.

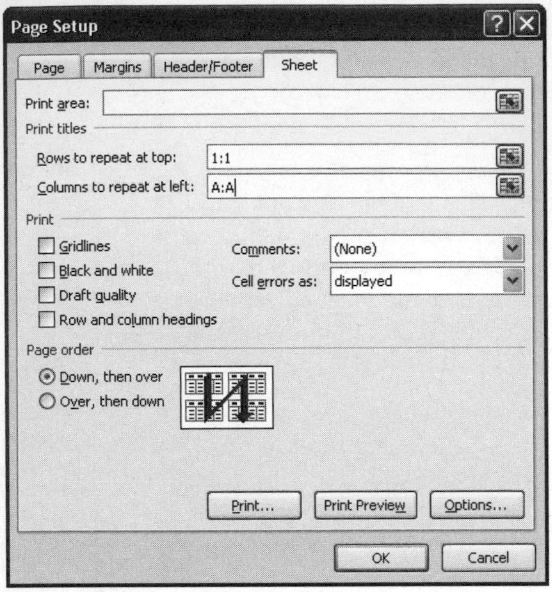

Figure 14-17:
The Page, Margins, and Header/Footer tabs provide options that are easier to configure than using the Page Layout ribbon tab. However, the Sheet tab includes a few options that you can't find anywhere else. In this example, Excel uses the "Print titles" section to ensure that every page in this printout will display the first row of the spreadsheet as well as the first column.

- **Row and column headings** prints the column headers (which contain the column letters) at the top of each page and the row headers (with the row numbers) on the left side of each page.

- **Black and white** tells Excel to render all colors as a shade of gray, regardless of your printer settings.

- **Draft quality** tells Excel to use lower-quality printer settings to save toner and speed up printing, assuming your printer has these features, of course.

- **Comments** lets you print the comments that you've added to a worksheet. Excel can either append them to the cells in the printout or add them at the end of the printout, depending on the option you select.

- **Cell errors** lets you configure how Excel should print a cell if it contains a formula with an error. You can choose to print the error that's shown (the standard option), or replace the error with a blank value, two dashes (--), or the error code #N/A (meaning not available). You'll learn much more about formulas in Chapter 15.

- **Page order** sets the way Excel handles a large worksheet that's too wide and too long for the printed page's boundaries. When you choose "Down, then over" (the standard option), Excel starts by printing all the rows in the first batch of columns. Once it's finished this batch, Excel then moves on to the next set of columns, and prints those columns for all the rows in your worksheet, and so on. When you chose "Over, then down," Excel moves across your worksheet first. That means it prints all the columns in the first set of rows. After it's printed these pages, it moves to the next set of rows, and so on.

Controlling Pagination

Sooner or later it will happen to you—you'll face an intimidatingly large worksheet that, when printed, is hacked into dozens of apparently unconnected pages. You could spend a lot of time assembling this jigsaw printout (using a bulletin board and lots of tape), or you could take control of the printing process and tell Excel exactly where to split your data into pages. In the following sections, you'll learn several techniques to do just that.

Page Breaks

One of Excel's often overlooked but surprisingly handy features is *manual page breaks*. The idea is you tell Excel explicitly where to start a new page. You can tell Excel to start a new page between subsequent tables on a worksheet (rather than print a page that has the end of the first one and the beginning of the next).

To insert a page break, move to the leftmost column (column A), and then scroll down to the first cell that you want to appear on the new page. Then, choose Page Layout → Page Setup → Breaks → Insert Page Break. You see a dotted line that indicates the dividing lines in between pages (Figure 14-18).

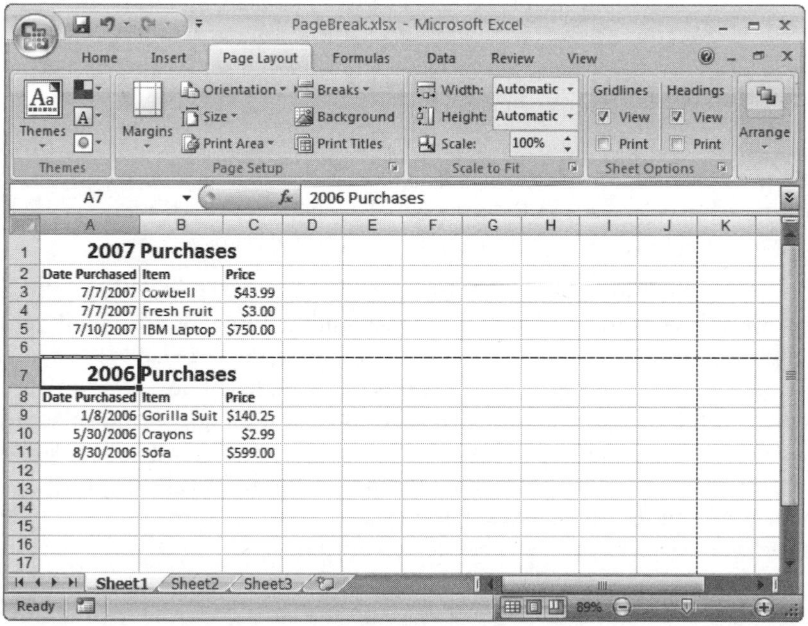

Figure 14-18:
Using a page break, you can make sure the second table ("2006 Purchases") always begins on a new page. The dotted line shows where one page ends and the new page starts. When you add a page break, you see a dotted line for it, and you see a dotted line that shows you where additional page breaks naturally fall, based on your margins, page orientation, and paper size settings.

Tip: There's no limit to how many page breaks you can add to a worksheet—if you have a dozen tables that appear one after the other, you can place a page break after each one to make sure they all start on a new page.

You can also insert page breaks to split your worksheet vertically into pages. This is useful if your worksheet is too wide to fit on one page, but you want to control exactly where the page break will fall. To do so, move to the first row, scroll to the column where the new page should begin, and then choose Page Layout → Page Setup → Breaks → Insert Page Break.

You can remove page breaks one at a time by moving to an adjacent cell and choosing Page Layout → Page Setup → Breaks → Remove Page Break. Or you can clear them all using Page Layout → Page Setup → Breaks → Reset All Page Breaks.

Scaling

Page breaks are a nifty feature for making sure your printouts are paginated just the way you want them. However, they can't help you fit more information on a page. They simply allow you to place page breaks earlier than they would ordinarily occur, so they fall in a more appropriate place.

If you want to fit more on a page, you need to shrink your information down to a smaller size. Excel includes a scaling feature that lets you take this step easily without forcing you to reformat your worksheet.

Scaling lets you fit more rows and columns on a page, by shrinking everything proportionally. For example, if you reduce scaling to 50 percent, you fit twice as many columns and rows on a page. (Keep in mind that the font size in the printout will be smaller, and it may be hard to read.) Conversely, you can use scaling to enlarge your data.

To change the scaling percentage, just type a new percentage into the Page Layout → Scale to Fit → Scale box. The data still appears just as big on your worksheet, but Excel shrinks or expands it in the printout. To gauge the effect, you can use the Page Layout view to preview your printout, as described on page 325.

Rather than fiddling with the scaling percentage (and then seeing what its effect is on your worksheet by trial and error), you may want to force your data to fit into a fixed number of pages. To do this, you set the values in the Page Layout → Scale to Fit → Width box and the Page Layout → Scale to Fit → Height box. Excel performs a few behind-the-scenes calculations and adjusts the scaling percentage accordingly. For example, if you choose one page tall and one page wide, Excel shrinks your entire worksheet so that everything fits into one page. This scaling is tricky to get right (and can lead to hopelessly small text), so make sure you review your worksheet in the Page Layout view before you print it.

Tip: Page Break Preview mode, described below, gives you yet another way to squeeze more data onto a single page.

Page Break Preview: A Bird's-Eye View of Your Worksheet

You don't have to be a tree-hugging environmentalist to want to minimize the number of pages you print out. Enter the Page Break Preview, which gives you a bird's-eye view of how an entire worksheet's going to print. Page Break Preview is particularly useful if your worksheet is made up of lots of columns. That's because Page Break Preview zooms out so you can see a large amount of data at once, and it uses thick blue dashed lines to show you where page breaks will occur, as shown in Figure 14-19. In addition, the Page Break Preview numbers every page, placing the label "Page X" (where "X" is the page number) in large gray lettering in the middle of each page.

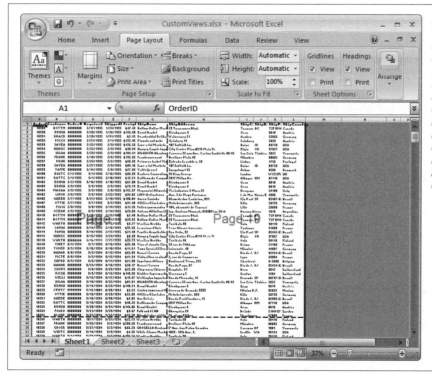

Figure 14-19:
This example shows a large worksheet in Page Break Preview mode. The worksheet is too wide to fit on one page (at least in portrait orientation), and the thick dotted line indicates that the page breaks after column G and after row 47. (Excel never breaks a printout in the middle of a column or row.)

To preview the page breaks in your data, select View → Workbook Views → Page Break Preview, or use the tiny Page Break Preview button in the status bar. A window appears, informing you that you can use Page Break Preview mode to move page breaks. You can choose whether you want to see this message again; if not, turn on the "Do not show this dialog again" checkbox before clicking OK.

Once you're in Page Break Preview mode, you can do all of the things you do in Normal view mode, including editing data, formatting cells, and changing the zoom percentage to reveal more or fewer pages. You can also click the blue dashed lines that represent page breaks, and drag them to include more or less rows and columns in your page.

Excel lets you make two types of changes using page breaks:

- **You can make *less* data fit onto a page.** To do so, drag the bottom page break up or the left-side page break to the right. Usually, you'll perform these steps if you notice that a page break occurs in an awkward place, like just before a row with some kind of summary or subtotal.

- **You can make *more* data fit onto a page.** To do so, drag the bottom page break down or the left-side page break to the left.

Of course, everyone wants to fit more information onto their printouts, but there's only so much space on the page. So what does Excel do when you expand a page by dragging the page break? It simply adjusts the scaling setting you learned about earlier (on page 336). The larger you make the page, the smaller the Scaling percentage setting becomes. That means your printed text may end up too tiny for you to read. (The text on your computer's display doesn't change, however, so you don't have any indication of just how small your text has become until you print out your data, or take a look at it in Page Layout view.)

Note: Scaling affects all the pages in your printout. That means when you drag one page break to expand a page, you actually end up compressing *all* the pages in your workbook. However, the page *breaks* don't change for other pages, which means you may end up with empty, unused space on some of the pages.

The best advice: If your goal is merely to fit more information into an entire printout, change the scaling percentage manually (page 336) instead of using the Page Break Preview. On the other hand, if you need to squeeze just a little bit more data onto a specific page, use the Page Break Preview.

CHAPTER 15

Building Basic Formulas

Most Excel fans don't turn to the world's leading spreadsheet software just to create nicely formatted tables. Instead, they rely on Excel's industrial-strength computing muscle, which lets you reduce reams of numbers to neat subtotals and averages. Performing these calculations is the first step to extracting meaningful information out of raw data.

Excel provides a number of different ways to build formulas, letting you craft them by hand or point-and-click them into existence. In this chapter, you'll learn about all of these techniques. You'll start by examining the basic ingredients that make up any formula, and then take a close look at the rules Excel uses when evaluating a formula.

Creating a Basic Formula

First things first: what exactly do formulas do in Excel? A *formula* is a series of mathematical instructions that you place in a cell in order to perform some kind of calculation. These instructions may be as simple as telling Excel to sum up a column of numbers, or they may incorporate advanced statistical functions to spot trends and make predictions. But in all cases, all formulas share the same basic characteristics:

• You enter each formula into a single cell.

• Excel calculates the result of a formula every time you open a spreadsheet or change the data a formula uses.

- Formula results are usually numbers, although you can create formulas that have text or Boolean (true or false) results.

- To view any formula (for example, to gain some insight into how Excel produced a displayed result), you have to move to the cell containing the formula, and then look in the *formula bar* (see Figure 15-1). The formula bar also doubles as a handy tool for editing your formulas.

- Formulas can evaluate a combination of numbers you input (useful when you want to use Excel as a handy calculator) or, more powerfully, the contents of other cells.

One of the simplest formulas you can create is this one:

    =1+1

The equal sign is how you tell Excel that you're entering a formula (as opposed to a string of text or numbers). The formula that follows is what you want Excel to calculate. Note that the formula doesn't include the *result*. When creating a formula in Excel, you write the question, and then Excel coughs up the answer, as shown in Figure 15-1.

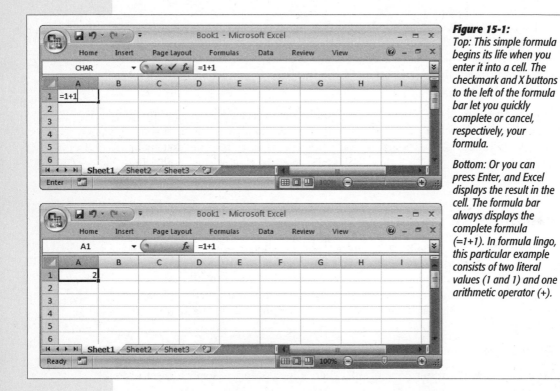

Figure 15-1:
Top: This simple formula begins its life when you enter it into a cell. The checkmark and X buttons to the left of the formula bar let you quickly complete or cancel, respectively, your formula.

Bottom: Or you can press Enter, and Excel displays the result in the cell. The formula bar always displays the complete formula (=1+1). In formula lingo, this particular example consists of two literal values (1 and 1) and one arithmetic operator (+).

All formulas use some combination of the following ingredients:

- **The equal sign** (=). Every formula must begin with the equal sign. It signals to Excel that the cell contains a formula, not just ordinary text.

- **The simple operators.** These ingredients include everything you fondly remember from high school math class, including addition (+), subtraction (−), multiplication (*), division (/), and exponentiation (^). Table 15-1 lists these ingredients, also known as *arithmetic operators*.

- **Numbers.** These ingredients are known as constants or *literal values*, because they never change (unless you edit the formula).

- **Cell references.** These references point to another cell, or a range of cells, that you need data from in order to perform a calculation. For example, say you have a list of 10 numbers. A formula in the cell beneath this list may refer to all 10 of the cells above it in order to calculate their average.

- **Functions.** Functions are specialized formulas built into Excel that let you perform a wide range of calculations. For example, Excel provides dedicated functions that calculate sums and averages, standard deviations, yields, cosines and tangents, and much more.

- **Spaces.** Excel ignores these. However, you can use them to make a formula easier to read. For example, you can write the formula *=3*5 + 6*2* instead of *=3*5+6*2*.

Table 15-1. Excel's Arithmetic Operators

Operator	Name	Example	Result
+	Addition	=1+1	2
−	Subtraction	=1−1	0
*	Multiplication	=2*2	4
/	Division	=4/2	2
^	Exponentiation	=2^3	8
%	Percent	=20%	0.20

Note: The percentage (%) operator divides a number by 100.

Excel's Order of Operations

For computer programs and human beings alike, one of the basic challenges when it comes to reading and calculating formula results is figuring out the *order of operations*—mathematician-speak for deciding which calculations to perform first when there's more than one calculation in a formula. For example, given the formula:

```
=10 - 8 * 7
```

the result, depending on your order of operations, is either 14 or –46. Fortunately, Excel abides by what's come to be accepted among mathematicians as the standard rules for order of operations, meaning it doesn't necessarily process your formulas from left to right. Instead, it evaluates complex formulas piece-by-piece in this order:

1. **Parentheses (any calculations within parentheses are always performed first)**

2. **Percent**

3. **Exponents**

4. **Division and Multiplication**

5. **Addition and Subtraction**

Note: When Excel encounters formulas that contain operators of equal *precedence* (that is, the same order of operation priority level), it evaluates these operators from left to right. However, in basic mathematical formulas, this has no effect on the result.

For example, consider the following formula:

    =5 + 2 * 2 ^ 3 - 1

To arrive at the answer of 20, Excel first performs the exponentiation (2 to the power of 3):

    =5 + 2 * 8 - 1

and then the multiplication:

    =5 + 16 - 1

and then the addition and subtraction:

    =20

To control this order, you can add parentheses. For example, notice how adding parentheses affects the result in the following formulas:

    5 + 2 * 2 ^ (3 - 1) = 13
    (5 + 2) * 2 ^ 3 - 1 = 55
    (5 + 2) * 2 ^ (3 - 1) = 28
    5 + (2 * (2 ^ 3)) - 1 = 20

You must always use parentheses in pairs (one open parenthesis for every closing parenthesis). If you don't, then Excel gets confused and lets you know you need to fix things, as shown in Figure 15-2.

Tip: Remember, when you're working with a lengthy formula, you can expand the formula bar to see several lines at a time. To do so, click the down arrow at the far right of the formula bar (to make it three lines tall), or drag the bottom edge of the formula bar to make it as many lines large as you'd like.

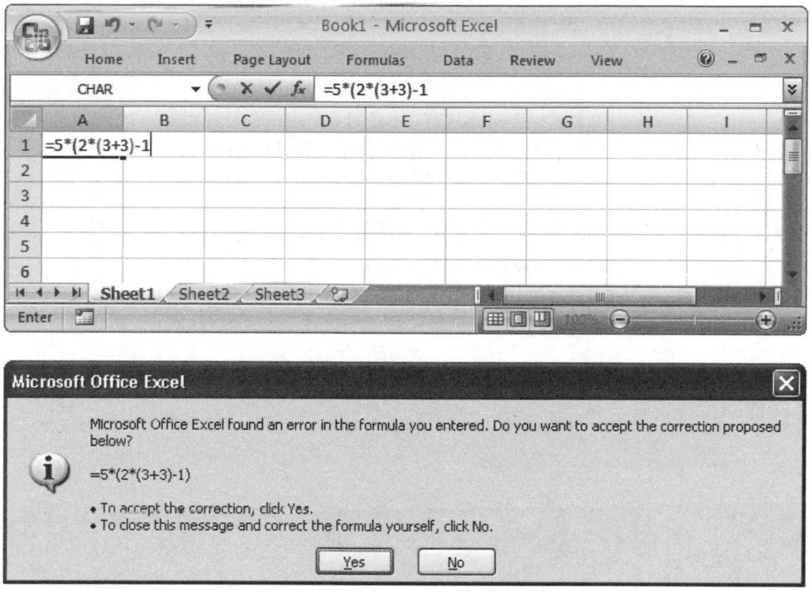

Figure 15-2:
Top: If you create a formula with a mismatched number of opening and closing parentheses (like this one), Excel won't accept it.

Bottom: Excel offers to correct the formula by adding the missing parentheses at the end. You may not want this addition, though. If not, cancel the suggestion, and edit your formula by hand. Excel helps a bit by highlighting matched sets of parentheses. For example, as you move to the opening parenthesis, Excel automatically bolds both the opening and closing parentheses in the formula bar.

Cell References

Excel's formulas are handy when you want to perform a quick calculation. But if you want to take full advantage of Excel's power, then you're going to want to use formulas to perform calculations on the information that's already in your worksheet. To do that you need to use *cell references*—Excel's way of pointing to one or more cells in a worksheet.

For example, say you want to calculate the cost of your Amazonian adventure holiday, based on information like the number of days your trip will last, the price of food and lodging, and the cost of vaccination shots at a travel clinic. If you use cell references, then you can enter all this information into different cells, and then write a formula that calculates a grand total. This approach buys you unlimited flexibility because you can change the cell data whenever you want (for example, turning your three-day getaway into a month-long odyssey), and Excel automatically refreshes the formula results.

Cell references are a great way to save a *ton* of time. They come in handy when you want to create a formula that involves a bunch of widely scattered cells whose values frequently change. For example, rather than manually adding up a bunch of subtotals to create a grand total, you can create a grand total formula that uses cell references to point to a handful of subtotal cells. They also let you refer to large groups of cells by specifying a *range*. For example, using the cell reference lingo you'll learn on page 348, you can specify all the cells in the first column between the 2nd and 100th rows.

Every cell reference points to another cell. For example, if you want a reference that points to cell A1 (the cell in column A, row 1), use this cell reference:

    =A1

In Excel-speak, this reference translates to "get the value from cell A1, and insert it in the current cell." So if you put this formula in cell B1, then it displays whatever value's currently in cell A1. In other words, these two cells are now linked.

Cell references work within formulas just as regular numbers do. For example, the following formula calculates the sum of two cells, A1 and A2:

    =A1+A2

Provided both cells contain numbers, you'll see the total appear in the cell that contains the formula. If one of the cells doesn't contain numeric information, then you'll see a special error code instead that starts with a # symbol. Errors are described in more detail on page 349.

GEM IN THE ROUGH

Excel As a Pocket Calculator

Sometimes you need to calculate a value before you enter it into your worksheet. Before you reach for your pocket calculator, you may like to know that Excel lets you enter a formula in a cell, and then use the result in that same cell. This way, the formula disappears and you're left with the result of the calculated value.

Start by typing your formula into the cell (for example =65*88). Then, press F2 to put the cell into edit mode. Next, press F9 to perform the calculation. Finally, just hit Enter to insert this value into the cell.

Remember, when you use this technique, you replace your formula with the calculated value. If your calculation is based on the values of other cells, then Excel won't update the result if you change those other cells' values. That's the difference between a cell that has a value, and a cell that has a formula.

How Excel Formats Cells That Contain Cell References

As you learned in Chapter 13, the way you format a cell affects how Excel displays the cell's value. When you create a formula that references other cells, Excel attempts to simplify your life by applying automatic formatting. It reads the number format that the *source cells* (that is, the cells being referred *to*) use, and applies that to the cell with the formula. If you add two numbers and you've formatted both with the Currency number format, then your result also has the Currency number format. Of course, you're always free to change the formatting of the cell after you've entered the formula.

Usually, Excel's automatic formatting is quite handy. Like all automatic features, however, it's a little annoying if you don't understand how it works when it springs into action. Here are a few points to consider:

• Excel copies only the number format to the formula cell. It ignores other details, like fonts, fill colors, alignment, and so on.

• If your formula uses more than one cell reference, and the different cells use different number formats, Excel uses its own rules of precedence to decide which number format to use. For example, if you add a cell that uses the Currency number format with one that uses the Scientific number format, then the destination cell has the Scientific number format. Sadly, these rules aren't spelled out anywhere, so if you don't see the result you want, it's best to just set your own formatting.

• If you change the formatting of the source cells *after* you've entered the formula, it won't have any effect on the formula cell.

• Excel copies source cell formatting only if the cell that contains the formula uses the General number format (which is the format that all cells begin with). If you apply another number format to the cell *before* you enter the formula, then Excel doesn't copy any formatting from the source cells. Similarly, if you change a formula to refer to new source cells, then Excel doesn't copy the format information from the new source cells.

Functions

A good deal of Excel's popularity is due to the collection of *functions* it provides. Functions are built-in, specialized algorithms that you can incorporate into your own formulas to perform powerful calculations. Functions work like miniature computer programs—you supply the data, and the function performs a calculation and gives you the result.

In some cases, functions just simplify calculations that you could probably perform on your own. For example, most people know how to calculate the average of several values, but when you're feeling a bit lazy, Excel's built-in AVERAGE( ) function automatically gives you the average of any cell range.

Note: Excel provides a detailed function reference that lists all the functions you can use (and how to use them). This function reference doesn't exactly make for light reading, though; for the most part, it's written in IRS-speak. You'll learn more about using this reference on page 356.

Every function provides a slightly different service. For example, one of Excel's statistical functions is named COMBIN( ). It's a specialized tool used by probability mathematicians to calculate the number of ways a set of items can be combined. Although this sounds technical, even ordinary folks can use COMBIN( ) to get some interesting information. You can use the COMBIN( ) function, for example, to count the number of possible combinations there are in certain games of chance.

The following formula uses COMBIN( ) to calculate how many different five-card combinations there are in a standard deck of playing cards:

    =COMBIN(52,5)

Functions are always written in all-capitals. (More in a moment on what those numbers inside the parentheses are doing.) However, you don't need to worry about the capitalization of function names because Excel automatically capitalizes the function names that you type in (provided it recognizes them).

Using a function in a formula

Functions alone don't actually *do* anything in Excel. Functions need to be part of a formula to produce a result. For example, COMBIN( ) is a function name. But it actually *does* something—that is, give you a result—only when you've inserted it into a formula, like so: *=COMBIN(52,5)*.

Whether you're using the simplest or the most complicated function, the *syntax*—or, rules for including a function within a formula—is always similar. To use a function, start by entering the function name. Excel helps you out by showing a pop-up list with possible candidates as you type, as shown in Figure 15-3. This handy feature is new to Excel 2007, and it's called Formula AutoComplete.

After you type the function name, add a pair of parentheses. Then, inside the parentheses, put all the information the function needs to perform its calculations.

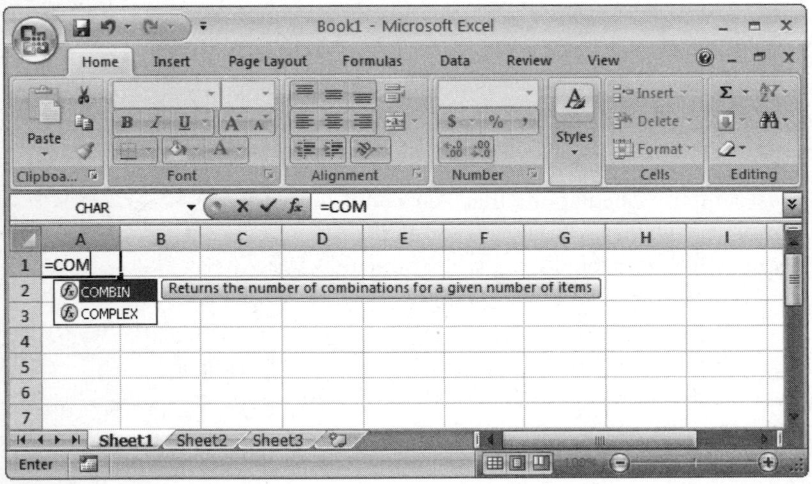

Figure 15-3:
After you type =COM, Excel helpfully points out that it knows only two functions that start that way: COMBIN( ) and COMPLEX( ). If your fingers are getting tired, then use the arrow keys to pick the right one out of the list, and then click Tab to pop it into your formula. (Or, you can just double-click it with the mouse.)

In the case of the COMBIN( ) function, Excel needs two pieces of information, or *arguments*. The first is the number of items in the set (the 52-card deck), and the second's the number of items you're randomly selecting (in this case, 5). Most functions, like COMBIN( ), require two or three arguments. However, some functions can accept many more, while a few don't need any arguments at all. Once again, Formula AutoComplete guides you by telling you what arguments you need, as shown in Figure 15-4.

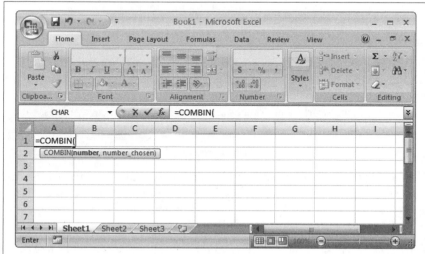

Figure 15-4:
When you type the opening parentheses after a function name, Excel automatically displays a tooltip indicating what arguments the function requires. The argument you're currently entering is shown bolded in the tooltip. The argument names aren't crystal clear, but if you already know how the function works, they're usually enough to jog your memory.

Once you've typed this formula into a cell, the result (2598960) appears in your worksheet. In other words, there are 2,598,960 different possible five-card combinations in any deck of cards. Rather than having to calculate this fact using probability theory—or, heaven forbid, trying to count out the possibilities manually—the COMBIN( ) function handled it for you.

Note: Even if a function doesn't take any arguments, you still need to supply an empty set of parentheses after the function name. One example is the RAND( ) function, which generates a random fractional number. The formula =RAND( ) works fine, but if you forget the parentheses and merely enter *=RAND*, then Excel displays an error message *(#NAME?)* that's Excelian for: "Hey! You got the function's name wrong." See Table 15-2 on page 351 for more information about Excel's error messages.

Using cell references with a function

One of the particularly powerful things about functions is that they don't necessarily need to use literal values in their arguments. They can also use cell references. For example, you could rewrite the five-card combination formula (mentioned previously) so that it specifies the number of cards that'll be drawn from the deck based on a number that you've typed in somewhere else in the spreadsheet.

Assuming this information's entered into cell B2, the formula would become:

```
=COMBIN(52,B2)
```

Building on this formula, you can calculate the probability (albeit astronomically low) of getting the exact hand you want in one draw:

```
=1/COMBIN(52,B2)
```

You could even multiply this number by 100 or use the Percent number style to see your percentage chance of getting the cards you want.

Using cell ranges with a function

In many cases, you don't want to refer to just a single cell, but rather a *range* of cells. A range is simply a grouping of multiple cells. These cells may be next to each other (say, a range that includes all the cells in a single column), or they could be scattered across your worksheet. Ranges are useful for computing averages, totals, and many other calculations.

To group together a series of cells, use one of the two following reference operators:

- **The comma (,) separates more than one cell.** For example, the series *A1, B7, H9* is a cell range that contains three cells. The comma's known as the *union operator*. You can add spaces before or after a comma, but Excel just ignores or removes them (depending on its mood).

- **The colon (:) separates the top-left and bottom-right corners of a block of cells.** You're telling Excel: "Hey, use *this* block of cells in my formula." For example, *A1:A5* is a range that includes cells A1, A2, A3, A4, and A5. The range *A2:B3* is a grid that contains cells A2, A3, B2, and B3. The colon is the *range operator*—by far the most powerful way to select multiple cells.

Tip: As you might expect, Excel lets you specify ranges by selecting cells with your mouse, instead of typing in the range manually. You'll see this trick later in this chapter on page 353.

You can't enter ranges directly into formulas that just use the simple operators. For example, the formula *=A1:B1+5* doesn't work, because Excel doesn't know what to do with the range A1:B1. (Should the range be summed up? Averaged? Excel has no way of knowing.) Instead, you need to use ranges with functions that know how to use them. For instance, one of Excel's most basic functions is named SUM( ); it calculates the total for a group of cells. To use the SUM( ) function, you enter its name, an open parenthesis, the cell range you want to add up, and then a closed parenthesis.

Here's how you can use the SUM( ) function to add together three cells, A1, A2, and A3:

```
=SUM(A1,A2,A3)
```

And here's a more compact syntax that performs the same calculation using the range operator:

```
=SUM(A1:A3)
```

A similar SUM( ) calculation's shown in Figure 15-5. Clearly, if you want to total a column with hundreds of values, then it's far easier to specify the first and last cell using the range operator rather than including each cell reference in your formula!

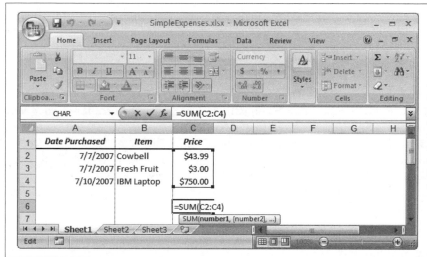

Figure 15-5:
Using a cell range as the argument in the SUM( ) function is a quick way to add up a series of numbers in a column. Note that when you enter or edit a formula, Excel highlights all the cells that formula uses with different colored borders. In this example, you see the range of cells C2, C3, and C4 in a blue box.

Formula Errors

If you make a syntax mistake when entering a formula (such as leaving out a function argument or including a mismatched number of parentheses), Excel lets you know right away. Moreover, like a stubborn school teacher, Excel won't accept the formula until you've corrected it. It's also possible, though, to write a perfectly legitimate formula that doesn't return a valid answer. Here's an example:

```
=A1/A2
```

If both A1 and A2 have numbers, this formula works without a hitch. However, if you leave A2 blank, or if you enter text instead of numbers, then Excel can't evaluate the formula, and it reminds you with an error message.

Excel lets you know about formula errors by using an *error code* that begins with the number sign (#) and ends with an exclamation point (!), as shown in Figure 15-6. In order to remove this error, you need to track down the problem and resolve it, which may mean correcting the formula or changing the cells it references.

When you click the exclamation mark icon next to an error, you see a menu of choices (as shown in Figure 15-6):

- **Help On This Error** pops open Excel's online help, with a (sometimes cryptic) description of the problem and what could have caused it.

- **Show Calculation Steps** pops open the Evaluate Formula dialog box, where you can work your way through a complex formula one step at a time.

- **Ignore Error** tells Excel to stop bothering you about this problem, in any worksheet you create. You won't see the green triangle for this error again (although you'll still see the error code in the cell).

- **Edit in Formula Bar** brings you to the formula bar, where you can change the formula to fix a mistake.

- **Error Checking Options** opens up the Excel Options dialog box, and brings you to the section where you can configure the settings Excel uses for alerting you about errors. You can turn off *background error checking,* or change the color of the tiny error triangles using the settings under the Error Checking heading. (Background error checking is the feature that flags cells with tiny green triangles when the cells contain a problem.) You can also tell Excel to start paying attention to errors you previously told it ignore by clicking the Reset Ignored Errors button.

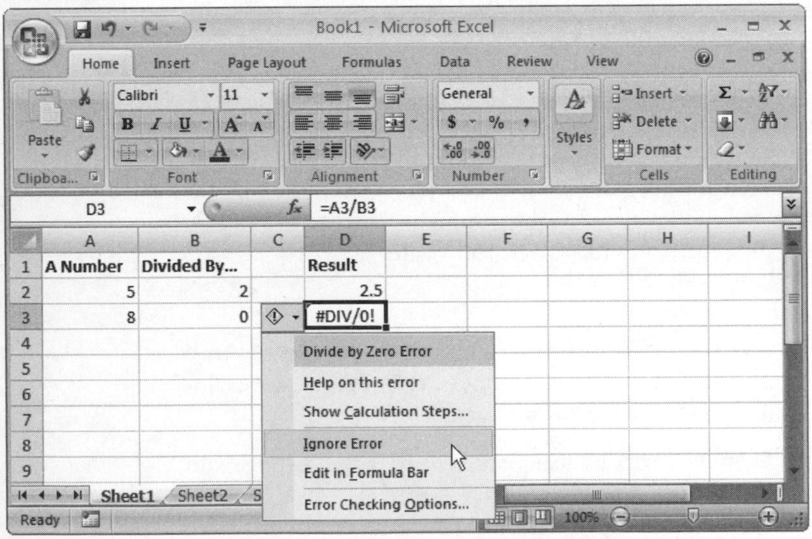

Figure 15-6:
When Excel spots an error, it inserts a tiny green triangle into the cell's top-left corner. When you move to the offending cell, Excel displays an exclamation mark icon next to it (a smart tag). Hover over the exclamation mark to view a description of the error (which appears in a tooltip), or click the exclamation icon to see a list of menu options.

Table 15-2 lists most of the error codes that Excel uses.

Table 15-2. Excel's Error Codes

Error Code	Description
#VALUE!	You used the wrong type of data. Maybe your function expects a single value and you submitted a whole range. Or, more commonly, you might have used a function or created a simple arithmetic formula with a cell that contains text instead of numbers.
#NAME?	Excel can't find the name of the function you used. This error code usually means you misspelled a function's name, although it can indicate you used text without quotation marks or left out the empty parentheses after the function name.
#NUM!	There's a problem with one of the numbers you're using. For example, this error code appears when a calculation produces a number that's too large or too small for Excel to deal with.
#DIV/0	You tried to divide by zero. This error code also appears if you try to divide by a cell that's blank, because Excel treats a blank cell as though it contains the number 0 for the purpose of simple calculations with the arithmetic operators. (Some functions, like AVERAGE( ), are a little more intelligent and ignore blank cells.)
#REF!	Your cell reference is invalid. This error most often occurs if you delete or paste over the cells you were using, or if you try to copy a cell from one worksheet to another.
#N/A	The value isn't available. This error can occur if you try to perform certain types of lookup or statistical functions that work with cell ranges. For example, if you use a function to search a range and it can't find what you need, you may get this result. Sometimes people enter a #N/A value manually in order to tell Excel to ignore a particular cell when creating charts and graphs. The easiest way to do this is to use the NA( ) function (rather than entering the text #N/A).
########	This code isn't actually an error condition—in all likelihood, Excel has successfully calculated your formula. However, the formula can't be displayed in the cell using the current number format. To solve this problem, you can widen the column, or possibly change the number format if you require a certain number of fixed decimal places.

Logical Operators

So far, you've seen the basic arithmetic operators (which are used for addition, subtraction, division, and so on) and the cell reference operators (used to specify one or more cells). There's one final category of operators that's useful when creating formulas: *logical operators*.

Logical operators let you build conditions into your formulas so the formulas produce different values depending on the value of the data they encounter. You can use a condition with cell references or literal values.

For example, the condition A2=A4 is true if cell A2 contains the same value as cell A4. On the other hand, if these cells contain different values (say 2 and 3), then the formula generates a false value. Using conditions is a stepping stone to using conditional logic. Conditional logic lets you perform different calculations based on different scenarios.

For example, you can use conditional logic to see how large an order is, and provide a discount if the total order cost's over $5,000. Excel *evaluates* the condition, meaning it determines if the condition's true or false. You can then tell Excel what to do based on that evaluation.

Table 15-3 lists all the logical operators you can use to build formulas.

Table 15-3. *Logical Operators*

Operator	Name	Example	Result
=	Equal to	1=2	FALSE
>	Greater than	1>2	FALSE
<	Less than	1<2	TRUE
>=	Greater than or equal to	1>=1	TRUE
<=	Less than or equal to	1<=1	TRUE
<>	Not equal to	1<>1	FALSE

You can use logical operators to build standalone formulas, but that's not particularly useful. For example, here's a formula that tests whether cell A1 contains the number 3:

```
=(A2=3)
```

The parentheses aren't actually required, but they make the formula a little bit clearer, emphasizing the fact that Excel evaluates the condition first, and then displays the result in the cell. If you type this formula into the cell, then you see either the uppercase word TRUE or FALSE, depending on the content in cell A2.

On their own, logical operators don't accomplish much. However, they really shine when you start combining them with other functions to build conditional logic. For example, you can use the SUMIF( ) function, which totals the value of certain rows, depending on whether the row matches a set condition. Or you can use the IF( ) function to determine what calculation you should perform.

The IF( ) function has the following function description:

```
IF(condition, [value_if_true], [value_if_false])
```

In English, this line of code translates to: If the condition is true, display the second argument in the cell; if the condition is false, display the third argument.

Consider this formula:

```
=IF(A1=B2, "These numbers are equal", "These numbers are not equal")
```

This formula tests if the value in cell A1 equals the value in cell B2. If this is true, you'll see the message "These numbers are equal" displayed in the cell. Otherwise, you'll see "These numbers are not equal."

> **Note:** If you see a quotation mark in a formula, it's because that formula uses text. You must surround all literal text values with quotation marks. (Numbers are different: You can enter them directly into a formula.)

People often use the IF( ) function to prevent Excel from performing a calculation if some of the data is missing. Consider the following formula:

```
=A1/A2
```

This formula causes a divide-by-zero error if A2 contains a 0 value. Excel then displays an error code in the cell. To prevent this from occurring, you can replace this formula with the conditional formula shown here:

```
=IF(A2=0, 0, A1/A2)
```

This formula checks if cell A2 is empty or contains a 0. If so, the condition is true, and the formula simply gives you a 0. If it isn't, the condition is false, and Excel performs the calculation A1/A2.

Formula Shortcuts

So far, you've learned how to build a formula by entering it manually. That's a good way to start out because it forces you to understand the basics of formula writing. But writing formulas by hand is a drag; plus, it's easy to type in the wrong cell address. For example, if you type A2 instead of A3, you can end up with incorrect data, and you won't necessarily notice your mistake.

As you become more comfortable with formulas, you'll find that Excel gives you a few tools—like point-and-click formula creation and the Insert Function button—to speed up your formula writing and reduce your mistakes. You'll learn about these features in the following sections.

> **Note:** In previous versions of Excel, the Insert Function dialog box was almost exactly the same, except it was known as the Function wizard.

Point-and-Click Formula Creation

Instead of entering a formula by typing it out letter-by-letter, Excel lets you create formulas by clicking the cells you want to use. For example, consider this simple formula that totals the numbers in two cells:

```
=A1+A2
```

To build this formula by clicking, just follow these steps:

1. **Move to the cell where you want to enter the formula.**

   This cell's where the result of your formula's calculation will appear. While you can pick any cell on the worksheet, A3 works nicely because it's directly below the two cells you're adding.

2. **Press the equal sign (=) key.**

   The equal sign tells Excel you're going to enter a formula.

3. **Move to the first cell you want to use in your formula (in this case, A1).**

   You can move to this first cell by pressing the up arrow key twice, or by clicking it with the mouse. You'll notice that moving to another cell doesn't cancel your edit, as it would normally, because Excel recognizes that you're building a formula. When you move to the new cell, the cell reference appears automatically in the formula (which Excel displays in cell A3, as well as in the formula bar just above your worksheet). If you move to another cell, Excel changes the cell reference accordingly.

4. **Press the + key.**

   Excel adds the + sign to your formula so that it now reads =A1+.

5. **Finish the formula by moving to cell A2 and pressing Enter.**

   Again, you can move to A2 either by pressing the up arrow key or by clicking the cell directly. Remember, you can't just finish the formula by moving somewhere else; you need to press Enter to tell Excel you're finished writing the formula. Another way to complete your edit is to click the checkmark that appears on the formula bar, to the left of the current formula. Even experienced Excel fans get frustrated with this step. If you click another cell before you press Enter, then you won't move to the cell—instead, Excel inserts the cell into your formula.

Tip: You can use this technique with any formula. Just type in the operators, function names, and so on, and use the mouse to select the cell references. If you need to select a range of cells, then just drag your mouse until the whole group of cells is highlighted. You can practice this technique with the SUM( ) function. Start by typing =SUM(into the cell, and then selecting the range of cells you want to add. Finish by adding a final closing parenthesis and pressing Enter.

Point-and-Click Formula Editing

You can use a similar approach to edit formulas, although it's slightly trickier:

1. **Move to the cell that contains the formula you want to edit, and put it in edit mode by double-clicking it or pressing F2.**

   Excel highlights all the cells that this formula uses with a colored outline. Excel's even clever enough to use a helpful color-coding system. Each cell reference uses the same color as the outline surrounding the cell it's referring to. This can help you pick out where each reference is.

2. **Click the outline of the cell you want to change. (Your pointer changes from a fat plus sign to a four-headed arrow when you're over the outline.) With the mouse button still held down, drag this outline over to the new cell (or cells) you want to use.**

   Excel updates the formula automatically. You can also expand and shrink cell range references. To do so, put the formula-holding cell into edit mode, and then click any corner of the border that surrounds the range you want to change. Next, drag the border to change the size of the range. If you want to move the range, then click any part of the range border and drag the outline in the same way as you would with a cell reference.

3. **Press Enter or click the formula bar checkmark to accept your changes.**

   That's it.

FREQUENTLY ASKED QUESTION

Showing and Printing Formulas

How in the world do I print out formulas that appear in my cells?

When you print a worksheet, Excel prints the calculated value in each cell rather than any formula that happens to be inside a cell. Usually, that's what you want to have happen. But in some cases, rather than a printout of the formula's results, you want a record of the calculations used to generate the results.

Excel gives you a view setting so you can get this record. Just choose Formulas → Formula Auditing → Show Formulas. Now, Excel displays the formula's contents instead of its results—but on the current worksheet only. Excel also widens the columns so they can show more information (as formulas tend to be longer than their results). Repeat this process, and then uncheck the setting to return to normal life.

The Formulas Tab

The ribbon is stocked with a few buttons that make formula writing easier. To take a look, click the Formulas tab.

The most important part of the Formulas tab is the Function Library section at the left. It includes the indispensable Insert Function button, which you'll take for a spin in the next section. It also includes many more buttons that arrange Excel's vast catalog of functions into related categories for easier access. Figure 15-7 shows how it works.

The Function Library divides its functions into the following categories:

- **AutoSum** has a few shortcuts that let you quickly add, average, or otherwise deal with a list of numbers.

- **Recently Used** has exactly what you'd expect—functions that you've recently chosen from the Function Library. If you're just starting out with functions, you see that Excel fills the Recently Used list with a small set of commonly used functions, like SUM( ).

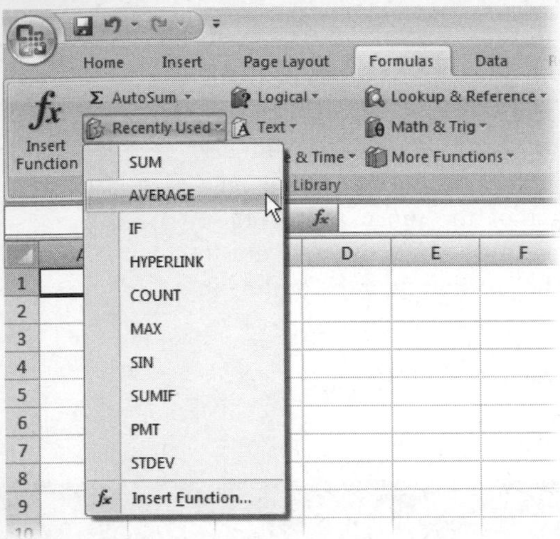

Figure 15-7:
Each button in the Function Library section (other than Insert Function) pops up a mini menu of function choices. Choose one, and Excel inserts that function into the current formula. You can use this technique to find functions that you've used recently, or to browse the main function categories.

- **Financial** functions let you track your car loan payments and calculate how many more years until you can retire rich.

- **Logical** functions let you create conditional logic for even smarter spreadsheets that make calculation decisions.

- **Text** functions manipulate words, sentences, and other non-numeric information.

- **Date & Time** functions perform calendar math and can help you sort out ages, due dates, and more.

- **Lookup & Reference** functions perform the slightly mind-bending feat of searching for information in other cells.

- **Math & Trig** functions are the mathematic basics, including sums, rounding, and all the other high-school trigonometry you're trying to forget.

- **More Functions** groups together some heavy-duty Excel functions that are intended for specialized purposes. This category includes high-powered statistical and engineering functions.

Using the Insert Function Button

Excel provides more than 300 built-in functions. In order to use a function, however, you need to type its name in *exactly*. That means that every time you want to employ a function, you'll need to refer to this book, call on your own incredible powers of recollection, or click over to the convenient Insert Function button.

To use the Insert Function feature, choose Formulas → Function Library → Insert Function. However, formula pros skip straight to the action by clicking the *fx* button that appears just to the left of the formula bar. (Or, they press the Shift+F3 shortcut key.)

No matter which approach you use, Excel displays the Insert Function dialog box (shown in Figure 15-8), which offers three ways to search for and insert any of Excel's functions.

- If you're looking for a function, the easiest way to find one is to choose a category from the "Or select a category" drop-down list. For example, when you select the Math & Trig category, you see a list of functions with names like SIN( ) and COS( ), which perform basic trigonometric calculations.

- If you choose the Most Recently Used category, you'll see a list of functions you've recently picked from the ribbon or the Insert Function dialog box.

- If you're really ambitious, you can type a couple of keywords into the "Search for a function" text box. Next, click Go to perform the search. Excel gives you a list of functions that match your keywords.

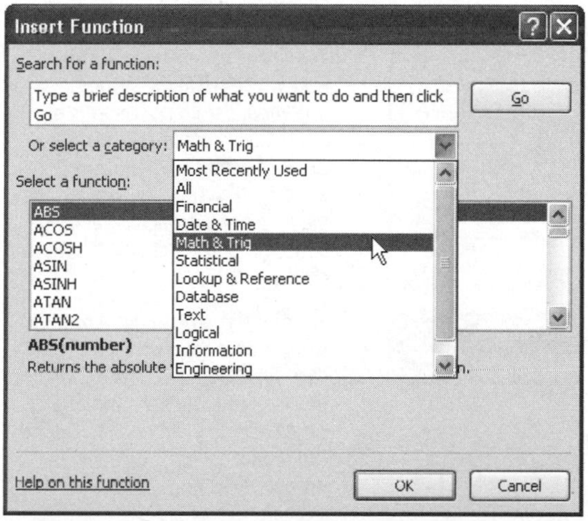

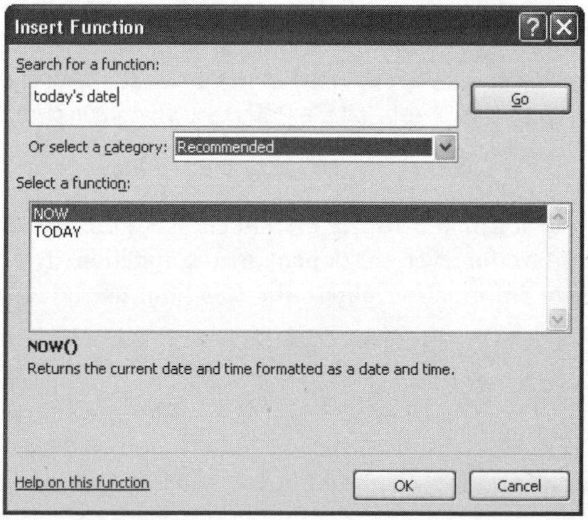

Figure 15-8:
Top: The Insert Function dialog box lets you quickly find the function you need. You can choose a category that seems likely to have the functions you're interested in.

Bottom: You can also try to search by entering keywords in the "Search for a function" box. Either way, when you click one of the functions in the list, Excel presents you with a description of the function at the bottom of the window.

When you spot a function that looks promising, click it once to highlight its name. Excel then displays a brief description of the function at the bottom of the window. For more information, you can click the "Help on this function" link in the bottom-left corner of the window. To build a formula using this function, click OK.

Excel then inserts the function into the currently active cell, followed by a set of parentheses. Next, it closes the Insert Function dialog box and opens the Function Arguments dialog box (Figure 15-9).

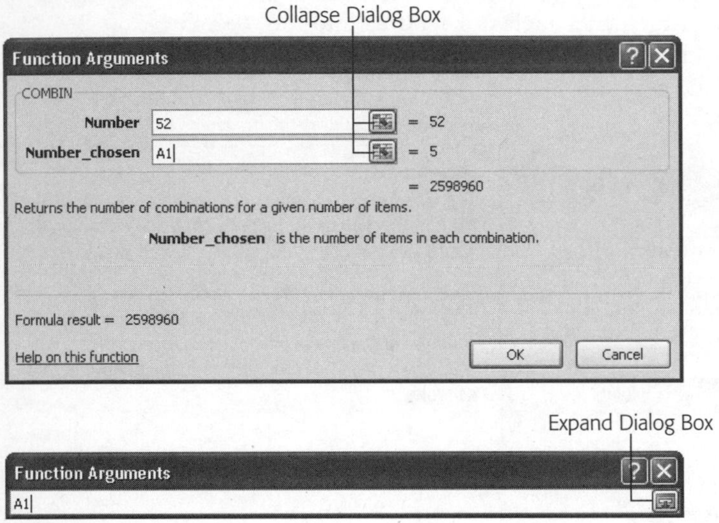

Figure 15-9:
Top: Here, the COMBIN( ) function has just been inserted via the Insert Function dialog box. Because the COMBIN( ) function requires two arguments (Number and Number_chosen), the Function Arguments dialog box shows two text boxes. The first argument uses a literal value (52), while the second argument uses a cell reference (A1). As you enter the arguments, Excel updates the formula in the worksheet's active cell, and displays the result of the calculation at the bottom of the Function Arguments dialog box.

Bottom: If you need more room to see the worksheet and select cells, you can click the Collapse Dialog Box icon to reduce the window to a single text box. Clicking the Expand Dialog Box icon restores the window to its normal size.

Note: Depending on the function you're using, Excel may make a (somewhat wild) guess about which arguments you want to supply. For example, if you use the Insert Function window to add a SUM( ) function, then you'll see that Excel picks a nearby range of cells. If this isn't what you want, just replace the range with the correct values.

Now you can finish creating your formula by using the Function Arguments dialog box, which includes a text box for every argument in the function. It also includes a help link for detailed information about the function, as shown in Figure 15-10.

To complete your formula, follow these steps:

1. **Click the text box for the first argument.**

   A brief sentence describing the argument appears in the Function Arguments dialog box.

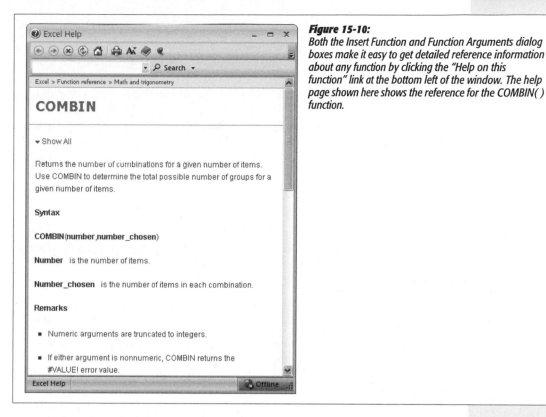

Figure 15-10:
Both the Insert Function and Function Arguments dialog boxes make it easy to get detailed reference information about any function by clicking the "Help on this function" link at the bottom left of the window. The help page shown here shows the reference for the COMBIN( ) function.

Some functions don't require any arguments. In this case, you don't see any text boxes, although you still see some basic information about the function. Skip directly to step 4.

2. **Enter the value for the argument.**

   If you want to enter a literal value (like the number 52), type it in now. To enter a cell reference, you can type it in manually, or click the appropriate cell on the worksheet. To enter a range, drag the cursor to select a group of cells.

   You may need to move the Function Arguments dialog box to the side to expose the part of the worksheet you want to click. The Collapse Dialog Box icon (located to the immediate right of each text box) is helpful since clicking it shrinks the window's size. This way, you'll have an easier time selecting cells from your worksheet. To return the window to normal, click the Expand Dialog Box icon, which is to the right of the text box.

3. **Repeat step 2 for each argument in the function.**

   As you enter the arguments, Excel updates the formula automatically.

4. **Once you've specified a value for every required argument, click OK.**

   Excel closes the window and returns you to your worksheet.

Copying Formulas

Sometimes you need to perform similar calculations in different cells throughout a worksheet. For example, say you want to calculate sales tax on each item in a product catalog, the monthly sales in each store of a company, or the final grade for each student in a class. In this section, you'll learn how Excel makes it easy with *relative cell references*. Relative cell references are cell references that Excel updates automatically when you copy them from one cell into another. They're the standard kind of references that Excel uses (as opposed to absolute cell references, which are covered in the next section). In fact, all the references you've used so far have been relative references, but you haven't yet seen how they work with copy-and-paste operations.

Consider the worksheet shown in Figure 15-11, which contains a teacher's grade book. In this example, each student has three grades: two tests and one assignment. A student's final grade is based on the following percentages: 25 percent for each of the two tests, and 50 percent for the assignment.

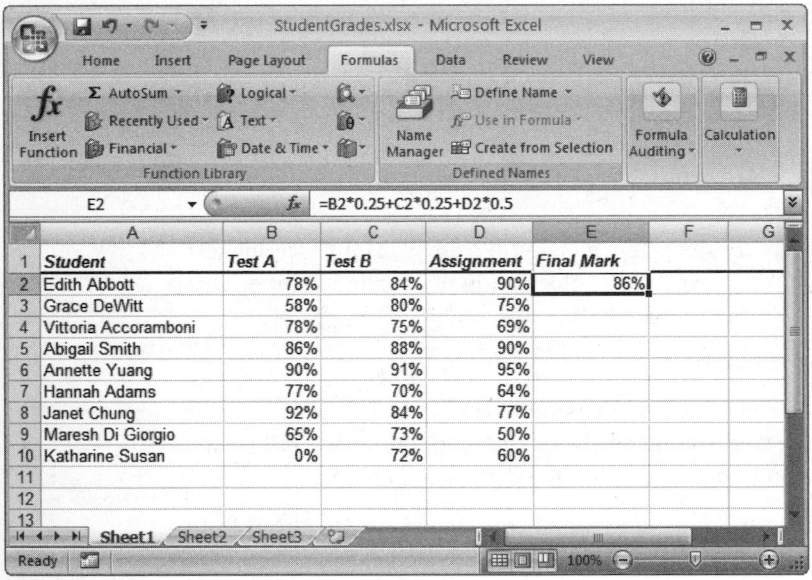

Figure 15-11:
This worksheet shows a list of students in a class, and calculates the final grade for each student using two test scores and an assignment score. So far, the only formula that's been added is for the first student (in cell E2).

The following formula calculates the final grade for the first student (Edith Abbott):

    =B2*25% + C2*25% + D2*50%

The formula that calculates the final mark for the second student (Grace DeWitt) is almost identical. The only change is that all the cell references are offset by one row, so that B2 becomes B3, C2 becomes C3, and D2 becomes D3:

    =B3*25% + C3*25% + D3*50%

You may get fed up entering all these formulas by hand. A far easier approach is to copy the formula from one cell to another. Here's how:

1. **Move to the cell containing the formula you want to copy.**

   In this example, you'd move to cell E2.

2. **Copy the formula to the clipboard by pressing Ctrl+C.**

   You can also copy the formula by choosing Home → Clipboard → Copy.

3. **Select the range of cells you want to copy the formula into.**

   Select cells E3 to E10.

4. **Paste in the new formulas by pressing Ctrl+V.**

   You can also paste the formula by choosing Home → Clipboard → Paste.

   When you paste a formula, Excel magically copies an appropriate version of the formula into each of the cells from E3 to E10. These automatic formula adjustments occur for any formula, whether it uses functions or just simple operators. Excel then automatically calculates and displays the results, as shown in Figure 15-12.

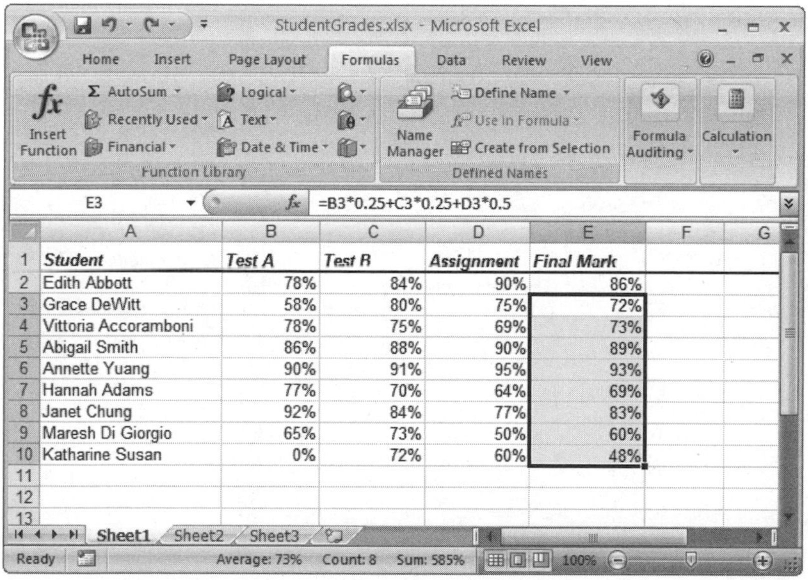

Figure 15-12:
When you paste the formula into one or more new cells, each Final Grade formula operates on the data in its own row. This means that you don't have to tweak the formula for each student. The formula bar shows the formula contained in cell E3.

Tip: There's an even quicker way to copy a formula to multiple cells by using the AutoFill feature introduced in Chapter 10. In the student grade example, you'd start by moving to cell E2, which contains the original formula. Then, you'd click the small square at the bottom-right corner of the cell outline, and drag the outline down until it covers all cells from E3 to E10. When you release the mouse button, Excel inserts the formula copies in the AutoFill region.

Absolute Cell References

Relative references are a true convenience since they let you create formula copies that don't need the slightest bit of editing. But you've probably already realized that relative references don't always work. For example, what if you have a value in a specific cell that you want to use in multiple calculations? You may have a currency conversion ratio that you want to use in a list of expenses. Each item in the list needs to use the same cell to perform the conversion correctly. But if you make copies of the formula using relative cell references, then you'll find that Excel adjusts this reference automatically and the formula ends up referring to the wrong cell (and therefore the wrong conversion value).

Figure 15-13 illustrates the problem with the worksheet of student grades. In this example, the test and assignment scores aren't all graded out of 100 possible points; each item has a different total score available (listed in row 12). In order to calculate the percentage a student earned on a test, you need to divide the test score by the total score available. This formula, for example, calculates the percentage for Edith Abbott's performance on Test B:

```
=B2/B12*100%
```

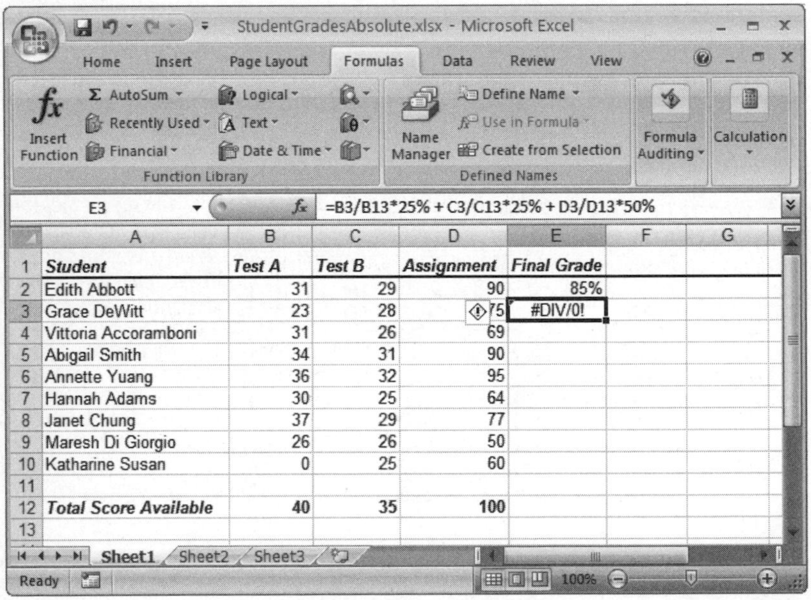

Figure 15-13:
In this version of the student grade book, both the tests and the assignment are graded on different scales (as listed in row 12). When you copy the Final Grade formula from the first row (cell E2) to the rows below it, Excel offsets the formula to use B13, C13, and D13—none of which provide any information. Thus a problem occurs— shown here as a divide-by-zero error. To fix this, you need to use absolute cell references.

To calculate Edith's final grade for the class, you'd use the following formula:

```
=B2/B12*25% + C2/C12*25% + D2/D12*50%
```

Like many formulas, this one contains a mix of cells that should be relative (the individual scores in cells B2, C2, and D2) and those that should be absolute (the possible totals in cell B12, C12, and D12). As you copy this formula to subsequent rows, Excel incorrectly changes all the cell references, causing a calculation error.

Fortunately, Excel provides a perfect solution. It lets you use *absolute cell references*—cell references that always refer to the same cell. When you create a copy of a formula that contains an absolute cell reference, Excel doesn't change the reference (as it does when you use *relative* cell references; see the previous section). To indicate that a cell reference is absolute, use the dollar sign ($) character. For example, to change B12 into an absolute reference, you would add the $ character twice, once in front of the column and once in front of the row, which changes it to $B$12.

Here's the corrected class grade formula (for Edith) using absolute cell references:

```
=B2/$B$12*25% + C2/$C$12*25% + D2/$D$12*50%
```

This formula still produces the same result for the first student. However, you can now copy it correctly for use with the other students. To copy this formula into all the cells in column E, use the same procedure described in the previous section on relative cell references.

UP TO SPEED

Creating an Exact Formula Copy

There's another way to copy a formula that prevents Excel from automatically changing the formula's cell references. The trick's to copy the formula itself rather than copy the whole cell (which is what you do when performing a basic copy-and-paste operation on a formula).

The process takes a few more steps, and it lets you paste only one copy at a time, but it can still come in handy if you don't want Excel to use relative references. Here's how it works:

1. First, move to the cell that contains the formula you want to copy.

2. Place this cell in edit mode by double-clicking it or pressing F2.

3. Select all the text in the cell. You can use the mouse, or you can use the arrow keys (just hold down Shift as you scroll from the beginning to the end of the cell).

4. Once you've selected the complete formula, press Ctrl+C to copy it.

5. Press Enter to leave edit mode once you're finished.

6. Move to the new cell, and press Ctrl+V to paste it.

Keep in mind that when you use this approach, you create an exact copy of the formula. That means this technique doesn't help in situations where some cell references need to be absolute, and others need to be relative.

Partially Fixed References

You might wonder why you need to use the $ character twice in an absolute reference (before the column letter *and* the row number). The reason is that Excel lets you create *partially* fixed references. To understand partially fixed references, it helps to remember that every cell reference consists of a column letter and a row number. With a partial fixed reference, Excel updates one component (say, the column part) but not the other (the row) when you copy the formula. If this sounds complex (or a little bizarre), consider a few examples:

- You have a loan rate in cell A1, and you want all loans on an entire worksheet to use that rate in calculations. If you refer to the cell as $A$1, then its column and row always stay the same when you copy the formula to another cell.

- You have several rows of loan information. The first column of a row always contains the loan rate for all loans on that row. In your formula cell, if you refer to cell $A1, then when you copy the formula across columns and rows, the row changes (2, 3, 4, etc.) but the column doesn't (A2, A3, A4, etc.).

- You have a table of loan rates organized by the length of the loan (10-year, 15-year, 20-year, etc.) along the top of a worksheet. Loans in each column are calculated using the rate specified at the top of that column. If you refer to the rate cell as A$1 in your first column's formula, then the row stays constant (1), but the column changes (B1, C1, D1, etc.) as you copy the formula across columns and down rows.

Tip: You can quickly change formula references into absolute or partially fixed references. Just put the cell into edit mode (by double-clicking it or pressing F2). Then, move through the formula until you've highlighted the appropriate cell reference. Now, press F4 to change the cell reference. Each time you press F4, the reference changes. If the reference is A1, for instance, it becomes $A$1, then A$1, then $A1, and then A1 again.

FREQUENTLY ASKED QUESTION

How Changing the Location of Cells Affects Formulas

OK, I know how Excel adjusts a formula when I copy it to another location. But what happens if I move cells around after I've created a formula?

No worries. It turns out that Excel is surprisingly intelligent. Consider the following simple formula:

    =B1+A2

If you cut and paste the contents of A2 to A3, Excel automatically updates your formula to point to the new cell, without complaining once. It also performs the same automatic cleanup if you drag the contents of a cell to another location (although if you simply make a duplicate copy of the cell, Excel won't change your formula). Excel is also on the ball when you insert and delete rows and columns.

If at any time Excel can't find your cells, the formula changes to show the error code #REF! You can then take a closer look at the formula to find out what really went wrong. For example, if you delete column B from your spreadsheet (by selecting the column and using the Home → Cells → Delete command), the formula changes to this:

    =#REF!+A2

Even though there's still a B1 cell in your worksheet (it's the cell that was formerly named C1), Excel modifies the formula to make it clear that you've lost your original data.

CHAPTER 16

Tables and Charts

Excel's grid-like main window gives you lots of freedom to organize your information. As you've seen in the chapters so far, tables of data can assume a variety of shapes and sizes-from a simple list of dishes your guests are bringing to a potluck dinner, to complex worksheets that track expenses.

Some tables are quite sophisticated, with multiple levels, subtotals, and summary information. But in many cases, your table consists of nothing more than a long list of data, with a single row at the top that provides descriptive column headings. These types of tables are so common that Excel provides a set of features designed exclusively for managing them. These tools let you control your tables in style-sorting, searching, and filtering your information with just a couple of mouse clicks.

Another handy way to organize-and analyze-data is with a chart. Charts depict data visually, so you can quickly spot overall trends. They're a fabulous way to help you find the meaning hidden in large amounts of data. You can create many different types of charts in Excel, including pie charts that present polling results, line charts that plot rising or declining assets over time, and three-dimensional area charts that show relationships between environmental conditions in a scientific experiment.

Note: This chapter gives you just a taste of what you can do with Excel's charting features. For the full story on charts, check out *Excel 2007: The Missing Manual*.

In this chapter, you'll learn about tables, how to create them, and how to make use of all their features. You'll also learn the basics of chart creation.

The Basics of Tables

An Excel table is really nothing more than a way to store a bunch of information about a group of items. Each item occupies a separate row, and different kinds of information about the item reside side by side in adjacent columns. In database terminology, the rows are *records*, and the columns of information are *fields*. For example, the records could represent customers, and the fields could contain things like name, address, purchase history, and so on.

Note: In previous versions of Excel, the tables feature was called *lists*. It's still the same feature, but Microsoft developers were so pleased with the improvements they added in Excel 2007 that they decided it deserved a whole new name.

Excel tables have a number of advantages over ordinary worksheet data:

- **They grow and shrink dynamically.** As you fill data into adjacent rows and columns, the table grows to include the new cells. And as a table changes size, any formulas that use the table adjust themselves accordingly. In other words, if you have a formula that calculates the sum of a column in a table, the range that the SUM( ) function uses expands when you add a new record to the table.

- **They have built-in smarts.** You can quickly select rows and columns, apply a custom sort order, and search for important records.

- **They excel (ahem) at dealing with large amounts of information.** If you need to manage vast amounts of information, you may find ordinary worksheet data a little cumbersome. If you put the same information in a table, you can simply apply *custom filtering*, which means you see only the records that interest you.

Creating a Table

Creating a table is easy. Here's how:

1. **Choose the row where you want your table to start.**

   If you're creating a new table, the worksheet's first row is a good place to begin. (You can always shift the table down later by putting your cursor in the top row, and then choosing Home → Cells → Insert → Insert Sheet Rows.) This first row is where you enter any column titles you want to use, as explained in the next step.

Note: Be careful when placing content in the cells directly *beneath* your table. If your table expands too far down, you'll run up against these filled-up cells. Although you can use commands like Home → Cells → Insert → Insert Sheet Rows to add some extra space when things get crowded, it's always better to start off with plenty of breathing room.

---

2. **Enter the column titles for your table, one column title for each category you want to create.**

   To create the perfect table, you need to divide your data into categories. For example, if you're building a table of names and addresses, you probably want your columns to hold the standard info you see on every form ever created: First Name, Last Name, Street, City, and so on. The columns you create are the basis for all the searching, sorting, and filtering you do. For instance, if you have First Name and City columns, you can sort your contacts by first name or by city.

   If you want, you can start to add entries underneath the column headings now (in the row directly below the column titles). Or just jump straight to the next step to create the table.

3. **Make sure you're currently positioned somewhere inside the table (anywhere in the column title row works well), and then choose Insert → Tables → Table.**

   Excel scans the nearby cells, and then selects all the cells that it thinks are part of your table. Once Excel determines the bounds of your table, the Create Table dialog box appears, as shown in Figure 16-1.

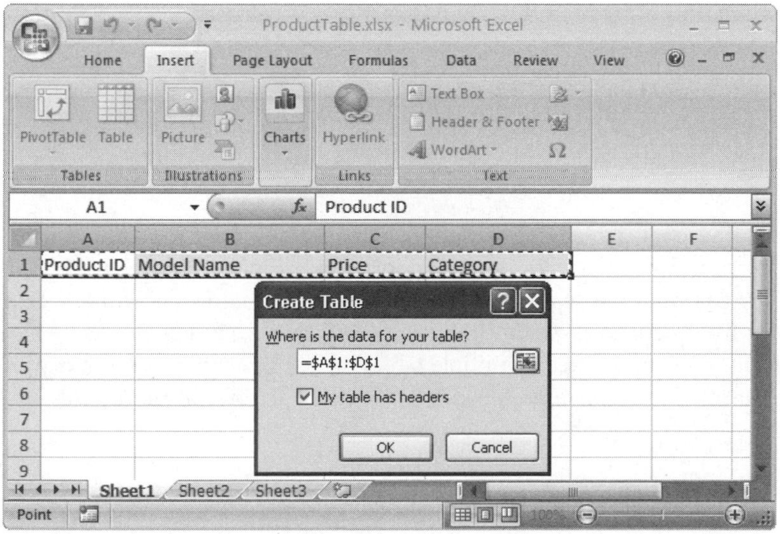

Figure 16-1:
The Create Table dialog box displays the cell references for the currently selected range. In this example, the selection includes only the headings (there's no data yet). You can change the range by typing in new information or by clicking the mini worksheet icon at the right end of the cell range box, which lets you select the range by dragging on the appropriate cells in the worksheet.

4. **Make sure the "My table has headers" checkbox is turned on. This option tells Excel you're using the first row just for column headers. Then click OK.**

   Excel transforms your cells into a table, like the one shown in Figure 16-2. You can tell that your ordinary range of cells has become a genuine table by the presence of a few telltale signs. First, tables start out with automatic formatting that gives each row a shaded background (alternating between blue and gray).

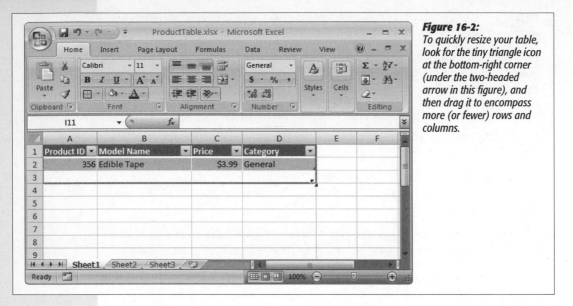

Figure 16-2:
To quickly resize your table, look for the tiny triangle icon at the bottom-right corner (under the two-headed arrow in this figure), and then drag it to encompass more (or fewer) rows and columns.

Second, the column headings appear in bold white letters on a dark background, and each one includes a drop-down arrow that you can use for quick filtering (a feature you'll explore on page 378).

If you create a table from a group of cells that don't include column titles, don't turn on the "My table has headers" checkbox. When you create the table, Excel adds a row of columns at the top with generic names like Column1, Column2, and so on. You can click these cells, and then edit the column titles, to be more descriptive.

Keep in mind that tables consist of exactly two elements: column headers (Figure 16-3) and rows. Tables don't support row headers (although there's no reason why you can't create a separate column and use that as a row title). Tables also have a fixed structure, which means that every row has exactly the same number of columns. You can create multiple tables on the same worksheet, but you're often better off placing them on separate worksheets so you can more easily manage them.

Formatting a Table

Every table starts out with some basic formatting, and you can use the ribbon and the Format Cells dialog box (as discussed in Chapter 13) to further change its appearance. However, Excel gives you an even better option—you can use *table styles*.

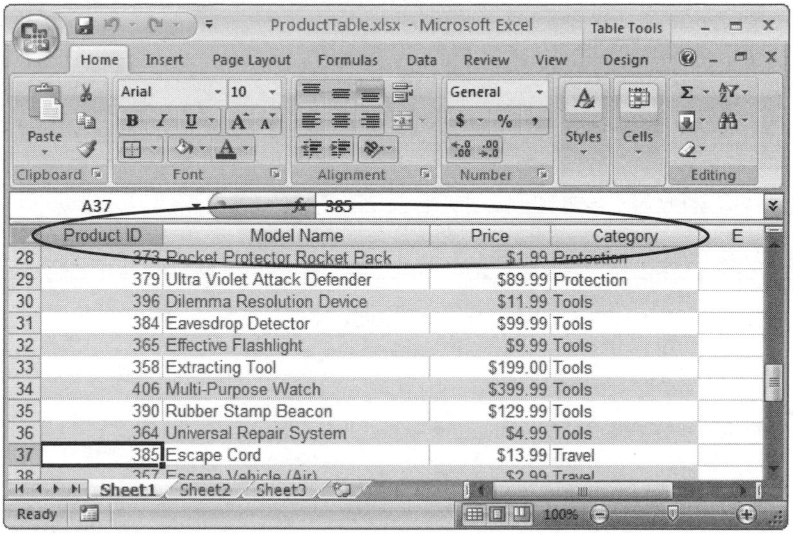

Figure 16-3:
Here's one unsung frill in every table. When you can't see the column headers any longer (because you've scrolled down the page), the column buttons atop the worksheet grid change from letters (like A, B, C) to your custom headers (like Product ID, Model Name, and Price). This way, you never forget what column you're in.

A table style is a collection of formatting settings that apply to an entire table. The nice part about table styles is that Excel remembers your style settings. If you add new rows to a table, Excel automatically adds the right cell formatting. Or, if you delete a row, Excel adjusts the formatting of all the cells underneath to make sure the *banding* (the alternating pattern of cell shading that makes each row easier to read) stays consistent.

When you first create a table, you start out with a fairly ordinary set of colors: a gray–blue combination that makes your table stand out from the rest of the worksheet. By choosing another table style, you can apply a different set of colors and borders to your table.

Note: Excel's standard table styles don't change the fonts in a table. To change fonts, select some cells, and then, from the ribbon's Home → Font section, pick the font you want.

To choose a new table style, head to the ribbon's Table Tools | Design → Table Styles section. You'll see a gallery of options as shown in Figure 16-4. As you move over a table style, Excel uses its live preview feature to change the table, giving you a sneak peak at how your table would look with that style.

Note: Notice that some table styles use banding, while others don't.

Table styles let you standardize and reuse formatting. They include a whole package of settings that tell Excel how to format different portions of the table, including the headers, first and last columns, the summary row, and so on.

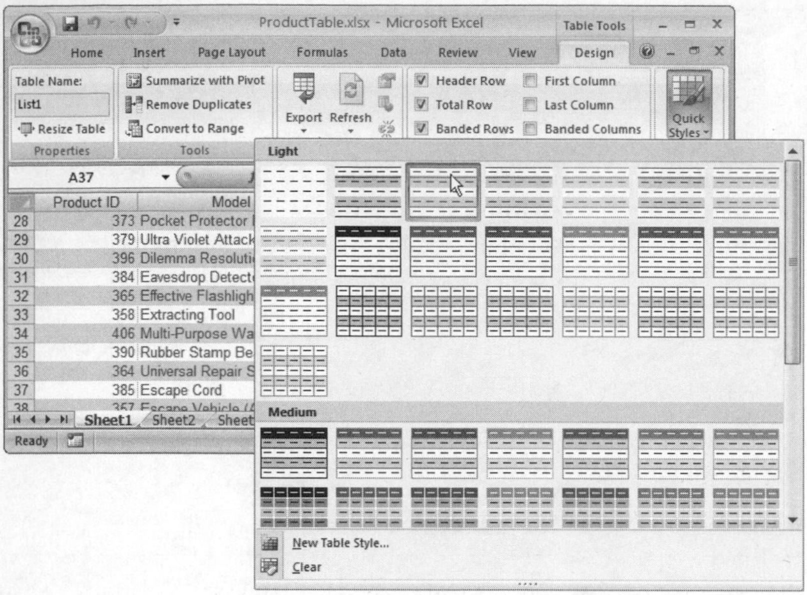

Figure 16-4:
Depending on your Excel window's width, in the ribbon, you may see the table style gallery. Or, if there's not enough room available, you see a Quick Styles button that you need to click to display a drop-down style gallery (as shown here).

Note: You can't edit the built-in table styles. However, you can change the table styles you create. In the table gallery, just right-click a style, and then choose Modify.

You'll notice that the built-in table styles have a limited set of colors. Excel limits them because table styles use colors from the current theme, which ensures that your table meshes well with the rest of your worksheet (assuming you've been sticking to theme colors elsewhere). To get different colors for your tables, you can change the theme by choosing from the Page Layout → Themes → Themes gallery. *Excel 2007: The Missing Manual* has more about themes.

Along with the table style and theme settings, you have a few more options to fine-tune your table's appearance. Head over to the ribbon's Table Tools | Design → Table Style Options section, where you see a group of checkboxes, each of which lets you toggle on or off different table elements:

- **Header Row** lets you show or hide the row with column titles at the top of the table. You'll rarely want to remove this option. Not only are the column headers informative, but they also include drop-down lists for quick filtering (page 378).

- **Total Row** lets you show or hide the row with summary calculations at the bottom of your table.

- **First Column** applies different formatting to the first column in your table, if it's defined in the table style.

- **Last Column** applies different formatting to the last column in your table, if it's defined in the table style.

- **Banded Rows** applies different formatting to each second row, if it's defined in the table style. Usually, the banded row appears with a background fill. Large-table lovers like to use banding because it makes it easier to scan a full row from right to left without losing your place.

- **Banded Columns** applies different formatting to each second column, if it's defined in the table style. Folks use banded columns less than banded rows, because people usually read tables from side to side (not top to bottom).

Editing a Table

Once you've created a table, there are three basic editing tasks you can perform:

- **Edit a record.** This part's easy. Just modify cell values as you would in any ordinary worksheet.

- **Delete a record.** First, go to the row you want to delete (you can be in any column). Then, choose Home → Cells → Delete → Delete Table Rows. Excel removes the row and shrinks the table automatically. For faster access that bypasses the ribbon altogether, just right-click a cell in the appropriate row, and then choose Delete → Table Rows.

- **Add a new record.** To add a record, head to the bottom of the table, and then type a new set of values just underneath the last row in the table. Once you finish typing the first value, Excel expands the table automatically, as shown in Figure 16-5. If you want to insert a row but don't want it to be at the bottom of the table, you can head to your chosen spot, and then choose Home → Cells → Insert → Insert Table Rows Above (or right-click and choose Insert → Table Rows Above). Excel inserts a new blank row immediately *above* the current row.

Note: Notice that when you insert or remove rows, you're inserting or removing *table* rows, not *worksheet* rows. The operation affects only the cells in that table. For example, if you have a table with three columns and you delete a row, Excel removes three cells, and then shifts up any table row underneath. Any information in the same row that exists *outside* the table is unaffected.

You may also decide to change the structure of your table by adding or removing columns. Once again, you'll find this task is like inserting or removing columns in an ordinary worksheet. (The big difference, as shown in Figure 16-6, is that any rows or columns *outside* your table remain unaffected when you add new rows or columns.)

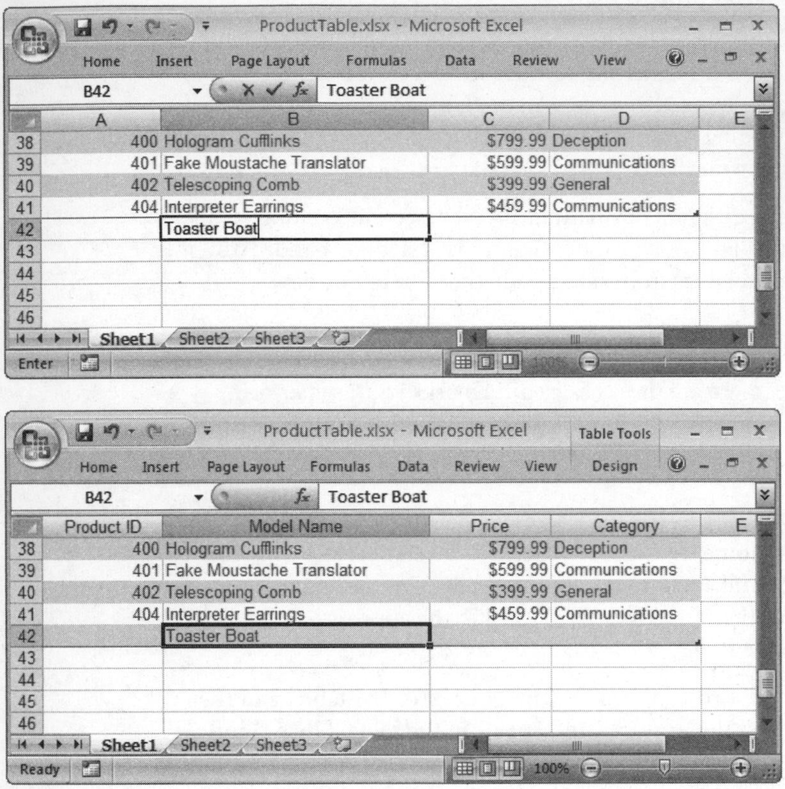

Figure 16-5:
Top: Here, a new record is being added just under the current table.

Bottom: Once you enter at least one column of information and move to another cell, Excel adds the new row to the table and formats it.

To add a column to the left of a column you're currently in, select Home → Cells → Insert → Insert Table Columns to the Left. Excel automatically assigns a generic column title, like Column1, which you can then edit. If you want to add a column to the right side of the table, just start typing in the blank column immediately to the right of the table. When you've finished your entry, Excel automatically merges that column into the table, in the same way that it expands to include new rows.

To delete a column, move to one of its cells, and then choose Home → Cells → Delete → Delete Table Column.

Finally, you can always convert your snazzy table back to an ordinary collection of cells. Just click anywhere in the table, and then choose Table Tools | Design → Tools → Convert to Range. But then, of course, you don't get to play with your table toys anymore.

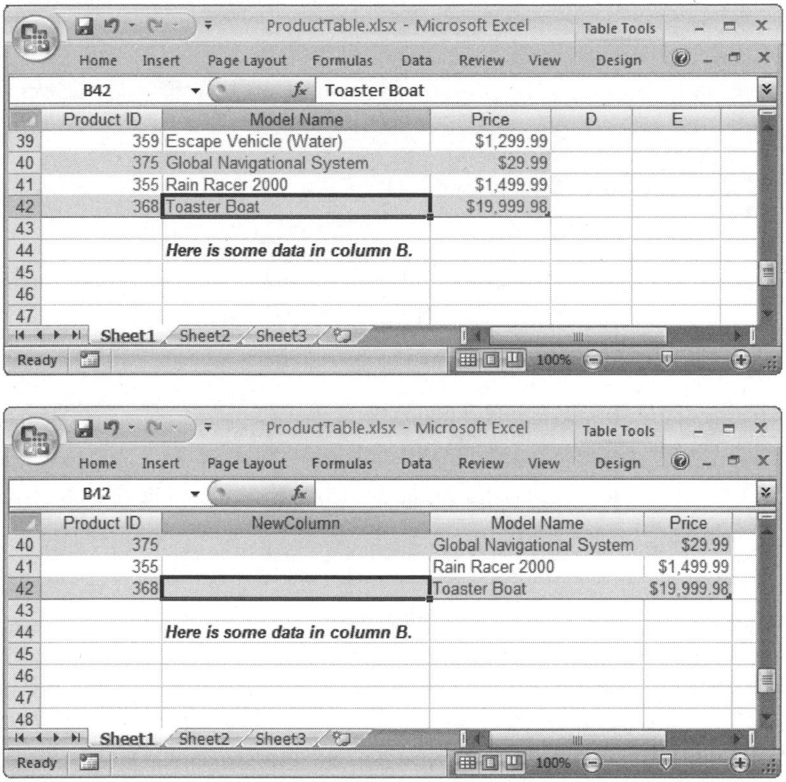

Figure 16-6:
Excel makes an effort to leave the rest of your worksheet alone when you change your table's structure. For example, when expanding a table vertically or horizontally, Excel moves cells out of the way only when it absolutely needs more space. The example here demonstrates the point. Compare the before (top) and after (bottom) pictures: Even though the table in the bottom figure has a new column, it hasn't affected the data underneath the table, which still occupies the same column. The same holds true when deleting columns.

Selecting Parts of a Table

Once you've created a table, Excel provides you with some nice timesaving tools. For example, Excel makes it easy to select a portion of a table, like an individual row or column. Here's how it works:

- **To select a column**, position your mouse cursor over the column header. When it changes to a down-pointing arrow, click once to select all the values in the column. Click a second time to select all the values plus the column header.

- **To select a row**, position your mouse cursor over the left edge of the row until it turns to a right-pointing arrow; then click once.

- **To select the entire table**, position your mouse at the top-left corner until it turns into an arrow that points down and to the right. Click once to select all the values in the table, and click twice to select all the values plus the column headers.

Figure 16-7 shows an example.

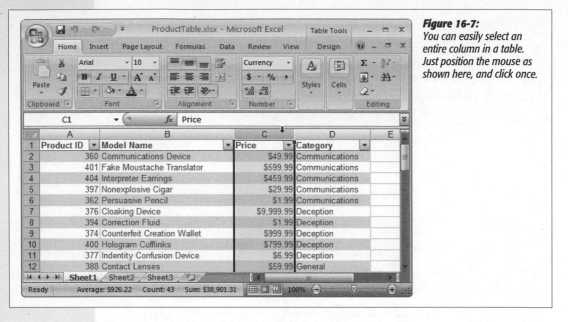

Figure 16-7:
You can easily select an entire column in a table. Just position the mouse as shown here, and click once.

Once you've selected a row, column, or the entire table, you can apply extra formatting or create a chart. However, changing a part of a table isn't exactly like changing a bunch of cells. For example, if you give 10 cells a hot-pink background fill, that's all you get—10 hot-pink cells. But if you give a column a hot-pink background fill, your formatting change may initially affect 10 cells, but every time you add a new value in that column, it also gets the hot-pink background. This behavior, in which Excel recognizes that you're changing parts of a table, and applies your change to new rows and columns automatically, is called *stickiness*.

Sorting and Filtering a Table

As you've seen, Excel tables make it easier to enter, edit, and manage large collections of information. Now it's time to meet two of the most useful table features:

- **Sorting** lets you order the items in your table alphabetically or numerically according to the information in a column. By using the correct criteria, you can make sure the information you're interested in appears at the top of the column, and you can make it easier to find an item anywhere in your table.

- **Filtering** lets you display only certain records in your table based on specific criteria you enter. Filtering lets you work with part of your data and temporarily hide the information you aren't interested in.

You can quickly apply sorting and filtering using the drop-down column headers that Excel adds to every table.

Note: Don't see a drop-down list at the top of your columns? A wrong ribbon click can inadvertently hide them. If you just see ordinary column headings (and you know you have a bona fide table), choose Data → Sort & Filter → Filter to get the drop-down lists back.

Applying a Simple Sort Order

Before you can sort your data, you need to choose a *sorting key*—the piece of information Excel uses to order your records. For example, if you want to sort a table of products so the cheapest (or most expensive) products appear at the top of the table, the Price column would be the sorting key to use.

In addition to choosing a sorting key, you also need to decide whether you want to use ascending or descending order. Ascending order, which is most common, organizes numbers from smallest to largest, dates from oldest to most recent, and text in alphabetical order. (If you have more than one type of data in the same column—which is rarely a good idea—text appears first, followed by numbers and dates, then true or false values, and finally error values.) In descending order, the order is reversed.

To apply a new sort order, choose the column you want to use for your sort key. Click the drop-down box at the right side of the column header, and then choose one of the menu commands that starts with the word "Sort." The exact wording depends on the type of data in the column, as follows:

- **If your column contains numbers**, you see "Sort Smallest to Largest" and "Sort Largest to Smallest".

- **If your column contains text**, you see "Sort A to Z" and "Sort Z to A" (see Figure 16-8).

- **If your column contains dates**, you see "Sort Oldest to Newest" and "Sort Newest to Oldest".

When you choose an option, Excel immediately reorders the records, and then places a tiny arrow in the column header to indicate that you used this column for your sort. However, Excel doesn't keep re-sorting your data when you make changes or add new records (after all, it would be pretty distracting to have your records jump around unexpectedly). If you make some changes and want to reapply the sort, just go to the column header menu and choose the same sort option again.

If you click a second column, and then choose Sort Ascending or Sort Descending, the new sort order replaces your previous sort order. In other words, the column headers let you sort your records quickly, but you can't sort by more than one column at a time.

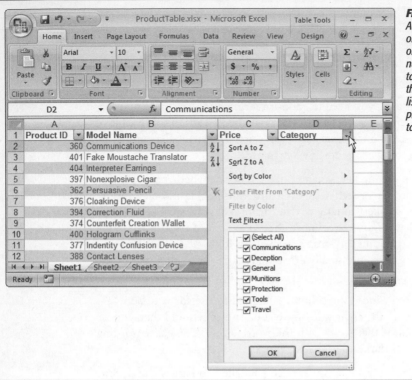

Figure 16-8:
A single click is all it takes to order records in ascending order by their category names. You don't need to take any action to create these handy drop-down lists—Excel automatically provides them for every table.

Sorting with Multiple Criteria

Simple table sorting runs into trouble when you have duplicate values. Take the product table sorted by category in Figure 16-8, for example. All the products in the Communications category appear first, followed by products in the Deception category, and so on. However, Excel doesn't make any effort to sort products that are in the *same* category. For example, if you have a bunch of products in the Communications category, then they appear in whatever order they were in on your worksheet, which may not be what you want. In this case, you're better off using *multiple sort criteria.*

With multiple sort criteria, Excel orders the table using more than one sorting key. The second sorting key springs into action only if there are duplicate values in the first sorting key. For example, if you sort by Category and Model Name, Excel first separates the records into alphabetically ordered category groups. It then sorts the products in each category in order of their model name.

To use multiple sort criteria, follow these steps:

1. **Move to any one of the cells inside your table, and then choose Home → Editing → Sort & Filter → Custom Sort.**

   Excel selects all the data in your table, and then displays the Sort dialog box (see Figure 16-9) where you can specify the sorting keys you want to use.

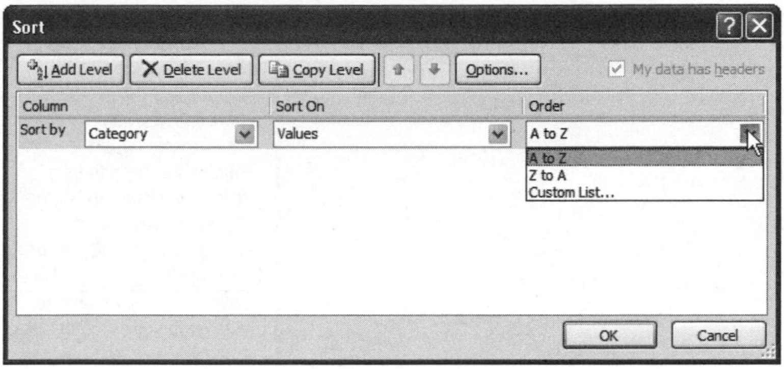

Figure 16-9:
To define a sorting key, you need to fill in the column you want to use (in this example, Category). Next, pick the information you want to use from that column, which is almost always the actual cell values (Values). Finally, choose the order for arranging values, which depends on the type of data. For text values, as in this example, you can pick A to Z, Z to A, or Custom List (page 379).

Note: You can use the Home → Editing → Sort & Filter → Custom Sort command with any row-based data, including information that's not in a table. When you use it with non-table data, Excel automatically selects the range of cells it believes constitutes your table.

2. **Fill in the information for the first sort key in the Column, Sort On, and Order columns.**

Figure 16-9 shows how it works.

3. **If you want to add another level of sorting, click Add Level, and then follow the instructions in step 2 to configure it.**

You can repeat this step to add as many sorting levels as you want (Figure 16-10). Remember, it makes sense to add more levels of sorting only if there's a possibility of duplicate value in the levels you've added so far. For example, if you've sorted a bunch of names by last name, you want to sort by first name, because some people may share the same last name. However, it's probably not worth it to add a third sort on the middle initial, because very few people share the same first and last name.

4. **Optionally, click the Options button to configure a few finer points about how your data is sorted.**

For example, you can turn on case-sensitive sorting, which is ordinarily switched off. If you switch it on, *travel* appears before *Travel*.

5. **Click OK.**

Excel sorts your entire table based on the criteria you've so carefully specified (Figure 16-11).

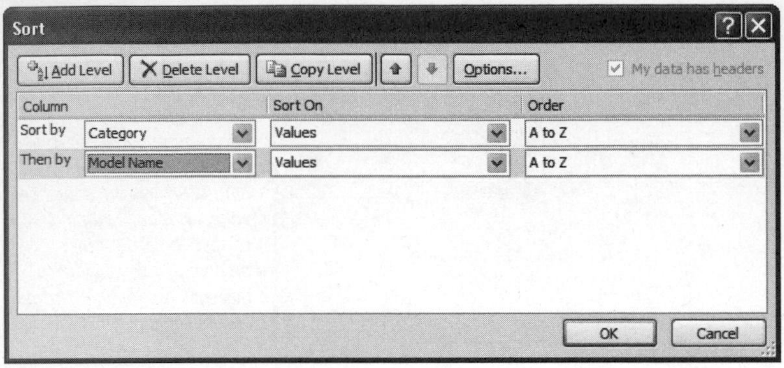

Figure 16-10:
This example shows two sorting keys: the Category column and the Model Name column. The Category column may contain duplicate entries, which Excel sorts in turn according to the text in the Model Name column. When you're adding multiple sort keys, make sure they're in the right order. If you need to rearrange your sorting, select a sort key, and then click the arrow buttons to move it up the list (so it's applied first) or down the list (so it's applied later).

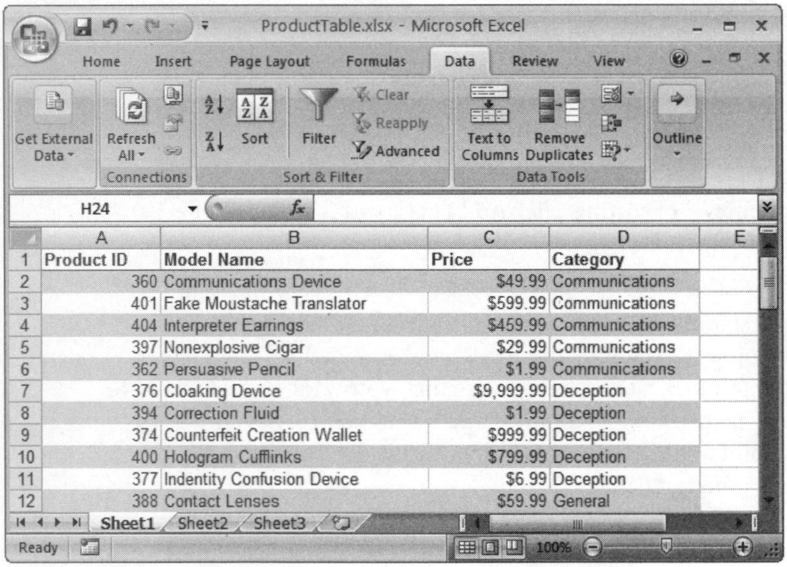

Figure 16-11:
The worksheet shows the following sort's result: alphabetically ordered categories, each of which contains a subgroup of products that are themselves in alphabetical order.

Filtering with the List of Values

Sorting is great for ordering your data, but it may not be enough to tame large piles of data. You can try another useful technique, *filtering*, which lets you limit the table so it displays only the data that you want to see. Filtering may seem like a small convenience, but if your table contains hundreds or thousands of rows, filtering is vital for your day-to-day worksheet sanity. Here are some situations where filtering becomes especially useful:

Sorting with a Custom List

Most of the time, you'll want to stick with the standard sorting orders. For example, you'll put numbers in numeric order, dates in chronological order, and text in alphabetical order. But not always. For example, you may have good reason to arrange the categories in Figure 16-11 in a different order that puts more important categories at the top of the table. Or, you may have text values that have special meaning and are almost always used in a specific non-alphabetical order, like the days of the week (Sunday, Monday, Tuesday, and so on) or calendar months (January, February, March, April, and so on).

You can deal with these scenarios with a custom list that specifies your sort order. In the Order column, choose Custom List. This choice opens the Custom List dialog box, where you can choose an existing list or create a new one by selecting NEW LIST and typing in your values. (Page 241 has more on creating specialized lists.) Figure 16-12 shows an example.

Custom list sorting works best when you have a relatively small number of values that never change. If you have dozens of different values, it's probably too tedious to type them all into a custom list.

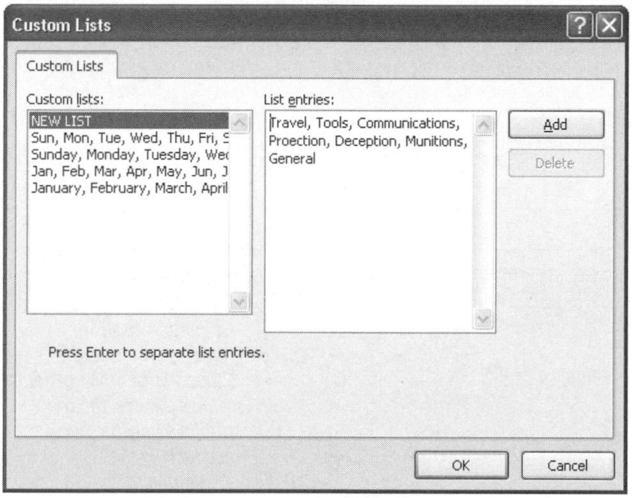

Figure 16-12:
Using a custom list for your sort order, you can arrange your categories so that Travel always appears at the top, as shown here. Once you've finished entering a custom list, click Add to store the list for future use.

- To pluck out important information, like the number of accounts that currently have a balance due. Filtering lets you see just the information you need, saving you hours of headaches.

- To print a report that shows only the customers who live in a specific city.

- To calculate information like sums and averages for products in a specific group.

Automatic filtering, like sorting, uses the drop-down column headings. When you click the drop-down arrow, Excel shows a list of all the distinct values in that column. Figures 16-13 and 16-14 show how filtering works on the Category column.

To remove a filter, open the drop-down column menu, and choose Clear Filter.

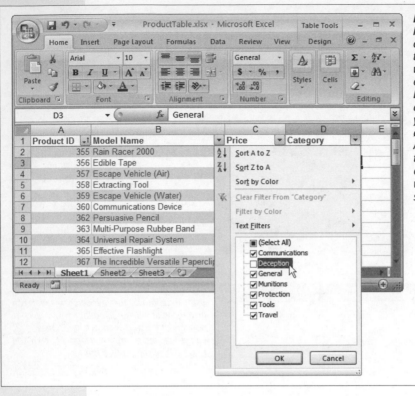

Figure 16-13:
Initially, each value has a checkmark next to it. Clear the checkmark to hide rows with that value. (In this example, products in the Deception category won't appear in the table.) Or, if you want to home in on just a few items, clear the Select All checkmark to remove all the checkmarks, and then choose just the ones you want to see in your table, as shown in Figure 16-14.

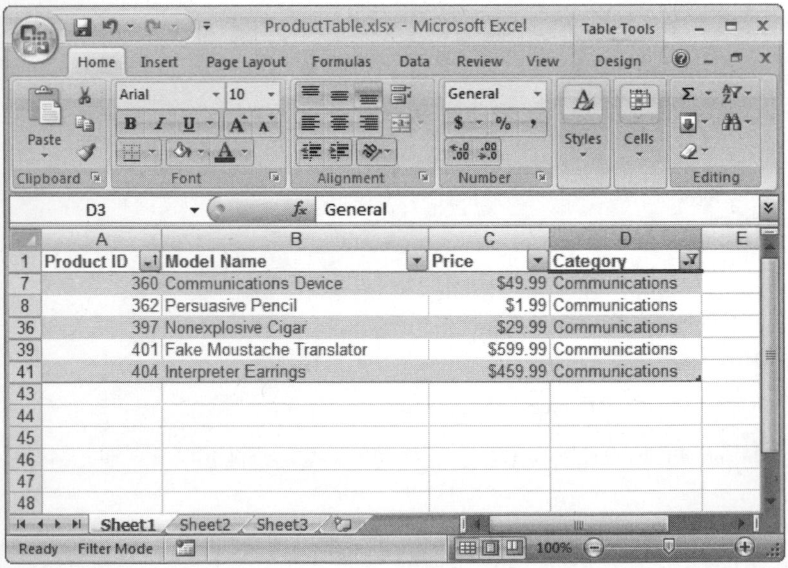

Figure 16-14:
If you select Communications and nothing else from the Category list in the product table example, the table displays only the five products in the Communications category.

Creating Smarter Filters

The drop-down column lists give you an easy way to filter out specific rows. However, in many situations you'll want a little more intelligence in your filtering. For example, imagine you're filtering a list of products to focus on all those that top $100. You could scroll through the list of values, and remove the checkmark next to every price that's lower than $100. What a pain in the neck that would be.

Thankfully, Excel has more filtering features that can really help you out here. Based on the type of data in your column (text, a number, or date values), Excel adds a wide range of useful filter options to the drop-down column lists. You'll see how this all works in the following sections.

Filtering dates

You can filter dates that fall before or after another date, or you can use preset periods like last week, last month, next month, year-to-date, and so on.

To use date filtering, open the drop-down column list, and choose Date Filters. Figure 16-15 shows what you see.

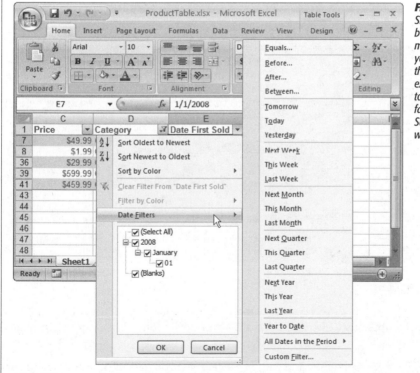

Figure 16-15:
Shown here is the mind-boggling array of ready-made date filtering options you can apply to a column that contains dates. For example, choose Last Week to see just those dates that fall in the period Sunday to Saturday in the previous week.

Filtering numbers

For numbers, you can filter values that match exactly, numbers that are smaller or larger than a specified number, or numbers that are above or below average.

To use number filtering, open the drop-down column list, choose Number Filters, and then pick one of the filter options. For example, imagine you're trying to limit the product list to show expensive products. You can accomplish this quite quickly with a number filter. Just open the drop-down column list for the Price column, and then choose Number Filters → Greater Than Or Equal To. A dialog box appears where you can supply the $100 minimum (Figure 16-16).

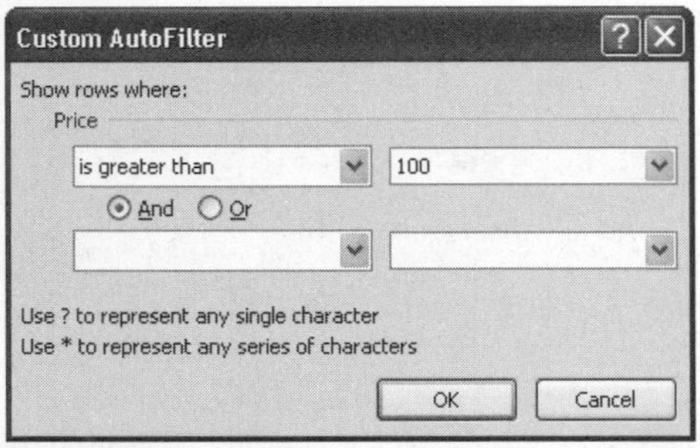

Figure 16-16:
This dialog box lets you complete the Greater Than Or Equal To filter. It matches all products that are $100 or more. You can use the bottom portion of the window (left blank in this example) to supply a second filter condition that either further restricts (choose And) or supplements your matches (choose Or).

WORKAROUND WORKSHOP

The Disappearing Cells

Table filtering's got one quirk. When you filter a table, Excel hides the rows that contain the filtered records. In fact, all Excel really does is shrink each of these rows to have a height of 0 so they're neatly out of sight. The problem? When Excel hides a row, it hides all the data in that row, *even if the data is not a part of the table.*

That property means that if you place a formula in one of the cells to the right of the table, then this formula may disappear from your worksheet temporarily when you filter the

table! This behavior is quite a bit different from what happens if you delete a row, in which case cells outside the table aren't affected.

If you frequently use filtering, you may want to circumvent this problem by putting your formulas underneath or above the table. Generally, putting the formulas above the table is the most convenient choice because the cells don't move as the table expands or contracts.

Filtering text

For text, you can filter values that match exactly, or values that contain a piece of text. To apply text filtering, open the drop-down column list, and then choose Text Filters.

If you're performing filtering with text fields, you can gain even more precise control using wildcards. The asterisk (*) matches any series of characters, while the question mark (?) matches a single character. So the filter expression *Category equals T** matches any category that starts with the letter T. The filter expression *Category equals T????* matches any five-letter category that starts with T.

Charting 101

Excel provides a dizzying number of different chart types, but they all share a few things. In this section, you'll learn about basic Excel charting concepts that apply to almost all types of charts; you'll also create a few basic charts.

Note: All charts are *not* created equal. Depending on the chart type you use, the scale you choose, and the data you include, your chart may suggest different conclusions. The true chart artist knows how to craft a chart to draw out the most important information. As you become more skilled with charts, you'll acquire these instincts, too.

To create a chart, Excel needs to translate your numbers into a graphical representation. The process of drawing numbers on a graph is called *plotting*. Before you plot your information on a chart, you should make sure your data's laid out properly. Here are some tips:

- Structure your data in a simple grid of rows and columns.

- Don't include blank cells between rows or columns.

- Include titles, if you'd like them to appear in your chart. You can use category titles for each column of data (placed in the first row, atop each column) and an overall chart title (placed just above the category-title row).

Tip: You can also label each row by placing titles in the far-left column, if it makes sense. If you're comparing the sales numbers for different products, list the name of each product in the first column on the left, with the sales figures in the following columns.

If you follow these guidelines, you can expect to create the sort of chart shown in Figure 16-17.

To create the chart shown in Figure 16-17, Excel performs a few straightforward steps. First, it extracts the text for the chart title from cell A1. Next, it examines the range of data (from $14,000 to $64,000) and uses it to set the value—or Y-axis—scale. You'll notice that the scale starts at $0, and stretches up to $80,000 in order to give your data a little room to breathe. (You could configure these numbers manually, but Excel automatically makes common-sense guesses like these by looking at the data you're asking it to chart.) After setting the vertical scale, Excel adds the labels along the bottom axis (also known as the X-axis or category axis), and draws the columns of appropriate height.

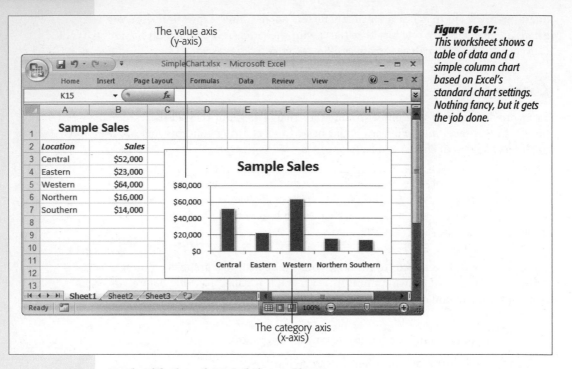

The value axis
(y-axis)

The category axis
(x-axis)

Figure 16-17:
This worksheet shows a table of data and a simple column chart based on Excel's standard chart settings. Nothing fancy, but it gets the job done.

Embedded and Standalone Charts

The chart in Figure 16-17 is an *embedded* chart. Embedded charts appear in a worksheet, in a floating box alongside your data. You can move the chart by dragging the box around your worksheet, although depending on where you put it, you may obscure some of your data.

Your other option is to create a *standalone* chart, which looks the same but occupies an entire worksheet. That means that your chart data and your chart are placed on separate worksheets. *Excel 2007: The Missing Manual* teaches you how to create standalone charts.

Usually, you'll use an embedded chart if you want to create printouts that combine both your worksheet data and one or more charts. On the other hand, if you want to print the charts separately, it's more convenient to use standalone charts. That way, you can print an entire workbook at once and have the charts and the data on separate pages.

Tip: If you use embedded charts, you still have the option of printing just the chart, sized so that it fills a full sheet of paper. Simply select the chart and then choose Office button → Print.

Charts Get a Facelift

If you've worked with charts in a previous version of Excel, you'll notice that Excel 2007 adds some serious eye candy. Overall, the types of charts you can create and the options to plot your data are the same as in previous versions. However, the *rendering engine*, the system that turns your data into lines and shapes, is completely new.

Along with the new rendering engine, Excel 2007 also changes the way you create your charts. Gone is the frumpy Chart Wizard. Now, the ribbon provides quick chart creation and easy-access options for changing every aspect of a chart, from its gridlines to its legend.

Creating a Chart with the Ribbon

So how do you create a chart like the one shown in Figure 16-17? Easy—all it takes is a couple of clicks in the ribbon. Here's how it works:

1. **Select the range of cells that includes the data you want to chart, including the column and row headings and any chart title.**

   If you were using the data shown in Figure 16-17, you'd select cells A1 to B7.

   For speedier chart building, just position your cursor somewhere inside the data you want to chart. Excel then automatically selects the range of cells that it thinks you want. Of course, it never hurts to remove the possibility for error by explicitly selecting what you want to use before you get started.

Charting a Table

You can use the Excel table feature (discussed on page 366) with charts. Tables and charts make a perfect match. Tables grow and shrink dynamically in size as you add or delete records. If a chart's bound to a table, the chart updates itself as you add new information or remove old data.

You've already learned how to build a new chart using an existing table. (Just move inside the table, and then make a selection from the ribbon's Insert → Charts section). But even if you've already created the chart with an ordinary range of cells, you can still use a table—all you need to do is convert the linked range to a table.

In the sales report example shown in Figure 16-17, here's what you'd need to do:

1. Select the range of cells that contain all the data, not including the chart's title (cells A2 to B7).

2. Select Insert → Tables → Table.

Now, as you add new items to the table, Excel adds them to the chart immediately.

When you chart a table, you also gain the ability to use other features, like easier sorting and filtering. You can use sorting to determine the order that items appear within a chart (which is occasionally useful), and you can use filtering to hide rows and to chart only a portion of the data (which is often indispensable). If you apply a filter condition that shows only the three best performing regions, the chart updates itself so that it shows only this data. You'll find this technique particularly handy when you're creating charts that use multiple series.

Tip: And for even *easier* charting, start by creating an Excel table—as described earlier in this chapter—to hold the data you want to chart. Then, if you position yourself somewhere inside the table and create a new chart, Excel automatically selects all the data. It also automatically updates the chart if you add new rows or remove existing data.

2. **Head to the ribbon's Insert → Charts section. You'll see a separate button for each type of chart (including column charts, line charts, pie charts, and so on). Click the type you want.**

When you choose a chart type, you get a drop-down list of subtypes (Figure 16-18).

Figure 16-18:
Under each chart choice are yet more subtypes, which add to the fun. If you select the Column type (shown here), you'll get subtypes for two- and three-dimensional column charts, and variants that use cone and pyramid shapes. If you hover over one of these subtypes, a box appears with a brief description of the chart.

The different chart types are explained in more detail in *Excel 2007: The Missing Manual*. For now, it's best to stick to some of the more easily understood choices, like Bar, Column, or Pie. Remember, the chart choices are just the starting point, as you'll still be able to configure a wide range of details that control things like the titles, colors, and overall organization of your chart.

3. **Click the subtype you want.**

Excel inserts a new embedded chart alongside your data, using the standard options (which you can fine-tune later).

UNDER THE HOOD

How Excel Anchors Charts

Although charts appear to float above the worksheet, they're actually anchored to the cells underneath. Each corner of the chart is anchored to one cell (these anchor points change, of course, if you move the chart around). This fact becomes important if you decide to insert or delete rows or columns anywhere in your worksheet.

For example, consider the chart shown in Figure 16-17. Its top edge is bound to row 2, and its bottom edge is bound to row 12. Similarly, its left edge is bound to column C, and its right edge to column I. That means if you insert a new row above row 2, the whole chart shifts down one row. If you insert a column to the left of column C, the whole chart shifts one column to the right.

Even more interesting is what happens if you insert rows or columns in the area that the chart overlaps. For example, if you insert a new row between the current row 10 and row 11, the chart stretches, becoming one row taller. Similarly, if you delete column D, the chart compresses, becoming one column thinner.

If it bugs you, you can change this sizing behavior. First, select the chart and head to the ribbon's Chart Tools | Format → Size section. Then, click the dialog launcher (the square-with-an-arrow icon in the bottom-right corner). When the Size and Properties dialog box appears, choose the Properties tab. You'll see three "Object positioning" options. The standard behavior is "Move and size with cells", but you can also create a chart that moves around the worksheet but never resizes itself ("Move but don't size with cells") and a chart that's completely fixed in size and position ("Don't move or size with cells").

Note: If you don't want to make *any* choices, you can actually build a chart with one key press. Just highlight your data and press F11. This step creates a column chart on a new worksheet. Although you can't undo this operation, you can always delete the new chart worksheet and start over.

The Chart Tools Ribbon Tabs

When you select a chart, Excel adds three new tabs to the ribbon under the Chart Tools heading. These tabs let you control the details of your charts:

- **Design.** This tab lets you change the chart type and the linked data that the chart uses.

- **Layout.** This tab lets you configure individual parts of the chart. You can add shapes, pictures, and text labels, and you can configure the chart's gridlines, axes, and background.

- **Format.** This tab lets you format individual chart elements, so you can transform ordinary items into eye candy. You can adjust the font, fill, and borders uses for chart titles and shapes, among other things.

In this chapter, you'll spend most of your time using the Chart Tools | Design tab.

Printing Charts

How you print a chart depends on the type of chart you've created. In this chapter, you've learned how to create embedded charts. You can print embedded charts either with worksheet data or on their own. (Standalone charts, which occupy separate worksheets, always print on separate pages.)

You can print embedded charts in two ways. The first approach is to print your worksheet exactly as it appears on the screen, with a mix of data and floating charts. In this case, you'll need to take special care to make sure your charts aren't positioned over any data you need to read in the printout. To double-check, use Page Layout view (choose View → Workbook Views → Page Layout View).

You could also print out the embedded chart on a separate page, which is surprisingly easy. Just click the chart to select it, and then choose Office Button → Print (or Office Button → Print → Print Preview to see what it'll look like). When you do so, Excel's standard choice is to print your chart using landscape orientation, so that the long edge of the page is along the bottom, and the chart's wider than it is tall. Landscape is usually the best way to align a chart, especially if it holds a large amount of data, so Excel automatically uses landscape orientation no matter what page orientation you've configured for your worksheet. If you want to change the chart orientation, select the chart, then choose Page Layout → Page Setup → Orientation → Portrait. Now your chart uses upright alignment, just as you may see in a portrait-style painting.

Note: If you select an orientation from the Page Layout → Page Setup → Orientation list while your chart is selected, you *don't* end up configuring the orientation for the worksheet itself. Instead you configure the embedded chart's orientation when you print it out on a separate page. If you want to configure the orientation for the whole worksheet, make sure nothing else is selected when you choose an orientation.

Excel also includes some page setup options that are specific to charts. To see these options, head to the Page Layout → Page Setup section, click the dialog launcher in the bottom-right corner to show the Page Setup dialog box, and then choose the Chart tab (which appears only when you've got a chart currently selected). You'll see an option to print a chart using lower print quality ("Draft quality"), and in black and white instead of color ("Print in black and white").

Part Three:
PowerPoint 2007

3

Creating a Basic Presentation

If you've never seen a PowerPoint presentation, you're in a pretty select group. With legions of folks all over the world pounding out an estimated *30 million PowerPoint slides every day*, PowerPoint's the runaway leader in the field of presentation programs, leaving competitors like Corel Presentations and Apple's Keynote in the dust. PowerPoint has become so ubiquitous that it's even managed to work its way into the English language: *powerpointless*, as many audience members can attest, describes a PowerPoint presentation that has bulleted text, graphics, animated slide transitions—everything except a good reason for existing.

So how do you improve a program that's so wildly successful? If you're Microsoft, you completely redesign it. As described in the introduction, PowerPoint 2007 looks completely different from its previous incarnation, PowerPoint 2003. The menus, wizards, and most of the toolbars and panes that a generation of Power-Pointilists grew up with have been replaced by the ribbon (Figure 17-1). And that's just the tip of the redesign iceberg.

This chapter will familiarize you with the major changes by walking you through the creation of a basic bullets-and-background slideshow presentation. You'll learn how to create a new slideshow, choose a look and feel, add text and slides, print speaker notes and handouts, and finally, how to unveil your masterpiece.

The good news is you can still do the same things in PowerPoint 2007 that you could do in earlier versions—and a few more, besides. You can still design beautiful slideshows that contain bulleted lists, pictures, and sound clips. You can still deliver your slideshows in person, on CD, or on an unattended kiosk.

What's new in PowerPoint 2007 is *how* you do all of these things.

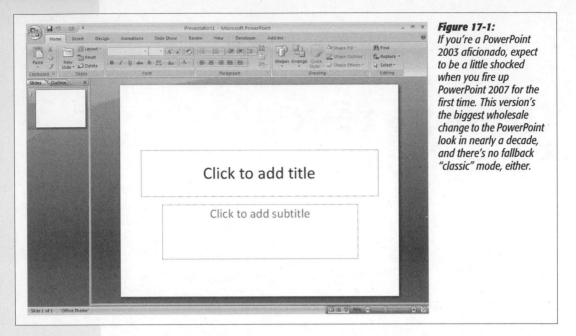

Figure 17-1:
If you're a PowerPoint 2003 aficionado, expect to be a little shocked when you fire up PowerPoint 2007 for the first time. This version's the biggest wholesale change to the PowerPoint look in nearly a decade, and there's no fallback "classic" mode, either.

If you're familiar with PowerPoint 2003 or an earlier version of the program, this book will help you make the transition from the old, familiar way of doing things to the new, improved way. (You'll even see tips and tricks that were buried so deep inside menus and toolbars in PowerPoint 2003 that you probably didn't know they were there.)

On the other hand, if you're brand new to PowerPoint—or even to presentation programs in general—then you're in luck, because this book shows you how to build basic to bowl-'em-over presentations for work, school, or whatever you're involved in.

FROM THE FIELD

Presentation vs. Slideshow

Microsoft's help files, as well as most PowerPoint books, use the terms *presentation* and *slideshow* interchangeably. But a very important distinction exists between the two.

A *slideshow* is a collection of slides but a *presentation* is everything that goes into delivering the slideshow to your audience. A presentation includes not just the slideshow, but speaker notes, printed handouts, and—most important of all—*you*, the presenter.

In other words, no matter how cool your slides are, they aren't your presentation. Your slides are nothing more than tools you use to deliver your message. If you keep this distinction in mind, you'll keep your focus on the message—where it belongs—and off the tricky stuff you can do with PowerPoint. For your audience's sake, avoid bringing yet another powerpointless presentation into the world!

What You Can Do with PowerPoint 2007

PowerPoint was originally designed to help business professionals create and deliver electronic slideshows (sales presentations, mostly). But over the years, as Microsoft piled on the options, folks began discovering new ways to use the program.

Here's a short list of what you can create using PowerPoint 2007:

- **Multimedia presentations.** Use PowerPoint to create slideshows that you—the presenter—can run in front of an audience on a computer screen (for small groups) or a digital projector (for a packed conference hall). The kinds of presentations that fit into this group include business and sales presentations, workshop and conference sessions, academic lectures, in-class reports, courtroom summations, and church choir programs. The sky's the limit. Anytime you need to stand in front of a group and present information, you can use a PowerPoint slideshow to get your point across.

- **Kiosk presentations.** Presentations that run unattended, are perfect for trade shows, department store product demonstrations—even (believe it or not) weddings and funerals.

- **Printed documents.** It's not a full-fledged page-layout program like Quark XPress, but PowerPoint 2007 comes with templates for popular printables (like certificates of achievement and calendars). It also gives you more control over layout than earlier versions of the program.

What's New in PowerPoint 2007

Nearly all the changes Microsoft made to PowerPoint 2007 affect the way the program looks and behaves; in other words, the changes affect how you do things in PowerPoint 2007. The most sweeping of these include:

- **A completely redesigned interface.** The difference you notice right away is the tabbed *ribbon* (Figure 17-2), which replaces all of the old, pre–PowerPoint 2007 menus and toolbars. Instead of wasting time trying to remember if the option you want is hiding on a toolbar or a menu or a pane or a dialog box or somewhere else entirely, in PowerPoint 2007, you reach *all* options from the ribbon.

- **New file formats.** The files you'll create in PowerPoint 2007 bear a different file extension than the ones you created in earlier versions of the program. The good news is that the new XML-based file formats tend to be smaller and more recoverable than the old ones. The bad news is that you can't edit PowerPoint 2007 files in an earlier version of the program unless you download and install a special converter program (page 396 has details).

- **Tighter integration among Office programs.** Microsoft gave all of the Office programs a face lift, not just PowerPoint. The result is that all Office programs share similar elements. For example, the Office button (the old File menu)

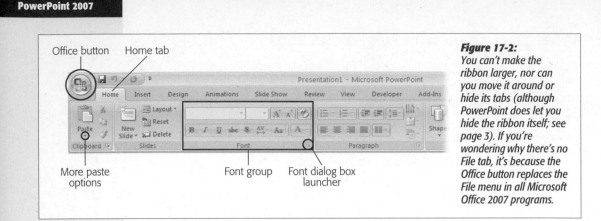

Office button   Home tab

More paste options

Font group   Font dialog box launcher

Figure 17-2:
You can't make the ribbon larger, nor can you move it around or hide its tabs (although PowerPoint does let you hide the ribbon itself; see page 3). If you're wondering why there's no File tab, it's because the Office button replaces the File menu in all Microsoft Office 2007 programs.

appears in the same spot in all Office programs, and certain options—like the ones you use to create charts and diagrams—look and behave pretty much the same way in PowerPoint as they do in Word and Excel.

- **Improved graphics.** All Office programs share a single, new-and-improved graphics engine that not only makes the charts, diagrams, and other visuals you create in PowerPoint look better (*much* better), but makes them easier to create, too (Figure 17-3).

- **More look-and-feel options.** PowerPoint 2007 comes with more and better-looking templates and slide layouts than earlier versions of the program.

FROM THE FIELD

When Not to Use PowerPoint

It's easy to get caught up in the trappings associated with giving a presentation: the slideshow, the handouts, the speaker notes, and so on. But you can give a fantastic, memorable presentation without any of these supporting tools. *You*—what you have to say and how you say it—are the reason people are filing into the room.

PowerPoint's supposed to *support* your presentation, not *be* your presentation.

So before you even fire up the program, ask yourself these questions:

- **Do I really need slides?** PowerPoint slides are great for keeping key points ("Our company's going down in flames") in front of your audience during your presentation. They're also great for making direct appeals ("Please be happy with your 50 percent pay cut"). What they're *not* good for is delivering a bunch of dense

information, such as the in-depth analysis of the last five years' worth of sales activity that led to your conclusion.

- **Do I really need speaker notes?** If you're planning to deliver a lengthy presentation, having your speaker notes cued up to match your slides can save you lots of hair-pulling. But if you're planning a short presentation, you know your material backwards and forwards, or you simply prefer to use 3×5 cards to jog your memory, then speaker notes may not be worth the time it takes to set them up.

- **Do I really need handouts?** Use printouts of your slides when you want to leave lots of specific instructions or actionable items with your audience. If that's not the case, skip the handouts (most end up in the circular file the minute the presentation's over anyway).

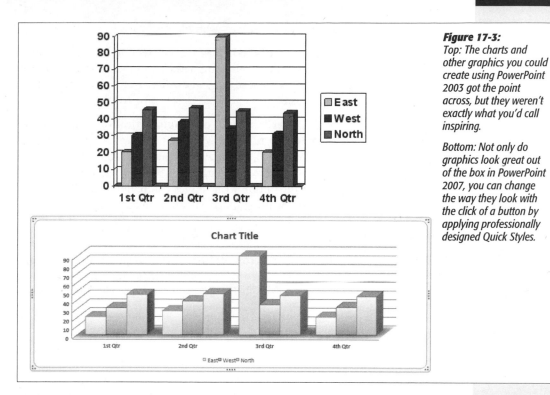

Figure 17-3:
Top: The charts and other graphics you could create using PowerPoint 2003 got the point across, but they weren't exactly what you'd call inspiring.

Bottom: Not only do graphics look great out of the box in PowerPoint 2007, you can change the way they look with the click of a button by applying professionally designed Quick Styles.

New File Formats

The files you create using PowerPoint 2007 bear different file extensions than the files you created using PowerPoint 2003 or an earlier version of the program. The "x" in the new PowerPoint 2007 file names reflects the new, XML-based file format. Table 17-1 shows you the differences.

Table 17-1. Old and New File Extensions for the Files You Create in PowerPoint

PowerPoint 2007 File Extension	Description	Old (pre-2007) File Extension
.pptx	Presentation	.ppt
.potx	Template	.pot
.ppsx	Show	.pps
.ppam	Add-in	.ppa
.pptm	Macro-enabled presentation	.ppt

Note: The PowerPoint portion of this book is based on *PowerPoint 2007: The Missing Manual* (O'Reilly). That book is a comprehensive reference covering every program feature, including geeky pursuits like adding video and animations to your slides and writing macros (mini-programs that automate your slideshows). Although you'll probably never need to do these things—and never want to—*PowerPoint 2007: The Missing Manual* has everything you need to know.

The implications of the new file formats are twofold:

- **Because the new file formats are based on XML, they tend to be more compact than PowerPoint 2003.** A smaller file is good news if you intend to deliver your presentation by email or on CD. Also, these new files are easier to recreate in the event of a computer crash.

- **The files you create with PowerPoint 2007 *can't* automatically be edited in earlier versions of the program.** Fortunately, Microsoft offers a compatibility pack that lets folks running Office 2003 open PowerPoint 2007 files; to download and install it, visit *www.microsoft.com/office/preview/beta/converter.mspx*. PowerPoint 2007 also gives you the option to save files compatible with PowerPoint 2003 and earlier versions of the program (see the box on page 422).

Improved Graphics

Microsoft overhauled the part of Microsoft Office that lets you create charts, diagrams, and pictures in PowerPoint, Word, and other Office programs. Not only is creating graphics easier in PowerPoint, the results, as you saw in Figure 17-3, are much more impressive.

More Theme Options

Like harvest-gold stoves and avocado shag carpeting, the design templates that came with PowerPoint 2003 were beginning to show their age. So Microsoft created a bunch of new design templates (they're called *Office themes* now) that look a little more up-to-date. Unlike the old PowerPoint-only design templates, you can apply the Office themes to any file you create using an Office program, from a PowerPoint slideshow to a Word document or Excel spreadsheet. (That's good news for folks who want to create matching backup reports in Word and matching spreadsheets in Excel to hand out at the end of their PowerPoint presentations.) Also new in PowerPoint 2007 is the ability to create multiple slides with the same layout faster with reusable slide masters (Chapter 21).

Beginning a New Presentation

You've got two basic choices when it comes to creating a new presentation:

- **You can start from scratch, using a blank canvas.** If you're familiar with earlier incarnations of the PowerPoint program, or if you're interested in learning the ins and outs of PowerPoint quickly, then you'll probably want to choose this option. (As daunting as "from scratch" sounds, you don't have to do all the work yourself; page 404 shows you how to apply a canned look and feel—or *theme*—to your new presentation.)

- **You can create a new presentation based on an existing template, theme, or
  presentation.** A *template* is a generic presentation file designed for you to reuse.
  Complete with themes (see the box on page 404), background images, and even
  generic content (such as page numbers and placeholder text), templates let you
  jump-start your presentation by giving you everything you need *except* your
  specific content. If you're creating a presentation for your local school board,
  for example, then you'll need to add the content that describes your findings,
  conclusions, and suggestions.

Templates are the better option when you need to crank out a presentation in a
jiffy. PowerPoint comes with a handful of professionally designed templates and
themes, but you can also create presentations based on a template, theme, or
presentation that you've previously created, or one that you've found online
and downloaded onto your computer.

Creating a New Presentation from Scratch

When you launch PowerPoint, the program starts you off with a brand-new presentation cleverly named Presentation1 (Figure 17-4).

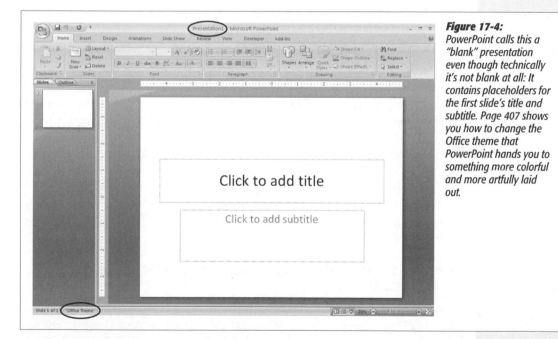

Figure 17-4:
*PowerPoint calls this a
"blank" presentation
even though technically
it's not blank at all: It
contains placeholders for
the first slide's title and
subtitle. Page 407 shows
you how to change the
Office theme that
PowerPoint hands you to
something more colorful
and more artfully laid
out.*

Typically, you dive right in, adding a look and feel, text, pictures, and so on to the
blank presentation PowerPoint hands you. But if you've closed or saved your free-
bie, here's how you create an additional blank presentation:

1. **Select Office button → New.**

   The New Presentation window (Figure 17-5) appears.

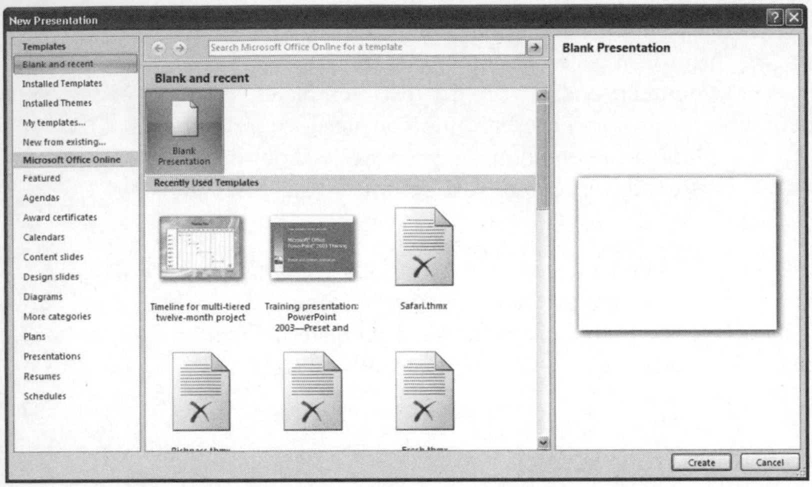

Figure 17-5:
Because folks typically want to create a new presentation either from scratch or based on a favorite (and, therefore, recently used) template, the "Blank and recent" option is automatically selected. But you can choose instead to create a presentation based on an existing presentation, or on a theme or template you've created or downloaded from the Web.

2. On the left side of the New Presentation window, make sure the "Blank and recent" option is selected.

   If it's not, click it to select it.

3. In the New Presentation window, double-click Blank Presentation (Figure 17-5). Or you can click Blank Presentation and then click Create.

   Either way, a new blank presentation named Presentation2 (or Presentation3, or Presentation4 depending on how many new presentations you've created since you launched the program) appears in your PowerPoint workspace.

Tip: To create a new blank presentation without going through the New Presentation window, press Ctrl+N.

To find out how to add content and design elements to your newly created presentation, zip down to page 410. Page 421 shows you how to save your new presentation.

Creating a Presentation from an Existing Template, Theme, or Presentation

PowerPoint lets you get a jump on your new presentation by starting with an existing template, theme, or presentation and then filling in your content. You can choose from the many templates and themes that come with PowerPoint, or you can go online and search for a specific template or theme that matches your needs. You can also reuse any of the templates, themes, or presentations that you (or your co-workers) have previously created. The following sections describe each of your options.

From an existing template

A *template* is a generic presentation designed (by Microsoft, by a third-party vendor, by you, or by whoever created the template) to be used again and again. Templates help you crank out presentations quickly, because all the design work has been done for you. All you have to do is add your content: the text, charts, graphics, and other elements that convey your particular message.

Templates vary widely, but all contain predefined *themes* (color schemes, background images, title and bullet point layouts, and text fonts). Some templates contain additional format and design elements and even some generic or placeholder content. Some templates are businesslike, with sober colors and artwork; some are whimsical, with wacky fonts and brightly colored balloons all over the place. The template motifs you can find are nearly endless, which makes it relatively easy to choose a template that fits the mood and structure you want to create for your presentation.

WORD TO THE WISE

The Trouble with Templates

The downside to using PowerPoint's pre-built templates is that you can end up with a presentation that looks exactly like the one Bob in Accounting presented last week. If that happens, then not only do you look bad, but your audience may tune out, assuming they've heard the same message before.

Another potential downside to using templates is that you may be tempted to shoehorn your presentation into the template—which is almost never a good idea.

Just keep in mind that to create an effective presentation, you need to focus first and foremost on your message, and *then* choose a template (or a theme, described on page 407) that supports your message. You may also want to consider tweaking the template—adjusting the font or replacing the background image with a tasteful gradient, for example—both to fit your message and to help ensure your presentation is as original and memorable as you are.

PowerPoint gives you four different options for creating a new presentation using an existing template: Recently used templates, Installed Templates, "My templates" (templates you've saved yourself), and Microsoft Office Online. The option you choose depends on where you want PowerPoint to hunt for the template, as described in the following sections.

Recently used templates. PowerPoint keeps track of the templates you apply to your presentations and displays the last few in a list. So if you tend to use the same two or three templates to create all your presentations, chances are you'll find this option the easiest.

Here's how to create a new presentation using a template you recently applied to another presentation:

1. **Select Office button → New.**

   The New Presentation window appears.

---

2. **In the left side of the New Presentation window, make sure the "Blank and recent" option is selected. (If it's not, click to select it.)**

3. **In the middle of the New Presentation window, scroll through the template thumbnails.**

Tip: Mousing over a template briefly displays the location of the template (for example, *C:\Program Files\Microsoft Office\Templates\QuizShow.potx* for a built-in template stored on your computer, or Office Website for a template located on Microsoft's Web server). You might find this information useful if, for example, you're hunting for a template you remember finding online.

4. **Click to select the template you want to base your new presentation on.**

   In the right side of the New Presentation window, a preview appears (see Figure 17-6). Depending on whether the selected template is stored on your computer or on Microsoft's Web server, PowerPoint displays a Create or Download button, respectively, at the bottom of the New Presentation window.

5. **Click Create (or Download).**

   The New Presentation window disappears. (If you clicked Download, then a Downloading Template message flashes briefly on the screen.) PowerPoint then loads the selected template into a new presentation it names Presentation1 (or Presentation2, or Presentation3, depending on how many presentations you've created since you launched PowerPoint).

Figure 17-6:
To see a larger version of a tiny template thumbnail—as well as to display any available identifying information, such as the template's file size and popularity rating—simply click to select the template.

Installed templates. When you installed PowerPoint, you automatically installed a handful of professionally designed templates, including templates that let you set up photo albums (Classic Photo Album and Contemporary Photo Album), corporate-style slideshows (Corporate Presentation), layouts for print publications (Pitchbook), animated question-and-answer tutorials (Quiz Show), and big-screen slideshows (Wide Screen Presentation 16×9).

To use one of these built-in templates to create a new presentation, follow these steps:

1. **Select Office button → New.**

   The New Presentation window appears.

2. **In the left side of the New Presentation window, click Installed Templates.**

   Several template thumbnails appear in the middle of the New Presentation window.

3. **Click a template to select it.**

   A larger version of the template appears in the preview area (the right side) of the New Presentation window.

4. **Click Create.**

   The New Presentation window disappears, and you see a new presentation file based on the template you selected. Figure 17-7 shows you an example.

Tip: Instead of clicking a template and then clicking Create, you can save a step by simply double-clicking the template.

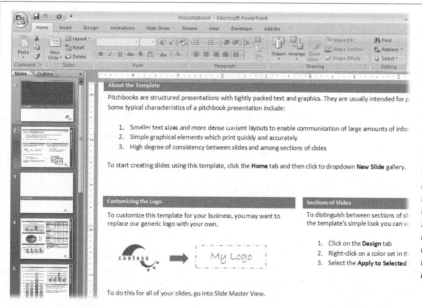

Figure 17-7:
Templates are nothing more than presentations for which someone (the template author) has defined Slide and Title masters. Masters, which you'll learn all about in Chapter 21, define the way your slides look overall (like this crisp, clean background) as well as the way your text looks (the color and font). Templates also typically include helpful slide layouts and content, like the attractive section headings and replaceable text shown here.

My templates. Each time you create your own template or download a template from Microsoft's Web site (below), PowerPoint automatically stores the template in a special directory on your computer similar to this one: *C:\Documents and Settings\[Your Name]\Application Date\Microsoft\Templates*.

To use one of these templates to create a new presentation, follow these steps:

1. **Select Office button → New.**

   The New Presentation window appears.

2. **On the left side of the New Presentation window, click "My templates."**

   The New Presentation window vanishes, and the New Presentation dialog box shown in Figure 17-8 appears.

3. **In the New Presentation dialog box, select the template you want to use and click OK.**

   The New Presentation dialog box disappears, and PowerPoint displays a new presentation file based on the template you selected.

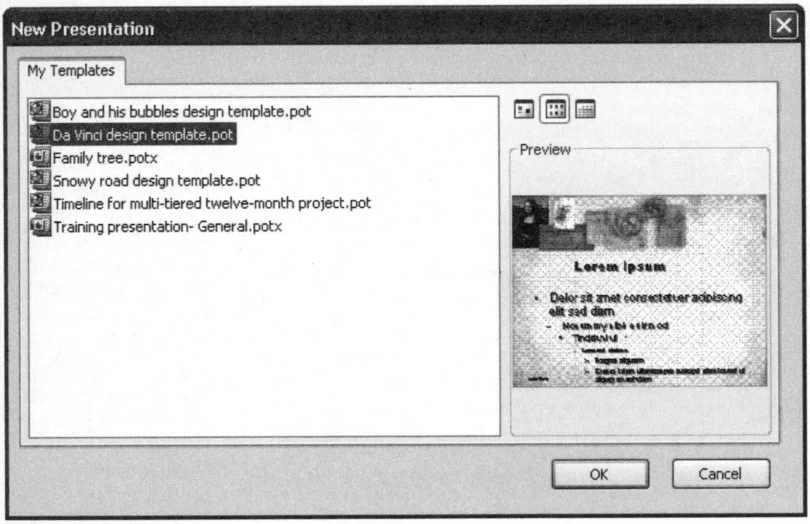

Figure 17-8:
PowerPoint stores the templates you create—or that you download from Microsoft's Office Online Web site—in a special folder so that you won't confuse them with PowerPoint's built-in templates. To change how the template icons appear, choose from Large Icons (which makes the template names easier to read), List (shown here), and Details (which displays the date the template was created).

Online. Although lots of Web sites offer PowerPoint templates for download, you should check Microsoft's Office Online Web site first for a couple of reasons. One, Microsoft's templates are free; and two, checking Microsoft's site is one-click easy, as described next.

Tip: Because Microsoft lets its customers upload templates willy-nilly, the quantity and quality of the templates you find on its site can vary widely. Figure 17-9 shows how to weed out customer-submitted templates, leaving only those designed by official Microsofties.

1. **Select Office button → New.**

   The New Presentation window appears.

2. **On the left side of the New Presentation window, under Microsoft Office Online, choose the type of template you're looking for, such as Brochures or Content Slides.**

   Template thumbnails appear in the center of the New Presentation window (Figure 17-9).

3. **Click a template thumbnail to select it; then click Download.**

   A validation message box appears, letting you know that Microsoft is gearing up to check your copy of PowerPoint to make sure it's not bootlegged. (If Microsoft doesn't find a legitimately purchased copy of PowerPoint on your computer, then you won't be able to download templates.)

4. **In the validation message box, click Continue.**

   Microsoft checks out your copy of PowerPoint. If it passes muster, a Downloading Template message appears briefly, after which PowerPoint displays a new presentation file based on the template you selected.

The rest of this chapter shows you how to add text and change the look of your newly created presentation.

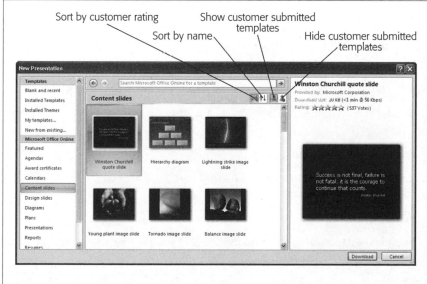

Sort by customer rating

Sort by name

Show customer submitted templates

Hide customer submitted templates

Figure 17-9:
For finer control over the templates you see, select Rating Sort (which displays the most popular templates first, as determined by other PowerPoint fans), Name Sort (which displays named templates in alphabetical order), Show Customer Submitted (which displays all templates, including the ones other PowerPoint folks have uploaded), or Hide Customer Submitted (which shows only those templates created by Microsoft).

The Difference Between Templates and Themes

In PowerPoint 2007, you have two separate and distinct ways to customize your presentations—*templates* and *themes*.

- **Templates.** A template is any presentation you plan to reuse. You tell PowerPoint—and remind yourself and your coworkers—that you plan to reuse it by saving it in the special template file format, .potx. Templates typically define custom slide layouts and, in some cases, generic content. Every template has a theme.

- **Themes.** A theme tells PowerPoint what color to use for your slides' titles, subtitles, body text, background, and so forth. It also describes which fonts and graphic effects to use; for example, some themes automatically add shadows to title text and blurring to the shapes you add to your slides.

From an existing (built-in) theme

If you know which theme you want to apply to the new presentation you're creating, then you can save a click or two by applying it when you create the presentation file. (The alternative is to create the presentation file and *then* apply the theme, as described on page 407.)

To create a new presentation based on one of the themes that comes with PowerPoint:

1. **Select Office button → New.**

   The New Presentation window appears.

2. **On the left side of the New Presentation window, click Installed Themes.**

   Several theme thumbnails appear in the middle of the New Presentation window.

3. **Click a theme to select it.**

   A larger version of the theme appears in the preview area (the right side) of the New Presentation window.

4. **Click Create.**

   The New Presentation window disappears and you see a new presentation based on the theme you selected. Figure 17-10 shows you an example.

Tip: Instead of clicking a theme and then clicking Create, you can save a step by simply double-clicking the theme.

Figure 17-10:
Unlike applying a template to a newly created presentation, applying a theme doesn't start you out with custom slide layouts or content. Instead—as you can see by the single slide shown here—themes give you coordinated color, font, and background effects. PowerPoint automatically applies these effects to each new slide you create.

From an existing presentation

If you've already got a presentation on your computer—created in any version of PowerPoint—then you can load that presentation into PowerPoint 2007 and use it as the basis of a new presentation.

You've got two options for loading an existing presentation: the New From Existing Presentation window, which is a good choice if you've never used PowerPoint before; and the Open window, which is handy if you're familiar with PowerPoint.

Note: A third, quickie alternative exists for creating a new presentation from an existing one—but this alternative works only if you've recently edited the existing presentation. To try it out, click the Office button and then, from the list of Recent Documents that appears, choose an existing document. After PowerPoint opens the document, immediately save it (Office button → Save As) with a different name.

The New from Existing Presentation window

If you're new to PowerPoint, then you'll appreciate the New from Existing Presentation window, which simplifies the process of opening an existing presentation. And unlike using the Open window, using the New from Existing Presentation window automatically generates a new file name, so you don't have to worry about accidentally overwriting your original presentation.

To create a presentation using the New from Existing Presentation window:

1. **Select Office button → New.**

   The New Presentation window appears.

2. **Click "New from existing."**

   The New from Existing Presentation window appears.

3. **Select the file you want to open, as described in Figure 17-11, and then click Create New.**

The New from Existing Presentation window disappears, and the presentation you selected appears in your PowerPoint workspace. PowerPoint gives the presentation a new, generic name (PowerPoint2, PowerPoint3, and so on) to remind you to rename the file before you save it. (Page 421 shows you how to rename files.)

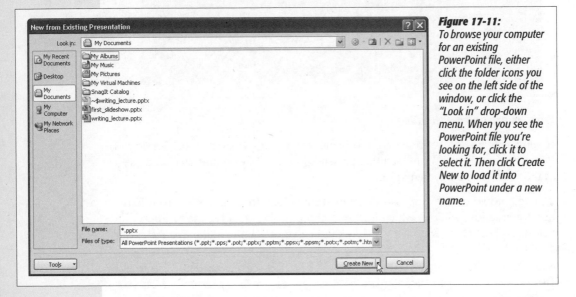

Figure 17-11:
To browse your computer for an existing PowerPoint file, either click the folder icons you see on the left side of the window, or click the "Look in" drop-down menu. When you see the PowerPoint file you're looking for, click it to select it. Then click Create New to load it into PowerPoint under a new name.

The Open window

The Open window gives you more options for opening an existing presentation than the New from Existing window does. You'll find these options useful in certain situations, such as when you want to protect an existing presentation by opening it in read-only mode, read through all the slides to make sure it's the one you want, and *then* save a copy.

To open an existing presentation using the Open window:

1. **Choose Office button → Open (or press Ctrl+O).**

The Open window shown in Figure 17-12 appears.

2. **Select the file you want to open, either by clicking the folder icons you see on the left side of the window, or by clicking the "Look in" drop-down menu. When the PowerPoint file you're looking for appears in the list, click it to select it.**

Tip: To see a preview of each file on the right side of the Open window as you select it, click the Open window's Views icon (Figure 17-12) and select Preview.

Views

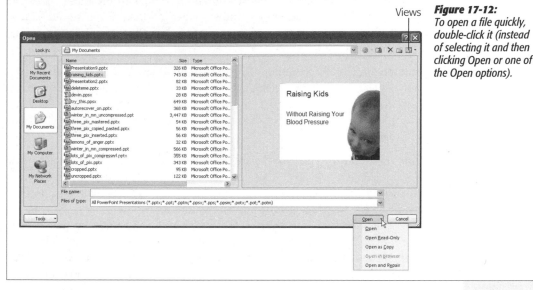

Figure 17-12:
To open a file quickly,
double-click it (instead
of selecting it and then
clicking Open or one of
the Open options).

3. **Choose one of the following options:**

   • **Open.** Opens the selected file.

   • **Open → Open Read-Only.** Opens a protected version of the file that lets you make changes to the presentation, but doesn't let you save them unless you specify a new filename.

   • **Open → Open as Copy.** Opens the presentation file, but renames it *Copy(1)filename.pptx.*

   • **Open → Open in Browser.** Opens the selected HTML file in Internet Explorer (or your default browser).

   • **Open → Open and Repair.** Tells PowerPoint to fix a corrupted file before it tries to open it.

   The file you selected appears in your PowerPoint workspace.

Choosing a Theme for Your Presentation

No matter which approach you use to create a presentation—from scratch, from an existing presentation, from a template, or from a built-in theme—once you have a presentation, you can change how it looks in one fell swoop by changing its *theme.*

A *theme* is a collection of characteristics including colors, fonts, and graphic effects (such as whether the shapes you add to your slides have drop shadows). For example, applying the built-in Deluxe theme turns your background a tasteful shade of blue and displays your title text (which appears in the Corbel font) in an attractively contrasting, gently shadowed shade of yellow—all thanks to the theme. You can change all of these characteristics individually, of course, as you'll see in Chapter 20. But applying themes gives you more bang for your buck in several important ways:

- **Using themes is quicker than changing individual settings one at a time.** Applying a theme is a two-click proposition. Changing the dozen-plus settings controlled by a theme would exercise your click finger a lot more than that. And themes save you time you'd otherwise spend figuring out which colors look good together.

- **Using themes helps ensure a decent-looking, readable slide.** Consistency is an important design principle: it sets the tone for your presentation and lets your audience focus on your message. When you change settings manually, you can end up with a distracting mishmash of colors and fonts on a single slide or across slides. Not so with themes. Once you apply a theme, the theme takes control of your settings. If you change the background color of your slides, then the theme automatically changes the title and subtitle fonts to compatible colors—colors that aren't just readable against your new background, but attractive, too.

- **Using themes lets you create a consistent look and feel across Microsoft Office-produced materials.** You can use the same themes you use in PowerPoint in Word and Excel, too. When you apply the same theme to your Word documents, Excel spreadsheets, and PowerPoint slides, you end up with a consistently presented, harmonious whole.

Here's how to apply a theme to a PowerPoint presentation:

1. **Click the Design tab.**

   The design tools appear, complete with a Theme gallery (Figure 17-13). (For more on PowerPoint 2007's new ribbon, check out page 2.)

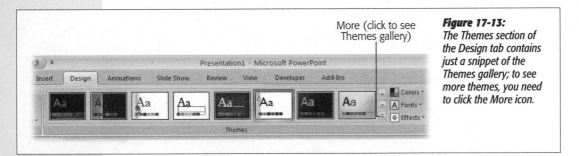

More (click to see Themes gallery)

Figure 17-13:
The Themes section of the Design tab contains just a snippet of the Themes gallery; to see more themes, you need to click the More icon.

2. **Click the More icon at the bottom-right corner of the Themes section (Figure 17-13).**

   Additional themes appear in the gallery, as shown in Figure 17-14.

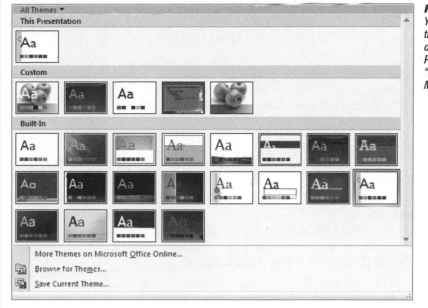

Figure 17-14:
*You can find additional
themes on the Web and
download them into
PowerPoint by clicking
"More Themes on
Microsoft Office Online."*

3. **Mouse over the themes in the gallery one by one.**

   PowerPoint previews each theme as you mouse over it (Figure 17-15) so you
   can get an idea of how each will look applied to your presentation's content and
   layout.

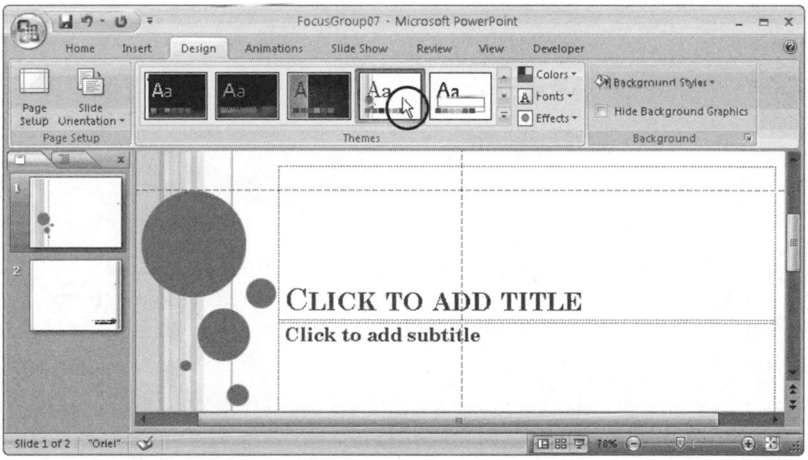

Figure 17-15:
*No more clicking Preview
or Apply and waiting
around: simply mousing
over a theme
temporarily applies it to
your presentation. To
apply the theme for
good, click the theme to
select it. If you change
your mind, you can
revert back to your
presentation's original
theme by applying the
Office Theme theme.*

Note: If you mouse over a theme and PowerPoint doesn't immediately preview it on your slide, wait a
few seconds: the process is quick, but it's not instantaneous.

---

4. **Click a theme to select it.**

PowerPoint applies the selected theme to all of the existing slides in your presentation, as well as all the new slides you create.

Tip: PowerPoint lets you apply a theme to only selected slides. Applying more than one theme to a slide-show is useful when you're creating a distinct before-and-after presentation or other multi-section slide-show and want each section to look distinct. For details, check out Chapter 20.

Adding Text

You'll want to add at least some text to most, if not all, PowerPoint presentations you create. (See the box on page 412 for advice on how much prose to add to your presentation.) Knowing that, the PowerPoint designers made it easy for you to add text to your slides. The following sections show you how.

Adding Text to an Existing Text Box

When you start to work with a new presentation, the ribbon displays the Home tab (Figure 17-16).

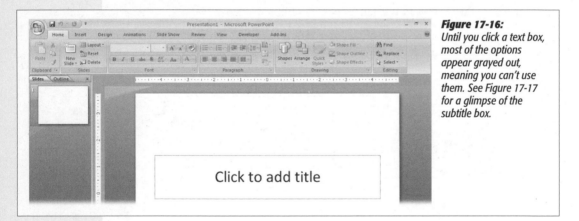

Figure 17-16:
Until you click a text box, most of the options appear grayed out, meaning you can't use them. See Figure 17-17 for a glimpse of the subtitle box.

Blank presentations come complete with title and subtitle placeholder text boxes. To replace the placeholder text in either of these two text boxes with your own text, simply click inside the placeholder and begin typing. When you do, two things happen:

- **PowerPoint displays the Drawing Tools | Format tab and, on the Home ribbon, activates many of the text formatting options (Figure 17-17).** You can use these options to change the font, size, and color of your text, turn your text into a right-justified paragraph or a bullet point, and much more. (Chapter 19 describes your options in detail.)

- **Resize and transform handles appear at the corners and edges of the text box** (**Figure 17-17**). Tiny white *resize handles*, which are square on the edges of the text box and circular on the corners, let you stretch or shrink your text box by dragging them. The circular green *transform handle* appears above the top of your text box and lets you tilt it. Drag the handles to tilt or resize your text box.

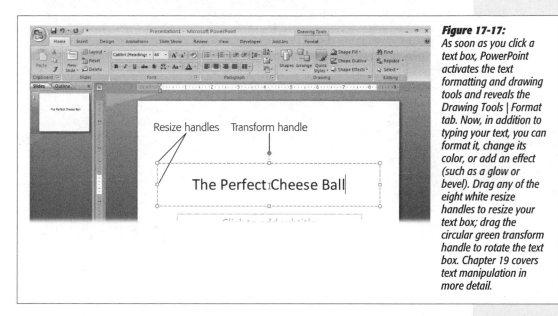

Figure 17-17:
As soon as you click a text box, PowerPoint activates the text formatting and drawing tools and reveals the Drawing Tools | Format tab. Now, in addition to typing your text, you can format it, change its color, or add an effect (such as a glow or bevel). Drag any of the eight white resize handles to resize your text box; drag the circular green transform handle to rotate the text box. Chapter 19 covers text manipulation in more detail.

Adding a New Text Box

You're not limited to the placeholder text boxes PowerPoint starts you off with: you can add as many additional text boxes to your slides as you like.

To add a new text box to a slide:

1. **Click the Insert tab.**

   The Insert tab (Figure 17-18) appears.

Figure 17-18:
As you can see in the Text section of the Insert tab, PowerPoint makes it easy to add not just text boxes, but headers, footers, date- and timestamps, and more.

The Evils (or Not) of Text

There are two schools of thought when it comes to using text in PowerPoint presentations. One says text is king; the other advises PowerPointers to use as little text as possible. Here's the rationale for each approach:

- **Text rules—always has, always will.** According to the more-bullets-the-better crowd, a presentation *is* text. Period. It's how we think, it's what we're used to, and it helps us organize our thoughts, reactions, and questions.

- **Text distracts.** The other school of thought is that it's nearly impossible for audiences to read more than a couple of words on a slide, even if they're sitting up front and wearing their glasses. And if your audience *does* read your slides, that means they're busy reading and forming opinions instead of paying attention to the actual presentation (which is *you*). Using a lot of text may result in ineffective and boring brain dumps disguised as presentations.

So which approach should you take? In a perfect world, you'd have time to create super-compelling graphics that beautifully complement your presentation. You'd deliver the message of your presentation by engaging your audience with your wit, knowledge, body language, and persuasive powers. You'd use text sparingly and appropriately: to pose questions (which you'd answer in your talk) and to hammer home main points.

Ultimately, you get to make the call. As long as you choose an approach that supports your presentation goals, you're golden.

2. **On the Insert tab, click Text Box.**

   In the status bar at the bottom of the screen, PowerPoint displays a helpful hint ("Click and drag to insert a text box"). When you mouse over your slide, you notice that your cursor looks like a tiny down arrow.

3. **On the slide, click where you want your new text box to appear.**

   A text box appears with the cursor handily positioned inside (Figure 17-19). The Drawing Tools | Format tab pops up, and on the Home tab, PowerPoint activates most of the formatting options, ready for you to format your text.

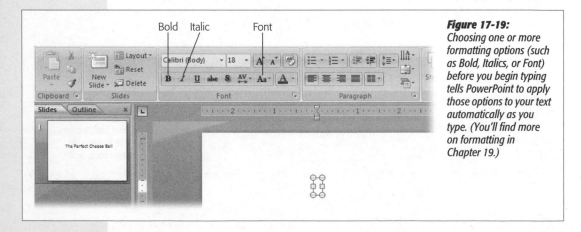

Figure 17-19:
Choosing one or more formatting options (such as Bold, Italics, or Font) before you begin typing tells PowerPoint to apply those options to your text automatically as you type. (You'll find more on formatting in Chapter 19.)

Note: Alternatively, you can click and drag to draw the outline of your text box before you begin typing. It's another step, but it'll help you get an idea of how much space your text will take up on your slide *before* you actually type it in.

4. **Type your text.**

   The text box expands automatically to accommodate your text.

DESIGN TIME

Using Text Effectively

If you choose to include text in your presentation, then keep these tips in mind:

- **Distill.** Your audience's eyes will glaze over if you hit them with a barrage of text on every slide, so you want to distill your message into as few words as possible. (Three to six bullets and a dozen or so words per slide is a good guideline.) In other words, reserve text for the few salient points you want your audience to take home with them. When you need back-up documentation, examples, supporting facts and figures, and so on, distribute hard-copy handouts–don't try to cram the information onto your slides.
- **Carefully consider word placement.** The Space Shuttle Columbia disaster a few years back put PowerPoint in the limelight for a sobering reason: In a PowerPoint presentation delivered to NASA officials *before* the disaster, engineers mentioned the problem that, ultimately, contributed to the tragic breakup of the shuttle over Texas in 2003. But the crucial information was buried in an avalanche of bullet points near the end of a long presentation, and none of the decision-makers in the audience realized its significance. Moral of the story: reserve the first and last slides of your presentation for critical information.

Adding More Slides

When you create a new blank presentation, PowerPoint spots you one slide. But in most cases, you'll want your presentation to contain a lot more slides than that. Fortunately, adding a new slide is easy, as you'll see in the following sections.

PowerPoint gives you two options: adding a slide with layout identical to the current slide, and specifying a different slide layout. A *slide layout* is a description of what content appears where on a slide. For example, applying a Title Slide layout to a slide positions title and subtitle text placeholders near the middle of your slide, and nothing else. Applying a Title and Content layout positions a title text placeholder near the top of a slide, and an object placeholder beneath that.

To add a slide with a layout identical to the current slide:

1. **Select any non-title slide.**

   PowerPoint doesn't automatically duplicate title slides for a pretty obvious reason: 99 percent of the time, you don't want two title slides in a single presentation. For the one percent of the time when that's exactly what you want, add a slide, and then change the slide's layout to Title Slide as shown on page 469.

2. **Click the Home tab.**

The ribbon you see in Figure 17-20 appears.

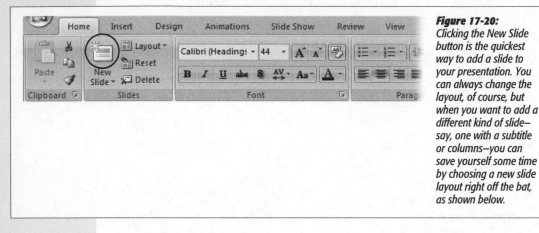

Figure 17-20:
Clicking the New Slide button is the quickest way to add a slide to your presentation. You can always change the layout, of course, but when you want to add a different kind of slide—say, one with a subtitle or columns—you can save yourself some time by choosing a new slide layout right off the bat, as shown below.

3. **Click the New Slide button.**

PowerPoint inserts a new slide after the current slide. If that's not what you want (for example, if you want to add a slide to the beginning of your presentation), then you can easily change the order of your slides. Page 490 shows you how.

Tip: PowerPoint gives you another way to add a new slide with a layout similar to the current slide. In the Slides pane (at the left side of your workspace, as shown in Figure 17-19), you can right-click the page after which you want to create a new slide. Then, from the menu that appears, select Duplicate.

To add a slide with a different layout:

1. **On the Home tab, click the down-arrow next to New Slide.**

A menu similar to the one you see in Figure 17-21 appears.

2. **Click to select the slide layout you want. Your choices include Title Slide, Title and Content, Section Header, Two Content, Comparison, Title Only, Blank, Content with Caption, and Picture with Caption.**

PowerPoint adds your new slide after the current slide.

Tip: To make an exact copy of the current slide—content and all—make sure you have the slide selected in the Slides pane, and then press Ctrl+D.

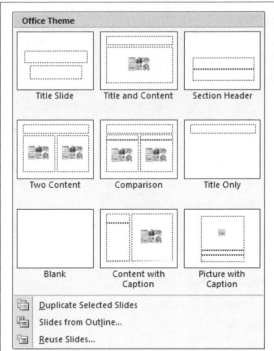

Figure 17-21:
The appearance and number of slide layouts you see in this menu depend on the theme (and template, if any) you've applied to your presentation. If you add a slide and then change your mind, you can either click Undo (Ctrl+Z), or delete the slide by choosing Home → Delete.

Moving Around Inside a Presentation

Moving around your presentation when you only have one slide isn't much of an issue. But once you start adding slides, you'll want a way to hop quickly from your first slide to your last. You'll also want to jump to specific slides in the middle of your presentation; for example, to tweak a particular slide's layout, to add content, or to delete it.

PowerPoint gives you several ways to flip through your presentation. This section acquaints you with the easiest and most useful options: using your workspace scroll bar, using the View pane on the left side of the screen, and using the Home tab's Find function.

Navigating with the Scroll Bar

In PowerPoint, you see a scroll bar on the right side of your workspace similar to the one in Figure 17-22.

To scroll through your presentation, all you need to do is click the scroll bar and drag up (to scroll toward the beginning of your presentation) or down (to scroll toward the end). As you go, PowerPoint displays each slide in turn.

Tip: To flip forward (or back) through your presentation one slide at a time, click the Next Slide (or Previous Slide) arrow shown in Figure 17-22.

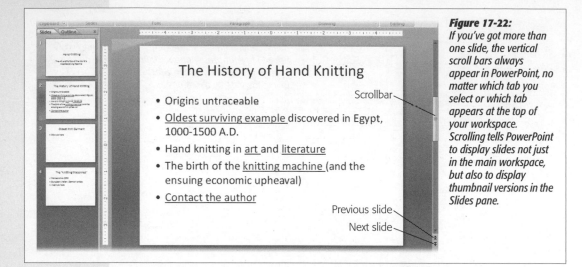

Figure 17-22:
*If you've got more than
one slide, the vertical
scroll bars always
appear in PowerPoint, no
matter which tab you
select or which tab
appears at the top of
your workspace.
Scrolling tells PowerPoint
to display slides not just
in the main workspace,
but also to display
thumbnail versions in the
Slides pane.*

Navigation with the Slides and Outline Tabs

Slides and Outline tabs are not views (they both appear in Normal view) but are
tabs that let you see slide thumbnails or an outline of your slideshow, respectively,
in the Slides (Figure 17-23) or Outline (Figure 17-24) pane.

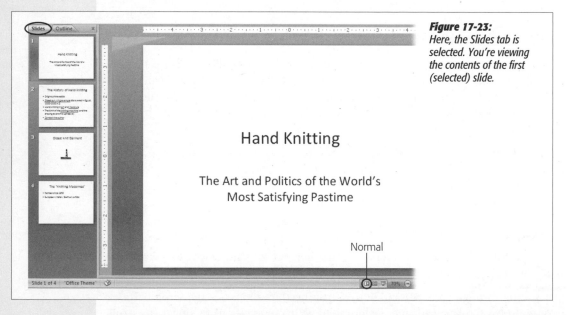

Figure 17-23:
*Here, the Slides tab is
selected. You're viewing
the contents of the first
(selected) slide.*

PowerPoint assumes you want to use Slides view until you tell it otherwise. To
change views, click the Outline tab shown in Figure 17-24. To switch back to Slides
view, click the Slides tab.

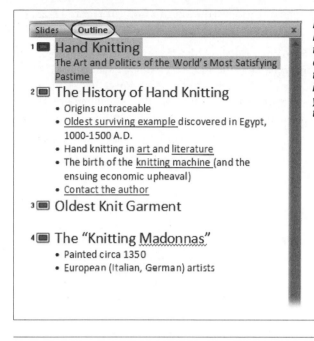

Figure 17-24:
Here's the same presentation in outline form. To banish the View pane altogether, click the X in the upper-right corner. To resize it, simply drag the resize handle on the right side of the pane. (In keeping with its new-and-improved design philosophy, PowerPoint doesn't let you make the View pane larger than one-quarter of the total interface.)

Note: If you don't see the View pane at all, select View → Normal (or click the Normal icon shown in Figure 17-23) to display it.

Using Find

When you've got a lot of slides and you're looking for one containing a specific word or phrase, you'll want to bypass Views in favor of the Find function. Similar to the Find feature in other Windows programs, PowerPoint's Find function lets you search for specific words quickly and easily. Here's how to use it.

1. **Press Ctrl+F.**

   The Find dialog box appears (Figure 17-25).

Figure 17-25:
Another way to display this Find box is to head to the Editing section of the Home tab and then click the Find button. Chapter 18 shows you how to use the more advanced Find functions, including Replace, which lets you automatically replace the text you find with different text.

2. In the "Find what" box, type in the text you want to find (in Figure 17-25, the text is *marshmallow*).

If you like, you can click to turn on the "Match case" checkbox (which tells PowerPoint to look for *marshmallow* but not *Marshmallow, MARSHMALLOW,* or *MaRsHmAlLoW*) or the "Find whole words only" checkbox (which tells PowerPoint to look for *marshmallow* but not *chocolatemarshmallowgraham*). When you finish, click Find Next.

PowerPoint displays the slide containing your text. If it doesn't find a match, it shows this message: "PowerPoint has finished searching the presentation. The search item wasn't found."

Adding Speaker Notes

Speaker notes are optional text notes you can type into PowerPoint. You can associate a separate speaker note with each slide of your presentation. Your audience can't see speaker notes, but you can. You may find speaker notes useful:

- **While you're putting your presentation together.** If you know you need to add a graphic to slide six and a couple of bullet points to slide 33, then you can jot down reminders to yourself in the Speaker Notes pane (Figure 17-26). Then, before you put your presentation to bed, you can view your speaker notes and double-check that you've caught everything.

- **While you're delivering your presentation.** You can set up your presentation so that your audience sees your slideshow on the screen while you see your notes (on your own computer monitor). Or, if you're the tactile type, you may prefer to print out your speaker notes and keep them with your during your presentation.

To add speaker notes for a particular slide, click in the Speaker Notes pane (Figure 17-26) and type away.

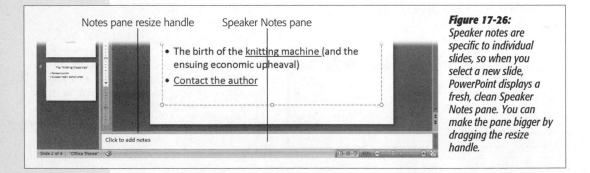

Figure 17-26:
Speaker notes are specific to individual slides, so when you select a new slide, PowerPoint displays a fresh, clean Speaker Notes pane. You can make the pane bigger by dragging the resize handle.

Note: If you don't see the Speaker Notes pane, then click the Speaker Notes pane's resize bar at the bottom of the workspace and drag upward, as shown in Figure 17-27.

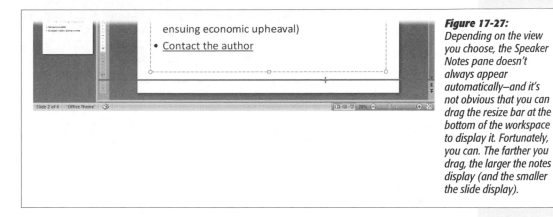

Figure 17-27:
Depending on the view you choose, the Speaker Notes pane doesn't always appear automatically—and it's not obvious that you can drag the resize bar at the bottom of the workspace to display it. Fortunately, you can. The farther you drag, the larger the notes display (and the smaller the slide display).

Creating and Printing Handouts

You don't have to do anything special to create handouts in PowerPoint. That's because *handouts* in PowerPoint are nothing more than slides printed one or more to a page.

To print handouts:

1. **Select Office button → Print → Print Preview.**

   The Print Preview tab appears, and PowerPoint's best guess at how you want your handouts printed appears in the workspace.

FROM THE FIELD

Handouts: Killing Trees Unnecessarily?

If you think your audience will benefit from printouts of your slides, then by all means, go for it. Say your presentation slides consist of graphic images accompanied by a few well-placed questions. What you want is a participatory, interactive presentation. Your audience should listen to you and jot down the answers to those questions—and what better way to encourage this interaction than to pass out hard copies of each slide?

But for some presentations, slide printouts are pretty worthless. Instead, you're going to want to give your audience printouts containing facts, figures, contact information, and other in-depth supporting information that you didn't have room for in your actual presentation.

One way to jump-start the process of creating truly useful handouts is to pull your PowerPoint presentation text into Word 2007 (assuming you have a copy installed on your computer). Using your presentation text as a starting point, you can add information until you've built handouts your audience will actually take back to their homes and offices.

To pull your slides into a Word document, click Office button → Publish → Create Handouts in Microsoft Office Word.

---

2. **Click the "Print what" drop-down box and then, from the menu that appears, choose how you want PowerPoint to print your handouts (Figure 17-28).**

   PowerPoint redisplays the handouts preview based on your selection.

3. **Click Print.**

   The familiar Print dialog box appears.

Note: Chapter 24, which shows you how to print your presentation, walks you through the Print dialog box step by step.

---

4. **Click OK.**

   PowerPoint prints your handouts.

5. **Click Close Print Preview (Figure 17-28) to dismiss the Print Preview tab and return to your workspace.**

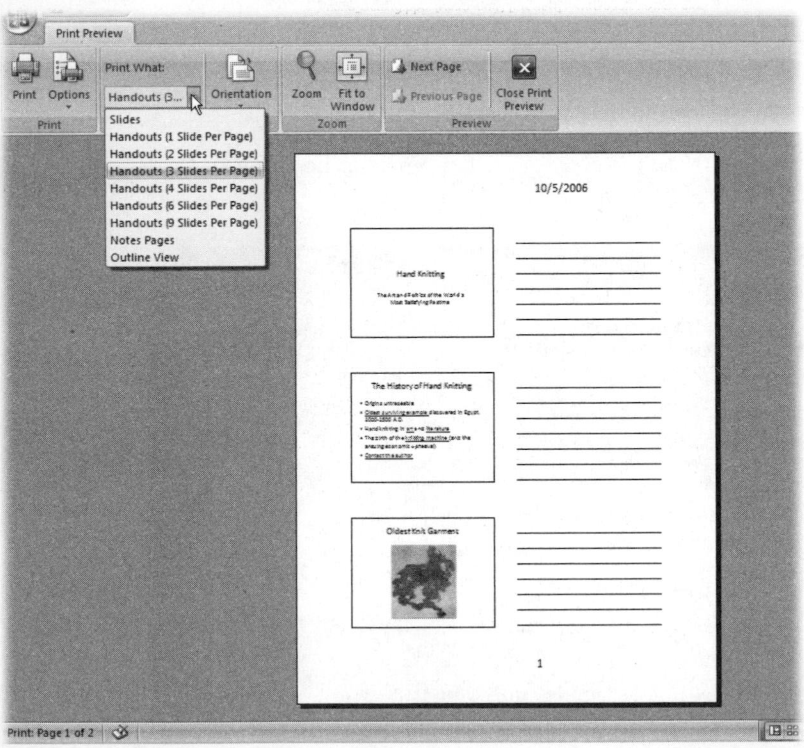

Figure 17-28:
You can tell PowerPoint to print up to nine slides per page. Here, you see the effect of printing three per page, which is a nice compromise: large enough to read the slides, but roomy enough for note taking.

Saving and Closing a Presentation

Lightning storms hit, coffee cups spill, and power cords work themselves out of walls (especially if you have a dog who likes to chase squeaky toys). After you've created a new presentation file and spent some time working on it, you'll want to save it every so often so that when your system crashes, you can recover your work. And if you're like most folks, you'll also want to save and close your presentation each time you wrap up a work session.

Saving and closing a PowerPoint presentation are both straightforward tasks. If you're familiar with any other Windows programs, then you'll recognize most of the steps.

To save a newly created presentation:

1. **Select Office button → Save.**

   The Save As dialog box appears (Figure 17-29).

Note: Alternatively, you can press Ctrl+S or click the Save button (the little diskette icon) that appears in the Quick Access toolbar.

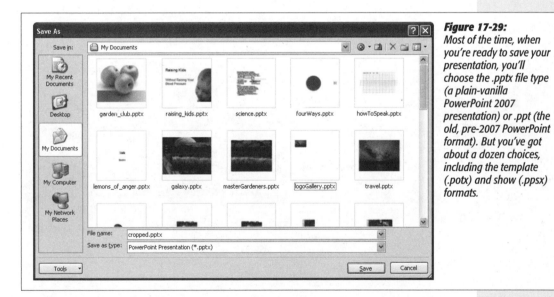

Figure 17-29:
Most of the time, when you're ready to save your presentation, you'll choose the .pptx file type (a plain-vanilla PowerPoint 2007 presentation) or .ppt (the old, pre-2007 PowerPoint format). But you've got about a dozen choices, including the template (.potx) and show (.ppsx) formats.

2. **Click the "Save in" drop-down box to choose a directory to store your file in. In the File name field, type a new name for your file.**

   Shoot for short, unique, and memorable; you don't want to have to spend a lot of time hunting for your file a week from now.

3. **Click the "Save as Type" drop-down box to select a file format. Most of the time, you'll choose the .pptx format.**

The box below explains your options. For example, to save your presentation as a template that you can use over and over, choose .potx.

4. **Click Save.**

The Save As dialog box disappears and PowerPoint saves the file in the format you specified.

To *close* a presentation, simply select Office → Close. When you do, PowerPoint closes your presentation with no fanfare. If you've never saved this particular file, however, a dialog box pops up asking you if you want to save the changes you made. Click Yes to display the Save As dialog box shown in Figure 17-29 and proceed as described above.

UP TO SPEED

PowerPoint 2007 File Types

PowerPoint 2007 (and Office 2007 more generally) introduces a slew of new file types, complete with unfamiliar file extensions. Here they are, in a nutshell:

• **.pptx** (PowerPoint 2007 presentation). Most of the time, you want to save your file in this format.

• **.potx** (PowerPoint 2007 template). Lets you save a presentation as a reusable design template.

• **.potm** (PowerPoint 2007 macro-enabled design template). Lets programmers save a macro-filled presentation as a design template.

• **.ppsx** (PowerPoint 2007 show). Lets you save this file as a PowerPoint show that folks can run using the PowerPoint viewer, as described in Chapter 23.

• **.ppsm** (PowerPoint 2007 macro-enabled show). Lets programmers save a macro-filled presentation as a show.

• **.ppam** (PowerPoint 2007 add-in). Lets programmers save presentations that actually add to PowerPoint's interface.

• **.pptm** (PowerPoint 2007 macro-enabled presentation). Lets programmers save presentations that contain macros.

• **.thmx** (Microsoft Office Theme). Lets you save your presentation as a reusable collection of colors, fonts, and graphic effects so that you can apply it to another PowerPoint slideshow, Word document, or Excel spreadsheet.

• **.ppt** (PowerPoint 2003—and earlier—presentation). Lets you save your presentation in a form that folks running PowerPoint 2003 can edit.

PowerPoint 2007 also handles the same file types as earlier versions, including .ppt, .pps, .htm, and so on.

Running a Presentation

Chapter 23 shows you everything you need to know about setting up and running special types of presentations: for example, recording narration, hiding certain slides, and creating stand-alone presentations that run on kiosks. But for running through a basic presentation on your very own computer, the process is simple:

1. **Press F5 or click the Slideshow icon you see at the bottom of the screen, as shown in Figure 17-30.**

   PowerPoint replaces your workspace with a full-screen version of your slide-show, beginning with the currently selected slide.

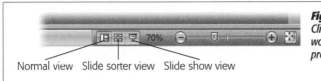

Figure 17-30:
Clicking the Slideshow icon at the bottom of your workspace is one of the easiest ways to run your presentation.

Normal view Slide sorter view Slide show view

Tip: Pressing Shift+F5 and clicking the Slideshow icon both tell PowerPoint to run your slideshow beginning at the current slide (not necessarily the *first* slide). To run your slideshow from the beginning, you have three choices: press F5, click the Slideshow icon, or select Slide Show → Start Slide Show → From Beginning.

---

2. **Click the forward and backward arrows that appear at the bottom of the screen (Figure 17-31) to step through your presentation. (Figure 17-31 describes how to end the presentation before the last slide.)**

   After the last slide, PowerPoint displays a black screen containing the words "End of slide show, click to exit."

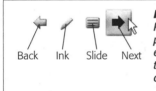

Back   Ink   Slide   Next

Figure 17-31:
PowerPoint displays ghosted controls (Back, Ink, Slide, and Next) when you run a presentation. Mousing over these controls highlights them so you can see where to click. To end your slideshow immediately without having to flip through every last slide, you have two choices: either hit Esc or click the Slide icon and then, from the menu that appears, choose End Show.

3. **Click anywhere on the screen (or press the Space bar or Enter).**

   PowerPoint returns you to your workspace.

CHAPTER 18

Editing Slides

Text is the heart and soul of an effective PowerPoint presentation. But coming up with just the right words—and organizing them in just the right way—isn't always easy. Just as you would if you were constructing a presentation using a flip chart or overhead transparencies, you jot down a few bullet points, read through what you've written, think of a few additional points, change your mind, and end up deleting, rearranging, and editing your material over and over again until you've got every word on every page (*slide*) exactly right.

Fortunately, PowerPoint can help. In addition to the standard cut, copy, and paste operations, this chapter shows you how to use PowerPoint's Search and Replace feature to find words and phrases buried in long presentations and change (or delete) them quickly. And if spelling's not your speciality, PowerPoint can help you check it.

Editing Text

When you change the text on a PowerPoint slide—when you cut it, copy it, replace it, or move it around—what you're doing is *editing* your text. To see most of the editing tools PowerPoint offers, all you have to do is take a look at the ribbon's Home tab (Figure 18-1). The following sections describe each editing tool in detail.

Note: In contrast, when you change the way your text *looks*—when you make it bold, italicize it, choose a different font or background color for it, and so on—what you're doing is *formatting*. Chapter 19 tells you all you need to know about formatting text.

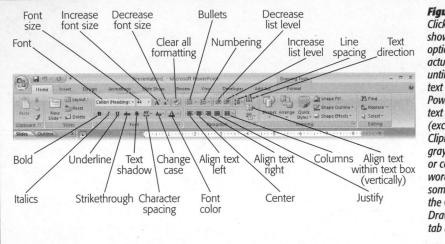

Figure 18-1:
Clicking the Home tab shows you your editing options, but you can't actually use any of them until you click inside a text box. When you do, PowerPoint activates the text editing options (except Paste and Clipboard, which remain grayed out until you cut or copy text; in other words, until you have something to paste from the Clipboard) and the Drawing Tools | Format tab appears.

Selecting Text

Before you can do anything to the text on your slides, you first have to select it. Text can appear in any of three places on a slide: in one of the title or subtitle placeholder text boxes that PowerPoint automatically adds to your slide; in a text box that you've added to a slide (page 411), or in a shape that you've added to a slide (check out *PowerPoint 2007: The Missing Manual* for more on this).

To select text:

1. **Click anywhere in an existing text box, placeholder text box, or on a shape.**

   PowerPoint highlights the outline of the text box you clicked in. In addition, PowerPoint displays the Drawing Tools/Format context tab and activates the text-related options in the Home tab—underlining, font size, alignment, and so on.

Note: When you click in a placeholder text box (one that says *Click to add title* or *Click to add subtitle*), PowerPoint erases the placeholder text. (Placeholder text doesn't appear in Slide Show view, nor does it appear when you run your slideshow; it's just there to remind you to type your own text.)

---

2. **Drag to select as much text as you like.**

   Alternatively, you can press Shift and use the arrow keys (or click again). Or double-click to quickly select a single word. To select *discontinuous* words or phrases, press Ctrl while you select each word or phrase.

   Whichever method you use, PowerPoint highlights the text you select.

Note: For a brief second after you select text, a see-through mini-toolbar appears next to your cursor. Because the mini-toolbar doesn't let you edit text—instead, it lets you format your text—it's covered in Chapter 19.

Cutting Text

As you edit and reorganize the content of your slideshow, you may run into a situation where you want to remove text from one slide and either ditch it permanently or reserve it so that you can paste it back into your slideshow later (on a different slide, perhaps).

Cutting text was designed for just such situations. When you cut text, you remove it from your slide and stow it away for safekeeping on the Office Clipboard. You can then choose to paste the cut text back onto the original slide or another slide; if you don't, eventually the Office Clipboard simply discards it. The box on the next page tells you more about the Clipboard.

To cut text:

1. **Select the text you want to cut (see the previous section).**

   PowerPoint highlights the selected text.

2. **Choose Home → Clipboard › Cut (the Cut icon looks like a tiny pair of scissors, as shown in Figure 18-1), or press Ctrl+X.**

   PowerPoint removes the selected text from your slide and adds it to the Clipboard.

Tip: Another way to cut text is to right-click your selection and then, from the menu that appears, choose Cut.

UP TO SPEED

The Ins and Outs of the Office Clipboard

The Office Clipboard that PowerPoint uses is the same clipboard that all the other Microsoft Office programs use: Word, Excel, Access, and so on. The Clipboard acts as a kind of virtual shoebox. Its job is to store the bits of information you've cut or copied from all of your Office programs (up to 24 pieces of information total) so that you can paste them in later, should you want to.

For example, say you copy some text from a Word document. Because Word automatically stores all cut and copied text on the Office Clipboard, you can paste that copied text onto a PowerPoint slide quickly and easily. You can go the other way, too, copying content from a PowerPoint slide and pasting it into a Word or Excel document.

You paste information from the Clipboard using Paste, Paste Special, and Clipboard options (as described in this chapter).

Copying Text

When you *copy* text, you tell PowerPoint to place a copy of the text on the Office Clipboard so that you can replicate it later—either by pasting it onto the same slide, onto another slide, or into another document (such as a Word document) altogether. Copying text is useful for those times when you need to repeat lengthy or tricky-to-spell words or phrases throughout your presentation.

To copy text:

1. **Select the text you want to copy (page 426).**

   PowerPoint highlights the selected text.

2. **Choose Home → Clipboard → Copy (the Copy icon looks like two tiny identical documents, as shown in Figure 18-1), or press Ctrl+C.**

   PowerPoint adds the selected text to the Clipboard.

Tip: Another way to copy text is to right-click your selection and then, from the menu that appears, choose Copy.

Pasting Text

When you *paste* text, what you're actually doing is telling PowerPoint to take a hunk of information you've already placed on the Clipboard—either by cutting or copying—and slap that information onto your slide. So in order to paste something, you must first cut or copy it.

Note: The text you paste into your slides doesn't have to be only text you've copied or cut from within PowerPoint. You can paste stuff you've cut or copied in Word, Excel, or any other Office program (and most non-Office programs, too).

The Clipboard can hold up to 24 separate pieces of information, so you have two options when it comes to pasting: You can quickly paste the last thing you cut or copied, or you can hunt through the entire contents of the Clipboard and choose what you want to paste. After you cut or copy a chunk of text once, you can paste it into your presentation as many times as you like.

Automatically pasting the last chunk of text you cut (or copied)

Like a lot of Microsoft programs, PowerPoint gives you a super-quick way to paste the last thing you cut or copied to the Clipboard. This procedure is one of the All Time Most Popular Office Tricks.

Here's how you do it:

1. **Click to position your cursor in the text box where you want your pasted text to appear.**

   PowerPoint highlights the outline of the text box you clicked in.

2. **Either click the Paste icon (which looks like a little clipboard behind a document, as shown in Figure 18-2), or choose Home → Paste → Clipboard → Paste. Keyboard jockeys save time by pressing Ctrl+V.**

   PowerPoint pastes the last thing you cut or copied onto your slide, and a tiny Paste Options icon appears briefly near your cursor.

Note: You can also right-click in the slide where you want to paste your item and then, from the menu that appears, choose Paste.

Choosing what to paste

Use this option when you want to paste multiple bits of information, or when you can't remember how long ago you cut (or copied) the text you want to paste.

To choose the text you want to paste into a slide:

1. **Click in the text box where you want your pasted text to go.**

   PowerPoint highlights the outline of the text box you clicked in.

2. **Click the Clipboard dialog box launcher.**

   The Clipboard task pane appears on the left side of your screen as shown in Figure 18-2.

3. **In the Clipboard task pane, click to select the text you want to paste.**

   PowerPoint pastes the selected text onto your slide.

4. **To close the Clipboard task pane, click the X in the upper-right corner of the pane.**

Figure 18-2:
If you've been busy copying and cutting, then you may have filled up the Clipboard. In that case, you'll need to use the scroll bars to scroll down through the contents of the Clipboard and find what you're looking for. Clicking Paste All pastes the entire contents of the Clipboard to wherever you've positioned your cursor, beginning with the first cut (or copied) item and ending with the last.

Choosing how to paste

In most situations, simply pasting text onto your slides the standard way is what you want. But PowerPoint gives you a few additional options for pasting certain types of information onto your slides. For example, when you want to be able to use PowerPoint's picture-formatting options to edit the pasted text, you'll want to paste it directly onto your slide as a picture.

To choose how to paste text onto your slides:

1. **Click the down arrow next to Paste and then, from the menu that appears, choose Paste Special.**

   The Paste Special window (Figure 18-3) appears.

2. **Choose how you want to paste the information onto your slide. Your options depend on the type of information you're pasting, but they include:**

   • **Pasting the information directly.** Turning on the radio box next to Paste, as shown in Figure 18-3, lets you choose one of several options including pasting the text as document object, pasting it as a picture, and pasting it as formatted text. Which option you want to choose depends on how you plan to format the text. For example, pasting text as a picture lets you use the options on PowerPoint's Picture Tools | Format contextual tab to format the text.

   • **Pasting a link to the information.** Turning on the radio box next to Paste Link lets you paste the text onto your slide, with a twist: double-clicking the pasted text lets you edit it not in PowerPoint, but in the program you used to create the text.

   After you've made your choice, click OK.

   PowerPoint pastes the most recently cut or copied text based on your selection.

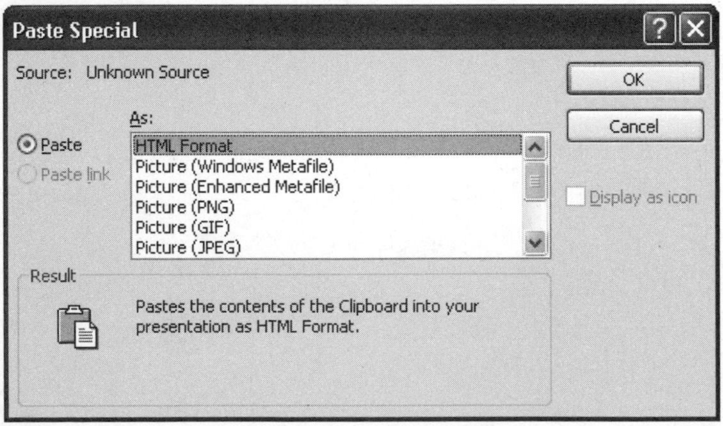

Figure 18-3:
The options the Paste Special window displays depend on the kind of information you cut (or copied), the program you were in when you cut (or copied) it, and whether or not the program you cut (or copied) it from is still running on your computer.

Moving Text

When all you want to do is move a bit of text from one spot on your slide to another spot on the same slide, you can certainly choose to cut the text and then paste it. But PowerPoint offers an easier way to accomplish the same thing: moving the text.

To move text:

1. **Select the text you want to move (page 426). Then, click your selection (but don't let go of your mouse button just yet).**

   The "moving" box you see in Figure 18-4 appears beneath your cursor.

2. **Drag the selection and drop it where you want it to appear.**

   The "moving" box disappears, and PowerPoint moves the text.

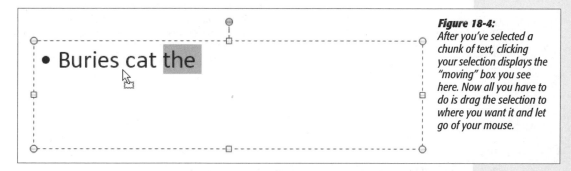

Figure 18-4:
After you've selected a chunk of text, clicking your selection displays the "moving" box you see here. Now all you have to do is drag the selection to where you want it and let go of your mouse.

Deleting Text

Unlike cutting text (page 427), which tells PowerPoint to save the text on the Clipboard in case you want to reuse it later, *deleting* text erases it completely. The only way to get deleted text back is to click Undo (see the next section).

To delete text:

1. **Select the text you want to delete (page 426).**

   PowerPoint highlights the selected text.

2. **Do one of the following:**

   • Press Delete. (PowerPoint deletes the selected text.)

   • Type some new text. (PowerPoint deletes the selected text and replaces it with your new text.)

Tip: To delete individual characters, position your cursor *after* the character you want to delete and press Backspace, or *before* the character you want to delete and press Delete.

Reversing an Action (Undo)

Undo is great for recovering from those slip-of-the-finger goofs everyone makes from time to time. Clicking the Undo button you see in the Quick Access toolbar (Figure 18-5) tells PowerPoint to reverse the last action you told it to take. If you cut some text and then select Undo, for example, PowerPoint puts the cut text back where it was (and removes the cut text from the Clipboard). If you paste some text and then select Undo, then PowerPoint removes the pasted text. If you just prefer pressing keys to using the mouse, you can reverse the last action by pressing Ctrl+Z.

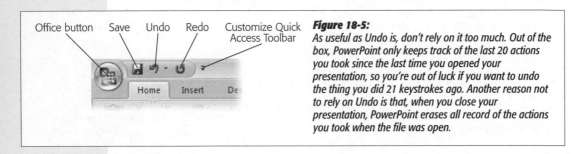

Office button   Save   Undo   Redo   Customize Quick
Access Toolbar

Figure 18-5:
As useful as Undo is, don't rely on it too much. Out of the box, PowerPoint only keeps track of the last 20 actions you took since the last time you opened your presentation, so you're out of luck if you want to undo the thing you did 21 keystrokes ago. Another reason not to rely on Undo is that, when you close your presentation, PowerPoint erases all record of the actions you took when the file was open.

Note: If you click Undo and then change your mind, you can undo the effects of Undo and reapply your action. To do so, just head to the Quick Access toolbar and click Redo or press Ctrl+Y.

Finding and Replacing Text Automatically

Imagine you're just putting the finishing touches on your presentation when you decide to check your email. There, in your virtual inbox, you see it: a memo informing you that Marketing just renamed the product you referred to throughout your presentation as "Sunny's Tomato Juice" to "Sunny's All-Natural Lycopene Infusion."

Fixing every occurrence by hand would take you forever, and you'd likely miss a few.

Fortunately, there's a better way. PowerPoint's Replace option can find all the occurrences of a particular word or phrase and replace them automatically with the text you specify.

Note: If you want to use Find without Replace—for example, if all you want to do is check to make sure that you've included a specific phrase in your presentation and don't want PowerPoint to swap it out for you—check out page 417.

To search for and replace text automatically:

1. **Press Ctrl+H or select Home → Editing → Replace.**

   The Replace dialog box shown in Figure 18-6 appears.

2. **In the "Find what" box, type in the word or phrase you want to search for.**

   For example, *Tomato Juice.*

3. **In the "Replace with" box, type in the text you want PowerPoint to substitute for the occurrences of "Find what" text it may (or may not) find.**

   All-Natural Lycopene Infusion, in this example.

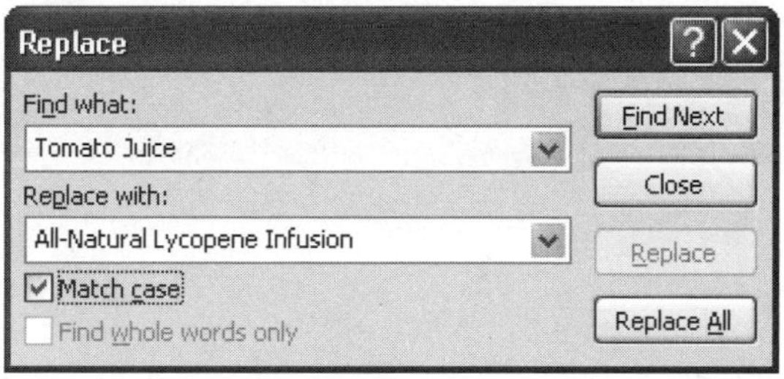

Figure 18-6:
Be sure to turn on the "Match case" checkbox as shown here if you want PowerPoint to look for a phrase that matches your "Find what" text exactly, capitalization and all.

4. **Click Replace All to tell PowerPoint to find and replace all occurrences of** *Tomato Juice* **(the text you typed in the "Find what" box) with** *All-Natural Lycopene Infusion* **(the contents of the "Replace with" box) in one fell swoop.**

   Or click Find Next to tell PowerPoint to flip to the first slide in your presentation containing the "Find what" text and select it. If you want to replace the text, click Replace. To search for additional occurrences, click Find Next again.

Warning: PowerPoint doesn't find occurrences of text buried inside pictures, charts, or diagrams, because these occurrences aren't text at all (to PowerPoint, at least). Using PowerPoint's Find and Replace options only helps you find (and replace) text in text boxes and shapes.

---

5. **Repeat Steps 2–4 for every word or phrase you want to replace.**

6. **If you repeat the steps until PowerPoint reaches the end of your presentation, the message "PowerPoint has finished searching the presentation" appears. Click OK to dismiss message.**

7. **When you're finished finding and replacing text, click Close.**

   The Replace dialog box disappears.

Replacing Fonts

In addition to letting you replace text, PowerPoint also lets you swap the fonts you've applied to text. Replacing fonts is useful when you're trying to match a font you've used in your slideshow to the font you've used in an Excel chart, or to the font your company (or client) uses in its marketing materials.

There's only one small caveat: Replacing fonts is a one-shot deal. You can't tell PowerPoint to replace a font only in certain text passages or certain slides. Instead, the program replaces the font wherever it finds it, from your first slide to your last.

To replace fonts:

1. Select Home → Editing → Replace → Replace Fonts.

2. From the "Replace" drop-down list that appears, choose the font you want to replace.

3. From the "With" drop-down list, choose the new font you want to apply to your slideshow text.

4. Click Replace. When you do, PowerPoint searches your entire slideshow for text formatted using the "Replace" font and applies the "With" font to that text.

Checking Spelling

Spelling errors are never a good thing. At best, they can give your audience the impression that you don't pay attention to details. At worst, they can actually prevent your audience from understanding what you're talking about. And make no mistake about it: the typo that no one but the former English teacher noticed when it appeared on a hard-copy handout is obvious to everyone when it's four feet high and splashed across a projector screen.

Note: Spell checkers' suggestions aren't always right, and they can miss errors, too. What's more, studies suggest that some folks actually make *more* mistakes when they use spell checkers than when they don't because they rely on the tool instead of their own proofreading skills. A spell checker can be a time-saver, but it's no substitute for carefully reading through your presentation.

PowerPoint gives you two choices when it comes to spell checking your presentation. You can check as you go, automatically, or wait until you're finished with your presentation and then run the check manually.

Setting up spelling

Whether you choose automatic spell checking or manual, you want to give Power-Point a heads-up on what kinds of special words to look out for—words like company-specific acronyms, passwords, or other non-words that you want PowerPoint to skip during a spell check. To set spelling options:

1. Select Office button → PowerPoint Options.

   The PowerPoint Options window appears.

2. On the left side of the PowerPoint Options window, click the Proofing category to select it.

3. **Turn on the checkbox next to one or more of the following:**

   - **Ignore words in UPPERCASE.** You want to choose this option if you use a lot of acronyms, like FUBAR.

   - **Ignore words that contain numbers.** This option is useful if, say, you're a system administrator who peppers presentations with passwords like *edgar123*.

   - **Ignore Internet and file addresses.** This option tells the spell checker not to flag computer-era "words" such as *www.oreilly.com* and *myFile.txt*.

   - **Flag repeated words.** Catches mistakes mistakes that the human eye often misses.

4. **Click OK.**

   The PowerPoint Options window disappears, returning you to your slides.

WORD TO THE WISE

Contextual Spelling (and Why It's Not Reliable, Either)

Spell checking is great for catching misspelled words (such as *mispelled*). But it's useless when it comes to catching *misused* words, which are at least as common as—and can tarnish your well-polished presentation even more than—glaring typos.

Take, for example, the phrase *more then this*. Because *then* is a legitimate, correctly spelled word, the PowerPoint spell checker doesn't flag it and suggest the correct word for this phrase, *than*.

PowerPoint does offer an option called *contextual spelling* which can help catch this sort of grammar error.

When you turn on contextual spelling, the PowerPoint spell checker examines words in the context of their neighbors to see if it can spot common grammar mistakes. For example, the spell checker correctly flags *then* in the phrase *More then this*. It even suggests *than*, which is in fact the correct spelling. As long as you're aware that no contextual spell checker can catch every grammatical error.

Here's how to turn it on: Choose Office → PowerPoint Options → Proofing, turn on the checkbox next to "Use contextual spelling," and then click OK.

Automatic (continuous) spell checking

Out of the box, PowerPoint assumes you want it to flag misspelled words automatically, as you type, by underlining them with a wavy red line. Figure 18-7 shows you an example.

Note: If you see an obvious misspelling on a slide but don't see a wavy underline, someone turned off automatic spell checking. To turn it on again, select Office → PowerPoint Options → Proofing. Then make sure the radio box next to "Check spelling as you type" is turned *on,* and the one next to "Hide spelling errors" is turned *off.*

To correct a misspelling, right-click the misspelled word.

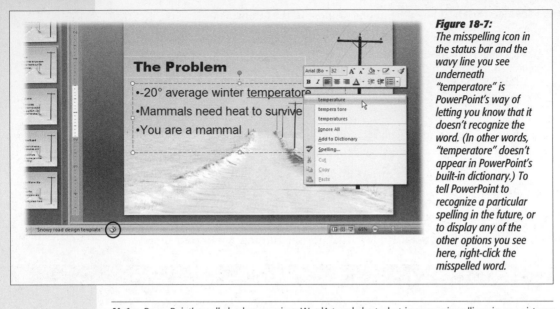

Figure 18-7:
The misspelling icon in the status bar and the wavy line you see underneath "temperatore" is PowerPoint's way of letting you know that it doesn't recognize the word. (In other words, "temperatore" doesn't appear in PowerPoint's built-in dictionary.) To tell PowerPoint to recognize a particular spelling in the future, or to display any of the other options you see here, right-click the misspelled word.

Note: PowerPoint's spell checker examines WordArt and charts, but ignores misspellings in any pictures (such as bitmaps) or graphs that you add to your slides.

From the context menu that appears (Figure 18-7), click to choose one of the following options:

- **One of the suggested correct spellings.** (In the example in Figure 18-7, the suggested correct spellings are *temperature*, *tempera tore*, and *temperatures*.) PowerPoint's built-in dictionary contains quite a few common words, so unless you're using trademarked names or jargon, chances are good you'll find the correct spelling listed for the word you've misspelled.

  When you choose a word, the context menu disappears. On the slide, PowerPoint replaces the misspelled version with the corrected version you chose.

- **Ignore All.** Tells PowerPoint to ignore this misspelled word each time it encounters it in this presentation. Choose this option when you're using an "illegitimate" word that you don't want PowerPoint to recognize a year from now, such as company-specific code name you know will be retired after the presentation you're currently working on.

  When you choose this option, the context menu disappears, as does the red wavy line beneath the misspelled word. PowerPoint doesn't flag additional occurrences of the misspelling (if it encounters them) in this presentation.

- **Add to Dictionary.** Tells PowerPoint to ignore this particular spelling when it appears in any presentation (technically, any presentation to which you've attached a custom dictionary; see the box on page 438 for more information).

This is the option you want to use for teachers' names, company acronyms, and other words you know you'll be using in more than one presentation.

When you choose this option, the context menu disappears, as does the red wavy line beneath the misspelled word. PowerPoint doesn't flag additional occurrences of this new word (assuming it encounters them) in *any* presentation.

- **Spelling.** Tells PowerPoint to display the Spelling dialog box shown in Figure 18-8.

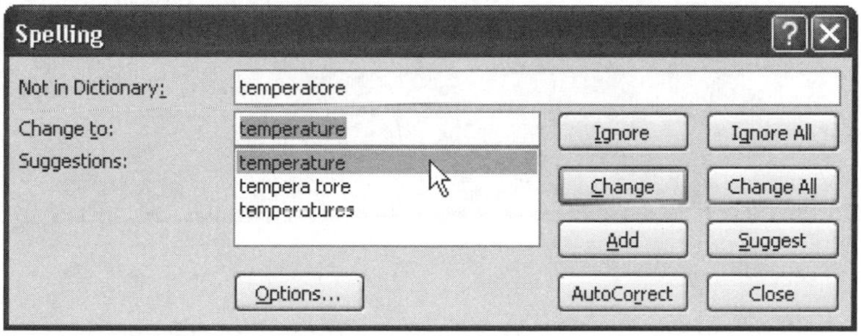

Figure 18-8:
The options you can choose from in this dialog box change depending on whether or not you've selected a suggested spelling. Here, the suggested spelling temperature is selected, so PowerPoint activates all of the options. If you don't select a suggested spelling, then the only available options are Resume, Ignore All, Add, Suggest, Options, and Close.

In the Spelling dialog box, you tell PowerPoint how to handle the misspelled word. Your options include:

- **Ignore.** Tells PowerPoint to ignore this particular occurrence of the misspelling, but to highlight any additional occurrences it finds in this presentation.

- **Ignore All.** Tells PowerPoint to ignore every existing occurrence of the misspelling in this presentation.

- **Change.** Tells PowerPoint to swap the selected suggestion (in Figure 18-8, *temperature*) for this particular occurrence of the misspelling.

- **Change All.** Tells PowerPoint to swap the selected suggestion for every existing occurrence of the misspelling.

- **Add.** Tells PowerPoint to add the "misspelled" word to the custom dictionary you choose (see the box on the following page).

- **Suggest.** Tells PowerPoint to cough up additional suggested spellings.

- **AutoCorrect.** Tells PowerPoint to keep an eye out for this misspelling in the future, and automatically substitute the selected suggestion if you misspell the same word the same way again.

- **Close.** Closes the Spelling dialog box without taking any additional action.

- **Options.** Tells PowerPoint to display the PowerPoint Options window, which lets you customize the way PowerPoint checks spelling.

Cleaning Up the Custom Dictionary

PowerPoint uses two separate dictionaries to check your spelling: a "real" dictionary (one that you can't change) and a custom dictionary (one called *custom.dic* that you *can* change).

Say, for example, that you accidentally added the word *persnicketty* to the custom dictionary when what you wanted to add was *persnickety*.

In PowerPoint 2007, the process of cleaning up erroneous custom spellings is easier than in previous versions. To delete a word from *custom.dic*, follow these steps:

1. Choose Office button → PowerPoint Options.

2. In the PowerPoint Options window that appears, click Proofing to select it.

3. Select Custom Dictionaries.

4. In the Custom Dictionaries dialog box that pops up, make sure the checkbox next to the custom dictionary you want to use is turned on, and then click Edit Word List.

5. In the dialog box that appears, click to select the word(s) you want to delete, and then click Delete to get rid of the word and OK to dismiss the dialog box.

Manual spell checking

Some folks find automatic spell checking (page 435) more distracting than helpful. They either resent those wavy red underlines distracting them while they're busy trying to concentrate, or they just get so used to seeing the underlines that they ignore them and end up leaving in misspellings.

If either of these reactions sounds familiar, you'll want to turn off automatic spell checking and run the tool yourself, when you've finished composing your text and are ready to begin proofreading in earnest.

To turn off automatic spell checking:

1. **Select Office button → PowerPoint Options → Proofing.**

   The PowerPoint Options window (Figure 18-9) appears showing all the spelling and automatic spelling options.

2. **Turn off the checkbox next to "Check spelling as you type" and then click OK.**

   The PowerPoint Options window disappears.

To check the spelling of your presentation manually:

1. **Click the Review tab.**

   The reviewing tools appear (Figure 18-10).

2. **Click Spelling.**

   Up pops the Spelling window shown back in Figure 18-8.

3. **Spell check your presentation following the instructions on page 434.**

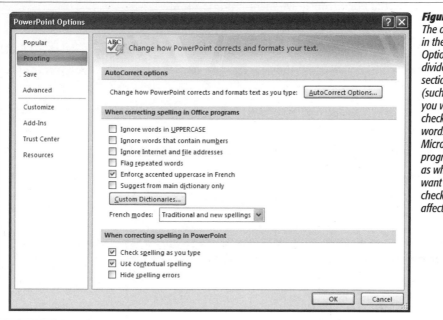

Figure 18-9:
The options you set here in the PowerPoint Options window are divided into labeled sections. Some settings (such as whether or not you want the spell checker to flag repeated words) affect all Microsoft Office programs; others (such as whether or not you want automatic spell checking turned on) affect PowerPoint only.

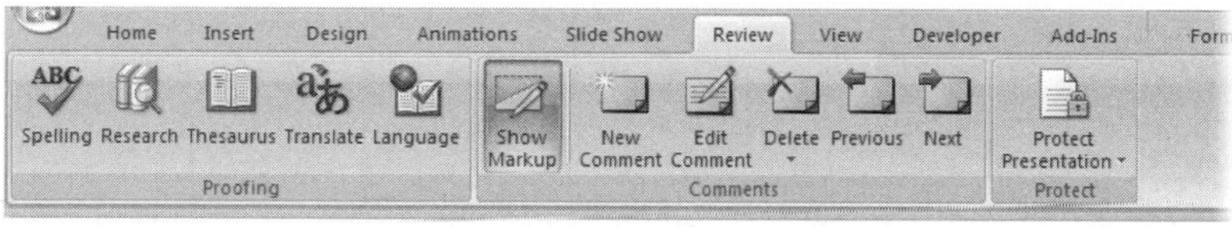

Figure 18-10:
The Review tab shows you all the options you're likely to need after you've finished creating your presentation, when you're ready to read through and tweak it. To bypass the Review tab altogether and skip directly to the Spelling window, press F7.

Adding Special Characters

Because PowerPoint comes complete with a slew of fonts and character sets, you can add all kinds of special characters to your slides without having to have a souped-up keyboard. Mathematical signs, foreign currency symbols, umlauts, schwas, superscripted characters, and happy faces are just some of the special characters—or *symbols*—at your disposal. If for no other reason than to accent those *e*'s in résumé, you want to familiarize yourself with inserting special characters.

Here's how you do so:

1. **Click in a text box and position your cursor where you want to insert the special character. Select Insert → Text → Symbol.**

    The Symbol dialog box appears (Figure 18-11).

2. **From the Font drop-down menu, choose a font.**

   The special characters you see vary depending on the font you choose, not just in appearance but in number.

3. **From the Subset drop-down menu, choose the type of symbol you're interested in.**

   Alternatively, you can scroll through the symbol window to find the symbol you're looking for.

4. **Choose the symbol you want to insert, and then click Insert.**

   PowerPoint inserts the selected symbol.

5. **Click Close to dismiss the Symbol dialog box.**

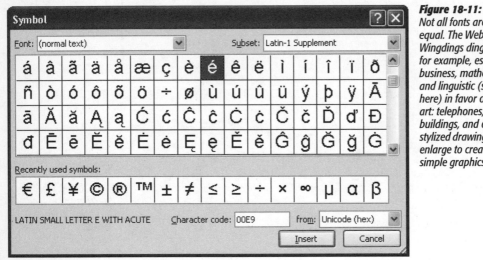

Figure 18-11:
Not all fonts are created equal. The Webdings and Wingdings dingbat fonts, for example, eschew the business, mathematical, and linguistic (shown here) in favor of vector art: telephones, hearts, buildings, and other stylized drawings you can enlarge to create clean, simple graphics.

CHAPTER 19

Formatting and Aligning Your Text

Content may be king, but presentation is queen. You're going to spend a lot of time choosing just the right text to add to your slides, so don't blow all that hard work by ignoring the way your text looks. If your text is hard to read or conveys a message counter to the point you're trying to make—if you choose whimsical, candy-colored fonts for a presentation introducing your company's expanded line of funeral services, for example—you're going to confuse (or even lose) your audience.

This chapter shows you how to format your text effectively. You'll find out how to choose fonts, colors, and special effects (such as underlining and shadowing) that support and strengthen your message (Figure 19-1), and how to avoid the effects that detract from it (Figure 19-2).

Automating Text Formatting

PowerPoint gives you more options for formatting text than a normal human being will ever need—everything from the basic (bold, italics, underlining) to the wacky (beveling, stacking, 3-D rotation). And it gives you two ways to take advantage of these options: automatically, and manually.

- **Automatic.** If you haven't finished adding text to your slides, you can turn on one or more of PowerPoint's automatic formatting features to tell the program to catch basic formatting and punctuation goofs for you as you type.

- **Manual.** If you've already added text to your slides or want to apply fancy effects, you'll need to format your text manually—either by applying individual effects one at a time, or by applying one of PowerPoint 2007's predesigned styles.

Figure 19-1:
Effectively formatted text is easy to read and it subliminally reinforces the message you're trying to drive home. Here, a solid, "respectable" font, a sober blue-and-tan-and-white color scheme, and spare, businesslike layout all contribute to the seriousness of the message.

Figure 19-2:
Anyone who's spent time in corporate America has suffered through at least one presentation like this. While it's true that your message (and your audience) should dictate the formatting choices you make, getting carried away is never a good idea. Too many formatting bells and whistles can affect your message more negatively than no formatting at all.

Less Is More

As you format your presentation, make sure you keep the following three goals in mind:

Readability.

Readability.

Readability.

Specialty formatting—like drop-shadows, bevels, and text that runs up and down instead of left to right—is the Power-Point equivalent of swearing: If you use it sparingly and appropriately, it gets your audience's attention. Use it frequently or indiscriminately, and it'll turn your audience off and reflect poorly on your skills as a communicator.

One way to keep your slides readable is to remember that your slides should *aid* you in giving your presentation; they shouldn't *be* your presentation.

Instead of automatically typing out a bunch of bullet points, consider displaying something on your slide that grabs your audience's attention, such as a drawing, a photo (*www.istockphoto.com* is a great source), or a provocative question. Then let your audience focus on this simple, powerful visual while you explain how it relates to your message—using as many words as you need to. (Chances are your audience will remember a striking photo or a single, stark, provocatively worded question much better than a bunch of text.)

If you *do* decide to go the text route, keep it readable by sticking to three or four bullet points per slide; try to limit each bullet point to five or six words; and size the text at 32 points or larger.

In most cases, you'll want to use both automatic and manual formatting. The following sections show you how.

Using AutoFormat

You can tell PowerPoint to catch certain formatting errors—like typing a hyphen when you meant to type a dash—and replace them with the correct punctuation or symbol automatically. You can also tell the program to automatically format text that threatens to spill over its bounding placeholder box.

Note: AutoFormat isn't retroactive. In other words, turning on AutoFormat options doesn't affect existing text; it affects only the text you add to your slides *after* you turn on AutoFormat. To see how to manually format existing text, flip to page 448.

To turn on automatic formatting options:

1. **Choose Office button → PowerPoint Options (it's at the bottom of the Office menu).**

   The PowerPoint Options window appears.

2. **Select the Proofing panel, and then click the AutoCorrect Options button.**

   The AutoCorrect dialog box opens (Figure 19-3).

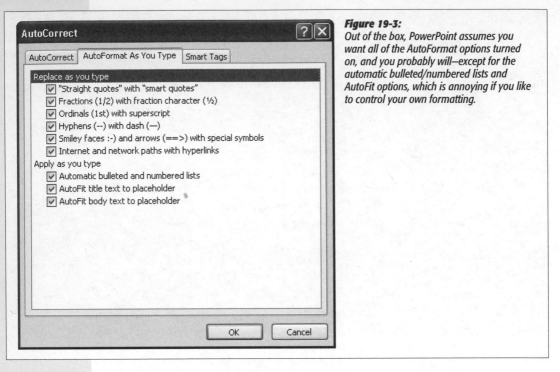

Figure 19-3:
Out of the box, PowerPoint assumes you want all of the AutoFormat options turned on, and you probably will—except for the automatic bulleted/numbered lists and AutoFit options, which is annoying if you like to control your own formatting.

3. **Click the AutoFormat As You Type tab.**

   This tab is where you control which items PowerPoint fixes on the fly. Turn on the checkbox next to one or more of the options that are described in the list that follows.

   - **"Straight quotes" with "smart quotes."** Popular with perfectionists, this option tells PowerPoint to substitute slightly curved quotation marks for the usual straight ones. (Here's where the "smart" part comes in: If you type "A dog named 'Sam,'" the first single and double smart quotes curve attractively to the right, and the final single and double smart quotes curve left. Plain old straight quotes, on the other hand, don't change their appearance based on position.)

   - **Fractions (1/2) with fraction character (½).** Turns the serviceable *1/2* (or *1/4*, or *3/4*, and so on) into a tiny, easier-to-read *½* (or *¼*, or *¾*) symbol.

   - **Ordinals (1st, 2nd, and so on) with superscript.** Tells PowerPoint to superscript the *st*, *nd*, *rd*, and *th* portions of *1st*, *2nd*, *3rd*, *4th*, *5th*, and so on.

   - **Hyphens (--) with dash (—).** Tells PowerPoint to turn two short hyphens in a row into a single long *em* dash.

   - **Smiley faces :-) and arrows ==> with special symbols.** Tells PowerPoint to turn homemade smiley emoticons and arrows into actual smiley and arrow symbols, as shown in Figure 19-4.

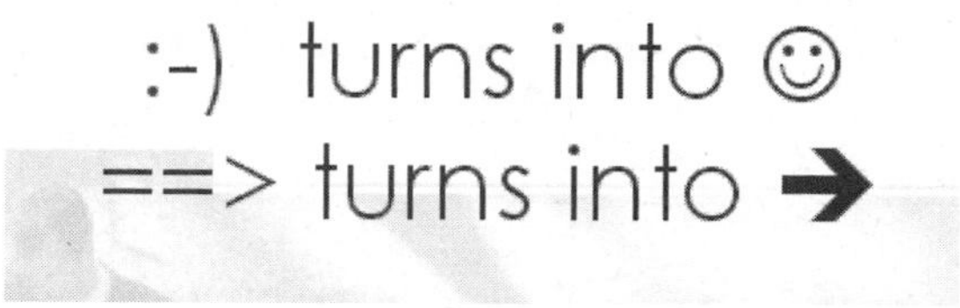

:-) turns into ☺

==> turns into ➔

Figure 19-4:
The standard substitutions you see here work for most folks, but if you prefer, you can turn them off by unchecking their boxes (Figure 19-3).

- **Internet and network paths with hyperlinks.** Tells PowerPoint to automatically turn any Web and email addresses you add to your slides (like *http:// www.oreilly.com*, *www.missingmanuals.com*, and *yourEmail@yourISP.net*) into clickable hyperlinks.

- **Automatic bulleted and numbered lists.** Tells PowerPoint to format your text as a bulleted or numbered list automatically when you type in a sentence beginning with either * or 1. (You find out all about lists on page 458.)

- **AutoFit title text to placeholder.** Tells PowerPoint to try to keep your title text inside its placeholder bounds. Typically, you want to select this option for two reasons: Overflowing text boxes are hard to select, and wordy titles don't do your presentation any good. When you do select this option, PowerPoint shrinks your font size and squeezes your line spacing automatically as soon as the text you type overflows your title placeholder box.

Note: Because titles, by definition, are supposed to stand out and be readable, PowerPoint doesn't automatically reduce your font size lower than the smallest size allowed by whoever designed the theme you're using (usually somewhere around size 40)—no matter how much title text you type in. But *you* can reduce your type as small as you want. Page 450 shows you how.

- **AutoFit body text to placeholder.** Tells PowerPoint to restrict your subtitle text to its placeholder bounding box, no matter how much text you type. If you type so much text that you spill over the placeholder, PowerPoint automatically shrinks the text font and line spacing to make it fit. Don't choose this option if you tend to be wordy, because as long as you keep typing, PowerPoint keeps shrinking your text until it's too small to read. Because the auto-shrunken text fits neatly into its placeholder box, you may not notice how small it's become. Thirty-two-point text is about as small as you want on a slide.

Using AutoFit

PowerPoint's AutoFit options let you control how you want your text to fit into the title and text placeholders you add to your slides. (Do you want your text to spill over? Shrink to fit?) AutoFit options also let you control whether you want to split giant wads of text into multiple columns, or break it up and put it on multiple slides.

Whether you've turned the automatic AutoFit options for title and body text on or off, PowerPoint always recognizes when text overflows its bounding box and lets you choose how you want to handle it by popping up the AutoFit Options icon shown in Figure 19-5.

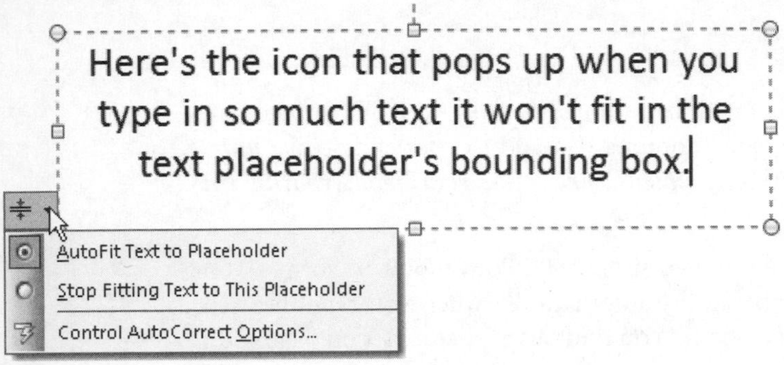

Here's the icon that pops up when you type in so much text it won't fit in the text placeholder's bounding box.

AutoFit Text to Placeholder

Stop Fitting Text to This Placeholder

Control AutoCorrect Options…

Figure 19-5:
There are two kinds of people in the world: those who appreciate the AutoFit Options icon springing to life every few minutes, and those who hate it. If you're the latter, simply click outside the text box to dismiss the icon. Otherwise, take advantage of the suggestions that this icon's menu provides. After all, the icon appears only when your text is running amok.

To select an AutoFit option:

1. **Click in a title or subtitle placeholder. Begin typing and continue until the text overflows the placeholder (the bounding box).**

   PowerPoint displays a tiny AutoFit Options icon at the lower left of your place-holder (see Figure 19-5).

2. **Click the AutoFit Options icon.**

   A menu similar to the one in Figure 19-5 appears. The actual options you see depend on the kind of text box you're working with, as well as how much text you've typed in and how you've formatted it.

3. **Choose one of the following options:**

   • **AutoFit Text to Placeholder.** Tells PowerPoint to shrink the text until it all fits neatly inside its bounding box (for text placeholders), or—if you're working with a title placeholder—to reduce the font size no lower than size 30. Choosing this option helps you keep your text within PowerPoint's sug-gested layout bounds (which, in turn, helps make sure your text is both read-able and attractively laid out).

   • **Stop Fitting Text to This Placeholder.** Springs the font size of your text back to its original point size. You want to choose this option in cases where you're trying to create a specific, nontraditional effect. Maybe you want to display a simple drawing using an extra-large character from a dingbat font (such as Webdings).

   • **Split Text Between Two Slides.** Tells PowerPoint to create a new slide and move half of the text to a similar placeholder on the new slide.

- **Continue On a New Slide.** Tells PowerPoint to create a new blank slide. As you continue to type, the new text flows onto the newly created slide in an unbroken stream.

- **Change to Two Columns.** Tells PowerPoint to reformat your text as a two-column layout. (For more on columns and slide layouts, zip ahead to page 457.)

- **Control AutoCorrect Options.** Displays the AutoCorrect dialog box you saw back in Figure 19-3, which lets you change your AutoFit settings.

Tip: If you want to change (or just look at) your AutoFit settings without waiting for PowerPoint to kick up the AutoFit Options icon, no problem—just right-click your text box. Then, from the context menu that appears, choose Format Text Effects to display the Format Text Effects dialog box. In the Format Text Effects dialog box, click the Text Box tab. Figure 19-6 shows you the result.

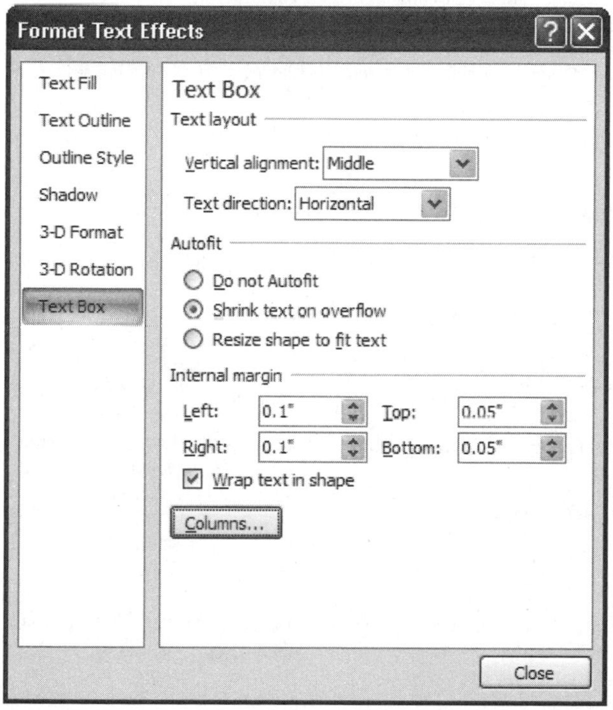

Figure 19-6:
The handiest way to deal with a ton of text is to wait until it overflows your text box and take one of PowerPoint's AutoFit suggestions. But if you're the impatient type—or if you know you're going to be adding a lot of text and want to resize the text box sooner rather than later—then the Format Text Effects dialog box, shown here, offers some of the same AutoFit options.

Manually Formatting Text Appearance

While PowerPoint's automatic formatting options help with the grunt work of formatting the text on your slides, you should do some of the formatting yourself. After all, the program has no way of knowing which words or phrases you want to emphasize—which, when you get right down to it, is what formatting is all about.

PowerPoint conveniently displays all of its text formatting options on the Home tab (Figure 19-7). A handful of the most commonly used formats also appear when you right-click text or when you select it, as shown in Figure 19-8.

Note: If you're the kind of person who simply can't stand pop-ups, you can turn off the mini-toolbar. To do so, select Office button → PowerPoint Options and then, in the PowerPoint Options window that appears, select Popular and turn off the "Show Mini Toolbar on selection" checkbox.

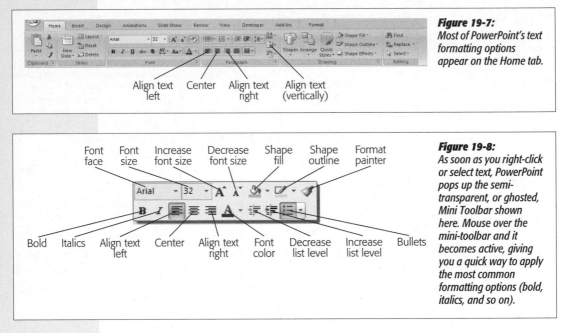

Figure 19-7:
Most of PowerPoint's text formatting options appear on the Home tab.

Figure 19-8:
As soon as you right-click or select text, PowerPoint pops up the semi-transparent, or ghosted, Mini Toolbar shown here. Mouse over the mini-toolbar and it becomes active, giving you a quick way to apply the most common formatting options (bold, italics, and so on).

Using the options you find on the Home tab, you can format individual characters and words by changing their color, font size, font, underlining, shadowing, and so on. You can format paragraphs by indenting them, turning them into bulleted or numbered lists, and by applying effects to them, such as rotating them or turning them into diagrams. The following sections show you how.

Changing the Font

PowerPoint's *fonts* (what printers used to call *typefaces*) determine how text looks: spidery, staid, clunky, old-fashioned, funky, and so on. Arial, Helvetica, and Times Roman are three common fonts, although PowerPoint offers a lot more than that.

FREQUENTLY ASKED QUESTION

Troubleshooting Fonts

Can using exotic fonts cause problems in PowerPoint?

Yes. Say you create a presentation using the SuperFancy font you downloaded from the Web and installed on your computer. You copy your presentation to your laptop and hop on a plane. When you arrive at your client's office, ready to give your spiel, you discover that the text of your presentation appears totally different from the way you created it. The problem? You forgot to install SuperFancy on your laptop, so PowerPoint substituted a *system font* (one of the factory-installed fonts that come with all operating systems). To avoid this problem, you've got two choices:

- **Use a standard font such as Arial, Times New Roman, or Courier New.** These fonts are pretty run-of-the-mill, it's true, but they're 99.9 percent

likely to be installed on every computer—and at least *you're* the one choosing them (and not Power-Point).

- **Embed your special font directly into your PowerPoint presentation.** This option lets your audience see exactly what you intended them to see. On the downside, embedding swells the size of your PowerPoint presentation, which becomes an issue if you intend to deliver it over the Web, and may cause problems in older versions of the program. *PowerPoint 2007: The Missing Manual* teaches you how to embed fonts.

(The actual number of fonts you can apply to your text in PowerPoint depends on how many fonts you have installed on your computer. For more information, see the box above.)

To change the font:

1. **Click in a text box.**

   The Drawing Tools | Format contextual tab appears, and PowerPoint activates the formatting options on the Home tab.

2. **Select the characters you want to format.**

   The characters appear highlighted, and you see a ghosted mini-toolbar.

3. **Choose Font, either in the Home → Font group or from the mini-toolbar.**

   A list of fonts similar to the one you see in Figure 19-9 appears.

4. **Select a font.**

   PowerPoint automatically reformats the selected text.

Note: Although they're common in the print world, *serif* fonts (fonts with fancy little feet on the letters) tend to be harder to read on computer screens than *sans-serif* (literally, "without serif") fonts. Sans-serif fonts—like Calibri—look clearer onscreen.

Figure 19-9:
PowerPoint doesn't raise a fuss if you choose a different font for every single character on your slide, but you should stick with one or two fonts per presentation (unless you like the ransom note look). Out of the box, the program assumes you want to use the Calibri font.

Changing Font Size

PowerPoint gives you two different ways to change the size of your font: You can increase or decrease your font by choosing from a list, or you can type a specific font size (such as 38). If you're like most folks, you'll want to increase or decrease your font size, eyeball the result, and repeat until you achieve the look you want. But when you need to match the font size on one slide to the size on another, the quickest approach is to specify the number directly using the drop-down menu shown in Figure 19-10.

Tip: Have pity on the folks in the back row (or, if you'll be delivering your slideshow over the Web, the folks with small monitors) and keep your font size as large as possible. A quick way to tell if your font's big enough is to print out a slide and drop it face-up on the floor. If you're standing over it and can't read it easily, your font is too small.

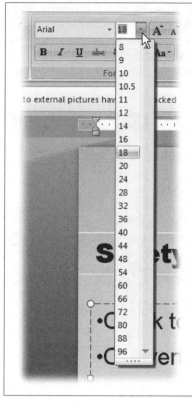

Figure 19-10:
If you don't see the particular font size you're looking for, no problem. Instead of clicking the arrow next to the Font box, click the displayed font (here, 18), type your own font size, and press Return. PowerPoint obediently applies any size you specify, from ridiculously small (1) to ridiculously large (999).

To change font size:

1. **Click in a text box.**

   The Drawing Tools | Format context tab pops up, and PowerPoint activates the formatting options on the Home tab.

2. **Select the characters you want to format.**

   The characters appear highlighted, and the mini-toolbar appears.

3. **In either the Home → Font group or on the mini-toolbar, choose a font size option.**

   You have three choices:

   • **Increase font size.** Clicking this option (the one with the "A" followed by the up-arrow) bumps up the font size to the next-highest size on the list.

   • **Decrease font size.** Clicking this option (the "A" followed by the down-arrow) shrinks font size to the next-lowest size on the list.

- **Font size menu.** Clicking this option (a drop-down box displaying a number) shows the list you see in Figure 19-10, from which you can choose the precise font size you want. Rolling your mouse over the list shows you immediately, right on the slide, what your text looks like in each font. When you find the size you want, click it to apply the previewed changes to your slide.

POWER USERS' CLINIC

The New Font Dialog Box

The Font dialog box offers a one-stop shop for all font-related settings described in this chapter: font and size, bolding and underlining, coloring and shadowing, super-scripting and subscripting, and more.

Using the Font dialog box saves you time if you're used to using it in older versions of PowerPoint, or if you want to make a bunch of font changes all at once.

To display the Font dialog box, either click the Font dialog launcher (the little down-arrow in the bottom-right corner of the Home tab's Font section, as shown in Figure 19-7) or right-click in a text box and then, from the context menu that appears, choose Font.

To use the Font dialog box to change an underline from a solid to a dashed one, click the Font tab, and then choose the dashed style you want from the "Underline style" drop-down box. To change the color of an underline, from the Font tab, head to the "Underline color" drop-down box and choose a color.

Bolding, Italicizing, and Underlining Text

Three of the easiest and most common ways to draw attention to text are to bold, italicize, or underline the text (Figure 19-11). These effects look and behave pretty much the same in PowerPoint as they do in most word-processing programs, including Microsoft Word.

To bold, italicize, or underline text:

1. **Click in a text box.**

   The Drawing Tools | Format contextual tab pops up, and PowerPoint activates the formatting options on the Home tab.

2. **Select the characters you want to format.**

   The characters appear highlighted, and the mini-toolbar appears.

3. **Choose one or more of the formatting options in the Home → Font group or from the mini-toolbar: Bold, Italicize, or Underline. (The Underline option isn't available on the mini-toolbar.)**

Tip: If you prefer keyboard shortcuts, after you've selected the text you want to format, you can press Ctrl+B (to make it bold), Ctrl+I (to italicize it), or Ctrl+U (to underline it). Pressing the same two keys again removes the effect.

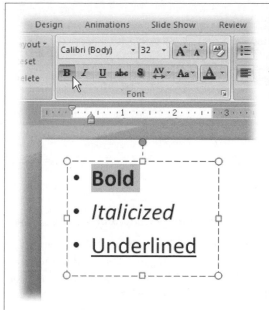

Changing Text Color and Background Color

PowerPoint lets you change the color of your text (and its background) from basic black to puce, chartreuse, chocolate mousse, or any other hue you come up with. You can color all of it, just a word or two for emphasis, or change the background color of the text box. You can also apply a gradient effect that makes your text look as though a light's shining on it (the following section shows you how).

Note: Color's a moot point if you intend to fax or print your presentation on a black-and-white printer. In that case, you want to make sure your slides look good in *grayscale*, which you do by choosing View → Color/Grayscale → Grayscale. Because grayscale adds shades of gray to plain black-and-white, it's the best way to print a non-colored version of a color presentation.

To change text and text background color:

1. **Click in a text box.**

   The Drawing Tools | Format context tab pops up, and PowerPoint activates the formatting options on the Home tab.

2. **Select the characters you want to format.**

   The characters appear highlighted, and the mini-toolbar appears.

3. **Click the drop-down arrow next to the Font Color icon that appears in the mini-toolbar or in the Home → Font group.**

   The color picker you see in Figure 19-12 appears.

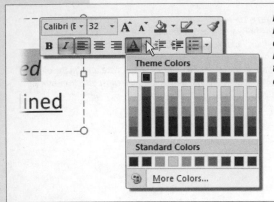

Figure 19-12:
Here, you see the basic color picker that appears when you choose Font Color from the Mini Toolbar, or when you select Font from the Font section of the Home tab. Most of the time, these basic options are all you need. But if you like, you can apply a special text effect, as described below.

4. **Choose a color from either the Theme or Standard sections of the color picker.**

   Choosing a color from the Theme section makes sure the color of your text coordinates attractively with the other colors in your theme, like the background color of your slide. If you choose a color from the Standard section, there's no guarantee it will look good with the other elements on your slide.

Adding Special Text Effects

In addition to basic bolding, italicizing, and underlining, you can add all kinds of special effects to your text, as you can see in Figure 19-13. You find the special effects options on the Font and WordArt Styles sections of the Home tab.

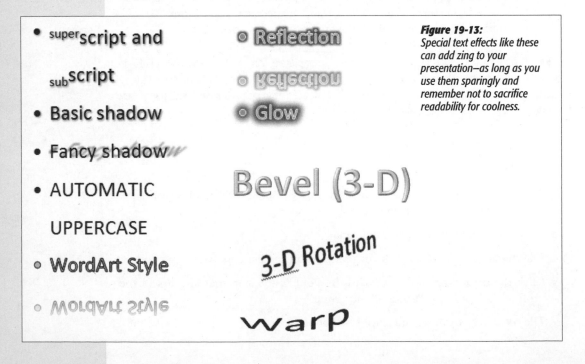

Figure 19-13:
Special text effects like these can add zing to your presentation—as long as you use them sparingly and remember not to sacrifice readability for coolness.

To add a special effect to your text, simply select the text, and then click the effect on the ribbon.

- **Add a superscript or subscript.** If your presentation covers chemistry or some other scientific field, you'll need to subscript and superscript characters (think H_2O). On the Home tab, click the Font dialog launcher and then, in the Font dialog box that appears, make sure the Font tab is selected and then turn on the checkbox next to Superscript or Subscript.

- **Add a shadow.** Select Home → Font → Text Shadow. When you do, Power-Point automatically adds a shadow to your text. For a more sophisticated shadow effect, right-click your selection, choose Format Text Effects, and then, in the Format Text Effects dialog box that appears, click Shadow (see Figure 19-14). Click Presets to choose from a handful of standard shadows; then, if you want, you can use the other options to tweak the standard shadow.

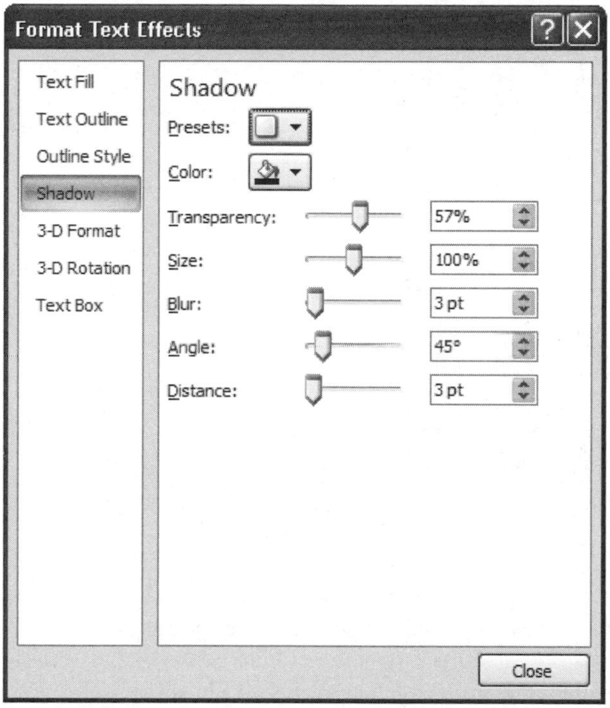

Figure 19-14:
Shadows tend to make skinny fonts unreadable, but they can effectively draw attention to short headings displayed in plump, bold fonts. Click Presets to choose from a gallery of attractive, predesigned shadow options; then click Size, Angle, Distance, or any of the other options shown here to customize the predesigned look.

- **Change text case.** You can tell PowerPoint to format the case of your text automatically, which is useful for fixing capitalization goofs. Click Home → Font → Change Case (the "AAa" button). From the menu that appears, choose one of the following: "Sentence case" (uppercases the first word of each line and adds a period after last word); "lowercase" (changes all characters to lowercase), UPPERCASE (changes all characters to uppercase); Capitalize Each Word (uppercases first letter of each word); or "tOGGLE cASE" (reverses the existing capitalization). This last option is rarely useful *unless* you just typed in a bunch of text with the caps lock key on by mistake.

- **Apply a pre-crafted effect (Quick Style).** The Quick Styles section of the Home tab offers a gallery of text effects including outlined fonts, glows, and reflections. To see them all, click the down arrow next to the Quick Styles option. The result is the full gallery of effects shown in Figure 19-15. Clicking an effect applies it directly to your text.

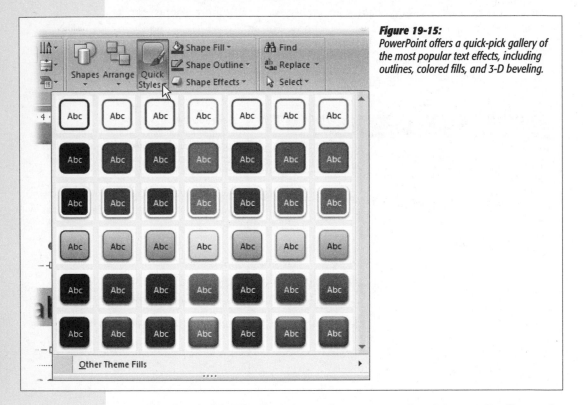

Figure 19-15:
PowerPoint offers a quick-pick gallery of the most popular text effects, including outlines, colored fills, and 3-D beveling.

- **Add a beveled (3-D) effect.** To get the most out of applying a 3-D effect, make sure your text is large and blocky. 3-D doesn't do much for skinny, light-colored characters. Then go to Home → Drawing → Quick Styles → Text Effects → Bevel and, from the gallery that appears, click to choose a bevel option.

- **Add a 3-D rotation effect.** Another effect that looks better applied to shapes than to text, the 3-D rotation effect reformats your text in 3-D form and then slants it based on the perspective you choose. On the Drawing section of the Home tab, select Shape Effects → 3-D Rotation and then, from the gallery that appears, click to choose the option you want.

Manually Aligning and Indenting Text

To effectively convey your message on a slide, your text must above all be readable. After all, your audience may have to read it across a large conference room, or on a small laptop monitor. Make things easier on your audience's eyes by making sure your words are neatly and attractively lined up.

Aligning Text and Creating Columns

Neatly arranged text can mean the difference between an easy-to-read, professional-looking slide, and a jumbled mess.

PowerPoint gives you two ways to align text:

- **You can align text with respect to its bounding placeholder box.** For example, you can center heading text inside its box or position it flush left or flush right. If you've got a paragraph's worth of text, you can *justify* it (add spaces between the words so the ends of each line up) or turn it into two or more columns.

- **You can align a text placeholder box with respect to the slide it's on.** This type of alignment's called *layout*, and it's covered on page 469.

This section shows you how to align text with respect to its bounding placeholder box.

To align text:

1. **Click in a text box.**

   The Drawing Tools | Format contextual tab pops up, and PowerPoint activates the formatting options on the Home tab.

2. **Go to Home → Paragraph and choose an alignment option.**

   You can see examples in Figure 19-16, left:

   - **Align Text Left.** Positions text at the top left of the bounding box.

   - **Center.** Positions text at the top center of the bounding box.

   - **Align Text Right.** Positions text at the top right of the bounding box.

Note: Unless you tell it different, PowerPoint assumes you want to align text at the top of the bounding box. Choosing Align Text Left, for example, has the effect of aligning your text at the left *and top* of the bounding box. (The distinction becomes important when your text box is really big.)

   - **Justify.** Adds spaces between your words so that the left and right edges of your sentences line up nicely.

   - **Columns.** Lets you split your text into one, two, or three columns. Simply click the number of columns you'd like, and PowerPoint reformats your text immediately. Clicking More Columns lets you choose four or more columns, and lets you adjust the space between your columns.

Tip: If you need absolutely precise layouts (because, for example, you're mocking up a program interface or a printable brochure), you can align text in a text box by setting internal margins (left, right, top, and bottom). To do so, in the Home tab, click Alignment → More Options to display the Format Text Effects dialog box with the Text Box option selected (Figure 19-16, right).

- **Align Text.** Click Align Text to position text at the top, middle, or bottom of a bounding box.

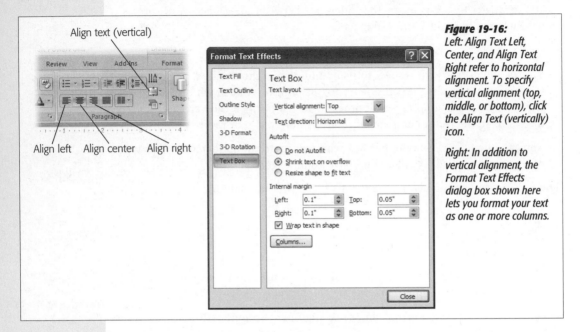

Figure 19-16:
Left: Align Text Left, Center, and Align Text Right refer to horizontal alignment. To specify vertical alignment (top, middle, or bottom), click the Align Text (vertically) icon.

Right: In addition to vertical alignment, the Format Text Effects dialog box shown here lets you format your text as one or more columns.

Tip: PowerPoint offers one additional, seldom-used alignment option, the Distributed alignment option, which (like Justify) lines up the left and right edges of your text, but (unlike Justify) stretches out the last (*orphaned*) line so that it, too, lines up left and right. To apply the Distributed alignment option, first select your text. Then, on the Home tab, click the Paragraph dialog launcher and, in the Paragraph dialog box that appears, head to the Alignment drop-down box and choose Distributed.

Creating Lists

For better or worse PowerPoint slides and bulleted lists are practically synonymous. The fact is, lists (both bulleted and numbered) like the ones you see in Figure 19-17 are a natural fit for PowerPoint because they let you organize information clearly and concisely.

In fact, when you find yourself adding a lot of lists to your slides, let PowerPoint format them for you automatically. After you do, each time you type in an asterisk or a number followed by some text and then the Enter key, PowerPoint automatically changes the asterisk to a basic bullet and types in a new bullet (or number).

GEM IN THE ROUGH

Copying Formatting with the Format Painter

You've spent half an hour tweaking, testing, and perfecting, and at long last, your slide headings are perfectly formatted. PowerPoint gives you an easy way to copy your formatting and apply it to new headings using the Format Painter (the icon shaped like a little paintbrush that appears both on the Home → Clipboard group, and on the mini-toolbar).

To copy formatting using the Format painter:

1. Click anywhere on the text that has formatting you want to copy.

2. Click the Format Painter. (Notice that, when you mouse over your slide, your cursor turns into a little paintbrush).

3. Click the text you want to format.

To copy formatting to a bunch of different text elements in one fell swoop:

1. Click anywhere on the text that has formatting you want to copy.

2. Double-click the Format Painter. (Once again, your cursor turns into a little paintbrush).

3. Click-drag or double-click to select the text element. As you select, PowerPoint applies the copied formatting to that element. You can repeat this step as many times as you like.

4. When you're finished, click the Format Painter icon again or press Esc. Your icon turns back into a pointer.

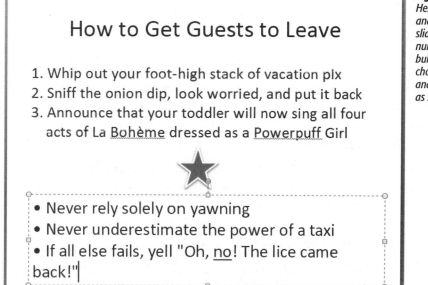

Figure 19-17:
Here they are, the bread and butter of PowerPoint slides the world over: numbered lists and bulleted lists. You can choose different bullet and numbering schemes, as shown in Figure 19-19.

To turn on automatic list formatting, select Office → PowerPoint Options → Proofing → AutoCorrect Options → AutoFormat As You Type and then turn on the checkbox next to "Automatic bulleted and numbered lists."

Of course, you can always turn a series of sentences into a list manually. Here's how:

1. **Click in a text box.**

   The Drawing Tools | Format context tab pops up, and PowerPoint activates the formatting options on the Home tab.

2. **Select the text you want to turn into a list. Then, go to Home → Paragraph and click one of the list buttons shown in Figure 19-18.**

   These buttons are toggles. Clicking once adds the bullets or numbering; clicking again removes it.

   - **Bullets.** The program applies bullets to the beginning of each selected word or sentence.

   - **Numbering.** The program applies sequential numbers (beginning with number 1) to the beginning of each selected word or sentence.

Bulleted list   Numbered list

Figure 19-18:
Clicking either the Bullets or Numbering option automatically applies a standard bullet (or numbering) scheme to the text you've selected. If you prefer to customize the standard scheme, instead of clicking the button itself, click the tiny down arrow beside it to see a menu of different styles.

Tip: An alternative—and faster—way to display bullet and numbering options is to right-click your text and then, from the menu that appears, choose Bullets or Numbering.

Customizing bulleted lists

PowerPoint lets you customize your bulleted lists by choosing one of several built-in bullet graphics, or by using your own image for the bullet. You can also resize and recolor your bullets. Here's how.

1. **Select the list you want to customize. Go to Home → Paragraph, and then click the down arrow next to the Bullets button.**

   A list of bullet options appears (Figure 19-19).

2. **Click a bullet option.**

   PowerPoint automatically reformats your list based on the option you chose.

3. **If you don't see a bullet you like, from the option list, choose Bullets and Numbering.**

   The Bullets and Numbering dialog box appears with the Bullets tab already selected (Figure 19-20).

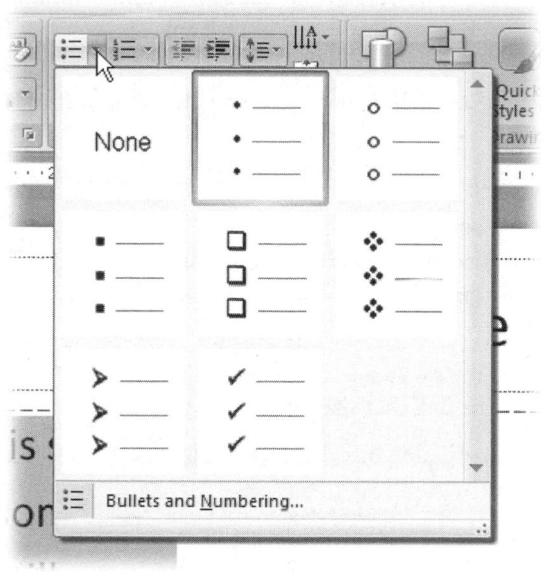

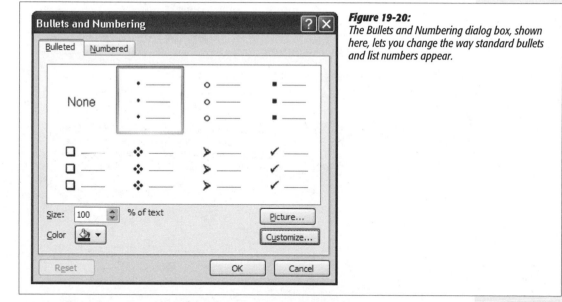

Figure 19-19:
Most of the time, one of these standard bullet options will fit the bill. But for those times when you want to substitute an itty-bitty globe or daisy for the standard dot, choose Bullets and Numbering to see additional options.

Figure 19-20:
The Bullets and Numbering dialog box, shown here, lets you change the way standard bullets and list numbers appear.

4. In the Bullets and Numbering dialog box, click Customize. In the Symbol dialog box that appears, select a symbol and click OK, and then Close.

The Symbol dialog box disappears and PowerPoint returns you to the Bullets and Numbering dialog box, where a new bulleted option appears featuring the symbol you selected. Click OK to apply the new bullet to your selection.

After you click OK, you're back in the Bullets and Numbering dialog box. If you like, you can now change the color and size of your bullets, as described in the next two steps.

5. **To change the color of your bullets, click Color. Select a color swatch from the color picker.**

   The Bullets and Numbering dialog box redisplays all the bullet options using the color you just selected.

6. **If you like, you can change the size of your bullets. In the Bullets and Numbering dialog box, click to increase and decrease the "Size % of text" counter, or type your own number.**

   100% means the bullet appears the same size as the largest upper-case letter of text, 50% means the bullet appears half that size, and so on.

7. **When the Bullets and Numbering dialog box displays the precise bullet option you want, click OK.**

   PowerPoint applies your customized bulleting scheme to your selection.

Customizing numbered lists

This procedure is a lot like customizing a bulleted list.

1. **Select the numbered list you want to tweak. Go to Home → Paragraph → Numbering and click the down arrow.**

   A slew of numbering options appears (Figure 19-21).

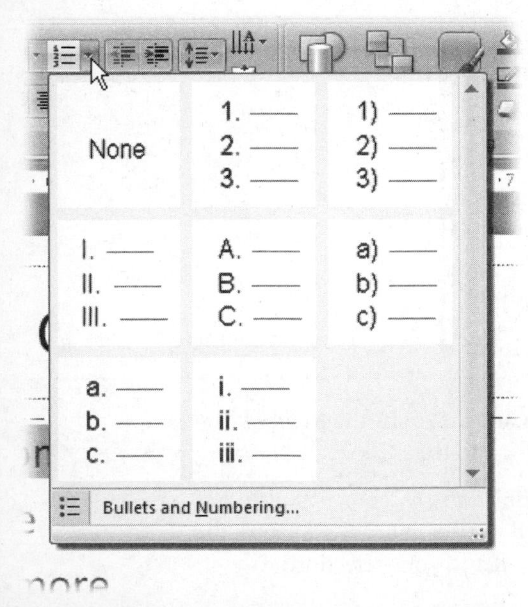

Figure 19-21:
Here are the most popular numbering schemes. (If you're wondering, choosing "None" just indents the list.) Click Bullets and Numbering to color, resize, or choose a new starting number for your list.

2. Click a numbering option.

PowerPoint automatically reformats your list based on the option you chose.

3. To change the color of a list number, select Bullets and Numbering. When the Bullets and Numbering dialog box appears (Figure 19-22), click Color, and then select a color swatch from the color picker that appears.

The Bullets and Numbering dialog box redisplays all of the list number options using the color you just selected.

4. If you like, you can specify how large you want your number to appear in relation to your text: In the Bullets and Numbering dialog box, select the numbering option you want to resize, and then click to increase and decrease the "Size % of text" counter, or type your own number.

100% means the number appears the same size as largest uppercase letter of text; 50% means the number appears half that size; and so on.

5. If you like, you can change the first number in your list from 1 to something else. From the Bullets and Numbering dialog box, click the "Start at" box and then click the counter or type in your own starting number.

The options in the dialog box change automatically.

6. When the Bullets and Numbering dialog box shows the customized numbering option you want, click to select it, and then click OK.

PowerPoint applies your customized numbering scheme to your selection.

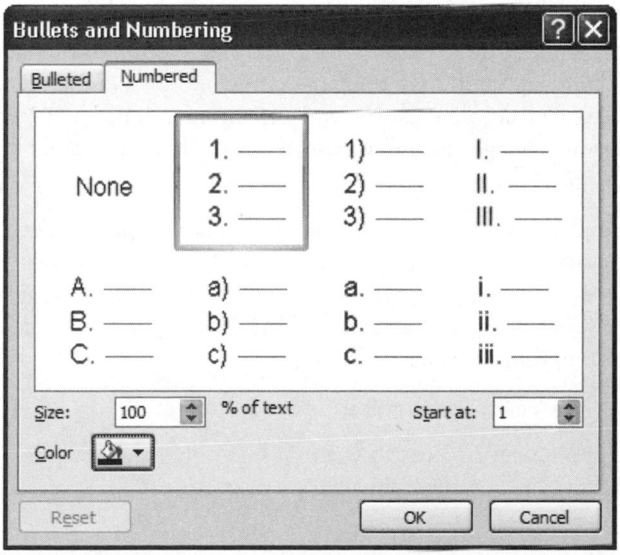

Figure 19-22:
Because details matter, PowerPoint lets you choose from a variety of list-numbering options.

Changing Indents

Unlike a word processing program, the text you add to your slides typically doesn't need a whole lot of special indenting. After all, one of the first rules of creating a great PowerPoint presentation is to keep your text brief—which means multiple paragraphs are out (and with them, the need to fiddle with your indents).

But if you *do* need to change the indentation—if you want to adjust the spacing between a bullet and its associated list item, for example—then you can.

Here's how it works: An *indent* is the space PowerPoint automatically leaves before the first line of every paragraph you add to a slide. Out of the box, PowerPoint assumes an indent of half an inch, but the program gives you three ways to change that setting:

- **Choose Home → Paragraph → Decrease List Level or Home → Paragraph → Increase List Level.** Selecting Home → Paragraph → Decrease List Level decreases the indent for the currently selected text box by one-half inch (or whatever you've set the indent to; see the third bullet below). Home → Paragraph → Increase List Level increases the indent by one-half inch (or whatever you've sent the indent to). Your text redisplays automatically. PowerPoint doesn't apply your changes to any unselected text or any other text boxes on your slide.

Note: If you select a list item and then choose Home → Paragraph → Decrease List Level or Home → Paragraph → Increase List Level, PowerPoint demotes or promotes the list item, adjusting text size as appropriate.

- **Turn on rulers and drag your indents where you want them.** Figure 19-23 shows you the rulers, indents, and tab stops you see when you turn on rulers (View → Ruler). Selecting text and then dragging an indent tells PowerPoint to redisplay your selected text automatically based on the new indent. (PowerPoint doesn't apply your changes to any unselected text, or to any other text boxes on your slide.)

- **Use the Paragraph dialog box to specify a numeric value (in percentages of inches) for indentations.** To see the Paragraph dialog box shown in Figure 19-24, click the dialog box launcher at the bottom of the Paragraph group (or right-click selected text and then chose Paragraph from the shortcut menu. The indentation options include:

  - **Before text.** Indents the entire paragraph from the left margin.

  - **Special.** Lets you apply your indents to the first line only, to every line but the first line (hanging), or to none of the text.

  - **By.** Lets you choose the width of the indent. PowerPoint displays width options in tenths of an inch, but you can type in hundredths of an inch if you like.

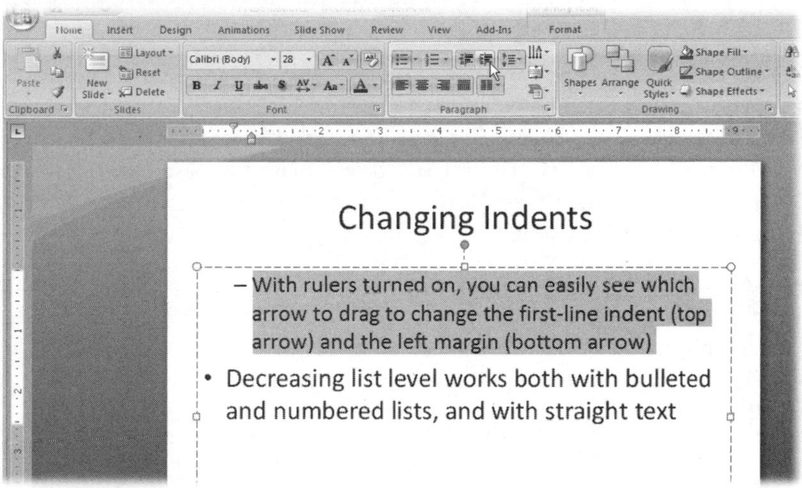

Figure 19-23:
In this example, the top paragraph has just been demoted. The top triangle you see in the ruler is the first line indent; the bottom arrow is the indent for the remaining lines in the paragraph. Drag the square to move both in one fell swoop.

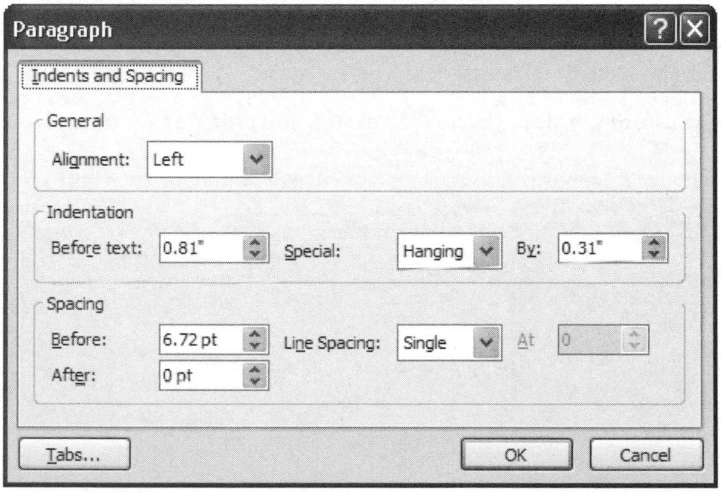

Figure 19-24:
The alignment you choose affects your indents. If you set the Alignment field to Left, for example, your indents start at the left; if it's set to Center, your indents start from where your text is centered.

Changing Tab Stops

A *tab* is the amount of space PowerPoint leaves when you press the Tab key. For example, you can scoot the first sentence of a paragraph over by clicking in front of the first word in the paragraph and pressing Tab, and you can scoot an entire list over by selecting the list and pressing Tab. You can also use tabs to create columns.

Note: You don't *have* to use tabs to create columns; in fact, PowerPoint has a special columns option you can use (page 457), and it's a lot easier to work with for columns.

Out of the box, PowerPoint sets tab stops every inch, but you can set your tab stops wherever you like. PowerPoint gives you two ways to do that:

- **Turn on rulers and drag your tab stops where you want them.** Figure 19-23 shows you the rulers, indents, and tab stops you see when you turn on rulers (View → Show/Hide → Ruler). Selecting text and then dragging a tab stop tells PowerPoint to redisplay your selected text automatically based on the new tab stop. (PowerPoint doesn't apply your changes to unselected text, or to any other text boxes on your slide.)

- **Use the Tab dialog box to specify a numeric value (in percentages of inches) for tab stops.** To see the Tabs dialog box shown in Figure 19-25, click the Home → Paragraph dialog box launcher and then, in the Paragraph dialog box that appears, click Tabs. The tab options you can set include:

  — **Add a tab stop.** Click to choose a number in the Tab stop position field, and then click Set.

  — **Delete a tab stop.** Select the tab stop you want to delete, and then click Clear.

  — **Delete all the tab stops for this slideshow.** Click Clear All.

  — **Change how far apart PowerPoint places its built-in tab stops.** Change the number in the Default tab stops field.

  — **Change a custom tab stop.** Delete the tab stop and create a new one.

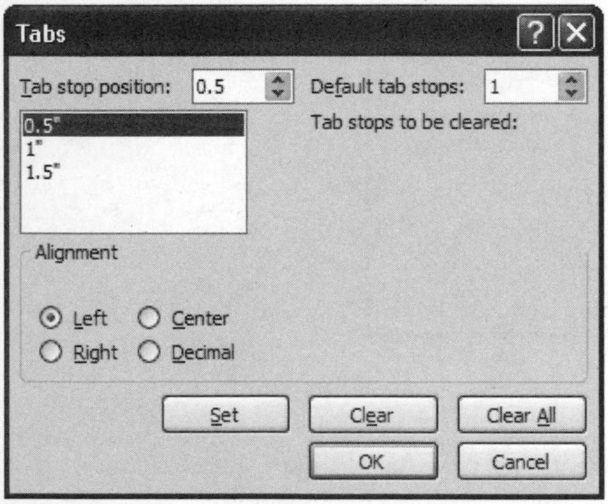

Figure 19-25:
After you add, change, or delete a tab stop, click OK to apply the change and dismiss the dialog box.

Changing Text Direction

Most languages read left to right, so most of the time, that's the way you want to display your text. But PowerPoint lets you rotate your text so that it reads top-to-bottom, right-to-left, left-to-right, upside down—pretty much any direction you like. PowerPoint gives you two options for changing the direction of your text: using the Text Direction option, and using the Size and Position dialog box.

Using the Text Direction option

This option is the one to use if you want to rotate text all the way to the left or all the way to the right, or to stack your text from the top of your text box to the bottom. (Typing your text first and *then* changing its direction is much easier than changing the direction of a text box and then typing in your text.)

1. **Click anywhere in a text box. Choose Home → Paragraph → Text Direction (the A with arrows icon). From the menu that appears, choose one of the following options (see examples of each in Figure 19-26):**

   • **Horizontal.** Basic left to right.

   • **Rotate all text 90°.** Positions text on the right side of the slide, rotating each letter so that the text reads from top to bottom.

   • **Rotate all text 270°.** Positions text on the left side of the slide, rotating each letter so that the text reads from bottom to top.

   • **Stacked.** Stacks letters on top of each other, from top to bottom, without rotating any letters.

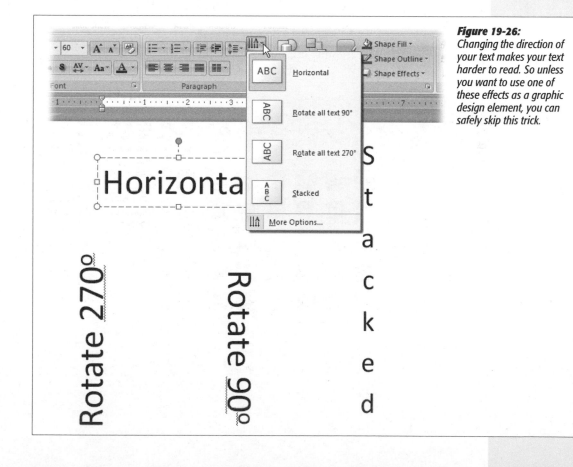

Figure 19-26:
Changing the direction of your text makes your text harder to read. So unless you want to use one of these effects as a graphic design element, you can safely skip this trick.

2. Because PowerPoint doesn't automatically change the size of your text box when it repositions your text, you may have to resize your text box yourself to make your text readable in its jaunty new position.

   If you don't remember how to resize a text box, see page 411.

Formatting Text Boxes

In addition to formatting the *text* on your slides, you can also format the text *boxes* that surround the text by applying options such as visible borders, colored backgrounds, and 3-D effects. These options don't change the text inside the text boxes, just the text boxes themselves. Formatting a text box is a good way to draw your audience's attention to a specific bit of text.

To format a text box:

1. Click anywhere in the text box you want to format. Choose Home → Drawing → Quick Styles.

   The gallery of effects you see in Figure 19-27 appears. As you mouse over each effect, PowerPoint previews the effect for you on your slide.

2. Click to choose the effect you want.

   On your slide, PowerPoint automatically formats your text box.

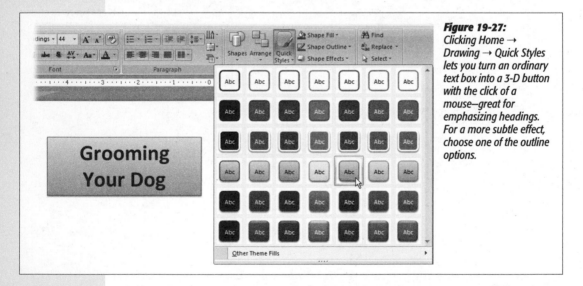

Figure 19-27:
Clicking Home → Drawing → Quick Styles lets you turn an ordinary text box into a 3-D button with the click of a mouse—great for emphasizing headings. For a more subtle effect, choose one of the outline options.

Formatting and Laying Out Your Slides

In the previous chapter, you learned how to massage text into perfectly indented paragraphs, columns, and lists. Now it's time for the big picture. This chapter shows you how to format slides using *layouts,* and how to reapply a *theme* (see page 407) or *color scheme* (a list of coordinating font colors). Finally—and most important when you're in a time crunch—you'll learn how to turn on Power-Point's automatic formatting options.

Changing Slide Layout

Each time you create a slide—by creating a new presentation, or by adding a slide to an existing presentation—PowerPoint gives that slide a layout such as the Title Slide layout, with one title text placeholder near the top and one subtitle text place-holder near the middle of the slide. But you can change the layout of your slide at any time, either before you've added content to it or after. PowerPoint gives you several options for changing slide layout:

- **Apply canned layouts to your slides.** You can tell PowerPoint to put a title at the top of a slide and two content placeholders (for text, pictures, and so on) side-by-side in the body of the slide.

- **Change orientation.** You can change a *landscape* orientation (where the slide's wider than it is tall) to a *portrait* orientation (where the slide's taller than it is wide).

- **Reposition elements.** You can drag text boxes and other objects (such as pictures) around on your slide to reposition them.

Applying a Canned Layout

PowerPoint offers nine canned layouts you can use. Most of the time, you're going to want to apply these layouts before you add text to your slides, but you can apply them after, as well.

To apply a canned layout to your slide:

1. **Create a new slide (page 413). Click any blank spot on your new slide.**

   Make sure you don't click a text placeholder, picture, diagram, or other object.

2. **Choose Home → Slides → Layout.**

   A layout gallery based on the template or theme you've applied to your slide-show appears. (You can also display the layout gallery by right-clicking the slide or the slide thumbnail you see in the Slides pane and then, from the context menu that appears, mousing over the Layout option.)

3. **From the layout gallery, click to choose the layout thumbnail you want to apply to your slide (Figure 20-1).**

   Mousing over any thumbnail in the gallery pops up the name of that thumbnail option. Typically, your options include:

   - **Title Slide.** One title placeholder near the top of the slide, and one subtitle placeholder.

   - **Title and Content.** One title placeholder and one large content placeholder.

   - **Section Header.** Similar to the Title Slide layout, but with a contrasting background. (Useful for alerting your audience that you're starting a new section of your slideshow.)

   - **Two Content.** One title placeholder and two content placeholders, each containing an icon you can click to add a diagram, chart, picture, or other content.

   - **Comparison.** Similar to the Two Content layout, but with extra placeholders for headings.

   - **Title Only.** One title placeholder.

   - **Blank.** No text placeholders at all.

   - **Content with Caption.** One title placeholder and one placeholder containing an icon you can click to add a diagram, chart, picture, or other content (see Figure 20-1).

   - **Picture with Caption.** One title placeholder and one placeholder you can click to add a picture.

   PowerPoint automatically applies the layout to your slide.

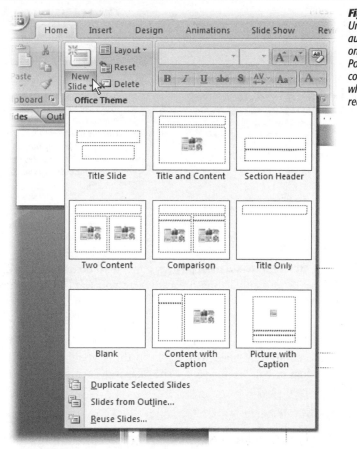

Switching Orientation from Landscape to Portrait (and Back)

Unless you tell it otherwise, PowerPoint assumes you want your presentation to appear in *landscape* form; that is, with slides that appear wider than they are tall. But you can change this orientation to *portrait* if you like. For example, if you intend to print your presentation, staple the pages, and hand it out to your audience, then you may want to switch to portrait so your audience can flip through the pages more easily.

To choose an orientation, go to Design → Page Setup → Slide Orientation and choose either Portrait or Landscape. Figure 20-2 shows you an example of each.

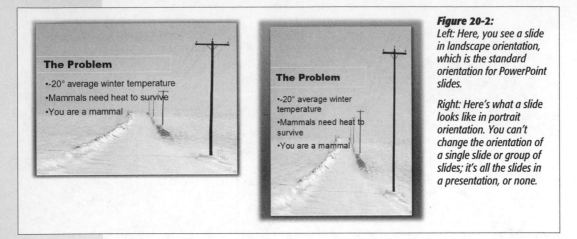

Figure 20-2:
Left: Here, you see a slide in landscape orientation, which is the standard orientation for PowerPoint slides.

Right: Here's what a slide looks like in portrait orientation. You can't change the orientation of a single slide or group of slides; it's all the slides in a presentation, or none.

Repositioning Text Boxes

PowerPoint gives you different ways to reposition the text boxes (and other objects) on your slides. You can either drag objects where you want them, or use the Size and Position dialog box.

Dragging typically works best when you have only a few objects on your slide. If you've got a bunch of objects (especially if they're overlapping), or if the text box you want to move is so completely filled with text you think you'll have trouble selecting its border to drag it, you'll want to use the Size and Position dialog box and save yourself some aggravation.

To reposition a text box by dragging:

1. **Click inside the text box you want to reposition and mouse over the outline of the text box.**

   PowerPoint changes your cursor from an arrow to the double-arrow cross you see in Figure 20-3.

2. **Click the text box outline.**

   The dashed outline turns solid.

3. **Drag the text box where you want it and release the mouse.**

   PowerPoint redraws the text box where you put it.

Tip: For finer control over the position of your text box: As soon as you see both the double-headed arrow cursor shown in Figure 20-3 and a solid text box outline, press the arrow keys on your keyboard to move the text box up, down, left, or right. To move the text box in even tinier increments, hold down Ctrl while you press the arrow keys.

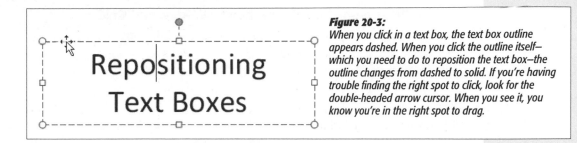

Figure 20-3:
When you click in a text box, the text box outline appears dashed. When you click the outline itself— which you need to do to reposition the text box—the outline changes from dashed to solid. If you're having trouble finding the right spot to click, look for the double-headed arrow cursor. When you see it, you know you're in the right spot to drag.

Tip: If you drag a bunch of stuff around on a slide and then change your mind and want to put it back the way it was, there's an easy way to revert to your original. Choosing Home → Slides → Reset tells PowerPoint to change your slide back to its original layout.

To reposition a text box using the Size and Position dialog box:

1. **Click anywhere inside the text box you want to reposition. Go to Drawing Tools | Format, and click the Size dialog launcher.**

   The Size and Position dialog box pictured in Figure 20-4 appears.

2. **On the Position tab, use the Horizontal box to tell PowerPoint how many inches to position the top-left corner of the text box from the left edge of the slide.**

   PowerPoint moves your text box left and right so you can gauge the effects on your slide in real-time.

3. **Use the Vertical box to tell PowerPoint how many inches to position the top-left corner text box from the top of the slide.**

   PowerPoint moves your text box up and down so you can gauge the effects on the slide in real-time.

4. **When you're satisfied with the position of your text box, click Close.**

   The Size and Position dialog box disappears.

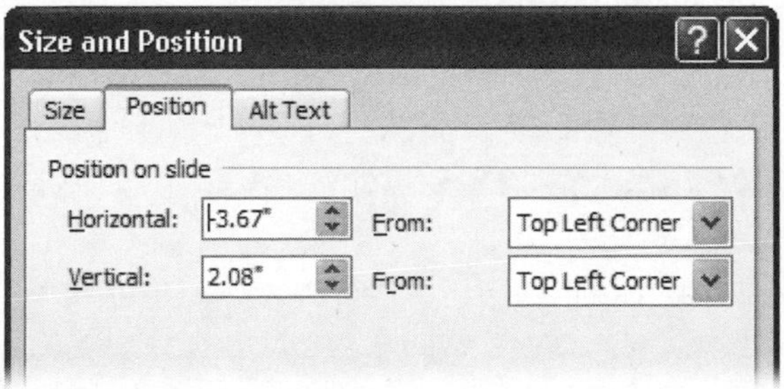

Figure 20-4:
The Position tab of the Size and Position dialog box lets you specify precisely how you want to position your text boxes and other elements, which is especially useful if you're using PowerPoint to create a program interface mock-up. If you like, you can tell PowerPoint to calculate the Horizontal and Vertical amounts you specify based on the center of your slide (instead of the top-left corner).

Help for Positioning Text Boxes: Zoom, Guides, and Grid

Whether you prefer dragging or using the Size and Position dialog box, there are times you'll need a little help positioning your text boxes and other objects—especially if your eyesight's not the best. PowerPoint offers that help in the form of the zoom, guides, and grid.

• **Zoom.** The *zoom* tool magnifies your slide, making it easier for you to distinguish between the boundaries of different objects on a cluttered slide. To use this tool, drag the zoom slider in the status bar at the bottom of the PowerPoint window. You can also click the + or - signs to zoom in or out, respectively.

• **Guides.** *Guides* in PowerPoint consist of two movable (draggable) crosshairs, one horizontal and the other vertical (Figure 20-5). Guides don't show up when you run your presentation; they appear only when you're working with your slides, to help you align text boxes and other objects. To display the guides, click Alt + F9. To make them disappear, click Alt + F9 again.

As you drag a guide, PowerPoint pops up a little direction arrow and the number of inches the guide currently is away from the center of your slide, helping you align stuff exactly 2.5 inches left of center, for example.

• **Grid.** PowerPoint's *grid* (Figure 20-5) gives you a bunch of visual reference points you can use to line up text boxes and other objects. To display the grid, select View → Show/Hide → Gridlines.

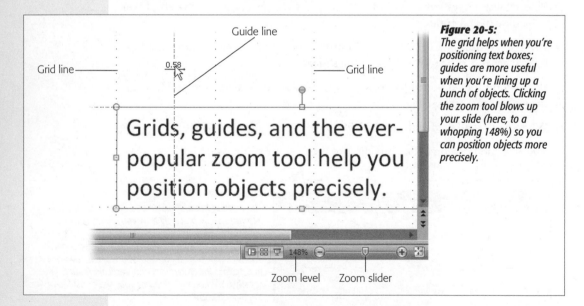

Figure 20-5:
The grid helps when you're positioning text boxes; guides are more useful when you're lining up a bunch of objects. Clicking the zoom tool blows up your slide (here, to a whopping 148%) so you can position objects more precisely.

Changing Background Color

In most cases, you won't want to change the background color of your slides. Instead, you'll rely on the professionally designed themes that come with Power-Point, which coordinate text and background color and effects into an aesthetically pleasing package.

Of course, there's an exception or two to every rule. In the case of background color, one exception to the don't-change-it rule is when you need to match your presentation to a specific (non-PowerPoint) corporate or organizational palette, such as the one your Marketing department uses for brochures and four-color ads.

WORD TO THE WISE

Building a Better Background

You're the boss when it comes to choosing a background color and effect for your slides. But keep these tips in mind:

- **Go dark—and be consistent.** Dark backgrounds tend to look good in presentations delivered onscreen, while light (or white) backgrounds are best saved for printed materials. Whichever you choose, though—light or dark—just make sure you stick with it. Changing backgrounds from slide to slide is one of the quickest ways to confuse your audience. (In the interest of free choice, you'll find instructions in this section for changing individual slide backgrounds. But it's still not a good idea.)

- **If you apply a background gradient, be careful how you arrange your text on top of it.** Few things shout "this is my first PowerPoint presentation" louder than text spanning a background that ranges from light to dark. No matter what color you make your text, part of it will be unreadable. If you *do* decide on a funky background, think like a book- or CD-cover stylist and confine your text to the area of the slide that contrasts best with your text.

Another exception is if you've monkeyed with your font color as described on page 453. Because the human eye sees color in a relative context, black text (for example) appears different depending on whether you set it against a white background, a pink background, or a dark blue background. So when you change the color of your text, you may want to adjust the background color of your slide, too, until you find a combination that looks good to you.

To change the background color of one, some, or all of the slides in a presentation:

1. **In the Slides pane (see Figure 20-6), Ctrl-click to select the slides you want to change.**

   You can skip this step if you want to change the background of the currently selected slide only. To select all of the slides in a presentation press Ctrl+A.

2. **Choose Design → Background Styles.**

   A gallery of background color options, complete with cool gradient effects, appears (Figure 20-7).

Figure 20-6:
If you don't see the Slides pane on the left side of your PowerPoint window, you—or someone else who has access to your computer—may have turned it off. In that case, head down to the Status bar and click Normal (or select View → Presentation Views → Normal). If your Slides pane doesn't look similar to this one, make sure the Slides tab is selected.

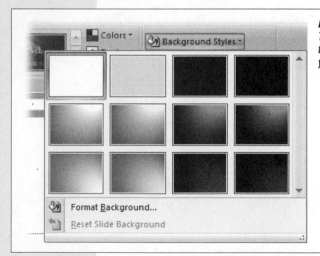

Figure 20-7:
The background options PowerPoint offers are ones that coordinate with the theme you've applied to your presentation.

Note: Another way to see basic background options is to right-click a blank spot on your slide and then, from the menu that appears, choose Background Styles.

3. **From the gallery, click to choose an option.**

The gallery disappears, and PowerPoint applies the new color-and-gradient background to all the currently selected slides.

Note: PowerPoint doesn't police you. If you apply a black background to a slide containing black text, your text becomes unreadable—and PowerPoint doesn't warn you in advance.

If you don't see a color option you like in the gallery, you can choose from a broader selection:

1. **In the Background Styles gallery, choose Format Background.**

The Format Background dialog box opens.

2. **On the Fill tab, turn on the radio button next to "Solid fill."**

The options you see in Figure 20-8 appear.

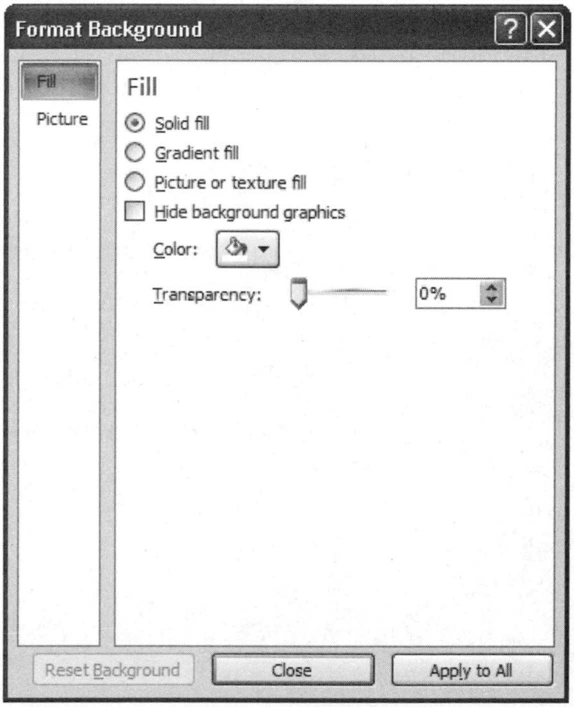

Figure 20-8:
Click Color to display a color picker that lets you choose a new background color (see Figure 19-12 for an example). Most of the time, you'll want to stick with one of the Theme colors PowerPoint offers. After all, the whole point of themes is to help you create tasteful presentations. But if you prefer, you can always head to the bottom of the color picker and click "More colors" to apply your own custom-blended background color.

3. Click the Color drop-down box to display a color picker, from which you can choose the color you want.

In most cases, you should stick with a color in the Themes Colors section, so that your background color coordinates with the theme you've applied to your presentation. (You can see how to reapply a theme on page 481.)

4. If you want to vary the tint of your color, drag the transparency slider. You can also change the percentage in the Transparency box.

Whether you drag the transparency slider or use the transparency box, Power-Point automatically previews the transparency effect on the slide.

5. When you're satisfied with the color and transparency you've chosen, click Close (to dismiss the Format Background dialog box and apply your new background to the currently selected slides) or Apply to All (to dismiss the Format Background dialog box and apply your new background to every slide in your presentation).

Adding a Gradient Effect

A solid colored background, like the ones you learned to apply in the previous section, sometimes do the trick. But some folks think a *gradient* effect (Figure 20-9) looks a bit more sophisticated. Instead of a single color, gradients blend multiple bands of color for mild to wild effects. All of the basic background options that PowerPoint suggests (Figure 20-7) include gradients, but you can apply your own custom gradient effect quickly and easily.

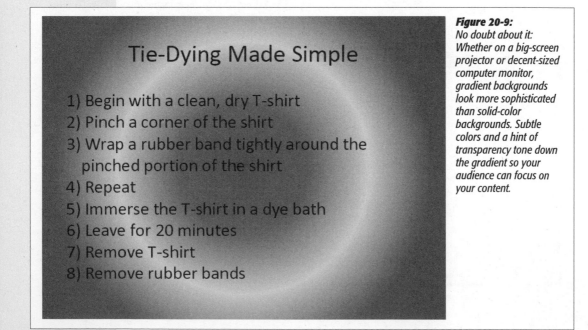

Figure 20-9:
*No doubt about it:
Whether on a big-screen
projector or decent-sized
computer monitor,
gradient backgrounds
look more sophisticated
than solid-color
backgrounds. Subtle
colors and a hint of
transparency tone down
the gradient so your
audience can focus on
your content.*

To apply a gradient effect to your background:

1. **Choose Design → Background → Background Styles.**

   A gallery of background color options appears, complete with cool gradient effects.

2. **In the gallery, choose Format Background.**

   The Format Background dialog box appears.

3. **On the Fill tab, turn on the radio box next to "Gradient fill."**

   PowerPoint applies a basic fill to your slide, and the gradient-related options you see in Figure 20-10 appear.

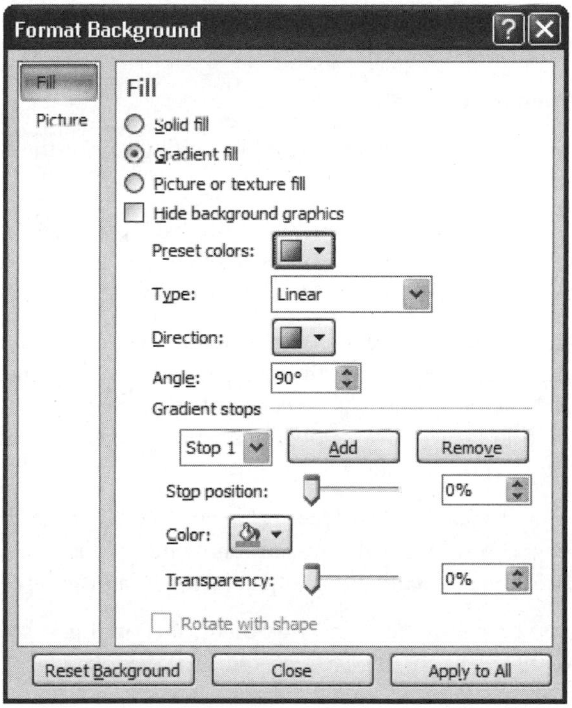

Figure 20-10:
PowerPoint gives you a dizzying array of options you can apply to create customized gradient effects.

4. **Click the down arrow next to "Preset colors."**

   A gallery of preset gradient options appears (Figure 20-11).

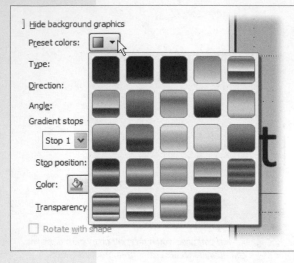

Figure 20-11:
This black-and-white screenshot doesn't do justice to the color-drenched gradient presets, or precreated gradient effects, that PowerPoint offers.

5. **Click to choose one of the gradient presets.**

If you like, you can customize the preset you selected by adding one of the following options:

- **Hide background objects.** Tells PowerPoint not to display background graphics on top of your gradient (assuming you've added background graphics to your slides). See *PowerPoint 2007: The Missing Manual* for details.

- **Type.** Lets you choose from among Linear (straight bands), Radial (bulls-eye bands), Rectangular (rectangular bands), Path (rectangular bulls-eye bands), or "Shade from title." Shade from title tells PowerPoint to display the gradient radiating from the title area outward; otherwise, the gradient radiates from the bottom right corner of the slide.

- **Direction.** Available only if you choose a type of Linear, Radial, or Rectangle, this option lets you choose from thumbnails showing gradient bands running in different directions (straight across, up at an angle, and so on).

- **Angle.** Available only if you choose the Linear gradient, this option lets you choose the angle at which the bands appear (45 percent is diagonal; 90 percent is straight across).

- **Gradient stops.** Click Add to tell PowerPoint to display an additional gradient band (10's the max). To delete one of the gradient bands you begin with, choose one from the drop-down box and then click Remove.

- **Color.** Click the down arrow next to this option to display a color picker and choose a color to apply to your gradient.

- **Stop position.** Drag the slider (or click the arrows) next to this option to tell PowerPoint where to begin your gradient's color bands.

- **Transparency.** Drag the slider (or click the arrows) next to this option to fade your gradient, from 100 percent (see-through) to 0 percent (completely opaque).

- **Rotate with shape.** Normally, choosing this option tells PowerPoint to rotate the gradient bands along with the shape—but when you apply a gradient background effect to a slide, PowerPoint deactivates (grays out) this radio box.

When you're satisfied with your gradient effect, choose Close to apply it to the currently selected slide or "Apply to All" to apply it to all of the slides in your presentation.

Reapplying Themes, Colors, and Fonts

It's great having the freedom to apply your own custom colors, fonts, and effects—until you make so many changes that your presentation looks like something your three-year-old might have created. Luckily, if that happens, you can reapply PowerPoint's professionally designed themes, color schemes or fonts to your presentation, which clears most of your changes and lets you start over from scratch. Reapplying themes is also a great way to try out new looks.

Warning: Because many themes feature different fonts, your text may appear misaligned after you reapply a theme or font. To avoid having to flip through slides and fix misaligned text, apply the theme you want before you've filled all 600 of your intricately laid-out slides with text.

Reapplying a Theme

Themes contain information that tells PowerPoint what fonts, colors, images, and layouts to apply to your presentation. You can reapply a theme after you've added content to your slides, but be aware that depending on the theme you choose to reapply, you may have to go back through your slides and eyeball them to make sure they look okay. (Different fonts and sizes can make a presentation that looked great in one theme look terrible in another.)

To reapply a theme:

1. **If you want to reapply a theme to one or more slides—but not *all* the slides in your presentation—select the slides you want to change.**

   Page 490 shows you how to select multiple slides.

2. **In the Design → Themes group, right-click the theme you want to reapply.**

   A shortcut menu appears.

Tip: Thanks to real estate constraints, the Design tab shows only a handful of themes. To see all of the themes you can apply to your slideshow, click the down arrow next to the displayed themes. Mousing over a theme tells PowerPoint to preview the theme in real time on your slide.

---

3. **From the shortcut menu, choose one of the following:**

   - **Apply to All Slides.** Applies the theme to every slide in your presentation.

   - **Apply to Selected Slides.** Applies the theme only to those slides you've selected.

   PowerPoint reapplies the selected theme.

Warning: A reapplied theme does *not* always overwrite the custom background you've added to your presentation. To delete a background effect you've applied to a slide, click the Reset Background button in the Format Background dialog box (Figure 20-10).

Reapplying a Color Scheme

Professionally designed themes—including the ones that come with PowerPoint—typically come with multiple color combinations, or *schemes*. These color schemes tell PowerPoint which colors to use for heading text, regular text, hyperlinks, slide backgrounds, and more. All of these colors were chosen by the theme designers to look good together, so choosing one of the theme-sanctioned color schemes ensures you of a reasonably attractive result.

If you decide halfway through creating a presentation that you'd like it to appear in different colors, or if you've experimented with changing font colors (page 453) and want to put your presentation back to the way it was, then you can do so by reapplying a color scheme.

To reapply a color scheme:

1. **Choose Design → Themes → Colors.**

   A gallery of color schemes similar to the one you see in Figure 20-12 appears.

2. **Click to choose one of the color schemes.**

   The gallery disappears. On your slide, PowerPoint changes the color of your background and text based on the color scheme you chose.

Reapplying a Font

There are two reasons you may want to reapply a font to your presentation:

- You've done a bit of experimenting with fonts, changing the text on the first couple of slides to one font, the text on the next couple of slides to a different font, and so on. Now you're unhappy with the helter-skelter results and want to reapply a single, consistent font.

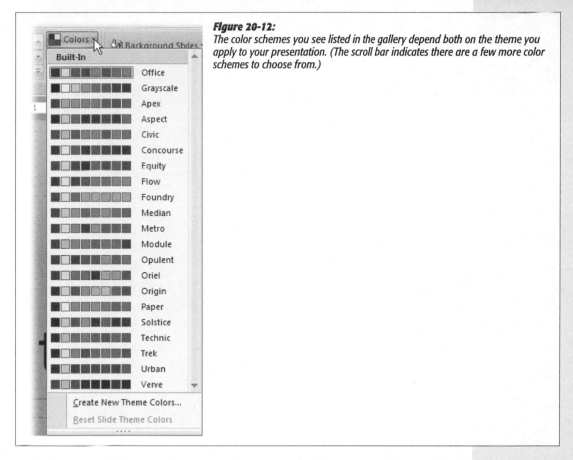

Figure 20-12:
The color schemes you see listed in the gallery depend both on the theme you apply to your presentation. (The scroll bar indicates there are a few more color schemes to choose from.)

- You've assembled your presentation from several other presentations—either ones you've done yourself, or ones you've cadged from the office stockpile—and now you want to unify all these disparate-looking slides by applying a consistent font.

To reapply a font to all of the text in your slideshow, go to Design → Themes → Fonts. Then, in the Fonts gallery, simply click to choose the font you want to reapply.

CHAPTER 21

Editing Your Slideshow

If you want to give a great presentation, then you have to practice. But if you're like most folks, every time you fire up PowerPoint, clear your throat, and start rehearsing, you find a few places in your slideshow that need tweaking. For example, you may realize that you've duplicated information on a couple of slides. Or maybe you discover that you've forgotten to cover a critical point, or decide that a small graphic on each slide would reinforce your message. Or, worst of all, you realize that the way you've organized your content is all wrong.

In this chapter, you'll see how to make all these changes and more. You'll learn to reorder your slides as easily as you shuffle a pack of cards. You can add, delete, move, duplicate, and renumber slides, and even copy slides from other slideshows. You'll also see how to control the overall look and feel of your presentation by editing its behind-the-scenes slide masters.

Viewing Multiple Slides

When you're adding text and graphics to an individual slide, as described in Chapter 17, you're concerned with just one slide at a time—the slide you're working on. Not so when you want to edit your slideshow as a whole. In that case, you need a way to spread all your slides out in front of you (virtually speaking) so you can see what you've got and then decide which slides you want to delete, duplicate, move, and so on.

PowerPoint gives you two handy ways to see most (if not all) of your slides at once: the Slides pane that appears in Normal view (Figure 21-1), and Slide Sorter view (Figure 21-2)

I've Got Good News and Bad News...

Most presentations fit into one of three broad categories, and thinking about which category your message falls into helps you organize your content effectively: *good news, bad news*, and *here's some stuff you should know*.

- **Good news.** The classic example of a good news presentation is the sales pitch, where the good news is that your widget will bring health, wealth, and increased productivity to every customer smart enough to buy it.

  If you're giving a good news presentation, then consider placing your main point—the benefit your audience can expect—both at the beginning and end of your presentation. Always finish a good news presentation by telling your audience specifically what they need to do, to receive the benefit—for example, call a certain number to place an order.

- **Bad news.** Layoffs, budget cuts, and a new freeway displacing a neighborhood's homes are all examples of bad news presentations.

To prepare your audience for bad news, state the problem first in the most sober terms possible. "Our company's losing so much money we're nearly out of business," for example. Spend the middle of your presentation elaborating on the problem and describing possible alternatives, and then place your main point—the bad news you want your audience to accept—at the end of your presentation. Always finish a bad news presentation by reminding your audience how they can salvage some benefit from the bad news you're laying on them. ("The company is offering a generous severance package and help finding a new job," for example.)

- **Here's some stuff you should know.** This type of presentation isn't likely to engender a strong reaction in your audience, either good or bad. "Human Resources just changed the process for switching HMOs," for example. For neutral, informative topics like these, you need only place your main point at the beginning of your presentation.

Slides Pane

PowerPoint assumes you want to see the Slides pane (Figure 21-1) until you tell it otherwise. The Slides pane is mighty handy: When you right-click individual slides in the Slides pane, you can delete them, duplicate them, move them, and so on, as described in the following pages.

To get rid of the Slides pane, click the X in the upper-right corner. To bring it back again, click the Normal icon or choose View → Normal. If you don't see a bunch of thumbnails, check to make sure you've selected the Slides tab.

Slide Sorter View

For situations where you only need to see three or four slides at a time, the Slides pane is the way to go. But if you need to work with more slides at a time—for example, if you need to move slides 1–5 to the end of a 25-slide presentation—then you need to switch to Slide Sorter view (Figure 21-2).

To switch from one-slide-at-a-time Normal view to Slide Sorter view, either click the Slide Sorter icon or select View → Presentation Views → Slide Sorter.

Tip: Double-clicking a slide in Slide Sorter view pops you back to Normal view with the slide you double-clicked front and center, ready for you to edit.

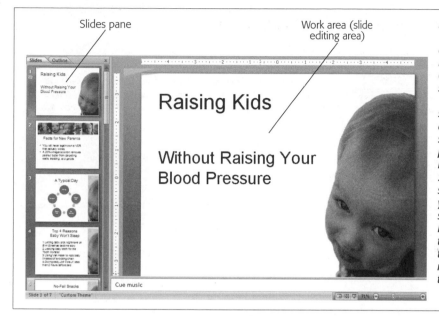

Figure 21-1:
When you click to select a slide in the Slides pane, PowerPoint displays the editable version of the slide in the work area. The number of slides you see in the Slides pane depends on how many slides are in your presentation, and how big you've made the Slides pane. Make it skinny, for example, and you'll see a lot more slides—but then PowerPoint has to make them really tiny to fit them all in. Drag the right edge of Slides pane to resize it.

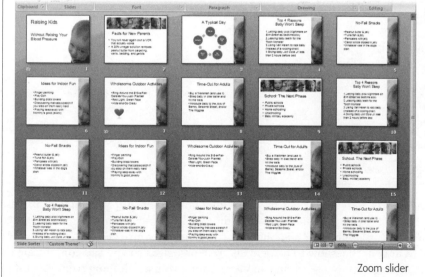

Figure 21-2:
An expanded version of the Slides pane in Slide Sorter view lets you see and work with about 20 slides at once (or more if you zoom out). When you have more than that, scroll bars appear in Slide Sorter view so you can scroll around and see them all.

Adding, Deleting, and Moving Slides

The best way to begin creating a PowerPoint presentation is to start with an outline, either a hand-sketched one or one created in a word processor (such as Microsoft Word). That way your material is pretty much organized before you begin putting your slides together (Figure 21-3).

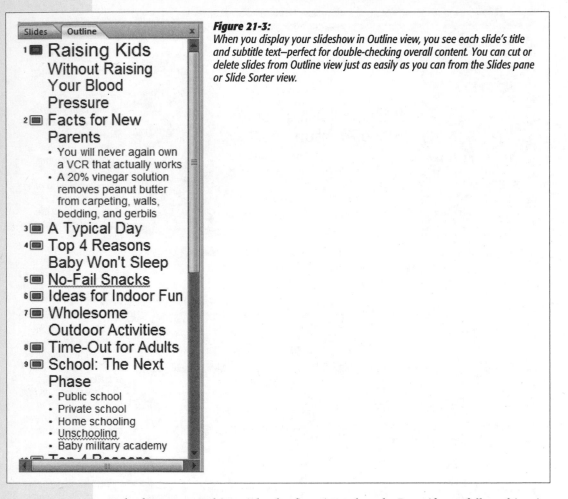

Figure 21-3:
When you display your slideshow in Outline view, you see each slide's title and subtitle text—perfect for double-checking overall content. You can cut or delete slides from Outline view just as easily as you can from the Slides pane or Slide Sorter view.

Nobody gets everything right the first time, though. Even if you follow this wise design practice, you'll find yourself adding, deleting, and moving the individual slides that make up your slideshow as you rehearse your presentation. After all, you want your slideshow to be tight and well organized so you can concentrate on your message without worrying about repeating yourself, leaping from one unrelated topic to another, or leaving out main points altogether.

Adding Blank Slides

You can easily add a blank slide to your slideshow. (You can also bring in a slide from another slideshow, as shown on page 493.) When you create a new blank slide, PowerPoint lets you choose one of several popular layouts. For example, you can create a title slide or a slide containing two columns of text.

Note: Each of the layout options that PowerPoint offers corresponds to a *slide master*, which serves as a template for creating predesigned slides.

To add a slide to your slideshow:

1. **In the Slides pane, click to select the slide *after* which you want to add a new slide.**

   When you want to add a slide at the very beginning of your slideshow, add it after your first slide. Then move it to first position, as described on page 490.

2. **Go to Home → Slides and click the down arrow next to New Slide.**

   A layout gallery similar to the one in Figure 21-4 appears.

3. **Click to choose one of the canned layouts. (You can always change the layout of the slide later if it's not exactly what you want.)**

   PowerPoint creates a new blank slide based on your layout choice and displays the slide in your workspace, ready for you to edit.

Note: PowerPoint gives you two additional, super-quick ways to add a slide. You can either click Home → Slides → New Slide (instead of the down-arrow next to New Slide), or—in either the Normal view's Slides pane or Slide Sorter view—you can right-click a slide and then, from the context menu that appears, choose New Slide. These methods don't let you choose a new layout, though; both simply create a basic Title and Content slide. To change to a different layout, right-click the newly added slide and choose Layout.

Deleting Slides

As you might expect, deleting a slide neatly excises it from your slideshow. After you delete a slide, it's gone; the only way to get it back is to click Undo, and *that* only works if you click Undo soon after you delete the slide. (PowerPoint only "undoes" so many actions per work session, as explained on page 432.)

If you're sure you want to delete the slide, then in the Slides pane that appears in Normal view, click to select the slide and then either click Home → Delete, or press the Delete key. Alternatively, in the Slides pane (or in Slide Sorter view), right-click the slide you want to delete and then choose Delete Slide from the shortcut menu that appears.

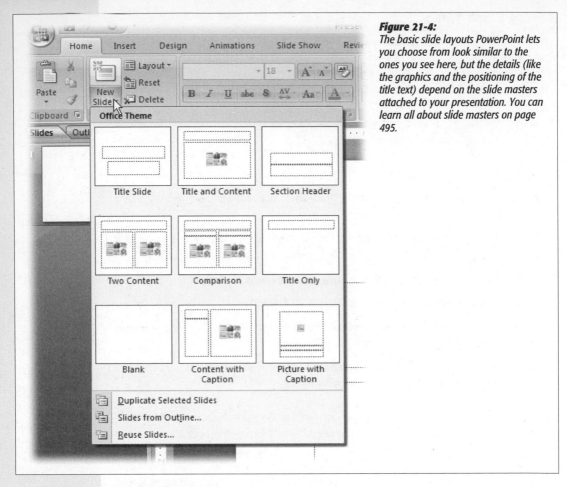

Figure 21-4:
The basic slide layouts PowerPoint lets you choose from look similar to the ones you see here, but the details (like the graphics and the positioning of the title text) depend on the slide masters attached to your presentation. You can learn all about slide masters on page 495.

Moving Slides

Rearranging slides in PowerPoint has the same effect as rearranging transparencies—but because you shuffle them using your mouse, you can't accidentally drop them all over the floor.

To move one or more slides from one position in your slideshow to another:

1. **In Slide Sorter view, click to select the slide (or slides) you want to move.**

   To select multiple contiguous slides, click the first slide, then Shift-click the last slide. When you do, PowerPoint automatically highlights all the slides in between. To select multiple noncontiguous slides, Ctrl-click each slide separately.

2. **Drag your selection.**

   As you move your mouse, PowerPoint displays a line between slides (see Figure 21-5) to let you know where it will place your selection when you let go of your mouse.

Tip: If you can't drag your selection, check to make sure you've let go of the Ctrl and Shift keys. If you forget and keep one of them pressed down, then PowerPoint won't let you drag your selection.

3. **When the line appears where you want to put your selection, let go of your mouse.**

   PowerPoint removes your selection from its original position and inserts it into your slideshow at the point where you dropped it.

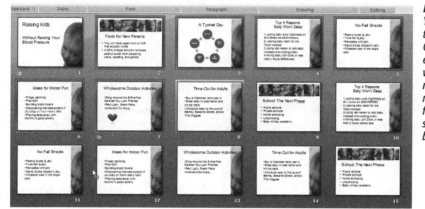

Figure 21-5:
You can move slides in the Slides pane or Outline view, too, but it's easier in Slide Sorter view since you can see more slides. You can move slides before your first slide, after your last slide, or anywhere in between.

Duplicating Slides

If you do much work with PowerPoint, then you'll probably run into a situation eventually where you want to create two similar slides through duplicating. For example, maybe the last slide in your show reiterates what was on the first slide. Duplicating is also a handy way to experiment with the formatting or content of one slide and keep a good copy in case your editing efforts go haywire. In situations like these, you'll find it easier to duplicate a slide and then tweak the duplicate than to create two similar slides from scratch.

You can duplicate slides in the Slides pane, Outline view, or Slide Sorter view. To do so, select the slide (or slides) you want to duplicate, and then choose Home → Slides → New Slide → Duplicate Selected Slides. You can also right-click your selection and then select Duplicate Slide from the shortcut menu. PowerPoint duplicates the selected slide (or slides) and places the duplicate immediately after the selection.

Another (slower) way to duplicate slides is to copy and paste them, as described next.

Cutting, Copying, and Pasting Slides

PowerPoint's cut, copy, and paste commands are an alternative way to move and duplicate slides. There's nothing new to memorize, since these commands work exactly the same way as the cut, copy, and paste commands in other programs. You may also prefer the precision of clicking-and-picking to dragging slides around using your mouse.

To cut slides:

1. **In Normal, Outline, or Slide Sorter view, select the slide (or slides) you want to cut. Right-click the selection and then choose Cut from the shortcut menu (or click the selection and then press Ctrl+X).**

   The selection disappears. If you're in Slide Sorter view, a blinking vertical line appears in the spot where the selection used to be.

To copy slides:

1. **In either Normal or Slide Sorter view, select the slide (or slides) you want to copy. Right-click the selection and then choose Copy from the shortcut menu (or click the selection and then press Ctrl+C).**

To paste slides that you've cut or copied:

1. **Still in Normal or Slide Sorter view, click between the two slides where you want to paste your cut or copied slides.**

   A blinking line appears where you click.

2. **Press Ctrl+V or choose Home → Paste.**

   PowerPoint pastes in the most recently cut or copied slides and renumbers all of the slides in your slideshow.

UP TO SPEED

Make the ^&$*@! Clipboard Go Away

Every time you cut, copy, or paste stuff on your slides, you're using the Office Clipboard—a fact that you may be unaware of until it slaps you in the face.

If you do a lot of cutting, copying, and pasting, then Power-Point takes it upon itself to display the Clipboard pane, unceremoniously bumping your Slides pane out of the way and shrinking your workspace, which can be unnerving.

You'll find the Clipboard pane useful if, for example, you want to paste a line of text you copied two minutes ago into a new slide. You can grab the text and plunk it onto a slide even if you've cut and pasted other things in the meantime.

But most of the time, you'd probably rather have the screen space back. You can temporarily dismiss the clipboard by clicking the X in the upper-right corner, but it'll just pop up again.

To get the Clipboard to leave you alone until you summon it, head to the bottom of the Clipboard pane and click Options. Then, in the pop-up menu, turn off the checkbox next to Show Office Clipboard Automatically. Should you want to bring the Clipboard back into view, go to the Home tab, and then click the Clipboard dialog box launcher.

Inserting Slides from Other Slideshows

If you create a lot of PowerPoint slideshows, then you'll be happy to know there's an easy way to grab slides from one slideshow and put them into another. Taking slides from other PowerPoint slideshows is useful not just for reusing chunks of slideshows that you've put together yourself, but also for borrowing from presentations that other folks have created.

Of course, you can always open both slideshows, hunt around in slideshow #2 for the slides you want to copy, copy them, and then paste them into slideshow #1, exactly as described on page 492. But there's an easier approach—the Reuse Slides command.

To insert a slide from another slideshow:

1. **Open the slideshow into which you want to insert a slide from another slideshow.**

2. **In the Slides pane in Normal view, click to select the slide you want the new slide to appear** *after.*

    If you skip this step, then PowerPoint assumes you want to add a new slide after the first slide of your main slideshow.

3. **Choose Home → New Slide → Reuse Slides.**

    The Reuse Slides pane appears (Figure 21-6). Slideshow files you've previously borrowed from appear in a drop-down list.

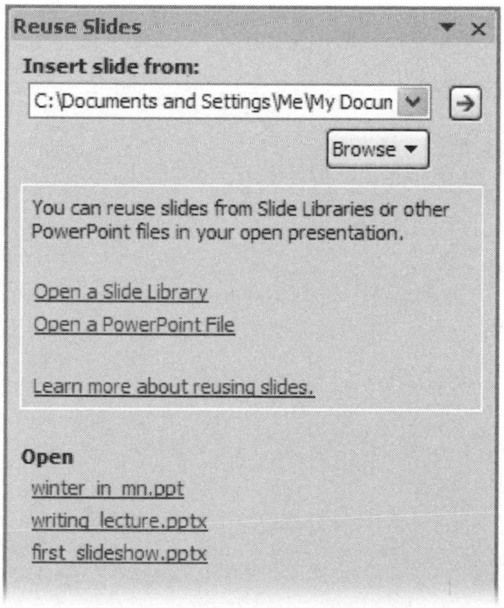

Reuse Slides   ▾ ✕

Insert slide from:

C:\Documents and Settings\Me\My Docun ▾ →

Browse ▾

You can reuse slides from Slide Libraries or other
PowerPoint files in your open presentation.

Open a Slide Library
Open a PowerPoint File

Learn more about reusing slides.

Open

winter_in_mn.ppt
writing_lecture.pptx
first_slideshow.pptx

Figure 21-6:
The Reuse Slides pane gives you several ways to choose the slideshow you want to borrow slides from.

4. **From the "Insert slide from" drop-down menu, choose the slideshow you want to borrow from.**

   Alternatively, you can head to the bottom of the Reuse Slides pane, right under where it says Open, and click the name of the recently opened PowerPoint file you want to borrow from.

Tip: You can click Browse → Browse File (or click the "Open a PowerPoint File" link) to look for Power-Point files on your computer, using an Open dialog box like the one in Figure 17-9.

   In the Reuse Slides pane, a Slide Sorter view of the selected slideshow appears (Figure 21-7).

5. **Click the slide you want to add to your slideshow.**

   PowerPoint adds the slide to your slideshow *after* the currently selected slide.

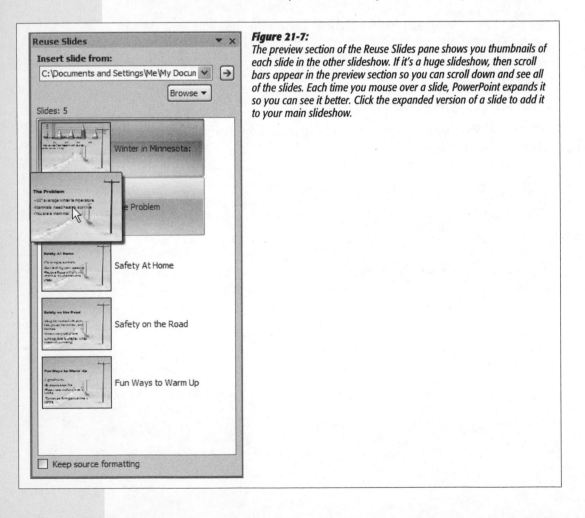

Figure 21-7:
The preview section of the Reuse Slides pane shows you thumbnails of each slide in the other slideshow. If it's a huge slideshow, then scroll bars appear in the preview section so you can scroll down and see all of the slides. Each time you mouse over a slide, PowerPoint expands it so you can see it better. Click the expanded version of a slide to add it to your main slideshow.

Editing Slide and Layout Masters

Slide masters and layout masters determine the initial look of every single slide in your slideshow. For example, if you place one background image, three text place-holders, and a date-and-time footer on a slide master, then every slide in your slideshow will contain the same background image, the same three text placehold-ers positioned in the same spots, and the same date-and-time footer.

In fact, you've been using slide masters without even knowing it. Whenever you choose a theme for your presentation, you're actually applying a set of slide mas-ters. A *theme* (page 407) is nothing more than a collection of masters. More specif-ically, a theme includes a *slide master* and a handful of *layout masters* packaged in a special file format (*.thmx*) so that you can easily apply them to different presenta-tions.

The purpose of slide masters is to help you create an attractive, cohesive-looking slideshow: Make a change once, and it appears on dozens of slides instantly. And because PowerPoint lets you override the slide master by editing individual slides directly, you're not locked into an all-or-nothing look.

But if you want to tweak a theme or create your own—in other words, if you want to add the same color scheme, formatting, or object (graphic, text, background, and so on) to multiple slides—then you need to learn to how masters work. Fortu-nately, editing PowerPoint's masters is just as easy as editing any other slide. The only difference is that you're not editing an individual slide—you're setting up a sort of blueprint that you can then apply to any number of slides.

PowerPoint has a few different types of masters, which makes sense because the different presentation elements—slides, notes, handouts—require slightly differ-ent kinds of formatting. To understand masters in PowerPoint, all you need to know is what each one does:

- **Slide master.** A *slide master* is a visual blueprint of how you want to format all the slides in your slideshow. Add a blue background and your company logo to your slide master, for example, and every single slide in your slideshow will have a blue background and that logo. Although most of the time one slide master per slideshow will do you just fine, you can create additional slide mas-ters if you like.

- **Layout master.** A *layout master* expands on the slide master to let you tell Pow-erPoint how you want specific types of slides to look. In other words, you can apply different formatting to Title slides, Title and Text slides, Title and Con-tent slides, Comparison slides, and so on. For example, say you have a slide master similar to the one described in the previous paragraph. If you put an italicized header on the Title and Content layout master, then that header (in addition to the blue background and logo) automatically appears on every slide you format using the Title and Content layout. Then you're free to use, say, a bold header (not italicized) on Title slides, since that's a different layout.

The Right Way to Add Graphics to Slide Masters

Slide masters and layouts give you a lot of power. Make a change once, and PowerPoint applies it to every slide on your slideshow—whether it's a scrap of text, a graphic, or a color and formatting effect.

But before you go crazy applying textured backgrounds and logos, you need to think about these two important design considerations:

- **Always leave blank spots for your titles and subtitles.** Ever notice how, on most CD and book covers that contain graphics, the designers leave a blank spot for the title? They do this for one very

simple reason: Generally speaking, text looks awful—if not downright unreadable—when you plaster it over a busy background.

- **Apply the same look and feel (but not necessarily the same images and formatting) to all your slides.** Your title page is a good place to go a bit wild with backgrounds, textures, colors, and fonts. But for the meat of your presentation—your text and content slides—you want your audience to focus on your message, not your skill with Clip Art.

PowerPoint automatically attaches one slide master and several layout masters to every presentation you create. To edit them, you have to switch into Slide Master view. You use the same steps whether you're editing a slide master or one of the layout masters:

1. **Create a new presentation (or open an existing one). Select View → Presentation Views → Slide Master.**

   PowerPoint displays the slide master in your workspace, ready for editing (Figure 21-8). The Master Slide tab appears and, on the left side of the screen where the Slides pane usually sits, you see instead the Thumbnail view of the slide master and the layout masters.

2. **Mouse over the thumbnails on the left side of the screen to see a description of each layout. Then click to choose the slide master or layout you want to edit.**

   - **[Name of Theme] Slide Master.** All of the changes you make to this grand-daddy slide master affect each of the slides in your slideshow. The changes you make to this slide master affect all of the associated layout masters, too.

   - **[Name of Content] Layout.** These masters are your layout masters. Edits you make to them affect only those slides that have that particular layout applied to them. Your choices include Title Slide, Title and Content (a title plus some text), Section Header, Two Content (two-column), Comparison (another two-column option, this time with column headings), Title Only, Blank, Content with Caption, and Picture with Caption.

   After you make your choice, PowerPoint displays the selected slide master or layout master in the workspace.

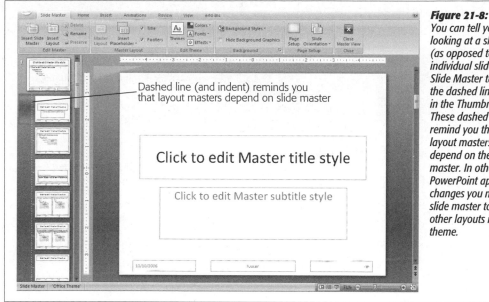

Figure 21-8:
You can tell you're looking at a slide master (as opposed to an individual slide) by the Slide Master tab and by the dashed lines you see in the Thumbnail view. These dashed lines remind you that the layout masters all depend on the slide master. In other words, PowerPoint applies any changes you make to the slide master to all of the other layouts in the theme.

Note: When you want to add text to a slide master (because, for example, you want to add the same quote or slogan to each of your slides), you need to insert a new text placeholder. Typing text inside an existing text placeholder doesn't affect what you see on your slides when you run your slideshow. Instead, it appears only when you're editing your slides.

3. **Edit the slide master or layout master.**

   Everything you can add to a regular slide—text, special effects, background colors, and so on—you can add to a slide master or layout master. On the Slide Master tab, you see options for changing the theme, theme-related fonts, effects, colors, and background of your slide master or layout master. You can also click the Home tab or mini-toolbar (to format text) or the Insert tab (to insert text boxes and other objects). Figure 21-9 shows you an example of editing the Title and Text Content layout master.

4. **When you're finished editing the master, click Close Master View.**

   PowerPoint scoots you back to the slide editing workspace, where you see that PowerPoint has automatically updated all of the slides that correspond to the slide master or layout master you just changed (Figure 21-10).

Figure 21-9:
The Title and Text Content Master has been edited to change the font of the title and to include a graphic. You can change the formatting of the text placeholders that PowerPoint gives you, but you can't change the text itself. (Well, you can, but PowerPoint won't apply the changed text to your slides.) To add text to a slide master or layout master, you need to add your own text box and then type in your text.

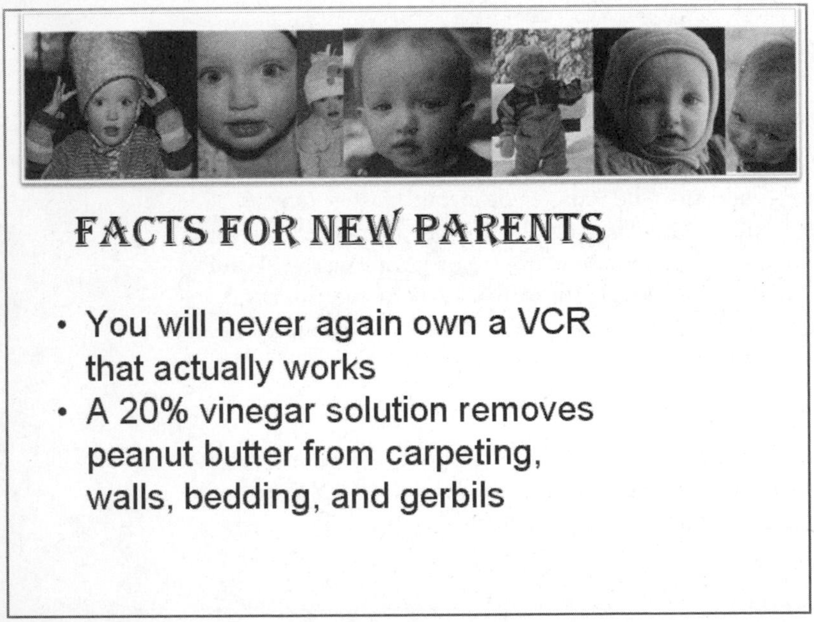

Figure 21-10:
This slide was created using the Title and Text layout, so it reflects the changes made in the Title and Text Content Master, as shown in Figure 21-9. The title is in a funky font and a graphic strip appears across the top of the slide.

Applying Multiple Slide Masters

PowerPoint lets you apply multiple slide masters to your slideshow. You don't want to go crazy and apply a different slide master to every single slide because that would counteract the whole time-saving point of slide masters. Still, in some situations—like when you want to format the sections of a long presentation differently—the ability to apply multiple slide masters comes in handy.

To apply a new slide master to one or more slides:

1. **In the Slide pane, select the slides to which you want to apply a new slide master. Go to Design → Themes and click the down arrow next to the thumbnails.**

   The Themes gallery appears. Mousing over each theme shows you a live preview, right there on your slide.

2. **In the Themes gallery, right-click the theme you want to apply to your slides and, from the shortcut menu, choose how you want to apply the theme. Your choices are:**

   • **Apply to selected slides.** Applies the selected theme only to the slides you've highlighted in the Slides pane.

   • **Apply to matching slide.** Applies the selected theme only to those slides that share a layout with the slides you've selected.

   • **Apply to all slides.** Applies the selected theme to all of the slides in your slideshow.

   PowerPoint reformats your slideshow based on your selection.

3. **Repeat steps 1–2 once for each slide master you want to apply to your slideshow.**

Tip: If you change your mind immediately after applying a slide master, then press Ctrl+Z or click Undo to tell PowerPoint to reverse your change.

Adding Headers and Footers

You can add any recurring text to the top or bottom of every slide in your slideshow, every handout, and every page of your speaker notes. PowerPoint gives you an efficient way to add recurring information to your presentation: built-in header and footer placeholders. And here's the best part: Simply by turning on a checkbox, you can choose to hide or show your headers or footers when you go to print your presentation.

Adding Footers to Your Slides

PowerPoint lets you add headers to your *handouts* using the "Header and Footer" dialog box, but you can't add headers to your *slides* this way. If you want to add a header to your slides, add it to the slide master, as described on page 495.

To add footers to your slides using the "Header and Footer" dialog box:

1. **In the Slides pane (Normal view), select the slides to which you want to apply a footer.**

   You can skip this step if you want all of the slides in your slideshow (or all of your slides *except* your title slide) to have a footer.

2. **Choose Insert → Text → Header & Footer.**

   The Header and Footer dialog box shown in Figure 21-11 appears.

3. **On the Slide tab, choose what you want to appear on your slides.**

4. **Your options include:**

   • **Date and time.** Turning on the checkbox next to this option lets you choose the current date and time, which PowerPoint can either update automatically (turn on the "Update automatically" radio box) or not (turn on the radio box next to Fixed). Choosing "Update automatically" also lets you specify the format in which you want the date and time to appear, the language, and the calendar type.

   • **Slide number.** Turn on the checkbox next to this option to tell PowerPoint to add automatically generated numbers to your slides.

   • **Footer.** Turning on the checkbox next to this option activates a text box into which you can type the text you want to appear at the bottom of your slides.

   As you choose options, PowerPoint automatically highlights the corresponding footer placeholder in the Preview section of the "Header and Footer" dialog box (see Figure 21-11).

5. **If you don't want your date, slide number, or text box footer to appear on your title slide, then turn on the checkbox next to "Don't show on title slide."**

6. **If you want to apply your date, slide number, and text box footer only to those slides you selected in step 1 above, then click Apply. Otherwise, click Apply All to tell PowerPoint you want the information to appear on every slide in your slideshow (except, possibly, your title slide; see step 4).**

   The "Header and Footer" dialog box disappears, and PowerPoint applies your footer options to your slides.

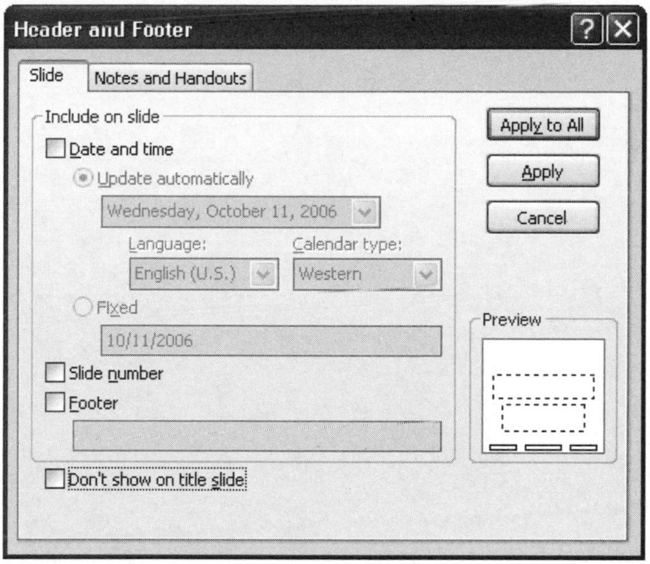

Figure 21-11:
After you tell PowerPoint to add the date and time, custom footer text, or automatically generated page numbers using the Header and Footer dialog box shown here, you can tweak the appearance of your header or footer content in Slide Master view (page 496).

Adding Headers and Footers to Notes Pages and Handouts

The "Header and Footer" dialog box lets you apply a date- and timestamp, automatically generated page numbers, and the same header and footer text to your notes pages and handout pages.

Choose Home → Insert → Header & Footer, and then click the "Notes and Handouts" tab to select it. Your options are identical to the ones described on page 500 with the addition of a Header checkbox, which lets you type in the text you want to appear in the upper-left corner of your notes and handout pages. When you're done choosing what you want to appear in your header and footer, click Apply to All.

The "Header and Footer" dialog box disappears, and PowerPoint applies your footer options to your notes and handout pages.

CHAPTER 22

Adding Charts, Diagrams, and Tables

Making your point visually is almost always more effective than slapping up a bunch of bullet points or a column full of numbers. That's why PowerPoint lets you create awesome charts, diagrams, and tables. Many new PowerPointers avoid these tools out of intimidation. That's a shame, because a good bar chart, Venn diagram, or data table can communicate more information than a dozen slides full of bullet points—with far fewer droopy eyelids.

Microsoft has seriously upgraded PowerPoint 2007's charting, diagramming, and table-creation tools. There's a new graphics engine, dozens of new diagram types, and galleries of professionally designed pick-and-click styles. You can even preview the styles live on your charts, diagrams, and tables before applying them. In short, you've got no excuse for leaving eye-popping, effective visuals out of your presentation. This chapter gets you making great-looking charts, diagrams, and tables *fast*.

Tip: PowerPoint's new tools are really Microsoft Office's new tools. In other words, the way you create charts, diagrams, and tables in Word and Excel is pretty darn similar to the way you create them in Power-Point, and the result is identical-looking visuals.

Creating Charts

You can talk numbers until you're blue in the face, but when you *really* want to get your audience's attention—and get your point across in the shortest time possible—you need a chart.

Sometimes referred to as a *graph*, a *chart* is nothing more than a visual representation of a bunch of numbers. The ubiquitous pie chart (Figure 22-1) breaks up a circular area into easy-to-understand, color-coded wedges, each of which represents a numerical quantity. PowerPoint 2007 lets you add punch to your presentations with the same bar charts, line charts, scatter graphs, and so on that PowerPoint 2003 offered. Only now they're better looking, since Microsoft Excel has replaced PowerPoint 2003's Microsoft Graph program.

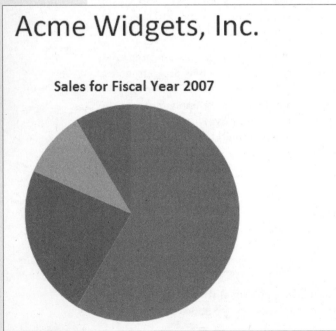

Acme Widgets, Inc.

Sales for Fiscal Year 2007

- 1st Qtr
- 2nd Qtr
- 3rd Qtr
- 4th Qtr

Figure 22-1:
Charting is an art unto itself, as all liars and statisticians are well aware. PowerPoint doesn't care whether the numbers you chart are accurate or whether your chart makes your conclusions dangerously misleading—it leaves those judgments up to you.

Note: You don't need to have Excel installed on your computer to create charts. If PowerPoint 2007 finds Excel on your PC, it uses Excel. Otherwise, it falls back on the built-in graphics program, Microsoft Graph. See the box on page 509 for the full scoop.

Creating a chart in PowerPoint is a straightforward process. You tell the program which type of chart you want to create (pie chart, bar chart, and so on), you type a few rows of data into an Excel (or Graph) spreadsheet, and then you apply a predesigned Chart Style and Chart Layout. Bingo—instant chart. And if you've never seen a chart built with an Office 2007 program, you'll be amazed how good it looks.

Choosing a Chart Type

PowerPoint's charts look great, but they're not all suited to every type of information. Do you know which one to choose? The chart type you pick affects how PowerPoint interprets your information, which affects your audience's conclusions. So choose a chart type based on what you're trying to communicate, not on what PowerPoint lets you do.

Charting is both art and science, and it's far too complex to tackle in a book about PowerPoint. Consider the following descriptions in deciding which type of chart to create:

- **Bar chart.** One of the most popular types of charts, the bar chart depicts numbers—like dollars, products sold, or the number of times something happened—using big, thick, hard-to-miss rectangles. Bar charts show numbers in the context of time. They can show how many field goals each high school's football team scored over the last five seasons. Bar charts can be *stacked*, which means PowerPoint stacks all of the data from all of the categories into one bar per event; or they can be *clustered*, which means that each data category gets its own bar for each event.

- **Column chart.** A column chart's the same as a bar chart, but lying on its side (with x- and y-axis labels flipped to match). Fancy types of column charts include *cylinder, cone,* and *pyramid*.

- **Line chart.** Line charts show noncumulative data horizontally, over time, so you can track performance. Consider a line chart if, for example, you're trying to show the progression of your company's quarter-by-quarter performance over the past fiscal year, compared with your two closest competitors' performances over that same period of time. Similar to bar charts, line charts track numbers in relation to time. But unlike bar charts, which clump the data for specific events (like field-goal totals for those five football seasons), line charts show a continuous intersection of activity. Thus, if it's events you're interested in comparing, then use a bar chart; when it's a continuous progression of up-and-down movement, use a line chart.

- **Pie chart.** Because pie charts show percentage values as slices of a circle, this type of chart makes sense only if you have a single column of numbers that add up to 100. For example, you can use a pie chart if you're trying to show how much of every dollar raised for your charity goes to overhead, to individual programs, and so on.

- **Scatter chart.** Use a scatter chart when you're working with data that neither occurs at regular intervals nor belongs to a series. Sometimes referred to as *XY charts* or *scatter graphs*, scatter charts show information as points distributed around an x-y axis—think darts thrown at a dartboard. The dots give a quick visual showing the relationship between the data represented by the x and y axes. You might use a scatter chart to plot the relationship between the prices of ovens and how long the ovens last. Scatter charts are popular with scientists.

- **Area, bubble, doughnut, stock, surface, and radar charts.** Theoretically, you can graph any data you want any way you want, and in this spirit PowerPoint offers the doughnut, stock, radar, and other specialty graphs. For example, a radar graph is useful for comparing the aggregate values of a bunch of data series. Say you want to compare the vitamin levels of three different brands of orange juice. Creating a radar chart lets your audience see at a glance which brand of juice contains the most Vitamin C, Vitamin D, Vitamin A—*and* which is the most nutritious overall.

Tip: Remember, though, the more complicated a graph is, the harder it is for your audience to understand it—even if you're there in person to explain it. And complexity totally defeats the purpose of a graph. Most of the time you should stick with the bar, column, line, and pie charts.

Figures 22-2 and 22-3 show you the different configuration your numbers and headings need to work with the different kinds of charts PowerPoint lets you create.

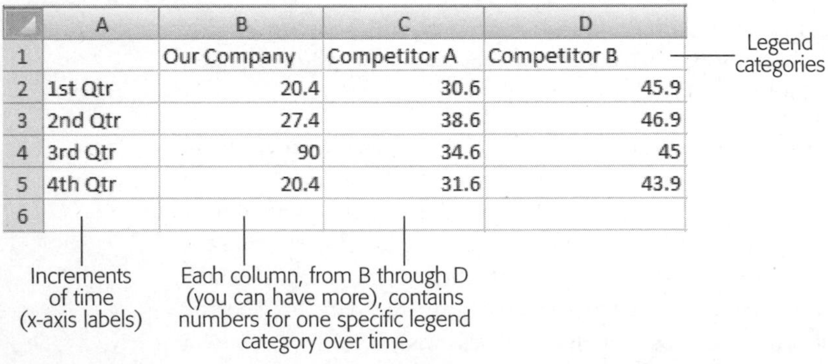

	A	B	C	D
1		Our Company	Competitor A	Competitor B
2	1st Qtr	20.4	30.6	45.9
3	2nd Qtr	27.4	38.6	46.9
4	3rd Qtr	90	34.6	45
5	4th Qtr	20.4	31.6	43.9
6				

Legend categories

Increments of time (x-axis labels)

Each column, from B through D (you can have more), contains numbers for one specific legend category over time

Figure 22-2:
The mocked-up data PowerPoint starts you off with would be a lot more useful if the program gave you a clue of how to interpret each cell. Here's how your data needs to appear for the Bar, Column, and Line charts (the ones that, along with Pie charts, you're most likely to use).

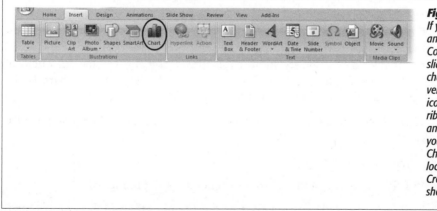

	A	B
1		Handknits - Skilled Labor Breakdown
2	Spinning	20
3	Dyeing	10
4	Knitting	55
5	Finishing	15
6		

PowerPoint uses the B1 cell for the title

Each row, from row 2 down, represents one piece of the pie

Legend categories

Figure 22-3:
Because pie charts can deal with only one category of numbers (in chart-speak, one data series), you need to arrange your figures as shown here for PowerPoint to graph your pie chart correctly. Also double-check your data range as described in the box on page 510, since PowerPoint doesn't always extrapolate correctly.

Creating a Chart

To create a chart, first tell PowerPoint what type of chart you want, and then feed it some data. The steps that follow explain how.

Note: Creating a chart is pretty simple, as you'll see in the following steps. But if you're new to Excel or spreadsheets in general, it's useful to walk through the process visually. A screencast at *www. missingmanuals.com* shows you how to create a chart in PowerPoint, complete with accompanying narration that explains each step.

---

1. **Go to Insert → Illustrations → Chart (Figure 22-4).**

   The Insert Chart dialog box (Figure 22-5) appears.

Figure 22-4:
If you've applied a Title and Content or Two Content layout to the slide you're adding your chart to, you'll see two versions of the Chart icon: one on the Insert ribbon (as shown here) and one in the center of your slide. Clicking the Chart icon in either location displays the Create Chart dialog box shown in Figure 22-5.

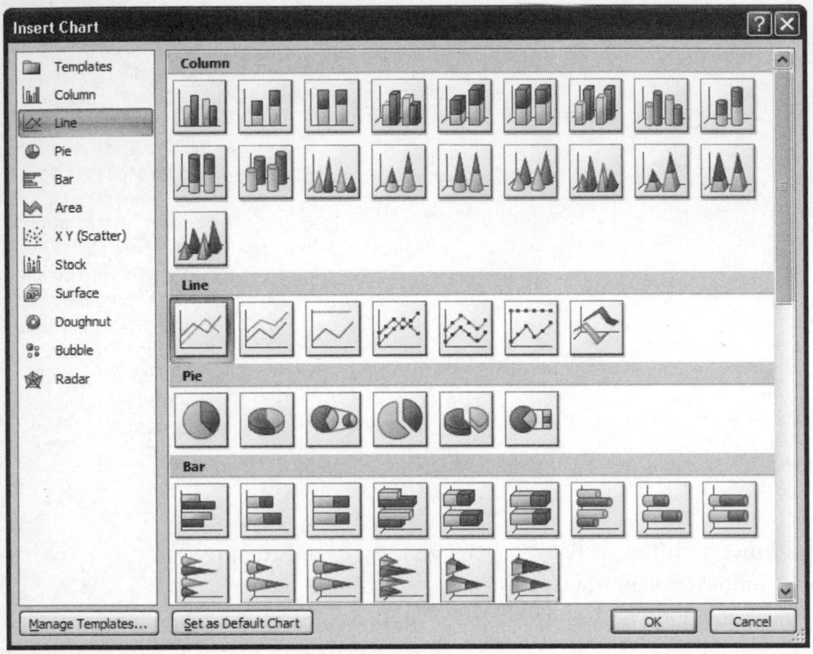

Figure 22-5:
The Insert Chart dialog box offers dozens of different types of charts. PowerPoint doesn't support live previews for charts the way it does for just about everything else, but it does display short descriptions as you mouse over each chart icon.

2. **Choose the kind of chart you want to add to your slide, and then click OK.**

   To find one you like, zip to the left side of the Insert Chart dialog box (Figure 22-5) and click a category (such as Bar, Area, or Doughnut), which whisks you straight to the section you're interested in. Or, if you prefer, you can use the scroll bar to browse leisurely through all the chart options.

Note: You can also double-click a chart type to add it to your slide.

   Once you click OK, PowerPoint shrinks to half size and scoots over to make room for Excel, which appears on the right side of your screen complete with placeholder data displayed in an Excel spreadsheet titled "Chart in Microsoft Office PowerPoint." In PowerPoint, the Chart Tools | Design, Chart Tools | Layout, and Chart Tools | Format tabs appear (Figure 22-6).

3. **Replace the mocked-up data you see in Excel with the real data you want to chart.**

   To do so, you can:

   • Click in each cell and type your own numbers and headings.

   • If you've already got a spreadsheet containing the numbers you want to chart, you can copy the cells from that spreadsheet and paste them into the spreadsheet PowerPoint gives you. (For quick tips on pasting from Excel, see the box on page 512.)

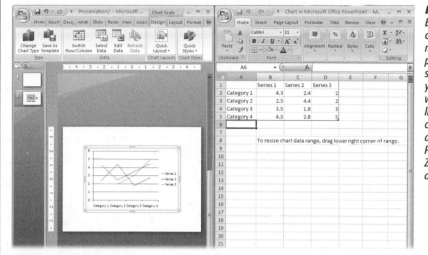

Figure 22-6:
Excel starts you off with a column or two of mocked-up data—one piece of information per spreadsheet cell—so that you can get a feel for what your chart will look like. To expand the tiny chart preview PowerPoint displays on your slide, in PowerPoint either click Zoom a few times or drag the Zoom slider.

FREQUENTLY ASKED QUESTION

Creating Charts Without Excel

PowerPoint uses Excel to do all its charting now. But I don't have Excel, just PowerPoint. Does that mean I can't do charts?

Microsoft Office comes with both programs, so lots of people who use Office have both PowerPoint and Excel installed on their computers. But not everyone who installs Office chooses to install both programs—and some folks choose to buy just PowerPoint, not the entire Office suite.

If you *do* have both PowerPoint and Excel installed on your computer, creating a chart in PowerPoint automatically kicks Excel into gear, as shown in this chapter.

But if you *don't* have Excel installed, you can still create charts. Here's why: when PowerPoint can't find Excel, it automatically launches Microsoft Graph, the same charting

and drawing program that came with PowerPoint 2003. Microsoft Graph doesn't offer the same bells and whistles that Excel does—which is why Microsoft replaced it with Excel in PowerPoint 2007—but you *can* use it to do the same basic things. For example, you can click in Microsoft Graph data cells to type in your own numbers and column headings, just the way you can in Excel.

This book focuses on creating charts in *PowerPoint* (and not Excel), so all of the instructions work the same for you as they do for someone who has Excel installed—even if what you see on your screen looks slightly different from the figures in this book. But if you run into a snag, then click the Microsoft Graph spreadsheet and choose Help → Microsoft Graph Help.

As you add, change, and delete data in the Excel spreadsheet, Excel's data range outline automatically changes to encompass your new data columns and headings, and your PowerPoint chart updates automatically to reflect your changes.

4. **When you're finished adding data, check to make sure the data range bounding box surrounds your entire data range, including your column and row headings.**

If it doesn't, drag the lower right corner of the data range bounding box so it covers all your cells (but no additional blank rows or columns).

5. **Click anywhere on your PowerPoint slide.**

   PowerPoint whisks you back to slide-editing mode and updates your chart with the data you just gave it.

Tip: If your spreadsheet accidentally disappears (perhaps you clicked the X in the upper-right corner by mistake), you can get it back again by selecting your chart and then choosing Chart Tools | Design → Data → Edit Data.

GEM IN THE ROUGH

Trying Data On for Size

PowerPoint lets you pinpoint the perfect chart by "trying out" different sets of data. This is useful if you want to experiment to find out which of several sets of data translates to the most dramatic chart.

Here's how it works:

1. Create a chart as described on page 507.

2. Choose Chart Tools | Design → Data → Select Data to display your spreadsheet (if it isn't visible already) and to display the Select Data Source dialog box.

3. In your spreadsheet, create another complete set of data; then click the new data range and drag to outline

your newly created columns and rows. Notice that PowerPoint automatically adjusts the Select Data Source dialog box to reflect your changes.

4. In the Select Data Source dialog box, click OK to tell PowerPoint to update your chart using your new data.

5. Repeat steps 3 and 4 for as many sets of data as you have. After you've decided to stick with one, don't bother deleting the others from your spreadsheet. Leave them there in case you change your mind.

Customizing Charts with Prebuilt Layouts and Styles

PowerPoint 2007 gives you the option of choosing both a canned Chart Layout and a canned Chart Style scheme. You simply pick one of PowerPoint's professionally designed Chart Layout schemes, some of which show the legend on the side of the chart, some at the bottom, and so on. Then you pick one Chart Style scheme, which sets the colors, data point markers, and a background for your chart.

Applying prebuilt Chart Layouts

Since you're going to be working on your chart's appearance, give yourself a nice big view. If PowerPoint isn't maximized on your computer screen, click the Maximize button in the upper-right corner of the window to maximize it. Then follow these steps:

1. **On your slide, click your chart to select it.**

   PowerPoint displays the Chart Tools contextual tab.

---

2. Go to Chart Tools | Design tab.

You see tools for formatting your chart's looks (Figure 22-7).

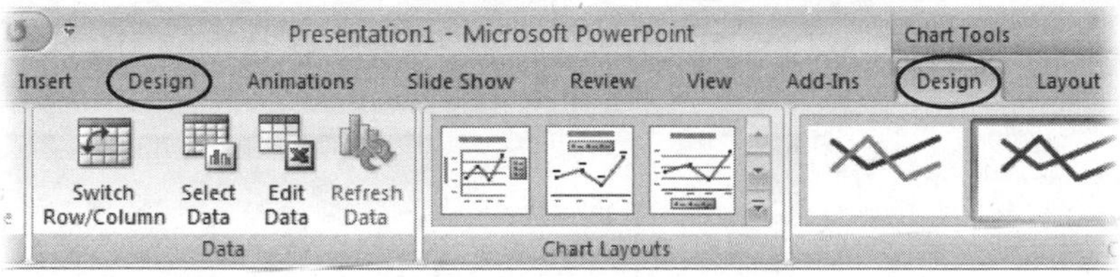

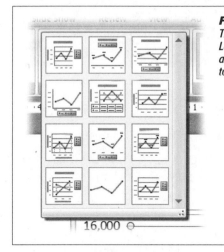

Figure 22-7:
Confusingly, when you select a chart, two Design tabs appear: the regular Design tab, and the Chart Tools | Design contextual tab, which appears above the ribbon. PowerPoint also highlights the contextual tab to make it stand out a bit. The Chart Tools | Design tab is specifically for working with your chart.

3. Click the Chart Layout gallery to expand it (Figure 22-8). Then click to choose the layout you want to apply to your chart.

PowerPoint redisplays your chart based on the layout you chose.

Figure 22-8:
The Chart Layout gallery varies depending on the type of chart you choose. Layouts define where chart elements such as titles, legends, and data and axis labels appear. This gallery shows the layouts that PowerPoint can apply to Line charts.

Applying prebuilt Chart Styles

The Chart Style schemes that come with PowerPoint give you a quick way to choose the color of your chart's data elements, as well as your chart's background. Because all of the colors in the Chart Style schemes are professionally designed to coordinate with each other, your chart looks good no matter which one you choose— and no matter how many data elements you're charting.

Excel: The Least You Need to Know

If you're on a tight deadline and don't have time to read through the Excel portion of this book, here are some tips to help you put together a decent-looking chart in Power-Point and then get on with your life:

Copy and paste cell data from an existing spreadsheet. You've already got a spreadsheet containing the data you want to chart, and you don't want to retype it into the spreadsheet PowerPoint provides. Copy and paste the data. Here's how:

1. In the Excel spreadsheet PowerPoint opened (the one titled "Chart in Microsoft Office PowerPoint"), choose Office button → Open and open a new spreadsheet (the spreadsheet containing the data you want to chart).

2. In the newly opened spreadsheet, drag to select the data you want to copy, and then choose Home → Copy (or press Ctrl+C) to copy it.

3. In the "Chart in Microsoft Office PowerPoint" sheet, click in cell A1, and then choose Home → Paste or press Ctrl+V to paste the data.

Delete the contents of cells. To clear out the contents of cells you don't want to chart (and don't want to see), drag to select the cells; then right-click the selection and choose Clear Contents from the shortcut menu

Widen columns. If you type text into two side-by-side cells, you may not be able to read all the text in the first cell. To widen the first cell's column, click the edge of the column header and drag to widen the entire column.

Insert and delete rows and columns. To insert a row or column, right-click the cell after which you want to add a row or column and then choose Insert from the shortcut menu. When the Insert dialog box opens, turn on the radio box next to "Entire row" (to insert a row) or "Entire column" (to insert a column).

To add data to your chart, you may have to delete a row or column. Right-click the row or column heading (the actual letter or number of the row or column, as opposed to a cell in the row or column) and then choose Delete from the shortcut menu.

To apply a Chart Style:

1. **On your slide, click your chart to select it. Then go to Chart Tools | Design tab.**

   Tools for formatting your chart's appearance show up on the ribbon.

2. **Click to expand the Chart Styles gallery (Figure 22-9). From the Chart Styles gallery, click to choose the style you want to apply to your chart.**

   PowerPoint redisplays your chart based on the style you chose.

Customizing chart titles

If you customize nothing else about your chart, you need to customize your title. That's because even though every chart needs a title, PowerPoint doesn't automatically assign one. You'll want to decide where to display your title, too.

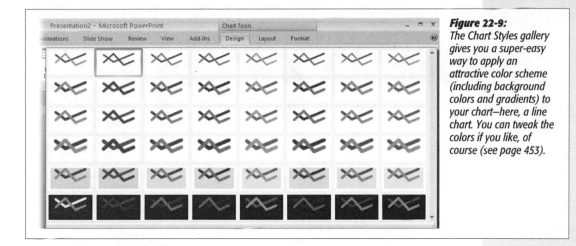

Figure 22-9:
The Chart Styles gallery gives you a super-easy way to apply an attractive color scheme (including background colors and gradients) to your chart—here, a line chart. You can tweak the colors if you like, of course (see page 453).

Creating Diagrams

Microsoft really upped the ante when it comes to using diagrams in your presentations. PowerPoint 2007 lets you create more types of diagrams than earlier versions of the program, they look snazzier, and they're easier to create and update. In some cases, when you tweak one section of a diagram, PowerPoint automatically redraws the rest of it to match.

In this section, you'll see two ways to create a diagram: by choosing a diagram type and filling in the text, or by converting an existing text list into a diagram. Then you'll learn to add a quick, professional-looking style to your diagram.

FREQUENTLY ASKED QUESTION

When to Diagram

Now you tell me about diagrams! I've just typed a list of all one hundred employees in my company on a PowerPoint slide. I see now the names would work better in an organizational chart. Is it too late?

Well, if you were using PowerPoint 2003, the answer would be yes. If you wanted to add a certain type of diagram to a slide—an organizational chart, for example—you had to add it to your slide first, and then fill in the employees' names later. In fact, you can still do it that way in PowerPoint 2007, if you want.

But you may run into a situation where you're adding text to a slide and *then* realize that a diagram would make more sense. Say you realize you've just typed a list that would be much more effective as a chevron diagram—one that shows a series of steps, for example, or that shows some other type of relationship. PowerPoint 2007 lets you experiment by turning that list into a diagram with the click of a button. See Figure 22-10 for an example. For instructions, flip to page 516.

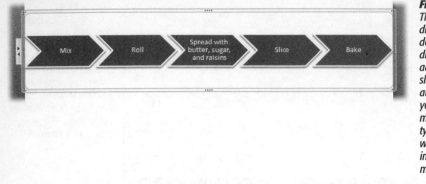

Figure 22-10:
This horizontal chevron diagram is just one of dozens of different diagrams that you can add to your PowerPoint slides. Because your audience needs to read your diagrams easily, no matter which diagram type you choose, you'll want to keep the individual steps to no more than a handful.

Adding Diagrams to Slides

Adding a diagram to a slide is simple. All you need to do is select a diagram type and click a button, as the following steps show.

1. **Select the slide to which you want to add a diagram. Go to Insert → Illustrations → SmartArt.**

   If you used a layout such as Title and Content, Comparison, or Content with Caption, then you can click the Insert SmartArt Graphic icon in the center of your slide. Either way, the Choose a SmartArt Graphic dialog box you see in Figure 22-11 appears.

2. **Click one of the diagram categories you see on the left side of the dialog box.**

   Diagram types related to that category appear in the middle of the dialog box.

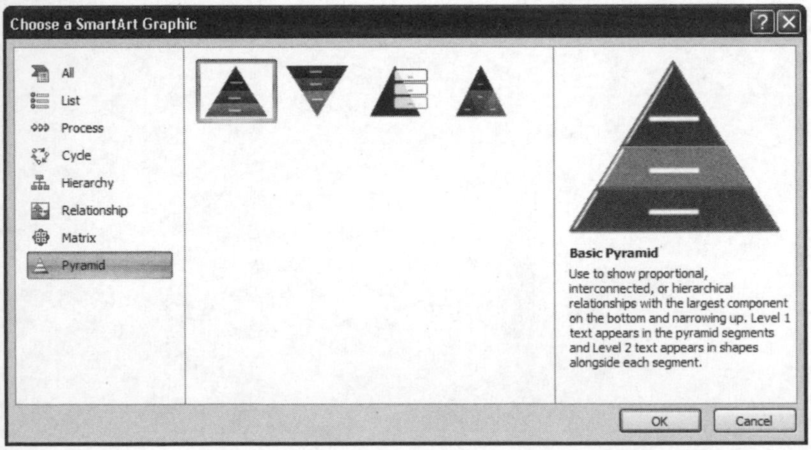

Figure 22-11:
PowerPoint 2007 offers a lot more diagrams than earlier versions of the program. If you're not familiar with one of the more exotic diagrams, click it. When you do, PowerPoint displays a helpful description on the right side of the Choose a SmartArt Graphic dialog box.

3. **Double-click a diagram type to add it to your slide.**

   Instead of double-clicking, you can click a diagram type (to see a helpful description) and then, when you're satisfied you want to add it to your slide, click OK.

PowerPoint displays the SmartArt Tools | Design and Format contextual tabs (Figure 22-12), and the selected chart appears on your slide, complete with a diagram text edit pane (see Figure 22-13 for an example)

4. **On your slide, add text to the diagram shapes by clicking in one of the place-holder text boxes.**

   PowerPoint highlights the diagram shape you clicked and activates the cursor so that you can begin typing.

Note: You can also click in the diagram's text edit pane as shown in Figure 22-13. If you're a fast typist and have several items to type, this method is for you.

---

5. **Type your text. Repeat for each diagram shape.**

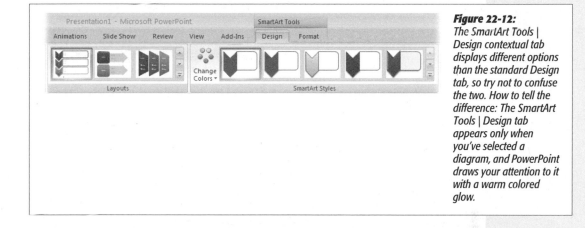

Figure 22-12:
The SmartArt Tools | Design contextual tab displays different options than the standard Design tab, so try not to confuse the two. How to tell the difference: The SmartArt Tools | Design tab appears only when you've selected a diagram, and PowerPoint draws your attention to it with a warm colored glow.

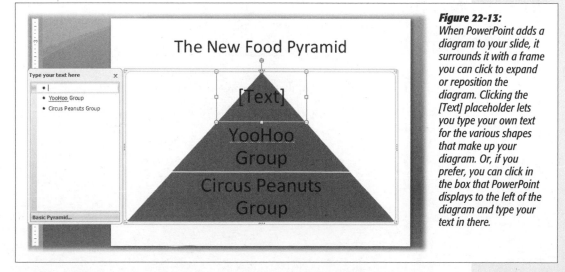

Figure 22-13:
When PowerPoint adds a diagram to your slide, it surrounds it with a frame you can click to expand or reposition the diagram. Clicking the [Text] placeholder lets you type your own text for the various shapes that make up your diagram. Or, if you prefer, you can click in the box that PowerPoint displays to the left of the diagram and type your text in there.

Turning Lists into Diagrams

If you find yourself creating a bulleted or numbered list (see Chapter 19) and realize it would be more effective as a diagram, you're in luck. PowerPoint 2007 lets you convert a list directly to a diagram. With the click of a button, you can even try out different diagram types until you find one that presents your list in the most compelling format.

To convert a list into a diagram:

1. **First, add a bulleted or numbered list on your slide.**

   You can type right on the slide, or paste in some text from another program.

2. **Right-click the list and then choose "Convert to SmartArt" from the shortcut menu (Figure 22-14).**

   PowerPoint displays a list of diagram types to choose from.

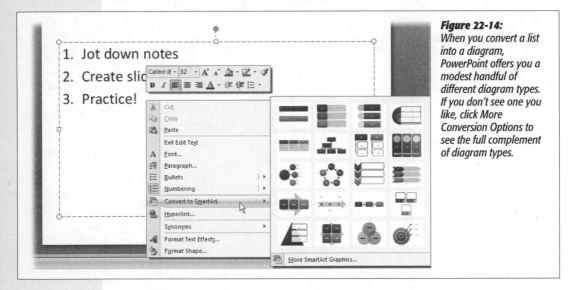

Figure 22-14:
When you convert a list into a diagram, PowerPoint offers you a modest handful of different diagram types. If you don't see one you like, click More Conversion Options to see the full complement of diagram types.

3. **Click to choose the type of diagram you want to create.**

   PowerPoint adds the selected diagram to your slide, pre-filled with your list data (Figure 22-15).

Figure 22-15:
Click the frame PowerPoint displays around a diagram, and you can resize the diagram as a whole by dragging the sides or corners. Clicking the individual elements lets you modify the shapes independently. To edit diagram text, click either of the arrows on the left side of the frame to display the diagram text edit pane.

Applying Prebuilt Styles and Color Themes to Diagrams

Applying a predesigned look-and-feel to your diagram lets you turn out an attractive diagram in no time flat. To counter the accusations of cookie cutter slides lobbed at earlier versions of the program, PowerPoint 2007 offers a wide range of predesigned SmartArt Styles, which you can dress up with an optional color theme. For a couple of clicks, you get a great-looking diagram that's unlikely to look like the ones Bob in Accounting churns out.

To apply a SmartArt Style and optional color theme to your diagram:

1. **Click to select the diagram you want to format.**

   The SmartArt Tools contextual tab appears.

2. **Click the SmartArt Tools | Design tab.**

   The SmartArt Tools/Design tab (flip back to Figure 22-12) appears. Next, you'll apply a SmartArt Style to your diagram.

3. **Go to SmartArt Tools | Design → SmartArt Styles and click the down-arrow.**

   The SmartArt Styles gallery appears (Figure 22-16).

4. **Click the SmartArt Style you want to apply to your diagram.**

   PowerPoint redisplays your diagram based on your selection.

5. **To choose a color theme for your diagram, go to SmartArt Tools | Design → SmartArt Styles → Change Colors.**

   The Primary Theme Colors gallery appears (Figure 22-17).

6. **Click to select a color theme.**

   PowerPoint redisplays your diagram based on the color theme you selected.

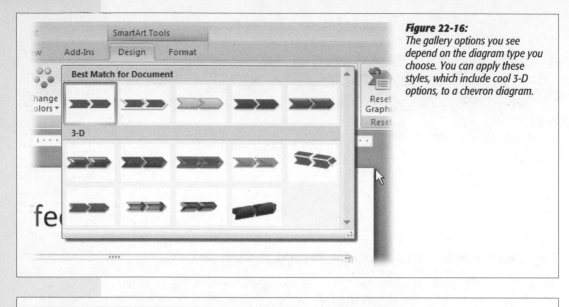

Figure 22-16:
The gallery options you see depend on the diagram type you choose. You can apply these styles, which include cool 3-D options, to a chevron diagram.

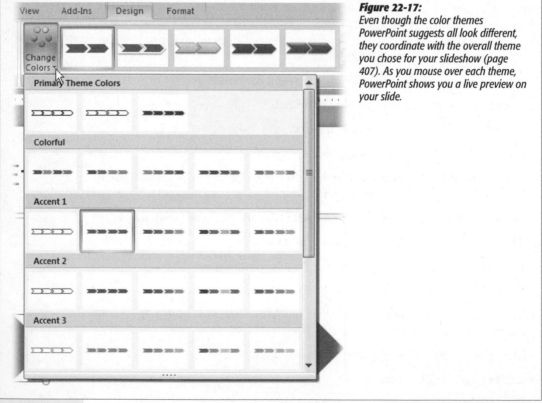

Figure 22-17:
Even though the color themes PowerPoint suggests all look different, they coordinate with the overall theme you chose for your slideshow (page 407). As you mouse over each theme, PowerPoint shows you a live preview on your slide.

Tweaking Diagrams

PowerPoint lets you change most elements of your diagram. For example, you can add titles, switch to a different type of diagram, or change the text in an existing diagram. You can also select your diagram to return to the SmartArt Tools contextual tab to adjust its design and color.

Adding titles

Oddly, when you create a diagram, PowerPoint doesn't start you out with a title placeholder. Instead, you have to insert and position your own text box, which you can see how to do on page 411. (If you've added your diagram to a slide that already contains a title, of course, you don't have to insert a new one.)

Switching to a different type of diagram

If you like, you can experiment with different diagram types to find one that presents your information in the most effective way possible. For example, if you've created a Basic Chevron diagram, you might find that switching to a Closed Chevron diagram demonstrates your conceptual point more effectively.

Just make sure the diagram you switch to fits your particular data. For example, a Multidirectional Cycle diagram implies a two-way relationship between diagram elements, while a Continuous Cycle implies a one-way repeating relationship. Because these two different types of diagrams communicate two very different messages, they're not interchangeable.

To switch to another diagram type:

1. **Click to select the diagram you want to change.**

   PowerPoint highlights the SmartArt Tools contextual tab.

2. **Go to SmartArt Tools | Design → Layouts and click the More button (the down-arrow).**

3. **A gallery of layouts appears.**

   If what you want doesn't appear, select More Layouts to show the "Choose a SmartArt Graphic" dialog box, which shows you the complete set of diagrams you can create in PowerPoint.

Note: To summon the "Choose a SmartArt Graphic" dialog box you can also right-click your diagram and then, from the menu that appears, choose Change Layout.

---

4. **Click a diagram type to select it, and then click OK.**

   PowerPoint redisplays your diagram based on the new type you just selected.

Changing diagram text

As your practice and hone your presentation, you'll probably find you need to change the text that appears in one or more diagram shapes. You can edit diagram text simply by clicking the text and typing, just as you edit the text in any text box—but there's an easier way. Displaying the diagram text edit pane (Figure 22-18) lets you see and edit all of the text in your diagram easily, without having to click from shape to shape.

To edit diagram text using the diagram text edit pane:

1. **If a text edit pane similar to the one you see in Figure 22-18 isn't already visible, right-click your diagram and then, from the context menu that appears, choose Show Text Pane.**

   The text edit pane appears.

2. **In the text edit pane, click the text you want to edit and begin typing.**

   PowerPoint automatically redisplays your diagram to reflect your changes.

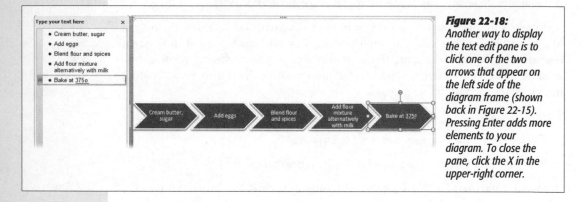

Figure 22-18:
Another way to display the text edit pane is to click one of the two arrows that appear on the left side of the diagram frame (shown back in Figure 22-15). Pressing Enter adds more elements to your diagram. To close the pane, click the X in the upper-right corner.

Creating Tables

Since ancient times, people have organized information into tables—rows and columns containing a number or bit of text in each cell. By now, you'd think working with tables would be a no-brainer.

It's not. Adding a table to your slideshow is easier in PowerPoint 2007 than it was in earlier versions of the program and the results are more impressive looking. But thanks to the overwhelming number of choices PowerPoint 2007 gives you, the process of adding a table can cause more headaches then ever. You start with four ways to create a table, plus you have dozens of ways to tweak every imaginable table element, from the lines that separate your columns to the shading that appears in your rows.

But nothing lets your audience compare figures better than a table. So eventually, you must create one. This section shows you the easiest way to create a table. Then, you'll see how to add the basics: data, a title, column headings, and so on.

Creating a Basic Table

PowerPoint gives you four different ways to create a table: by mousing over a grid, by typing your table dimensions into the Insert Table box, by drawing the table's outline on a slide, or by inserting an Excel table. Most of the time, you want to use one of the first two options, which are the quickest and easiest. (You can read about the other two methods in the boxes below and on pages 524.)

POWER USERS' CLINIC

Drawing Tables

Above, you see two ways to create a basic table: by mousing over a grid, or by typing in the number of columns and rows you want. These two table creation options are all most folks will ever need.

But suppose you're trying to work your table around other slide content and can't guess precisely how many rows and columns you need to create a table that *just* fits the space you have. PowerPoint's got your back: It lets you draw the outline of a table the size you want it, and then carve it up into rows and columns later.

1. If you like, go to the Table Tools | Design → Draw Borders group and click Pen Style, Pen Weight, and Pen Color to customize the table border you're about to draw. You can choose a border style of solid, dashed, or dotted; a border thickness; and a border color, respectively.

2. Choose Insert → Tables → Table → Draw Table.

3. Mouse over your slide. As you do, your cursor turns into a tiny pencil.

4. Drag to draw the outline of your table. As you drag, you create a dotted outline. When you let go of your mouse, PowerPoint replaces the dotted outline with a proper table frame.

5. Press Esc to turn off drawing.

6. Choose Table Tools | Layout → Merge → Split Cells Layout.

7. In the Split Cells dialog box that appears, type in the number of columns and rows you want your table to have; then click OK.

8. PowerPoint carves up your table based on the number of columns and rows you specified.

Whichever approach you choose, after you've created your table, you need to fill it with data and add a title and column headings. The following sections walk you through the entire process.

Creating rows and columns

To create a table, you start by telling PowerPoint how many rows and columns you want your table to have. PowerPoint gives you a gloriously easy way to do so—mousing over a grid to define the size and shape of your table.

Here's how:

1. **Select the slide where you want to place your table. Go to Insert → Tables → Table.**

   Up pops a menu similar to the one shown in Figure 22-19.

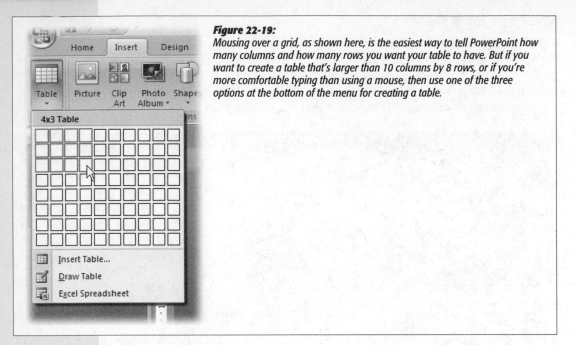

Figure 22-19:
Mousing over a grid, as shown here, is the easiest way to tell PowerPoint how many columns and how many rows you want your table to have. But if you want to create a table that's larger than 10 columns by 8 rows, or if you're more comfortable typing than using a mouse, then use one of the three options at the bottom of the menu for creating a table.

2. **Move your mouse over the grid to select your desired configuration of rows and columns.**

   PowerPoint highlights the cells your cursor passes over, and displays your proposed table dimensions at the top of the menu. In Figure 22-19, for example, the top of the menu reads "4x3 Table," corresponding to the four-column-by-three-row grid that's highlighted. On your slide, PowerPoint previews your table, which grows and shrinks as you highlight more and less of the grid. (The table preview shows the rows only, not the columns.)

3. **When your cursor reaches the bottom right cell of the table you want to create, click that cell.**

   PowerPoint adds a table to your slide containing the number of rows and columns you specified, and displays the Table Tools tab (see Figure 22-20).

Tip: Instead of using your mouse to tell PowerPoint how many columns and rows you want your table to have, you can go to Insert → Tables → Table → Insert Table to display the Insert Table dialog box (Figure 22-21) and type the number of columns and rows you want. When you finish, click OK to dismiss the dialog box and add your newly created table to your slide.

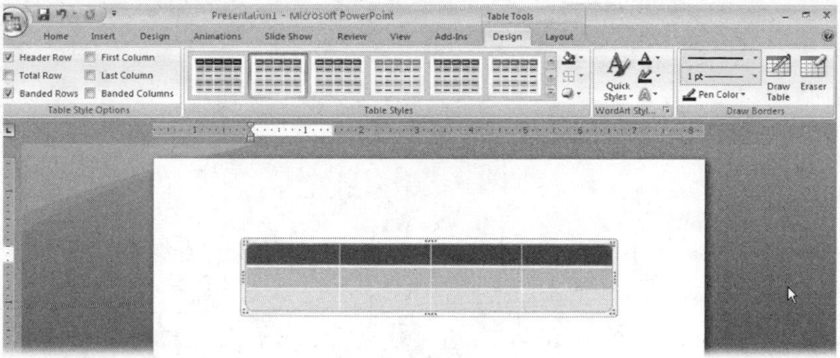

Figure 22-20:
Behold the basic table, complete with a header row (the darker-colored row) across the top. Unless you tell it different, PowerPoint lightly tints, or bands, every other row to make it easier for your audience to read your table. You see how to change both of these formatting effects starting on page 526.

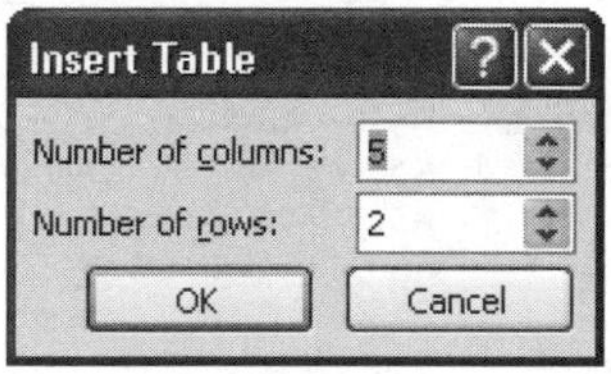

Figure 22-21:
To add a table to a slide, select Insert → Tables → Table → Insert Table. The Insert Table dialog box also pops up when you're working on a slide to which you've applied a content layout, and you click the table icon displayed in the center of the slide.

Selecting cells, rows, and columns

Before you can add data to a cell or format a cell, row, or column, you first have to select that cell, row, or column. To select a cell, simply click in the cell. To select multiple cells, click in one cell, and then drag your cursor to select additional cells. PowerPoint highlights cells as you mouse over them to let you know which cells you're selecting.

Tip: Another way to select multiple cells is to click in one cell, and then Shift-click in another. Doing so tells PowerPoint to select all the cells in between.

To select a column or a row:

1. **Mouse above the column you want to select (or to the left of the row you want to select).**

   Your cursor turns into a thick down-arrow (see Figure 22-22).

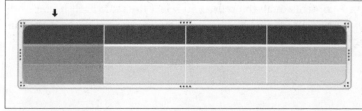

Figure 22-22:
As you mouse just above a column, wait for your cursor to change to a small arrow. When it does, click to select the column. Here you can see the tinting that PowerPoint uses to let you know you've successfully selected a column.

Inserting an Excel Table

PowerPoint has some nifty table tools, but nothing like Excel's sophisticated spreadsheet formulas. If you need to use calculations or scientific notation in your table, you can borrow these features from Excel. Just tell PowerPoint where you want to insert the table, pop into Excel, whip out your table, and then pop back to PowerPoint, where you find your newly created Excel table displayed on your slide. Here's the step-by-step:

1. Choose Insert → Tables → Table → Excel Spreadsheet. Excel's ribbon replaces PowerPoint's, and a blank Excel spreadsheet appears on your slide (Figure 22-23).

2. Create your table using the Excel tools.

3. Choose File → Close. Excel's ribbon disappears.

4. In the "Do you want to save the changes you made to your presentation?" dialog box that pops up, click Yes.

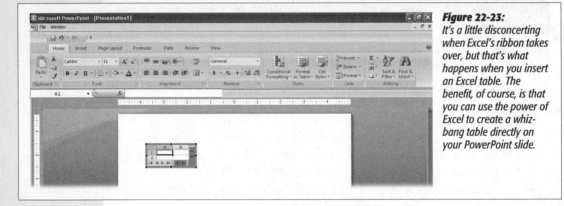

Figure 22-23:
It's a little disconcerting when Excel's ribbon takes over, but that's what happens when you insert an Excel table. The benefit, of course, is that you can use the power of Excel to create a whiz-bang table directly on your PowerPoint slide.

2. Click just above the column (or to the left of the row) you want to select.

   You can also click a cell in the column or row you want to select, and then click Table Tools | Layout → Table → Select → Select Column or Table Tools | Layout → Table → Select → Select Row.

   PowerPoint tints the column (or row) to let you know you've selected it.

Selecting entire tables

PowerPoint makes a distinction between selecting all the cells in a table, and selecting the table itself. You select all the rows and columns in a table if you want to delete or format the contents of all the cells. You select the table itself if you want to resize, reposition, or delete the table, or if you want to change the font of your table text by applying a table style (see page 526).

The previous section shows you how to select all the cells in a table. To select the table itself, click any cell in table you want to select. Then choose Table Tools | Layout → Table → Select → Select Table. You can also drag your cursor around your table to select it. (Or, if you prefer, right-click any cell in your table and then, from the context menu that appears, choose Select Table.)

Whichever way you go about it way, after you successfully select a table, PowerPoint highlights the table frame and turns your cursor into a four-headed arrow.

Warning: Clicking in a cell highlights the table frame, too, which can mistakenly lead you to think you've selected the table. But if you want to, say, delete or apply an effect (such as color) to your table as a whole, then you need to select the table as described above: simply clicking in a cell doesn't cut it.

Adding data

After you've added a table to your slide, you need to fill the cells with data. To do so, click in any cell and begin typing. To move to the next cell, press Tab or click in the next cell.

Adding a title

PowerPoint doesn't offer you any special way to add a title to your table. Instead, you simply add a text box, type in the title text you want, and then position the text box over your table. Chapter 17 shows you how to add and position text boxes.

Adding column headings

You add a column heading the same way that you add any other bit of data to a table cell—by clicking in the cell and then typing. But because most folks want to draw special attention to column headings, PowerPoint gives you a quick way to highlight them.

Here's how it works. When you create a table, PowerPoint highlights the first row (Figure 22-22) for you. But if the first row of your table doesn't appear highlighted—perhaps your co-workers has been fiddling with your presentation file—you can recover the highlighted effect by going to Table Tools → Design → Table Style Options and, in the Table Style Options group, turning on the Header checkbox.

PowerPoint tints the first row of your table an attractive color based on your table's style. It also automatically switches the color of the text in the first row to a contrasting color. See Figure 22-22 for an example. (Want to change these row highlights? See the next page.)

Tweaking Tables

Adding a basic table to your slide may be all you need. But once you type more than a couple rows' data, odds are good you'll need to insert a row here or resize a column there. Also, once you've got your table data typed in the way you want it, you may decide to spice up your table with a bit of formatting. You might want to change the color of your table so that it coordinates with your company's logo, or draw a big, thick border around a section of your table to draw attention to it.

PowerPoint lets you change virtually every element of your table, from the width of your rows and columns to the background color of each cell. This section shows you the most useful ways to work with table data and modify your table's appearance.

Applying prebuilt styles

The basic table you create in PowerPoint is just that—basic. To spice it up with a predefined collection of formatting effects including color, shading, and borders:

1. **Click any cell in your table. Then go to Table Tools | Design → Table Styles. In the Table Styles group, mouse over the style options.**

   As you mouse over each option, PowerPoint displays a live preview on your slide.

   To see a gallery of additional style options, click the down arrow in the Table Styles group.

2. **Click the style option you want to apply to your table.**

   PowerPoint redisplays your table based on the style you chose.

Highlighting rows and columns

Say you're showing your boss or your teacher an important table. You know she's going to have only a few minutes to examine it, so to emphasize the important numbers, you take a yellow pen and highlight them. PowerPoint lets you do something similar in the tables you add to your slides: you can highlight specific columns or rows (such as the totals row) or tell PowerPoint to lightly tint every other column or row for readability.

If you've had a chance to check out Figure 22-22, you've already seen how Power-Point applies header rows and banded rows to your table. In addition to tinting the first row of your table and lightly tinting every other row, you can tell PowerPoint to add a totals row, highlight the data in the first or last column, or band columns (instead of rows). Here's how:

- Click any cell in your table to select the table. Then choose your options from the Table Tools | Design tab → Table Style Options group.

You can choose from the following:

- **Header Row.** Tints the first row of the table and adjusts text color accordingly.

- **Total Row.** Draws a thicker line above the last row of data and bolds the last row of data.

- **Banded Rows.** Lightly tints every other row.

- **First Column.** Bolds all the data in the first column.

- **Last Column.** Bolds all the data in the last column.

- **Banded Columns.** Lightly tints every other column.

PowerPoint redisplays your table based on your choice. Figure 22-24 shows you an example.

Skeins sold	Wool	Cotton	Silk
Jan-March	5,000	3,000	2,523
Apr-June	5,250	3,500	3,110
July-Sep	6,500	4,200	4,239
Oct-Dec	7,333	6,430	5,274
Total Yearly Sales	24,203	17,250	15,280

Figure 22-24:
Turning on Total Row tells PowerPoint to add a thicker line, and bold the data and color the background in the last row of the table.

Inserting and deleting rows and columns

You've typed in twenty cells' worth of data when you realize you accidentally skipped a row. No sweat: simply insert a new blank row and type the skipped numbers.

To insert a row or a column, right-click one of the cells in your table and then, from the context menu that appears, choose Insert → Insert Above or Insert → Insert Below (to insert a row to the above or below your currently selected cell, respectively) or Insert → Insert Left or Insert → Insert Right (to insert a column to the left or right of your currently selected cell, respectively).

To delete a row or column, right-click any cell in the row or column you want to delete and then, from the context menu that appears, choose Delete Rows or Delete Columns. To delete multiple rows or columns, select them first; then right-click.

Changing the width of a row or column

Each table that you create begins with standard, consistently sized rows and columns. But depending on the content that you add to your cells, you may want to increase or decrease the width of a row or column. For example, if you type a column heading wider than the column width, PowerPoint assumes you want to break it up into two lines. If you don't agree, you can widen the column.

To adjust the width of a row or column:

1. **Click anywhere in your table.**

2. **Mouse over the cell border of the row or column you want to adjust.**

   Your cursor turns into the double-headed arrow cursor shown in Figure 22-25.

3. **Click the cell border and drag to adjust the row (or column) width.**

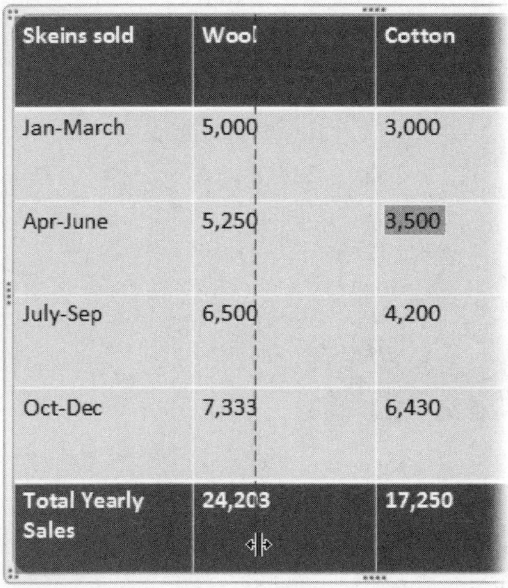

Skeins sold	Wool	Cotton
Jan-March	5,000	3,000
Apr-June	5,250	3,500
July-Sep	6,500	4,200
Oct-Dec	7,333	6,430
Total Yearly Sales	24,203	17,250

Figure 22-25:
Simply drag to adjust the width of a column, as shown here, or a row. You know you're exactly over a column border when you see the double-headed arrow.

Note: If you'd prefer to type numbers for the width and height of your rows or columns, you can. Just select the rows or columns you want to work with, then choose Table Tools | Layout → Table Size → Width or Table Tools | Layout → Table Size → Height and click the arrows to increase or decrease row (or column) size. As you adjust the numbers, PowerPoint automatically redraws your table.

Aligning data inside cells

Unless you tell it otherwise, PowerPoint assumes you want the text and numbers you type into your table cells to be top- and left-aligned. But you're free to change that to anything else you like. For example, text often looks nice when centered. Numbers are usually easier to read when right aligned.

Because most folks find vertical alignment options (top, center, and bottom) most useful, those are the options easiest to get to. But by using the Cell Text Layout dialog box described below, you can align your data eight ways to Sunday.

To realign data:

1. **Select the cells whose contents you want to realign.**

2. **Go to Table Tools | Layout → Alignment and choose Align Top, Center Vertically, or Align Bottom.**

   PowerPoint redraws your table using the alignment you selected.

3. **If vertical alignment isn't what you want, click Table Tools | Layout → Alignment → Cell Margins → Custom Margins.**

   The Cell Text Layout dialog box appears.

4. **In the Cell Text Layout dialog box, click the Internal Margins options to align your text the way you want it to appear.**

   PowerPoint redraws your table using the alignment options you selected.

To align the text in your data cells horizontally, follow the same steps, but adjust the internal left and right margins.

Merging (and splitting) cells

Depending on the data you're trying to present, you may want to merge cells (erase the border between cells) or split cells (add a border between cells). Merging cells is especially useful for creating a heading inside your table, as shown in Figure 22-26 (top). You want to consider splitting cells when you find yourself cramming more than one or two words, phrases, or sentences in a single cell (Figure 22-26, bottom).

To merge a cell, select the cells you want to merge and click Table Tools | Layout → Merge → Merge Cells. You can also right-click a selection and choose Merge Cells.

To split a cell, select the cell you want to split and then click Table Tools | Layout → Merge → Split Cells (or right-click the selected cell and choose Split Cells). In the Split Cells dialog box that appears, type in the number of columns and number of rows you want your newly split cell to have. When you finish, click OK.

Pros & Cons of Adding Visuals to a PowerPoint Presentation	
Table	Pro: Your teacher (boss) expects a table. Con: You don't have any relevant data (or any idea where to find some).
Chart	Pro: A process chart will get across your ideas succinctly and powerfully. Con: You've already got a chart you created in UNIX using X's and O's that you want to use.

Pros & Cons of Adding Visuals to a PowerPoint Presentation		
Table	Pro: Your teacher (boss) expects a table.	
	Con: You don't have any relevant data (or any idea where to find some.	
Chart	Pro: A process chart will get across your ideas succinctly and powerfully.	
	Con: You've already got a chart you created in UNIX using X's and O's that you want to use.	

Figure 22-26:
Top: The text in this table is okay, but its placement isn't particularly stellar.

Bottom: Here you see the same table, with two minor adjustments: the two cells in the top row were merged, and the two cells in the right column were each split. The result (after a bit of the cell alignment magic described on page 529) is attractive and professional looking.

Resizing Tables

PowerPoint gives you two options for resizing your table:

- **Drag to resize.** Dragging is the easiest approach, and it's the way to go if eyeballing the resulting size of your table is good enough. To resize your table by dragging, mouse over the dots you see on the corners and at the sides of your table frame (Figure 22-26). When your cursor in the right place, it turns into a two-headed arrow. As soon as you see the two-headed arrow, drag to resize your table.

- **Specify numbers for table width and height.** If you need to create a table of a very specific size—you want to match your table to a background image or a table on another slide, for example—you want to go this route. First, go to Table Tools | Layout → Table Size. Then use the Width and Height boxes to increase or decrease the current dimensions. (You can either click the arrows to dial up or down, or type a number in directly.)

Repositioning Tables

You move a table around on your slide similar to the way you move pictures, charts, and other objects—by dragging. Simply mouse over your table's frame until you see a four-headed arrow, and then drag to reposition your table.

Deleting Tables

You'll probably be surprised to learn that you *don't* delete a table the way you delete just about everything else in PowerPoint—by right-clicking it and then choosing Home → Delete. (Doing so deletes the slide on which the table appears.)

Instead, you need to select the table (page 524) and then press Delete.

You can also cut the table by selecting it and then choosing Home → Cut. (Technically speaking, cutting isn't the same things as deleting, but it's close enough. See page 427 for details.)

CHAPTER 23

Delivering Presentations

In the old days, giving a PowerPoint presentation almost always meant connecting your laptop to a computer projector. You'd stand in front of a live audience and use a remote control to click through each slide while you explained each of your points in detail. You can still give a "stand and deliver" presentation, but today you can also:

- Package your presentation for delivery on CD. This option is ideal for interactive, audience-paced presentations like tutorials or continuously running kiosk presentations.

- Email the presentation to your audience.

This chapter covers both of these presentation delivery options.

Note: You can also convert your presentation to a Web page, complete with clickable links that viewers can use to navigate your slideshow and even jump to other documents or Web sites. For more on these and other advanced features, see *PowerPoint 2007: The Missing Manual*.

Setting Up a Slideshow

After you've put together your slideshow—created slides, added text and graphics, and so on—you have to give PowerPoint a few instructions on how it should display the slideshow when it's show time. Say you're creating a slideshow that you want to run continuously on a kiosk, with no human intervention. You might want to tell to linger a few seconds longer on certain slides than on others. Or imagine that you have two monitors hooked up to your computer: one set into the wall of a conference room, and one on a laptop placed strategically where only you can see it. You can have PowerPoint display the slideshow on the wall monitor, and the speaker notes on the laptop.

Using the Slide Show tab (Figure 23-1), you can set these options and more. The following sections show you how.

Figure 23-1:
The Slide Show tab offers a grab-bag of options you can set to tell PowerPoint how you want your slideshow to appear when it runs on a computer.

Choosing a Slideshow Mode

The first thing to do when you're setting up your slideshow is to decide which mode you want your slideshow to run in: full-screen, browser, or kiosk. Your choice affects the way folks can interact with your slideshow while it's running, as well as which other options you can set.

Full-screen mode

Full-screen mode (Figure 23-2) is the way to go if you'll be the one giving your presentation. As the name implies, in full-screen mode slideshows take up the entire screen. Depending on the PowerPoint options you've set, ghosted controls appear in the lower-left corner of a full-screen slideshow. Other ways you can interact with a full-screen slideshow running include keyboard shortcuts and a right-click menu (page 545).

The program assumes you want full-screen mode unless you tell it different. But if you (or a coworker) has set your slideshow to another mode and you want to set it back, here's how:

1. **Choose Slide Show → Set Up → Set Up Slide Show.**

   The Set Up Show dialog box (Figure 23-3) appears.

2. **Turn on the radio button next to "Presented by a speaker (full screen)."**

Browser mode

When you set up a slideshow to run in browser mode, your slides don't take over the entire screen; instead, they appear in a self-contained window (see Figure 23-4). A specialized right-click menu appears (page 545), offering choices that folks running your presentation might find handy—printing your slides, for example. Designed to be relatively easy for non-PowerPoint folks to figure out how to run, browser mode is an option for slideshows you're planning to distribute by CD or email.

Top 4 Reasons
Baby Won't Sleep

1. Letting baby pick *Nightmare on Elm Street* as bedtime story
2. Leaving baby teeth for the Tooth Monster
3. Using Van Halen to rock baby (instead of a rocking chair)
4. Giving baby *Jolt Cola Jr.* less than 2 hours before bed

Figure 23-2:
Full-screen mode is the way to go if you plan to run your slideshow yourself, because it gives you the most options for interacting with your slideshow. Pressing Esc ends the presentation.

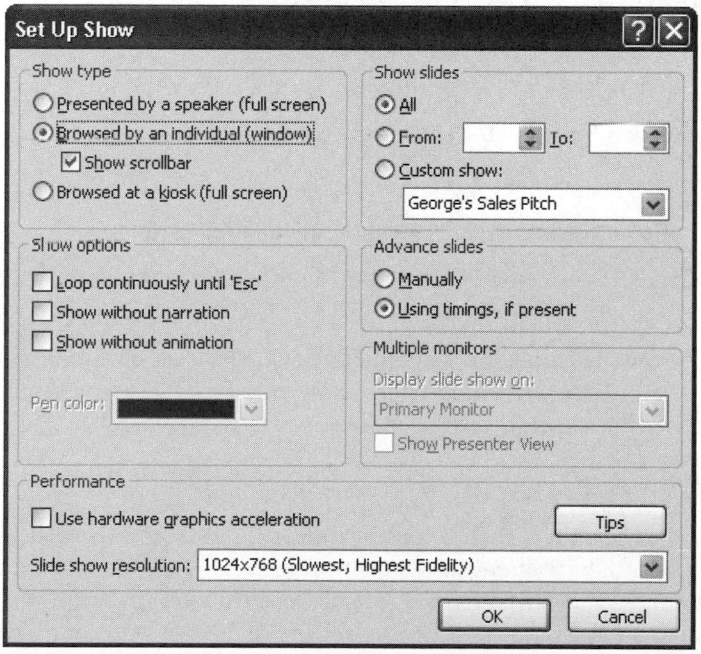

Set Up Show

Show type
- ○ Presented by a speaker (full screen)
- ◉ Browsed by an individual (window)
  - ☑ Show scrollbar
- ○ Browsed at a kiosk (full screen)

Show options
- ☐ Loop continuously until 'Esc'
- ☐ Show without narration
- ☐ Show without animation

Pen color: [black ▼]

Show slides
- ◉ All
- ○ From: [ ] To: [ ]
- ○ Custom show:
  - George's Sales Pitch ▼

Advance slides
- ○ Manually
- ◉ Using timings, if present

Multiple monitors
Display slide show on:
Primary Monitor ▼
☐ Show Presenter View

Performance
- ☐ Use hardware graphics acceleration   [Tips]
- Slide show resolution: 1024x768 (Slowest, Highest Fidelity) ▼

[OK] [Cancel]

Figure 23-3:
The Set Up Show dialog box lets you set useful but relatively seldom-used options that wouldn't fit on the Slide Show tab.

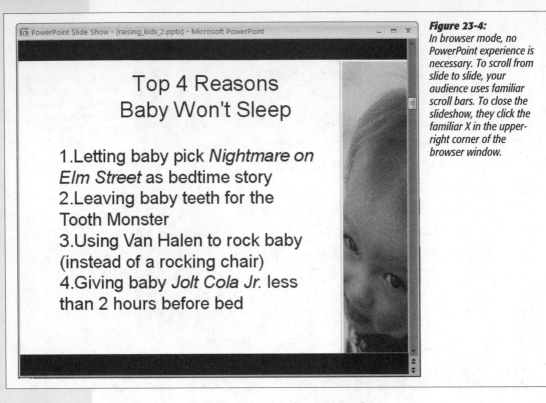

Figure 23-4:
In browser mode, no PowerPoint experience is necessary. To scroll from slide to slide, your audience uses familiar scroll bars. To close the slideshow, they click the familiar X in the upper-right corner of the browser window.

To set up your slideshow to run in browser mode:

1. **Choose Slide Show → Set Up → Set Up Slide Show.**

   The Set Up Show dialog box appears.

2. **Turn on the radio button next to "Browsed by an individual (window)."**

3. **For your audience's sake, also make sure the Show Scrollbar checkbox, which now becomes available, is turned on.**

   If you leave this option turned off, your audience won't see an obvious way to scroll through your slides. They must either know to right-click (which displays a menu of options) or sit there frustrated.

Kiosk mode

If you're planning to let your slideshow run unattended, kiosk mode is what you want. In kiosk mode, there are no ghosted controls or right-click menus—which means there's nothing built-in that your audience can click to start your slideshow, stop it, hop from one slide to the next, or otherwise interact with your slides. After all, since there won't be a presenter, you don't want to include presenter controls and risk someone wandering by and fiddling with them.

But what no presenter controls also means is that if you set up your slideshow to run in kiosk mode, you must set automatic timings (page 539) so your slideshow plays automatically all the way through before looping around again.

To set up your slideshow to run in kiosk mode:

1. **Choose Slide Show → Set Up → Set Up Slide Show.**

   The Set Up Show dialog box appears.

2. **Turn on the radio button next to "Browsed at a kiosk (full screen)."**

   Typically, you'll save kiosk-mode slideshows as self-running PowerPoint shows (page 546).

Tip: Pressing Esc stops a slideshow running in kiosk mode, so if you're setting up a kiosk slideshow to run automatically and want to prevent folks from inadvertently stopping it in its tracks the second you turn your back, make sure you hide the keyboard.

Hiding Individual Slides

First, make sure your slideshow includes all the slides you want to show—and none that you don't. To eliminate a slide from a particular slideshow, you don't have to delete it from the presentation—you can choose to hide it temporarily. That way, you can always take it out of hiding when you want to use it again.

Say you're giving a presentation to management. One of your slides is quite high-tech—a complicated chart and some head-busting equations. Since this level of detail may confuse your audience, you can hide that slide. If someone in your audience happens to ask a pertinent question during the presentation, you can display the slide manually, as described in the table on page 545. The same slide may be appropriate for the engineers you're giving the same presentation to later in the week, so you can bring it out of hiding for that show.

Note: Because hiding a slide doesn't delete it, don't rely on hiding to conceal sensitive or proprietary information. There's always a chance that you (or someone else running your slideshow) could unhide it accidentally. Instead, either delete the slide or create a custom slideshow (page 541).

To hide a slide:

1. **In the Slides pane in Normal view, select the slide (or slides) you want to hide.**

   If you don't see thumbnails of your slides on the left side of your screen, choose View → Presentation Views → Normal to restore the Slides pane.

2. **Click Slide Show → Set Up → Hide Slide.**

   In the Slides pane, the number of your newly hidden slide appears with a line through it (Figure 23-5).

3. **The next time your presentation runs, PowerPoint skips the hidden slide(s).**

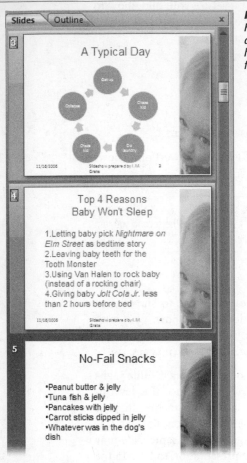

Figure 23-5:
Hide Slide is a toggle option, so clicking Hide Slide while you've got a visible slide selected hides the slide. Clicking it while you've got a hidden slide selected unhides the slide. You can also hide slides from Slide Sorter view.

Setting Up a Speaker Notes Screen

Pros use teleprompters for a reason: they work. When your brain goes blank and you forget an important point, having an electronic cheat sheet that only you can see can save your presentation (and your reputation as a confident, extemporaneous speaker). PowerPoint offers the next best thing to a teleprompter: It lets you run your slideshow on one monitor, and your speaker notes on another. While your audience is looking at your slides or at you, you can sneak a peek at your notes. And because you're not fumbling with 3×5 cards, no one will be the wiser.

To set up a presenter view, first connect two different monitors to the computer you intend to run your presentation on. (A laptop computer counts as one monitor.) Once the monitors are plugged in, open the presentation you want to set up as a presenter view. Then go to Slide Show → Monitors and turn on the checkbox next to Use Presenter View.

Click the down-arrow next to Show Presentation On (which has now become available), and then, from the list that appears, choose the monitor on which you want your *slideshow* to appear. Your speaker notes appear on the monitor you're using to follow these steps.

Setting Up Automatic Timing

You've got two choices when it comes to clicking through your slides at showtime: you can click through each slide manually, or you can set up an automatic slideshow by telling PowerPoint when to go from one slide to the next. An automatic slideshow is useful if, for example, you're delivering your presentation on a kiosk, or if you have exactly 40 minutes to give your presentation and need PowerPoint to keep you on track. Also, if you've done a presentation many times, you may be able to give your spiel and let PowerPoint change the slides automatically, at just the right moment.

The key to setting up an automatic slideshow is to rehearse your presentation. You run through it just as you would in front of a live audience, while PowerPoint's virtual stopwatch keeps track of how many seconds you spend on each slide. Then, if you're satisfied with the pacing, you tell PowerPoint to keep those timings.

Tip: Instead of painstakingly rehearsing your presentation, you can assign each slide, say, a minute and a half (or any amount of time you choose). In the Slides pane, select a slide. Then select Animations → Transition to This Slide, turn on the "Automatically after" checkbox, and type the amount of time you want the currently selected slide to remain onscreen. (Make sure you turn off On Mouse Click.) Repeat for the remaining slides in your slideshow. Alternatively, for each slide you can type the amount of slide time you want in the Rehearsal dialog box (Figure 23-6).

To rehearse your presentation and set timings:

1. **Click Slide Show → Set Up → Rehearse Timings.**

   PowerPoint begins a full-screen version of your slideshow and displays the Rehearsal toolbar (Figure 23-6).

Figure 23-6:
Rehearsing your timing not only helps you cement in your mind what you're going to say and how you're going to say it, it also lets you know whether you have enough slides to fill your allotted speaking time (or too many).

2. **Step through your presentation as you normally would, speaking aloud and gesturing to a pretend audience.**

   Hopping around slides in your slideshow affects your rehearsal timings. For example, clicking Repeat to back up to an earlier slide stops the overall slideshow clock, which doesn't start up again until you return to (or pass) the slide you were on when you clicked Repeat.

Typing the number of a particular slide and then pressing Enter to hop directly to that slide resets the current slide clock even if you've already timed that slide; meanwhile, the overall slideshow clock keeps on ticking away.

If the phone rings, the dog barks, your boss steps in, or you're otherwise interrupted, head to the Rehearsal toolbar and click Pause to stop the clock. Then, after you've handled the interruption, click Pause again to resume your rehearsal where you left off.

3. **When you get to the last slide, take as long as you need to wrap up your presentation, and then press Esc.**

PowerPoint kicks up the dialog box you see in Figure 23-7.

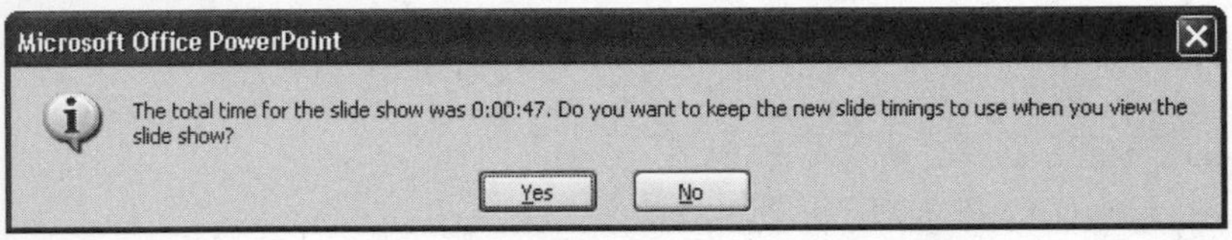

Figure 23-7:
If you're not sure you're happy with the pace at which you just rehearsed your presentation, choose Yes anyway. You can always rehearse again later—and when you do, PowerPoint will discard these timings and use your new timings.

Tip: You can also press Esc at any time to abort the rehearsal.

4. **Choose Yes if you want PowerPoint to flip through the slides at the pace you just rehearsed the next time you run your slideshow. Choose No if you want to flip through your slides manually, or if you've discovered during your rehearsal that you need to add or delete slides, rearrange your slideshow, or come up with a lot more banter.**

If you chose Yes, PowerPoint displays the Slide Sorter view showing your timings. (If you chose No, PowerPoint simply returns you to Normal view.)

5. **On the Slide Show tab, make sure Use Rehearsed Timings checkbox is turned on.**

The next time you start your slideshow, PowerPoint uses your rehearsed timings to click through your slides automatically.

Looping Continuously

Whether you choose to click through each slide yourself or use automatic timings (page 539) to tell PowerPoint how fast to move through each slide, you usually want to stop the slideshow after the last slide. But for those times when you *do* want your slideshow to loop continuously (to begin the slideshow over again the instant it finishes), you can do that by clicking Slide Show → Set Up → Set Up Slide Show to open the Set Up Show dialog box. Then, in the Show Options section, turn on the "Loop continuously until 'Esc'" checkbox. When you take down the show at the end of the day, just press the Esc key to stop the show and regain control of your laptop.

Note: If you set up your slideshow to run in kiosk mode (page 536), you don't have to tell PowerPoint to loop continuously—it assumes that's what you want. In fact, PowerPoint deactivates the "Loop continuously until 'Esc'" option.

Slideshows for Multiple Audiences

If you give a lot of presentations, you've probably found yourself creating one big comprehensive presentation on a particular topic, and then adjusting it for different audiences. For example, say you want to give slightly different variations of the same sales pitch to small-business owners, government acquisitions teams, and purchasing departments in large corporations. Say, too, that you want a ten-minute version of your presentation that skims the highlights for those times when all your potential clients will give you is ten minutes of their time. But you also want thirty-minute and hour-long versions that cover the technical features of your product.

You could reinvent the wheel by copying slides from one slideshow into another, reorganizing them, and saving the newly copied slides as a separate slideshow. But PowerPoint gives you an easier way to accomplish the same result. By creating a *custom slideshow*, you tell PowerPoint which subset of slides in your comprehensive presentation you want to designate as a new version. You even get to change the order the slides appear. Then you give your new version a meaningful name, like *small_business* or *ten_minute*, to remind you what situations to use it for.

Because you don't actually duplicate slides or files when you create a custom slideshow, you don't have to worry about carting around multiple PowerPoint files (or keeping them all updated and in synch).

Note: Unfortunately, you can't mix and match slides from different slideshows in the same custom slideshow. To create a new slideshow from a bunch of different slideshows, you need to copy and paste individual slides (page 492).

Creating a Custom Slideshow

The term *custom slideshow* is a little misleading. When you create a custom slideshow, you're not actually creating a new PowerPoint file; what you're creating is a new version of the original slideshow in the form of a named list of slides. The slides themselves stay right where they are, in the original slideshow, which is exactly what makes custom slideshows so useful. Since they're essentially nothing but lists of slides, no matter how many times the slides themselves change, your custom slideshows always stay automatically up-to-date.

Note: Additional ways to adjust the way your slideshow runs include hiding slides (page 537) and looping your slideshow continuously (page 540).

To create a custom slideshow:

1. **Select Slide Show → Start Slide Show → Custom Slide Show.**

   If you've created custom slideshows in this presentation before, their names appear here, along with the Custom Shows option. (If you haven't, only the Custom Shows option appears.)

2. **Select Custom Shows.**

   A Custom Shows dialog box similar to Figure 23-8 pops up.

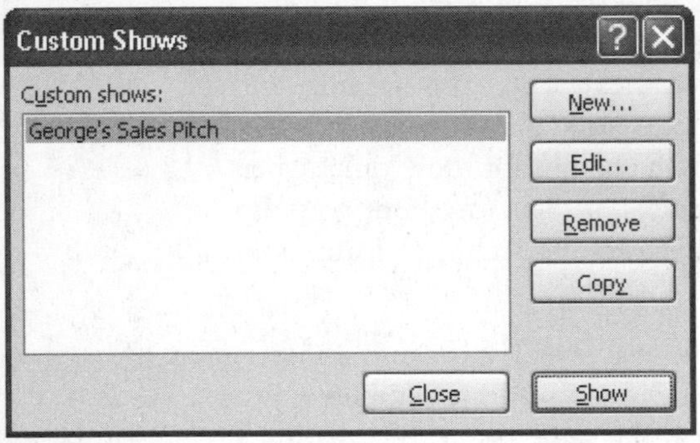

Figure 23-8:
If you haven't previously created any custom shows in this presentation file, you won't see any listed here, and all of the options except New appear grayed-out. To create a new custom show, click New.

3. **In the Custom Shows dialog box, click New.**

   The Define Custom Show dialog box appears (Figure 23-9).

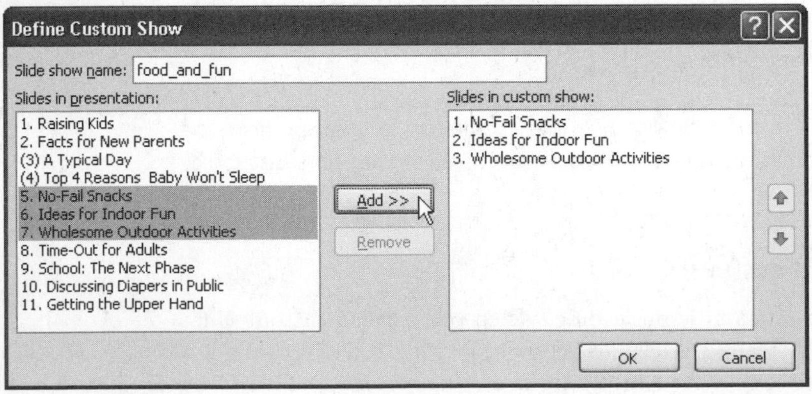

Figure 23-9:
PowerPoint lists each slide in your comprehensive slideshow along the left side of the Define Custom Show dialog box, ready for you to pick and choose which slides you want to add to your custom version. PowerPoint designates hidden slides with parentheses as you can see here on Slide 3.

4. **In the "Slide show name" box, type a name for your new custom slideshow.**

   Pick a short name that reminds you of either the content of the slideshow you're putting together, or the length (for example, *thirty_minute*). (In Figure 23-9, the custom slideshow's name is *food_and_fun*.) Instead of underlines between words, you can use spaces if you like.

5. **On the left side of the Define Custom Show dialog box, select the slide you want to add. Then click Add.**

   PowerPoint lists the slide in the "Slides in custom show" box on the right side of the dialog box. Repeat this step for each slide in the comprehensive slideshow that you want to add to your custom show.

Tip: To select multiple contiguous slides, click the first slide, and then Shift+click the last slide to select that slide plus all slides in between. To select multiple noncontiguous slides, click the first slide, then Ctrl+click each additional slide.

---

6. **If you like, you can change the order of the slides in your custom slideshow: in the "Slides in custom show" list, click the slide you want to reorder. Then press the Up or Down arrow to move the slide up or down in the custom show's organization (it doesn't affect their order in the actual presentation).**

   As you move each slide, PowerPoint renumbers all of the slides in your custom slideshow.

7. **When you're satisfied with your custom slideshow, click OK.**

   The Define Custom Show dialog box disappears, and the Custom Shows dialog box reappears with your new custom slideshow listed. You can test your custom slideshow at this point by clicking Show.

8. **Click Close to dismiss the Custom Show dialog box and return to normal editing mode.**

Editing a Custom Slideshow

Because a custom slideshow is nothing but a list of slides, you can't edit a custom slideshow's slide content directly. (To do that, you need to edit the content of the original slideshow's slides.) But you *can* add, delete, and reorder the slides that make up your custom slideshow.

To edit a custom slideshow:

1. **Go to Slide Show → Start Slide Show → Custom Slide Show → Custom Shows.**

   A list of custom shows appears.

2. **Click to select the name of the show you want to edit, and then choose one of the following options:**

- **Edit.** Lets you rename the custom show, and add, remove, and reorder slides.

- **Remove.** Deletes the custom slideshow.

- **Copy.** Copies the custom slideshow (good for creating additional versions that aren't too different from one you've selected).

3. **When you've finished editing your custom slideshow, click Close to dismiss the Custom Show dialog box and return to normal editing mode.**

FREQUENTLY ASKED QUESTION

The Poor Man's Custom Slideshow

All I want to do is show the first half of my slides. Do I have to go to all the trouble of setting up a custom slideshow just to do that?

If all you want to do is show the first half of your slideshow, the last half, or any other contiguous set of slides (for example, slides 4 through 22) in order, PowerPoint gives you a much quicker and easier option than creating a custom slideshow. Here's what you do:

1. Select Slide Show → Set Up → Set Up Slide Show.

2. In the Set Up Show dialog box that appears, head to the Show Slides section, turn on the From radio button, and then choose slide numbers in the From and To boxes.

3. Click OK to dismiss the Set Up Show dialog box. The next time you run your slideshow, PowerPoint will show only the specified slides.

Presenting Your Slideshow

The control you have when it comes time to present your slideshow depends on how you've chosen to set up your slideshow: as full-screen, browser, or kiosk mode (see page 534).

- **Full-screen mode.** Right-clicking your mouse while you're running a slideshow in full-screen mode kicks up a context menu that lets you choose how to present your slideshow, as you can see in Figure 23-10. But most folks find it quicker (and less distracting to the audience) to use the keyboard shortcuts described in Table 23-1. In addition, when you run a slideshow in full-screen mode, you see the ghosted controls shown back in Figure 23-2, and you can control your presentation with a remove control.

Tip: Even if you're not normally a keyboard shortcut fan, you may want to familiarize yourself with Table 23-1. That way, if you're in the middle of giving a presentation and you suddenly notice your slides racing by, for example, you'll know why (and what to do about it).

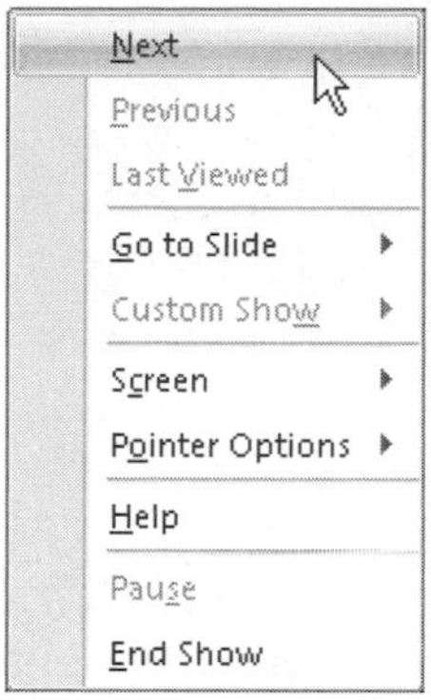

Figure 23-10:
Anything you can do with keyboard shortcuts, you can do with the context menu shown here. Trouble is, your audience has to sit through the menu selections, which may not do much for their concentration.

Next
Previous
Last Viewed

Go to Slide ▶
Custom Show ▶
Screen ▶
Pointer Options ▶
Help
Pause
End Show

Table 23-1. *Key Strokes for Navigating Your Slideshow*

To Do This	Press This
Go forward one slide	Enter, Space, Page Down, N, click, right-arrow, down-arrow
Back up one slide	Backspace, Page Up, P, left-arrow, up-arrow
Jump directly to a specific slide, even if it's hidden (page 537)	Type the slide number and then press Enter, or right-click the slide and, from the menu that appears, click the title of the slide you want to go to
Scroll back and forth through slides quickly	Roll the wheel on your mouse
Black out the presentation	B or . (period)
White out the presentation	W or , (comma)
End the slideshow	Esc or Ctrl+Break
Hide the cursor (pointer)	= (A to show pointer again)
Start drawing (annotating) electronically on a slide using your mouse or a graphics pen	Ctrl+P, then drag mouse (or stylus) to draw
Stop drawing and turn pen back into arrow pointer	Ctrl+A
Erase all the ink annotations on a slide	E
Pause a slideshow that's running automatically	S (Press S again or + to restart it)

- **Browser mode.** If you set up your slideshow to run in browser mode *and* told PowerPoint to show scroll bars (page 415), you can use the scroll bars in the browser window to scroll from slide to slide. Right-clicking shows a different context menu (shown in Figure 23-11) than the one that appears for full-screen presentations. Finally, only a few keyboard shortcuts work for browser-mode slideshows: Go forward one slide, Back up one slide, and End the slideshow (see Table 23-1) .

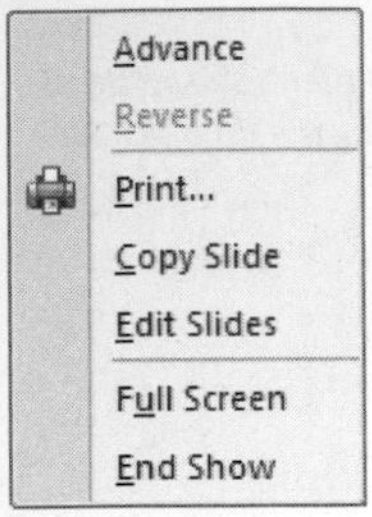

	Advance
	Reverse
🖶	Print...
	Copy Slide
	Edit Slides
	Full Screen
	End Show

Figure 23-11:
Right-clicking a slideshow set up to run in browser mode displays a different menu than the one that appears when you right-click a slideshow set up to run in full-screen mode.

- **Kiosk mode.** If you set up your slideshow to run in kiosk mode (page 536), no ghosted controls appear, and no right-click menu appears, either. What's more, none of the keyboard shortcuts shown in Table 23-1 work. Instead, you need to set up automatic timings (page 539) so that the slideshow runs through your slides automatically so that folks who stop by the kiosk can navigate your slideshow.

Creating PowerPoint Shows

A *PowerPoint show* is a version of your slideshow saved in a special format (.ppsx, .ppsm, or .pps) that folks who don't have PowerPoint installed on their computers can run. Instead, when you distribute a PowerPoint show—by burning it to CD, for example, by emailing it—all your recipients need to run your show is a copy of the *PowerPoint viewer*. The PowerPoint viewers is a freely downloadable Microsoft program that lets viewers run and print slideshows, but not edit them.

The difference between a slideshow saved as a PowerPoint show and the same slideshow saved as a PowerPoint presentation file is simply this: opening the show in PowerPoint or in the PowerPoint viewer runs it in slideshow mode; opening the presentation file in PowerPoint runs it in editing mode. Both shows and presentation files can be edited in PowerPoint.

Note: When you package your slideshow for CD, PowerPoint automatically throws in a copy of the free PowerPoint viewer so the recipient of your CD doesn't have to hunt one down herself. To run a slideshow that's on a CD, simply insert the disc into a computer's CD drive. Windows launches PowerPoint (or the PowerPoint viewer), and the show starts playing automatically.

To create a PowerPoint show:

1. **Choose Office button → Save As.**

   The Save As dialog box appears.

2. **From the "Save as type" drop-down menu, choose "PowerPoint Show(*.ppsx)".**

3. In the "File name" box, type the filename you want your file to have. In the "Save in" box, type the folder where you want to save your file. When you're done, click Save.

PowerPoint saves your show using the filename and folder you specified, and the Save As dialog box disappears.

Emailing Your Presentation

Thanks to PowerPoint 2007's new, more compact file formats, emailing presentation files is easier on your audience than ever. Emailing a presentation is especially easy if you have Outlook installed on your computer. You never have to leave the comfort of PowerPoint.

Note: If you don't have Outlook installed on your computer, you need to email your presentation the old-fashioned way. In your email program, create a new email message. Then fill in your recipients' email addresses, attach your presentation file (for example, myPresentation.pptx), and then send the email.

To email a presentation, make sure you've saved your presentation, and then choose Office button → Send → Email. Microsoft Outlook opens a blank email message with your presentation automatically attached. Customize the email message, type your recipients' email addresses, and click Send to send the message.

Packaging Presentations for CD

File-wise, creating a PowerPoint presentation can get messy fast. You've got your presentation file itself, of course, but depending on which elements and effects you've added to your slides, your presentation file may depend on additional files containing fonts, audio and clips, images, linked content, and so on. And if you've ever tried to make a quick copy of a presentation (for example, on your way out the door to catch a plane) you know how frustratingly hard this theoretically easy task is to pull off in reality.

Fortunately, PowerPoint can automate the process. When you package your presentation for CD, you tell PowerPoint to gather up all of the files you need to run your slideshow (complete with a copy of the PowerPoint viewer, if you like, to make sure they have everything they need to run the slideshow) and stick them in a single folder, which you can then store on your computer or, if you happen to have a CD burner connected to your computer, copy directly to disk.

Note: You can save more than one presentation to a CD (or to a named file). If you do, PowerPoint lets you specify what order you want your presentations to run in (see step 5 on page 549).

If you've created additional files such as supporting documentation, electronic brochures, or text scripts, you can tell PowerPoint to add them to the package, too. Supporting documentation helps offset the fact that your audience (and not you) will be running the slideshow. For example, if your slideshow is a tutorial, you can include self-tests, answer keys, instructional drawings, a bibliography, or anything else you want students to be able to refer to after they've worked through the tutorial.

To package a presentation for CD:

1. **Office button → Publish → Package for CD.**

   A Package for CD dialog box similar to Figure 23-12 appears.

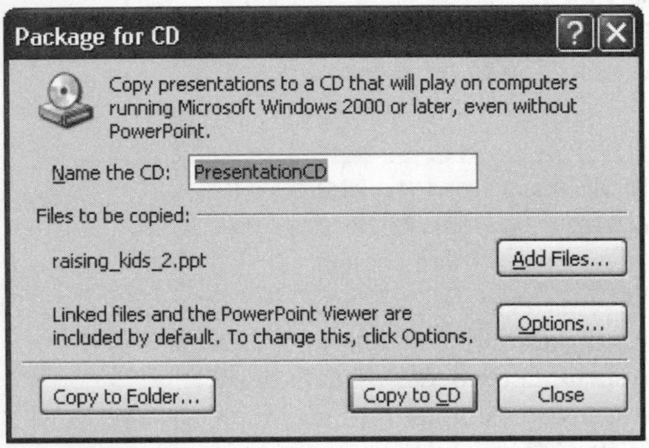

Figure 23-12:
The Package for CD option is a bit of a misnomer. Yes, you can use it to gather up all your presentation-related files and burn them to a CD—but you can also use it to organize the files in a single folder, an option you may find useful if you're hooked up to a network. Clicking Options displays the dialog box in Figure 23-13.

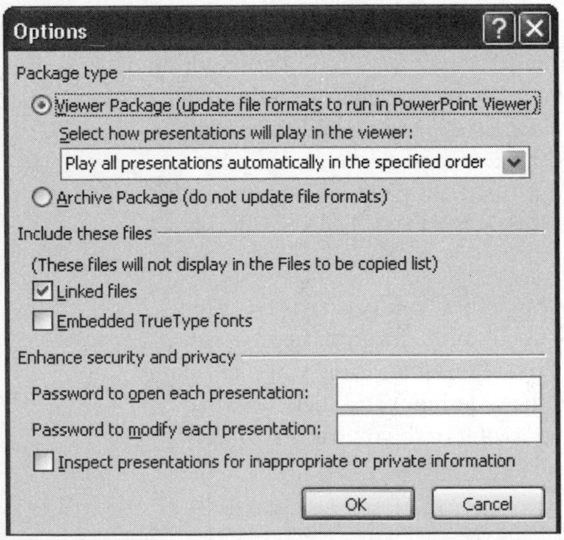

Figure 23-13:
Here's where you customize the way your audience runs your packaged presentation.

2. **In the Name the CD box, type the name you want to give your CD (or, if you're not planning to burn a CD, the name you want to give your presentation's file folder).**

   Your audience will see this name, so make sure it's both meaningful and appropriate.

3. **If you have supporting files you'd like to add to your CD (or to your folder), click Add Files. In the "File name" box, type the name of the file you want to add (or browse your computer to find the file). Then click Add.**

   The Add Files dialog box disappears, and PowerPoint adds the file to the list of things to burn to your CD.

4. **To tell PowerPoint how you want your audience to run your packaged presentation, click Options.**

   The Options dialog box opens (Figure 23-13).

5. **Turn on the Viewer Package radio button.**

   This popular option tells PowerPoint to include a copy of the PowerPoint viewer in your package, as well as an executable file that launches the viewer preloaded with your presentation as soon as your audience inserts the CD.

   If you choose this option, PowerPoint also lets you click the down arrow next to "Select how presentations will play in the viewer" and choose one of the following: "Play all presentations automatically in the specified order," "Play only the first presentation automatically," "Let the user select which presentation to view," or "Don't play the CD automatically."

   When you've finished setting options, click OK to close the Options dialog box.

6. **In the Package for CD dialog box, choose one of the following:**

   - **Copy to CD.** Choose this option if you want to copy your presentation files to a CD. Obviously, this option doesn't work unless you have a CD burner attached to your computer.

   - **Copy to Folder.** Choose this option if you want to copy your presentation files to a named folder on your own computer, or to a computer on your network.

   PowerPoint pops up a dialog box that lets you type in a name for your folder, as well as where on your computer (or network) you want to store it.

7. **Click Close.**

   PowerPoint saves your presentation to disk or to your computer.

CHAPTER 24

Printing Presentations

Most of the time, you'll deliver your PowerPoint presentations electronically, on a computer or digital projector. So with all these high-tech bits-and-bytes options, why on earth would you print your slides?

Here are three cool things you can do with printed slides:

- **Create a foolproof, fail-safe backup.** Printouts may not look as glamorous as full-color, widescreen slideshows, but they're invaluable when you have a technology meltdown. So when you reach your client's office with three minutes to spare and discover that your preschooler poured maple syrup into your laptop when you weren't looking, you at least have hard copies to work from.

- **Run off quick-and-dirty handouts.** For really useful audience handouts, you'll probably want to create separate supporting materials, as described on page 557. But to give your boss a quick outline of your presentation, printouts are the way to go.

- **Deliver your presentation in low-tech but effective ways like overhead transparencies.** You can't always control your presentation environment. For example, if you're in a location where an old overhead projector is all that's available, you can turn your presentation into overheads.

In addition to printing your slides, for some presentations you may want to print related materials like speaker notes for moral support behind the podium; a presentation outline, for double-checking that you've included all your important points; and even tent cards, for making your audience feel welcome. Another reason you might want to print a slide is because you've created a layout meant to be printed, such as an award certificate or a calendar. (See page 495 for the scoop on using Microsoft's own slide designs to create these and more printable layouts.)

Printing Slides (One Slide per Page)

The most straightforward to way to print your presentation is to print each individual slide on a separate piece of paper. You can keep paper printouts in a file, bring them with you to the presentation as a failsafe, or use them to practice your spiel or proof your slides (some errors are easier to spot in plain black and white).

When you commit your slides to paper, you have a few extra decisions to make. For example, onscreen slides don't usually have a footer with a page number and date, but that kind of information is mighty handy on a hard copy. You can also choose exactly which slides to print, whether to print in black and white or color, and more. The following tutorial walks you through all your options.

Tip: A super-fast way to print one slide per page is to select Office button → Print → Quick Print. But because choosing this option tells PowerPoint to begin printing immediately—without giving you a chance to inspect or change your print settings—you probably don't want to use it unless you've printed your presentation at least once following the steps in this section.

To print your slides:

1. **Choose Office button → Print → Print Preview.**

   The Print Preview tab (Figure 24-1) appears, along with a preview of your first slide. As you mouse over the preview, your cursor turns into a magnifying glass bearing either a plus sign (+), which tells PowerPoint to zoom in when you click, or a minus sign (−), which tells PowerPoint to zoom out when you click.

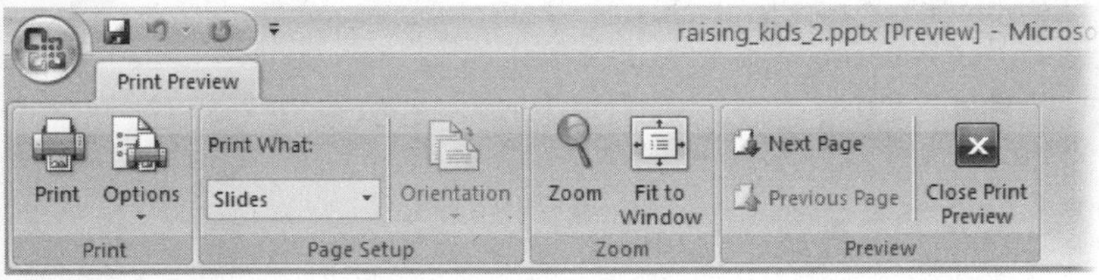

Figure 24-1:
Out of the box, PowerPoint assumes you want to print your presentation one slide per page, so that's what you get if you click the printer icon. But because printing a presentation is a time-consuming proposition, you'll want to set a few options before you actually tell PowerPoint to start printing.

2. **Make sure the word Slides appears in the Print What box.**

   If it doesn't, click the drop-down arrow next to Print What and, from the list of options that appears, choose Slides.

3. **Click Options → Header and Footer.**

   The Header and Footer dialog box (Figure 24-2) appears.

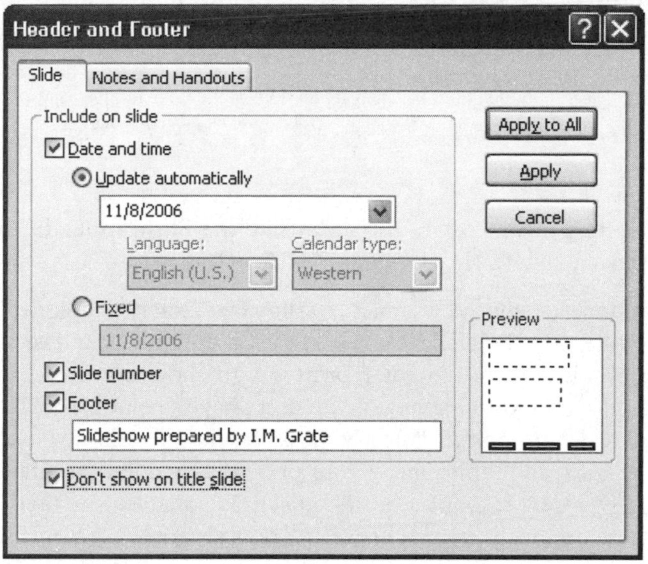

Figure 24-2:
As you turn on the checkboxes next to Date and Time, Slide Number, or Footer, PowerPoint adjusts the thumbnail in the Preview section to let you know where it intends to put each footer element: left, center, or right. Here, the checkboxes next to all three elements are turned on, so all three footer elements in the Preview area appear black. Turning off an element grays out its position in the Preview.

4. **Check to make sure the Slide tab is selected; if it isn't, click to select it.**

    This tab lets you set a host of printing options:

    • If you want to add a date, timestamp, or both to your footer, then turn on the checkbox next to Date and Time. Then choose either Update automatically (to tell PowerPoint to adjust the date or time so that it always matches today's, in which case you need to choose a date-and-time format from the drop-down list shown in Figure 24-2) or Fixed (in which case you need to type the fixed text you want PowerPoint to add to your footer).

    • If you want to add a consecutively numbered page number (beginning with 1) to the footer that appears on each page of your printout, then turn on the checkbox next to Slide number.

Tip: If you want to number your slides starting not from 1 but from, say, 21 (perhaps you're responsible for the second half of a 40-page presentation), click Close Print Preview to return to your presentation, and then choose Design → Page Setup → Page Setup. When the Page Setup dialog box opens, enter *21* in the "Number slides from" box.

    • If you want to add text to your footer, turn on the Footer checkbox and then, in the text box, type in the text you want to appear at the bottom of each page of your printout.

    • If you don't want your footer to appear on the first page of your presentation (most folks don't, because the first page usually contains the title of their presentation and nothing more), then turn on the checkbox next to "Don't show on title slide."

After you've chosen your settings, click Apply to All to tell PowerPoint to add your footer to each page of your document.

Tip: You can reformat your header and footer text by changing the font of the page number, say, or the color of the date. To do so, you need to edit your presentation's *Slide master*, which you learn all about in Chapter 21.

---

5. **To choose whether to print in color, grayscale (like the illustrations in this book), or plain black and white, click Options → Color/Grayscale.**

   From the list that appears, choose one of the following: Color, Grayscale, or Pure Black and White. As you click, you can see each option in the Preview pane. Choose Color when you need color printouts to show in public (this option uses a lot of ink). Choose Grayscale if you don't have a color printer, but want your printed slides to look as much as possible like they do in Power-Point. Choose Pure Black and White only if your presentation doesn't contain a lot of graphics and you want to print it out as quickly as possible. (See the box on page 556 for more on the differences between Grayscale and Pure Black and White.)

6. **Choose one or more of the following options, which determine how the slide appears on the page:**

   - **Options → Scale to Fit Paper.** Tells PowerPoint to stretch the content of your slide, leaving the tiniest of margins on all sides.

   - **Options → Frame Slides.** Tells PowerPoint to draw a thin black line around the content of each slide.

   - **Options → Print Hidden Slides.** Tells PowerPoint to print any slides you've previously earmarked as hidden (page 537). PowerPoint doesn't activate this option if your slideshow doesn't contain any hidden slides.

7. **Click Next Page and Previous Page to scroll through the preview of your presentation and make sure everything looks good.**

   Alternatively, you can use the scroll bars that appear in the Preview area to scroll through each slide. You want to make sure your slideshow looks good—right down to the headers, footers, and margins—*before* you've spent half an hour (and half an ink cartridge) printing it.

8. **If you spot a problem, then click Close Print Preview.**

   The Print Preview tab disappears, and you return to the main ribbon. Make any changes you want, and then choose Office button → Print → Print Preview. Repeat steps 2 through 8 until you're satisfied with how your presentation looks in preview mode.

9. **When you're ready to print, click the Print icon.**

   The Print dialog box you see in Figure 24-3 appears.

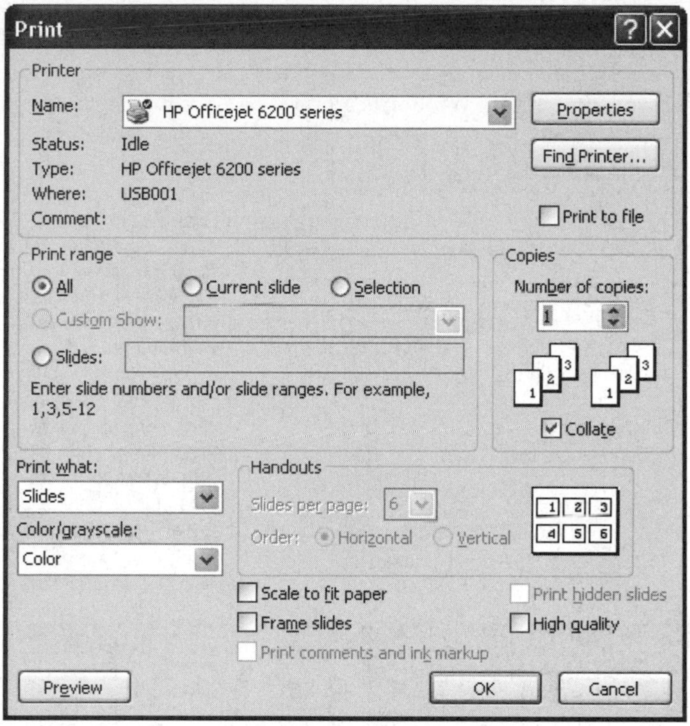

Figure 24-3:
Most of the options you see here are options you've already set in the Print Preview ribbon. (When you set them in the Print Preview ribbon, PowerPoint carries them over to this dialog box.) Two options that you do want to set (or double-check) here: which pages you want to print, and how many copies you want to print.

10. **Tell PowerPoint which pages you want to print by choosing one of the following options:**

   • **All.** Prints every page of your presentation. PowerPoint assumes you want this option, unless you tell it differently.

   • **Current slide.** Prints only the currently selected slide.

   • **Selection.** Prints a range of selected slides. PowerPoint doesn't activate this option until you select multiple slides in the Slides pane (see page 486).

   • **Custom show.** Prints a named subset of your slideshow called a custom show. To see how to create a custom show, flip back to page 541.

   • **Slides.** Lets you specify a print range, which may be contiguous (1–12) or noncontiguous (1, 2, 5, 6).

11. **Tell PowerPoint how many copies of your presentation you want to print in the "Number of copies" box.**

   If you want just one copy, then you can skip this step: PowerPoint assumes you want to print one copy unless you tell it differently.

12. **Click OK to print your presentation.**

The Print dialog box disappears, and PowerPoint sends your presentation to the printer. At the bottom of the PowerPoint interface you see the print status (Figure 24-4). If you notice that your presentation isn't printing the way you want, click the X icon to cancel printing.

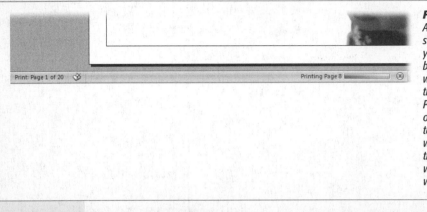

Figure 24-4:
After you click Print, a status bar appears to let you know PowerPoint's busy gearing up to print—which is a really a good thing, because printing a PowerPoint presentation of any length typically takes so long that, without feedback from the status bar, you might wonder if something was wrong.

UP TO SPEED

When to Go Gray

PowerPoint gives you three choices when it comes to printing your presentation: color, grayscale, and in pure black and white.

Here's when (and why) you would choose each:

- **Color.** If you have a color printer and you don't expect to make black-and-white copies of your printout—you're printing overhead transparencies, for example—you'll want to print in color. This option is the only one that prints slide backgrounds.

- **Grayscale.** If you don't have a color printer, or just want to print some inexpensive black-and-white handouts, then choose Grayscale. In this mode, PowerPoint prints graphic portions of your slides that it won't print in pure black and white. The quality of the images is like the black-and-white photographs in a newspaper.

- **Pure Black and White.** If you don't have a color printer, your presentation doesn't contain a lot of graphics (fills, patterns, shadows, backgrounds, and

so on), and you want to speed up the printing process, Pure Black and White is the way to go. When you print using this option, graphic fills and patterns won't appear in your printouts, and any shadow effects you've applied to non-text objects appear pitch black.

Keep in mind that unless you print in color, your slide backgrounds, background images, and text shadow effects *won't* appear in your printouts.

And finally, if you're still trying to decide between the grayscale and black-and-white, head back to your presentation proper and experiment with the many subtle shading variations PowerPoint offers, and *then* print your slides. Go to View → Color/Grayscale and choose either Grayscale or Pure Black and White. Doing so pops up either the Grayscale or Black and White tab, where you can select (and preview) several shading options.

Printer Problems

If you've printed a presentation from your computer using an earlier version of PowerPoint, then chances are you won't have any problems printing in PowerPoint 2007. But if this is your first time using PowerPoint 2007, you might run into a couple of snags. Here's what to look for:

- **You're trying to print to the wrong printer.** If you've ever had more than one printer hooked up to your computer, PowerPoint may be trying to print to the wrong one—even one that's no longer hooked up to your computer. To choose the right printer, in the Print dialog box, click the down arrow next to Name and then, from the drop-down menu that appears, choose the right printer. (If you don't see the name of the printer you're trying to print to, see the next point.)

- **PowerPoint doesn't know about your printer.** If you've hooked up a new printer recently, PowerPoint might not be aware of it. If you don't see the

name of your printer in the Name drop-down box, click Find Printer and follow the instructions that appear.

- **You've set options in your printing software that PowerPoint can't override.** Most printers let you set options, such as print quality, that PowerPoint can't override. To see these options, click Properties. (The dialog box that appears—and the printer options you can and can't override—depend on your printer's particular make and model.)

- **You've set options in the PowerPoint Options dialog box that override the options you set in the Print dialog box.** Choosing Office button → PowerPoint Options and clicking Advanced lets you set printing options (such as whether you want to print slides or handouts, color or grayscale) that PowerPoint uses to print your presentation no matter what you've set in the Print dialog box.

Handouts (Multiple Slides per Page)

In PowerPoint-ese, a *handout* is a printout designed to accompany your presentation. There are two major differences between printing handouts and printing slides: You can only print slides one per page, but you can print handouts anywhere from *one to nine* slides per page. Also, when you print handouts (even one slide per page), PowerPoint automatically adds a basic header and footer and leaves good-sized margins for note taking.

Theoretically, your audience can jot down notes on their handouts during your presentation and be left with useful information they can refer to days or weeks afterward. The problem with this theory is that most slides make terrible handouts—for two reasons:

- **Good slides are brief; good handouts aren't.** To be effective, the text on your slides needs to be brief, concise, and compelling. For example, short sentences that either ask questions or make controversial statements (which you, of course, answer or explain during your presentation). The same text on a handout, on the other hand, is only going to confuse the audience a week later.

- **Good slides are colorful; good handouts aren't.** Light-colored text on a nice dark background with a couple of tasteful graphics thrown in for good measure looks great onscreen. The same slide printed in black and white isn't going to look good at all—in fact, the background won't even print. And it goes without saying that any animated effects, sound clips, and interactive links that you've added to your slides aren't going to translate to printed form.

The best handouts provide detailed, lengthy, or dense background information that supports your slides—testimonials, reports, charts, graphics, and so on. Thus, creating really useful handouts is a lot harder than simply selecting a print option and then clicking Print. You have to double your efforts by creating handout material from scratch, most likely in another program like Microsoft Word. Power-Point lets you jump-start this process by selecting Office button → Publish → Create Handouts in Microsoft Office Word. Whether the results are worth the extra effort, only you—the presenter—can say.

On the other hand, when you're in a hurry, PowerPoint's quick-and-dirty version of handouts may be better than none at all.

Tip: One use for PowerPoint handouts that's often overlooked is as a practice aid. With multiple-slides-to-a-page handouts in front of you, you can easily practice your presentation on an airplane, on a bus, or even in a staff meeting—no laptop necessary.

To print handouts:

1. **Choose Office button → Print → Print Preview.**

   The Print Preview ribbon appears.

2. **In the "Print what" box, choose one of the following: Handouts (1 slide per page), Handouts (2 slides per page), and so on, all the way up to Handouts (9 slides per page).**

   A preview of your handout's configuration appears in the Preview area. Figure 24-5 shows an example.

3. **You can switch the orientation of your handout pages from Landscape to Portrait (or vice versa) by heading to the Print Preview tab and clicking Options → Portrait or Options → Landscape.**

   If you've chosen to print six slides per page or more, then you can tell Power-Point whether you want it to arrange the slides in horizontal rows or vertical columns. To do so, click Options → Printing Order and then choose either Horizontal or Vertical.

4. **You can change any of several other print settings explained beginning on page 552. When you're ready to print, click the Print icon.**

   The Print dialog box appears.

5. **Tell PowerPoint how many copies of your handout you want to print, and then click OK.**

   The Print dialog box disappears, and PowerPoint sends your presentation to the printer.

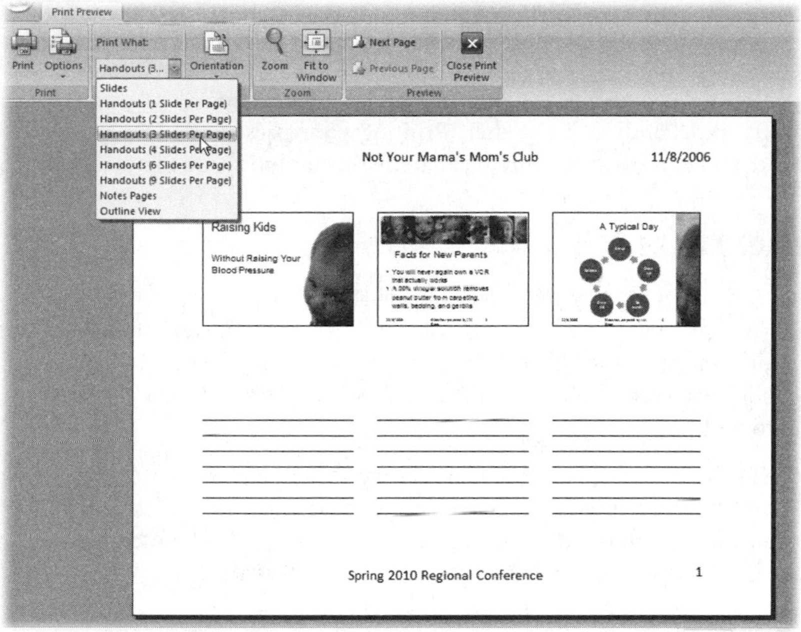

Figure 24-5:
The good thing about choosing to print three pages per slide is that PowerPoint gives you lines for note taking. (You get extra room on the page with other options, but no lines.) Notice that PowerPoint assumes you want your handouts to include page numbers. You can delete the page numbers by selecting Options → Header and Footer, clicking the Slide tab, and turning off the radio button next to Slide number.

Overhead Transparencies

Overhead transparencies, also known as *foils* or just plain *overheads*, are see-through sheets of plastic you slap onto an overhead projector. In the old, pre-PowerPoint days, overheads (and chalkboards) were the only means folks had to deliver presentations. But even today, with PowerPoint 2007 at your disposal, you may have occasion to print your presentation onto overheads.

For example, imagine you're on a plane, headed for the most important presentation of your entire career. You're settling into a taxi when you discover you left your laptop in the airport terminal. When you get to the conference center, there's not enough time to get your office to email a copy of the presentation and then wrestle it onto an unfamiliar computer. If the conference center has an overhead projector (most do) and you've got a stack of overheads in your briefcase, you're golden.

Printing out overheads isn't a lot of extra work. It involves the same steps you take to create a regular printout, with the following exceptions:

• **Replace the paper in your printer with a stack of overhead transparencies, available at any office supply store.** (You don't need a special printer or special ink.)

• **Consider printing your presentation on paper first to make sure it looks exactly the way you want it to.** It's often easier to spot goofs on paper printouts than onscreen.

- **If your slides have colored backgrounds, consider printing grayscale or black-and-white (page 556) versions.** Doing so leaves white space you'll appreciate if you tend to draw or jot notes on your transparencies while you're presenting.

- **If you're the one feeding the printer, watch it like a hawk. Transparencies tend to shift, slide, and stick together.** Printing your presentation in two or three batches makes it easier for you to catch missing and misprinted overheads.

Speaker Notes

Speaker notes, as you may recall from page 418, are notes you can attach to any slide of your presentation to remind yourself of things you want to say but don't want your audience to read, like "Remember to tell the joke about the priest, the rabbi, and the lawyer before you start this slide" or "Haul out the flip chart when you get to bullet #2."

Chapter 23 shows how you can set up an extra computer screen to display your speaker notes while you're running your presentation from your main computer (page 538). But in most cases, simply printing your speaker notes and keeping them with you while you give your presentation is sufficient.

To print speaker notes:

1. **Choose Office button → Print → Print Preview.**

   The Print Preview ribbon appears.

2. **From the Print What drop-down menu, choose Notes Pages.**

   The Notes pages you've attached to your slides appear in the Preview area (Figure 24-6).

Tip: If you'd like to add a header or footer before you print, check out page 499.

---

3. **To double-check your speaker notes, click Next Page and Previous Page (or use the scroll bars that appear next to the Preview area to flip through your notes pages).**

4. **When you're satisfied, click Print.**

   The Print dialog box appears. For help in setting Print options, such as choosing which pages to print or how many copies to print, head to page 552.

5. **Click OK.**

   PowerPoint prints your speaker notes.

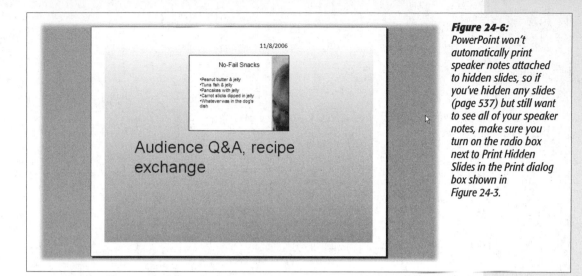

Figure 24-6:
*PowerPoint won't
automatically print
speaker notes attached
to hidden slides, so if
you've hidden any slides
(page 537) but still want
to see all of your speaker
notes, make sure you
turn on the radio box
next to Print Hidden
Slides in the Print dialog
box shown in
Figure 24-3.*

Presentation Outline

Printing an outline version of your presentation is useful for the same reason as examining your presentation in Outline view (Figure 24-7) is: It pares away all the formatting and lets you focus on the organization of your content, which is the heart of any good presentation. You might want to print an outline as a proofing tool, to help you double-check that you've included all the material you wanted to include. But you can also use a printed outline as a hard-copy backup of your presentation and even (in a pinch) as an audience handout.

To print an outline of your presentation, choose Office button → Print → Print Preview. From the "Print what" drop-down menu, choose Outline View (see Figure 24-7), and then follow the steps on page 552 to send your outline to the printer.

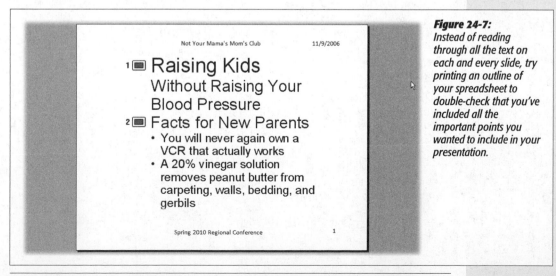

Figure 24-7:
*Instead of reading
through all the text on
each and every slide, try
printing an outline of
your spreadsheet to
double-check that you've
included all the
important points you
wanted to include in your
presentation.*

Images and Transitions

PowerPoint would have disappeared long ago if all you could do with it was slap bullet points on a screen. Drawings, photographs, and other pictures add meaning, sophistication, and polish to your slideshow. They also serve as powerful visual cues to help your audience understand a point, or recall something you've previously said. They can also tie a slideshow together (when you use similar design elements on each slide), and even help with branding (think logo in the corner of every single slide).

It's not surprising, then, that PowerPoint lets you add all manner of visual elements to your slides. You can use everything from simple graphics you draw right on a slide, to photographs and images created in another program, to the free clip art that comes with PowerPoint. This chapter shows you how to get drawings and pictures onto your slides.

You'll also learn how to add transitions from one slide to the next. If you're a movie buff, you're familiar with scene transitions such as jump cuts, dissolves, and tasteful fades. PowerPoint gives you lots of transitions to choose from, and this chapter shows you how to apply them to your slideshow.

Note: In addition to graphics, PowerPoint lets you add sound files to your slides-like music, sound effects, or your own voice-over narration. You can even put videos on slides. When you're ready to take on multimedia slides, consult a book like *PowerPoint 2007: The Missing Manual*, which also teaches you how to modify drawings and pictures.

When to Use a Graphic

Whether it's clip art, a scanned photo, a picture you drew yourself, or any other artwork, the images you add to your slides need to do more than just take up space. They need contribute to the overall message you're conveying.

Here are a few tips for making sure images carry their weight:

- **Use images to reduce slide text.** Instead of describing stuff with words, think visually and see if you can make your point with a picture. For example, instead of listing the countries where your company does business, display a map of the world with your countries shown in bright yellow. Instead of spelling out in text that you've developed a new product or hired a new employee, consider using a picture of the product or employee.

- **Use images for emphasis.** To a chart or diagram, add text on a shape like an arrow, callout, or simple rectangle to indicate the point you're trying to make.

- **Use specific, relevant images.** Don't pepper your slideshow with stock graphics like clocks, generic machinery, or employees in business suits. They add neither interest nor meaning, and after the third or fourth one, your audience will wonder if the rest of your presentation is canned, too.

- **Use images sparingly.** Humans tend to value what's scarce. Cram a bunch of images onto every slide in your presentation, and your audience is going to start ignoring them. Add one or two, and they'll catch your audience's attention.

Drawing on Slides

The Internet's filled with photos and art you can use in presentations but sometimes you need a picture that's so specific you need to sketch it yourself. Imagine you're a defense attorney building a PowerPoint slideshow to present at trial, and you want to describe the route your client took from his desk to the bank vault. You can use stock images of desks, customers, and the bank vault, but you need to draw your own arrows to show your client's route.

Or say you're giving a presentation to management that explains why your department is over budget. You've created a chart (which you learned how to do in Chapter 22) that clearly shows the problem, but your audience (management, remember), needs things spelled out more clearly. You can use PowerPoint's drawing tools to place a big red circle around the negative total. And, right where the chart shows your department's performance taking a nosedive in October, draw a cartoon balloon with the words "Plant #2 burned down 10/15."

If you're artistically challenged, don't worry. There's very little you have to draw freehand in PowerPoint (although you can if you want to). PowerPoint 2007 gives you special tools for drawing lines, curves, and some 80-odd standard shapes including banners, stars, flowchart symbols, and arrows (Figure 25-1). You can also add built-in visual effects—like gradients, shadows, and reflections—to your drawings, and connect shapes with special lines called *connectors* that adjust themselves automatically when you reposition the shapes they're connected to.

Note: The kinds of things you can draw haven't changed in PowerPoint 2007, but the way you draw them has. The shape gallery in PowerPoint 2007 replaces the AutoShapes toolbar that appeared in PowerPoint 2003 and earlier versions of the program.

Drawing Lines and Shapes

Drawing in PowerPoint means choosing what you want to draw from a gallery of lines and shapes and then dragging them over your slide.

1. **Click Insert → Illustrations → Shapes.**

   PowerPoint displays the shape gallery (Figure 25-1).

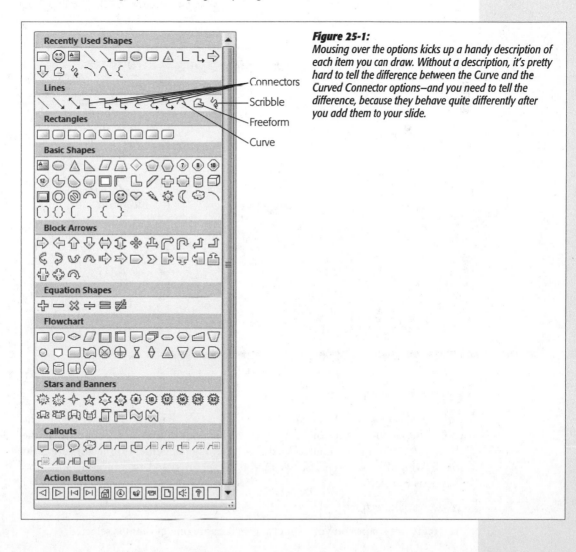

Figure 25-1:
Mousing over the options kicks up a handy description of each item you can draw. Without a description, it's pretty hard to tell the difference between the Curve and the Curved Connector options—and you need to tell the difference, because they behave quite differently after you add them to your slide.

2. **Click one of the line or shape options to select it and then move the mouse over your slide.**

   Your cursor turns into a giant + sign to let you know you can begin drawing.

3. **Click your slide where you want to begin drawing, and then drag your cursor. Let go of your mouse when your line or shape is the size you want it to be.**

   If you're drawing a curvy line, click where you want your line to curve, and then click again where you want your curved line to end. Keep clicking different parts of your slide to create a long curvy line. When you're finished drawing, press Esc.

   PowerPoint adds the line or shape to your slide (see Figure 25-2). The Drawing Tools | Format tab appears.

Figure 25-2:
PowerPoint's shape gallery lets you embellish your slides with everything from straight lines and curves to basic shapes, such as this circle/slash. Most of the time, lines and shapes aren't enough and you'll need to add text as shown here.

Drawing Connectors

Connectors are special lines you draw between two shapes to connect them. The cool thing about connectors is that when you reposition one (or both) of the shapes, PowerPoint automatically adjusts the connecting line. Connectors are great for drawings like flow charts, where you frequently need to add and reposition shapes as you work.

To draw a connector:

1. **Create two shapes on your slide, and make sure one of them is selected.**

2. Click Drawing Tools | Format → Illustrations → Shapes and choose a connector.

3. Move your mouse over the first shape.

The cursor turns into a big plus sign, and tiny red connection squares appear around the edge of your shape (Figure 25-3).

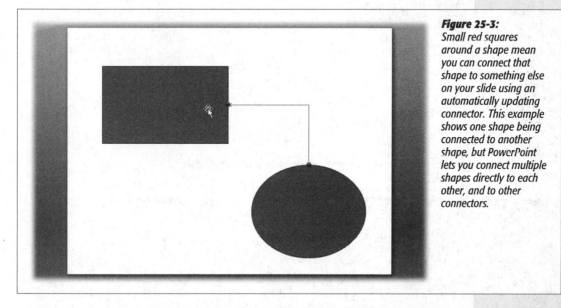

Figure 25-3:
Small red squares around a shape mean you can connect that shape to something else on your slide using an automatically updating connector. This example shows one shape being connected to another shape, but PowerPoint lets you connect multiple shapes directly to each other, and to other connectors.

4. Click one of the red connection squares on the first shape and drag toward the second shape.

PowerPoint displays red connection squares around the edge of your second shape.

5. When your cursor's over one of the red connection squares at the edge of your second shape, let go of the mouse button.

One red connector dot appears on each shape (Figure 25-4) to show where you've connected them.

You can tell PowerPoint to redraw, or *reroute*, an existing connector so it looks better. (Sometimes dragging the connected shapes around leaves the connector looking cramped or oddly bent.) To reroute a connector, select it and then, from the Drawing Tools | Format tab, choose Edit Shape → Reroute Connectors.

If you're still not happy with the way PowerPoint reroutes your connector, you can do it yourself. To move the connection from, say, the top of a shape to the bottom of the shape, click the connector and move it until the end of the connector snaps to the red connector square at the bottom of the shape.

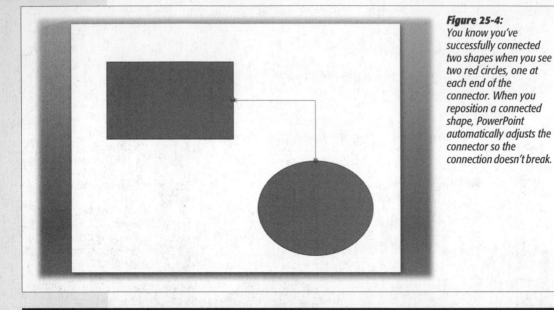

Figure 25-4:
You know you've successfully connected two shapes when you see two red circles, one at each end of the connector. When you reposition a connected shape, PowerPoint automatically adjusts the connector so the connection doesn't break.

GEM IN THE ROUGH

Tips for Faster Drawing

Using a computer program to draw anything more complicated than a quick callout or arrow can be tedious, no matter which program you're using—and PowerPoint is no exception. PowerPoint includes some shortcuts for faster, easier drawing, but it doesn't make them obvious.

So here they are, in no particular order:

- **Force perfection.** Pressing Shift while you draw a line or shape tells PowerPoint to force a line into a perfectly straight 45-degree angle, an oval into a perfect circle, a rectangle into a perfect square, and so on.

- **Draw more than one line or shape in a row (without having to reselect it over and over again).** After you finish drawing a line or shape, PowerPoint turns your cursor from a drawing instrument (+ sign) back into a regular point-and-click cursor (arrow). But to save some time, you can draw multiple lines or shapes without having to reclick the option every time: First, in the shape gallery, click the shape you want to draw. Then right-click that

shape and choose Lock Drawing Mode. Now you can draw as many shapes as you like, one right after the other. Choose another shape (or any other ribbon option) to revert back to normal, one-at-a-time drawing mode.

- **Tweak shapes instead of redrawing them.** When you add a shape to your slide, one or more tiny yellow diamonds usually appear along the shape's outline. To distort the shape—to make the arrow shape just a little pointier, for example, or to turn the smiley face into a frowny face—click one of the diamonds and drag.

- **Draw shapes from the center out (instead of from side to side).** Normally, when you add a shape to your slide and drag your cursor to resize it, PowerPoint draws the shape from left to right. But when you're trying to center your shapes along, say, a vertical line, press Ctrl as you drag. The Ctrl key tells PowerPoint to draw the shape starting at its center and extend equally on both sides.

Adding Pictures from Other Programs

Instead of drawing your own image directly onto your slide, as described on page 564, you can insert a scanned photo, digital picture, professionally drawn sketch, one of the stock images that come with Microsoft Office, or any other image you have stored on your computer.

The upside of using a canned picture, of course, is that it's easier than rolling your own. And depending on your artistic skills, the results could be more professional looking, too. The downside is that some folks are tempted to fill their presentations with generic images—dollar signs, handshakes, spinning globes, and so on—just because they have access to them. (See the box on page 572 for details.)

In this section, you see how to spice up your presentation with image files from your computer as well as from Microsoft Office's cache of free clip art. You also see how to create a super-quick slideshow consisting of nothing but captioned images called, appropriately enough, a photo album.

Inserting a Picture Stored on Your Computer

You can insert virtually any image file into your slideshow, from the common .jpg, .bmp, and .gif file formats to the less-well-known .cgm and .emz formats. The following steps walk you through the process:

1. **In the Slides tab in Normal view, select the slide to which you want to add an image.**

2. **Click Insert.**

   The Insert tab shown in Figure 25-5 appears.

Tip: If you applied a content layout to your slide, then clicking the picture icon (Figure 25-6) displayed in the center of the slide automatically shows you the Insert Picture dialog box.

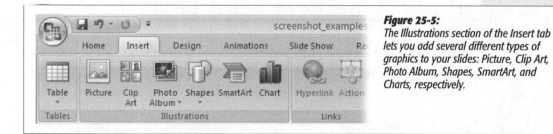

Figure 25-5:
The Illustrations section of the Insert tab lets you add several different types of graphics to your slides: Picture, Clip Art, Photo Album, Shapes, SmartArt, and Charts, respectively.

Figure 25-6:
Content layouts, including Title and Content, Picture with Caption, and Comparison, come complete with clickable icons you can use to add pictures to your slide quickly, without having to click around on tabs.

---

3. **From the Illustrations section of the Insert tabs, choose Picture.**

   The Insert Picture dialog box (Figure 25-7) appears.

4. **Browse your computer for the file you want to add to your slide by clicking the "Look in" drop-down box, or the icons listed on the left side of the Insert Picture dialog box. When the name of your file appears in the center of the dialog box, click it to select it.**

   PowerPoint places the name of your file in the File name box.

5. **Click Insert.**

   PowerPoint inserts the selected file onto your slide, and the Picture Tools | Format tab appears. Use the Picture Tools | Format Tab to do things like crop and resize your images.

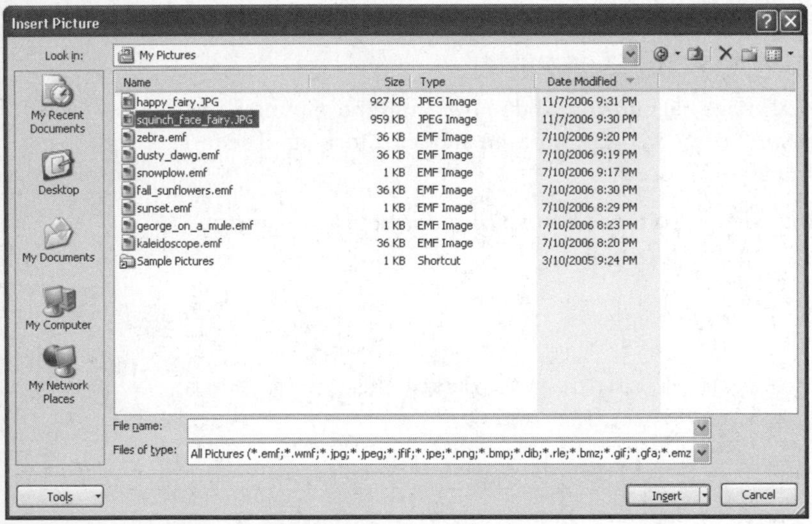

Figure 25-7:
The Insert Picture dialog box is similar to just about every other dialog box PowerPoint uses to let you add non-PowerPoint files to a PowerPoint presentation. PowerPoint recognizes almost any imaginable type of image file, including the popular ones (JPEG, GIF, and TIFF), and many you've never heard of.

Adding Built-in Clip Art Drawings

When you install PowerPoint 2007 or any other Microsoft Office program, you automatically install a pile of free, built-in drawings you can add to your slide-shows. Although some of the drawings are pretty cheesy, Microsoft maintains a large and growing online library of clip art drawings and photos (and animation and sound clips, too), some of which look downright sophisticated.

To add clip art to a slide:

1. **In the Slide tab in Normal view, select the slide you want to add clip art to. Then choose Insert → Illustrations → Clip Art.**

   The Clip Art pane you see in Figure 25-8 appears.

Finding the Perfect Clip Art

Using the Clip Art panel to find just the right piece of clip art for your slideshow can be a challenge. Here are a few tips that should help:

- **Look in all the right places.** If a basic search (for *nature* or *industry*, for example) doesn't bring back any thumbnails, click the down-arrow next to "Search in" and make sure the checkboxes next to all of the possible collections (file folders) are turned on.

- **Filter out animation and sound clips.** When you're looking for clip art, it's frustrating to get a bunch of search results—only to find they're all sound clips. To confine your searches to images, click the down-arrow next to "Results should be" and make sure the checkboxes next to "Clip Art" and "Photographs" are turned *on* (and that the checkboxes next to "Movies" and" Sounds" are turned *off*).

- **Look online.** If you've searched for clip art and come up empty-handed, click the "Clip art on Office Online," which whisks you to Microsoft's growing online library of clip art.

- **Add your own images.** If you've got your own drawings, photographs, or other image files already stored on your computer, you can add them to the Clip Art Organizer (a fancy name for "file folder") so you can use them the next time you go looking for clip art. Here's how: Click the "Organize clips" link you find at the bottom of the Clip Art pane and then, from the dialog box that appears, choose File → Add Clips to Organizer.

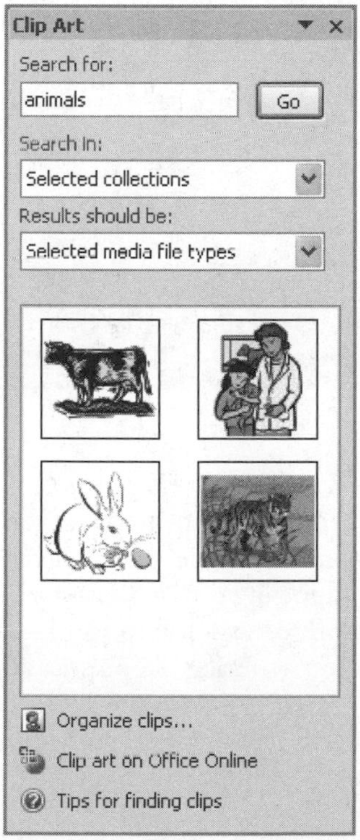

Figure 25-8:
As you can see from these representative thumbnails, there's a reason clip art isn't called high art. Still, depending on the effect you're after, clip art can be perfectly serviceable. Check out the box on the next page for ideas.

2. **In the "Search for" box, type a description of the picture you'd like to add to your slide and click Go.**

   In the results area of the Clip Art pane, PowerPoint displays thumbnails of all the clip art pictures that match your search word or phrase.

   To see all the clip art images stored on your computer, don't type anything; just click Go.

3. **Click a thumbnail to add that drawing to your slide.**

   PowerPoint places a copy of the drawing in the center of your slide, on top of whatever else already happens to be there. You can also drag the thumbnail from the Clip Art pane to the precise spot on your slide where you want it.

DESIGN TIME

Using Clip Art Creatively

Clip art is convenient, but sometimes the problem is, well, it *looks* like clip art. If you want people to take your presentation seriously, you must avoid having your slides look like you plunked down the first cheesy stock image you found. PowerPoint doesn't enforce good graphic design principles, but if you follow these no-fail tips, you can turn cheese into *fromage*:

- **Keep it small.** Try to keep your clip art small and off to one side of the slide, leaving the bulk of the space for text, as shown in Figure 25-9 (top).

- **Make it transparent.** Applying a 75% or higher transparency effect to backgrounds, clip art, and even the basic shapes you add to your slides lets text shine through. (See Figure 25-9, bottom.) If you use clip art, you need to avoid hard-to-read-text sitting on a busy background.

- **Not everything has to line up.** Sometimes, tilting an image just a little results in the rakish, attractive effect shown in Figure 25-10 (top).

- **Consider filled text boxes**. Applying a contrasting fill color to your text boxes doesn't just make text stand out; it also adds an appealing design element to your slides (Figure 25-10, top).

- **If all else fails, use contrasting text.** If you're using a strong, stylized image as a slide background, you can get away with pasting text on top—as long as you use a bold, contrasting font and color as shown in Figure 25-10 (bottom).

Slide Transitions

When you start with a blank presentation, advancing from one slide to the next is a simple on-or-off proposition—a slide is either 100 percent visible, or 100 percent hidden. There's nothing wrong with simple, but by applying a *slide transition*—a named effect that makes slide content fade, drop, swirl, or gallop into view—you can convey a mood that supports your presentation (sobriety, sophistication, whimsy, and so on).

Figure 25-9:
Top: The easiest way to add clip art—by tucking it out of the way, as shown here—gives a conservative result.

Bottom: Transparency can be hard to pull off. Too transparent, and your audience may think there's a water stain on the overhead screen; not transparent enough, and they won't be able to read your text. Still, in the right situation and with the right degree of transparency, it can be effective.

Note: Although PowerPoint lets you add slide transitions to individual slides, doing so can make your presentation look amateurish and disorganized. Instead, stick with the same slide transition to every slide. Doing so lets your audience focus on your content, not wondering which direction the next slide is going to come from.

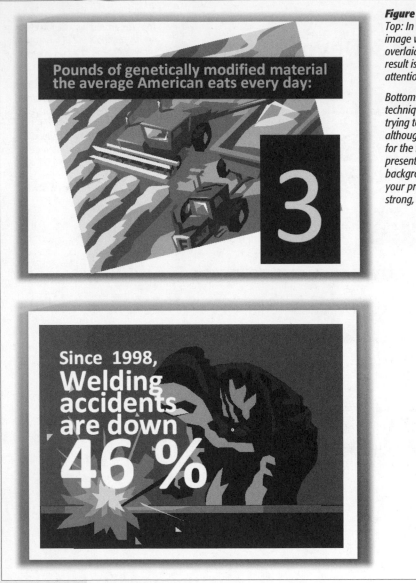

Figure 25-10:
Top: In this example, a clip art image was enlarged, rotated, and overlaid with filled text boxes. The result is both readable and attention grabbing.

Bottom: This text-on-image technique works best when you're trying to get across a single point, although it can also be effective for the first and last slides in your presentation. Make sure the background image is relevant to your presentation and choose a strong, clean font.

Types of Transitions

PowerPoint organizes its 50-plus built-in slide transitions into five different categories:

- **Fades and Dissolves.** The tasteful transitions in this category include Fade Smoothly, Fade Through Black, Cut, Cut Through Black, and Dissolve.

- **Wipes.** Wipe transitions make your slides appear from one or more directions, as though you were wiping slide content on with a rag. The impressive number of transitions in this category include Wipe Down, Wipe Left, Wipe Right, Wipe Up, Wedge, Uncover Down, Uncover Left, Uncover Right, Uncover Up, and many more.

- **Push and Cover.** Similar to Wipes transitions, these transitions make slide content appear from one or more directions. The difference is that Push and Cover transitions appear to push old slides out of the way as new slides appear. The transitions in this category include Push Down, Push Left, Push Right, Push Up, Cover Down, Cover Left, Cover Right, Cover Up, Cover Left-Down, Cover Left-Up, Cover Right-Down, and Cover Right-Up.

- **Stripes and Bars.** The transitions in this category cause slides to appear a strip or chunk at a time. They include Blinds Horizontal, Blinds Vertical, Checkerboard Across, Checkerboard Down, Comb Horizontal, and Comb Vertical.

- **Random.** This category includes two Stripes-and-Bars-like transitions, Random Bars Horizontal and Random Bars Vertical (both of which cause slides to appear one strip at a time). It also includes the Random transition, which tells PowerPoint to pick your transition. Because a good presenter consciously chooses every aspect of her presentation to support her message, you'll almost never want to use the Random transition.

Adding Transitions Between Slides

Transition effects look impressive, but adding them to your slideshow is no more difficult than, say, applying a font or choosing a bullet point style. Your tools are all in one place—the Animations tab shown in Figure 25-11. Open a slideshow with two or more slides in it, and then follow the steps described next.

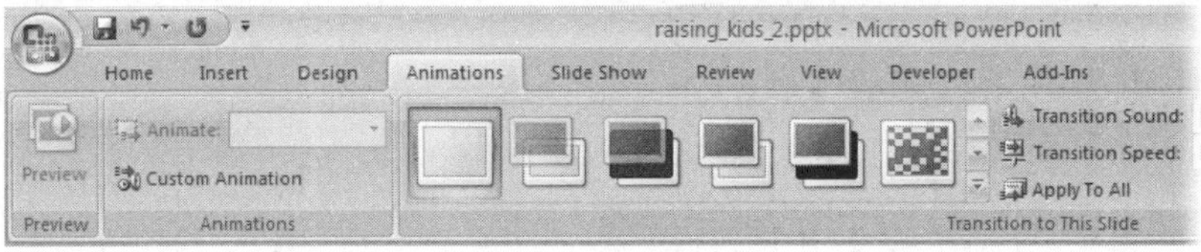

Figure 25-11:
Until you tell it otherwise, PowerPoint assumes you don't want a slide transition applied to any of your slides. The Animations tab shows you five popular slide transitions. You can mouse over them to get a description of each as well as an instant preview, or you can click More (the down arrow) to see the 52 additional slide transitions.

1. **In Normal view, select the second slide in your presentation (or the slide you want to add a transition *to*).**

   On the Slides tab, PowerPoint highlights the selected slide. The slide's contents appear in the slide editing area.

2. **On the Animations tab, head to the "Transition to This Slide" section and click the More down arrow on the far right.**

   A transition gallery similar to Figure 25-12 appears.

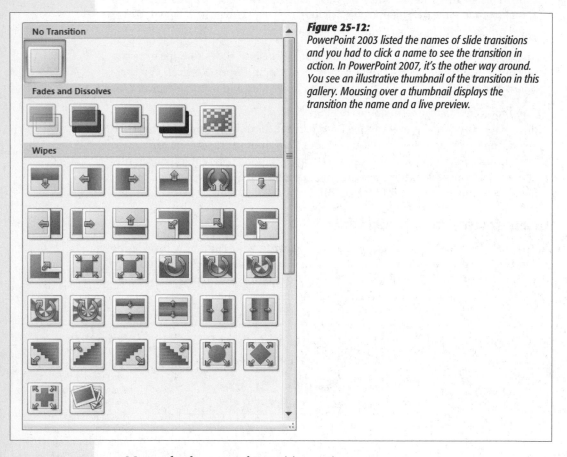

Figure 25-12:
PowerPoint 2003 listed the names of slide transitions and you had to click a name to see the transition in action. In PowerPoint 2007, it's the other way around. You see an illustrative thumbnail of the transition in this gallery. Mousing over a thumbnail displays the transition the name and a live preview.

3. **Mouse slowly over each transition option.**

   As your cursor passes over each transition option, PowerPoint displays the name of that option (such as Blinds Horizontal, Checkerboard Down, or Dissolve) and previews the option in the slide editing area.

4. **Click the transition you want.**

   PowerPoint previews the transition in the slide editing area. On the Slides tab, PowerPoint displays the star-shaped Play Animations icon directly beneath the slide number (Figure 25-13).

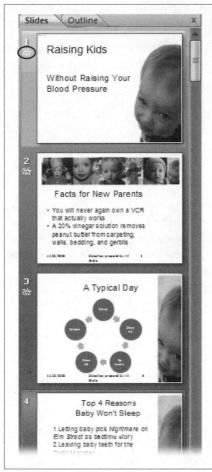

Figure 25-13:
A star displayed under a slide number on the Slides tab or in Slideshow View lets you know that PowerPoint has successfully applied an animated effect to that slide. Clicking the star previews the effect.

5. **To set transition speed, on the Animations ribbon, head to the Transition to this Slide section, and click the Transition Speed drop-down menu (Figure 25-11) and choose Slow, Medium, or Fast.**

   Out of the box, PowerPoint assumes you want your transition to move as quickly as possible.

6. **Tell PowerPoint how you want to advance from slide to slide.**

   If you want to do it manually, go to Animations → Transition to This Slide and turn on the On Mouse Click checkbox. To have slides advance automatically, turn on the Automatically After checkbox, and then enter the number of seconds you want PowerPoint to pause before it moves on.

7. **If you want every slide in your slideshow to have the same slide transition, select Animations → Transition to This Slide → Apply To All.**

   On the Slides tab, PowerPoint displays stars beneath every slide number. (If you change your mind after you apply a slide transition to your entire slideshow, click Undo.)

Note: If you've already applied a slide transition to all of the slides in your slideshow and then change how the transition looks, behaves, or sounds, you need to click Apply To All *again* to tell PowerPoint to update the transition for all of the slides.

---

8. **Run your slideshow to preview the transition.**

   PowerPoint gives you two additional ways to preview your slide transition: by heading to the Animations ribbon and clicking Preview → Preview, or heading to the Slides tab and clicking the star beneath the slide number. But make sure you run the entire slideshow, too, and not just that one slide; doing so lets you double-check that you've added the transition you want to the slides you want.

Part Four:
Access 2007

4

Creating Your First Database

Access is a tool for managing databases—carefully structured catalogs of information (a.k.a. data). Databases can store just about any type of information, including numbers, pages of text, and pictures. Databases also range wildly in size—they can handle everything from your list of family phone numbers to a ginormous product catalog for Aunt Ethel's Discount Button Boutique.

Access can help you organize all your information, but it can also be intimidating. Even though Microsoft has spent millions making Access 2007 easier to use, most people still see it as the most complicated Office program on the block—and they're probably right.

Access seems more daunting than any other Office program because of the way databases work. Quite simply, databases *need strict rules*. Other programs aren't as obsessive. For example, you can fire up Word and start typing a letter straight away. Or you can start Excel and launch right into a financial report. But Access isn't nearly as freewheeling. Before you can enter a stitch of information into an Access database, you need to create that database's *structure*. And even after you've defined that structure, you'll probably want to spend more time creating other useful tools, like handy search routines and friendly forms that you can use to simplify data lookup and data entry. All of this setup takes effort, and a good understanding of how databases work.

In the next several chapters, you'll learn how to design complete databases, maintain them, search for valuable nuggets of information, and build attractive forms for quick and easy data entry. Once you master Access's new style with the help of this book, you'll be able to build great databases in record time.

In this chapter, you'll conquer any Access resistance you may have and learn to create a simple but functional database. Along the way, you'll get acquainted with the slick new user interface and learn exactly what you can store in a database. You'll then be ready to tackle the fine art of database design, covered in more detail throughout the Access part of this book.

What You Can Do with Access

The modern world is filled with information. A Web search for a ho-hum topic like "canned carrots" nets more than a million Web pages. As a result, it's no surprise that people from all walks of life need great tools to store and manage information.

It's impossible to describe even a fraction of the different databases that Access fans create every day. But just to get you thinking like a database maven, here are some common types of information that you can store handily in an Access database:

- Catalogs of books, CDs, rare wine vintages, risqué movies, or anything else you want to collect and keep track of
- Mailing lists that let you keep in touch with friends, family, and co-workers
- Business information, like customer lists, product catalogs, order records, and invoices
- Lists of guests and gifts for weddings and other celebrations
- Lists of expenses, investments, and other financial planning details

Think of Access as a personal assistant that can help you organize, update, and find any type of information. This help isn't just a convenience—it also lets you do things you could never accomplish on your own.

Imagine you've just finished compiling a database for your collection of 10,000 rare comic books. On a whim, you decide to take a look at all the books written in 1987. Or just those that feature Aquaman. Or those that contain the words "special edition" in the title. Performing these searches with a paper catalog would take days. On an average computer, Access can perform all three searches in under a second.

Access is also the king of small businesses, because of its legendary powers of customization. After all, you can use virtually any database product to create a list of customer orders. But only Access makes it easy to build a full *user interface* for that database (as shown in Figure 26-1).

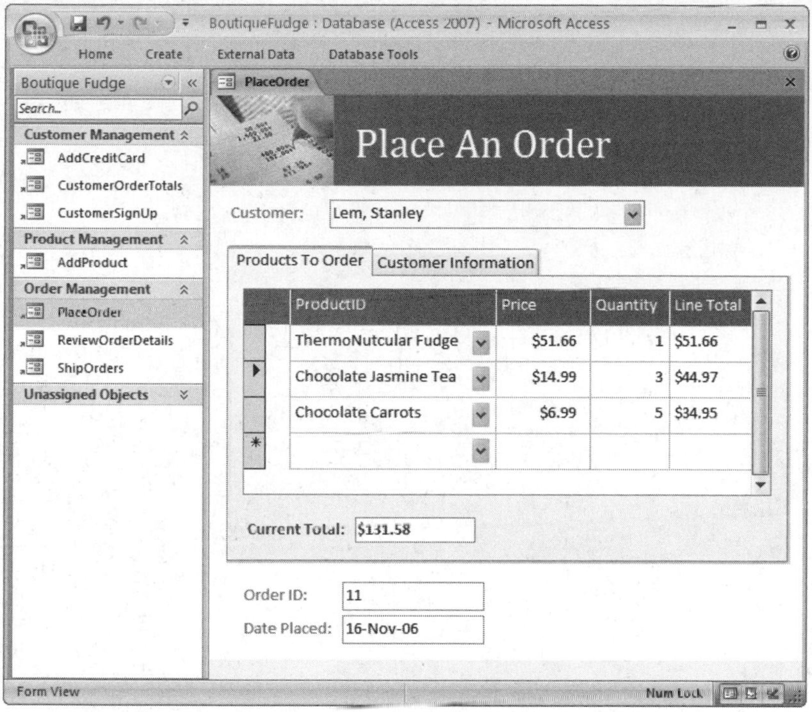

Figure 26-1:
This sales database includes handy forms that sales people can use to place new orders (shown here), customer service representatives can use to sign up new customers, and warehouse staff can use to review outgoing shipments. Best of all, the people who are using the forms in the database don't need to know anything about Access. As long as a database pro (like your future self, once you've finished this book) has designed these forms, anyone can use them to enter, edit, and review data.

The Two Sides of Access

As you'll see, there are actually two separate tasks you'll perform with Access:

- **Designing your database.** This task involves creating *tables* to hold data, *queries* that can ferret out important pieces of information, *forms* that make it easy to enter information, and *reports* that produce attractive printouts.

- **Dealing with data.** This task involves adding new information to the database, updating what's there, or just searching for the details you need. In order to do this work, you use the tables, queries, forms, and reports that you've already built.

Most of this book's dedicated to task #1—creating and perfecting your database. This job's the heart of Access, and it's the part that initially seems the most daunting. It's also what separates the Access masters from the neophytes.

Once you've finished task #1, you're reading to move on to task #2—actually *using* the database in your day-to-day life. Although task #1 is more challenging, you'll (eventually) spend more time on task #2. For example, you might spend a couple of hours creating a database to keep track of your favorite recipes, but you'll wind up entering new information and looking up recipes for *years* (say, every time you need to cook up dinner).

The Benefits of a Good Database

Many people use an address book to keep track of close friends, distant relatives, or annoying co-workers. For the most part, the low-tech address book works great. But consider what happens if you decide to store the same information in an Access database. Even though your contact list isn't storing Google-sized volumes of information, it still offers a few features that you wouldn't have without Access:

- **Backup.** If you've ever tried to decipher a phone number through a coffee stain, you know that sometimes it helps to have things in electronic form. Once you place all your contact information into a database, you'll be able to preserve it in case of disaster, and print up as many copies as you need (each with some or all of the information showing). You can even share your list with a friend who needs the same numbers.

- **Space.** Although most people can fit all the contacts they need into a small address book, a database ensures you'll never fill up that "M" section. Not to mention that there are only so many times you can cross out and rewrite the address for your itinerant Uncle Sy before you run out of room.

- **Searching.** An address book organizes contacts in one way—by name. But what happens once you've entered everyone in alphabetical order by last name, and you need to look up a contact you vaguely remember as Joe? Access can effortlessly handle this search. It can also find a matching entry by phone number, which is great if your phone gives you a log of missed calls and you want to figure out who's been pestering you.

- **Integration with other applications.** Access introduces you to a realm of timesaving possibilities, like mail merge. You can feed a list of contacts into a form letter you create in Word, and automatically generate dozens of individually addressed letters. You'll see how to do this in Chapter 34.

All these examples demonstrate solid reasons to go electronic with almost any type of information.

Access vs. Excel

Access isn't the only Office product that can deal with lists and tables of information. Microsoft Excel also includes features for creating and managing lists. So what's the difference?

Although Excel's perfectly good for small, simple amounts of information, it just can't handle the same *quantity* and *complexity* of information as Access. Excel also falters if you need to maintain multiple lists with related information (for example, if you want to track a list with your business customers, and a list of the orders they've made). Excel forces you to completely separate these lists, which makes it harder to analyze your data and introduces the possibility of inconsistent information. Access lets you set up strict *links* between tables, which prevents these problems.

Access also provides all sorts of features that don't have any parallel in the spreadsheet world, such as the ability to create customized search routines, design fine-tuned forms for data entry, and print a variety of snazzy reports.

Note: The Access portion of this book is based on *Access 2007: The Missing Manual* (O'Reilly). That book is a truly complete reference for Access 2007, covering every feature, including geeky stuff like XML, VBA, SQL Server, and other things you'll probably never encounter—or even want to. But if you get really deep into Access and want to learn more, *Access 2007: The Missing Manual* can be your trusted guide.

Access 2003 Menu Shortcuts

If you've worked with a previous version of Access, you may have trained yourself to use menu shortcuts—key combinations that open a menu and pick out the command you want. When you press Alt+E in Access 2003, the Edit menu pops open (in the main menu). You can then press the S key to choose the Paste Special command.

At first glance, it doesn't look like these keyboard shortcuts amount to much in Access 2007. After all, Access 2007 doesn't even have a main menu! Fortunately, Microsoft went to a little extra trouble to make life easier for longtime Access aficionados. You can still use your menu shortcuts, but they work in a slightly different way.

If you hit Alt+E in Access 2007, a tooltip appears over the top of the ribbon (Figure 26-2) that lets you know you've started to enter an Access 2003 menu shortcut. If you go on to press S, then you wind up at the familiar Paste Special dialog box, because Access knows what you're trying to do. It's almost as though Access has an invisible menu at work behind the scenes.

Of course, this feature can't help you out all the time. It doesn't work if you're trying to use one of the few commands that don't exist any longer. And if you need to see the menu to remember what key to press next, you're out of luck. Access just gives you the tooltip.

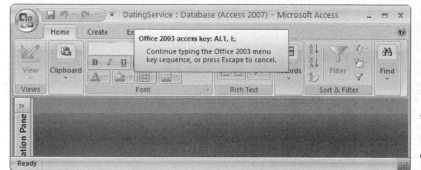

Figure 26-2:
By pressing Alt+E, you've triggered the "imaginary" Edit menu. You can't actually see it (because it doesn't exist in Access 2007). However, the tooltip lets you know that Access is paying attention. You can now complete your action by pressing the next key for the menu command.

Why Reinvent the Wheel?

Some Access veterans are understandably skeptical about the new Access interface. After all, we've had to suffer through some painful experiments. Past versions of Access have introduced kooky ideas like personalized menus that always seem to hide just the command you need, pop-up side panels that appear when you least expect them, and floating toolbars that end up strewn across the screen.

In reality, all the Office applications have been struggling to keep up with more than a decade's worth of new features. The menus in most Office programs haven't changed since Word 2.0 hit the scene in the early 1990s. In those days, a basic menu and a single toolbar were just the ticket, because the number of commands was relatively small.

Today, the Office programs are drowning in features—and they're crammed into so many different nooks and crannies that even pros don't know where to look.

That's where the new ribbon fits in. Not only can you easily understand and navigate it, it provides one-stop shopping for everything you need to do. Microsoft's user interface designers have a new mantra: *It's all in the ribbon*. In other words, if you need to find a feature, then look for it in one of the tabs at the top of the Access window. As you get accustomed to this new system, you'll find it not only helps you quickly use your favorite features, it also helps you discover new features just by browsing.

Understanding Access Databases

As you already know, a database is a collection of information. In Access, every database is stored in a single file. That file contains *database objects,* which are simply the components of a database.

Database objects are the main players in an Access database. Altogether, you have six different types of database objects:

- **Tables** store information. Tables are the heart of any database, and you can create as many tables as you need to store different types of information. A fitness database could track your daily running log, your inventory of exercise equipment, and the number of high-protein whey milkshakes you down each day, as three separate tables.

- **Queries** let you quickly perform an action on a table. Usually, this action involves retrieving a choice bit of information (like the 10 top-selling food items at Ed's Roadside Dinner, or all the purchases you made in a single day). However, you can also use queries to apply changes.

- **Forms** are attractive windows that you create, arrange, and colorize. Forms provide an easy way to view or change the information in a table.

- **Reports** help you print some or all of the information in a table. You can choose where the information appears on the printed page, how it's grouped and sorted, and how it's formatted.

- **Macros** are mini-programs that automate custom tasks. Macros are a simple way to get custom results without becoming a programmer.

- **Modules** are files that contain Visual Basic code. You can use this code to do just about anything—from updating 10,000 records to firing off an email. For more on Visual Basic, see *Access 2007: The Missing Manual.*

Access gurus refer to all these database ingredients as objects because you manage them all in essentially the same way. If you want to use a particular object, then you add it to your database, give it a name, and then fine-tune it. Later on, you can view your objects, rename them, or delete ones you don't want anymore.

Tip: Designing a database is the process of adding and configuring database objects. For those keeping score, an Access database can hold up to 32,768 separate objects.

In this chapter, you'll consider only the most fundamental type of database object: *tables*. But first, you need to learn a bit more about databases and the Access environment.

Getting Started

It's time to begin your journey and launch Access. You'll start at a spiffy Getting Started page (Figure 26-3).

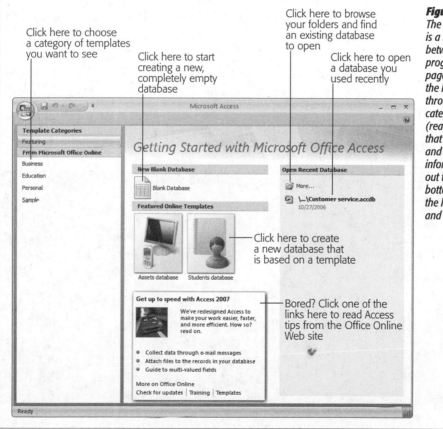

Click here to choose a category of templates you want to see

Click here to start creating a new, completely empty database

Click here to browse your folders and find an existing database to open

Click here to open a database you used recently

Click here to create a new database that is based on a template

Bored? Click one of the links here to read Access tips from the Office Online Web site

Figure 26-3:
The Getting Started page is a bit of a cross between a Windows program and a Web page. Use the links on the left to browse through different categories of templates (ready-to-go databases that you can download and fill with your own information). Or check out the links on the bottom, which show you the latest Access news and tips.

Using Someone Else's Database

Can I use an Access database I didn't design?

Although every database follows the same two-step process (first somebody creates it, and then people fill it with information), the same person doesn't need to perform both jobs. In fact, in the business world, different people often work separately on these two tasks.

For example, a summer student whiz kid at a beer store may build a database for tracking orders (task #1). The sales department can then use the database to enter new orders (task #2), while other employees look up orders

and fill them (also task #2). Warehouse staff can make sure stock levels are OK (again, task #2), and the resident accountant can keep an eye on total sales (task #2).

If task #1 (creating the database) is done well, task #2 (using the database) can be extremely easy. In fact, if the database is well designed, people who have little understanding of Access can still use it to enter, update, and look up information. Amazingly, they don't even need to know they're running Access at all!

The Getting Started page looks a little dizzying at first glance, but it really serves just three purposes:

- **It shows you recent content from Microsoft's Office Online Web site.** For example, you can read helpful articles about Access, find timesaving tips, or download updates. All links open in a separate browser window.

- **It lets you open a database you used recently.** Look for the Open Recent Database section on the right, which gives you a list.

- **It lets you create a new database.** You can start off with an empty database (use the Blank Database button), or you can try to find a ready-made *template* that fits the bill.

Templates: One Size Fits Some

Templates are prebuilt databases. Templates aim to save you the work of creating your database, and let you jump straight to the fine-tuning and data-entry stage.

As you might expect, there's a price to be paid for this convenience. Even if you find a template that stores the type of information you want to track, you might find that the predefined structure isn't quite right. For example, if you choose to use the Home Inventory template to track all the stuff in your basement, you might find that it's missing some information you want to use (like the projected resale

value of your stuff on eBay) and includes other details you don't care about (like the date you acquired each item). To make this template work, you'll need to change the design of your table, which involves the same Access know-how as creating one.

In this book, you'll learn how to build your own databases from the ground up. Once you're an Access master, you can spend many fun hours playing with the prebuilt templates and adapting them to suit your needs.

You may think that it would be nice to customize the Getting Started page. Access does let you do so, but it's not all that easy—and it's recommended only for organizations that want to standardize the Getting Started page to better suit their employees. A business could add links to a company Web site or a commonly used database template. If you're interested in this feature, you'll need another tool: the freely downloadable Access Developer's Toolkit, which you can search for at *http://msdn.microsoft.com*. (This tool wasn't yet released at the time of this writing.)

The Getting Started page is only the front door to the features in Access—there's lot more in store once you get rolling. You won't be able to try out other parts of the Access until you create a new database, and the next section shows you how.

Creating a New Database

In this chapter, you'll slap together a fairly straightforward database. The example's designed to store a list of prized bobblehead dolls. (For those not in the know, a bobblehead doll is a toy figure with an outsize head on a spring, hence the signature "bobbling" motion. Bobblehead dolls usually resemble a famous celebrity, politician, athlete, or fictional character.)

Tip: You can get the Bobblehead database, and all the databases in this book, on the Web. Check out page 14 in the Introduction for more details about www.*missingmanual..com*.

Here's how to create a blank new database:

1. **On the Getting Started page, click the Blank Database button.**

   A side panel appears on the right (see Figure 26-4).

2. **Type in a file name.**

   Access stores all the information for a database in a single file with the extension *.accdb* (which stands for Access database). Don't stick with the name Access picks automatically (like Database1.accdb). Instead, pick something more suitable. In this example, Bobblehead.accdb does the trick.

   As with any other file, Access files can contain a combination of letters, spaces, numbers, parentheses, hyphens (-), and the underscore (_). It's generally safest to stay away from other special characters, some of which aren't allowed.

Note: Depending on your computer settings, Windows may hide file extensions. Instead of seeing the Access database file MyScandalousWedding.accdb in file-browsing tools like Windows Explorer, you may just see the name MyScandalousWedding (without the .accdb part on the end). In this case, you can still tell the file type by looking at the icon. If you see a small Access icon next to the file name (which looks like a key), that's your signal that you're looking at an Access database. If you see something else (like a tiny paint palette), you need to make a logical guess about what type of file it is.

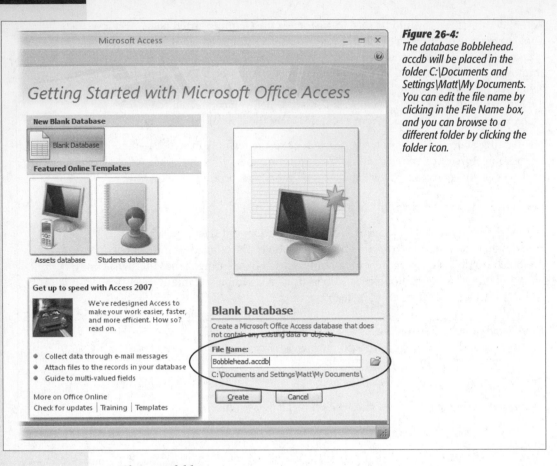

Figure 26-4:
The database Bobblehead.accdb will be placed in the folder C:\Documents and Settings\Matt\My Documents. You can edit the file name by clicking in the File Name box, and you can browse to a different folder by clicking the folder icon.

3. **Choose a folder.**

   Like all Office programs, Access assumes you want to store every file you create in your personal My Documents folder. If this isn't the case, click the folder icon to show the File New Database dialog box, browse to the folder you want (Figure 26-5), and then click OK.

4. **Click the Create button (at the bottom-right of the Access window).**

   Access creates your database file and then pops up a datasheet where you can get to work creating your first table.

   Once you create or open a database, the Access window changes quite a bit. An impressive-looking toolbar (the *ribbon*) appears at the top of your screen, and a navigation pane shows up on the left. You're now in the control center where you'll perform all your database tasks (as shown in Figure 26-6).

   The Introduction covers the basics of how the ribbon works. But first, it's time to consider how you can make use of your brand-new, empty database by adding a table.

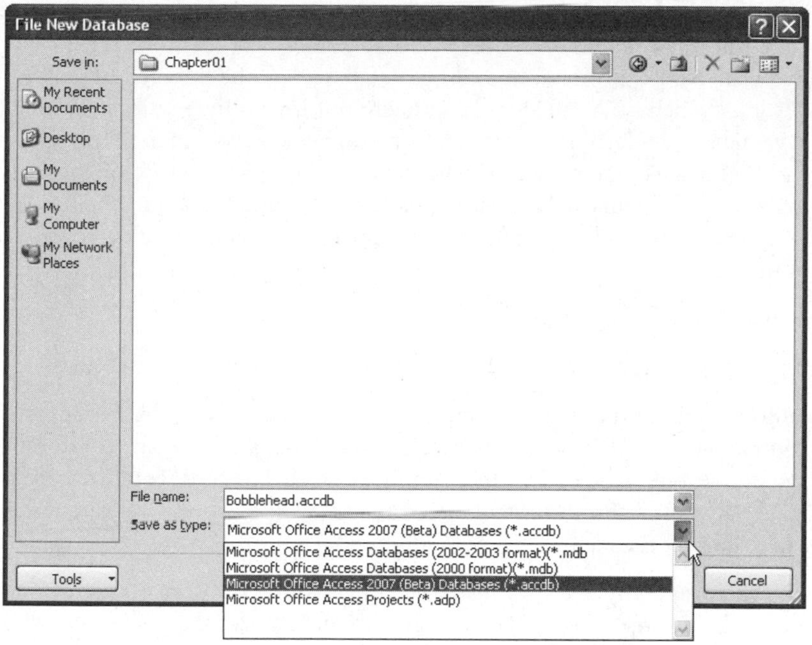

Figure 26-5:
The File New Database dialog box lets you choose where you'll store a new Access database file. It also gives you the option to create your database in the format used by previous versions of Access (.mdb). To do so, you need to choose either the 2000 or 2002-2003 format options from the "Save as type" list, as shown here. If you're running Windows Vista, you'll notice that the File New Database dialog box has a whole different look, but all the same features.

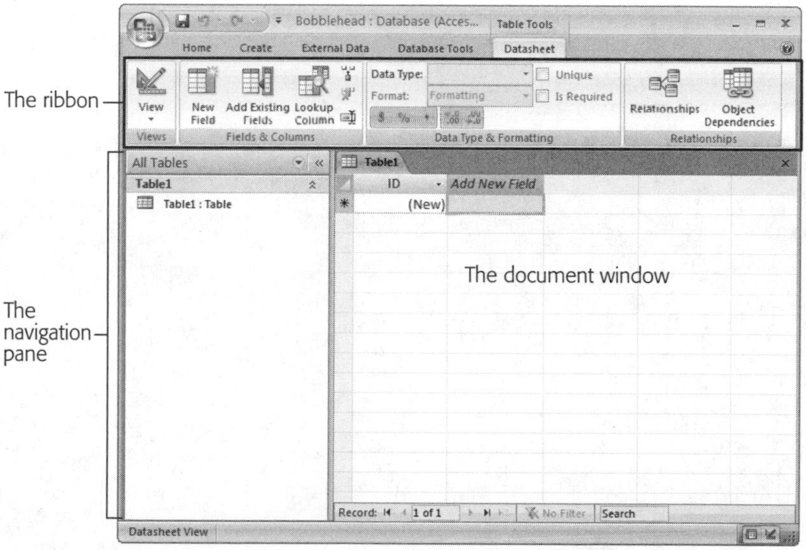

Figure 26-6:
The navigation pane on the left lets you see different items (or objects) in your database. You can use the navigation pane to jump from a list of products to a list of customers and back again. The ribbon along the top groups together every Access command. This ribbon's the mission control that lets you perform various tasks with your database.

Understanding Tables

Tables are information containers. Every database needs at least one table—without it, you can't store any data. In a simple database, like the Bobblehead database, a single table (which we'll call Dolls) is enough. But if you find yourself wanting to store several lists of related information, then you need more than one table. In the database BigBudgetWedding.accdb, you might want to keep track of the guests that you invited to your wedding, the gifts that you requested, and the loot that you actually received. In Chapter 30, you'll see plenty of examples of databases that use multiple tables.

Figure 26-7 shows a sample table.

Before you start designing this table, you need to know some very basic rules:

- **A table's nothing more than a group of *records*.** A record's a collection of information about a single thing. In the Dolls table, for example, each record represents a single bobblehead doll. In a Family table, each record would represent a single relative. In a Products table, each record would represent an item that's for sale. You get the idea.

- **Each record's subdivided into *fields*.** Each field stores a distinct piece of information. For example, in the Dolls table, one field stores the person on whom the doll's based, another field stores the price, another field stores the date you bought it, and so on.

- **Tables have a rigid structure.** In other words, you can't bend the rules. If you create four fields, *every* record must have four fields (although it's acceptable to leave some fields blank if they don't apply).

WORD TO THE WISE

Sharing Databases with Older Versions of Access

Older versions of Access don't use the .accdb format. If you try to open Bobblehead.accdb in Access 2003, you'll get nothing more than a blank stare and an error message.

Earlier versions of Access use the *.mdb* file format (which stands for Microsoft database). Although Access 2007 is happy using both .accdb and .mdb files, previous versions of Access recognize only .mdb. (And just to make life more interesting, the .mdb format actually has *three* versions: the really, really old original format, a retooled version that appeared with Access 2000, and the improved-yet-again version that Microsoft introduced with Access 2002 and reused for Access 2003.)

Here's what you need to know to choose the right format for your new databases. The standard .accdb format's the best choice if you don't need to worry about compatibility, because it has the best performance and a few extra features. But if you need to share databases with other versions of Access, skip the new kid on the block, and rely instead on the tested-and-true .mdb format.

To create an old-style .mdb database file in Access 2007, use the "Save as type" option shown in Figure 26-5. You can choose the Access 2002-2003 file format, or the even older Access 2000 format. (If you're set on going back any further, say the Access 95 format, your best bet's a time machine.)

Creating a Simple Table

When you first create a database, it's almost empty. But in order to get you started, Access creates your first database object—a table named Table1. The problem is, this table begins life completely blank, with no defined fields (and no data).

If you followed the steps to create a new database (page 589), you're already at the *Datasheet view* (Figure 26-7), which is where you enter data into a table. All you need to do is customize this table so that it meets your needs.

There are two ways to customize a table:

- **Design view** lets you precisely define all aspects of a table before you start using it. Almost all database pros prefer Design view, and you'll start using it in Chapter 27.

- **Datasheet view** is where you enter data into a table. Datasheet view also lets you build a table on the fly as you insert new information. You'll use this approach in this chapter.

The name of the table

A field named Character

A record

Dolls

ID	Character	Manufacturer	PurchasePrice	DateAcquired
1	Homer Simpson	Fictional Industries	$7.99	1/1/2008
2	Edgar Allan Poe	Hobergarten	$14.99	1/30/2008
3	Frodo	Magiker	$8.95	2/4/2008
4	James Joyce	Hobergarten	$14.99	3/3/2008
5	Jack Black	All Dolled Up	$3.45	3/3/2008
7	The Cat in the Hat	All Dolled Up	$3.77	3/3/2008
*	(New)			

Figure 26-7:
In a table, each record occupies a separate row. Each field is represented by a separate column. In this table, it's clear that you've added six bobblehead dolls. You're storing information for each doll in five fields (ID, Character, Manufacturer, PurchasePrice, and DateAcquired).

UP TO SPEED

Database Planning for Beginners

Many database gurus suggest that before you fire up Access, you should decide exactly what information you want to store by brainstorming. Here's how it works. First, determine the type of list you want by finishing this sentence "I need a list of …." (One example: "I need a list of all the bobblehead dolls in my basement.")

Next, jot down all your must-have pieces of information on a piece of paper. Some details are obvious. For example, for the bobblehead doll collection, you'll probably want to keep track of the doll's name, price, and date you bought it.

Other details, like the year it was produced, the company that created it, and a short description of its appearance or condition may require more thought.

Once you've completed this process and identified all the important bits of data you need, you're ready to create the corresponding table in Access. The bobblehead doll example demonstrates an important theme of database design: First you plan the database, and then you create it using Access. In Chapter 30, you'll learn a lot more about planning more complex databases.

The following steps show you how to turn a blank new table (like Table1) into the Dolls table using the Datasheet view:

1. **To define your table, you need to add your first record.**

   In this case, that means mentally picking a bobblehead doll to add to the list. For this example, you'll use a nifty Homer Simpson replica.

Note: It doesn't matter which doll you enter first. Access tables are *unsorted*, which means they have no underlying order. However, you can sort them any way you want when you need to retrieve information later on.

---

2. **In the datasheet's Add New Field column, type the first piece of information for the record (see Figure 26-8).**

   Based on the simple analysis you performed earlier (page 593), you know that you need to enter four fields of information for every doll. For the Homer Simpson doll, this information is: "Homer Simpson" (the name), "Fictional Industries" (the manufacturer), $7.99 (the price), and today's date (the purchase date). Although you could start with any field, it makes sense to begin with the name, which is clearly an identifying detail.

3. **Press Tab to move to the next field, and return to step 2.**

   Repeat steps 2 and 3 until you've added every field you need, being careful to put each separate piece of information into a different column.

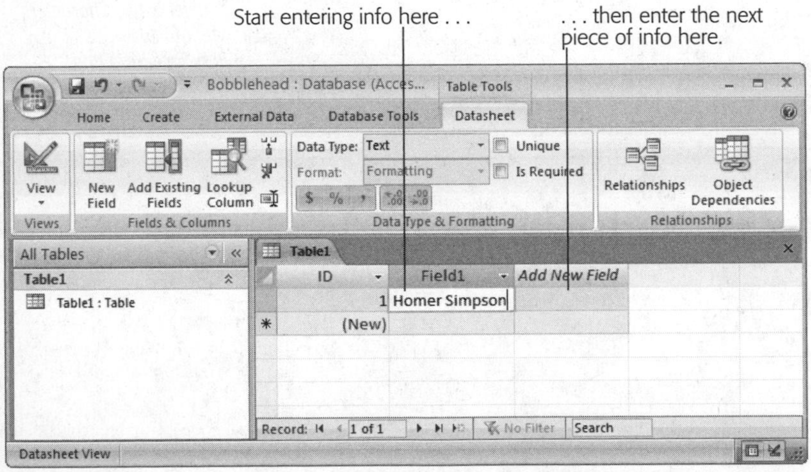

Figure 26-8:
To fill in your first record, start by entering something in the first field of information (like the doll name "Homer Simpson"). Then, hit Tab to jump to the second column, and then enter the second piece of information. Ignore the ID column for now—Access adds that to every table to identify your rows.

If you want to get a little fancier, include the currency symbol ($) when you enter the price, and make sure you put the data in a recognized date format (like *January 1, 2008* or *01-01-2008*). These clues tell Access what type of information you're putting in the column. (In Chapter 27, you'll learn how to take complete control of the type of data in each column and avoid possible misunderstandings.) Figure 26-9 shows the finalized record.

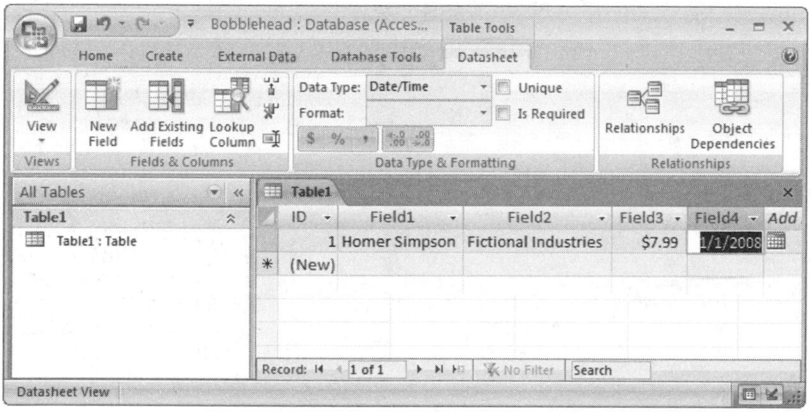

Figure 26-9:
The only problem with the example so far is that as you enter a new record, Access creates spectacularly useless field names. You'll see its choices at the top of each column (they'll have names like Field1, Field2, Field3, and so on). The problem with using these meaningless names is that they might lead you to enter a piece of information in the wrong place. You could all too easily put the purchase price in the date column. To prevent these slip-ups, you need to set better field names.

UP TO SPEED

Putting Big Values in Narrow Columns

A column can hold entire paragraphs of information, so you may find yourself running out of space once you start typing. This phenomenon isn't a problem (after all, you can just scroll through your field itself while you're editing it), but it *is* annoying. Most people prefer to see the entire contents of a column at once.

Fortunately, you don't need to suffer in silence with cramped columns. To expand a column, just position your mouse at the right edge of the column header. (To expand a column named Field1, move your mouse to the right edge

of the Field1 box.) Then, drag the column to the right to resize it as big as you want.

If you're just a bit impatient, there's a shortcut. Double-click the right edge of the column to resize it to fit the largest piece of information that's in the column (provided this doesn't stretch the column beyond the edge of the Access window). That way, you automatically get all the room you need.

Note: If you hit Tab without entering any information, you'll move to the next row and start inserting a new record. If you make a mistake, you can backtrack using the arrow keys.

4. **It's time to fix your column names. Double-click the first column title (like Field1).**

   The field name switches into Edit mode.

5. **Type in a new name, and then press Enter. Return to step 4.**

   Repeat this process until you've cleaned up all the field names. The proper field names for this example are Character, Manufacturer, PurchasePrice, and Date-Acquired. Figure 26-10 shows how it works.

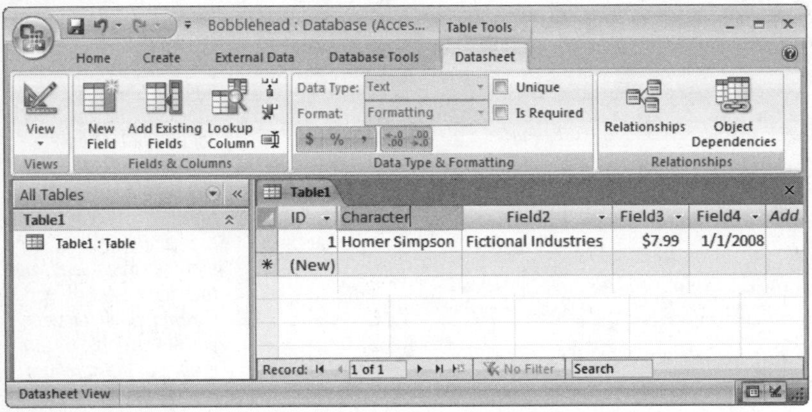

Figure 26-10:
To choose better field names, double-click the column title. Next, type in the real field name, and then press Enter. Page 640 has more about field naming, but for now just stick to short, text-only titles that don't include any spaces, as shown here.

Tip: Don't be too timid about tweaking your table. You can always rename fields later, or even add entirely new fields. (It's also possible to *delete* existing fields, but that has the drawback of also clearing out all the data that's stored in that field.)

6. **Choose Office button → Save (or use the Ctrl+S shortcut) to save your table.**

   Access asks you to supply a table name (see Figure 26-11).

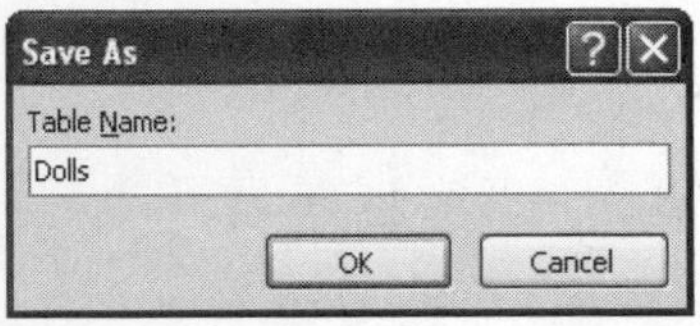

Figure 26-11:
A good table name's a short text title that doesn't have any spaces (like Dolls here).

7. **Type a suitable table name, and then click OK.**

   Congratulations! The table's now a part of your database.

Note: Technically, you don't need to save your table right away. Access prompts you to save it when you close the datasheet (by clicking the X at the document window's top-right corner), or when you close Access.

As you can see, creating a simple table in Access is almost as easy as laying out information in Excel or Word. If you're itching to try again, you can create *another* table in your database by choosing Create → Table from the ribbon. But before you get to that stage, it makes sense to take a closer look at how you edit your table.

Editing a Table

You now have a fully functioning (albeit simple) database, complete with one table, which in turn contains one record. Your next step's filling your table with useful information. This often-tedious process is *data entry*.

To fill the Dolls table, you use the same datasheet you used to define the table. You can perform three basic tasks:

- **Editing a record.** Move to the appropriate spot in the datasheet (using the arrow keys or the mouse), and then type in a replacement. You may also want to use Edit mode, which is described in the next section.

- **Inserting a new record.** Move down to the bottom of the table, to the row that has an asterisk (*) on the left. This row doesn't actually exist until you start typing in some information. At that point, Access creates the row and moves the asterisk down to the next row underneath. You can repeat this process endlessly to add as many rows as you want (Access can handle millions).

- **Deleting a record.** You have several ways to remove a record, but the easiest is to right-click the margin immediately to the left of the record, and then choose Delete Record. Access asks you to confirm that you really want to remove the selected record, because you can't reverse the change later on.

Edit mode

You'll probably spend a lot of time working with the datasheet. So settle in. To make your life easier, it helps to understand a few details.

As you already know, you can use the arrow keys to move from field to field or row to row. However, you might have a bit of trouble editing a value. When you start typing, Access erases any existing content. To change this behavior, you need to switch into *Edit mode* by pressing the F2 key; in Edit mode, your typing doesn't delete the stuff that's already in that field. Instead, you get to change or add to it. To switch out of Edit mode, you press F2 again. Figure 26-12 shows a closeup look at the difference.

Tip: You can also switch in and out of Edit mode by double-clicking a cell.

Edit mode also affects how the arrow keys work. In Edit mode, the arrow keys move through the current field. For example, to move to the next cell, you need to move all the way to the end of the current text, and then press the right arrow (→) key again. But in Normal mode, the arrow keys always move you from cell to cell.

Dolls				×
ID ▾	Character ▾	Manufacturer ▾	PurchasePrice ▾	
1	Homer Simpson	Fictional Industries	$7.99	
2	Edgar Allan Poe	Hobergarten	$14.99	
3	Frodo	Magiker	$8.95	
4	James Joyce	Hobergarten	$14.99	
5	Jack Black	All Dolled Up	$3.45	
* (New)				

Figure 26-12:

Top: Normal mode. If you start typing now, you'll immediately erase the existing text ("Hobergarten"). The fact that all the text in the field's selected is a big clue that you're about to wipe it out.

Bottom: Edit mode. The cursor shows where you're currently positioned in the current field. If you start typing now, you'll insert text in between "Hober" and "garten".

Dolls				×
ID ▾	Character ▾	Manufacturer ▾	PurchasePrice ▾	
1	Homer Simpson	Fictional Industries	$7.99	
2	Edgar Allan Poe	Hobergarten	$14.99	
3	Frodo	Magiker	$8.95	
4	James Joyce	Hobergarten	$14.99	
5	Jack Black	All Dolled Up	$3.45	
* (New)				

Shortcut keys

Power users know the fastest way to get work done is to use tricky keyboard combinations like Ctrl+Alt+Shift+*. Although you can't always easily remember these combinations, a couple of tables can help you out. Table 26-1 lists some useful keys that can help you whiz around the datasheet.

Table 26-2 lists some convenient keys for editing records.

WORD TO THE WISE

When in Doubt, Don't Delete

Most seasoned database designers rarely delete records from their databases. Every ounce of information is important.

For example, imagine you have a database that lists the products that a mail-order origami company has for sale. You might think it makes sense to delete products once they've been discontinued and can't be ordered anymore. But it turns out that it makes sense to keep these old product records around. For example, you might want to find out what product categories were the best sellers over the previous year. Or maybe a manufacturer issues a recall of asbestos-laced paper, and you need to track down everyone who ordered it. To perform either of these tasks, you need to keep your product records.

This hang-onto-everything rule applies to any kind of database. For example, imagine you're tracking student enroll-

ment at a top-flight culinary academy. When a class is finished, you can't just delete the class record. You might need it to find out if a student has the right prerequisites for another course, what teachers she's had in the past, and so on.

The same is true for employees who retire, promotions that end, items that you used to own but you've sold, and so on. You need them all (and you probably need to keep them indefinitely).

In many cases, you'll add extra fields to your table to help you separate old data from the new. For example, you can create a Discontinued field in the Products table that identifies products that aren't available anymore. You can then ignore those products when you build an order-placement form.

Table 26-1. *Keys for Moving Around the Datasheet*

Key	Result
Tab (or Enter)	Moves the cursor one field to the right, or down when you reach the edge of the table. This key also turns off Edit mode if it's currently switched on.
Shift+Tab	Moves the cursor one field to the left, or up when you reach the edge of the table. This key also turns off Edit mode.
→	Moves the cursor one field to the right (in Normal mode), or down when you reach the edge of the table. In Edit mode, this key moves the cursor through the text in the current field.
←	Moves the cursor one field to the left (in Normal mode), or up when you reach the edge of the table. In Edit mode, this key moves the cursor through the text in the current field.
↑	Moves the cursor up one row (unless you're already at the top of the table). This key also turns off Edit mode.
↓	Moves the cursor down one row (or it moves you to the "new row" position if you're at the bottom of the table). This key also turns off Edit mode.
Home	Moves the cursor to the first field in the current row. This key brings you to beginning of the current field if you're in Edit mode.
End	Moves the cursor to the last field in the current row. This key brings you to end of the current field if you're in Edit mode.
Page Down	Moves the cursor down one screenful (assuming you have a large table of information that doesn't all fit in the Access window at once). This key also turns off Edit mode.
Page Up	Moves the cursor up one screenful. This key also turns off Edit mode.
Ctrl+Home	Moves the cursor to the first field in the first row. This key doesn't do anything if you're in Edit mode.
Ctrl+End	Moves the cursor to the last field in the last row. This key doesn't do anything if you're in Edit mode.

Table 26-2. *Keys for Editing Records*

Key	Result
Esc	Cancels any changes you've made in the current field. This key works only if you use it in Edit mode. Once you move to the next cell, change is applied. (For additional cancellation control, try the Undo feature, described next.)
Ctrl+Z	Reverses the last edit. Unfortunately, the Undo feature in Access isn't nearly as powerful as it is in other Office programs. For example, Access allows you to reverse only one change, and if you close the datasheet, you can't even do that. You can use Undo right after you insert a new record to remove it, but you can't use the Undo feature to reverse a delete operation.
Ctrl+"	Copies a value from the field that's immediately above the current field. This trick's handy when you need to enter a batch of records with similar information. Figure 26-13 shows this often-overlooked trick in action.
Ctrl+;	Inserts today's date into the current field. The date format's based on computer settings, but expect to see something like 24-12-2007. You'll learn more about how Access works with dates on page 629.
Ctrl+Alt+Space	Inserts the default value for the field. You'll learn how to designate a default value on page 670.

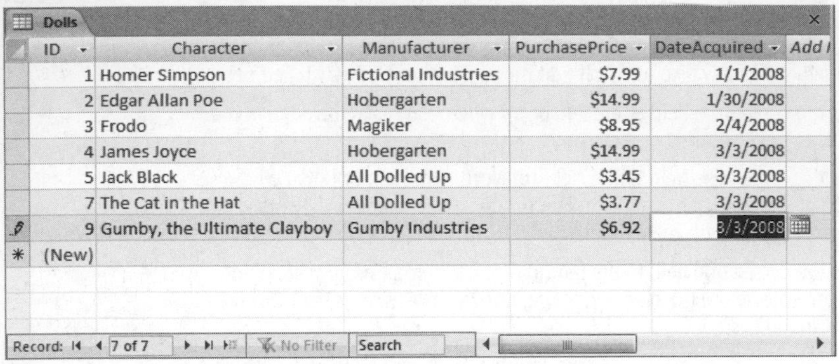

Dolls

	ID	Character	Manufacturer	PurchasePrice	DateAcquired	Add
	1	Homer Simpson	Fictional Industries	$7.99	1/1/2008	
	2	Edgar Allan Poe	Hobergarten	$14.99	1/30/2008	
	3	Frodo	Magiker	$8.95	2/4/2008	
	4	James Joyce	Hobergarten	$14.99	3/3/2008	
	5	Jack Black	All Dolled Up	$3.45	3/3/2008	
	7	The Cat in the Hat	All Dolled Up	$3.77	3/3/2008	
	9	Gumby, the Ultimate Clayboy	Gumby Industries	$6.92	3/3/2008	
*	(New)					

Record: 7 of 7 No Filter Search

***Figure 26-13:** An Access user has been on an eBay buying binge and needs to add several dolls at once. With a quick Ctrl+" keystroke, the acquire date from the previous record's pasted into the current field.*

Cut, copy, and paste

Access, like virtually every Windows program, lets you cut and paste bits of information from one spot to another. This trick's easy using just three shortcut keys: Ctrl+C to copy, Ctrl+X to cut (similar to copy, but the original content's deleted), and Ctrl+V to paste. When you're in Edit mode, you can use these keys to copy whatever you've selected. If you're not in Edit mode, the copying or cutting operation grabs all the content in the field.

Saving and Opening Access Databases

Unlike other programs, Access doesn't require that you save your work. It automatically saves any changes you make.

When you create a new database (page 589), Access saves your database file. When you add a table or another object to the database, Access saves the database again. And when you enter new data or edit existing data, Access saves the database almost instantaneously.

GEM IN THE ROUGH

Copying an Entire Record in One Step

Usually, you'll use copy and paste with little bits and pieces of data. However, Access has a little-known ability that lets you copy an *entire record*. To pull it off, follow these steps:

1. Click the margin to the left of the record you want to copy.
2. This selects the record. (If you want to copy more than one adjacent record, hold down Shift, and then drag your mouse up or down until they're all selected.)
3. Right-click the selection, and then choose Copy. This copies the content to the clipboard.
4. Scroll to the bottom of the table until you see the new-row marker (the asterisk).
5. Right-click the margin just to the left of the new-row marker, and then choose Paste.

Presto—an exact duplicate. (Truth be told, one piece of data doesn't match exactly. Access updates the ID column for your pasted record, giving it a new number. That's because every record needs to have a unique ID. You'll learn why on page 638.)

This automatic save process takes place behind the scenes, and you probably won't notice anything. But don't be alarmed when you exit Access and it doesn't prompt you to save changes, as *all changes are saved the moment you make them.*

Making Backups

The automatic save feature can pose a problem if you make a change mistakenly. If you're fast enough, you can use the Undo feature to reverse your last change (Figure 26-14). However, the Undo feature reverses only your most recent edit, so it's no help if you edit a series of records and then discover the problem. It also doesn't help if you close your table and then reopen it.

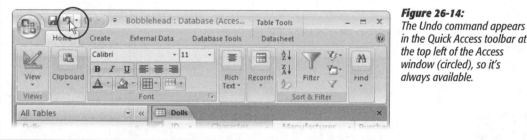

Figure 26-14:
The Undo command appears in the Quick Access toolbar at the top left of the Access window (circled), so it's always available.

Shrinking a Database

When you add information to a database, Access doesn't always pack the data as compactly as possible. Instead, Access is more concerned with getting information in and out of the database as quickly as it can.

After you've been working with a database for a while, you might notice that its size bloats up like a week-old fish in the sun. If you want to trim your database back to size, you can use a feature called *compacting*. To do so, just choose Office button → Manage → Compact and Repair Database. The amount of space you reclaim varies widely, but it's not uncommon to have a 10 MB database shrink down to a quarter of its size.

The only problem with the database compacting feature is that you need to remember to use it. If you want to keep your databases as small as possible at all times, you can switch on a setting that tells Access to compact the current database every time you close it. Here's how:

1. Open the database that you want to automatically compact.

2. Choose Office button → Access Options. Access opens the Access Options window where you can make a number of configuration changes.

3. In the list on the left, choose Current Database.

4. In the page on the right, turn on the "Compact on Close" checkbox.

5. Click OK to save your changes.

You can set the "Compact on Close" setting on as few or as many databases as you want. Just remember, it's not switched on when you first create a new database.

For these reasons, it's a good idea to make frequent database backups. To make a backup, you simply need to copy your database file to another folder, or make a copy with another name (like Bobblehead_Backup1.accdb). You can perform these tasks with Windows Explorer, but Access gives you an even easier option. Just choose Office button → Manage → Back Up Database, and Access creates a copy of your database for you, in the location you choose (Figure 26-15).

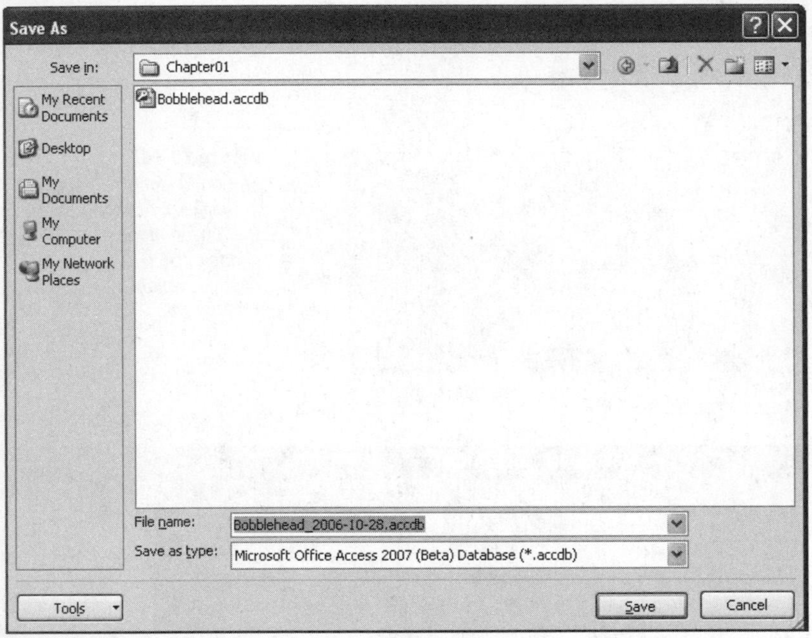

Figure 26-15:
When you choose Office button → Manage → Back Up Database, Access fills in a suggested file name that incorporates the current date. That way, if you have several backup files, you can pick out the one you want.

Note: It's still up to you to *remember* to back up your database. Access doesn't include an automatic backup feature, but you can use another tool to periodically copy your database file. One example is the Windows Task Scheduler that's included with most versions of Windows. (You can read a quick no-nonsense Task Scheduler tutorial at *www.pctechguide.com/tutorials/ScheduleTasks.htm*.)

Saving a Database with a Different Name or Format

If you want to save your database with a different name, in a different place, or using an older Access file format, you can use the trusty Save As command. Choose Office button → Save As, and then use one of the options in Figure 26-16.

Figure 26-16:
Make sure you click the right-pointing arrow next to the Save As menu command to see this submenu of choices. (Just clicking Save As performs the default option, which saves a copy of the currently selected database object, not your entire database.) Then, choose one of the options under the "Save the database in another format" heading.

Note that, once Access creates the new database file, that file's the one it keeps using. In other words, when you create a table or edit some data, Access updates the *new* file. (If you want to go back to the old file, you either need to open it in Access, or use Save As again.)

Opening a Database

Once you've created a database, it's easy to open it later. You can use any of these approaches:

- Double-click a database file. (You can browse to it using My Computer, Windows Explorer, or just plop in on your desktop.) Remember, Access databases have the file extension .accdb or .mdb.

- Launch Access, and then look for your database in the Open Recent Database section on the right of the Getting Started page. (The same list's available through the Office menu, as shown in Figure 26-17.)

- Launch Access, choose Office button → Open, and then browse for your Access database file.

When you open a database, you'll notice something a little bizarre. Access pops up a message bar with a scary-sounding security warning (Figure 26-18).

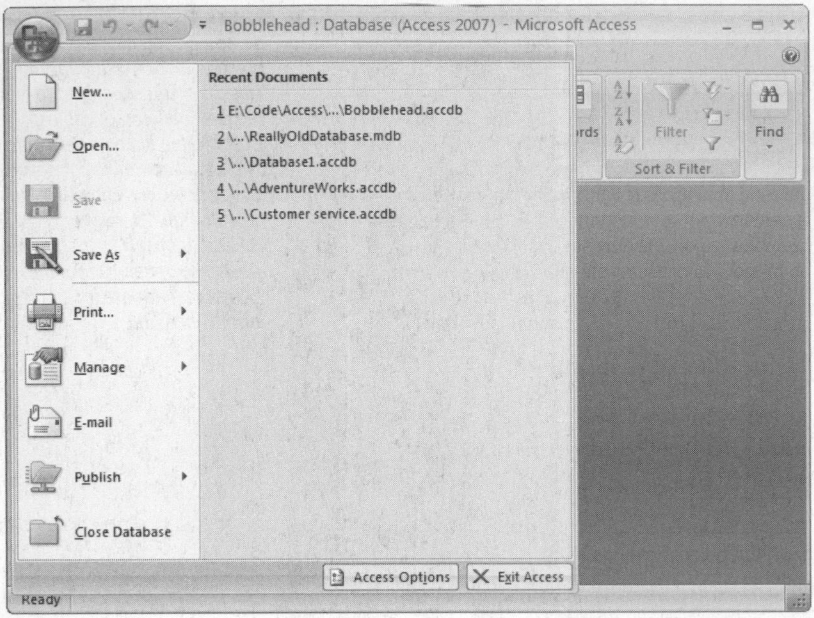

Figure 26-17:
The Office menu's Recent Documents list has the same list of files as the Open Recent Database section on the Getting Started page. But if you already have a database open, the Recent Documents list's more convenient, because you don't need to head back to the Getting Started page.

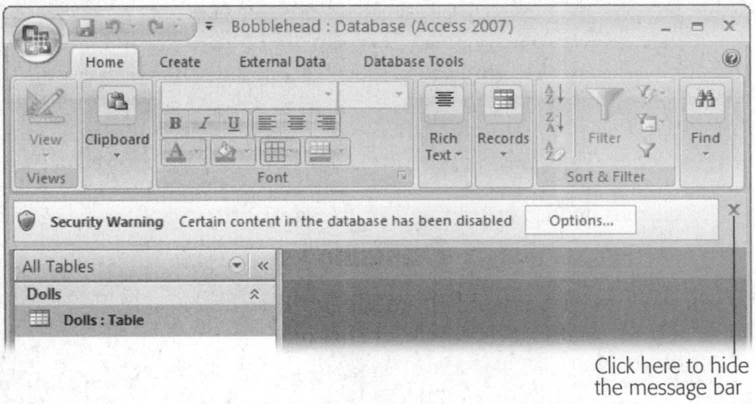

Figure 26-18:
This security warning tells you that Access doesn't trust your database—in other words, it's opened your file in a special safe mode that prevents your database from performing any risky operations.

Click here to hide
the message bar

The security warning's a bit confusing, because right now your database doesn't even *attempt* do anything risky. However, when you start using action queries (Chapter 31), it's a different story. At that point, you may want to reconfigure Access so it recognizes your files and learns to be a bit more trusting.

In the meantime, you're probably wondering what you should do about the message bar. Just click the X at the right side of the message bar to banish it. (It'll reappear the next time you open the database.)

FREQUENTLY ASKED QUESTION

What's with the .laccdb File?

I see an extra file with the extension .laccdb. What gives?

So far, you've familiarized yourself with the .accdb file type. But if you're in the habit of browsing around with Windows Explorer, you may notice another file that you didn't create, with the cryptic extension .laccdb. Along with Bobblehead. accdb, you may spot the mysterious Bobblehead.laccdb.

Access creates a .laccdb file when you open a database file and removes it when you close the database, so you'll see it only while you (or someone else) is browsing the database.

Access uses the .laccddb to track who's currently using the database. The *l* stands for *lock*, and it's used to make sure that if more than one person's using the database at once, people can't make changes to the same record at the same time (which could cause all manner of headaches).

Access 2007: The Missing Manual covers more on how Access works with multiple users. All you need to know is that it's safe to ignore the .laccddb file. You don't need to include it in your backups.

Opening More Than One Database at Once

Every time you use the Office button → Open command, Access closes the current database, and then opens the one you chose. If you want to see more than one database at a time, you need to fire up more than one copy of Access at the same time. (Computer geeks refer to this action as starting more than one *instance* of a program.)

It's almost embarrassingly easy. If you double-click another database file while Access is already open, then a second Access window appears in the taskbar for that database. You can also launch a second (or third, or fourth…) instance of Access from the Start menu, and then use Office button → Open to load up a different database in each one.

Opening a Database Created in an Older Version of Access

You can use the Office button → Open command to open an Access database that somebody created with a previous version of Access. (See the box "Sharing Databases with Older Versions of Access" on page 592 for more about different Access file formats.)

Access handles old database files differently, depending on just how old they are. Here's how it works:

- If you open an Access 2002-2003 file, you don't get any notification or warning. Access keeps the current format, and you're free to make any changes you want.

- If you open an Access 2000 file, you're also in for smooth sailing. However, if you change the design of the database, the new parts you add may not be accessible in Access 2000.

- If you open an older Access file (like one created for Access 97, 95, or 2.0), Access asks whether you want to convert the database or just open it (see Figure 26-19).

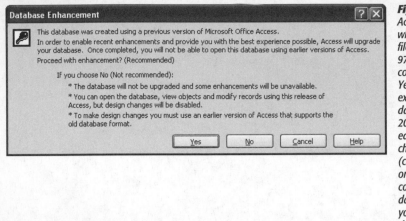

Figure 26-19:
Access gives you a choice when you open a database file that was created in Access 97, 95, or 2.0. If you choose to convert the database (click Yes), Access copies the existing database into a new database file, in Access 2002-2003 format. You can then edit this copy normally. If you choose to open the database (click No), Access opens the original file without making a copy. You can still edit existing data and add new data, but you can't change the database's design.

POWER USERS' CLINIC

Changing the Folder Access Uses for Databases

Access always assumes you want to store databases in the My Documents folder. And though you can choose a different location every time you save or open a database, if there's another folder you need to visit frequently, then it makes sense to make that your standard database storage location. You can configure Access to use this folder with just a few steps:

1. Choose Office button → Access Options. The Access Options window appears.

2. In the list on the left, choose Popular.

3. In the page on the right, look for the "Creating databases" heading. Underneath, you'll find a "Default database folder" text box. Type in the folder you want to use (like C:\MyDatabases), or click Browse to navigate to it.

When you're finished, click OK to save your changes.

Tip: You can always tell the current database's format by looking at the text in brackets in the Access window's title bar. If you open an Access 2002-2003 file, the title bar might read "Bobblehead: Database (Access 2002-2003 file format)".

When you open an old-school Access database, you'll notice something else has changed. When you open a table, it won't appear in a tabbed window (like the ones shown in Figure 26-22). Instead, the table opens in an ordinary window that can float wherever it wants *inside* the main Access window. This seems fine at first, until you open several tables at once. Then, you're stuck with some real clutter, as shown in Figure 26-20.

This somewhat unfriendly behavior is designed to be more like previous versions of Access. But don't worry—you can get back to the slick tabs even if you don't convert your database to the new format. All you need to do is set a single configuration option for your database:

Figure 26-20:
In an old-style Access database, different windows can overlap each other. It's not long before the table you want is buried at the bottom of a stack of windows.

1. Choose Office button → Access Options. The Access Options window appears.

2. In the list on the left, choose Current Database.

3. Under the Application Options heading, look for the Document Windows Options setting, where you can choose Overlapping Windows (the Access 2003 standard) or Tabbed Windows (the wave of the future).

4. Click OK.

5. Close and open your database so the new setting takes effect.

For a retro touch, you can use the same setting to make a brand new Access database use overlapping windows instead of tabs.

Creating Another Database

Creating a new database is the easiest task yet. You simply need to choose Office button → New. Access takes you back to the Getting Started page, where you can create a blank database by clicking the familiar Blank Database button, as described earlier (page 589).

The Navigation Pane

It's time to step back and take a look at what you've accomplished so far. You've created the Bobblehead database, and added a single database object: a table named Dolls. You've filled the Dolls table with several records. You don't have the fancy windows, reports, and search routines that make a database work really smoothly, but you do have the most important ingredient—organized data.

One issue you haven't tackled yet is how you manage the objects in your database. For example, if you have more than one table, you need a way to move back and forth between the two. That tool's the navigation pane, shown in Figure 26-21.

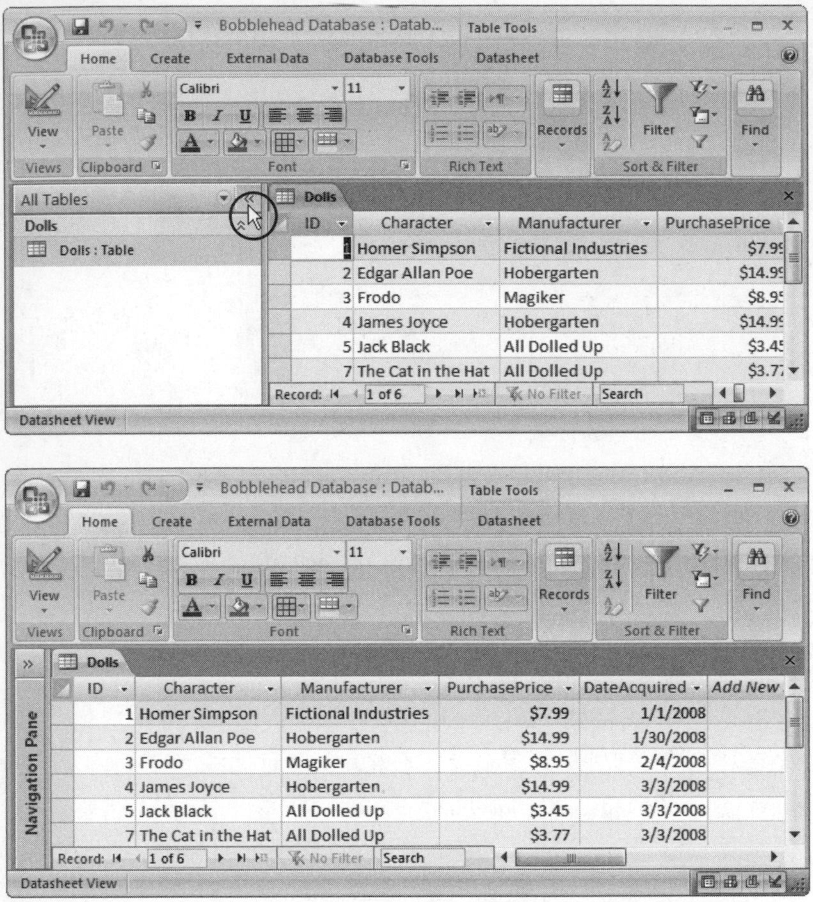

Figure 26-21:
Unhappy with the space consumed by the navigation pane? Click the Open/Close button in the top-right corner (top), and the navigation bar slides out of the way to give more room for the datasheet (bottom). Click the button again to expand it back into view.

Browsing Tables with the Navigation Pane

The navigation pane shows the objects (page 586) that are part of your database, and it lets you manipulate them. However, you don't necessarily see all your database objects at all times. The navigation pane has several different viewing modes, so you can home in on exactly what interests you.

When you first create a database, the navigation pane shows only the tables in your database. That's good enough for now—after all, your database doesn't contain anything but the tables you've created.

To really try out the navigation pane, you need a database with more than one table. To give it a whirl, choose Create → Table from the ribbon to add a new blank table. Follow all the steps on page 594 to define the table and insert a record or two.

Tip: Not sure what table to create? Try creating a Collectors table that tracks all the friends you know who share the same bobbleheaded obsession. Now try to come up with a few useful fields for this table (while remembering that there's no need to go crazy with the details yet), and then compare your version to the example in Figure 26-22.

Once you've added the new table, you see both the new table and the old in the navigation pane at the same time. If you want to open a table, then, in the navigation pane, just double-click it. If you have more than one datasheet open at once, then Access organizes them into tabs (see Figure 26-22).

If you open enough tables, eventually all the tabs you need won't fit. In this situation, Access adds tiny scroll buttons to the left and right of the tab strip. You can use these buttons to move through all the tabs, but it takes longer.

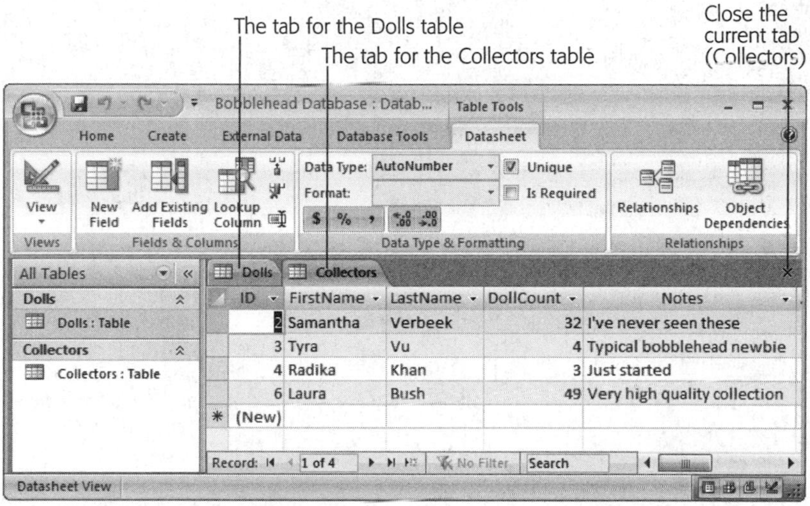

The tab for the Dolls table
The tab for the Collectors table
Close the current tab (Collectors)

Figure 26-22:
Using the navigation pane, you can open as many tables at once as you want. Access gives each datasheet a separate tabbed window. To move from one window to another, you just click the corresponding tab. If you're feeling a bit crowded, just click the X at the far right of the tab strip to close the current datasheet.

Managing Database Objects

So far, you know how to open a table using the navigation pane. However, opening tables isn't all you can do with the navigation pane. You can actually perform three more simple tasks with any database object that shows up in the navigation pane:

• **Rename it.** Right-click the object, and then choose Rename. Then, type in the new name, and then press Enter. Go this route if you decide your Dolls table would be better off named DollsInMyWorldRenownedCollection.

GEM IN THE ROUGH

Collapsing the Ribbon

Most people are happy to have the ribbon sit at the top of the Access window, with all its buttons on hand. However, serious data crunchers demand maximum space for their data. They'd rather look at another record of information than a pumped-up toolbar. If this preference describes you, then you'll be happy to find out you can *collapse* the ribbon, which shrinks it down to a single row of tab titles, as shown in Figure 26-23. To do so, just double-click any tab title.

Even when the ribbon's collapsed, you can still use all its features. Just click a tab. If you click Home, the Home tab pops up over your worksheet. As soon as you click the button you want in the Home tab (or click somewhere else in the Access window), the ribbon collapses itself again. The same trick works if you trigger a command in the ribbon using the keyboard, as described on page 6.

If you use the ribbon only occasionally, or if you prefer to use keyboard shortcuts, it makes sense to collapse the ribbon. Even when collapsed, the ribbon commands are available; it just takes an extra click to open the tab. On the other hand, if you make frequent trips to the ribbon, or if you're learning about Access and you like to browse the ribbon to see the available features, don't bother collapsing it. The extra space that you'll lose is well worth it.

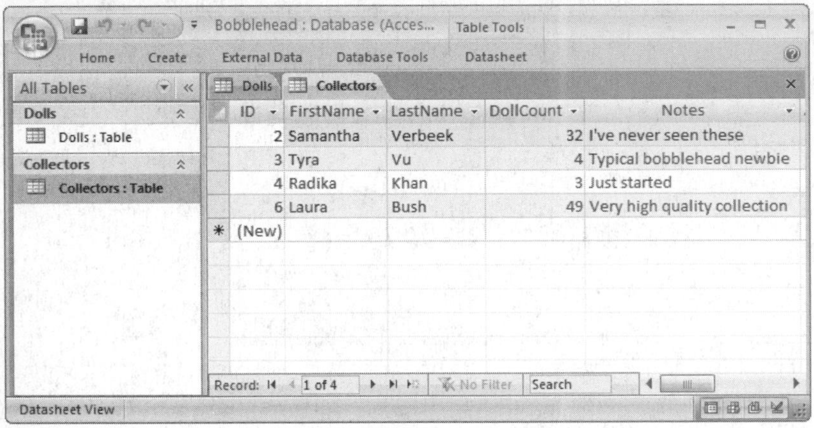

Figure 26-23:
Do you want to use every square inch of screen space for your data? You can collapse the ribbon (as shown here) by double-clicking any tab. Click a tab to pop it open temporarily, or double-click a tab to bring the ribbon back for good. And if you want to perform the same trick without raising your fingers from the keyboard, then you can use the shortcut key Ctrl+F1.

- **Create a copy.** Right-click the object, and then choose Copy. Right-click anywhere in the navigation pane, and then choose Paste. Access prompts you to supply the new copy's name. The copy-an-object feature's useful if you want to take an existing table and try redesigning it, but you're not ready to remove the original copy just yet.

- **Delete it.** Right-click the object, and then choose Delete. Access asks you to confirm this operation, because you can't reverse it.

Access gives you a few more options for transferring database objects and tucking them out of sight. You'll consider these features later in the book.

Creating a Shortcut to a Table

You probably already know that you can place a Windows shortcut on your desktop that points to your database file. To do so, just right-click your desktop, choose New → Shortcut, and then follow the instructions to pick your database file and choose a shortcut name. Now, any time you want to jump back into your database, you can double-click your shortcut.

You probably don't know that you can create a shortcut that opens a database *and* navigates directly to a specific table. In fact, this maneuver's even easier than creating a plain-vanilla shortcut. Just follow these steps:

1. Resize the Access window so it doesn't take up the full screen, and then minimize any other programs. This way, you can see the desktop behind Access, which is essential for this trick.

2. Find the table you want to use in the navigation pane. Drag this table out of Access and over the desktop.

3. Release the mouse button. Access creates a shortcut with a name like "Shortcut to Dolls in Bobblehead.accdb". Double-click this shortcut to load the Bobblehead database and open a datasheet right away for the Dolls table.

CHAPTER 27

Building Smarter Tables

In the previous chapter, you learned how to dish out databases and pop tables into them without breaking a sweat. However, there's bad news. The tables you've been creating so far aren't up to snuff.

Most significantly, you haven't explicitly told Access what *type* of information you intend to store in each field of your table. A database treats text, numbers, dates, and other types of information differently. If you store numeric information in a field that expects text, then you can't do calculations later on (like find the average value of your bobblehead dolls), and you can't catch mistakes (like a bobblehead with a price value of "fourscore and twenty").

To prevent problems like these, you need to define the *data type* of each field in your table. This is the central task you'll tackle in this chapter. Once you've mastered data types, you're ready to consider some of the finer points of database design.

Understanding Data Types

All data's not created equal. Consider the Dolls table you created in Chapter 26 (page 593). Its fields actually contain several different types of information:

- **Text.** The Character and Manufacturer fields.
- **Numbers.** The ID and PurchasePrice fields.
- **Dates.** The DateAcquired field.

You may naturally assume that the PurchasePrice field always includes numeric content, and the DateAcquired field always includes something that can be interpreted as a date. But if you haven't set the data types correctly, Access doesn't share your assumptions, and doesn't follow the same rules.

When you create a new field in Datasheet view, Access makes an educated guess about the data type by examining the information you've just typed in. If you type *44*, then Access assumes you're creating a number field. If you type *Jan 6, 2007*, then Access recognizes a date. However, it's easy to confuse Access, which leads to the problems shown in Figure 27-1.

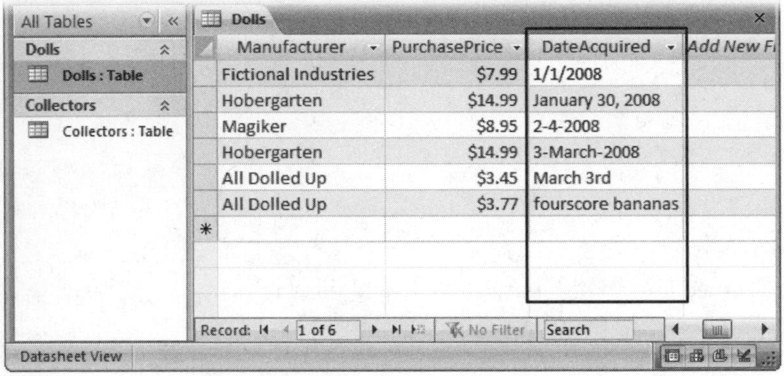

Figure 27-1:
Here, Access doesn't recognize the date format used for the DateAcquired field when it was created. As a result, Access treats that field as ordinary text. You can enter dates in several different formats (which makes the DateAcquired information harder to read and impossible to sort). You also let in completely nonsensical entries, like "fourscore bananas."

In order to prevent invalid entries, you need to tell Access what each field *should* contain. Once you set the rules, Access enforces them rigorously. You put these requirements in place using another window—the Design view of your table.

Design View

When you create a new database, Access starts you off with a single table and shows that table in Datasheet view. (As you learned last chapter, Datasheet view is the grid-like view where you can create a table *and* enter data.) To switch to Design view, right-click the tab name (like "Dolls: Table"), and then choose Design View. (Or you can use the Home → View command, the Table Tools | Datasheet → View command, or the View buttons at the bottom of the Access window. Figure 27-2 shows all your options. All of these commands do the same thing, so pick whichever approach seems most convenient.)

Note: If you've opened an old Access 2003 database, you won't see any tabs. Instead, you'll get a bunch of overlapping windows. You can remedy this problem and get your tabs back by following the instructions on page 606. Or, if you want to keep the overlapping windows, just use the view buttons or the ribbon to change views (instead of the right-click-the-tab-title approach described above).

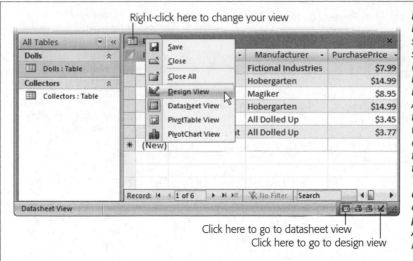

Right-click here to change your view

| Save |
| Close |
| Close All |
| Design View |
| Datasheet View |
| PivotTable View |
| PivotChart View |

Manufacturer	▾	PurchasePrice	▾
Fictional Industries		$7.99	
Hobergarten		$14.99	
Magiker		$8.95	
Hobergarten		$14.99	
All Dolled Up		$3.45	
All Dolled Up		$3.77	

* (New)

All Tables
Dolls
   Dolls : Table
Collectors
   Collectors : Table

Record: ⏮ ◀ 1 of 6 ▶ ⏭ ⏭ No Filter Search ◀ ▶

Datasheet View

Click here to go to datasheet view
Click here to go to design view

Figure 27-2:
Right-click the tab name to see this menu. You can switch to Design view (choose Design View) and back again (choose Datasheet View). Alternatively, you can use the tiny view buttons in the window's bottom-right corner to jump back and forth. (Don't worry about the other two view buttons. Those are used to analyze data in a pivot table, an advanced form of data presentation covered in Access 2007: The Missing Manual.)

If you switch to Design view on a brand-new table that you haven't saved yet, Access asks you for a table name. Access then saves the table before switching you to Design view.

Tip: For a handy shortcut, you can create a new table and automatically start in Design view. To do this, choose Create → Tables → Table Design. However, when you take this route, your table doesn't include the very important ID column, so you need to add one, as described on page 639.

While Datasheet view shows the content in your table, Design view shows only its *structure* (see Figure 27-3).

You can use Design view to add, rearrange, and remove fields, but you can't use it to add new records. In the Dolls table, you can use Design view to add a Quantity field to keep track of doll duplicates. However, you can't add your newly purchased Bono bobblehead without switching back to the Datasheet view. Design view isn't intended for data entry.

At first, Design view seems quite intimidating. To simplify what you're looking at, you should start by closing the Property Sheet box on the window's right side. (The Property Sheet lets you set a few highly technical table settings, none of which you need to consider right now.) To banish it, choose Table Tools | Design → Property Sheet. If you want to bring it back later, then just repeat the same command.

Organizing and Describing Your Fields

Design view allows you to rearrange the order of your fields, add new ones, rename the existing ones, and more. You can also do all these things in Datasheet view, but Access gurus usually find it's easier to work in Design view, because you won't be distracted by the data in the table.

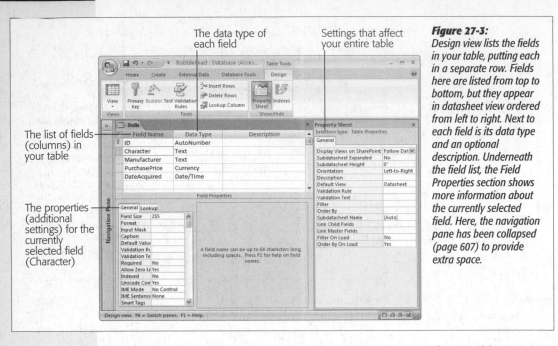

The data type of each field

Settings that affect your entire table

The list of fields (columns) in your table

The properties (additional settings) for the currently selected field (Character)

Figure 27-3:
Design view lists the fields in your table, putting each in a separate row. Fields here are listed from top to bottom, but they appear in datasheet view ordered from left to right. Next to each field is its data type and an optional description. Underneath the field list, the Field Properties section shows more information about the currently selected field. Here, the navigation pane has been collapsed (page 607) to provide extra space.

Here are a few simple ways you can change the structure of your table in Design view:

- **Add a new field to the end of your table.** Scroll to the last row of the field list, and then type in a new field name. This action's equivalent to adding a new field in Datasheet view.

- **Add a new field between existing fields.** Move to the field that's just *under* the place where you want to add the new field. Right-click the field, and then choose Insert Rows. Then, type a field name in the new, blank row.

- **Move a field.** Drag the gray square immediately to the left of the field you want to move, to the new position.

Note: Remember, the fields' order isn't all that important, because you can change the order in which you view the fields in Datasheet view. However, most people find it's easier to design a table if you organize the fields from the very start.

- **Delete a field.** Right-click the gray square immediately to the left of the field you want to remove, and then choose Delete Rows. Keep in mind that when you remove a field, you also wipe out any data that was stored in that field. This action isn't reversible, so Access prompts you to confirm it's really what you want to do.

- **Add a description for a field.** Type in a sentence or two in the Description column next to the appropriate field (see Figure 27-4).

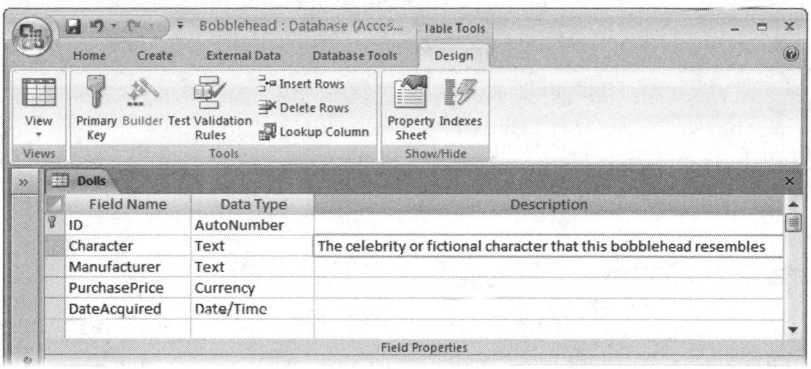

Figure 27-4:
Descriptions can help you remember what's what if you need to modify a table later on. Descriptions are a great idea if more than one person maintains the same database, in which case you need to make sure your fields are as clear as possible. Descriptions also appear in the status bar when you're entering information in a table (see Figure 27-5).

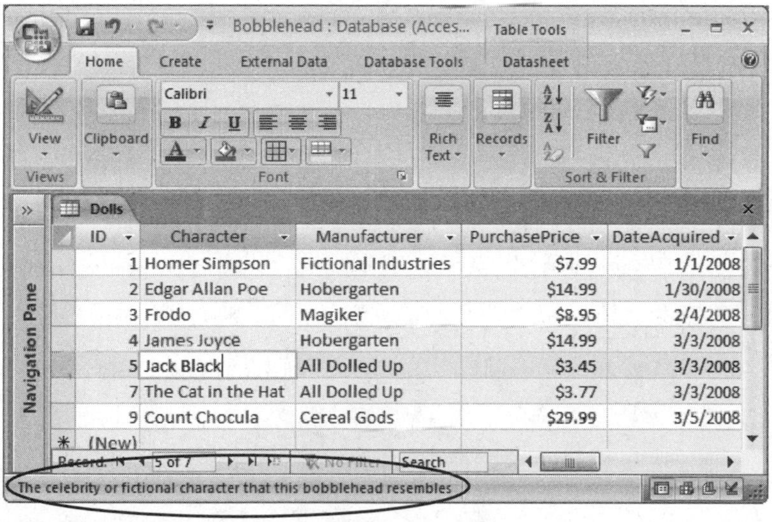

Figure 27-5:
The status bar text tells you what goes in this column, based on the field description. Sadly, this feature isn't as useful as it seems, because most people never think to look down in the status bar.

How Updates Work in Design View

Access doesn't immediately apply the changes you make in Design view. Instead, it waits until you close the table or switch back to Datasheet view. At that point, Access asks whether you want to save the table. (The answer, of course, is Yes.)

Sometimes, you may apply a change that causes a bit of a problem. You could try to change the data type of a field so that it stores numbers instead of text. (The box on page 621, "Changing the Data Type Can Lose Information," discusses this problem in more detail.) In this situation, you won't discover the problem until you close the table or switch back to the Datasheet view, which might be a little later than you expect.

If you've made a potentially problematic change and you just can't take the suspense, you're better off applying your update *immediately,* so you can see if there's a problem before you go any further. To do so, click the Quick Access toolbar's Save button (it's the diskette icon in the Access window's top-left corner), or just use the keyboard shortcut Ctrl+S. Access applies your change, and then saves the table. If it runs into a problem, Access tells you about it (and lets you choose how you want to fix it) before you do anything else with the table.

Access Data Types

Design view's a much more powerful place for defining a table than Datasheet view. As you'll see throughout this chapter, Design view allows you to tweak all sorts of details that are hidden in Datasheet view (or just awkward to change).

One of these is the *data type* of your field—a setting that tells Access what type of information you're planning to store. To change the data type, make a selection in the Data Type column next to the appropriate field (Figure 27-6). Here's where you separate the text from numbers (and other data types). The trick's choosing the best data type from the long list Access provides—you'll get more help in the following section.

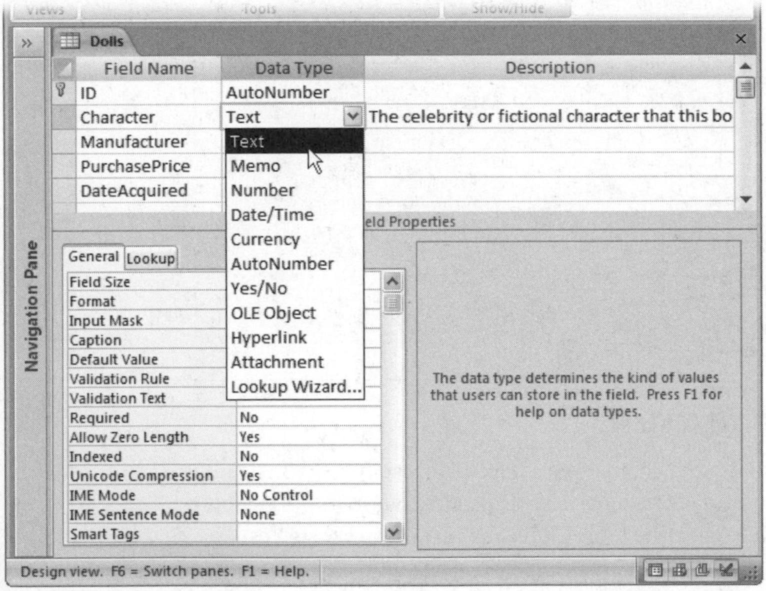

Figure 27-6:
To choose a data type, click the Data Type column next to the appropriate field. A drop-down list box appears, with 11 choices.

Depending on the data type you choose, there are other *field properties* that you can adjust to nail down your data type even more precisely. If you use a text data type, then you use field properties to set the maximum length. If you choose a decimal value, then you use field properties to set the number of decimal places. You set field properties in the Field Properties part of the Design view, which appears just under the field list. You'll learn more about field properties throughout this chapter (and you'll consider them again in Chapter 29).

The most important decision you'll make for any field is choosing its data type. The data type tells Access what sort of information you plan to store in that field. Access uses this information to reject values that don't make sense (see Figure 27-7), to perform proper sorting, and to provide other features like calculations, summaries, and filtering.

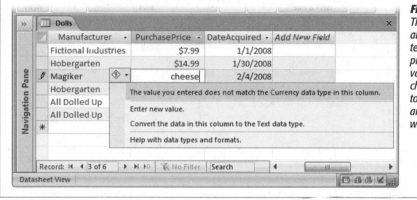

Figure 27-7:
This currency field absolutely does not allow text. Access lets you fix the problem by entering a new value (the right choice) or changing the field data type to text so that it allows anything (the absolutely wrong choice).

Note: A field can have only one data type. You can't create a field that can store two or three different data types, because Access wouldn't have enough information to manage the field properly. (Instead, in this situation, you probably need two separate fields.)

As you learned earlier, there are three basic types of data in the world: text, numbers, and dates. However, Access actually provides a whopping *11* data types, which include many more specialized choices. Before you pick the right data type, it's a good idea to review all your choices. Table 27-1 shows an overview of the first 10 menu options in the Data Type list. (The Lookup wizard choice isn't included, because it isn't a real data type. Instead, this menu option launches the Lookup wizard, which lets you set a list of allowed values. You'll learn more about this on page 689 in Chapter 29.)

The following sections describe each data type except for OLE Object, which is a holdover from the dark ages of Access databases. Each section also describes any important field properties that are unique to that data type.

Table 27-1. Access Data Types

Data Type	Description	Examples
Text	Numbers, letters, punctuation, and symbols, up to a maximum of 255 characters (an average-sized paragraph).	Names, addresses, phone numbers, and product descriptions. This data type's the most common.
Memo	Large amounts of unformatted text, up to 65,536 characters (an average-sized chapter in a novel).	Articles, memos, letters, arrest warrants, and other short documents.
Number	A variety of different kinds of numbers, including negative numbers and those that have decimal places.	Any type of number except dollar values. Stores measurements, counts, and percentages.
Currency	Similar to Number, but optimized for numbers that represent values of money.	Prices, payments, and expenses.
Date/Time	A calendar date or time of day (or both). Don't use this field for time *intervals* (the number of minutes in a song, the length of your workout session)—instead, use the Number data type.	Birthdates, order dates, ship dates, appointments, and UFO sighting times.
Yes/No	Holds one of two values: Yes or No. (You can also think of this as True or False.)	Fields with exactly two options, like male/female or approved/unapproved.
Hyperlink	A URL to a Web site, an email address, or a file path.	www.FantasyPets.com, noreplies@antisocial.co.uk, f:\Documents\Report.doc.
Attachment	One or more separate files. The content from these files is copied into the database.	Pictures, Word documents, Excel spreadsheets, sound files, and so on.
AutoNumber	Stores a number that Access generates when you insert a new record. Every record automatically gets a unique number that identifies it.	Used to uniquely identify each record, especially for a primary key (page 638). Usually, the field's named ID.
OLE Object	Holds embedded binary data, according to the Windows OLE (object linking and embedding) standard. Rarely used, because it leads to database bloat and other problems. The Attachment field's almost always a better choice.	Some types of pictures and documents from other programs. Mostly used in old-school Access databases. Nowadays, database designers use the Attachment data type instead of the OLE Object data type.

Text

Text is the all-purpose data type. It accepts any combination of letters, numbers, and other characters. So you can use a text field for a word or two (like "Mary Poppins"), a sentence ("The candidate is an English nanny given to flights of song."), or anything else ("@#$d sf_&!").

Changing the Data Type Can Lose Information

The best time to choose the data types for your fields is when you first create the table. That way, your table's completely empty, and you won't run into any problems.

If you add a few records, and *then* decide to change the data type in one of your fields, life becomes a little more complicated. You can still use Design view to change the data type, but Access needs to go through an extra step and *convert* the existing data to the new data type.

In many cases, the conversion process goes smoothly. If you have a text field that contains only numbers, you won't have a problem changing the data type from Text to Number. But in other cases, the transition isn't quite so seamless. Here are some examples of the problems you might run into:

- You change the data type from Text to Date, but Access can't interpret some of your values as dates.

- You change the data type from Text to Number, but some of your records have text values in that field (even though they shouldn't).

- You change the data type from Text to Number. However, your field contains fractional numbers (like 4.234), and you forget to change the Field Size property (page 626). As a result, Access assumes you want to use only whole numbers, and chops off all your decimal places.

The best way to manage these problems is to make a backup (page 601) before you make any drastic changes, and be on the lookout for changes that go wrong. In the first two cases in the list above, Access warns you that it needs to remove some values because they don't fit the data type rules (see Figure 27-8). The third problem's a little more insidious—Access gives you a warning, but it doesn't actually tell you whether or not a problem occurred. If you suspect trouble, switch to Design view, and then check out your data before going any further.

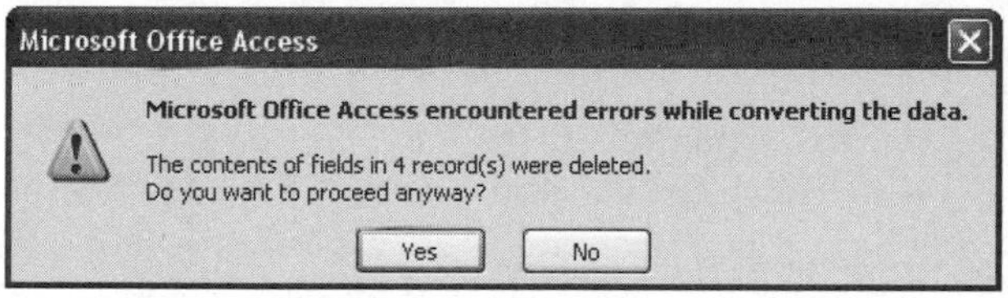

Figure 27-8:
Don't say you weren't warned. Here, Access lets you know (in its own slightly obscure way) that it can't make the change you want—modifying the data type of field from Text to Date—without throwing out the values in four records. The best course of action is to click No to cancel the change and then take a closer look at your table in Datasheet view to track down the problematic values.

Note: Because text fields are so lax, you can obviously enter numbers, dates, and just about anything else in them. However, you should use text only when you're storing some information that can't be dealt with using another data type, because Access always treats the contents of a text field as plain, ordinary text. In other words, if you store the number 43.99 in a text field, Access doesn't realize you're dealing with numbers, and it doesn't let you use it in a calculation.

Sometimes it seems that the Text data type's just too freewheeling. Fortunately, you can apply some stricter rules that deny certain characters or force text values to match a preset pattern. For example, Access usually treats phone numbers like text, because they represent a series of characters like 123-4444 (not the single number 1,234,444). However, you don't want to let people put letters in a phone number, because they obviously don't belong. To put this restriction into action, you can use input masks (page 675) and validation (page 680), two features discussed in Chapter 29.

Text length

Every text field has a *maximum length*. This trait comes as a great surprise to many people who aren't used to databases. After all, with today's gargantuan hard drives, why worry about space? Can't your database just expand to fit whatever data you want to stuff inside?

The maximum length matters because it determines how *densely* Access can pack your records together. For performance reasons, Access needs to make sure that an entire record's stored in one spot, so it always reserves the maximum amount of space a record might need. If your table has four fields that are 50 characters apiece, Access can reserve 200 characters worth of space on your hard drive for each record. On the other hand, if your fields have a maximum 100 characters each, Access holds on to twice as much space for each record, even if you aren't actually using that space. The extra space isn't a major issue (you probably have plenty of room on your computer), but the more spread out a database, the slower your searches.

The standard maximum length is 50, a good starting point. The box "Maximum Length Guidelines" (page 624) has some more recommendations.

To set the maximum length, enter a number in the Field Size box, in the Field Properties section (Figure 27-9). The largest maximum you're allowed is 255 characters. If you need to store a large paragraph or an entire article's worth of information, then you need the Memo data type instead (see below).

Tip: It's worthwhile being a little generous with maximum lengths to avoid the need to modify the database later on.

Memo

Microsoft designed the Memo data type to store large quantities of text. If you want to place a chapter from a book, an entire newspaper article, or just several paragraphs into a field, you need the Memo data type. The name's a little odd—although a memo field could certainly store the information from an inter-office memorandum, it's just as useful any time you have large blocks of text.

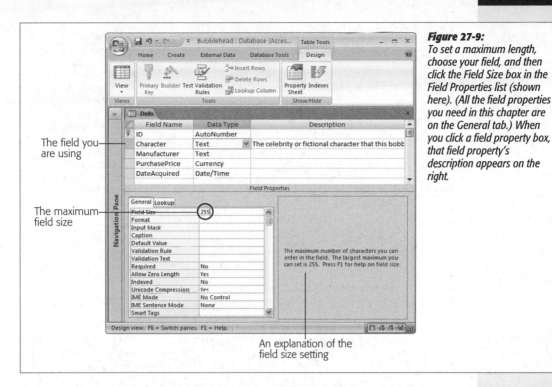

The field you are using

The maximum field size

An explanation of the field size setting

Figure 27-9:
To set a maximum length, choose your field, and then click the Field Size box in the Field Properties list (shown here). (All the field properties you need in this chapter are on the General tab.) When you click a field property box, that field property's description appears on the right.

When creating a memo field, you don't need to supply a maximum length, because Access stores the data in a memo field differently from other data types. Essentially, it stuffs memo data into a separate section, so it can keep the rest of the record as compact and efficient as possible, but accommodate large amounts of text.

A memo field tops out at 65,536 characters. To put it in perspective, that's about the same size as this chapter. If you need more space, then add more than one memo field.

Note: Technically, the 65,536 character limitation's a limitation in the Access user interface, not the database. If you program an application that uses your database, it could store far more—up to a gigabyte's worth of information in a memo field.

If you need to edit a large amount of text while you're working on the datasheet, then you can use the Zoom box (Figure 27-10). Just move to the field you want to edit, and then press Shift+F2.

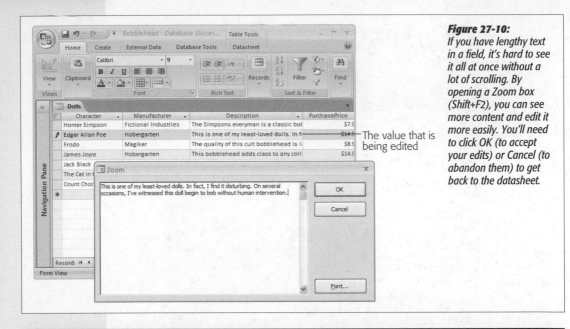

Figure 27-10:
If you have lengthy text in a field, it's hard to see it all at once without a lot of scrolling. By opening a Zoom box (Shift+F2), you can see more content and edit it more easily. You'll need to click OK (to accept your edits) or Cancel (to abandon them) to get back to the datasheet.

UP TO SPEED

Maximum Length Guidelines

Here are some recommended maximum lengths:

- **First names and last names.** 25 characters handles a first name, while 50 characters each plays it safe for a long, hyphenated last name.

- **Middle initial.** One character. (Sometimes common sense is right.)

- **Email address.** Go with 50 characters. Email addresses closer to 100 characters have turned up in the wild (Google "world's longest email address" for more), but they're unlikely to reach your database.

- **Cities, states, countries, and other places.** Although a Maori name for a hill in New Zealand tops out at over 80 characters (see *http://en. wikipedia.org/wiki/Longest_word_in_English*), 50 is enough for most practical purposes.

- **Street address.** A street address consists of a number, followed by a space, then the street name, another

space, and the street abbreviation (like Rd or St). Fifty characters handles it, as long as you put postal codes, cities, and other postal details in other fields.

- **Phone numbers, postal codes, credit card numbers, and other fixed-length text.** Count the number characters and ignore the placeholders, and set the maximum to match. If you want to store the phone number (123) 456-7890, make the field 10 characters long. You can then *store* the phone number as 1234567890, but use an input mask (page 675) to add the parentheses, spaces, and dash when you *display* it. This approach is better because it avoids the headaches that result from entering similar phone numbers in different ways.

- **Description or comments.** 255 characters fits three or four average sentences of information. If you need more, consider the memo data type instead (page 622).

Formatted text

Like a text field, the memo field stores *unformatted* text. However, you can also store *rich text* in a memo field—text that has different fonts, colors, text alignment, and so on. To do so, set the Text Format setting to Rich Text (rather than Plain Text).

To format part of your text, you simply need to select it and then choose a formatting option from the ribbon's Home → Font Home → Rich Text sections. However, most of the time you won't take this approach, because it's difficult to edit large amounts of text in the datasheet's narrow columns. Instead, use Shift+F2 to open a Zoom box, and then use the mini-toolbar (Figure 27-11).

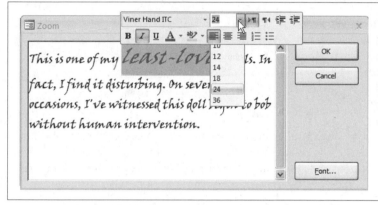

Figure 27-11:
To show the mini-toolbar, select some text, and then hover over it with the mouse. The mini-toolbar—a compact toolbar with formatting options—gradually fades into view. The mini-toolbar's sometimes a little finicky, and you may need to reselect the text more than once to get it to appear.

Tip: There's another, even easier way to get formatted text into a memo field. Create the text in a word processing program (like Word), format it there, and then copy and paste it into the field. All the formatting comes with it.

As neat as this feature may seem at first glance, it's rarely worth the trouble. Database purists believe that tables should store raw information and let other programs (or fancy forms) decide how to format it. The problem is that once you've created your formatted text, it can be quite a chore to maintain it. Just imagine having to change the font in 30,000 different records.

If you really do want to store formatted content, then consider linking your database to a separate document, like a Word file. In Access, you can do this in two ways:

• **Create a field that points to the file.** For example, c:\myfile\BonoBobblehead-Description.docx). For this trick, use the Text or Hyperlink data type (page 632).

• **Embed the file inside your database.** This way, it's impossible to lose the file (or end up pointing to the wrong location). However, you'll need to pull the file out every time you want to update it. To do this, you need to use the Attachment data type (page 633).

Number

The Number data type includes a wide variety of differently sized numbers. You can choose to allow decimal numbers, and you can use negative values (just precede the value with a minus sign). You should use the Number data type for every type of numeric information you have—except currency amounts, in which case the Currency data type (page 628) is a better match.

When you use numeric fields, you don't include information about the units you're using. You may have a field that represents a Weight in pounds, a Height in Meters, or an Age in Years. However, these fields contain only a number. It's up to you to know what that number signifies. If you think other people may be confused, consider explaining the units in the description (page 616), or incorporate it into the field name (like HeightInMeters).

Note: Your field should never, ever contain values like "44 pounds." Access treats this value as a text value, so if you make this mistake, you can't use all the important number crunching and validation tools you'll learn about later in this book.

Number size

As with a text field, when you create a number field, you need to set the Field Size property to make sure Access reserves the right amount of space. However, with numbers your options are a little more complicated than they are for ordinary text.

Essentially, numbers are divided into several subgroups, depending on whether or not they support fractional values (numbers to the right of a decimal point) and how many *bytes* of space Access uses to store them.

Note: A byte's a group of eight bits, which is the smallest unit of storage in the computer world. For example, a megabyte's approximately one million bytes.

Table 27-2 lists the different Field Size options you can choose for the Number data type, and explains when each one makes most sense. Initially, Access chooses Long Integer for all fields, which gives a fair bit of space but doesn't allow fractional values.

Table 27-2. Field Size Options for the Number Data Type

Field Size	Contains	When to Use It
Byte	An integer (whole number) from 0 to 255. Requires just one byte of space.	This size is risky, because it fits only very small numbers. Usually, it's safer to use Integer for small numbers and give yourself a little more breathing room.
Integer	An integer (whole number) from −32,768 to 32,767. Requires two bytes of space.	Useful if you need small numbers with no decimal part.

Table 27-2. *Field Size Options for the Number Data Type (continued)*

Field Size	Contains	When to Use It
Long Integer	An integer (whole number) from −2,147,483,648 to 2,147,483,647. Requires four bytes of space.	The Access standard. A good choice with plenty of room. Use this to store just about anything without hitting the maximum, as long as you don't need decimals.
Single	Positive or negative numbers with up to 38 zeroes and 7 decimal places of accuracy. Requires four bytes of space.	The best choice if you need to store fractional numbers or numbers that are too large to fit in a Long Integer.
Double	Positive or negative numbers with up to 308 zeroes and 15 decimal places of accuracy. Requires eight bytes of space.	Useful if you need ridiculously big numbers.
Decimal	Positive or negative numbers with up to 28 zeroes and 28 decimal places of accuracy. Requires eight bytes of space.	Useful for fractional numbers that have lots of digits to the right of the decimal point.

Note: Table 27-2 doesn't include Replication ID, because you use that option only with the AutoNumber data type (page 636).

Number formatting

The Field Size determines how Access stores your number in the table. However, you can still choose how it's *presented* in the datasheet. For example, 50, 50.00, 5E1, $50.00, and 5000% are all the same number behind the scenes, but people interpret them in dramatically different ways.

To choose a format, you set the Format field property. Your basic built-in choices include:

- **General Number.** Displays unadorned numbers, like 43.4534. Any extra zeroes at the end of a number are chopped off (so 4.10 becomes 4.1).

- **Currency and Euro.** Both options display numbers with two decimal places, thousands separators (the comma in $1,000.00), and a currency symbol. These choices are used only with the Currency data type (page 628).

- **Fixed.** Displays numbers with the same number of decimal places, filling in zeroes if necessary (like 432.11 and 39.00). A long column of numbers lines up on the decimal point, which makes your tables easier to read.

- **Standard.** Similar to Fixed, except it also uses thousands separators to help you quickly interpret large numbers like 1,000,000.00.

- **Percent.** Displays fractional numbers as percentages. For example, if you enter 0.5, that translates to 50%.

- **Scientific.** Displays numbers using scientific notation, which is ideal when you need to handle numbers that range widely in size (like 0.0003 and 300). Scientific notation displays the first non-zero digit of a number, followed by a fixed number of digits, and then indicates what power of ten that number needs to be multiplied by to generate the specified number. For example, 0.0003 becomes 3.00×10^{-4}, which displays as 3.00E-4. The number 300, on the other hand, becomes 3.00×10^{2}, or 3E2.

Tip: When using Fixed, Standard, Percent, or Scientific, you should also set the Decimal Places field property to the number of decimal places you want to see. Otherwise, you always get two.

- **A custom format string.** This is a cryptic code that tells Access exactly how to format a number. You need to type the format string you need into the Format box. For example, if you type in the weird-looking code #,##0, (including the comma at the end) Access hides the last three digits of every number, so 1 million appears as 1,000 and 15,000 as 15.

Note: Custom number formats aren't terribly common in Access (they're more frequently used with Excel). Later on, you'll learn about expressions (page 670), which let you do pretty much the same thing.

Currency

Currency's a slight variation on the Number data type that's tailored for financial calculations. Unlike the Number data type, here you can't choose a Field Size for the Currency data type—Access has a one-size-fits-all policy that requires eight bytes of storage space.

Note: The Currency data type's better than the Number data type because it uses optimizations that prevent rounding errors with very small fractions. The Currency data type's accurate to 15 digits to the left of the decimal point, and four digits to the right.

You can adjust the number of decimal places Access shows for currency values on the datasheet by setting the Decimal Places field property. Usually, it's set to 2.

The formatting that Access uses to display currency values is determined by the Regional and Language Options settings on your computer (page 631). However, these settings might produce results you don't want—for example, say you run an artisanal cereal business in Denmark that sells all its products overseas in U.S. dollars (not kroner). You can control exactly how currency values are formatted by setting the Format field property, which gives you the following options:

- **Currency.** This option is the standard choice. It uses the formatting based on your computer's regional settings.

- **Euro.** This option always uses the Euro currency symbol (€).

- **A custom format string.** This option lets you get any currency symbol you want (as described below). You need to type the format string you need into the Format box.

There's a simple recipe for cooking up format strings with a custom currency symbol. Start by adding the character for the currency symbol (type in whatever you want) and then add #,###.## which is Access code for "give me a number with thousands separators and two decimal places."

For example, the Danish cereal company could use a format string like this to show the U.S. currency symbol:

```
$#,###.##
```

Whereas a U.S. company that needs to display a Danish currency field (which formats prices like *kr 342.99*) would use this:

```
kr #,###.##
```

Note: Enterprising users can fiddle around with the number format to add extra text, change the number of decimal places (just add or remove the number signs), and remove the thousands separators (just take out the comma).

Date/Time

Access uses the Date/Time data type to store a single instant in time, complete with the year, month, day, and time down to the second. Behind the scenes, Access stores dates as numbers, which lets you use them in calculations.

Although Access always uses the same amount of space to store date information in a field, you can hide some components of it. You can choose to display just a date (and ignore any time information) or just the time (and ignore any date information). To do this, you simply need to set the Format field property. Table 27-3 shows your options.

Table 27-3. Date/Time Formats

Format	Example
General Date	2/23/2008 11:30:15 PM
Long Date	February 23, 2008 11:30:15 PM
Medium Date	23-Feb-08
Short Date	2/23/2008
Long Time	11:30:15 PM
Medium Time	11:30 PM
Short Time	23:30

Note: Both the General Date and Long Date show the time information only if it's not zero.

The format affects only how the date information's displayed—it doesn't change how you type it in. Access is intelligent enough to interpret dates correctly when you type any of the following:

- 2008-23-2 (the international year-month-day standard always works)

- 2/23/2008 (the most common approach, but you might need to flip the month and day on non-U.S. computers)

- 23-Feb-08

- Feb 23 (Access assumes the current year)

- 23 Feb (ditto)

To add date and time information, just follow the date with the time, as in 23-Feb-08 5:06 PM. Make sure to include the AM/PM designation at the end, or use a 24-hour clock.

If it's too much trouble to type in a date, then consider using the calendar smart tag instead. The smart tag is an icon that appears next to the field whenever you move to it, as shown in Figure 27-12.

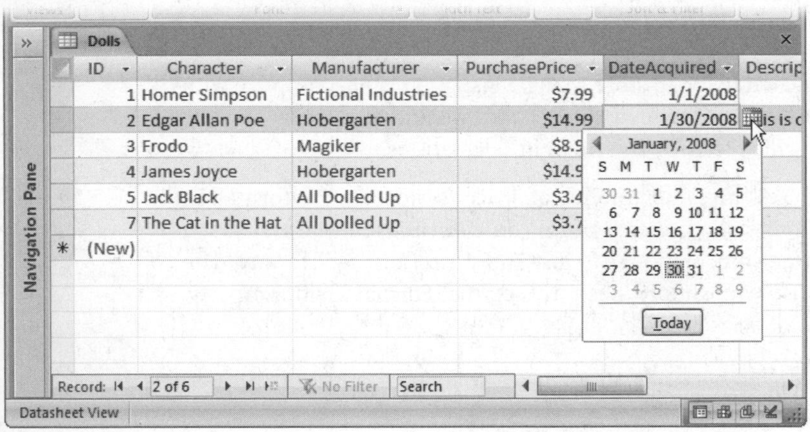

Figure 27-12:
Access automatically pops up the calendar smart tag for all date fields. Click the calendar icon to pop up a mini calendar where you can browse to the date you want. However, you can't use the calendar to enter time information.

Yes/No

A Yes/No field is a small miracle of efficiency. It's the leanest of Access data types, because it allows only two possible values: Yes or No.

When using a Yes/No field, imagine that your field poses a yes or no question by adding an imaginary question mark at the end of your field name. You could use a field named InStock to keep track of whether or not a product's in stock. In this case, the yes or no question is "in stock?" Other examples include Shipped (in a list of orders), Male (to separate the boys from the girls), and Republican (assuming you're willing to distinguish between only two political orientations).

Dating Your Computer

Windows has regional settings for your computer, which affect the way Microsoft programs display things like dates and currencies. In Access, the regional settings determine how the different date formats appear. In other words, on a factory-direct U.S. computer, the Short Date format shows up as 2/23/2008. But on a British computer, it may appear as 23/2/2008. Either way, the information that's stored in the database is the same. However, the way it appears in your datasheet changes.

You can change the regional settings, and they don't have to correspond to where you live—you can set them for your company headquarters on another continent, for instance. But keep in mind that these settings are global, so if you alter them, you affect all your programs.

To make a switch, head to Control Panel. (In Windows XP, click the Start menu and choose Settings → Control Panel.

In Windows Vista, click Start and look for the Control Panel option on the right side.) Once you've opened the Control Panel, double-click Regional and Language Options, which brings up a dialog box. The first tab has all the settings you want. The most important setting's in the first box, which has a drop-down list you can use to pick the region you want to use, like English (United States) or Swedish (Finland).

You can fine-tune the settings in your region, too. This makes sense only if you have particular preferences about how dates should be formatted that don't match the standard options. Click the Customize button next to the region box to bring up a new dialog box, and then click the Date tab (shown in Figure 27-13).

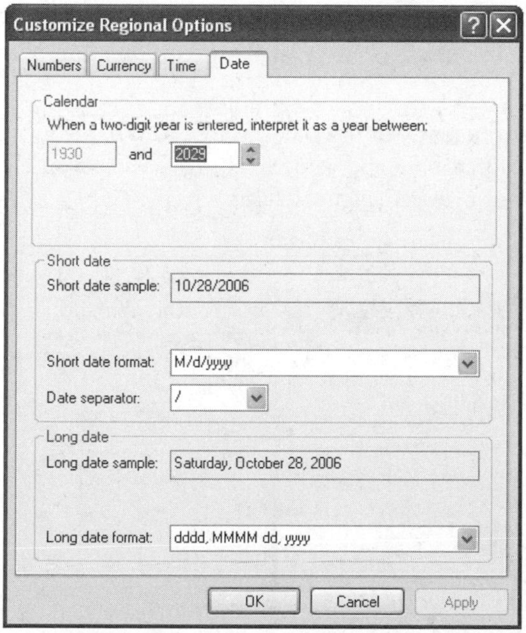

Figure 27-13:
The Customize Regional Options dialog box lets you customize how dates appear on your computer. Use the drop-down lists to specify the date separator; order of month, day, and year components in a date; and how Access should interpret two-digit years. You can mix and match these settings freely, although you could wind up with a computer that's completely counterintuitive to other people.

Although every Yes/No field is essentially the same, you can choose to format it slightly differently, replacing the words "Yes" and "No" with On/Off or True/False. You'll find these three options in the Format menu. However, it doesn't make much difference because on the datasheet, Yes/No fields are displayed with a checkbox, as shown in Figure 27-14.

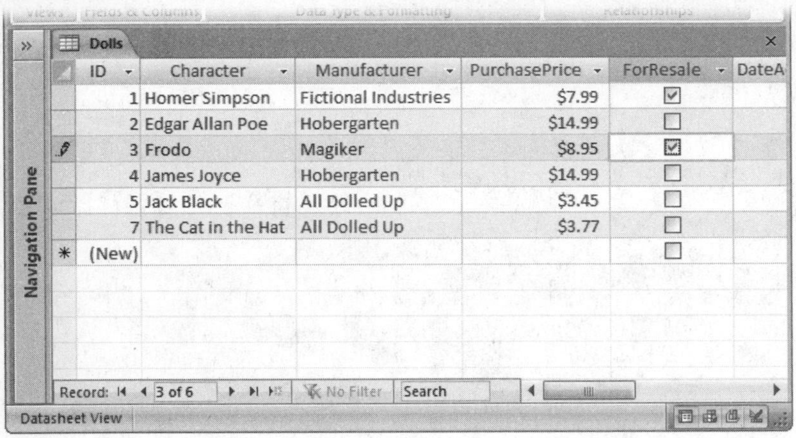

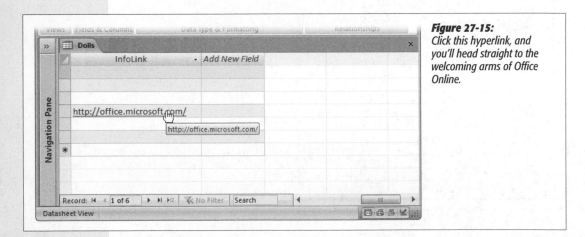

Figure 27-14:
In this example, ForResale is a Yes/No field. A checked checkbox represents Yes (or True or On). An unchecked checkbox represents No (or False or Off).

Hyperlink

The Hyperlink data type comes in handy if you want to create a clickable link to a Web page, file, or email address. You can mix and match any combination of the three in the same table.

Access handles hyperlinks a little differently in the Datasheet view. When you type text into a hyperlink field, it's colored blue and underlined. And when you click the link, Access pops it open in your browser (Figure 27-15).

Figure 27-15:
Click this hyperlink, and you'll head straight to the welcoming arms of Office Online.

One hyperlink field feature isn't immediately obvious. Hyperlink fields actually store more than one piece of information. Every hyperlink includes these three components:

- The text you see in the cell

- The destination you go to when you click the cell (the URL or file path)

- The text you see when you hover over the link with your mouse (the tooltip)

When you type a link into the datasheet, all three of these are set to the same value—what you just typed in. That is, when you type *http://www.FantasyPharmacologists.com*, the text you see, the URL link, and the tooltip are all set to hold the same content, which is the URL *http://www.FantasyPharmacologists.com*.

Most of the time, this approach is good, because it lets you quickly size up a link. However, you aren't limited to this strategy. If you want to set these three components to have different values, move to the value, and then hit Ctrl+K to pop up the Edit Hyperlink window (see Figure 27-16). Or right-click it, and then choose Hyperlink → Edit Hyperlink.

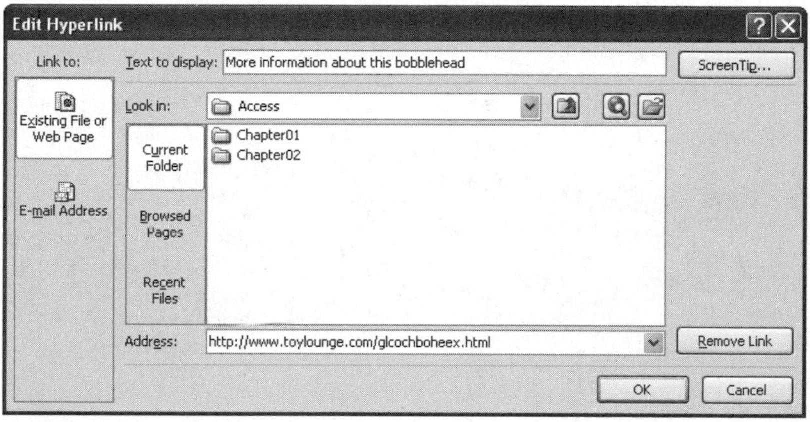

Figure 27-16:
Using the Edit Hyperlink window, you can change the text that appears in the cell (at the top of the window) and the page that Access opens when you click it (at the bottom). You can also create links that use email addresses (in which case Access opens the email program that's configured on your computer) or links to file paths (use the folder browsing area to pick the file you want).

Attachment

The Attachment data type's new in Access 2007. It lets you add files to your database record in much the same way that you tack on attachments to your email messages. Access stores the files you add to an attachment field as part of your table, embedded inside your database file.

The Attachment data type's a good choice if you need to insert a picture for a record, a short sound file, or even a document from another Office application, like Word or Excel. You could create a People table with a picture of each person in your contact list, or a product catalog with pictures of the wares you're selling. In these cases, attachments have an obvious benefit—because they're stored inside your database file, you'll never lose track of them.

However, attachments aren't as graceful with large files, or files you need to modify frequently. If you place a frequently modified document into an Access database, it isn't available on your hard drive for quick editing, printing, and searching. Instead, you'll need to fire up Access, and then find the corresponding record before you can open your document. If you want to make changes, then you'll also need to keep Access open so it can take the revised file and insert it back into the database.

Warning: Think twice before you go wild with attachments. As you've already learned, an Access database is limited to two gigabytes of space. If you start storing large files in your tables, you just may run out of room. Instead, store large documents in separate files, and then record the file name in a text or hyperlink field.

When you use the Attachment data type, make sure you set the Caption field property, which determines the text that appears in the column header for that field. (Often, you'll use the field name as the caption.) If you don't set a caption, the column header shows a paper clip but no text.

You'll recognize an attachment field in the datasheet because it has a paper clip icon next to it (Figure 27-17).

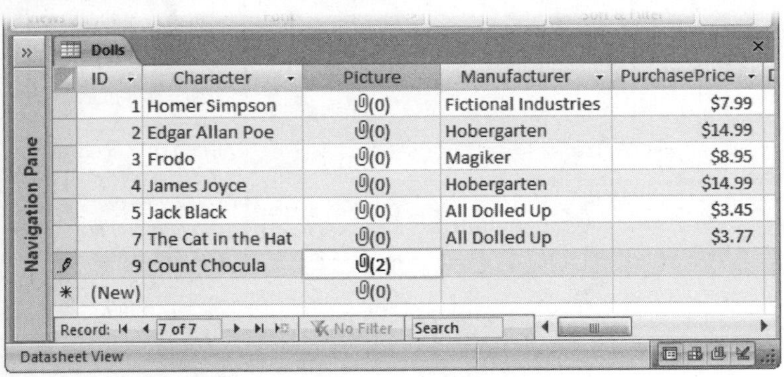

Figure 27-17:
Attachments are flagged with a paper clip icon and a number in brackets, which tells you how many files are attached. In this example, all the values in the Picture attachment field are empty except Count Chocula, which has two.

To attach a file or review the list of attached files, double-click the paper clip icon. You'll see the Attachments dialog box (see Figure 27-18).

Here's what you can do in the Attachments window:

- **Add a new attachment.** Click the Add button. Then browse to a new file, and then click OK. You'll see it appear at the bottom of the list.

- **Delete an attachment.** Select the attachment in the list, and then click Remove.

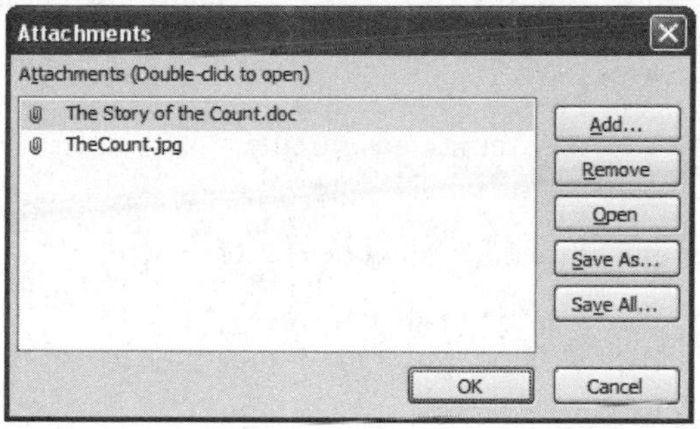

Figure 27-18:
The Attachments dialog box shows you all the files that are linked to your field.

- **Save a copy of an attachment.** Select the attachment, click Save, and then browse to a location on your computer. Or, click Save All to save copies of all the attachments in this field. If you change these copies, you don't change the attachment in the database.

- **Edit or view an attachment.** Select the attachment, and then click Open. Access copies the attachment to a temporary folder on your computer, where Internet content is cached. If you save the file, then Access notices the change, updates the attachment automatically, and then removes the file. If you close the Attachments window before you've closed the file, then Access warns you that your updates might not be reflected in the database. Figure 27-19 shows what happens.

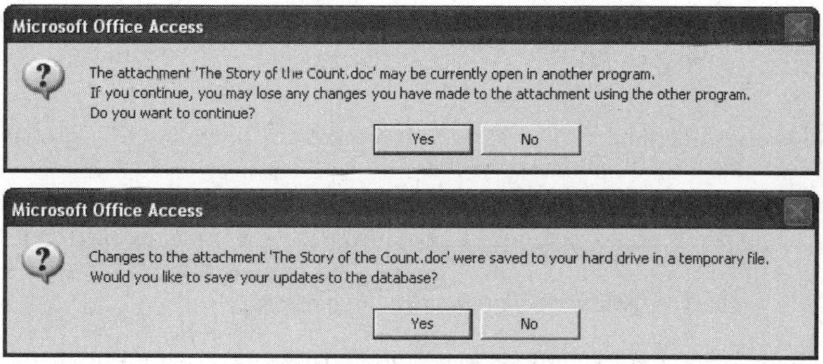

Figure 27-19:
Top: In this example, the file "The Story of the Count.doc" is still open. If you continue, then any changes you make (or any changes you've made so far and haven't saved) aren't reflected in the database.

Bottom: If Access notices you've saved your file since you first opened it, then Access also asks if you want to update the database with the last saved version. (To avoid such headaches, attach only files that you don't plan to edit.)

Unfortunately, the Attachment data type doesn't give you a lot of control. Here are some of its limitations:

- You can't restrict the number of attachments allowed in an attachment field. All attachment fields allow a practically unlimited number of attachments (although you can't attach two files with the same name).

- You also can't restrict the types of files used for an attachment.

- You can't restrict the size of the files used for an attachment.

AutoNumber

An AutoNumber is a special sort of data type. Unlike all the other data types you've seen, you can't fill in the value for an AutoNumber field. Instead, Access does it automatically whenever you insert a new record. Access makes sure that the AutoNumber value is unique—in other words, it never gives two records the same AutoNumber value.

Note: Every table can have no more than one AutoNumber field.

Ordinarily, the AutoNumber field looks like a *sequence* of numbers—Access tends to give the first record an AutoNumber value of 1, the second an AutoNumber of 2, and so on. However, the truth isn't so straightforward. Sometimes, Access skips a number. This skipping could happen when several people are using a database at once, or if you start adding a new record, and then cancel your action by pressing the Esc key. You may also delete an existing record, in which case Access never reuses that AutoNumber value. As a result, if you insert a new record and you see it's assigned an AutoNumber value of 401, then you can't safely assume that there are already 400 records in the table. The actual number's probably less.

Truthfully, an AutoNumber value doesn't represent anything, and you probably won't spend much time looking at it. The AutoNumber field's sole purpose is to make sure you have a unique way to point to each record in your table. Usually, your AutoNumber field's also the primary key for your table, as explained on page 638.

Using AutoNumbers without revealing the size of your table

AutoNumber values have one minor problem: they give a clue about the number of records in a table. You may not want a customer to know that your brand-new food and crafts company, Better Butter Sculptures, hasn't cracked 12 customers. So you'll be a little embarrassed to tell him he's customer ID number 6.

The best way to solve this problem is to start counting at a higher number. You can fool Access into generating AutoNumber values starting at a specific minimum. For example, instead of creating customer IDs 1, 2, and 3, you could create the ID values 11001, 11002, 11003. This approach also has the advantage of keeping your IDs a consistent number of digits, and it allows you to distinguish between IDs in different tables by starting them at different minimums. Unfortunately, in order to pull this trick off, you need to fake Access out with a specially designed query that requires some power-user skills beyond the scope of this book. (Budding power users should check out *Access 2007: The Missing Manual* for details.)

Fortunately, you can tell Access to generate AutoNumber values in a different way. You have two choices:

- **Random AutoNumber value.** To use random numbers, change the New Values field property from Increment to Random. Now you'll get long numbers for each record, like 212125691, 1671255778, and −1388883525. You might use random AutoNumber to create values that other people can't guess. (For example, if you have an Orders table that uses random values for the OrderID field, you can use those values as confirmation numbers.) However, random AutoNumbers are rarely used in the Access world.

- **Replication IDs.** Replication IDs are long, obscure codes like 38A94E7B-2F95-4E7D-8AF1-DB5B35F9700C that are statistically guaranteed to be unique. To use them, change the Field Size property from Long Integer to Replication ID. Replication IDs are really used only in one scenario—if you have separate copies of a database and you need to merge the data together in the future. The next section explains that scenario.

Both of these options trade the easy-to-understand simplicity of the ordinary AutoNumber with something a little more awkward, so evaluate them carefully before using these approaches in your tables.

Using Replication IDs

Imagine you're working at a company with several regional sales offices, each with its own database for tracking customers. If you use an ordinary AutoNumber field, then you'll end up with several customers with the same ID, but at different offices. If you ever want to compare data, you'll quickly become confused. And you can't combine all the data into one database for further analysis later on.

Access gives you another choice—a *replication ID*. A replication ID's a strange creation—it's an extremely large number (16 bytes in all) that's represented as a string of numbers and letters that looks like this:

```
38A94E7B-2F95-4E7D-8AF1-DB5B35F9700C
```

This ID's obviously more cumbersome than an ordinary integer. After all, it's much easier to thank someone for submitting Order 4657 than Order 38A94E7B-2F95-4E7D-8AF1-DB5B35F9700C. In other words, if you use the AutoNumber value for tracking or bookkeeping, then the replication ID's a bad idea.

However, the replication ID solves the problem described earlier, where multiple copies of the same database are being used in different places. That's because replication IDs are guaranteed to be *statistically unique*. In other words, there are so many possible replication IDs that it's absurdly unlikely that you'll ever generate the same replication ID twice. So even if you have dozens of separate copies of your database, and they're all managing hundreds of customers, you can rest assured that each customer has a unique customer ID. Even better, you can periodically fuse the separate tables together into one master database. (This process is called *replication*, and it's the origin of the term replication ID. You'll learn more about transferring data from one database to another in Chapter 34.)

Figure 27-20 shows a table that uses replication IDs.

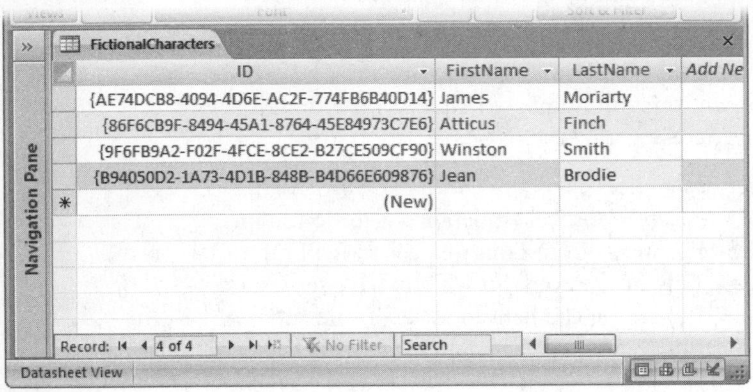

Figure 27-20:
This figure shows four records in the FictionalCharacters table, each with a statistically unique AutoNumber value.

The Primary Key

Design view also allows you to set a table's *primary key*, which is a field (or a combination of fields) that's unique for each record. Every table must have a primary key. To understand why the primary key's important, you need to consider a little bit more about how databases work. The box below has the full story.

UP TO SPEED

How Access Prevents Duplicate Records

In order to function correctly, a database program like Access needs to be able to tell the difference between each and every record in your table. In other words, you can't insert two records with *exactly* the same information. Databases are notoriously fussy, and they don't tolerate this sort of sloppiness.

The challenge of preventing duplicates isn't as easy as it seems. Access is designed to be blisteringly fast, and it can't afford to double-check your new record against every other record in the table to see if there's a duplicate. So instead, it relies on a *primary key*. As long as every record in a table

has a unique, never-duplicated primary key, you can't have two identical records. (At worst, they'll be two almost identical records that have the same information in all their other fields, but have different primary keys. And this is perfectly acceptable to Access.)

In an Employees table, the Social Security number could serve as the primary key. This method works well, because when you insert a new record, Access can check for duplicates by breezing through the list of Social Security numbers, which is much faster than scanning through the entire table.

Choosing a primary key is trickier than it seems. Imagine you have a list of friends (and their contact information) in a table named People. You may logically assume that you can create a primary key using a combination of first and last name. Unfortunately, that just won't do—after all, some address books have two Sean Smiths.

Your best solution's to *invent* a new piece of information. You can label every individual in your contact list with a unique ID number. Best of all, you can get Access to automatically create this number for you (and make sure that no two people get the same number), so you don't even need to think about it. That way, if you have two Sean Smiths, each one has a different ID. And even if Ferris Wheel Simpson decides to change his first name, the ID remains the same.

This approach is exactly the one Access uses when you create a table using the Datasheet view. Consider the Dolls table you built in Chapter 26. You'll notice that it includes a field named ID, which Access fills automatically. You can't set the ID value in a new record, or change it in an existing record. Instead, Access takes complete control, making sure each bobblehead has a different ID number. This behavior's almost always what you want, so don't try to change it or delete the ID field.

However, there's one exception. If you *create* a table in Design view by choosing Create → Tables → Table Design, then Access assumes you know what you're doing, and it doesn't create an ID field for you. You need to add an ID field (or something like it).

Creating Your Own Primary Key Field

If your database doesn't have an ID field (perhaps because you created it using the Create → Tables → Table Design command), it's up to you to create one and set the primary key.

Here's how to do it:

1. **Create a new field by typing a name in the Field Name column.**

   For automatically generated values, the name ID is the best choice. Some people prefer to be a little more descriptive (for example, BobbleheadID, CustomerID, and so on), but it's unnecessary.

2. **In the Data Type column, choose AutoNumber.**

   By choosing the AutoNumber data type, you make sure that Access generate a unique ID value for every new record you insert. If you don't want this process to happen, you can choose something else (like the Text or Number data type). You'll be responsible for entering your own unique value for each record, which is more work that it seems.

3. **Right-click the field, and then choose Primary Key.**

   This choice designates the field as the primary key for the table. Access doesn't allow duplicate values in this field.

Note: If you want to make a primary key that includes more than one field, then you need to take a slightly different approach. First, click the margin next to the field name, and then drag the mouse to select more than one field. Then, hold down Shift, and then right-click your selection. Now you can choose Primary Key.

UP TO SPEED

Why It's Important to Be Unique

You won't completely understand why it's so important for each record to have a unique ID number until you work with the more advanced examples in later chapters. However, one of the reasons is that other programs that use your database need to identify a record *unambiguously*.

To understand why there's a problem, imagine that you've built a program for editing the Dolls table. This program starts by retrieving a list of all your table's bobbleheads. It displays this list to the person using the program, and lets her make changes. Here's the catch—if a change is made, the program needs to be able to apply the change to the corresponding record in the database. And in order to apply the change, it needs some unique piece of information that it can use to locate the record. If you've followed the best design practices described above, the unique "locator" is the bobblehead's ID.

Six Principles of Database Design

With great power comes great responsibility. As a database designer, it's up to you to craft a set of properly structured tables. If you get it right, you'll save yourself a lot of work in the future. Well-designed databases are easy to enhance, simpler to work with, and lead to far fewer mind-bending problems when you need to extract information.

Sadly, there's no recipe for a perfect database. Instead, a number of recommendations can guide you on the way. In this section, you'll learn about a few of the most important.

Tip: Building a good database is an art that takes practice. For best results, read these guidelines, and then try building your own test databases.

---

1. Choose Good Field Names

Access doesn't impose many rules on what field names you can use. It lets you use 64 characters of your choice. However, field names are important. You'll be referring to the same names again and again as you build forms, create reports, and even write code. So it's important to choose a good name from the outset.

Here are some tips:

- **Keep it short and simple.** The field name should be as short as possible. Long names are tiring to type, more prone to error, and can be harder to cram into forms and reports.

- **CapitalizeLikeThis.** It's not a set-in-stone rule, but most Access fans capitalize the first letter of every word (known as CamelCase), and then cram them all together to make a field name. Examples include UnitsInStock and DateOf-Expiration.

- **Avoid spaces.** Spaces are allowed in Access field names, but they can cause problems. In SQL (the database language you'll use to search for data), spaces aren't kosher. That means you'll be forced to use square brackets when referring to field name that includes spaces (like [Number Of Guests]), which gets annoying fast. If you really must have spaces, then consider using underscores instead.

- **Be consistent.** You have the choice between the field names Product_Price and ProductPrice. Either approach is perfectly reasonable. However, it's not a good idea to mingle the two approaches in the same database—doing so's a recipe for certain confusion. Similarly, if you have more than one table with the same sort of information (for example, a FirstName field in an Employees table and a Customers table), use the same field name.

- **Don't repeat the table name.** If you have a Country field in a Customers table, it's fairly obvious that you're talking about the Country where the customer lives. The field name CustomerCountry would be overkill.

- **Don't use the field name Name.** Besides being a tongue-twister, Name is an Access keyword. Instead, use ProductName, CategoryName, ClassName, and so on. (This is one case where it's OK to violate the previous rule and incorporate the table name in the field name.)

You should also give careful thought to naming your tables. Once again, consistency is king. For example, database nerds spend hours arguing about whether or not to pluralize table names (like Customers instead of Customer). Either way's fine, but try to keep all your tables in line.

2. Break Down Your Information

Be careful that you don't include too much information in a single field. You want to have each field store a single piece of information. Rather than have a single Name field in a table of contacts, it makes more sense to have a FirstName and a LastName field.

There are many reasons for breaking down information into separate fields. First of all, it stops some types of errors. With a Name field, the name could be entered in several different ways (like "Last, First" or "First Last"). Splitting the name avoids these issues, which can create headaches when you try to use the data in some sort of automated task (like a mail merge). But more importantly, you can more easily work with data that's broken down into small pieces. Once the Name field's split into FirstName and LastName, you can perform sorts or searches on just one of these two pieces of information, which you couldn't otherwise do. Similarly, you should split address information into columns like Street, City, State, and Country—that way, you can far more easily find out who lives in Nantucket.

Figure 27-21 (top) shows an example of proper separation. Figure 27-21 (bottom) shows a dangerous mistake—an attempt to store more than one piece of information in a single field.

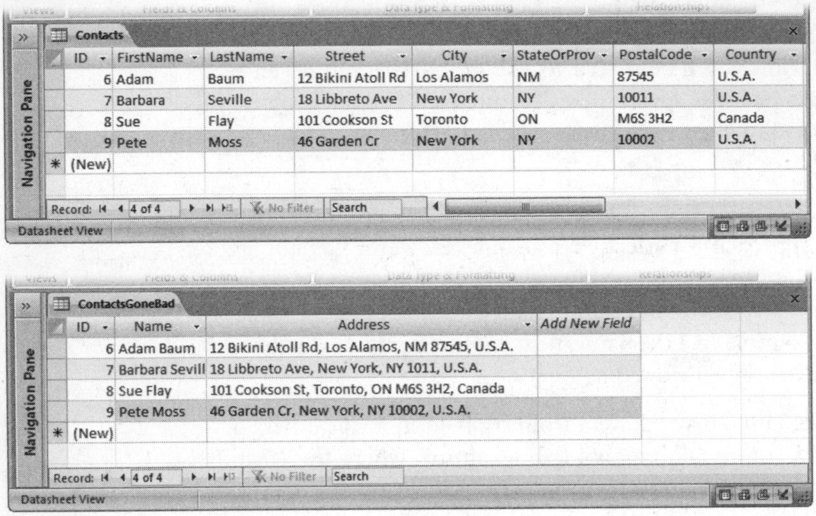

Figure 27-21:
This example shows the right way to subdivide information in the Contacts table (top), and the wrong way (bottom).

3. Include All the Details in One Place

Often, you'll use the same table in many different tasks. You may use the Dolls table to check for duplicates (and avoid purchasing the same bobblehead twice), to identify the oldest parts of your collection, and to determine the total amount of money you've spent in a given year (for tax purposes). Each of these tasks needs a slightly different combination of information. When you're calculating the total money spent, you aren't interested in the Character field that identifies the doll. When checking for a duplicate, you don't need the DateAcquired or Purchase-Price information.

Even though you don't always need all these fields, it's fairly obvious that it makes sense to put them all in the same table. However, when you create more detailed tables, you may not be as certain. It's not difficult to imagine a version of the Dolls table that has 30 or 40 fields of information. You may use some of these fields only occasionally. However, you should still include them all in the same table. All you'll see in this book, you can easily filter out the information you don't need from the datasheet, as well as in your forms and printed reports.

4. Avoid Duplicating Information

As you start to fill a table with fields, it's sometimes tempting to include information that doesn't really belong. This inclusion causes no end of headaches, and it's a surprisingly easy trap to fall into. Figure 27-22 shows this problem in action with a table that tries to do too much.

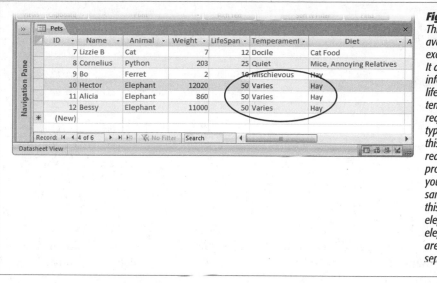

Figure 27-22:
*This table lists the
available pets at an
exotic animal breeder's.
It also lists some helpful
information about the
life expectancy,
temperament, and meal
requirements of each
type of animal. Initially,
this design seems fairly
reasonable. However, a
problem appears when
you have several of the
same type of animals (in
this case, three
elephants). Now the
elephant-specific details
are repeated three
separate times.*

Duplicate data like that shown in Figure 27-22 is inefficient. You can easily imagine a table with hundreds of similar records, needlessly wasting space repeating the same values over and over again. However, this concern's minor compared to the effort of updating that information, and the possibility of inconsistency. What happens if you want to update the life expectancy information for every elephant based on new studies? Based on the current design of the table, you need to change each record that has the same information. Even worse, it's all too easy to change some records but leave others untouched. The overall result's inconsistent data—information in more than one spot that doesn't agree—which makes it impossible to figure out the correct information.

This problem occurs because the information in the Pets table doesn't all belong. To understand why, you need to delve a little deeper into database analysis.

As a rule, every table in a database stores a single *thing*. In the Pets table, that thing is pets. Every field in a table is a piece of information about that thing.

In the Pets table, fields like Name, Animal, and Weight all make sense. They describe the pet in question. But the LifeSpan, Temperament, and Diet fields aren't quite right. They don't describe the individual pet. Instead, they're just standards for that species. In other words, these fields aren't based on the *pet* (as they should be)—they're based on the *animal type*. The only way to solve this problem is to create two tables: Pets and AnimalTypes (Figure 27-23).

It takes experience to spot fields that don't belong. And in some cases, breaking a table down into more and more sub-tables isn't worth the trouble. You could theoretically separate the address information (contained in fields like Street, City, Country, and PostalCode) from a Customers table, and then place it into a separate Addresses table. However, it's relatively uncommon for two customers to

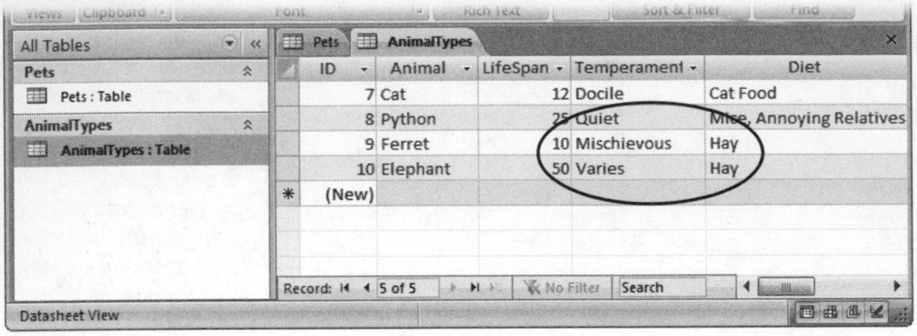

Figure 27-23:
Now the animal-specific information is maintained in one place, with no duplicates. It takes a little more work to get all the pet information you need—for example, to find out the life expectancy for Beatrice, you need to check out the Elephant record in the AnimalTypes table—but the overall design's more logical.

share the same address, so this extra work isn't likely to pay off. You'll consider how to define formal relationships between tables like Pets and AnimalTypes in Chapter 30.

Tip: Many database gurus find the best way to plan a database is to use index cards. To do this, start by writing down all the various types of information you need in your database. Then, set aside an index card for each table you expect to use. Finally, take the fields on the scrap paper, and write them down on the appropriate index cards, one at a time, until everything's set into neat, related groups.

---

5. Avoid Redundant Information

Another type of data that just doesn't belong is redundant information—information that's already available elsewhere in the database, or even in the same table, sometimes in a slightly different form. As with duplicated data, this redundancy can cause inconsistencies.

Calculated data's the most common type of redundant information. An Average-OrderCost field in a Customers table is an example. The problem here is that you can determine the price of an average order by searching through all the records in the Orders table for that customer, and averaging them. By adding an AverageOrderCost field, you introduce the possibility that this field may be incorrect (it may not match the actual order records). You also complicate life, because every time a customer places an order, you need to recalculate the average, and then update the customer record.

Note: Database gods do sometimes use calculated data as a performance-improving technique. However, this type of optimization's very rare in Access databases. It's more common in industrial-strength server-side databases that power large companies and Web sites.

Here are some more examples of redundant information:

- **An Age and a DateOfBirth field (in a People table).** Usually, you'll want to include just a DateOfBirth field. If you have both, then the Age field contains redundant information. But if you have only the Age field, you're in trouble—unless you're ready to keep track of birthdays and update each record carefully, your information will soon be incorrect.

- **A DiscountPrice field (in a Products table).** You should be able to calculate the discount price as needed based on a percentage. In a typical business, markups and markdowns change frequently. If you calculate 10 percent discounts and store the revised prices in your database, then you'll have a lot of work to do when the discount drops to nine percent.

6. Include an ID Field

As you learned earlier (page 638), Access automatically creates an ID field when you create a table in Datasheet view and sets it to be the primary key for the table. But even now that you've graduated to Design view, you should still add an ID field to all your tables. Make sure it uses the AutoNumber data type so Access fills in the numbers automatically, and set it to be the primary key.

In some cases, your table may include a unique field that you can use as a primary key. *Resist the temptation.* You'll always buy yourself more flexibility by adding an ID field. You never need to change an ID field. Other information, even names and social insurance numbers, may change. And if you're using table relationships, Access copies the primary key into other tables. If a primary key changes, you'll need to track down the value in several different places.

Note: It's a good idea to get into the habit of using ID fields in all your tables. In Chapter 30, you'll see the benefits when you start creating table relationships.

CHAPTER 28

Mastering the Datasheet

In Chapter 26, you took your first look at the datasheet—a straightforward way to browse and edit the contents of a table. As you've learned since then, the datasheet isn't the best place to build a table. (Design view's a better choice for database control freaks.) However, the datasheet *is* a great tool for reviewing the records in your table, making edits, and inserting new data.

Based on your experience creating the Dolls table (page 593), you probably feel pretty confident breezing around the datasheet. However, most tables are considerably larger than the examples you've seen so far. After all, if you need to keep track of only a dozen bobbleheads, then you really don't need a database—you'll be just as happy jotting the list down in any old spreadsheet, word processor document, or scrap of unused Kleenex.

On the other hand, if you plan to build a small bobblehead empire (suitable for touring in international exhibitions), you need to fill your table with hundreds or thousands of records. In this situation, it's not as easy to scroll through the mass of data to find what you need. All of a sudden, the datasheet seems more than a little overwhelming.

Fortunately, Access is stocked with datasheet goodies that can simplify your life. In this chapter, you'll become a datasheet expert, with tricks like sorting, searching, and filtering at your fingertips. You'll also learn a quick-and-dirty way to print a snapshot of the data in your table.

Note: It's entirely up to you how much time you spend using datasheets. Some Access experts prefer to create *forms* for all their tables (as described in Chapter 33). With forms, you can design a completely customized window for data entry. Designing forms takes more work, but it's a great way to satisfy your inner Picasso.

Datasheet Customization

Getting tired of the drab datasheet, with its boring stretch of columns and plain text? You can do something about it. Access lets you tweak the datasheet's appearance and organization to make it more practical (or suit it to your peculiar sense of style). Some of these customizations—like modifying the datasheet font—are shameless frills. Other options, like hiding or freezing columns, can genuinely make it easier to work with large tables.

Note: Access doesn't save formatting changes immediately (unlike record edits, which it stores as soon as you make them). Instead, Access prompts you to save changes the next time you close the datasheet. You can choose Yes to keep your customizations or No to revert to the table's last look and feel (which doesn't affect any edits you've made to the *data* in that table).

Formatting the Datasheet

Access lets you format the datasheet with eye-catching colors and fonts. Do these options make any difference to the way the datasheet works? Not really. But if your computer desktop looks more like a '60s revival party than an office terminal, then you'll enjoy this feature.

To find the formatting features, look at the ribbon's Home → Font section (see Figure 28-1).

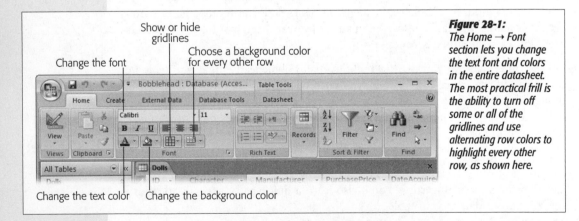

Show or hide
gridlines

Choose a background color
for every other row

Change the font

Change the text color   Change the background color

Figure 28-1:
The Home → Font section lets you change the text font and colors in the entire datasheet. The most practical frill is the ability to turn off some or all of the gridlines and use alternating row colors to highlight every other row, as shown here.

Every formatting change you make affects the entire table. You may think it's a nifty idea to apply different formatting to different columns, but Access doesn't let you. If this limitation's frustrating you, be sure to check out forms and reports later in this book. Both are more complicated to set up, but give you more formatting power.

Note: There's one other way you can use the ribbon's Home → Font section. If you have a field that uses the Memo data type and you've set your field to use rich text (page 625), then you can select some text inside your field, and change its formatting using the ribbon.

Customizing All Your Datasheets

Access lets you format only one table at a time. So if you find a formatting option you really like, you'll need to apply it separately to every table in your database.

However, you can set formatting options so that they automatically apply to every table in every database by configuring Access itself. To pull this trick off, follow these steps:

1. Choose Office button → Access Options to show the Access Options window.

2. Choose Datasheet from the list on the left.

3. On the right, you see the standard font, color, gridline, and column width options, which you can change to whatever you want.

When you change the datasheet formatting settings in the Access Options window, you change the *defaults* that Access uses. These settings determine the formatting that Access uses for new tables and any tables that aren't customized. When you customize a table, you override the default settings, no matter what they are.

If you set Access to use red text, but you format a specific table to use green text, the green text setting takes precedence. However, if you set a yellow background in the Access Options window, and you don't customize that detail for your table, then it automatically acquires the standard yellow.

Rearranging Columns

The fields in the datasheet are laid out from left to right, in the order you created them. Often, you'll discover that this order isn't the most efficient for data entry.

Imagine you've created a Customers table for a novelty pasta company. When a new customer registration ends up on your desk, you realize that the registration form starts with the name and address information, and then includes the customer's pasta preferences. Unfortunately, the fields on the datasheet are laid out in a completely different order. From right to left, they're arranged like this: ID, FreshPastaPreference, DriedPastaPreference, FirstName, LastName, Street, City, State, Country. (This organization isn't as crazy as it seems—it actually makes it easier for the people filling pasta orders to quickly find the information *they* want.) Because of this ordering, you need to skip back and forth just to enter the information from a single registration.

Fortunately, you can solve this problem without redesigning the table. Drag the columns you want to move to new positions, as shown in Figure 28-2.

The best part of this approach is that you don't need to modify the database's actual structure. If you switch to Design view after moving a few columns, you'll see that the field order hasn't changed. In other words, you can keep the exact same physical order of fields (in your database file) but organize them differently in Datasheet view.

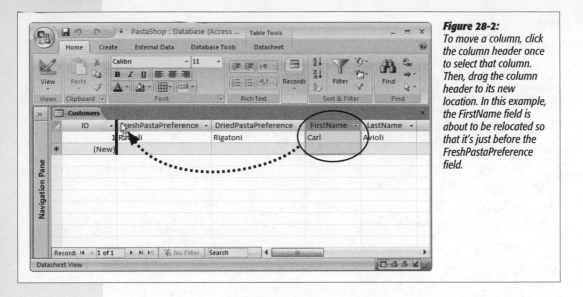

Figure 28-2:
To move a column, click the column header once to select that column. Then, drag the column header to its new location. In this example, the FirstName field is about to be relocated so that it's just before the FreshPastaPreference field.

Tip: Rearranging columns is a relatively minor change. Don't worry about shifting columns around to suit a specific editing job and then switching them back later on. Your changes don't affect the data in the database. If you want to use a particular column order for a one-time job, simply refrain from saving your changes when you close the datasheet.

Resizing Rows and Columns

As you cram more and more information into a table, your datasheet becomes wider and wider. In many cases, you'll be frustrated with some columns hogging more space than they need and others being impossibly narrow.

As you'd expect, Access lets you tweak column widths. But you probably haven't realized how many different ways you can do it:

- **Resize a single column.** Move the mouse to the column's right edge. Drag to the left (to shrink the column) or to the right (to make it larger).

- **Resize a column to fit its content.** Double-click the column edge. Access makes the column just wide enough to fit the field name or the largest value (whichever's larger). However, it doesn't make the column so wide that it stretches beyond the bounds of the window.

- **Resize several adjacent columns.** Drag the first column's header across the columns until you've selected them all. Then, drag the right edge of your selection to the left or the right. All the selected columns shrink or expand to fit the available space, sharing it equally.

- **Resize a column with pinpoint accuracy.** Right-click the column header, and then choose Column Width. You'll see the Column Width dialog that lets you set an exact width as a number (Figure 28-3).

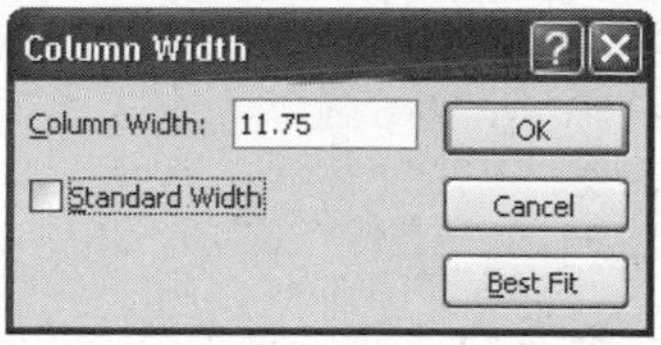

Figure 28-3:
The Column Width dialog box lets you set an exact width as a number. (The number doesn't actually have a concrete meaning—it's supposed to be a width in characters, but because modern Access uses proportional fonts, different characters are different sizes.) You can also turn on the Standard Width checkbox to reset the width to the standard narrow size, or click Best Fit to expand the column to fit its content (just as when you double-click the edge of the column).

Note: Remember, a column doesn't need to be wide enough to show all its data at once. You can scroll through a lengthy text field using the arrow keys, and if that's too awkward, use the Shift+F2 shortcut to show the full contents of the current field in a Zoom box.

Just as you can resize columns, you can also resize rows. The difference is that Access makes sure all rows have the same size. So when you make one row taller or shorter, Access adjusts all the other rows to match.

You'll mainly want to shrink a row to cram more rows into view at once. You'll want to enlarge a row mostly to show more than one line of text in each text field (see Figure 28-4).

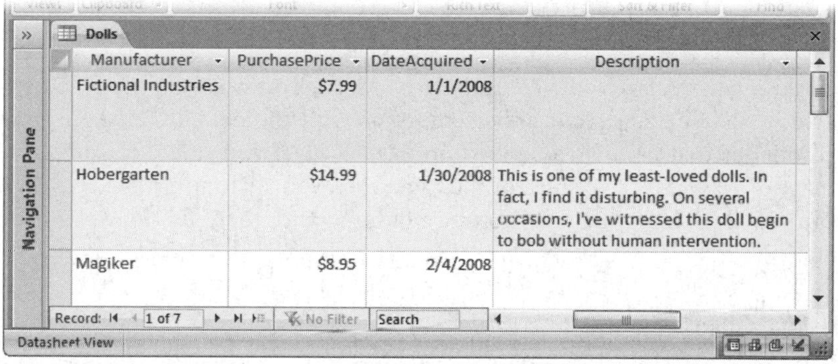

Figure 28-4:
If a row's large enough, Access wraps the text inside it over multiple lines, as shown here with the Description column.

Hiding Columns

Many tables contain so many columns that you can't possibly fit them all into view at the same time. This quality's one of the drawbacks to the datasheet, and often you have no choice but to scroll from side to side.

However, in some situations, you may not need to see all the fields at once. In this case, you can temporarily hide the columns that don't interest you, thereby homing in on the important details without distraction. Initially, every field you add to a table is out in the open.

To hide a column, select the column by clicking the column header. (You can also select several adjacent columns by clicking the column header of the first, and then dragging the mouse across the rest.) Then, right-click your selection, and then choose Hide Columns. The column instantly vanishes from the datasheet. (This sudden disappearance can be a little traumatic for Access newbies.)

Fortunately, the field and all its data remain just out of sight. To pop the column back into view, right-click any column header and choose Unhide Columns. Access then shows the Unhide Columns dialog box (Figure 28-5).

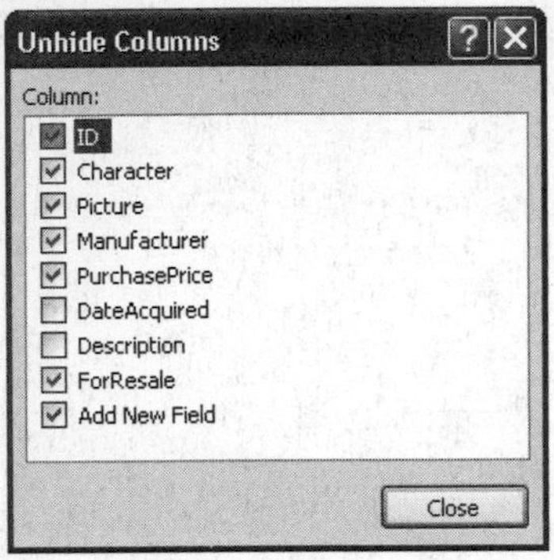

Figure 28-5:
Using the Unhide Columns dialog box, you can choose to make hidden columns reappear, and (paradoxically) you can hide ones that are currently visible. Every column that has a checkmark next to it is visible—every column that doesn't is hidden. As you change the visibility, Access updates the datasheet immediately. When you're happy with the results, click Close to get back to the datasheet.

Note: At the bottom of the field list, you'll see an entry named Add New Field. This "field" isn't really a field—it's the placeholder that appears just to the right of your last field in Datasheet view, which you can use to add new fields (page 615). If you're in the habit of adding fields using Design view (page 614), then you can hide this placeholder to free up some extra space.

If you add a new record while columns are hidden, you can't supply a value for that field. The value starts out either empty or with the default value (if you've defined one for that field, as described on page 670). If you've hidden a required field (page 668), you receive an error message when you try to insert the record. All you can do is unhide the appropriate column, and then fill in the missing information.

Freezing Columns

Even with the ability to hide and resize columns, you'll probably need to scroll from side to side in a typical datasheet. In this situation, you can easily lose your place. You might scroll to see more information in the Contacts table, but then forget exactly which person you're looking at. Access has one more feature that can help you by making sure important information is always visible—*frozen* columns.

A frozen column remains fixed in place at the Access window's left side at all times. Even as you scroll to the right, all your frozen columns remain visible (Figure 28-6). To freeze a column (or columns), select them, right-click the column header, and then choose Freeze Columns.

Tip: If you want to freeze several columns that aren't next to each other, start by freezing the column that you want to appear at the very left. Then, repeat the process to freeze the column that you want to appear just to the right of the first column, and so on.

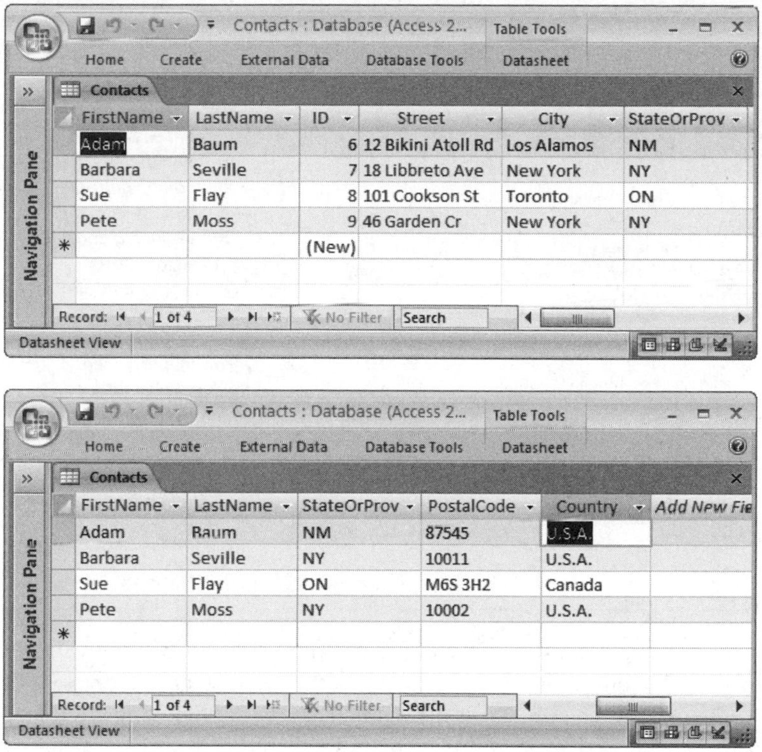

Figure 28-6:
Top: In this example, the FirstName and LastName field are frozen. They appear initially at the left. (The ribbon's collapsed in this figure to make more room, as described on page 610.)

Bottom: When you scroll to the side to see more information, the FirstName and LastName columns stay put.

Frozen columns must always be positioned at the left size of the datasheet. If you freeze a column that's somewhere else, Access moves it to the left side and then freezes it. You can move it back after you unfreeze the column using the column reordering trick on page 649. Keep in mind that while a column's frozen, you can't drag it to a different place.

To unfreeze columns, right-click a column header, and then choose Unfreeze All Columns.

Note: Eventually, you'll discover that the customizations provided by the datasheet aren't enough, or you'll need to customize the same table different ways for different people. These signs tell you that you need to step up to forms, a more advanced data display option described in Chapter 33.

Datasheet Navigation

In Chapter 26, you learned the basics of moving around the datasheet. Using your mouse and a few select keystrokes, you can cover a lot of ground. (Flip back to page 599 for a review of the different keys you can use to jump from place to place and perform edits.)

However, you haven't seen a few tricks yet. One's the timesaving record navigation buttons at the bottom of the datasheet (Figure 28-7).

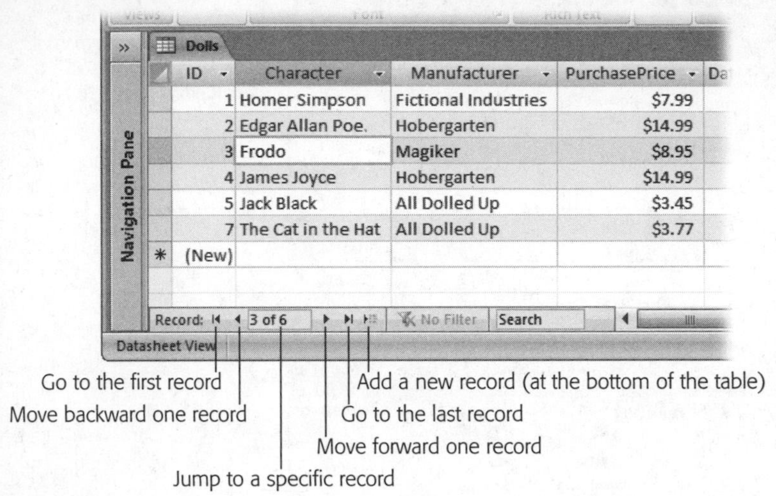

Figure 28-7:
You could easily overlook the navigation buttons at the bottom of the datasheet. These buttons let you jump to the beginning and end of the table, or, more interestingly, head straight to a record at a specific position. To do this, type the record number (like "4") into the box (where it says "3 of 6" in this example), and then hit Enter. Of course, this trick works only if you have an approximate idea of where in the list your record's positioned.

Several more datasheet features help you orient yourself when dealing with large amounts of data, including *sorting* (which orders the records so you can see what you want), *filtering* (which cuts down the data display to include only the records you're interested in), and *searching* (which digs specific records out of an avalanche of data). You'll try all these features out in the following sections.

Sorting

In some cases, you can most easily make sense of a lot of data by putting it in order. You can organize a customer list by last name, a product catalog by price, a list of wedding guests by age, and so on.

To sort your records, pick a column you want to use to order the records. Click the drop-down arrow at the right edge of the column header, and then choose one of the sort options at the top of the menu (see Figure 28-8).

Depending on the data type of field, you'll see different sorting options, as explained in Table 28-1. (You can also apply the same types of sort using the commands in the ribbon's Home → Sort & Filter section.)

In an unsorted table, records are ordered according to when they were created, so that the oldest records are at the top of the datasheet, and the newest at the bottom. Sorting doesn't change how Access stores records, but it does change the way they're displayed.

Tip: Use the Home → Sort & Filter → Clear All Sorts command to return your table to its original, unsorted order.

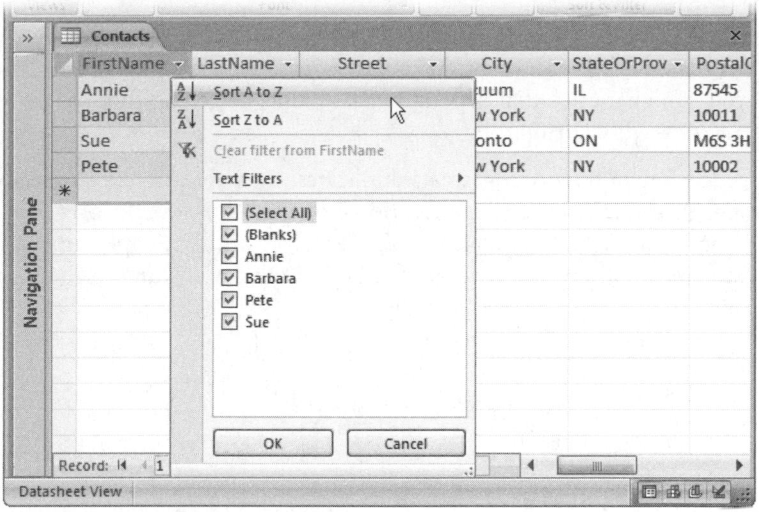

Figure 28-8:
This text field gives you the choice of sorting alphabetically from the beginning of the alphabet (A to Z) or backward from the end (Z to A). The menu also provides filtering options, which are described on page 657.

Table 28-1. *Sorting Options for Different Data Types*

Data Type	Sort Options	Description
Text, Memo, and Hyperlink	Sort A to Z Sort Z to A	Performs an alphabetic sort (like the dictionary), ordering letter by letter. The sort isn't case-sensitive, so it treats "baloney" and "Baloney" the same.
Number, Currency, and AutoNumber	Sort Smallest to Largest Sort Largest to Smallest	Performs a numeric sort, putting smaller numbers at the top or bottom.
Date/Time	Sort Oldest to Newest Sort Newest to Oldest	Performs a date sort, distinguishing between older dates (those that occur first) and more recent dates.
Yes/No	Sort Selected to Cleared Sort Cleared to Selected	Separates the selected from the unselected values.

Sorting is a one-time affair. If you edit values in a sorted column, then Access doesn't reapply the sort. Imagine you sort a list of people by FirstName. If you then edit the FirstName value for one of the records, changing "Frankie" to "Chen," Access *doesn't* relocate the row to the C section. Instead, the changed row remains in its original place until you resort the table. Similarly, any new records you add stay at the end of the table until the next sort (or the next time the table is opened). This behavior makes sense. If Access relocated rows whenever you made a change, you'd quickly become disoriented.

Note: The sorting order's one of the details that Access stores in the database file. The next time you open the table in Datasheet view, Access automatically applies your sort settings.

Sorting on multiple fields

If a sort finds two duplicate values, there's no way to know what order they'll have (relative to one another). If you sort a customer list with two "Van Hauser" entries in it, then you can guarantee that sorting by last name will bring them together, but you don't know who'll be on top.

If you want more say in how Access treats duplicates, then you can choose to sort based on more than one column. The traditional phone book, which sorts people by last name and *then* by first name, is a perfect example of this. People who share the same last name are thus grouped together and ordered according to their first name, like this:

```
...
Smith, Star
Smith, Susan
Smith, Sy
Smith, Tanis
...
```

In the datasheet, sorts are *cumulative*, which means you can sort based on several columns at the same time. The only trick's getting the order right. The following steps take you through the process:

1. **Choose Home → Sort & Filter → Clear All Sorts.**

   Access reverts your table to its original, unsorted order.

2. **Use the drop-down column menu to apply the sub-sort that you want for duplicates.**

   If you want to perform the phone book sort (names are organized by last name, then first name), you need to turn on sorting for the FirstName field. Page 655 explains the sorting options you'll see, depending on the data type.

3. **Use the drop-down column menu to apply the first level sort.**

   In the phone book sort, this is the LastName field.

You can extend these steps to create sorts on more fields. Imagine you have a ridiculously large compendium of names that includes some people with the same last *and* first name. In this case, you could add a third sort—by middle initial. To apply this sort, you'd switch sorting on in this order: MiddleInitial, FirstName, LastName. You'll get this result:

```
...
Smith, Star
Smith, Susan K
Smith, Susan P
Smith, Sy
...
```

Filtering

In a table with hundreds or thousands of records, scrolling back and forth in the datasheet is about as relaxing as a pneumatic drill at 3:00 a.m. Sometimes, you don't even need to see all the records at once—they're just a finger-tiring distraction from the data you're really interested in. In this case, you should cut the datasheet down to just the records that interest you, with *filtering*.

In order to filter records, you specify a condition that record must meet in order to be included in the datasheet. For example, an online store might pick out food items from a full product catalog, a shipping company might look for orders made last week, and a dating service might hunt down bachelors who don't live with their parents. When you apply a filter condition, you end up hiding all the records that don't match your requirements. They're still in the table—they're just tucked neatly out of sight.

Access has several different ways to apply filters. In the following sections, you'll start with the simplest, and then move on to the more advanced options.

Quick filters

A *quick filter* lets you choose what values you want to include and which ones you want to hide, based on the current contents of your table. To apply a quick filter, choose the column you want to use, and then click the drop-down arrow at the column header's right edge. You'll see a list of all the distinct values in that column. Initially, each value has a checkmark next to it. Clear the checkmark to hide records with that value. Figure 28-9 shows an example where a sort and filter are being used at the same time.

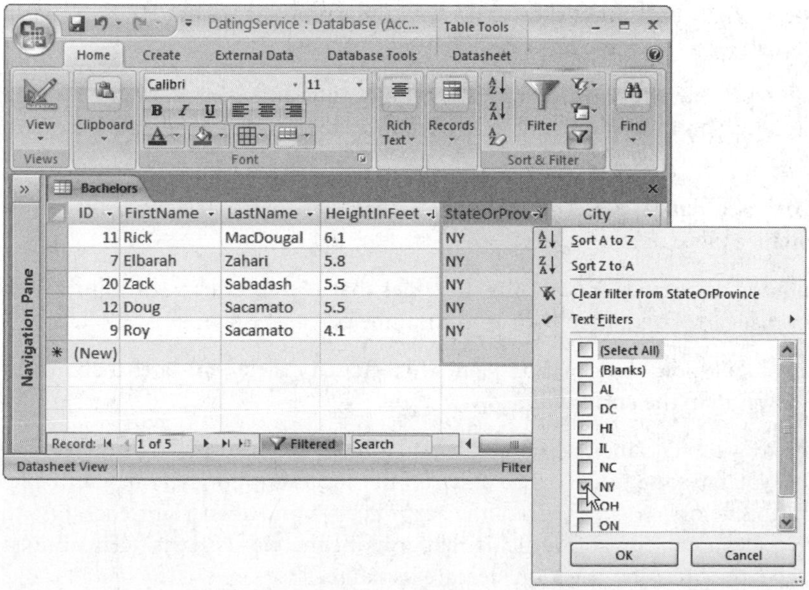

Figure 28-9:
This list of eligible bachelors is sorted first by height (in descending largest-to-smallest order), and then filtered to include only those hopefuls who live in the state of New York. A checkmark indicates that records that have this value are included in the datasheet. Others are hidden from view.

Note: To remove all the filters on a column (and show every record in the datasheet), click the drop-down button at the right edge of the column header, and then choose "Clear filter."

Not all data types support filtering. Data types that do include Number, Currency, AutoNumber, Text, Hyperlink, Date/Time, and Yes/No. Memo fields don't support quick filters (because their values are typically too large to fit in the drop-down list), but they do support other types of filters.

You can apply quick filters to more than one column. The order in which you apply the filters doesn't matter, as all filters are *cumulative*, which means you see only records that match all the filters you've set. You can even use quick filters in combination with the other filtering techniques described in the following sections. To remove your filters, choose Home → Sort & Filter → Remove Filter.

Tip: Quick filters work best if you have a relatively small number of distinct values. Limiting people based on the state they live in is a great choice, as is the political party they support or their favorite color. It wouldn't work as well if you wanted to cut down the list based on birth date, height, or weight, because there's a huge range of different possible values. (You don't need to give up on filtering altogether—rather, you just need to use a different type of filter.)

Filter by selection

Filter by selection lets you apply a filter based on any value in your table. This choice is handy if you've found exactly the type of record you want to include or exclude. Using filter by selection, you can turn the current value into a filter without hunting through the filter list.

Here's how it works. First, find the value you want to use for filtering in the datasheet. Right-click the value, and then choose one of the filter options at the end of the menu (see Figure 28-10).

All data types that support filtering allow you to filter out exact matches. But many also give you some additional filtering options in the right-click menu. Here's what you'll see for different data types:

- **Text-based data types.** You can filter values that match exactly, or values that contain a piece of text.

- **Numeric data types.** You can filter values that match exactly, or numbers that are smaller or larger than the current number.

- **Date data types.** You can filter values that match exactly, or dates that are older or newer than the current date.

Finally, to get even fancier, you can create a filter condition using only *part* of a value. If you have the value "Great at darts" in the Description field in your table of hopeful bachelors, you can select the text "darts," and then right-click just that text. Now you can find other fields that contain the word "darts." This utility is what gives the filter "by selection" feature its name.

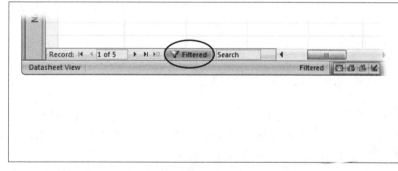

Figure 28-10:
Depending on the data type, you see slightly different filtering options. For a text field (like the City field shown here), you have the option to include only the records that match the current value (Equals "Chicago"), or those that don't (Does Not Equal "Chicago"). You also have some extra filtering options that go beyond what a quick filter can do— namely, you can include or exclude fields that simply contain the text "Chicago." That filter condition applies to values like "Chicagoland" and "Little Chicago."

Access makes it easy to switch filtering on and off at a moment's notice. Figure 28-11 shows how.

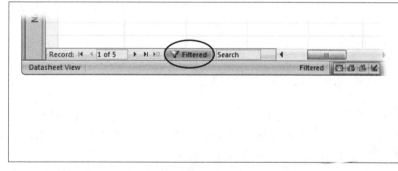

Figure 28-11:
Right next to the navigation controls at the bottom of your datasheet is a Filtered/Unfiltered indicator that tells you when filtering's applied. You can also use this box to quickly switch your filter on and off—clicking it once removes all filters, and clicking it again reapplies the most recent set of filters.

Filter by condition

So far, the filters you use have taken the current values in your table as a starting point. But if you're feeling confident with filters, you may be ready to try a more advanced approach: *filtering by condition*. When you use a filter by condition, you can define exactly the filter you want.

Imagine you want to find all the rare wine vintages in your cellar with a value of more than $85. Using the filter-by-selection approach, you need to start by finding a wine with a value of $85, which you can use to build your condition. But what if there isn't any wine in your list that has a price of exactly $85, or what if you just can't seem to find it? A quicker approach is defining the filter condition by hand.

Here's how it works. First, click the drop-down arrow at the right edge of the column header. But instead of choosing one of the quick filter options, look for a submenu with filtering options. This menu's named according to the data, so text fields include a Text Filters option, number fields have a Number Filters option, and so on. Figure 28-12 shows an example.

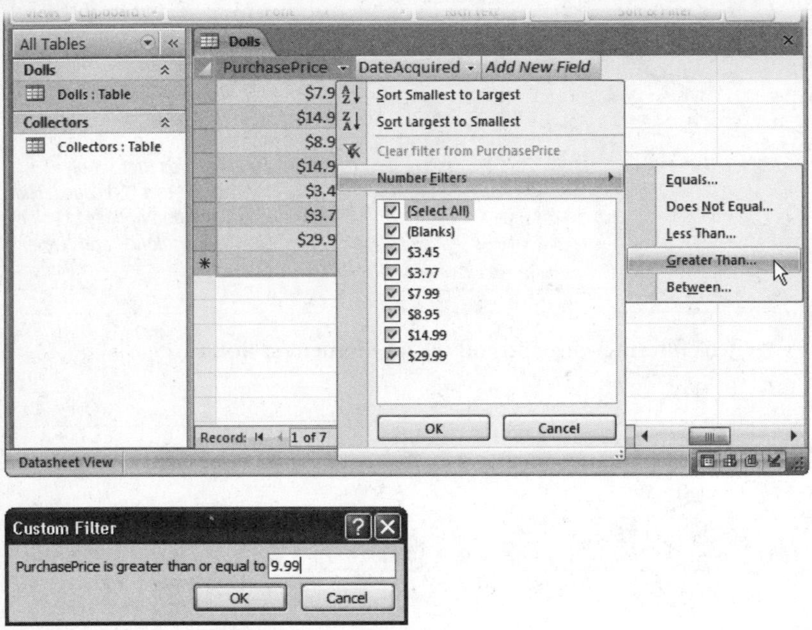

Figure 28-12:
Top: With a numeric field like this PurchasePrice field, filtering by condition lets you look at values that fall above a certain minimum.

Bottom: Once you've chosen the type of filter you want, you need to supply the information for that filter. If you choose Greater Than, then you need to supply the minimum number. Records that are equal to or larger than this value are shown in the datasheet.

Here's a quick overview that describes the extra options you get using filter by condition, depending on your data type:

- **Text-based data types.** All the same options as filter by selection, plus you can find values that start with specific text, or values that end with certain text.

- **Numeric data types.** All the same options as filter by selection, plus you can find values that are in a range, meaning they're greater than a set minimum but smaller than a set maximum.

- **Date data types.** All the same options as filter by selection, plus you can find dates that fall in a range, *and* you can chose from a huge list of built-in options, like Yesterday, Last Week, Next Month, Year to Date, First Quarter, and so on.

Searching

Access also provides a *quick search* feature that lets you scan your datasheet for specific information. Whereas filtering helps you pull out a batch of important records, searching's better if you need to find a single detail that's lost in the mountains of data. And while filtering changes the datasheet view by hiding some records, searching leaves everything as is. It just takes you to the data you want to see.

The quickest way to search is through the search box next to the record navigation controls (see Figure 28-13). Just type in the text you want to find. As you type, the first match in the table is highlighted automatically. You can press Enter to search for subsequent matches.

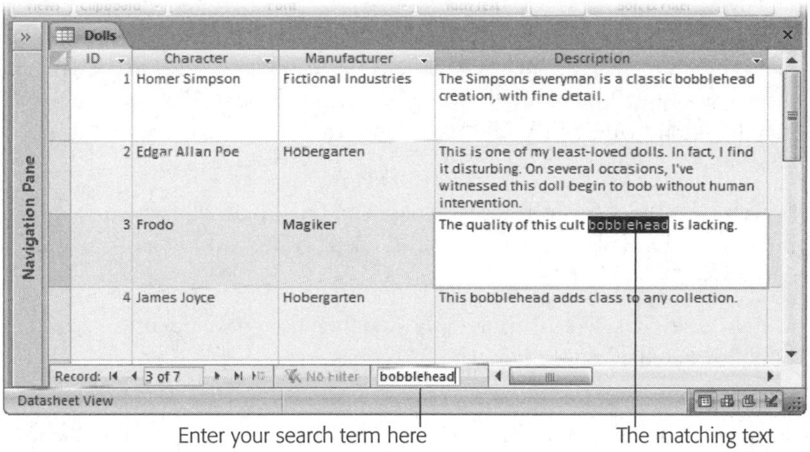

Figure 28-13:
Here, a search is being performed for the word "bobblehead." If you find a match, you can keep searching—just press Enter again to jump to the next match. In this example, pressing Enter sends Access to the next record's Description field.

Enter your search term here   The matching text

When performing a search, Access scans the table starting from the first field in the first record. It then goes left to right, examining every field in the current record. If it reaches the end without a match, then it continues to the next record and checks all of its values, and so on. When it reaches the end of the table, it stops.

If you want to change the way Access performs a search, you'll need to use the Find feature instead:

1. **Choose Home → Sort & Filter → Find. (Or, just use the shortcut Ctrl+F.)**

   The Find and Replace dialog box appears (Figure 28-14).

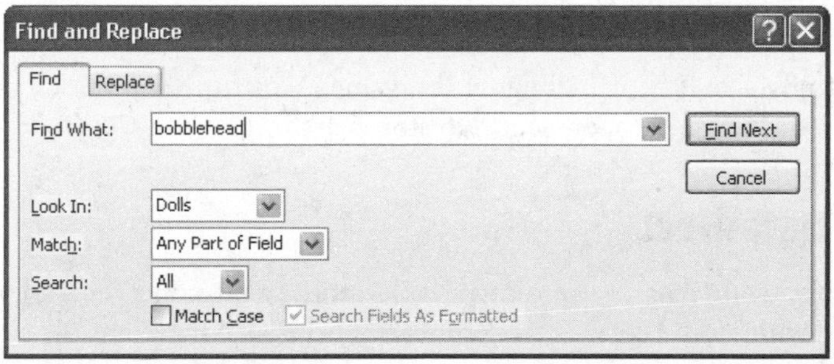

Figure 28-14:
The Find and Replace dialog box is the perfect tool for hunting for lost information.

2. Specify the text you're searching for in the Find What box, and then set any other search options you want to use:

- **Find What.** The text you're looking for.

- **Look In.** Allows you to choose between searching the entire table or just a single field.

- **Match.** lets you specify whether values need to match exactly. Use Whole Field to require exact matches. Use Start of Field if you want to match beginnings (so "bowl" matches "bowling"), or Any Part of Field if you want to match text anywhere in a field (so "bowl" matches "League of extraordinary bowlers").

- **Search.** Sets the direction Access looks: Up, Down, or All (which loops from the end of the table to beginning, and keeps going until it has traversed the entire table).

- **Match Case.** If selected, finds only matches that have identical capitalization. So "banana" doesn't match "BANANA."

- **Search Fields as Formatted.** If selected, means Access searches the value as it appears on the datasheet. For example, the number 44 may appear in a Currency field as $44.00. If you search for 44, you always find what you're looking for. But if you search for the formatted representation $44.00, you get a match only if you have Search Fields as Formatted switched on. In extremely large tables (with thousands of records), searches may be faster if you switch off Search Fields as Formatted.

Note: In order to turn off Search Fields as Formatted, you must choose to search a single field in the Look In box. If you are searching the entire table, then you must search the formatted values.

---

3. **Click Find Next.**

Access starts searching from the current position. If you're using the standard search direction (Down), Access moves from left to right in the current record, and then down from record to record until it finds a match.

When Access finds a match, it highlights the value. You can then click Find Next to look for the next match, or Cancel to stop searching.

Printing the Datasheet

If you want to study your data at the dinner table (and aren't concerned about potential conflicts with non-Access-lovers), nothing beats a hard copy of your data. You can dash off a quick printout by choosing File → Print from the menu while your datasheet's visible. However, the results you get will probably disappoint you, particularly if you have a large table.

Find and Replace

The search feature doubles as a powerful (but somewhat dangerous) way to modify records.

Initially, when the Find and Replace dialog box appears, it shows the Find tab. However, you can click the Replace tab to be able to find specific values and replace them with different text. All the settings for a replace operation are the same as for a find operation, except you have an additional text box, called Replace With, to supply the replacement text.

The safest way to perform a replace operation is to click the Find Next button to jump to the next match. At this point, you can look at the match, check that you really *do* want to modify it, and then click Replace to change the value and jump to the next match. Repeat this procedure to move cautiously through the entire table.

If you're a wild and crazy skydiving sort who prefers to live life on the edge, you can use the Replace All button to change every matching value in the entire table in a single step. Although this procedure's ridiculously fast, it's also a little risky. Replace operations can't be reversed (the Undo feature's no help here because it can reverse only a single record change), so if you end up changing more than you intend, there's no easy way back. If you're still seduced by the ease of a Replace All, consider creating a backup of your database file (page 601) before going any further.

The key problem's that Access isn't bothered about tables that are too wide to fit on a printed page. It deals with them by splitting the printout into separate pages. If you have a large table and you print it out using the standard Access settings, you could easily end up with a printout that's four pages wide and three pages long. Assembling this jigsaw is not for the faint of heart. To get a better printout, it's absolutely crucial that you *preview* your table before you print it, as described in the next section.

Print Preview

The print preview feature in Access gives you the chance to tweak your margins, paper orientation, and so on, before you send your table to the printer. This way, you can make sure the final printout's genuinely usable. To preview a table, open it (or select it in the navigation pane), and then choose Office button → Print → Print Preview.

The print preview shows a picture of what your data will look like once it's committed to paper. Unlike the datasheet view, the print preview *paginates* your data (Figure 28-15). You see exactly what fits on each page and how many pages your printout requires (and what content shows up on each page).

If you decide you're happy with what you see, then you can fire off your printout by choosing Print Preview → Print → Print from the ribbon. This opens the familiar Windows Print dialog box, where you can pick a printer and seal the deal.

When you're finished looking at the print preview window, choose Print Preview → Close Preview → Close Print Preview, or click one of the view buttons at the Access window's bottom-right corner to switch to Datasheet view or Design view.

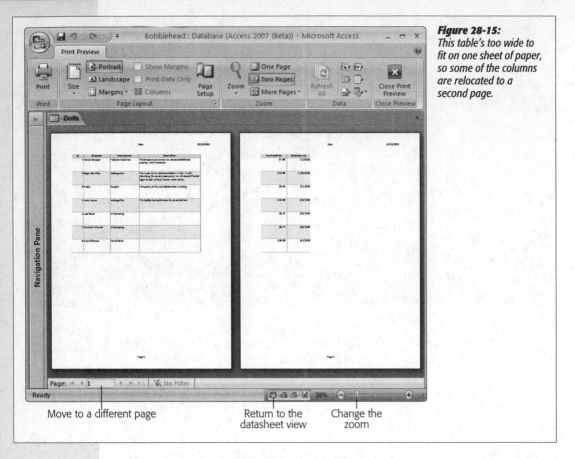

Figure 28-15:
This table's too wide to fit on one sheet of paper, so some of the columns are relocated to a second page.

Move to a different page   Return to the datasheet view   Change the zoom

Moving around the print preview

You can't change anything in the print preview window. However, you can browse through the pages of your virtual printout and see if it meets your approval.

Here's how you can get around in the preview window:

• Use the scroll buttons to move from one page to another. These buttons look the same as the scroll buttons in the datasheet, but they move from page to page, not record to record.

• To move from page to page, you can use the scroll bar at the side of the window or the Page Up and Page Down keys.

• To jump in for a closer look, click anywhere on the preview page (you'll notice that the mouse pointer has become a magnifying glass). This click magnifies the sheet to 100 percent zoom, so you can more clearly see the text and details. To switch back to full-page view, click the page or click the mouse pointer again.

- To zoom more precisely, use the zoom slider that's in the status bar's bottom-right corner. Slide it to the left to reduce your zoom (and see more at once), or slide it to the right to increase your zoom (and focus on a smaller portion of your page).

- To see two pages at once, choose Print Preview → Zoom → Two Pages. To see more, choose Print Preview → Zoom → More Pages, and then pick the number of pages you want to see at once from the list.

Changing the page layout

Access provides a small set of page layout options that you can tweak using the ribbon's Print Preview → Page Layout section in the print preview window. Here are your options:

- **Size.** Lets you use different paper sizes. If you're fed up with tables that don't fit, you might want to invest in some larger stock (like legal-sized paper).

- **Portrait** and **Landscape.** Let you choose how the page is oriented. Access, like all Office programs, assumes you want to print out text using standard *portrait* orientation. In portrait orientation, pages are turned upright so that the long edge is along the side and the short edge is along the top. It makes perfect sense for résumés and memos, but it's pure madness for a wide table, because it guarantees at least some columns will be rudely chopped off and relocated to different pages. *Landscape* orientation makes more sense in this case, because it turns the page on its side, fitting fewer rows per page but many more columns.

- **Margins.** Lets you choose the breathing space between your table and the edges of the page. Margins is a drop-down button, and when you click it, you see a menu with several common margin choices (Normal, Narrow, and Wide). If none of those fit the bill, then click the Page Setup button, which opens a Page Setup dialog box where you can set the exact width of the margin on each side of the page.

Fine-Tuning a Printout

Based on the limited page layout options, you might assume that there's not much you can do customize a printout. However, you actually have more control than you realize. Many of the formatting options that you've learned about in this chapter also have an effect on your printout. By applying the right formatting, you can create a better printout.

Here are some pro printing tips that explain how different formatting choices influence your printouts:

- **Font.** Printouts use your datasheet font and font size. Scale this down, and you can fit more in less space.

- **Column order and column hiding.** Reorder your columns before printing out to suit what you want to see on the page. Even better, use column hiding (page 651) to conceal fields that aren't important.

- **Column widths and row height.** Access uses the exact widths and heights that you've set on your datasheet. Squeeze some columns down to fit more, and expand rows if you have fields with large amounts of text and you want them to wrap over multiple lines.

- **Frozen columns.** If a table's too wide to fit on your printout, then the frozen column is printed on each part. For example, if you freeze the FirstName field, you'll see it on every separate page, so you don't need to line the pages up to find up who's who.

- **Sort options.** They help you breeze through data in a datasheet—and they can do the same for a printout. Apply them before printing.

- **Filter options.** These are the unsung heroes of Access printing. Use them to get just the important rows. That way, your printout has exactly what you need.

The only challenge you face when using these settings is the fact that you can't set them from the print preview window. Instead, you have to set them in the datasheet, jump to the print preview window to see the result, jump back to the datasheet to change them a little bit more, jump back to the print preview window, and so on. This process can quickly get tiring.

Tip: Don't spend too much time tweaking the formatting options to create the perfect printout. If you have a large table that just can't fit gracefully into a page, you probably want to use reports, which are described in Chapter 32. They provide much more formatting muscle, including the ability to split fields over several lines, separate records with borders, and allow large values to take up more space by gently bumping other information out of the way.

CHAPTER 29

Blocking Bad Data

Even the best database designer has spent a sleepless night worrying about the errors that could be lurking in a database. Bad data's a notorious problem—it enters the database, lies dormant for months, and appears only when you discover you've mailed an invoice to customer "Blank Blank" or sold a bag of peanuts for –$4.99.

The best way to prevent these types of problems is to stop bad data from making it into your database in the first place. In other words, you need to set up validation rules that reject suspicious values as soon as someone types them in. Once bad data's entered your database, it's harder to spot than a blueberry in a swimming pool.

This chapter covers the essential set of Access data validation tools:

- **The basics** include duplicates, required fields, and default values.

- **Input masks** format ordinary text into patterns, like postal codes and phone numbers.

- **Validation rules** lay down strict laws for unruly fields.

- **Lookups** limit values to a list of preset choices.

Data Integrity Basics

All of Access's data validation features work via the Design view you learned about in Chapter 27. To put them in place, you choose a field and then tweak its properties. The only trick's knowing what properties are most useful. You've already seen some in Chapter 27, but the following sections fill in a few more details.

Tip: Remember, Access gives you three ways to switch to Design view. You can right-click the table tab title and then choose Design View from the menu, use the Home → View button on the ribbon, or use the tiny view buttons at the Access window's bottom-right corner. And if you're really impatient, then you don't even need to open your table first—just find it in the navigation pane, right-click it there, and then choose Design View.

Preventing Blank Fields

Every record needs a bare minimum of information to make sense. However, without your help, Access can't distinguish between critical information and optional details. For that reason, every field in a new table is optional, except for the primary-key field (which is usually the ID value). Try this out with the Dolls table from Chapter 26; you'll quickly discover that you can add records that have virtually no information in them.

You can easily remedy this problem. Just select the field that you want to make mandatory in Design view, and then set the Required field property to Yes (Figure 29-1).

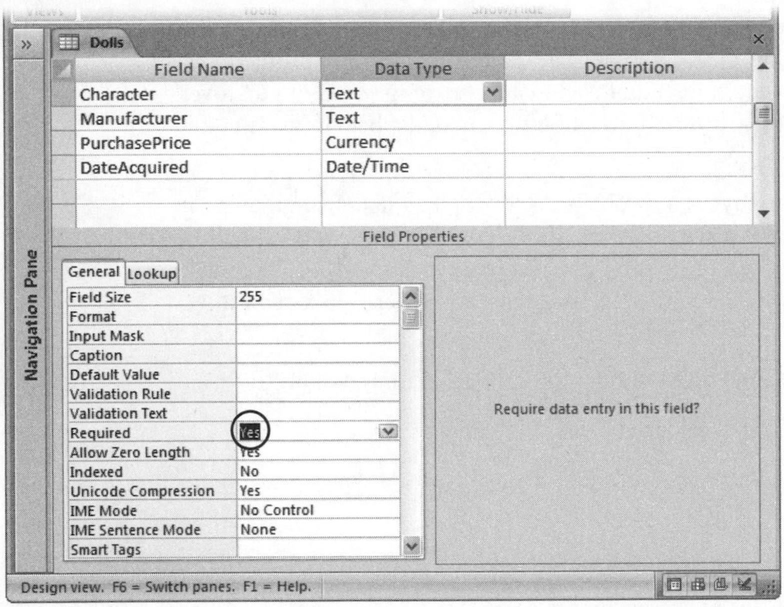

Figure 29-1:
The Required field property tells Access not to allow empty values (called nulls in tech-speak).

Access checks the Required field property whenever you add a new record or modify a field in an existing record. However, if your table already contains data, there's no guarantee that it follows the rules.

Imagine you fill the Dolls table with a few bobbleheads before you decide that every record requires a value for the Character field. You switch to Design view, choose the Character field, and then flip the Required field property to Yes. When you save the table (by switching back to Datasheet view or closing the table), Access gives you the option of verifying the bobblehead records that are already in the table (Figure 29-2). If you choose to perform the test and Access finds the problem, it gives you the option of reversing your changes (Figure 29-3).

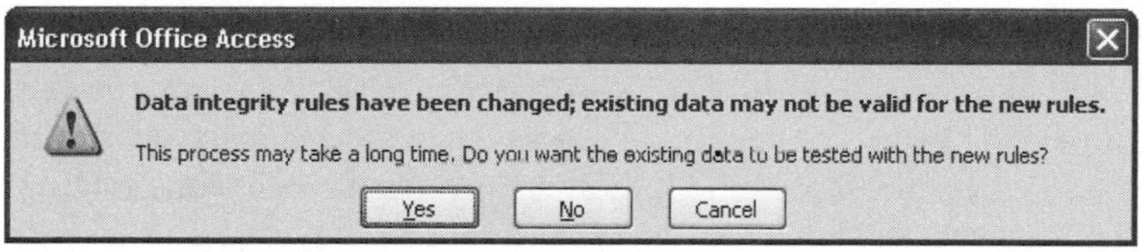

Figure 29-2:
It's a good idea to test the data in your table to make sure it meets the new requirements you put into place. Otherwise, invalid data could still remain. Don't let the message scare you—unless you have tens of thousands of records, this check doesn't take long.

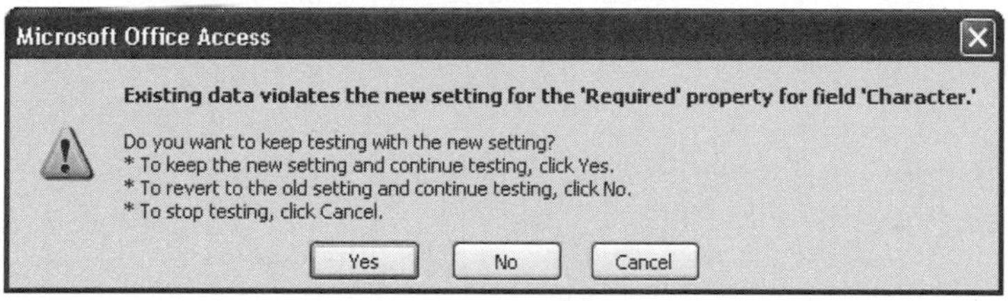

Figure 29-3:
If Access finds an empty value, then it stops the search and asks you what to do about it. You can keep your changes (even though they conflict with at least one record)— after all, at least new records won't suffer from the same problem. Your other option is to reset your field to its more lenient previous self. Either way, you can track down the missing data by performing a sort on the field in question (page 654), which brings empty values to the top.

WORD TO THE WISE

Don't Require Too Much

You'll need to think very carefully about what set of values you need, at a minimum, to create a record.

For example, a company selling Elvis costumes might not want to accept a new outfit into their Products table unless they have every detail in place. The Required field property's a great help here, because it prevents half-baked products from showing up in the catalogue.

On the other hand, the same strictness is out of place in the same company's Customers table. The sales staff needs the flexibility to add a new prospect with only partial information. A potential customer may phone and leave only a mailing address (with no billing address, phone number, email information, and so on). Even though you don't have all the information about this customer, you'll still need to place that customer in the Customers table so that he or she can receive the monthly newsletter.

As a general rule, make a field optional if the information for it isn't necessary or might not be available at the time the record is entered.

Blank values and empty text

Access supports this Required property for every data type. However, with some data types you might want to add extra checks. That's because the Required property prevents only blank fields—fields that don't have any information in them at all. However, Access makes a slightly bizarre distinction between blank values and something called *empty text*.

A blank (null) value indicates that no information was supplied. Empty text indicates that a field value was supplied, but it just happens to be empty. Confused yet? The distinction exists because databases like Access need to recognize when information's missing. A blank value could indicate an oversight—someone might just have forgotten to enter the value. On the other hand, empty text indicates a conscious decision to leave that information out.

Note: To try this out in your datasheet, create a text field that has Required set to Yes. Try inserting a new record, and leaving the record blank. (Access stops you cold.) Now, try adding a new record, but place a single space in the field. Here's the strange part: Access automatically trims out the spaces, and by doing so, it converts your single space to empty text. However, you don't receive an error message because empty text isn't the same as a blank value.

The good news is that if you find this whole distinction confusing, then you can prevent both blank values *and* empty text. Just set Required to Yes to stop the blank values, and set Allow Zero Length to No to prevent empty text.

Note: A similar distinction exists for numeric data types. Even if you set Required to Yes, you can still supply a number of 0. If you want to prevent that action, then you'll need to use the validation rules described later in this chapter (page 680).

Setting Default Values

So far, the fields in your tables are either filled in explicitly by the person who adds the record or left blank. But there's another option—you can supply a *default value*. Now, if someone inserts a record and leaves the field blank, Access applies the default value instead.

You set a default value using the Default Value field property. For a numeric AddedCost field, you could set this to be the number 0. For a text Country field, you may use the text "U.S.A." as a default value. (All text values must be wrapped in quotations marks when you use them for a default value.)

Access shows all your default values in the new-row slot at the bottom of the datasheet (Figure 29-4). It also automatically inserts default values into any hidden columns (page 651).

Access inserts the default value when you create a new record. (You're then free to change that value.) You can also switch a field back to its default value using the Ctrl+Alt+Space shortcut while you're editing it.

Figure 29-4:
This dating service uses four default values: a default height (5.9), a default city (New York), a default state (also New York), and a default country (U.S.A.). This system makes sense, because most of their new entries have this information. On the other hand, there's no point in supplying a default value for the name fields.

Four default values

Tip: One nice feature is that you can use the default value as a starting point for a new record. For example, when you create a new record in the datasheet, you can edit the default value, rather than replacing it with a completely new value.

You can also create more intelligent *dynamic* default values. Access evaluates dynamic default values whenever you insert a new record, which means that the default value can vary based on other information. Dynamic default values use *expressions* (specialized database formulas) that can perform calculations or retrieve other details. One useful expression, *Date( )*, grabs the current date that's set on your computer. If you use Date( ) as the default value for a date field (as shown in Figure 29-5), then Access automatically inserts the current date whenever you add a new record.

Preventing Duplicate Values with Indexes

Any table's first rule is that each record it contains must be unique. To enforce this restriction, you need to choose a primary key (page 638), which is one or more fields that won't ever be duplicated in different records.

Here's the catch. As you learned in Chapter 27, the safest option's to create an ID field for the primary key. So far, all the tables you've seen have included this detail. But what if you need to make sure *other* fields are unique? Imagine you create an Employees table. You follow good database design principles and identify every record with an automatically generated ID number. However, you also want to make sure that no two employees have the same Social Security number (SSN) to prevent possible errors—like accidentally entering the same employee twice.

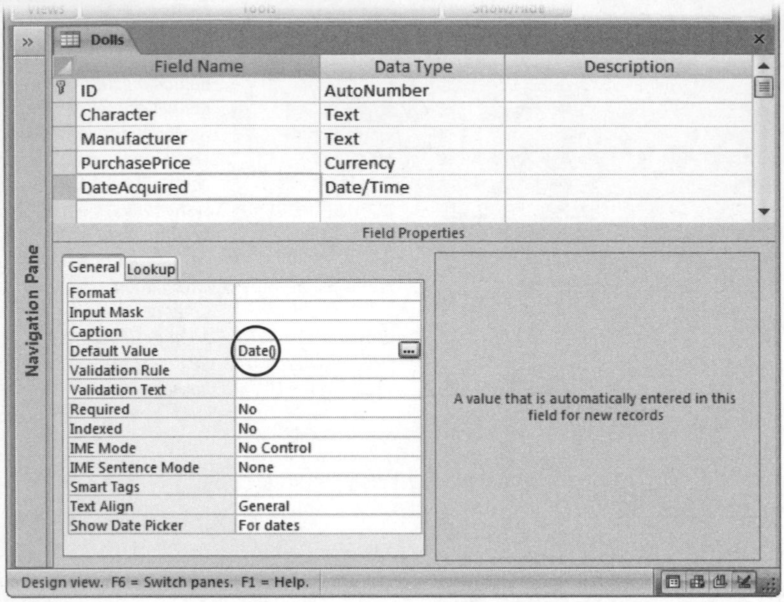

Figure 29-5:
If you use the Date( ) function as the default value for the DateAcquired field in the bobblehead table, then every time you add a new bobblehead record, Access fills in the current date. You decide whether you want to keep that date or replace it with a different value.

Note: For a quick refresher about why ID fields are such a good idea, refer to page 638. In the Employees table, you certainly could choose to make the SSN the primary key, but it's not the ideal situation when you start linking tables together (Chapter 30), and it causes problems if you need to change the SSN later on (in the case of an error), or if you enter employee information before you've received the SSN.

You can force a field to require unique values with an *index*. A database index is analogous to the index in a book—it's a list of values (from a field) with a cross-reference that points to the corresponding section (the full record). If you index the SocialSecurityNumber field, Access creates a list like this and stores it behind the scenes in your database file:

SocialSecurityNumber	Location of Full Record
001-01-3455	...
001-02-0434	...
001-02-9558	...
002-40-3200	...

Using this list, Access can quickly determine whether a new record duplicates an existing SSN. If it does, then Access doesn't let you insert it.

How Indexes Work

It's important that the list of SSNs is *sorted*. Sorting means the number 001-01-3455 always occurs before 002-40-3200 in the index, regardless of where the record's physically stored in the database. This sorting's important, because it lets Access quickly check for duplicates. If you enter the number 001-02-4300, then Access needs to read only the first part of the list. Once it finds the next "larger" SSN (one that falls later in the sort, like 001-02-501), it knows the remainder of the index doesn't contain a duplicate.

In practice, all databases use many more optimizations to make this process blazingly fast. But there's one key principle—without an index, Access would need to check the entire table. Tables aren't stored in sorted order, so there's no way Access can be sure a given SSN isn't in there unless it checks every record.

So how do you apply an index to a field? The trick's the Indexed field property, which is available for every data type except Attachment and OLE Object. When you add a field, the Indexed property's set to No, which means Access doesn't create a field. To add an index and prevent duplicates, you can change the Indexed property in Design view to Yes [No Duplicates]. The third option, Yes [Duplicates OK], creates an index but lets more than one record have the same value. This option doesn't help you catch repeated records, but you can use it to speed up searches.

Note: As you know from Chapter 27 (page 638), primary keys also disallow duplicates, using the same technique. When you define a primary key, Access automatically creates an index on that field.

When you close Design view after changing the Indexed field property, Access prompts you to save your changes. At this point, it creates any new indexes it needs. You can't create a no-duplicates index if you already have duplicate information in your table. In this situation, Access gives you an error message when you close the Design window and it attempts to add the index.

Multifield indexes

You can also use indexes to prevent a *combination* of values from being repeated. Imagine you create a People table to track your friends and their contact information. You're likely to have entries with the same first or last name. However, you may want to prevent two records from having the same first *and* last name. This limitation prevents you from inadvertently adding the same person twice.

Note: This example could cause endless headaches if you honestly *do* have two friends who share the same first and last names. In that case, you'll need to remove the index before you're allowed to add the name. You should think carefully about legitimate reasons for duplication before you create any indexes.

To ensure that a combination of fields is unique, you need to create a *compound index*, which combines the information from more than one field. Here's how to do it:

1. **In Design view, choose Table Tools | Design → Show/Hide → Indexes.**

   The Indexes window appears (Figure 29-6). Using the Indexes window, you can see your current indexes and add new ones.

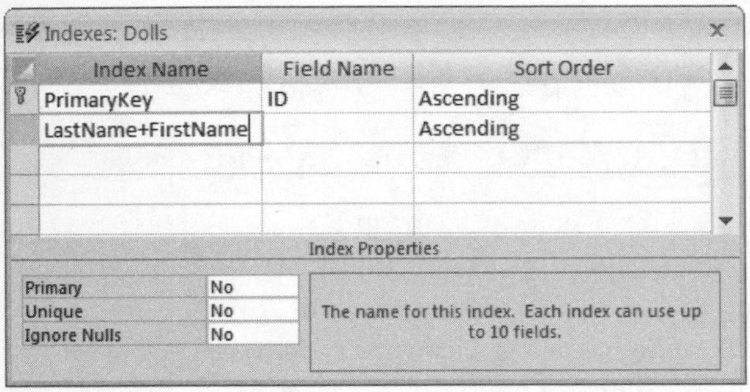

Figure 29-6:
The Indexes window shows all the indexes that are defined for a table. Here, there's a single index for the ID field (which Access created automatically) and a compound index that's in the process of being created.

2. **Choose a name for your index. Type this name into the first blank row in the Index Name column.**

   The index name has no real importance—Access uses it to store the index in the database, but you don't see the index name when you work with the table. Usually, you'll use the name of one or both of the fields you're indexing (like Last-Name+FirstName).

3. **Choose the first field in the Field Name column in the same row (like Last-Name).**

   It doesn't matter which field name you use first. Either way, the index can prevent duplicate values. However, the order does affect how searches use the index to boost performance.

4. **In the area at the bottom of the window, set the Unique box to Yes.**

   This creates an index that prevents duplicates (as opposed to one that's used only for boosting search speeds).

   You can also set the Ignore Nulls box to Yes, if you want Access to allow duplicate blank values. Imagine you want to make the SSN field optional. However, if an SSN number *is* entered, then you want to make sure it doesn't duplicate any other value. In this case, you should Ignore Nulls to Yes. If you set Ignore Nulls to No, then Access lets only one record have a blank SSN field, which probably isn't the behavior you want.

Note: You can also disallow blank values altogether using the Required property, as described on page 668.

Ignore the Primary box (which identifies the index used for the primary key).

5. **Move down one row. Leave the Index Name column blank (which tells Access it's still part of the previous index), but choose another field in the Field Name column (like FirstName).**

If you want to create a compound index with more than two fields, then just repeat this step until you've added all the fields you need. Figure 29-7 shows what a finished index looks like.

You can now close the Indexes window.

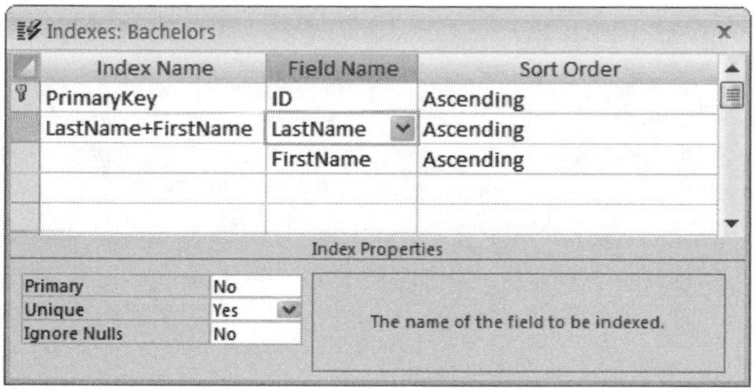

Figure 29-7:
Here's a compound index that prevents two people from sharing the same first and last names.

Input Masks

As you've already learned, databases prize *consistency*. If you have a field named Height, you better be sure every value in that field uses the same type of measurements; otherwise, your data's not worth its weight in sock lint. Similarly, if you have a PhoneNumber field, you better make sure every phone number has the same format. If some phone numbers are written with dashes, spaces, and parentheses (like *(844) 547-1123*), while others are a bit different (say *847-547-1123*), and a few leave out the area code information altogether (*547-1123*), then you've got a small problem on your hands. Because of the lack of consistency, you'll have a hard time working with this information (say, searching for a specific phone number or sorting the phone numbers into different categories based on area code).

To help you manage values that have a fixed pattern—like phone numbers—you can use an *input mask*. Essentially, an input mask (or just *mask* for short) gives you a way to tell Access what pattern your data should use. Based on this pattern, Access changes the way values are entered and edited to make them easier to understand and less error-prone. Figure 29-8 shows how a mask lets Access format a series of characters as they're being typed into a field.

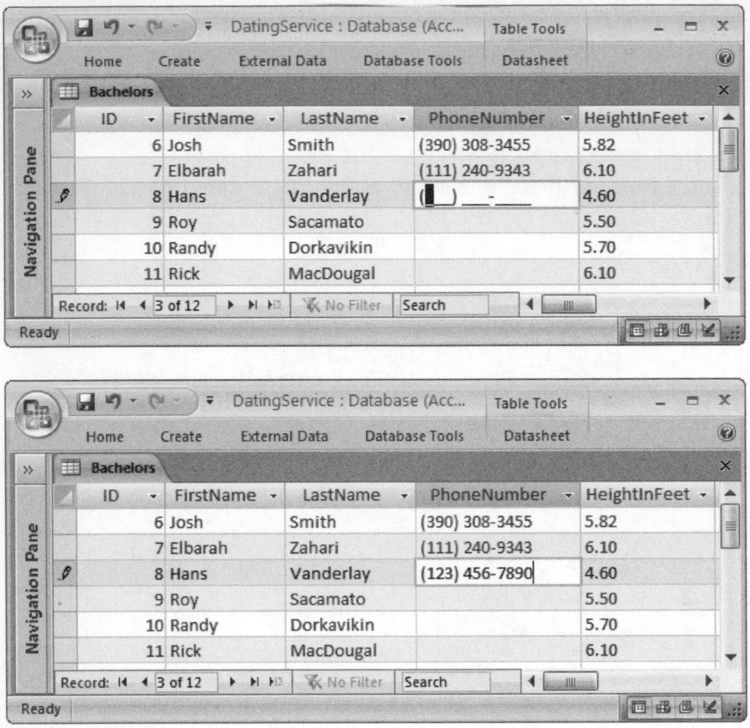

Figure 29-8:
Top: Here's a PhoneNumber field with a mask that's ready to go. So far, the person entering the record hasn't typed anything. The PhoneNumber field automatically starts out with this placeholder text.

Bottom: The mask formats the numbers as you type. If you type 1234567890 into this phone number mask, then you see the text (123) 456-7890. Behind the scenes, the databases stores 1234567890, but the information's presented in the datasheet using a nicely formatted package. That package is the mask.

You can add a mask to any field that uses the Text data type. Masks give you several advantages over ordinary text:

- **Masks guide data entry.** When empty, a masked edit control shows the placeholders where values need to go. A phone number mask shows the text (___) ___-____ when it's empty, clearly indicating what type of information it needs.

- **Masks make data easier to understand.** You can read many values more easily when they're presented a certain way. Most people can pick out the numbers in this formatted Social Security number (012-86-7180) faster than this unformatted one (012867180).

- **Masks prevent errors.** Masks reject characters that don't fit the mold. If you're using the telephone mask, you can't use letters.

- **Masks prevent confusion.** With many types of data, you have several ways to present the same information. You can enter phone numbers both with and without area codes. By presenting the mask with the area code placeholder, you're saying that this information's required (and where it goes). It's also obvious that you don't need to type in parentheses or a dash to separate numbers, because those details are already there. You'll see the same benefit if you use masks with dates, which can be entered in all sorts of different combinations (Year/Month/Day, Month-Day-Year, and so on).

Masks are best suited for when you're storing numeric information in a text field. This scenario occurs with all sorts of data, including credit card numbers, postal codes, and phone numbers. These types of information shouldn't be stored in number fields, because they aren't meant to be interpreted as a single number. Instead, they're meant to be understood as a series of digits. (If you do make the mistake of storing a phone number in a number field, you'll find out that people can type in perfectly nonsensical phone numbers like 0 and –14 because these are valid numbers, even if they aren't valid phone numbers. But an input mask on a text field catches these errors easily.)

Masks can't help you with more sophisticated challenges, like data values that have varying lengths or subtle patterns. For instance, a mask doesn't help you spot an incorrect email address.

Note: Text and Date/Time are the only data types that support masks.

Using a Ready-Made Mask

The easiest way to get started with masks is to use one of the many attractive options that Access has ready for you. This method's great, because it means you don't need to learn the arcane art of mask creation.

Here's what you need to do to pick out a prebuilt mask:

1. **In Design view, select the text field where you want to apply the mask.**

   For this test, try a PhoneNumber field.

2. **Look for the Input Mask field property. Click inside the field.**

   When you do, a small ellipsis (…) button appears at the left edge, as shown in Figure 29-9.

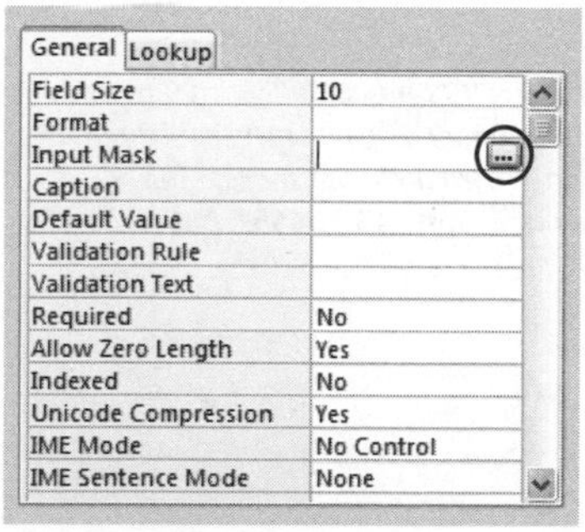

Figure 29-9:
The ellipsis (...) button (circled) is just the way Access tells you that you don't need to fill in this value by hand. Instead, you can click the ellipsis and pop up a wizard (like the Input Mask wizard) or some sort of helpful dialog box.

3. **Click the ellipsis button.**

The Input Mask wizard starts (see Figure 29-10).

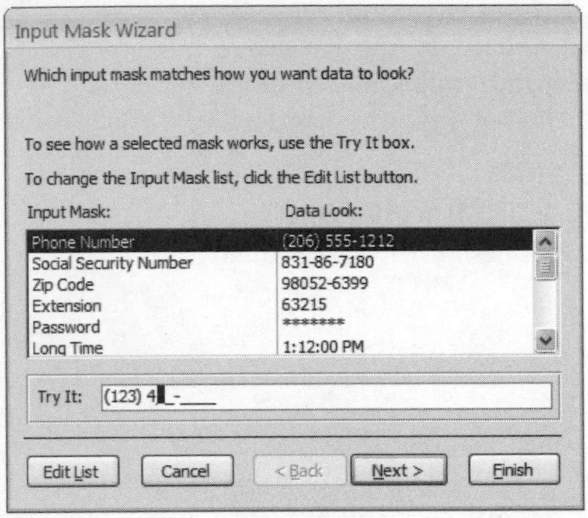

Figure 29-10:
The Input Mask wizard starts with a short list of commonly used masks. Next to every mask, Access shows you what a sample formatted value looks like. Once you select a mask, you can try using it in the Try It text box. The Try It text box gives you the same behavior that your field will have once you apply the mask.

4. **Choose the mask you want from the list of options.**

In this case, choose the first item in the list (Phone Number).

Note: Don't see what you want? You'll need to create your own (an advanced topic covered in *Access 2007: The Missing Manual*). If you see one that's close but not perfect, select it. You can tweak the mask in the wizard's second step.

---

5. **Click Next.**

The wizard's second step appears (see Figure 29-11).

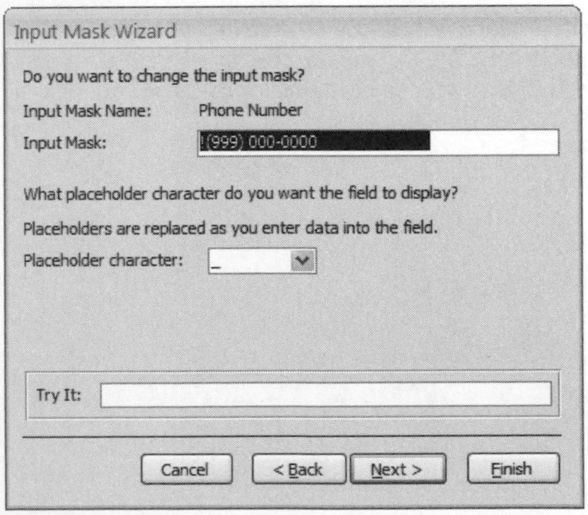

Figure 29-11:
The phone number mask is !(999) 000-000. Each 9 represents an optional number from 0 to 9. Each 0 represents a required number from 0 to 9. So according to this mask, (123) 456-7890 is a valid phone number, as is 123-4567, but (123) 456 isn't.

6. **If you want, you can change the mask or the placeholder character.**

   To change the mask, you'll need to learn what every mask character means (see *Access 2007: The Missing Manual* for details).

   You use the placeholder to show the empty slots where you enter information. The standard choice is the underscore. Optionally, you can use a space, dash, asterisk, or any other character by typing it in the "Placeholder character" box.

7. **Click Next.**

   If you're adding a mask to a text field, then the wizard's final step appears (see Figure 29-12).

   If you're adding a mask to a date field, then Access doesn't need to ask you how to store the information—it already knows. In this case, you can jump to step 9 and click Finish.

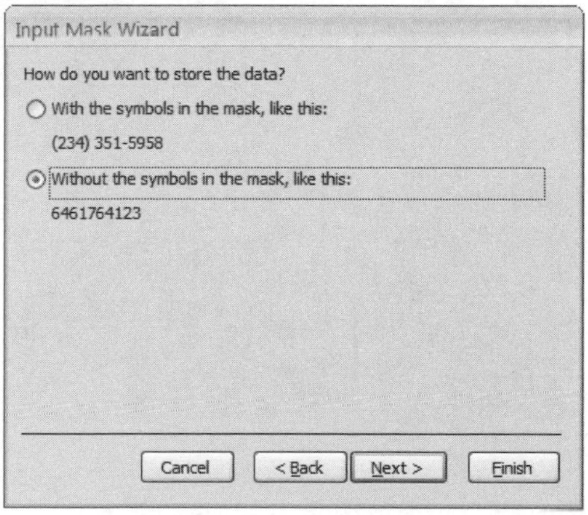

Figure 29-12:
The final step lets you choose how the data in your field is chosen—with or without the mask symbols.

8. **Choose how you want to store the value in this field.**

   The standard choice is to store just the characters you've typed in (in other words, everything you type into the field). If you use this option, the placeholders aren't included. For example, the phone number (416) 123-4567 is stored as *4161234567*. This option saves a little space, and it also lets you change the mask later on to present the information in a slightly different way.

   You could also store the mask complete with all the extra characters. Then a phone number's stored complete with hyphens, dashes, and spaces, like *(416) 123-4567*. This approach isn't nearly as flexible because you can't change the mask later.

9. **Click Finish.**

   The final mask appears in the Input Mask field property.

Before going any further, you may want to make sure that the length you've reserved for your field matches the mask. In the phone number example, you need a Field Size of 10 if you've chosen to store unformatted values (because there are 10 digits), or a Field Size of 14 for the whole shebang, complete with placeholders (one dash, one space, and two parentheses).

10. **Switch back to the Datasheet view, and click Yes when Access asks you to save changes.**

    Your input mask is now in place.

Note: Access uses the input mask information to control how you enter information in the datasheet. However, it's possible to circumvent the mask by entering the information in other ways. You could, for instance, create a form (as described in Chapter 33), and switch off the mask. A mask's not an absolute guarantee against invalid data—if you want such a guarantee, then you need a validation rule instead.

POWER USERS' CLINIC

Adding Your Mask to the Mask List

Sometimes you may create a mask that's so useful you want to use it in many different tables in your database (and maybe even in different databases). While you can certainly copy your mask to every field that needs to use it, Access has a nicer option—you can store your mask in its *mask list*. That way, the mask shows up whenever you run the Input Mask wizard, right alongside all Access's other standard masks.

To add your mask to the list, head to the Input Mask field property (for any field), and then click the ellipsis button to fire up the Input Mask wizard. Then, click the Edit List button, which pops up a handy window where you can edit the masks that Access provides, and add your own (Figure 29-13).

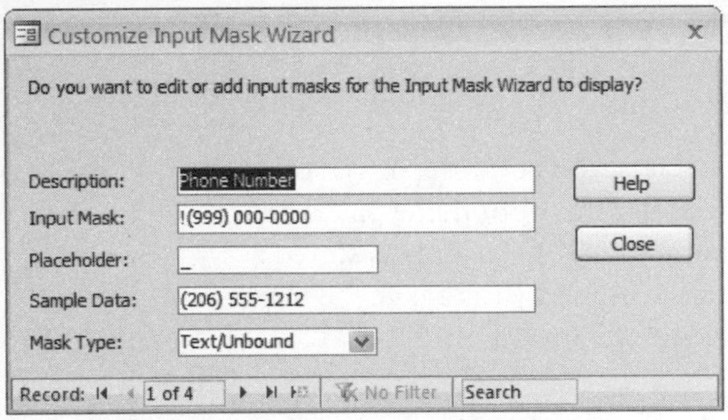

Figure 29-13:
To add your own mask, use the record scrolling buttons (at the bottom of the window) to scroll to the end. Or you can use this window to change a mask. For example, the prebuilt telephone mask doesn't require an area code. If that's a liberty you're not willing to take, then replace it with the more restrictive version (000) 000-0000.

Validation Rules

Input masks are a great tool, but they apply to only a few specific types of information—usually fixed-length text that has a single, unchanging pattern. To create a truly bulletproof table, you need to use more sophisticated restrictions, like making sure a number falls in a certain range, checking that a date hasn't yet occurred, or verifying that a text value starts with a certain letter. *Validation rules* can help you create all these restrictions.

A validation rule's premise is simple. You set up a restriction that tells Access which values to allow in a field and which ones are no good. Whenever someone adds a new record or edits a record, Access makes sure the data lives up to your validation rules. If it doesn't, then Access presents an error message and forces you to edit the offending data and try again.

Applying a Field Validation Rule

Each field can have a single validation rule. The following set of steps show you how to set one up. You'll start out easy, with a validation rule that prevents a numeric field from accepting 0 or any negative number (and in the following sections you'll hone your rule-writing abilities so you can tackle other data types).

Here's how to add your validation rule:

1. **In Design view, select the field to which you want to apply the rule.**

   All data types—except Memo, AutoNumber, and OLE Object—support validation. The validation rule in this example works with any numeric data type (like Number or Currency).

2. **In the Validation Rule field property, type a validation expression (Figure 29-14).**

   An expression's a bit of SQL that performs a check on the data you've entered. Access performs its validation check when you finish entering a piece of data, and try to navigate to another field or another record. For example, *>0* is a validation rule that forces the value in a Number field to be larger than 0. You'll learn more validation rules in the following sections.

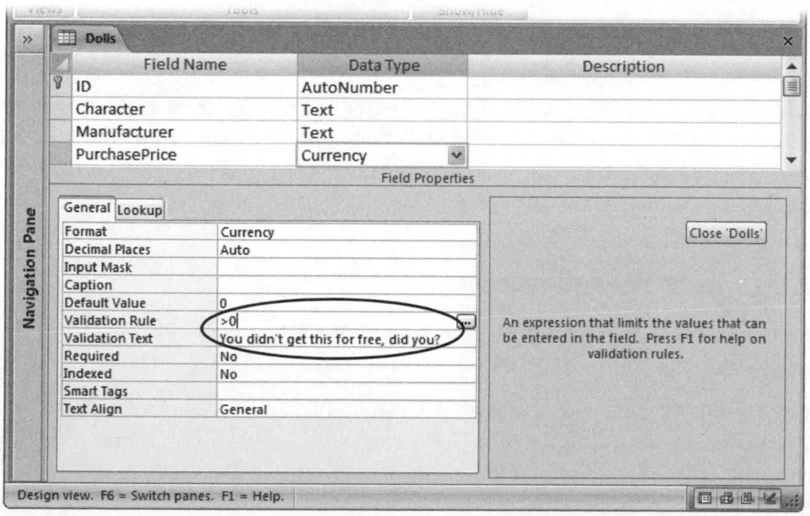

Figure 29-14:
Here, the Validation Rule property prevents impossible prices, and the Validation Text provides an error message.

3. **Type some error-message text in the Validation Text field property.**

If you enter a value that fails the validation check, then Access rejects the value and displays this error text in a dialog box. If you don't supply any text, then Access shows the validation rule for the field (whatever you entered in step 2), which is more than a little confusing for most mere mortals.

4. **Right-click the tab title, and then choose Datasheet View.**

If your table has existing records, Access gives you the option of checking them to make sure they meet the requirements of your validation rule. You decide whether you want to perform this check, or skip it altogether.

Once you're in Datasheet view, you're ready to try out your validation rule (Figure 29-15).

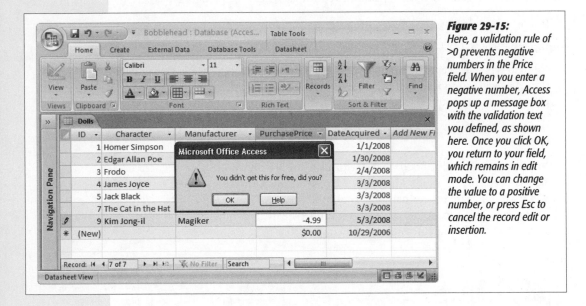

Figure 29-15:
Here, a validation rule of >0 prevents negative numbers in the Price field. When you enter a negative number, Access pops up a message box with the validation text you defined, as shown here. Once you click OK, you return to your field, which remains in edit mode. You can change the value to a positive number, or press Esc to cancel the record edit or insertion.

Note: Just because your table has validation rules doesn't mean the data inside *follows* these rules. A discrepancy can occur if you added records before the validation rules came into effect. (You learned about the same potential problem with required fields on page 668.) To avoid these headaches, set up your validation rules before you start adding data.

Writing a Field Validation Rule

As you can see, it's easy enough to apply a validation rule to a field. But *creating* the right validation rule takes more thought.

Although validation's limited only by your imagination, Access pros turn to a few basic patterns again and again. The following sections give you some quick and easy starting points for validating different data types.

Note: Access uses your validation rule only if a field contains some content. If you leave it blank, then Access accepts if without any checks. If this isn't the behavior you want, then just set the Required property to Yes to make the field mandatory, as described on page 668.

Validating numbers

For numbers, the most common technique's to check that the value falls in a certain range. In other words, you want to check that a number's less than or greater than another value. Your tools are the comparison signs < and >. Table 29-1 shows some common examples.

Table 29-1. Expressions for Numbers

Comparison	Sample Expression	Description
Less than	<100	The value must be less than 100.
Greater than	>0	The value must be greater than 0.
Not equal to	<>42	The value can be anything except 42.
Less than or equal to	<=100	The value must be less than or equal to 100.
Greater than or equal to	>=0	The value must be greater than or equal to 0.
Equal to	=42	The value must be 42. (Not much point in asking anyone to type it in, is there?)
Between	Between 0 and 100	The value must be 0, 100, or somewhere in between.

Validating dates

As with numbers, date validation usually involves checking to see if the value falls within a specified range. Here, your challenge is making sure that your date's in the right format for an expression. If you use the validation rule >*Jan 30, 2007*, Access is utterly confused, because it doesn't realize that the text (Jan 30, 2007) is supposed to represent a date. Similarly, if you try >*1/30/07*, then Access assumes the numbers on the right are part of a division calculation.

To solve this problem, use Access universal date syntax, which looks like this:

    #1/30/2007#

A universal date always has the date components in the order month/day/year, and it's always bracketed by the # symbol on either side. Using this syntax, you can craft a condition like >*#1/30/2007#*, which states that a given date must be larger than (fall after) the date January 30, 2007. January 31, 2007 fits the bill, but a date in 2006 is out.

The universal date syntax can also include a time component, like this:

    #1/30/2007 5:30PM#

Note: When comparing two dates, Access takes the time information into consideration. The date #1/30/2007# doesn't include any time information, so it's treated as though it occurs on the very first second of the day. As a result, Access considers the date value #1/30/2007 8:00 AM# larger, because it occurs eight hours later.

Once you've learned the universal date syntax, you can use any of the comparison operators you used with numbers. You can also use these handy *functions* to get information about the current date and time:

- **Date( )** gets the current date (without any time information, so it counts as the first second of the day).

- **Now( )** gets the current instant in time, including the date and time information.

Note: A function's a built-in code routine that performs some task, like fetching the current date from the computer clock.

Table 29-2 has some examples.

Table 29-2. *Expressions for Dates*

Comparison	Sample Expression	Description
Less than	<#1/30/2007#	The date occurs before January 30, 2007.
Greater than	>#1/30/2007 5:30 PM#	The date occurs after January 30, 2007, or on January 30, 2007, after 5:30 p.m.
Less than or equal to	<=#1/30/2007#	The date occurs before January 30, 2007, or on the first second of January 30, 2007.
Greater than or equal to	>=#1/30/2007#	The date occurs on or after January 30, 2007.
Greater than the current date	>Date( )	The date occurs today or after.
Less than the current date	<Date( )	The date occurs yesterday or before.
Greater than the current date (and time)	>Now( )	The date occurs today after the current time, or any day in the future.
Less than the current date (and time)	<Now( )	The date occurs today before the current time, or any day in the past.

Validating text

With text, validation lets you verify that a value starts with, ends with, or contains specific characters. You perform all these tasks with the *Like* operator, which compares text to a pattern.

This condition forces a field to start with the letter R:

```
Like "R*"
```

The asterisk (*) represents zero or more characters. Thus, the complete expression asks Access to check that the value starts with R (or r), followed by a series of zero or more characters.

You can use a similar expression to make sure a piece of text ends with specific characters:

```
Like "*ed"
```

This expression allows the values *talked*, *walked*, and *34z%($)#ed*, but not *talking*, *walkable*, or *34z%($)#*.

For a slightly less common trick, you can use more than one asterisk. The following expression requires that the letter *a* and *b* appear (in that order but not necessarily next to each other) somewhere in a text field:

```
Like "*a*b*"
```

Along with the asterisk, the Like operator also supports a few more characters. You can use ? to match a single character, which is handy if you know how long text should be or where a certain letter should appear. Here's the validation rule for an eight-character product code that ends in 0ZB:

```
Like "?????0ZB"
```

The # character plays a similar role, but it represents a number. Thus, the following validation rule defines a product code that ends in 0ZB and is preceded by five numbers:

```
Like "#####0ZB"
```

And finally, you can restrict any character to certain letters or symbols. The trick's to put the allowed characters inside square brackets.

Suppose your company uses an eight-character product code that always begins with A or E. Here's the validation rule you need:

```
Like "[AE]???????"
```

Note that the [AE] part represents one character, which can be either A or E. If you wanted to allow A, B, C, D, you'd write [ABCD] instead, or you'd use the handy shortcut [A-D], which means "allow any character from A to D, including A and D."

Here's one more validation expression, which allows a seven-letter word, and doesn't allow numbers or symbols. It works by repeating the [A-Z] code (which allows any letter) seven times:

```
Like [A-Z][A-Z][A-Z][A-Z][A-Z][A-Z][A-Z]
```

As you can see, text validation expressions aren't always pretty. Not only can they grow to ridiculous sizes, but there are lots of restrictions they can't apply. You can't, for instance, let the length of the text vary between a minimum and maximum that you set. And you can't distinguish between capitalized and lowercase letters.

Combining validation conditions

No matter what the data type, you can also *combine* your conditions in two different ways. Using the *And* keyword, you can create a validation rule that enforces two requirements. This trick's handy, because each field can have at most a single validation rule.

To use the And keyword, just write two validation rules and put the word And in between. It doesn't matter which validation rule's first. Here's a validation rule that forces a date to be before today but later than January 1, 2000:

```
<Date( ) And >#1/1/2000#
```

You can also use the Or keyword to accept a value if it meets either one of two conditions. Here's a validation rule that allows numbers greater than 1000 or less than −1000:

```
>1000 Or <-1000
```

Creating a Table Validation Rule

Field validation rules always apply to a single field. However, database designers often need a way to compare the values in different fields. Suppose you have an Orders table that logs purchases from your monogrammed sock store. In your Orders table, you use two date fields: DateOrdered and DateShipped. To keep everything kosher, you need a validation rule that makes sure DateOrdered falls *before* DateShipped. After all, how can you ship a product out before someone orders it?

Because this validation rule involves two fields, the only way to put it in place is to create a validation rule for the whole table. Table validation rules can use all the tricks you've learned about so far, *and* they can pull the values out of any field in the current record.

Here's how to create a table validation rule:

1. **In Design view, choose Table Tools | Design → Show/Hide → Property Sheet.**

   A box with extra settings appears on the right side of the window (Figure 29-16).

Note: You can create only a single validation rule for a table. This limit might sound like a problem, but you can get around it by using the And keyword (page 686) to yoke together as many conditions as you want. The validation rule may be a little difficult to read, but it still works without a hitch.

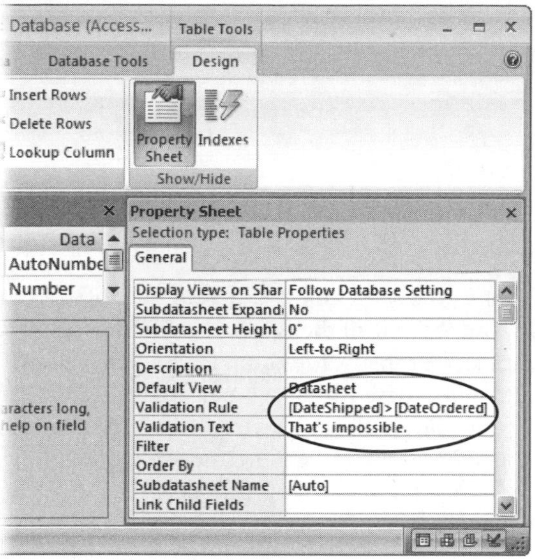

Figure 29-16:
The Property Sheet shows some information about the entire table, including the sorting (page 654) and filtering settings (page 657) you've applied to the datasheet, and the table validation rule. Here, the validation rule prevents orders from being shipped before they're ordered.

2. **In the Property Sheet tab, set the Validation Rule.**

   A table validation rule can use all the same keywords you learned about earlier. However, table validation rules usually compare two or more fields. The validation rule *[DateOrdered] < [DateShipped]* ensures that the value for the DateOrdered field is older than that used for the DateShipped.

   When referring to a field in a table validation rule, you need to include square brackets around your field names. That way, Access can tell the difference between fields and functions (like the Date( ) function you learned about on page 671).

3. **Set the Validation Text.**

   This message is the error message that's shown if the validation fails. It works the same as the validation text for a field rule.

   When you insert a new record, Access checks the field validation rules first. If your data passes the test (and has the right data types), then Access checks the table validation rule.

Tip: Once you set the table validation rule, you might want to close the Property Sheet to get more room in your design window. To do so, choose Table Tools | Design → Show/Hide → Property Sheet.

Lookups

In a database, minor variations can add up to big trouble. Suppose you're running International Cinnamon, a multinational cinnamon bun bakery with hundreds of orders a day. In your Orders table, you have entries like this:

```
Quantity  Product
10        Frosted Cinnamon Buns
24        Cinnamon Buns with Icing
16        Buns, Cinnamon (Frosted)
120       FCBs
...
```

(Other fields, like the ID column and the information about the client making the order, are left out of this example.)

All the orders shown here amount to the same thing: different quantities of tasty cinnamon and icing confections. But the text in the Product column's slightly different. This difference doesn't pose a problem for ordinary human beings (for example, you'll have no trouble filling these orders), but it does create a small disaster if you want to analyze your sales performance later. Since Access has no way to tell that a Frosted Cinnamon Bun and an FCB are the same thing, it treats them differently. If you try to total up the top-selling products or look at long-range cinnamon sales trends, then you're out of luck.

Note: This example emphasizes a point that you've seen before. Namely, databases are strict, no-nonsense programs that don't tolerate minor discrepancies. In order for your databases to be useful, you need to make sure you store top-notch information in them.

Lookups are one more tool to help standardize your data. Essentially, a lookup lets you fill a value in a field by choosing from a ready-made list of choices. Used properly, this tool solves the problem in the Orders table—you simply need a lookup that includes all the products you sell. That way, instead of typing the product name in by hand, you can choose Frosted Cinnamon Buns from the list. Not only do you save some time, but you also avoid variants like FCBs, thereby ensuring that the orders list is consistent.

Access has two basic types of lookup lists: lists with a set of fixed values that you specify, and lists that are drawn from a linked table. In the next section, you'll learn how to create the first type. Then, in Chapter 30, you'll graduate to the second.

Note: The following data types don't support lookups: Memo, Date/Time, Currency, AutoNumber, Yes/No, OLE Object, Hyperlink, and Attachment.

Creating a Simple Lookup with Fixed Values

Simple lookups make sense if you have a simple, short list that's unlikely to change. The state prefix in an address is a perfect example. In this case, there's a set of just 50 two-letter abbreviations (AL, AK, AZ, and so on).

To try out the process in the following list of steps, you can use the Bachelors table included with the online examples for this chapter (look for the DatingService. accdb database file). Or, you can jump straight to the completed lookup by checking out the DatingServiceLookup.accdb file:

1. **Open the table in Design view.**

   If you're using the DatingService.accdb example, then open the Bachelors table.

2. **Find the field where you want to add the lookup.**

   In the Bachelors table, it's the State field.

3. **Make sure your field has the correct data type.**

   Text and Number are the most common data types that you'll use in conjunction with the lookup feature.

4. **Choose Lookup Wizard from the data type list.**

   This action doesn't actually change your data type. Instead, it tells Access you want to run the Lookup wizard based on the current data type. When you select this option, the first step of the Lookup wizard appears (Figure 29-17).

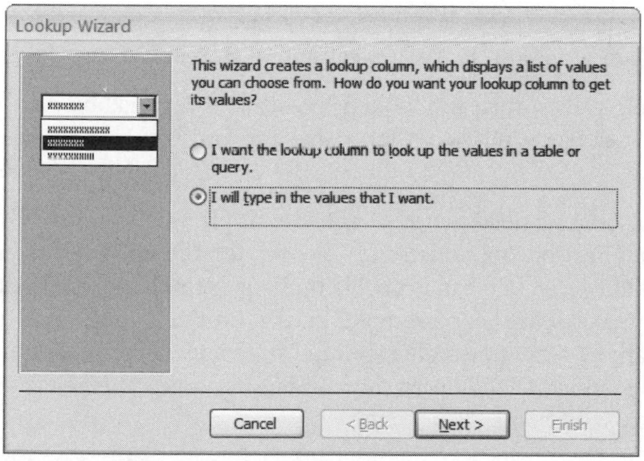

Figure 29-17:
First you choose the source of your lookup: fixed values or data from another table.

5. **Choose "I will type in the values that I need".**

   Page 709 describes your other choice: drawing the lookup list from another table.

6. **Click Next.**

The second step of the wizard gives you the chance to supply the list of values that should be used, one per row (Figure 29-18). In this case, it's a list of abbreviations for the 50 U.S. states.

You may notice that you can supply multiple columns of information. For now, stick to one column. You'll learn why you may use more on page 709.

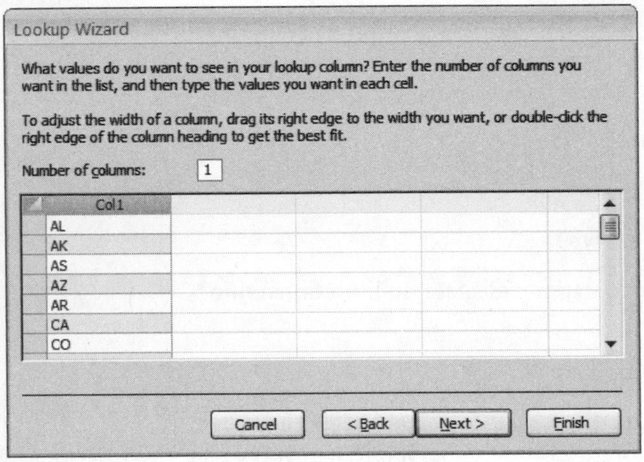

Figure 29-18:
This lookup includes the abbreviations for all the American states. This list's unlikely to change in the near future, so it's safe to hardcode this rather than store it in another table.

7. **Click Next.**

The final step of the Lookup wizard appears.

8. **Choose whether or not you want the lookup column to store multiple values.**

If you allow multiple values, then the lookup list displays a checkbox next to each item. You can select several values for a single record by checking more than one item.

In the State field, it doesn't make sense to allow multiple values—after all, a person can physically inhabit only one state (discounting the effects of quantum teleportation). However, you can probably think of examples where multiple selection does make sense. For example, in the Products table used by International Cinnamon, a multiple-value lookup would let you create an order for more than one product. (You'll learn more about multiple value selections and table relationships in Chapter 30.)

9. **Click Finish.**

Switch to Datasheet view (right-click the tab title, and then choose Datasheet View), and then save the table changes. Figure 29-19 shows the lookup in action.

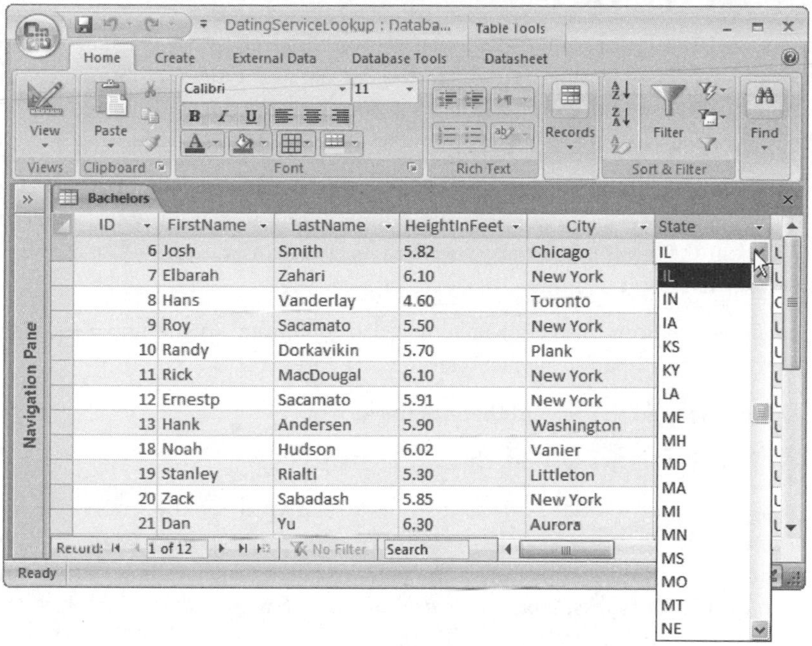

Figure 29-19:
When you move to a field that has a lookup, you'll see a down-pointing arrow on the right side. Click this arrow, and a drop-down list appears with all your possibilities. Choose one to insert it into the field.

UP TO SPEED

Creating a Lookup That Uses Another Table

In the previous example (on page 689), you created a lookup list that's stored as part of your field settings. This is a good approach, but it's not the best solution. A much more flexible approach is to store the lookup list in a separate table.

There are several reasons to use a separate table:

- **It allows you to add, edit, and remove items,** all by simply editing the lookup table. Even if you think you have a set of fixed, unchanging values, it's a good idea to consider a separate table. For example, the set of state abbreviations in the previous section seem unlikely to change—but what if the dating service goes international, and you need to add Canadian provinces to the list?

- **It allows you to reuse the same lookup list in several different fields** (either in the same table, or in different tables). That beats endless copy-and-paste operations.

- **It allows you to store extra information.** For example, maybe you want to keep track of the state abbreviation (for mailing purposes) but show the full state name (to make data entry easier). You'll learn how to perform this trick on page 709.

Table-based lookups are a little trickier, however, because they involve a table *relationship*: a link that binds two tables together and (optionally) enforces new restrictions. Chapter 30 is all about relationships, which are a key ingredient in any practical database.

Adding New Values to Your Lookup List

When you create a lookup that uses fixed values, the lookup list provides a list of *suggestions*. You can choose to ignore the lookup list and type in a completely different value (like a state prefix of ZI), even if it isn't on the list. This design lets you use the lookup list as a timesaving convenience without limiting your flexibility.

In many cases, you don't want this behavior. In the Bachelors table, you probably want to prevent people from entering something different in the State field. In this case, you want the lookup to be an error-checking and validation tool that actually stops entries that don't belong.

Fortunately, even though this option's mysteriously absent in the Lookup wizard, it's easy enough to add after the fact. Here's what you need to do:

1. **In Design view, go to the field that has the lookup.**

2. **In the Field Properties section, click the Lookup tab.**

    The Lookup tab provides options for fine-tuning your lookup, most of which you can configure more easily in the Lookup wizard. In the Row Source box, for example, you can edit the list of values you supplied. (Each value's on the same line, in quotation marks, separated from the next value with a semicolon.)

3. **Set the Limit to List property to Yes.**

    This action prevents you from entering values that aren't in the list.

4. **Optionally, set Value List Edits to Yes.**

    This action lets people modify the list of values at any time. This way, if something's missing from the lookup list, you can add it on the fly (Figure 29-20).

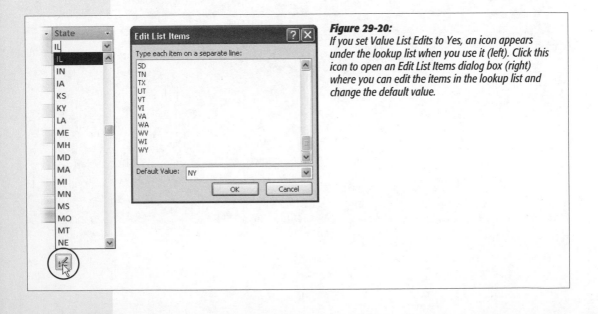

Figure 29-20:
If you set Value List Edits to Yes, an icon appears under the lookup list when you use it (left). Click this icon to open an Edit List Items dialog box (right) where you can edit the items in the lookup list and change the default value.

Linking Tables with Relationships

The tables you've seen so far lead lonely, independent lives. You don't find this isolation with real-world databases. Real databases have their tables linked together in a web of *relationships*.

Suppose you set out to build a database that can manage the sales of your custom beadwork shop. The first ingredient's simple enough—a Products table that lists your merchandise—but before long you'll need to pull together a lot more information. The wares in your Products table are sold in your Orders table. The goods in your Orders table are mailed out and recorded in a Shipments table. The people in your Customers table are billed in your Invoices table. All these tables—Products, Orders, Shipments, Customers, and Invoices—have bits of related information. As a result, if you want to find out the answer to a common question (like, "How much does Jane Malone owe?" or "How many beaded wigs did we sell last week?"), you'll need to consult several tables.

Based on what you've learned so far, you already know enough to nail down the design for a database like this one. But relationships introduce the possibility of inconsistent information. And once a discrepancy creeps in, you'll never trust your database the same way again.

In this chapter, you'll learn how to *explicitly* define the relationships between tables. This process lets you prevent common errors, like data in different tables that doesn't sync up. It also gives you a powerful tool for browsing through related information in several tables.

Relationship Basics

One of any database's key goals is to break information down into distinct, manageable pieces. In a well-designed database, you'll end up with many tables. Although each table records something different, you'll often need to travel from one table to another to get all the information you want.

To better understand relationships (of the non-romantic kind, anyway), consider an example. The following section demonstrates two ways to add information to the bobblehead database: one that risks redundant data, and one that avoids the problem by properly using a relationship.

Redundant Data vs. Related Data

Think back to the Dolls table you created in Chapter 26 to store a list of bobblehead dolls. One of the Dolls table's pieces of information is the Manufacturer field, which lists the name of the company that created each doll. Although this seems like a simple-enough detail, it turns out that to properly assess the value of a bobblehead, you need to know a fair bit more about the manufacturing process. You may want to know things like where the manufacturing company's located, how long it's been in business, and if it's had to fight off lawsuits from angry customers.

If you're feeling lazy, you could add all this information to the Dolls table, like so (the grayed-out columns are the new ones):

ID	Character	Manufacturer	Manufacturer-Location	Manufacturer-OpeningYear	Manufacturer-Lawsuits	PurchasePrice
342	Yoda	MagicPlastic	China	2003	No	$8.99

Your first reaction to this table is probably to worry about the clutter of all these fields. But don't panic—in the real world, tables must include all the important details, so they often grow quite wide. (That's rule #3 of data design, from page 642.) So don't let the clutter bother you. You can use techniques like column hiding (page 651) to filter out the fields that don't interest you.

Although column clutter isn't a problem, another issue lurks under the surface in this example—redundant data. A well-designed table should list only one type of thing. This version of the Dolls table breaks that rule by combining information about the bobblehead *and* the bobblehead manufacturer.

This situation seems innocent enough, but if you add a few more rows, things don't look as pretty:

ID	Character	Manufacturer	Manufacturer-Location	Manufacturer-OpeningYear	Manufacturer-Lawsuits	PurchasePrice
342	Yoda	MagicPlastic	China	2003	No	$8.99
343	Dick Cheney	Rebobblicans	Taiwan	2005	No	$28.75
344	Tiger Woods	MagicPlastic	China	2003	No	$2.99

Once you have two bobbleheads that were made by the same company (in this case, MagicPlastic), you've introduced duplicate data, the curse of all bad databases. (You'll recognize this as a violation of rule #4 of good database design, from page 642.) The potential problems are endless:

- If MagicPlastic moves its plants from China to South Korea, you'll need to update a whole batch of bobblehead records. If you were using two tables with related data (as you'll see next), you'd have just one record to contend with.

- It's all too easy to update the manufacturer information in one bobblehead record but miss it in another. If you make this mistake, you'll wind up with *inconsistent* data in your table, which is even worse than duplicate data. Essentially, your manufacturer information will become worthless because you won't know which record has the correct details, so you won't be able to trust anything.

- If you want to track more manufacturer-related information (like a contact number) in your database, you'll have to update your Dolls table and edit *every single record*. Your family may not see you for several few weeks.

- If you want to get information about manufacturers (but not dolls), you're out of luck. For example, you can't print out a list of all the bobblehead manufacturers in China (at least not easily).

It's easy to understand the problem. By trying to cram too many details into one spot, this table fuses together information that would best be kept in two separate tables. To fix this design, you need to create two tables that use *related data*. For example, you could create a Dolls table like this:

ID	Character	Manufacturer	PurchasePrice
342	Yoda	MagicPlastic	$8.99
343	Dick Cheney	Rebobblicans	$28.75
344	Tiger Woods	MagicPlastic	$2.99

And a separate Manufacturers table with the manufacturer-specific details:

ID	Manufacturer	Location	OpeningYear	Lawsuits
1	MagicPlastic	China	2003	No
2	Rebobblicans	Taiwan	2005	No

This design gives you the flexibility to work with both types of information (dolls and manufacturers) separately. It also removes the risk of duplication. The savings are small in this simple example, but in a table with hundreds or thousands of bobblehead dolls (and far fewer manufacturers), the difference is dramatic.

Now, if MagicPlastic moves to South Korea, you need to update the Location field for only one record, rather than many instances in an overloaded Dolls table.

You'll also have an easier time building queries (Chapter 31) that combine the information in neat and useful ways. (For example, you could find out how much you've spent on all your MagicPlastic dolls and compare that with the amounts you've spent for dolls made by other manufacturers.)

Note: Access includes a tool that attempts to spot duplicate data in a table and help you pull the fields apart into related tables. (To try it out, choose Database Tools → Analyze → Analyze Table.) Although it's a good idea in theory, this tool really isn't that useful. You'll do a much better job of spotting duplicate data and creating well designed tables from the start if you understand the duplicate-data problem yourself.

Matching Fields: The Relationship Link

This bobblehead database shows you an example of a *relationship*. The telltale sign of a relationship is two tables with matching fields. In this case, the tip-off's the Manufacturer field, which exists in both the Dolls table and the Manufacturers table.

Note: In this example, the fields that link the two tables have the same name in both tables: Manufacturer. However, you don't have to do it this way. You can give these fields different names, so long as they have the same data type.

Using these linked fields, you can start with a record in one table and look up related information in the other. Here's how it works:

- **Starting at the Dolls table,** pick a doll that interests you (let's say Yoda). You can find out more information about the manufacturer of the Yoda doll by looking up "MagicPlastic" in the Manufacturers table.

- **Starting at the Manufacturers table,** pick a manufacturer (say, Rebobblicans). You can now search for all the products made by that manufacturer by searching for "Rebobblicans" in the Dolls table.

In other words, a relationship gives you the flexibility to ask more questions about your data, and get better answers.

Linking with the ID Column

In the previous example, the Dolls and Manufacturers tables are linked through the Manufacturer field, which stores the name of the manufacturing company. This seems like a reasonable design—until you spend a couple of minutes thinking about what might go wrong. And databases experts are known for spending entire weeks contemplating inevitable disasters.

Here are two headaches that just may lie in store:

- **Two manufacturers have the same company name.** So how do you tell which one made a doll?

- **A manufacturer gets bought out by another company and changes its name.** All of a sudden, there's a long list of records to change in the Dolls table.

You might recognize these problems, because they're similar to the challenges you faced when you tackled primary keys (page 638). As you learned, it's difficult to find information that's guaranteed to be unique and unchanging. Rather than risk problems, you're better off just relying instead on an AutoNumber field, which stores an Access-generated ID number.

Interestingly enough, you use the same solution when linking tables. To refer to a record in another table, you shouldn't use just any piece of information—instead, you should use the unique ID number that points to the right record. Here's a redesigned Dolls table that gets it right by changing the Manufacturer field to ManufacturerID:

ID	Character	ManufacturerID	PurchasePrice
342	Yoda	1	$8.99
343	Dick Cheney	2	$28.75
344	Tiger Woods	1	$2.99

If you take a look back at the Manufacturers table (page 695), then you can quickly find out that the manufacturer with the ID value 1 is MagicPlastic.

This design's the universal standard for databases. However, it does have two obvious drawbacks:

- The person adding records to the Dolls table probably doesn't know the ID of each manufacturer.

- When you look at the Dolls table, you can't tell what manufacturer created each doll.

To solve both these problems, use a *lookup*. Lookups show the corresponding manufacturer information in the Dolls table, and they also let you choose from a list of manufacturers when you add a record or edit the ManufacturerID field. (You saw how to use lookups with value lists on page 692. You'll learn how to use lookups to bring together related tables, like Dolls and Manufacturers, on page 698.)

The Parent-Child Relationship

No, this isn't a detour into feel-good Dr. Phil psychology. Database nerds use the labels *parent* and *child* to identify the two tables in a relationship, and keep track of which one's which.

Here's the analogy. As you no doubt know, in the real world a parent can have any number of children. However, a child has exactly one set of parents. The same rule works for databases. In the bobblehead database, a single manufacturer record can be linked to any number of doll records. However, each doll record refers to a single manufacturer. So according to the database world's strange sociology, Manufacturers is a parent table and Dolls is a child table. They're linked by a *parent-child relationship*.

Tip: Don't think too hard about the parent-child analogy. It's not a perfect match with biological reality. For example, in the bobblehead database, you may create a manufacturer that doesn't link to any dolls (in other words, a parent with no children). You still call that record a parent record, because it's part of the parent table.

It's important to realize that you can't swap the parent and child tables around without changing your relationship. It's *incorrect* to suggest that Dolls is the parent table and Manufacturers is the child table. You can see that such a suggestion would break the parent-child analogy: a single doll can't have more than one manufacturer, and a manufacturer isn't limited to creating a single doll. In order to prevent problems and all-around fuzzy thinking, you need to know exactly which table's the parent and which one's the child.

Tip: If you have trouble identifying which table's the parent, there's a simple rule to steer you right. The child table always contains a piece of identifying information from the parent table. In the bobblehead database, the Dolls table contains the ManufacturerID field. On the other hand, the Manufacturer table doesn't have any doll information.

If you have database-savvy friends, you'll hear the term parent-child relationship quite a bit. The same relationship is also called a *one-to-many* relationship (where *one* is the parent and *many* represents the children, because a single parent record in one table can link to several child records in the other).

Note: Relationships are so common in modern-day databases that software like Access is often described as a *relational database management system* (RDBMS). A database without relationships is about as common as a beachfront resort in Ohio.

Using a Relationship

The relationship between Dolls and Manufacturers is *implicit*, which is a fancy way of saying that you know the relationship exists, but Access doesn't. Database pros aren't satisfied with this arrangement. Instead, they almost always define their relationships *explicitly*. When you create an explicit relationship, you clearly tell Access how two tables are related. Access then stores the information about that relationship in the database file.

You have good reasons to bring your relationships out into the open. Once Access knows about a relationship, it can enforce better error checking. It can also provide handy features for browsing related data and editing linked fields. You'll see all these techniques in the following sections. But first, you need to learn how to define a relationship.

Defining a Relationship

You can try out the following steps with the Bobblehead.accdb file, which is included with the online examples for this chapter. It contains the Dolls and Manufacturers tables, in their original form (with no relationships defined). The BobbleheadRelationships.accdb database file shows the final product: two tables with the right relationship.

Here's what you need to do to set up a relationship:

1. **Every relationship links two fields, each in a different table. Your first step is to identify the field you need to use in the parent table.**

   In a well-designed database, you use the primary-key field (page 638) in the parent table. For example, in the Manufacturers table, you use the ID column, which uniquely identifies each manufacturer.

2. **Open the child table in Design view. (The quickest way is to right-click it in the navigation pane, and then choose Design View.)**

   In this example, the child table is Dolls.

3. **Create the field you need in the child table, if it's not there already.**

   Each child record creates a link by storing a piece of information that points to a record in the parent table. You need to add a new field to store this information, as shown in Figure 30-1.

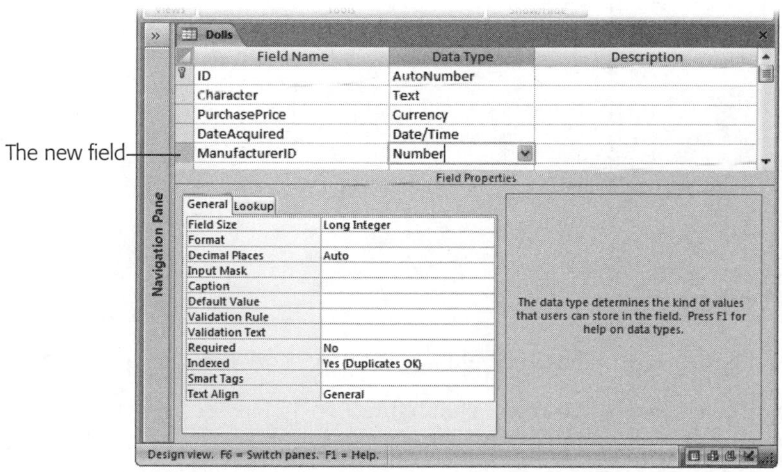

The new field

Figure 30-1:
In the Dolls table, you need a field that identifies the manufacturer for that doll. It makes sense to add a new field named ManufacturerID. Set the data type to Number, and the Field Size to Long Integer, so it matches the ID field in the Manufacturers table. After you add this field, you need to fill it with the right information. (Each doll record should have the ID number of the corresponding manufacturer.)

Note: The fields that you link in the parent and child tables must have consistent data types. However, there's one minor wrinkle. If the parent field uses the AutoNumber data type, then the child field should use the Number data type instead (with a Field Size of Long Integer). Behind the scenes, an AutoNumber and a Long Integer actually store the same numeric information. But the AutoNumber data type tells Access to fill in the field with a new, automatically-generated value whenever you create a record. You obviously don't want this behavior for the ManufacturerID field in the Dolls table.

4. **Close both tables.**

   Access prompts you to save your changes. Your tables are now relationship-ready.

5. **Choose Database Tools → Show/Hide → Relationships.**

   Access opens a new tab named Relationships. This tab's a dedicated window where you can define the relationships between all the tables in your database. In this example, you'll create a just a single relationship, but you can use the Relationships tab to define many more.

   Before Access lets you get to work in the Relationships tab, it pops up a Show Table dialog box asking what tables you want to work with (see Figure 30-2).

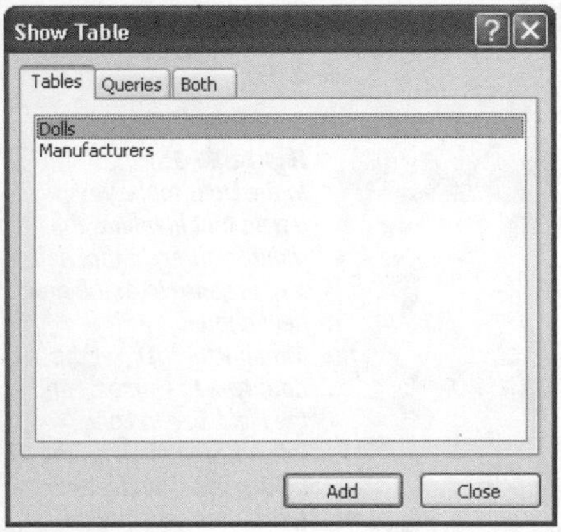

Figure 30-2:
You can add as many tables as you want to the Relationships tab. Be careful not to add the same table twice (it's unnecessary and confusing).

6. **Add both the parent table and child table to your work area.**

   It doesn't matter which one you choose first. To add a table, select it in the list, and then click Add (or just double-click it).

   Access represents each table in the Relationships tab by a small box that lists all the table fields. If relationships are already defined between these tables, they'll appear as connecting lines.

7. **Click Close.**

You can now arrange the tables in the Relationships tab (see Figure 30-3). The Relationships tab shows a *database diagram*—it's the canvas where you add relationships by "drawing" them on.

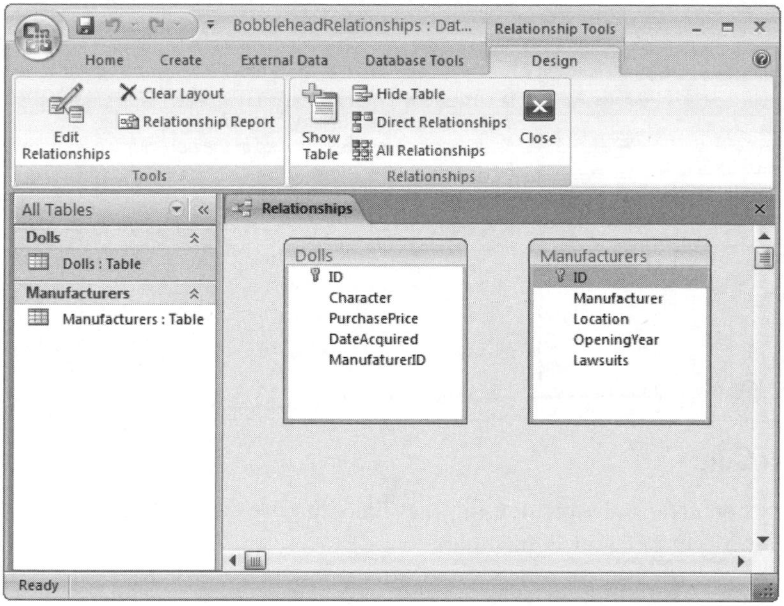

Figure 30-3:
You can drag the tables you've added to any place in the window. If you have a database that's thick with relationships, this ability lets you arrange them so that the relationships are clearly visible. To remove a table from the diagram, right-click it, and then choose Hide Table. To add another table, right-click the blank space, and then choose Show Table to pop up the Show Table dialog box.

Tip: Access gives you a shortcut if you need to rework the design of a table that's open in the Relationships tab. Just right-click the table box, and choose Design Table.

8. **To define your relationship, find the field you're using in the parent table. Drag this field to the field you want to link it to in the child table.**

   In this case, you're linking the ManufacturerID field in the Dolls table (the child) to the ID field in the Manufacturers table (the parent). So drag ManufacturerID (in the Dolls box) over to ID (in the Manufacturers box).

Tip: You can drag the other way, too (from the child to the parent). Either way, Access creates the same relationship.

   When you release the mouse button, the Edit Relationships dialog box appears (see Figure 30-4).

9. **If you want to prevent potential errors, then put a checkmark in the Enforce Referential Integrity option. (It's always a good idea.)**

   This setting turns on enhanced error checking, which prevents people from making a change that violates the rules of a relationship (like creating a doll that points to a nonexistent manufacturer). You'll learn more about referential integrity and the two settings for cascading changes on page 704. For now, it's best to switch on the Enforce Referential Integrity option and leave the others unchecked.

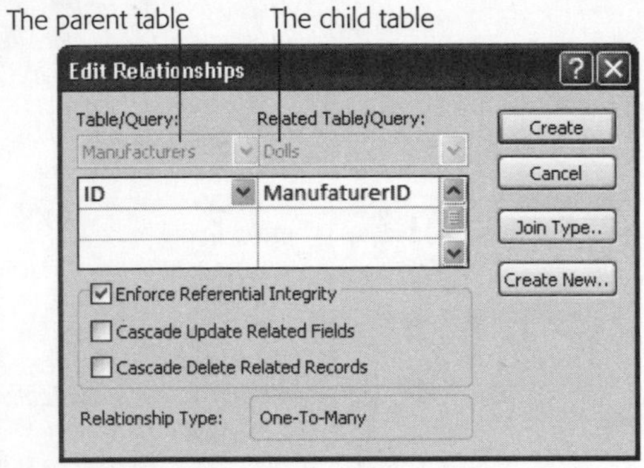

The parent table   The child table

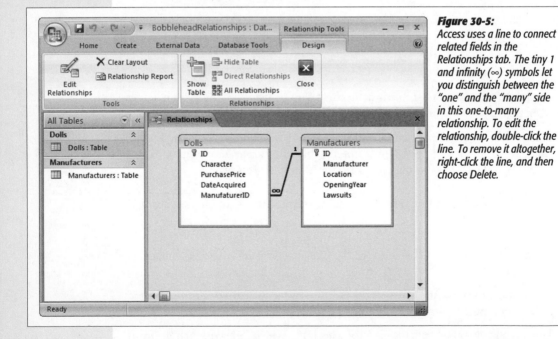

Figure 30-4:
Access is clever enough to correctly identify the parent table (shown in the Table/Query box) and the child table (shown in the Related Table/Query box) when you connect two fields. Access identifies the field in the parent table because it has a primary key (page 638) or a unique index (page 671). If something isn't quite right in the Edit Relationships dialog box, then you can swap the tables or change the fields you're using to create the relationship before continuing.

10. **Click Create.**

This action creates the relationship that links the two tables. It appears in the diagram as a line (Figure 30-5).

Figure 30-5:
Access uses a line to connect related fields in the Relationships tab. The tiny 1 and infinity (∞) symbols let you distinguish between the "one" and the "many" side in this one-to-many relationship. To edit the relationship, double-click the line. To remove it altogether, right-click the line, and then choose Delete.

Tip: If you chose Enforce Referential Integrity (in step 9), Access checks to make sure any existing data in the table follows the relationship rules. If it finds some that doesn't, then it alerts you about the problem and refuses to continue. At this point, the best strategy's to create the relationship without referential integrity, correct the invalid data, and then edit the relationship later to turn on referential integrity.

11. **Close the Relationships tab. (You can click the X in the tab's top-right corner, or choose Relationship Tools | Design → Relationships → Close.)**

    Access asks whether or not you want to save the Relationships tab's layout. Access is really asking you whether you want to save the relationship diagram you've created. No matter what you choose, the relationship remains in the database, and you can use it in the same way. The only difference is whether you'll be able to quickly review or edit the relationship in the Relationships tab.

    If you choose to keep the relationship diagram, the next time you switch to the Relationships tab (by choosing Database Tools → Show/Hide → Relationships), you see the same arrangement of tables. This feature's handy.

    If you choose not to keep the relationship diagram, it's up to you to recreate the diagram next time by adding the tables you want to see and arranging them in the window (although you won't need to redefine the relationships). This process takes a little more work.

Tip: Many database pros choose to save their database diagram, because they want to see all their relationships at once in the Relationships tab, just the way they left them. However, real-world databases often end up with a tangled web of relationships. In this situation, you may choose *not* to save a complete diagram so you can focus on just a few tables at once.

Editing Relationships

The next time you want to change or add relationships, you'll follow the same path to get to the Relationship window (choose Database Tools → Show/Hide → Relationships).

If you choose to save a relationship diagram (in step 11 in the previous section), the tables you added appear automatically, just as you left them. If you want to work with tables that aren't in any relationships yet, you can add them to the diagram by right-clicking anywhere in the blank area, and then choosing Show Table.

If you choose *not* to save your relationship diagram, you can use a few shortcuts to put your tables back on display:

- Drag your tables right from the navigation pane, and then drop them in the Relationships tab.

- Choose Relationship Tools | Design → Relationships → All Relationships to show all the tables that are involved in *any* relationships you've created previously.

- Add a table to the diagram, select it, and then choose Relationship Tools | Design → Relationships → Direct Relationships to show the tables that are linked to *that* table.

As you already know, you can use the Relationships tab to create new relationships. You can also edit the relationships you've already created. To do so, right-click the line that represents the relationship, and then choose Edit Relationship. (This takes some nimble finger-clicking. If you don't see the Edit Relationships option in the menu, you've just missed the line.) To remove a relationship, right-click the relationship line, and then choose Delete.

Note: Usually, you edit a relationship to change the options for referential integrity, which you'll learn about in the next section.

Referential Integrity

Now that you've gone to the work of defining your relationship, it's time to see what benefits you've earned. As in the real world, relationships impose certain restrictions. In the database world, these rules are called *referential integrity*. Taken together, they ensure that related data's always consistent.

Note: Referential integrity comes into action only if you switched on the Enforce Referential Integrity option (page 702) for your relationship. Without this detail, you're free to run rampant and enter inconsistent information.

In the bobblehead example, referential integrity requires that every manufacturer you refer to in the Dolls table must exist in the Manufacturer table. In other words, there can never be a bobblehead record that points to a nonexistent manufacturer. That sort of error could throw the hardiest database software out of whack.

To enforce this rule, Access disallows the following three actions:

- Adding a bobblehead that points to a nonexistent manufacturer.

- Deleting a manufacturer that's linked to one or more bobblehead records. (Once this record's removed, you're left with a bobblehead that points to a non-existent manufacturer.)

- Updating a manufacturer by changing its ID number, so that it no longer matches the manufacturer ID in the linked bobblehead records. (This updating isn't a problem if you use an AutoNumber field, because you can't change AutoNumber values once you've created the record.)

Note: If you need to add a new doll made by a new manufacturer, you must add the manufacturer record first, and *then* add the doll record. There's no problem if you add manufacturer records that don't have corresponding doll records—after all, it's perfectly reasonable to list a manufacturer even if you don't have any of the dolls they've made.

Along with these restrictions, Access also won't let you remove a table if it's in a relationship. You need to delete the relationship first (using the Relationships window) and *then* remove the table.

Blank values for unlinked records

It's important to realize that there's one operation you can perform that doesn't violate referential integrity: creating a bobblehead that doesn't point to *any* manufacturer. You do this by leaving the ManufacturerID field blank (which database nerds refer to as a *null value*). The only reason you'll leave the ManufacturerID field blank is if the manufacturer record doesn't exist in your database, or if the information doesn't apply. Perhaps the bobblehead wasn't created by any manufacturer but was created by an advanced space-faring alien race and left on this planet for you to discover.

If this blank-value back door makes you nervous, then you can stop it. Just set the Required field property (page 668) on the ManufacturerID field in the Dolls table. This setting ensures that every bobblehead in your Dolls table has legitimate manufacturer information. This technique's important when related information isn't optional. A sales company shouldn't be able to place an order or create an invoice without linking to the customer who made the order.

Cascading deletes

The rules of referential integrity stop you cold if you try to delete a parent record (like a manufacturer) that other child records (like dolls) link to. However, there's another option—and it's much more drastic. You can choose to blow away all related child records whenever you delete a parent. For example, this would allow you to remove a manufacturer and wipe out all the dolls that were produced by that manufacturer.

Warning: Cascading deletes are risky. It's all too easy to wipe out way more records than you intend, and if you do there's no going back. Even worse, the Undo feature can't help you reverse this change. So proceed with caution.

To turn on this option, you need to switch on the Cascade Delete Related Records setting when you create your relationship (Figure 30-4). You can also modify the relationship later on to add this setting.

Once you've switched this option on, you can try it out by deleting a manufacturer, as shown in Figure 30-6.

Cascading updates

Access also provides a setting for cascading updates. If you switch on this feature (by going to the Edit Relationships dialog box, and then choosing Cascade Update Related Fields), Access copies any change you make to the linked field in the parent record to all the children.

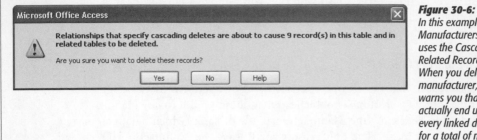

Figure 30-6:
In this example, the Dolls-Manufacturers relationship uses the Cascade Delete Related Records setting. When you delete a manufacturer, Access warns you that you'll actually end up deleting every linked doll record, for a total of nine records.

FREQUENTLY ASKED QUESTION

Switching Off Referential Integrity

Are there any situations where you don't want to enforce referential integrity?

In most cases, referential integrity's the ultimate database safety check, and no one wants to do without it—especially if the database includes mission-critical information for your business. Remember, referential integrity prevents only inconsistent data. It still lets you leave a field blank if there's no related record that you want to link to.

The only time you may decide to dodge the rules of referential integrity is when you're using *partial copies* of your database. This situation usually happens in a large business that's using the same database at different sites.

Consider an extremely successful pastry sales company with six locations. When a customer makes an order at your downtown location, you add a new record in the Orders table, and fill in the CustomerID (which links to a full record in the Customers table). But here's the problem. The full customer record may not be in your copy of the database—instead, it's in one of the databases at another site, or at company headquarters. Although the link in the Orders table's valid, Access assumes you've made a mistake because it can't find the matching customer record.

In this situation, you may choose to turn off referential integrity so you can insert the record. If you do, then be sure to enter the linked value (in this case, the CustomerID) very carefully to avoid errors later on.

With the bobblehead database, a cascading update lets you change the ID of one of your manufacturers. When you change the ID, Access automatically inserts the new value into the ManufacturerID field of every linked record in the Dolls table. Without cascading updates, you can't change a manufacturer's ID if there are linked doll records.

Cascading updates are safer than cascading deletes, but you rarely need them. That's because if you're following the rules of good database design, you're linking based on an AutoNumber ID column (page 636). Access doesn't let you edit an AutoNumber value, and you don't ever need to. (Remember, an AutoNumber simply identifies a record uniquely, and it doesn't correspond to anything in the real world.)

On the other hand, cascading updates come in handy if you're working with a table that hasn't been designed to use AutoNumber values for links. If the Dolls and Manufacturers table were linked based on the manufacturer name, then you need cascading updates—it makes sure that child records are synchronized whenever a manufacturer name's changed. Cascading updates are just as useful if you have linked records based on Social Security numbers, part numbers, serial numbers, or other codes that aren't generated automatically and are subject to change.

WORD TO THE WISE

Use Cascading Deletes with Care

Cascade Delete Related Records is the nuclear option of databases, so think carefully about whether it makes sense for you. This setting makes it all too easy to delete records when you should really be *changing* them.

If you're dropping a customer from your customer database, then it doesn't make sense to remove the customer's payment history, which you need to calculate your total profit. Instead, you're better off modifying the customer record to indicate that this record isn't being used anymore. You could add a Yes/No field named Active to the customer record, and set this field to No to flag customer accounts that aren't currently in use, without removing them.

You should also keep in mind that cascading deletes are just a convenience. They don't add any new features. If you don't switch on Cascade Delete Related Fields, you can still remove linked records, as long as you follow the correct order. If you want to remove a manufacturer, then start by removing any linked bobbleheads, or changing those bobbleheads to point to a different manufacturer (or have no manufacturer at all) by modifying the ManufacturerID values. Once you've taken this step, you can delete the manufacturer record without a problem.

Navigating a Relationship

Relationships aren't just useful for catching mistakes. Relationships also make it easier for you to browse through related data. *Access 2007: The Missing Manual* teaches you how to create search routines that pull together information from related tables. But even without this technique, Access provides some serious relationship mojo in the datasheet.

Here's how it works. If you're looking at a parent table in the datasheet, then you can find the related child records for any parent record by clicking the plus box that's just at the left of the row (Figure 30-7).

Figure 30-7:
Curious to find out what dolls you have from MagicPlastic? Just click the plus box (circled).

This drops a *subdatasheet* into view, which shows just the related records (Figure 30-8). You can use the subdatasheet to edit the doll records here in exactly the same way as you would in the full Dolls datasheet. You can even add new records.

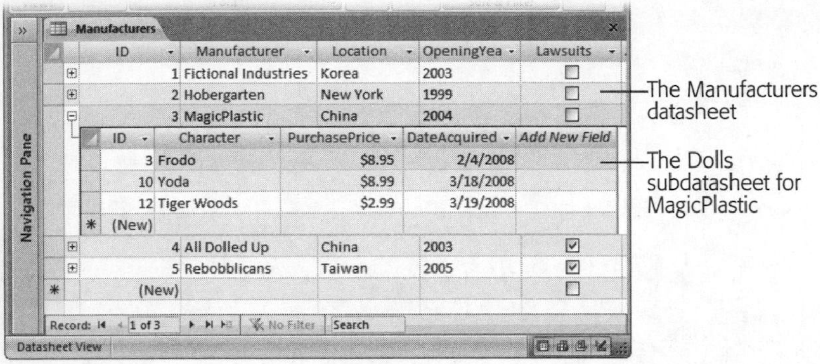

Figure 30-8:
The subdatasheet's really a filtered version of the ordinary Dolls datasheet. It shows only the records that are linked to the manufacturer you chose. The subdatasheet has all the same view settings (like font, colors, column order) as the datasheet for the related table.

Note: You can open as many subdatasheets as you want at the same time. The only limitation is that the records in a subdatasheet don't show up if you print the datasheet (page 662).

A parent table may be related to more than one child table. In this case, Access gives you a choice of what table you want to use when you click the plus box. Imagine you've created a Customers table that's linked to a child table of customer orders (Orders), and a child table of billing information (Invoices). When you click the plus box, Access doesn't know which table to choose, so it asks you (see Figure 30-9).

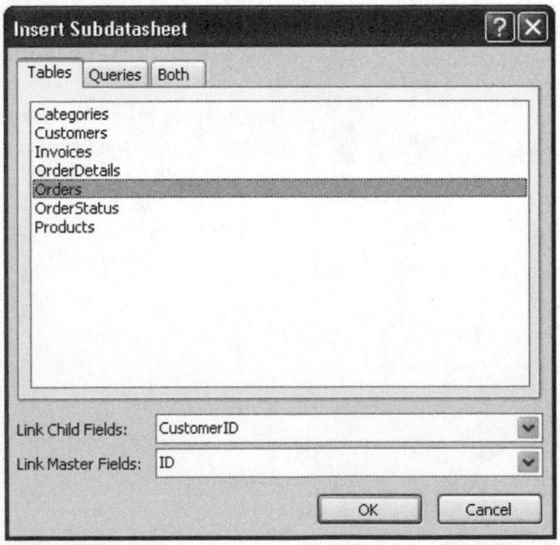

Figure 30-9:
When Access doesn't know which table to use as a subdatasheet, it lets you pick from a list of all your tables. In this case, only two choices make sense. Choose Orders to see the customer's orders, or Invoices to see the customer's invoices. When you select the appropriate table in the list, Access automatically fills in the linked fields in the boxes at the bottom of the window. You can then click OK to continue.

Note: You have to choose the subdatasheet you want to use only once. Access remembers your setting and always uses the same subdatasheet from that point on.

As you create more elaborate databases, you'll find that your tables are linked together in a chain of relationships. One parent table might be linked to a child table, which is itself the parent of another table, and so on. This complexity doesn't faze Access—it lets you drill down through all the relationships (see Figure 30-10).

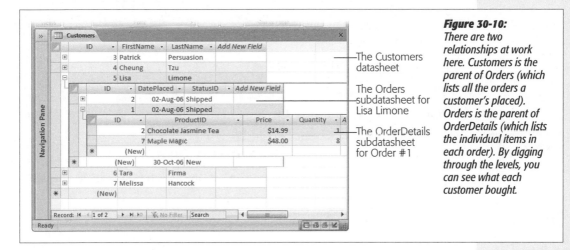

Figure 30-10:
There are two relationships at work here. Customers is the parent of Orders (which lists all the orders a customer's placed). Orders is the parent of OrderDetails (which lists the individual items in each order). By digging through the levels, you can see what each customer bought.

Lookups with Related Tables

So far, you've seen how relationships make it easier to review and edit your records. But what about when you add your records in the first place? Relationships are usually based on an unhelpful AutoNumber value. When you create a new doll, you probably won't know that 3408 stands for Bobelle House O' Dolls. Access stops you from entering a manufacturer ID that isn't linked to anyone at all, but it doesn't help you choose the ID value you want.

Fortunately, Access has a technique to help you out. In the previous chapter, you learned about *lookups* (page 688), a feature that provides you with a list of possible values for a column. When creating a lookup, you can supply a list of fixed values, or you can pull values from another table. You could create a lookup for the ManufacturerID field in the Dolls table that uses a list of ID values drawn from the Manufacturers table. This type of lookup helps a bit—it gives you a list of all the possible values you can use—but it still doesn't solve the central problem. Namely, the befuddled people using your database won't have a clue what ID belongs to what manufacturer. You still need a way to show the manufacturer name in the lookup list.

Happily, *lookup lists* provide just this feature. The trick is to create a lookup that has more than one column. One column holds the information (in this case, the manufacturer name) that you want to display to the person using the database.

The other column has the data you want to use when a value's picked (in this case, the manufacturer ID).

Note: Access is a bit quirky when it comes to lookups. It expects you to add the lookup, and *then* the relationship. (In fact, when you set up a lookup that uses a table, Access creates a relationship *automatically*.) So if you've been following through with the examples on your own, then you'll need to *delete* the relationship between the Dolls and Manufacturers tables (as described on page 703) before you go any further.

The following steps show how you can create a lookup list that links the Dolls and Manufacturers tables:

1. **Open the child table in Design view.**

   In this example, it's the Dolls table.

2. **Select the field that links to the parent table, and, in the Data Type column, choose the Lookup Wizard option.**

   In this example, the field you want is ManufacturerID.

3. **Choose "I want the lookup column to look up the values in a table or query" and then click Next.**

   The next step shows a list of all the tables in your database, except the current table.

4. **Choose the parent table, and then click Next.**

   In this case, you're after the Manufacturers table. Once you select it and move to the next step, you'll see a list of all the fields in the table.

FREQUENTLY ASKED QUESTION

Refreshing a Lookup

I just added a record, but it doesn't appear in my lookup. Why not?

Access fills in your lookup lists when you first open the table. For example, when you open the Dolls table, Access gets a list of manufacturers ready to go. However, sometimes you might have both the table that *uses* the lookup and the table that *provides* the lookup data open at the same time. In this situation, the changes you make in the table that provides the lookup won't appear in the table that uses the lookup.

To see how this works, open both the Dolls and Manufacturers tables at once. (They'll appear in separate tabs.) In the Manufacturers table, add a new manufacturer. Now, switch back to the Dolls table and try using the ManufacturerID lookup. You'll notice that the lookup list doesn't show the new record.

Fortunately, there's an easy to solution. You can tell Access to refresh the lookup list at any time by choosing Home → Records → Refresh All. Try that out in the Dolls table, and you'll see the updated list of manufacturers appear in the lookup.

---

5. **Add the field you use for the link and another more descriptive field to the list of Selected Fields (Figure 30-11). Click Next to continue.**

   In this case, you need to add the ID field and the Manufacturer field.

Tip: In some cases, you might want to use more than one field with descriptive information. For example, you might grab both a FirstName and LastName field from a FamilyRelatives table. But don't add too much information, or the lookup list will become really wide in order to fit it all in. This looks a bit bizarre.

---

6. **Choose a field to use for sorting the lookup list (Figure 30-12), and then click Next.**

   In this example, the Manufacturer field's the best choice to sort the list.

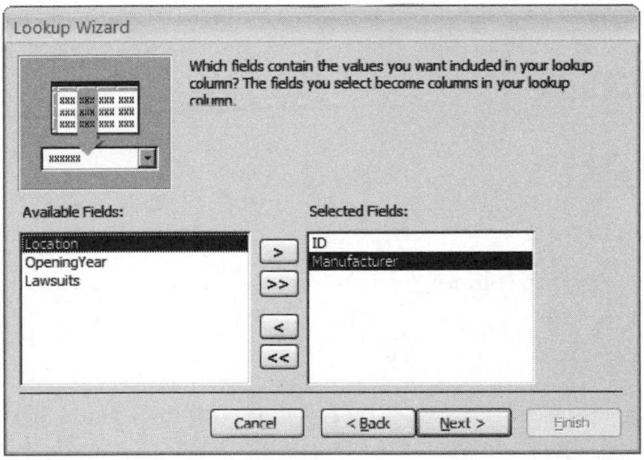

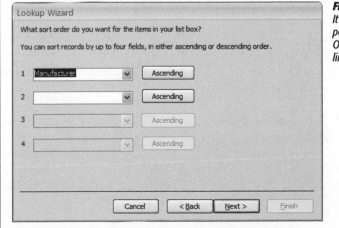

Figure 30-11:
The secret to a good lookup is getting two pieces of information: the primary key (in this case, the ID field) and a more descriptive value (in this case, the manufacturer's name). The ID field's the piece of information you need to store in the doll record, while the Manufacturer field's the value you'll show in the lookup list to make it easier to choose the right manufacturer.

Figure 30-12:
It's important to sort the lookup list, so that the person using it can find the right item quickly. One links students to classes, and the other links teachers to classes.

---

7. **The next step shows a preview of your lookup list (Figure 30-13). Make sure the "Hide key column" option's selected, and then click Next.**

Although the primary-key field has the value that links the two tables together, it doesn't mean much to the person using the database. The other, descriptive field's more important.

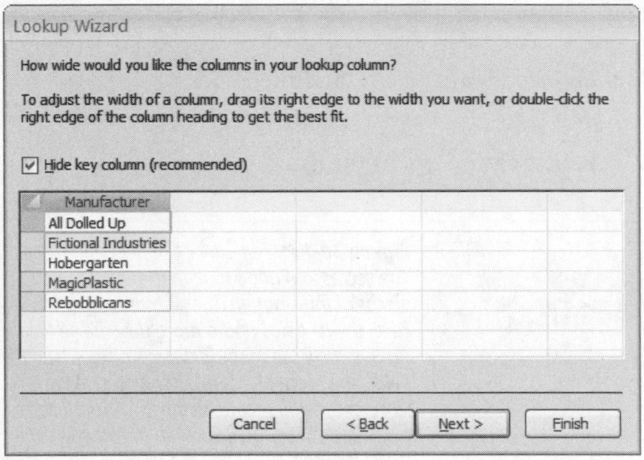

Figure 30-13:
Here, the lookup list shows the manufacturer name (the Manufacturer field) and hides the manufacturer ID (the ID field).

8. **Choose a name for the lookup column.**

Usually, it's clearest if you keep the name of the field that uses the lookup (in this case, ManufacturerID).

The final step also gives you an option named Allow Multiple Values. If you check this, then the lookup list shows a checkbox next to each item, so that you can pick several at once. (In this example, you can create a doll that has more than one manufacturer.)

9. **Click Finish.**

Now, Access creates the lookup for the field and prompts you to save the table. Once you do, Access creates a relationship between the two tables you've linked with your lookup column. Here, Access creates a parent-child relationship between Manufacturers and Dolls, just as you did yourself on page 699.

Note: The relationships that Access creates don't enforce referential integrity, because Access doesn't know if your records can live up to that strict standard. You can have a doll that points to a nonexistent manufacturer. If this possibility seems dangerously lax, you can edit your relationship using the Relationships tab (as described on page 703). Begin by adding both the Dolls and the Manufacturers table to the relationships diagram. Then, right-click the relationship line in between, and then choose Edit Relationship. Finally, switch on the Enforce Referential Integrity checkbox, and then click OK.

Now, if you switch to the design view of the Dolls table, you can use your lookup when you're editing or adding records (Figure 30-14).

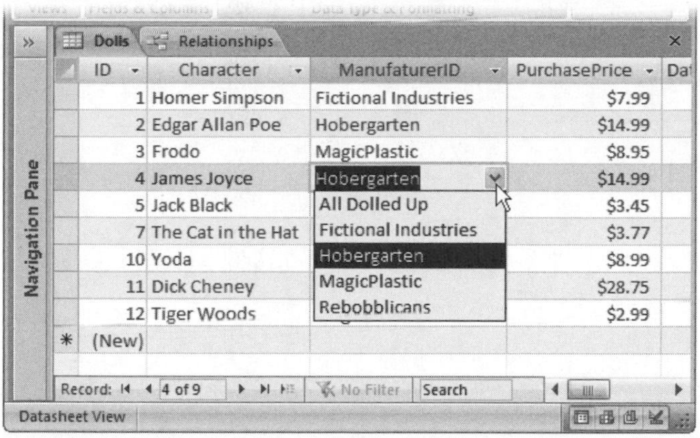

Figure 30-14:
Even though the Dolls table stores an ID value in the ManufacturerID field behind the scenes, that's not how it appears on your datasheet. Instead, you see the related manufacturer name. Even better, if you need to add a new record or change the manufacturer that's assigned to an existing one, then you can pick the manufacturer from the list by name.

FREQUENTLY ASKED QUESTION

Printing Your Relationship

Why is the Office button → Print command disabled when I'm looking at the Relationships tab?

Once you've created your relationships, you might want to have a printed copy at your fingertips. You can't print the contents of the Relationships tab directly, but you *can* convert it into a report, which is a specialized database object that lets you create a printout whenever you want. (You'll learn how to create reports in Chapter 33.)

To create a report for your relationships, first arrange all the tables to your liking in the Relationships tab. Then, choose Relationship Tools | Design → Tools → Relationship Report. A preview window appears, which looks more or less the

same as the current contents of the Relationships tab. You can then choose Office button → Print to send it to the printer.

When you close the relationship report, Access asks you if you want to save it permanently in your database. Usually, you won't bother, because you can easily regenerate the report whenever you need it. However, if you have a complex database and you want to print several different diagrams (each showing a different group of relationships), you may decide to save your relationship report for later use. You'll learn more about reports in Chapter 32.

CHAPTER 31

Queries: Reusable Searches

In a typical database, with thousands or millions of records, you may find it quite a chore finding the information you need. In Chapter 28, you learned how to go on the hunt using the tools of the datasheet, including filtering, searching, and sorting. At first glance, these tools seem like the perfect solution for digging up bits of hard-to-find information. However, there's a problem: The datasheet features are *temporary*.

To understand the problem, imagine you're creating an Access database for a mail-order food company named Boutique Fudge. Using datasheet filtering, sorting, and column hiding, you can pare down the Orders table so it shows only the most expensive orders placed in the past month. (This information's perfect for targeting big spenders or crafting a hot marketing campaign.) Next, you can apply a different set of settings to find out which customers order more than five pounds of fudge every Sunday. (You could use this information for more detailed market research, or just pass it along to the Department of Health.) But every time you apply new datasheet settings, you lose your previous settings. If you want to jump back from one view to another, then you need to painstakingly reapply all your settings. If you've spent some time crafting the perfect view of your data, this process adds up to a lot of unnecessary extra work.

The solution to this problem's to use *queries*: ready-made search routines that you store in your database. Even though the Boutique Fudge company has only one Orders table, it may have dozens (or more) queries, each with different sorting and filtering options. If you want to find the most expensive orders, then you don't need to apply the filtering, sorting, and column hiding settings by hand—instead, you can just fire up the MostExpensiveOrdersLastMonth query, which pulls out just the information you need. Similarly, if you want to find the fudge-a-holics, then you can run the LargeRepeatFudgeOrders query.

Queries are a staple of database design. In this chapter, you'll learn to design and fine-tune the simplest and most common type of query: the *select query*, which retrieves a subset of information from a table. Once you've retrieved this information, you can print or edit it using a datasheet, in the same way you interact with a table.

In addition to using queries to retrieve data, you can also use them to *change* data. Queries that take this more drastic step—whether it's deleting, updating, or adding records—are known collectively as *action queries*. You'll get a quick introduction to action queries at the end of this chapter.

Query Basics

As the name suggests, queries are a way to ask *questions* about your data, like what products net the most cash, where do most customers live, and who ordered the embroidered toothbrush? Access saves each query in your database, like any other database object (page 586). Once you've saved a query, you can run it any time you want to take a look at the live data that meets your criteria.

Queries' key feature is their amazing ability to reuse your hard work. Queries also introduce some new features that you don't have with the datasheet alone:

• **Queries can combine related tables.** This feature's insanely useful because it lets you craft searches that take related data into account. In the Boutique Fudge example, you can use this feature to create queries that find orders with specific product items, or orders made by customers living in specific cities. Both these searches need relationships, because they branch out past the Orders table to take in information from other tables (like Products and Customers).

• **Queries can perform calculations.** The Products table in the Boutique Fudge database lists price information, along with the quantity in stock. A query can multiply these details, and then add a column that lists the calculated value of the product you have on hand.

• **Queries can automatically apply changes.** If you want to find all the orders made by a specific person and reduce the cost of each one by 10 percent, then a query can apply the entire batch of changes in one step. This action requires a different type of query, an *action query*, which you'll learn about later in this chapter.

Creating Queries

Access gives you three ways to create a query:

• **The Query wizard** gives you a quick-and-dirty way to build a simple query. However, this option also gives you the least control.

Note: If you decide to use the Query wizard to create your query, then you'll probably want to refine your query later on using Design view.

- **Design view** offers the most common approach to query building. It provides a handy graphical tool that you can use to perfect any query.

- **SQL view** gives you a behind-the-scenes look at the actual query *command*, which is a piece of text (ranging from one line to more than a dozen) that tells Access exactly what to do. The SQL view's where many Access experts hang out; for more information on the world of SQL, see *Access 2007: The Missing Manual*.

Creating a Query in Design View

The best starting point for query creation's the Design view. The following steps show you how it works. (To try this out yourself, you can use the BoutiqueFudge. accdb database that's included with the downloadable samples for this chapter.) The final result—a query that gets the results that fall in the first quarter of 2007—is shown in Figure 31-6.

Here's what you need to do:

1. **Choose Create → Other → Query Design.**

   A new design window appears, where you can craft your query. But before you get started, Access pops open the Show Table dialog box, where you can choose the tables that you want to work with (Figure 31-1).

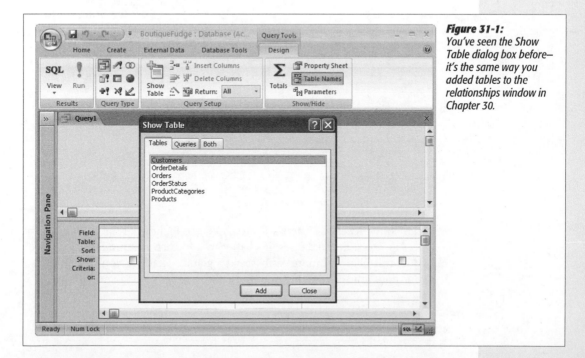

Figure 31-1:
You've seen the Show Table dialog box before—it's the same way you added tables to the relationships window in Chapter 30.

2. **Select the table that has the data you want, and then click Add (or just double-click the table).**

   In the Boutique Fudge example, you need the Orders table.

   Access adds a box that represents the table to the design window. You can repeat this step to add several related tables, but for now stick with just one.

3. **Click Close.**

   The Show Table dialog disappears, giving you access to the Design view for the query.

4. **Select the fields you want to include in your query.**

   To select a field, double-click it in the table box (Figure 31-2). Take care not to add the same field more than once, or that column shows up twice in the results. If you're using the Boutique Fudge example, then make sure you choose at least the ID, DatePlaced, and CustomerID fields.

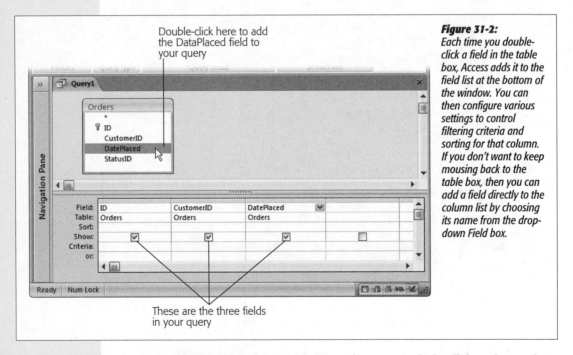

Double-click here to add the DataPlaced field to your query

These are the three fields in your query

Figure 31-2:
Each time you double-click a field in the table box, Access adds it to the field list at the bottom of the window. You can then configure various settings to control filtering criteria and sorting for that column. If you don't want to keep mousing back to the table box, then you can add a field directly to the column list by choosing its name from the drop-down Field box.

You can double-click the asterisk (*) to choose to include *all* the columns from a table. However, in most cases, it's better to add each column separately. Not only does this help you more easily see at a glance what's in your query, it also lets you choose the column order, and use the field for sorting and filtering.

Note: A good query includes only the fields you absolutely need. Keeping your query lean ensures it's easier to focus on the important information (and easier to fit your printout on a page).

5. **Arrange the fields from left to right in the order you want them to appear in the query results.**

   When you run the query, the columns appear in the same order as they're listed in the column list in Design view. (Ordinarily, this system means the columns appear from left to right in the order you added them.) If you want to change the order, then all you need to do is drag (as shown in Figure 31-3).

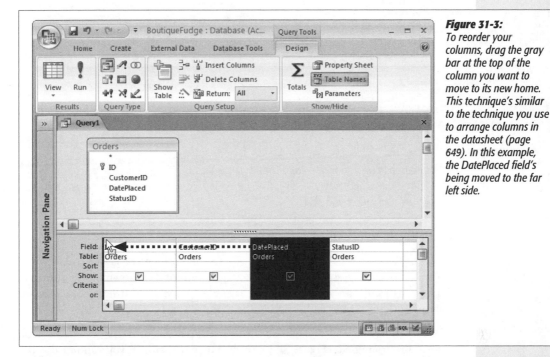

Figure 31-3:
To reorder your columns, drag the gray bar at the top of the column you want to move to its new home. This technique's similar to the technique you use to arrange columns in the datasheet (page 649). In this example, the DatePlaced field's being moved to the far left side.

6. **If you want to hide one or more columns, then clear the Show checkbox for those columns.**

   Ordinarily, Access shows every column you've added to the column list. However, in some situations you want to work with a column in your query, but not actually display its data. Usually, it's because you want to use the column values for sorting or filtering.

7. **Choose a sort order.**

   If you don't supply a sort order, then you'll get the records right from the database in whatever order they happen to be. This convention usually (but not always) means the oldest records appear first, at the top of the table. To sort your table explicitly, choose the field you want to use to sort the results, and then, in the corresponding Sort box, choose a sorting option. In the current example, the table's sorted by date in descending order, so that the most recent orders are first in the list (Figure 31-4).

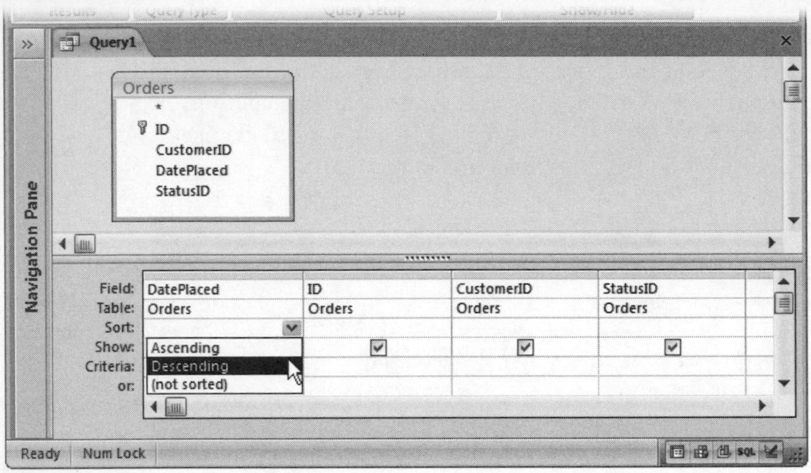

Figure 31-4:
Choose Ascending if you want to sort a text field from A-Z, a numeric field from lowest to highest, or a date field from oldest to most recent. Choose Descending to use the reverse order. Page 654 has more information about sorting and how it applies to different data types.

Field:	DatePlaced	ID	CustomerID	StatusID
Table:	Orders	Orders	Orders	Orders
Sort:				
Show:	Ascending	✓	✓	✓
Criteria:	Descending			
or:	(not sorted)			

Tip: You can sort based on several fields. The only trick's that your columns need to be ordered so that the first sorting criteria appears first (to the left) in the column list. Use the column rearranging trick from step 5 to make sure you've got it right.

8. **Set your filtering criteria.**

   Filtering (page 657) is a tool that lets you focus on the records that interest you and ignore all the rest. Filtering cuts a large swath of data down to the information you need, and it's the heart of many a query. (You'll learn much more about building a filter expression in the next section.)

   Once you have the filter expression you need, place it into the Criteria box for the appropriate field (Figure 31-5). In the current example, you can put this filter expression in the Criteria box for the DatePlaced field to get the orders placed in the first three months of the year:

   ```
   >=#1/1/2007# And <=#3/31/2007#
   ```

   You aren't limited to a single filter—in fact, you can add a separate filter expression to each field. If you want to use a field for filtering but not display it in the results, then clear the Show checkbox for that field.

9. **Choose Query Tools | Design → Results → Run.**

   Now that you've finished the query, you're ready to put it into action. When you run the query, you'll see the results presented in a datasheet (complete with lookups on linked fields), just like when you edit a table. (Figure 31-6 shows the result of the query on the Orders table.)

   You can switch back to Design view by right-clicking the tab title and then choosing Design View.

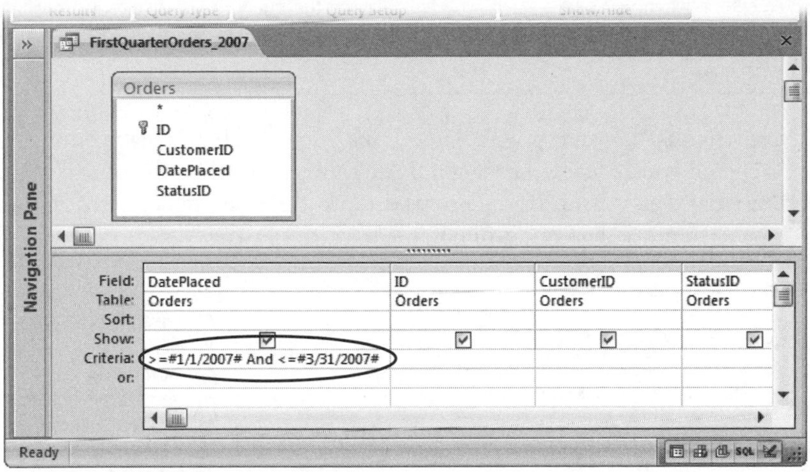

Figure 31-5:
Here's a filter that finds orders made in a date range (from January 1 to March 31, in the year 2007). Notice that when you use an actual hard-coded date as part of a condition (like January 1, 2007 in this example), you need to bracket the date with the # symbols. For a refresher about date syntax, refer to page 683.

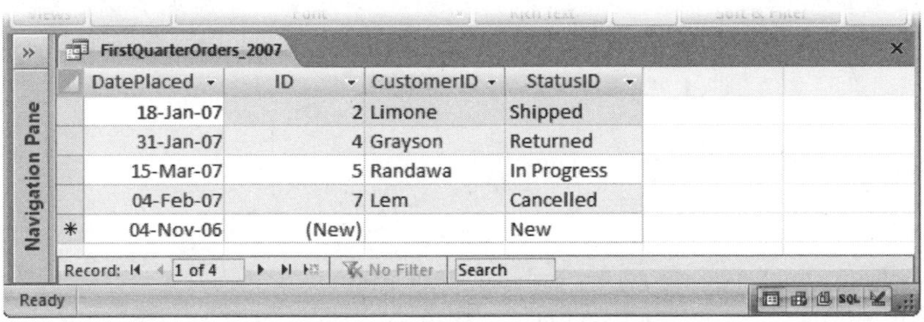

Figure 31-6:
Here are the results of a query that shows orders placed within a specific date range. You can use the datasheet window to review or print your results, or you can edit information just as you would in a table datasheet.

Note: The datasheet for your query acquires any formatting you applied to the datasheet of the underlying table. If you applied a hot-pink background and cursive font to the datasheet for the Orders table, then the same settings apply to any queries that use the Orders table. However, you can change the datasheet formatting for your query just as you would with a table.

10. **Save the query.**

You can save your query at any time using the keyboard shortcut Ctrl+S. If you don't, then Access automatically saves your query when you close the query tab (or your entire database). Of course, you don't *need* to save your query. Sometimes you might create a query for a specific, one-time-only task. If you don't plan to reuse the query, then there's no point in cluttering up your database with extra objects.

The first time you save your query, Access asks for a name. Use the same naming rules that you follow for tables—refrain from using spaces or special characters, and capitalize the first letter in each word. A good query describes the view of data that it presents. One good choice for the example shown in Figure 31-6 is FirstQuarterOrders_2007.

Note: Remember, when you save a query, you aren't saving the query *results*—you're just saving the query *design*, with all its settings. That way, you can run the query any time to get the live results that match your criteria.

Once you've created a query, you'll see it in your database's navigation pane (Figure 31-7). If you're using the standard All Tables view, then the query appears under the table that it uses. If a query uses more than one table, then the same query appears in more than one group in the navigation pane.

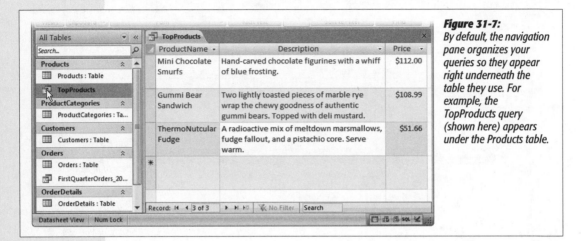

Figure 31-7:
By default, the navigation pane organizes your queries so they appear right underneath the table they use. For example, the TopProducts query (shown here) appears under the Products table.

You can launch the query at any time by double-clicking it. Suppose you've created a query named TopProducts that grabs all the expensive products in the Products table (using the filter criteria *>50* on the Price field). Every time you need to review, print, or edit information about expensive products, you run the TopProducts query. To fine-tune the query settings, right-click it in the navigation pane, and then choose Design View.

Access lets you open your table and any queries that use it at the same time. (They all appear in separate tabs.) However, you can't modify the design of your table until you close all the queries that use it.

If you add new records to a table while a query's open, then the new records don't automatically appear in the query. Instead, you'll need to run your query again. The quickest way is to choose Home → Records → Refresh → Refresh All. You can also close your query and open it again, because Access runs your query every time you open it in Datasheet view.

Note: Remember, a query's a *view* of some of the data in your table. When you edit your query results, Access changes the data in the underlying table. On the other hand, it's perfectly safe to rename, modify, and delete queries—after all, they're there to make your life simpler.

Building filter expressions

The secret to a good query's getting the information you want, and nothing more. To tell Access what records it should get (and which ones it should ignore), you need a *filter expression*.

The filter expression defines the records you're interested in. If you want to find all the orders that were placed by a customer with the ID 1032, you could use this filter expression:

```
=1032
```

To put this filter expression into action, you need to put it in the Criteria box under the CustomerID field.

Technically, you could just write *1032* instead of *=1032*, but it's better to stick to the second form, because that's the pattern you'll use for more advanced filter expressions. It starts with the *operator* (in this case, the equals sign) that defines how Access should compare the information, followed by the *value* (in this case, 1032) you want to use to make the comparison.

WORD TO THE WISE

Don't Get Confused by Lookups

As you know, lookups change the way values appear on the datasheet. If you add a lookup on the CustomerID field in the Orders table, then you don't see a cryptic number like 1032. Instead, you see some descriptive information, like the name *Hancock, John*.

However, when you write your filter expression, you need to remember what information's actually stored in the field. So the CustomerID filter expression *=1032* works fine, but *=Hancock, John* doesn't, because the name information's actually stored separately. (It's in the Customers table, not the Orders table.)

Sometimes, you really *do* want to create a filter expression that uses linked information. You may want to find records in the Orders table using a customer name instead of a customer ID, because you don't have the ID value handy. In this situation, you have two choices:

- You can look up the ID value you need in the Customers table before you start. Then, you can use that value when you build your query for the Orders table.

- You can use a *join query* to get the name information from the Customers table, and display it alongside the rest of your order details. Join queries are a fairly sophisticated maneuver; *Access 2007: The Missing Manual* teaches you how to use them.

If you're matching text, then you need to include quotation marks around your value. Otherwise, Access wonders where the text starts and stops:

```
="Harrington Red"
```

Instead of using an exact match, you can use a range. Add this filter expression to the OrderTotal field to find all the orders worth between $10 and $50:

```
<50 And >10
```

This condition's actually two conditions (less than 50 and greater than 10), which are yoked together by the powerful *And* keyword (page 686). Alternatively, you can use the *Or* keyword if you want to see results that meet any one of the conditions you've included (page 686).

Date expressions are particularly useful. Just remember to bracket any hardcoded dates with the # character (page 683). If you add this filter condition to the DatePlaced field, then it finds all the orders that were placed in 2007:

```
<#1/1/2008# And >#12/31/2006#
```

This expression works by requiring that dates are earlier than January 1, 2008, but later than December 31, 2006.

Tip: With a little more work, you could craft a filter expression that gets the orders from the first three months of the *current* year, no matter what year it is. This trick requires the use of the functions Access provides for dates. See page 670 for more details.

UP TO SPEED

Filter Syntax

If filters seem uncannily familiar, there's a reason. Filters have exactly the same syntax as the validation rules you used to protect a table from bad data (page 680). The only difference is the way Access interprets the condition. A validation rule like *<50 And >10* tells Access a value shouldn't be allowed unless it falls in the desired range (10 to 50).

But if you pop the same rule into a filter condition, it tells Access you aren't interested in seeing the record unless it fits the range. Thanks to this similarity, you can use all the validation rules you saw on pages 682 to 688 as filter conditions.

Getting the top records

When you run an ordinary query, you see *all* the results that match your filter conditions. If that's more than you bargained for, you can use filter expressions to cut down the list.

However, in some cases, filters are a bit more work than they should be. Imagine a situation where you want to see the top 10 most expensive products. Using a filter condition, you can easily get the products that have prices above a certain threshold. Using sorting, you can arrange the results so the most expensive items turn up at the top. However, you can't as easily tell Access to get just 10 records and then stop.

In this situation, the query Design view has a shortcut that can help you out. Here's how it works:

1. **Open your query in Design view (or create a new query and add the fields you want to use).**

   This example uses the Products table, and includes the ProductName and Price fields.

2. **Sort your table so that the records you're most interested in are at the top.**

If you want to find the most expensive products, then add a descending sort (page 654) on the Price field.

3. **In the Query Tools | Design → Query Setup → Return box, choose a different option (Figure 31-8).**

The standard option's All, which gets all the matching records. However, you can choose 5, 25, or 100 to get the top 5, 25, or 100 matching records, respectively. Or, you can use a percentage value like 25 percent to get the top quarter of matching records.

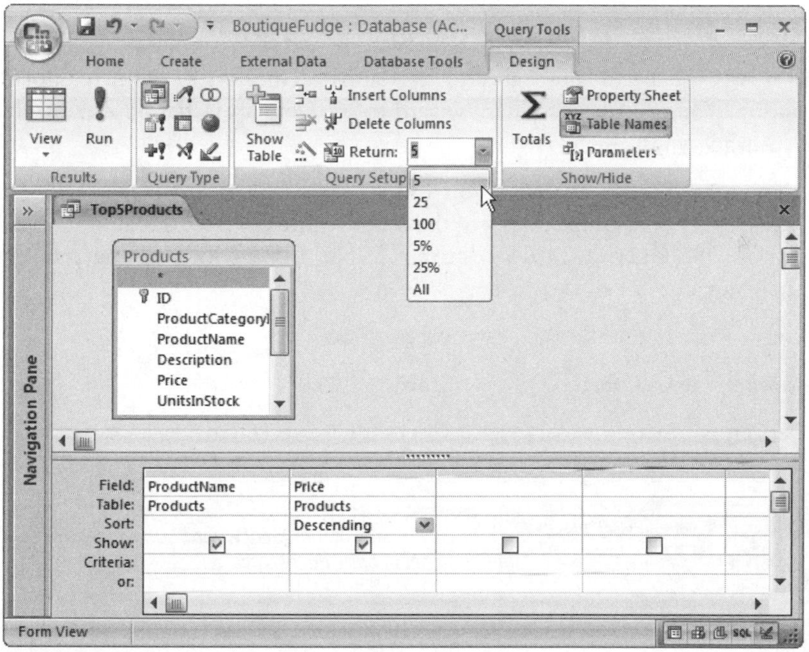

Figure 31-8:
If you don't see the number you want in the list, just type it into the Return box on your own. There's no reason you can't grab the top 27 most expensive products.

Note: For the Query Tools | Design → Query Setup → Return box to work, you must choose the right sort order. To understand why, you need to know a little more about how this feature works. If you tell Access to get just five records, it actually performs the normal query, gets all the records, and arranges them according to your sort order. It then throws everything away except for the first five records in the list. If you've sorted your list so that the most expensive products are first (as in this example), you're left with the top five budget-busting products in your results.

4. **Run your query to see the results (Figure 31-9).**

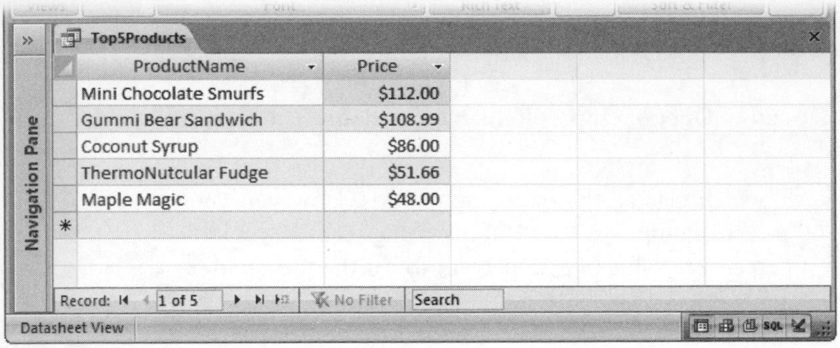

Figure 31-9:
*Here are the top five
most expensive products.*

Creating a Simple Query with the Query Wizard

Design view's usually the best place to start constructing queries, but it's not the only option. You can use the Query wizard to give you an initial boost, and then refine your query in Design view.

The Query wizard works by asking you a series of questions, and then creating the query that fits the bill. Unlike many of the other wizards in Access and other Office applications, the Query wizard's relatively feeble. It's a good starting point for query newbies, but not an end-to-end performer.

Here's how you can put the Query wizard to work:

1. **Choose Create → Other → Query Wizard.**

   Access gives you a choice of several different wizards (Figure 31-10).

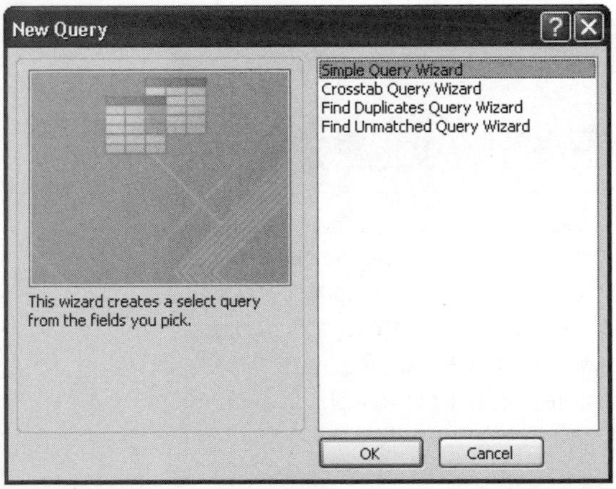

Figure 31-10:
*In the first step of the Query wizard, you choose from a
small set of basic query types.*

2. **Choose a query type. The Simple Query wizard's the best starting point for now.**

   The Query wizard includes a few common kinds of queries. With the exception of the crosstab query, there's nothing really unique about any of these choices. You'll learn to create them all using Design view:

- **Simple Query Wizard** gets you started with an ordinary query, which displays a subset of data from a table. This query's the kind you created in the previous section.

- **Crosstab Query Wizard** generates a crosstab query, which lets you summarize large amounts of data using different calculations. You can find more on this advanced topic in *Access 2007: The Missing Manual*.

- **Find Duplicates Query Wizard** is similar to the Simple Query wizard, except it adds a filter expression that shows only records that share duplicated values. If you forgot to set a primary key or create a unique index for your table (page 671), then this can help you clean up the mess.

- **Find Unmatched Query Wizard** is similar to the Simple Query wizard, except it adds a filter expression that finds unlinked records in related tables. You could use this to find an order that isn't associated with any particular customer.

3. **Click OK.**

   The first step of the Query wizard appears.

4. **In the Tables/Queries box, choose the table that has the data you want. Then, add the fields you want to see in the query results, as shown in Figure 31-11.**

   For the best control, add the fields one at a time. Add them in the order you want them to appear in the query results, from left to right.

   You can add fields from more than one table. To do so, start by choosing one of the tables, add the fields you want, and then choose the second table and repeat the process. This process really makes sense only if the tables are related.

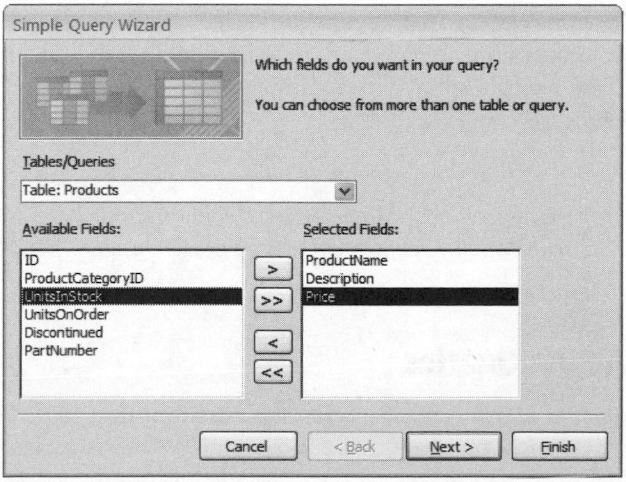

Figure 31-11:
To add a field, select it in the Available Fields list, and then click the > arrow button (or just double-click it). You can add all fields at once by clicking the >> arrow button, and you can remove fields by selecting them in the Selected Fields list and then clicking <. In this example, three fields are included in the query.

5. **Click Next.**

   If your query includes a numeric field, the Query wizard gives you the choice of creating a summary query that arranges rows into groups, and calculates information like totals and averages. If you get this choice, pick Detail and then click Next.

   The final step of the Query wizard appears (Figure 31-12).

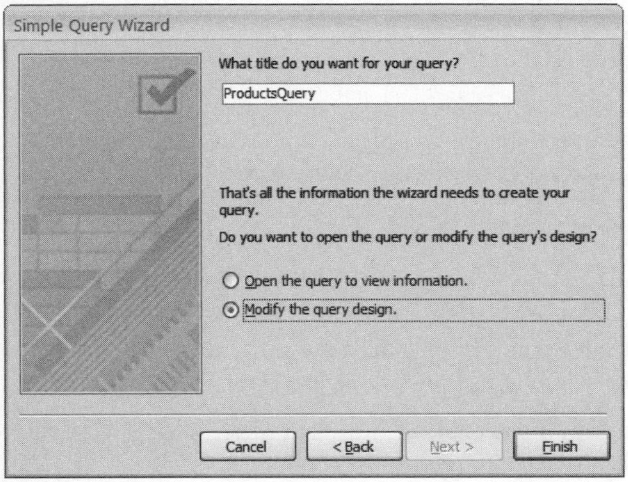

Figure 31-12:
In the last step, you choose the name for your query, and decide whether you want to see the results right away or refine it further in Design view.

6. **Supply a query name in the "What title do you want for your query?" box.**

7. **If you want to fine-tune your query, then choose "Modify the query design". If you're happy with what you've got, then choose "Open the query to view information" to run the query.**

   One reason you may want to open your query in Design view is to add filter conditions (page 657) to pick out specific rows. Unfortunately, you can't set filter conditions in the Query wizard.

8. **Click Finish.**

   Your query opens in Design view or Datasheet view, depending on the choice you made in step 7. You can run it by choosing Query Tools | Design → Results → Run.

Understanding Action Queries

Action queries aren't quite as useful as select queries, because they tend to be less flexible. You create an ideal query once, and reuse it over and over. Select queries fit the bill, because you'll often want to review the same sort of information (last week's orders, top-selling products, class sizes, and so on). But action queries are trickier, because they make *permanent* changes.

In most cases, a change is a one-time-only affair, so you don't have any reason to hang onto an action query that just applies the same change all over again. And even if you do need to modify some details regularly (like product prices or warehouse stocking levels), the actual values you set aren't the same each time. As a result, you can't create an action query that can apply your change in an automated fashion.

But before you skip this chapter for greener pastures, it's important to consider some cases where action queries are surprisingly handy. Action queries shine if you have:

• **Batch tasks that you want to repeatedly apply.** Some tasks *can* be repeated exactly. You may need to copy a large number of records from one table to another, delete a batch of old information, or update a status field across a group of records. If you need to perform this kind of task over and over again, action queries are a perfect timesaver.

• **Complex or tedious tasks that affect a large number of records.** Every once in a while, a table needs a minor realignment. You may decide that it's time to increase selling prices by 15 percent, or you may discover that all orders linked to customer 403 really should point to customer 404. These are one-off tasks, but they affect a large number of records. To polish them off, you need to spend some serious time in the datasheet—or you can craft a new action query that makes the change more efficiently. When you're done, you decide whether you delete the action query, or save it in case you want to modify and reuse your work later on.

Testing Action Queries (Carefully)

In the wrong hands, action queries are nothing but a high-tech way to shoot yourself in the foot. They commit changes (usually to multiple records), and once you've applied the changes, you can't reverse them. Some database fans avoid action queries completely.

If you do decide to use action queries (and there are plenty of handy tricks you can accomplish with them), then you need to take the right precautions. Most importantly, before you use an action query, make a database backup! This step's especially crucial when you're creating a new action query, because it may not always generate the result you expect. To make a backup, you can copy your .accdb database file (just like you would any other file; one way is to right-click it, and then select Copy). If you don't want to mess with Windows Explorer, then you can create a backup without leaving Access by selecting the Office button → Manage → Back Up Database (page 601).

Tip: It's always easier to make a backup than to clean up the wake of changes left by a rampaging action query.

Backups are great for disaster recovery, but it's still a good idea to avoid making a mistake in the first place. One safe approach is to start by creating a select query. You can then make sure your query's selecting the correct records before taking the next step and converting it into an action query (by choosing one of the action query types in the Query Tools | Design → Query Type section of the ribbon).

The Action Query Family

Access has four types of action queries:

- **An update query** changes the values in one or more records.

- **An append query** selects one or more records, and then adds them to an existing table.

- **A make-table query** selects one or more records, and then creates a new table for them.

- **A delete query** deletes one or more records.

If this brief introduction to action queries has piqued your interest, grab a copy of *Access 2007: The Missing Manual* for the lowdown on how to create them.

CHAPTER 32

Creating Reports

There are many reasons to create a hard copy of your lovingly maintained Access data. With a good printout, you can:

- **Carry your information without lugging your computer around.** For example, you can take an inventory list while you go shopping.

- **Show your information to non-Access users.** For example, you can hand out product catalogs, order forms, and class lists to other people.

- **Review details outside the office.** For example, you can search for mistakes while you're on the commuter train home.

- **Impress your boss.** After all, it's difficult to argue with 286 pages of raw data.

In Chapter 28 you learned how to print the raw data that's in a table, straight from the datasheet. This technique is handy, but it provides relatively few features. You don't have the flexibility to deal with large blocks of information, you can't fine-tune the formatting of different fields, and you don't have tools like grouping and summarizing that can make the information easier to understand. As you've probably already guessed, Access provides another printing feature that fills in these gaps. It's called *reports*, and it allows you to create a fine-tuned blueprint that tells Access exactly how it should prepare your data for the printer.

Reports are specialized database objects, much like tables and queries. As a result, you can prepare as many reports as you need, and keep them on hand indefinitely. Life isn't as easy if you stick to the datasheet alone. For example, if you're using the bobblehead database, you may want to print a list of bobblehead dolls with the doll's name and manufacturer information for your inventory list, and a separate list with prices for your budgeting process. To switch back and forth between these two types of printouts using the datasheet, you have to manually rearrange and hide columns *every time*. Reports don't suffer from this problem, because each report is saved as a separate database object. So if you want to print your inventory list, you simply run the DollInventory report. If you want the budgeting details, you fire up the DollPrices report.

To see one reason why reports are insanely better than ordinary datasheet printouts, compare Figure 32-1 (which shows a datasheet printout) and Figure 32-2 (which puts the same data into a simple report). Notice how the datasheet printout has both wasted space and missing information.

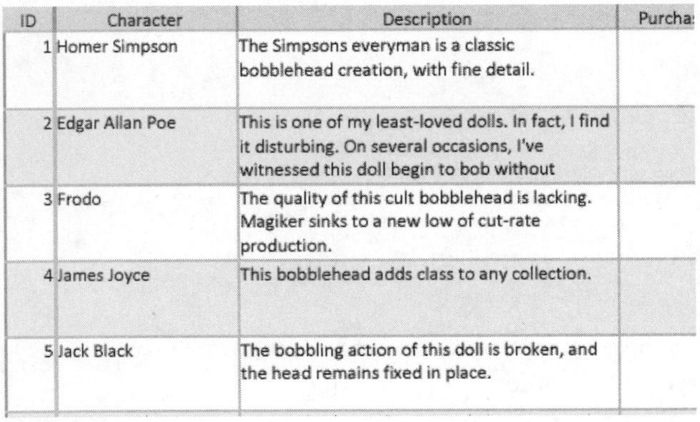

ID	Character	Description	Purcha:
1	Homer Simpson	The Simpsons everyman is a classic bobblehead creation, with fine detail.	
2	Edgar Allan Poe	This is one of my least-loved dolls. In fact, I find it disturbing. On several occasions, I've witnessed this doll begin to bob without	
3	Frodo	The quality of this cult bobblehead is lacking. Magiker sinks to a new low of cut-rate production.	
4	James Joyce	This bobblehead adds class to any collection.	
5	Jack Black	The bobbling action of this doll is broken, and the head remains fixed in place.	

Figure 32-1:
Ordinary printouts are notoriously bad at dealing with large amounts of data in a single column. Consider the Description field in this Dolls table. Every record has the same-sized box for its description, which fits three short lines. If the information is larger than the available space (as it is for the Edgar Allan Poe doll), it's chopped off at the end. If the information is smaller (as with the James Joyce doll), you have some wasted white space to look at.

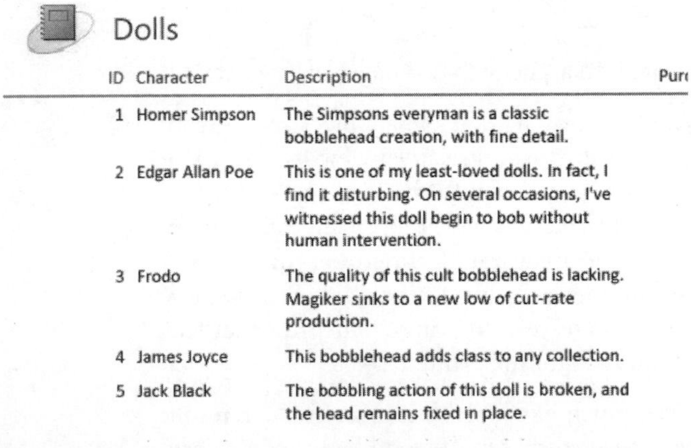

Dolls

ID	Character	Description	Pur(
1	Homer Simpson	The Simpsons everyman is a classic bobblehead creation, with fine detail.	
2	Edgar Allan Poe	This is one of my least-loved dolls. In fact, I find it disturbing. On several occasions, I've witnessed this doll begin to bob without human intervention.	
3	Frodo	The quality of this cult bobblehead is lacking. Magiker sinks to a new low of cut-rate production.	
4	James Joyce	This bobblehead adds class to any collection.	
5	Jack Black	The bobbling action of this doll is broken, and the head remains fixed in place.	

Figure 32-2:
In a typical report, you size the column widths, but the height of each row depends on the amount of information in the record. That means each row is just large enough to show all the text in the Description field. Best of all, you don't need to apply any special settings to get this behavior. Reports do it automatically.

Report Basics

You can take more than one path to create a report. Experienced report writers (like you, once you've finished this chapter) often choose to create a report from scratch. Report newbies (like you, right now) usually generate a quick report with a single click. This section covers the simplest method for generating a report.

Creating a Simple Report

It takes just two steps to create a simple report, and a few more to fine-tune it. If you want to try out this technique for yourself, open the Boutique Fudge database (included with the downloadable content for this chapter, explained on page 14) or a database of your creation, and follow these steps:

1. **In the navigation pane, select the table you want to use for your new report.**

    This example uses the Products table from the Boutique Fudge database. You can also create a report that's based on a query. See *Access 2007: The Missing Manual* for more about this trick.

2. **Choose Create → Reports → Report.**

    A new tab appears with a simple, automatically generated report. This report arranges information in a table, with each field in the table (or query) occupying a separate column. The Report view looks somewhat like the datasheet, except for the fact that it has nicer formatting and uses space more efficiently, as shown in Figure 32-2.

    When you first create a report, the fields are arranged from left to right in the same order that they live in the table. It doesn't make any difference if you've rearranged the columns in the datasheet. However, any columns you've hidden in the datasheet (page 651) are left out of the report.

Note: You can fine-tune exactly which data appears in your report by removing columns you don't want and adding new columns. Page 736 has more about this trick.

---

3. **Resize the columns smaller or larger until you have the balance you want.**

    To resize a column, first click the column header to select it. (A dotted line will appear around the column.) Next, move the mouse to the right-side of the column header, so that it changes into the two-way resize pointer. Finally, drag the column border to the left (to make it smaller) or to the right (to make it larger). Figure 32-3 shows this process in action.

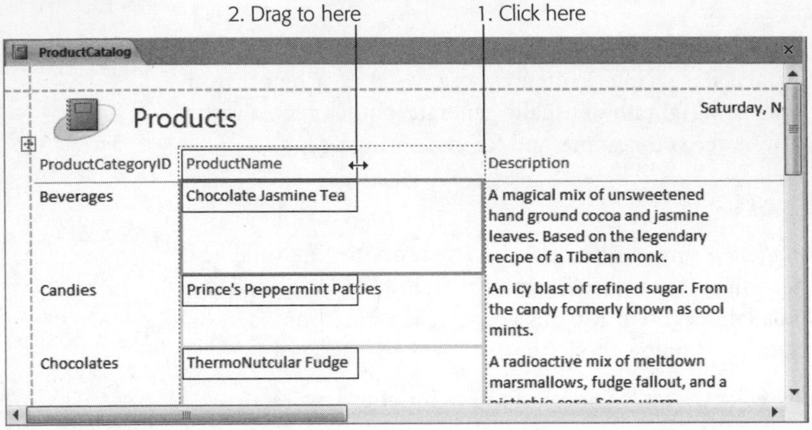

2. Drag to here   1. Click here

Figure 32-3:
Drag the edge of the column to the desired width. A black box shows you the new width. When you release the mouse button, Access changes the column width and moves all the following columns accordingly. To prevent the last column from leaking off the edge of the page, you may need to shrink some columns after you expand others.

Note: You'll see a dotted line on the right side of your report that indicates the edge of the page. You can resize a column right off the edge of the page—which may make sense if you have dozens of columns, and the only way you can deal with them is to create a printout that's two pages wide. Generally, though, it's better to make sure all your fields fit the width of the page, and turn the page sideways using landscape orientation (page 665) if you need to accommodate more columns.

4. **Arrange the columns in the order you want by dragging them.**

   To move a column, click the column heading, and then drag the column to a new position.

Tip: You can also move columns with the keyboard. Just click to select the right column, and then use the left and right arrow keys to hop from one spot to the next.

5. **Optionally, you can tweak the formatting by changing fonts, colors, and borders.**

   The quickest way to change the formatting of your report is to select the appropriate part (by clicking), and then use the buttons in the Report Layout Tools | Formatting → Font section of the ribbon. Using this technique, you can change how titles, column headers, and data appear. Page 749 has more on this technique.

6. **Add the finishing touches.**

   Now's the time to change the headings, add a logo, and apply page numbers. You'll learn how to fill in these details starting on page 740.

7. **Optionally, choose Office button → Print to print the report now.**

   You can also adjust the print settings in Print Preview mode (choose Office button → Print → Print Preview), as described on page 742.

8. **Save your report to use later.**

   You can save your report at any time by pressing Ctrl+S. If you close the report tab without saving it, Access prompts you to make the save. Either way, you need to supply a name for your report.

   It's possible to create reports that have the same names as tables or other database objects. For example, you could create a Products report that shows information about the Products table. However, in practice it's usually better to pick a more specific report name (like ProductsByCategory, ProductListForDealers, and Top50Products). The report shown in Figure 32-2 and elsewhere in this chapter is named ProductCatalog.

Arranging a Report

You've already learned how you can shuffle columns around in a report. However, that's not all you can move. You can also add space between the rows (see Figure 32-4) and adjust all the following elements:

- **The logo** (in the top-left corner). In a new report, the logo looks like a notebook with a circle around it.

- **The report title** (right next to the logo). To start out, this is the name of the table or query on which the report is based (like Products).

- **The date and time** (which is updated every time you open the report). Initially, this appears in the top-right corner.

- **The page number**. This appears at the center-bottom of each page. In Layout view, Access treats the report as though all the data occupies one page, so you need to scroll to the end to find this element.

- **The report data** (after the title). To change where the table in the report first appears on the page, click one of the column headers, and then drag it down (to add space between the title and the report data) or up (to remove the space).

- **The totals** (at the bottom of some columns). Access automatically adds calculations for numeric fields. For example, when the ProductCatalog report is first created, Access adds a total at the bottom of the Price column that indicates how much it costs to buy one of each product. (This total is of dubious value— to change it, select the column, and then pick another summary option from Report Layout Tools | Formatting → Grouping & Totals → Totals menu.)

Tip: You can also remove most elements by selecting them, and then pressing the Delete key. This trick is handy if you don't want to see details like page numbers, dates, or totals.

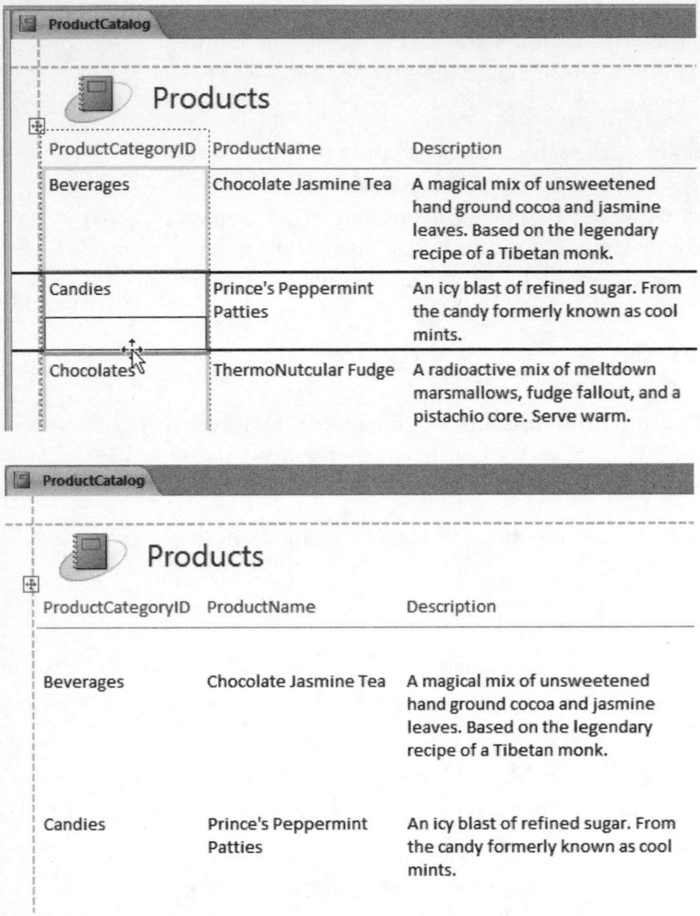

Figure 32-4:
Top: To add space between the rows, click a value in one of the rows, and drag it down.

Bottom: All the rows are adjusted to have the same spacing.

Adding and Removing Fields

If you're tired of merely rearranging columns, you may want to try adding ones that aren't already included or removing existing ones that you don't want. Removing a field is easy: just click to select it, and then press Delete. (You can try out this technique with the Discontinued field in the ProductCatalog report.)

When you create a simple report using the quick creation technique described on page 733, you usually end up with all the fields you need. However, there are two reasons why you may need to add an additional field that isn't already in the report:

- **You want to add a field that's hidden in the Datasheet view (page 651).** When you create a new report, hidden fields are left out.

- **You want to add a field with related information from a linked table.** For example, you could add fields from the ProductCategories table to show information about the category that each product is in.

To add a new field, you need the help of the Field List pane (see Figure 32-5). To show it, choose Report Layout Tools | Formatting → Controls → Add Existing Fields.

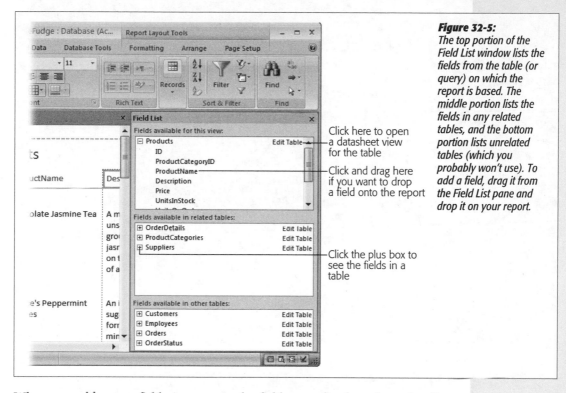

Figure 32-5:
The top portion of the Field List window lists the fields from the table (or query) on which the report is based. The middle portion lists the fields in any related tables, and the bottom portion lists unrelated tables (which you probably won't use). To add a field, drag it from the Field List pane and drop it on your report.

When you add a new field, Access uses the field name for the column heading, which isn't always what you want. Maybe you'd prefer *Product Name* (with a space) to *ProductName*. Or maybe you'd like to shorten *ProductCategoryID* to just *Category*. After all, the report shows the name instead of the numeric category ID, because the ProductCategoryID field uses a lookup (page 709). Fortunately, renaming the column headers is easy. Just double-click one to switch it into edit mode. You can then edit the existing text or replace it altogether.

The Many Views of a Report

Just like tables and queries, you can use several different views to change a report. When you create a report using the quick creation technique described earlier, you begin in Layout view, which is an ideal starting place for report builders. But depending on the task at hand, you may choose to switch to another view.

Adding Pictures to Reports

Can I store pictures in a table and show them in a report?

Many tables include embedded pictures using the Attachment data type (page 633). You can use this technique to store employee photos, product pictures, or supplier logos. Depending on the type of picture, you may then want to include them in your printouts.

It is possible to show your pictures in a report (and even print them), provided you meet the following requirements:

- **Your picture is stored in an attachment field.** (See page 633 for more information about the attachment data type.)

- **Your picture is stored in a standard picture format (think .bmp, .jpg, .gif, .tif, .wmf, and so on).** If you have another type of file in an attachment field, you just see the icon of the related application (like Microsoft Word for a .doc file) in your report.

- **Your picture is the first attachment.** If you have more than one attachment, when you select the row in the report, tiny arrow buttons appear above that you can use to move from one attachment to another. But it's way too much work to do this with all your records before you print a report.

The Dolls table in the bobblehead database Products table fits the bill, which lets you create a report like the one shown in Figure 32-6.

Alternatively, you can show the file name or the file type of an attachment in a report. To do this, you need to use the Field List pane (Figure 32-5). For example, if you have an attachment field named Picture, it appears with a plus button next to it in the Field List pane. Click the plus button, and you'll see the three Picture-related details you can display in a report: *Picture.FileData* (the attachment content itself, which is the image), *Picture.FileName* (the name of the file), and *Picture.FileType* (the type of file). If you want to show these details, just drag them onto your report.

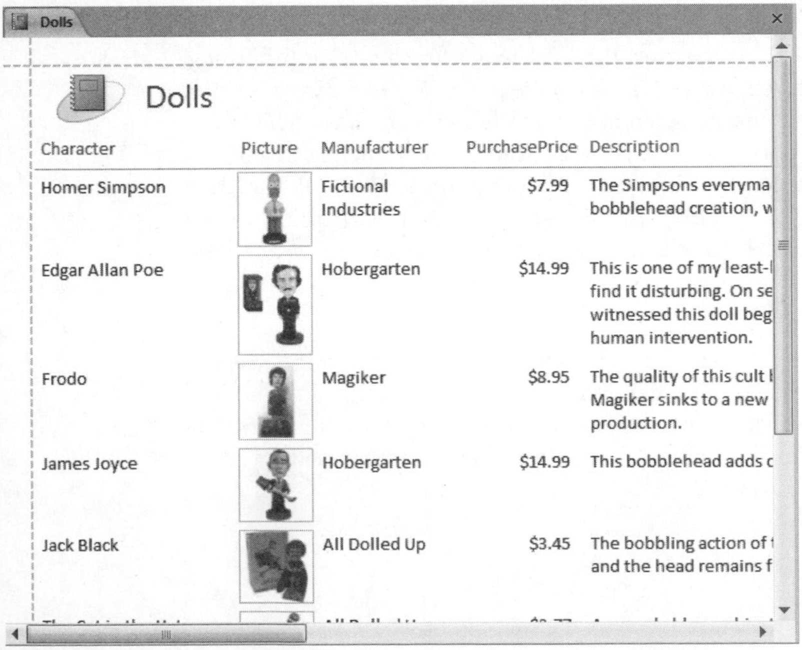

Figure 32-6:
You can see this in the sample Bobblehead database examples for this chapter. (They're available on the "Missing CD" page at www.missingmanuals.com.) The report is named DollsWithPictures.

You have four viewing options:

- **Layout View.** Shows what the report will look like when printed, complete with the real data from the underlying table. You can use this view to format and rearrange the basic building blocks of the report.

- **Report View.** Looks almost the same as Layout view but doesn't allow you to make changes. If you double-click a report in the navigation pane, Access opens it in Report view so you can see the data it contains without accidentally changing its design. One common reason to use Report view is to copy portions of your report to the clipboard, so you can paste them into other programs (like Microsoft Word). Figure 32-7 shows how that works.

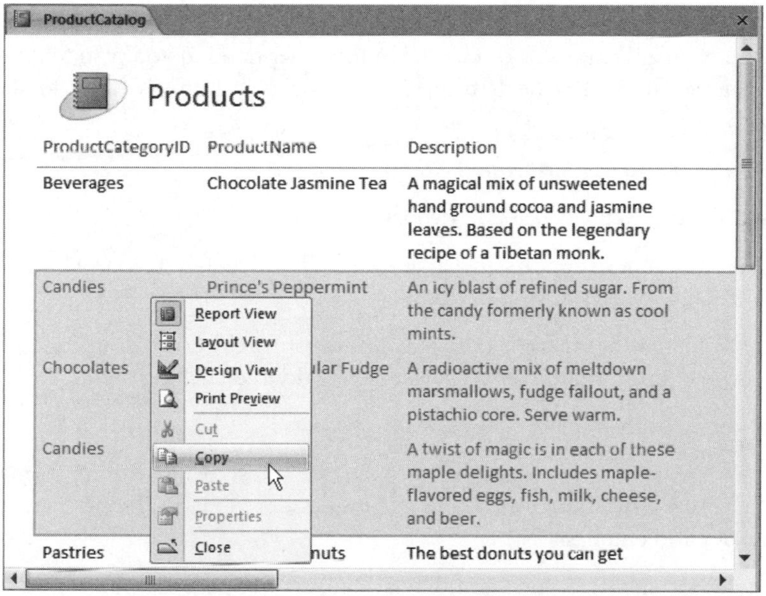

Figure 32-7:
To select a bunch of rows, click in the margin on the left next to the first row you want to select, and then drag down to highlight the rows you want. Then, right-click the highlighted portion, and choose Copy to transfer it to the clipboard, so it's ready for pasting into other Windows applications.

Note: If you want to transfer the entire content of a report, you should consider the export features described on page 743.

- **Print Preview.** Shows a live preview of your report, just like Layout view and Report view. The difference is that the preview is *paginated* (divided into print pages), so you can figure out how many pages your printout needs and where the page breaks fall. You can also change print settings (like page orientation) and export the complete report, as described on page 743.

- **Design View.** Shows a template view where you can define the different sections of your report. It's not nearly as intuitive as Layout view, but it does give you complete, unrestrained flexibility to customize your report. Access experts often begin creating a report in Layout view and then add more exotic effects in Design view. Learn more about Design view in *Access 2007: The Missing Manual*.

You can switch from one view to another by right-clicking the report tab title, and then choosing the appropriate view from the pop-up menu. (Or, you can use the Home → Views → View menu or the view buttons in the bottom-right corner of the Access window. It's just a matter of personal preference.)

After you've closed your report, you can reopen it in the view of your choice. Just right-click the report in the navigation pane, and then choose the appropriate view. Or double-click the report in the navigation pane to open it in Report view.

Creating a Report from Scratch

So far, you've learned how to quickly create a report based on a table or a query. However, you have another choice—you can start with a blank slate and explicitly add each field you want. Both approaches are equally valid. You may prefer to use the quick creation technique when you want to build a report that closely follows the structure of an existing table or query. On the other hand, if you plan to create a report that uses just a few fields from a table, you may find it's easier to start from scratch.

Here's how you create a report from the bottom up:

1. **Choose Create → Reports → Blank Report.**

   A new, empty report appears in Layout view. The Field List appears on the right, with all the tables in your database.

2. **Add the fields you want from the appropriate table, either by dragging them from the Field List onto the report surface or by double-clicking them.**

3. **Format the columns.**

   When you create a report from scratch, the columns start off with no formatting at all. You'll need the formatting techniques described in the next section to add color and emphasis.

4. **Add any other elements you want, like a logo, a title, page numbers, and the date.**

   When you create a simple report, you get all these ingredients for free. Fortunately, it's just as easy to add them to a report you're building from scratch. Just head to the Report Layout Tools | Formatting → Controls section of the ribbon (see Figure 32-8).

Printing, Previewing, and Exporting a Report

Once you've created the perfect report, it's time to share it with rest of the world. Most commonly, you'll choose to print it.

Printing a report is easy—simply choose Office button → Print. But before you inadvertently fire off an 87-page customer list in jumbo 24-point font, it's a good idea to preview the end result. Access makes it easy with its integrated Print Preview feature.

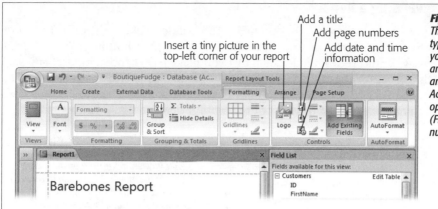

Insert a tiny picture in the top-left corner of your report

Add a title

Add page numbers

Add date and time information

Figure 32-8:
The logo and title typically sit at the top of your report. You can use any picture for the logo and any text for the title. Access gives you more options for the date (Figure 32-9) and page number (Figure 32-10).

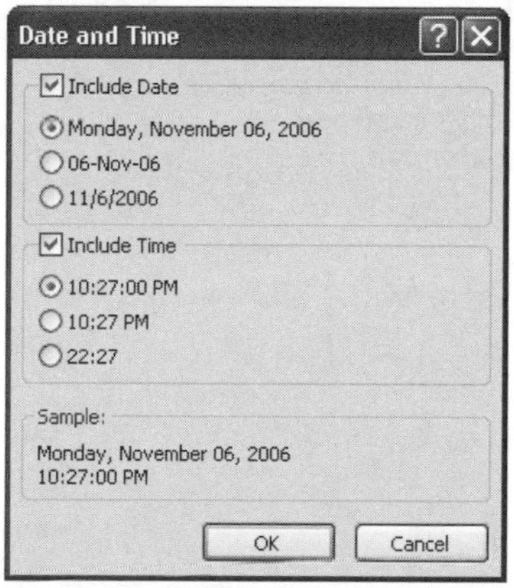

Figure 32-9:
When adding date information, you can choose whether to include the date, the time, or both. You also pick the format. Once you've added the date information, you can change the font, borders, and colors, as with any other report element.

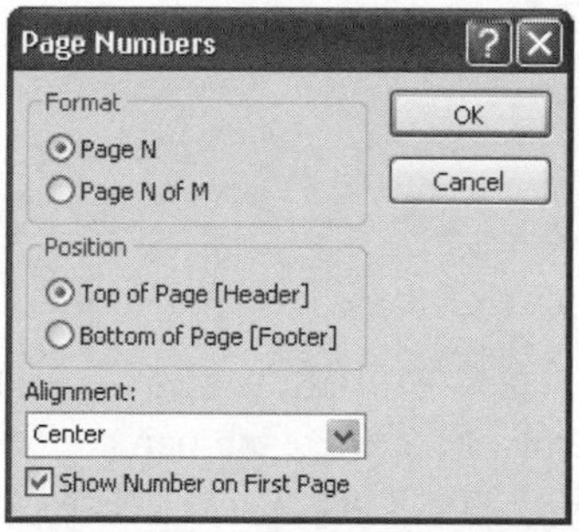

Figure 32-10:
With page numbers, you can choose the format, the position, and the alignment. (The position determines whether the page numbers appear above or below the report data. Although you can drag the page numbers around after you add them, Access will shift the report data to make room, based on your choice.)

Tip: You don't need to open your report to print it. Just select it in the navigation pane, and then choose Print from the Office menu. But beware—when you use this shortcut you don't get the chance to preview the result and make sure it's what you want before it pops out of the printer.

Previewing a Report

To get a preview of what your printed report will look like, right-click the report tab title and then choose Print Preview, or choose Office button → Print → Print Preview. Print Preview mode doesn't let you make any changes or select any part of the report. You're limited to zooming in and out, and moving from page to page (see Figure 32-11). When you're finished looking at your print preview, choose Print Preview → Close Preview → Close Print Preview.

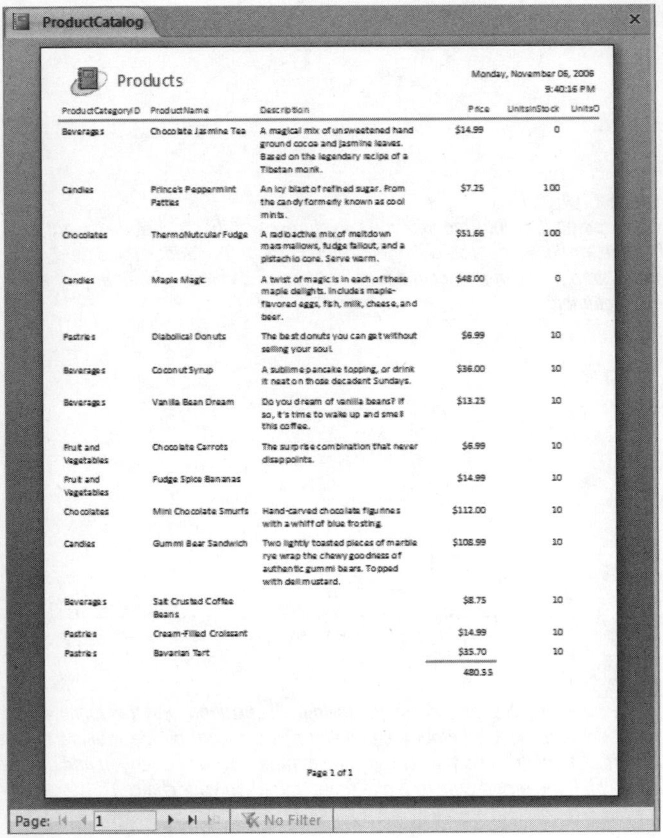

Figure 32-11:
In Print Preview mode, to zoom in, click once with the mouse. Click again to zoom back out to the full page view. You can also use the page navigation buttons at the bottom of the window to move from one page to the next, and the zoom slider (not shown) for more precise zooming. But the most useful commands appear in the ribbon, which lets you tweak the print settings and export your report results to another type of file.

In Print Preview mode, the ribbon changes dramatically. The tabs you've grown to know and love disappear, and Access replaces them with a single tab named Print Preview. (This is the same Print Preview tab you saw when you previewed a datasheet printout in Chapter 28.) You can use all the same techniques that you learned on page 664 to move around the preview, see multiple pages at once (which lets you study where page breaks occur), and change the page margins and paper orientation.

For example, the Portrait and Landscape buttons let you quickly switch between the standard portrait orientation (which places the short edge at the top of the page) and landscape (which rotates the page, placing the long edge at the top).

Portrait fits more rows, while landscape fits more columns. Generally, portrait is best, provided it can fit all your columns. If portrait mode doesn't fit all your columns, you can try using landscape orientation, a smaller font size (page 749), narrower margins, or a larger type of paper.

Note: Reports always use your standard paper size (which is usually 8.5 × 11 inches, or letter size) when you first create them. However, if you change the size, the new size setting is stored with the report. That means the next time you open your report, it still has the customized paper size. The same applies for the paper orientation setting.

Access has two extra options that aren't provided in a normal datasheet print preview:

- **Use the Print Data Only button** to produce a streamlined printout that leaves out details like column headers and titles. This option is rarely useful, because the resulting printout is harder to read.

- **Use the Columns button** to fit more report data on a page. This option works only if your report is much narrower than the page width. For example, if your report is less than half the width of the page, you can double-up by using two columns. You'll need half the number of pages.

Tip: You can change a lot of the page layout settings (like margins and paper orientation) without heading to the print preview. You'll find many of the same buttons in the Report Layout Tools | Page Setup tab of the ribbon, which appears whenever you have your ribbon in Layout view.

Exporting a Report

The Print Preview tab is a bit of an oddity, because it includes a few commands that don't have anything to with printing your report. The commands in the Print Preview → Data section let you take a snapshot of the current report data, and then *export* it into some other type of file so you can view it outside of Access or work with it in another program. This technique is a great one to use if you want to share some data with other people (read: impress the boss).

Although Access supports many different formats for exporting a report, you'll use just a few with reports. (The others are more useful when you're exporting pure data from a table or query, as explained in Chapter 34.) The useful formats for exporting reports include:

- **Word.** This option transforms your report into a document you can open in Microsoft Word. However, the format Access uses is a bit clumsy. (It separates each column with tabs and each line with a hard return, which makes it difficult to rearrange the data after the fact in Word.) A nicer export feature would put the report data into a Word table, which would make it far easier to work with.

- **HTML Document.** This option transforms your report into a rich HTML document, suitable for posting on the Web or just opening straight from your hard drive. The advantage of this format is that all you need to view it is a Web browser (and who doesn't have one of those?). The only drawback is that the formatting, layout, and pagination of your report won't be preserved exactly, which is a disadvantage if someone wants to print the exported report.

- **Snapshot Viewer.** This option creates a .snp snapshot file, which anyone can open to view and print the fully formatted report. In order to view the snapshot file, you need Microsoft's free Snapshot Viewer program. (To download it, surf to *http://office.microsoft.com* and search for "Snapshot Viewer.") Although the Snapshot Viewer works perfectly well, most people prefer to use the more standard PDF format (next in the list), which provides the same features. (Truthfully, the Snapshot Viewer is a bit of a holdover from earlier versions of Office.)

- **PDF or XPS.** This option lets you preserve your exact report formatting (so your report can be printed), and it lets people who don't have Access (and possibly don't even have Windows) view your report. The only disadvantage is that this feature isn't included in the basic Access package. Instead, you need to install a free add-in to get it (you'll see how on page 746). For more information about the PDF and XPS formats, see the box "Learning to Love PDFs" below.

UP TO SPEED

Learning to Love PDFs

You've probably heard about PDF, Adobe's popular format for sharing formatted, print-ready documents. PDFs are used to pass around product manuals, brochures, and all sorts of electronic documents. Unlike a document format such as .xlsx, PDF files are designed to be viewed and printed, but not edited.

The best part about PDFs is that they can be viewed on just about any type of computer and operating system using the free Adobe Reader. You can download Adobe Reader at *www.adobe.com/products/acrobat/readstep2.html*, but you probably don't need to. Most computers already have

Adobe Reader installed, because it comes bundled with so many different programs (usually so you can view their electronic documentation). It's also used widely on the Web.

PDF isn't the only kid on the block. Microsoft's newest operating system, Windows Vista, includes its own electronic paper format called XPS (XML Paper Specification). In time, as XPS is integrated into more and more products, it may become a true PDF competitor. But for now, PDF is dramatically more popular and widespread, so it's the one to stick with.

No matter which format you use, the process is essentially the same:

1. **If you're not already in Print Preview mode, right-click the report tab title, and then choose Print Preview.**

2. **Click one of the buttons in the Print Preview → Data section of the ribbon, depending on the format you want to use for your export.**

   For example, choose Print Preview → Data → Word to copy the results of your report into a Word-compatible document. Some of the options are stored under the Print Preview → Data → More menu, and you won't see a PDF export option until you install the PDF add-in (as described in the next section).

3. **Choose a name for the destination file (Figure 32-12).**

   The destination file is the place where the exported data will be stored.

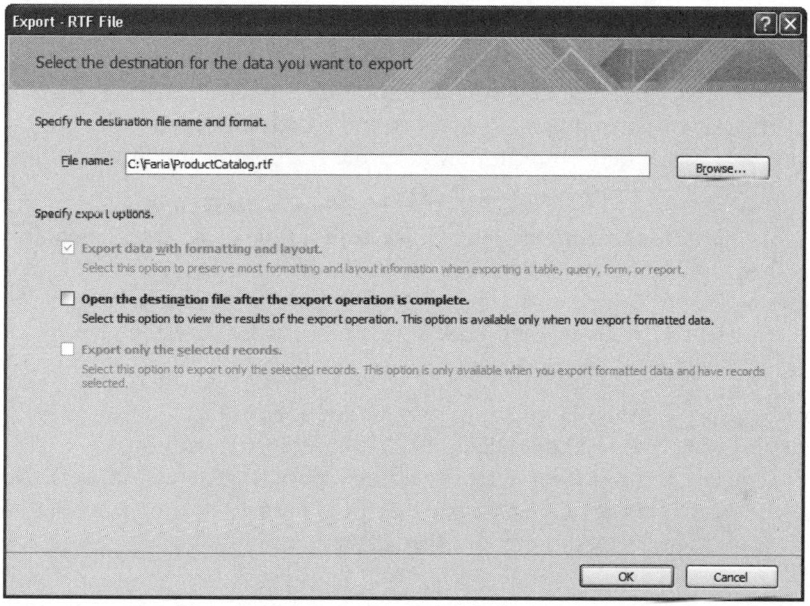

Figure 32-12:
Access assumes you want a name that matches your report (for example, ProductCatalog.rtf if the ProductCatalog report is exported to a rich text document that can be opened in Word). However, you can change the file name to whatever you want.

4. **If you wish to open your exported file in the related program, check the setting "Open the destination file after the export operation is complete."**

   Say you're exporting a Word document and you choose this option; Access will export the data, launch Word, and load up the document. This is a good way to make sure your export operation worked as expected. This option works only if you have the program you need on your computer.

5. **Click OK to perform the export.**

   Ignore the other two checkboxes, which are grayed out. They apply only to export operations that work with other database objects.

Note: Remember, exporting a report is like printing a report. Your exported file contains the data that existed at that moment in time. If you decide a week later that you need more recent data, you need to export your report again.

---

6. **Choose whether or not you want to save your export settings.**

By saving your export settings, you can quickly repeat your export operation later on. For example, if you export to a Word document and save the export settings, you can export the report data tomorrow, next week, or a year in the future.

Tip: You don't need to open your report in order to export it. Instead, you can use all the commands you need straight from the navigation pane. Just right-click the report name, and then choose Export to show a menu of all your export options, from PDF files to HTML pages. You'll also see a few options that don't appear in the Export tab of the ribbon, including options for exporting the report to older, almost forgotten database and spreadsheet products like dBase, Paradox, and Lotus 1-2-3.

Getting the "Save As PDF" Add-in

To export a report as a PDF file, you need the "Save As PDF or XPS" add-in. To get it, surf to *www.microsoft.com/downloads*, and search for "PDF". The links will lead you to a page where you can download the add-in and install it with just a couple clicks.

Once you install the add-in, all your Office applications will have the ability to export their documents in PDF format. In an Access report, you work this magic by choosing Print Preview → Data → PDF or XPS while you've got a report in Print Preview mode. Or, you can right-click your report in the navigation pane, and then choose Export → PDF or XPS.

When you export a PDF file, you get a few extra options in the "Publish as PDF or XPS" dialog box (Figure 32-13). PDF files can be exported with different resolution and quality settings (which mostly affect reports that have pictures). Normally, you use higher-quality settings if you're planning to print your PDF file because printers use higher resolutions than computer monitors.

The "Publish as PDF or XPS" dialog box gives you some control over the quality settings with the "Optimize for" options. If you're just exporting a PDF copy so other people can *view* the information in your report, choose "Minimum size (publishing online)" to save some space. On the other hand, if there's a possibility that the people reading your PDF may want to print it out, choose "Standard (publishing online and printing)" instead. You'll export a slightly larger PDF file that will make for a better printout.

Tip: Getting the "Save As PDF or XPS" add-in is a bit of a hassle, but it's well worth the effort. In previous versions of Access, people who wanted to create PDF files had to get another add-in or buy the expensive full version of the Adobe Acrobat software. The "Save As PDF or XPS" feature was originally slated for inclusion in Office (with no add-in required), but antitrust concerns caused an ultra-cautious Microsoft to keep it out. Best of all, the add-in gives you PDF-saving abilities in other Office applications, like Word, Excel, and PowerPoint.

Finally, if you want to publish only a portion of your report as a PDF file, click the Options button to open a dialog box with yet a few more settings. You can choose to publish just a fixed number of pages rather than the full report.

Different Ways to Export Data

Is it better to export the results of a report, or the entire contents of a table?

There are several ways to transport data out of Access. You can take data directly from a table, or you can export the results of a query or a report. So which approach is best?

Generally, the easiest option is to get data straight from the appropriate table (as described in Chapter 34). However, in a few cases it makes more sense to use a report:

- You want to use the unique arrangement of columns that you've defined in a report. (For example, you may not want the full Products table—instead, the ProductCatalog report lays out exactly what you need.)

- You want to use the filtering, sorting, or grouping settings that you've applied to a report. These advanced options are discussed in depth in *Access 2007: The Missing Manual.*

- You want to take advantage of the formatting you've applied to a report. Depending on what exporting option you use, you may be able to keep formatting details like fonts. If you export to a PDF file, HTML document, or snapshot, all the formatting remains in place. If you export to an Office application like Word or Excel, only some of the formatting is retained. But if you export a table or a query, you get the data only, and it's up to you to make it look nice all over again.

In Chapter 34, you'll take a closer look at how to export tables and queries.

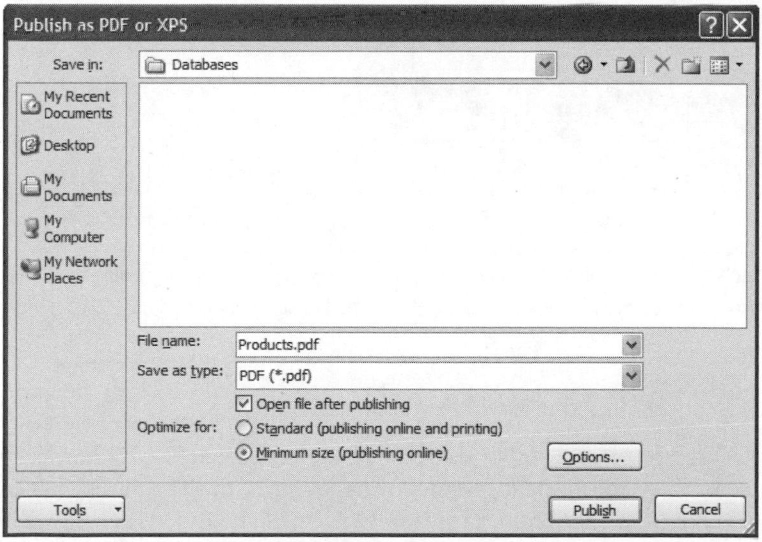

Figure 32-13:
The "Publish as PDF or XPS" dialog box looks a lot like the Export As dialog box, except it has a Publish button instead of an Export button. You can turn on the "Open file after publishing" checkbox to tell Access to open the PDF file in Adobe Reader (assuming you have it installed) after the publishing process is complete, so you can check the result.

Formatting a Report

So far, you've learned to create simple reports that show all the information you want in a compact table. The only problem with these reports is that they all look the same. If you're working in a cubicle farm for a multinational insurance company, this drab sameness is probably a good thing. But those who still have a pulse may want to jazz up their reports with borders, exotic fonts, and a dash of color.

The quickest way to apply formatting is to use one of the prebuilt AutoFormats (shown in Figure 32-14) from the Report Layout Tools | Formatting → AutoFormat → AutoFormat list. Each AutoFormat applies a combination of fonts, colors, and border settings. AutoFormats let you transform the entire look of your report in one step, but they don't give you the fine-grained control to apply exactly the details you want.

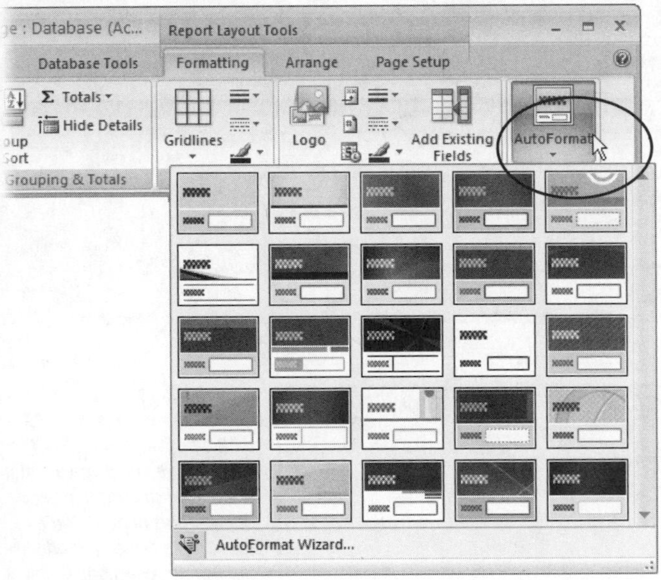

Figure 32-14:
Click the drop-down arrow (circled) to see all the available AutoFormats. (Or, if you have a really large monitor, the AutoFormat previews appear right in the ribbon.) Each thumbnail preview shows the colors and a bit of the background that the format uses, but you need to apply it before you can really see what it looks like.

Note: Remember, in order to format a report, it needs to be in Layout view. If you double-click a report in the navigation pane, it opens in Report view. Right-click the tab title, and then choose Layout View to switch over.

You can do a couple other things with AutoFormat:

• To apply just *part* of an AutoFormat, choose Report Layout Tools | Formatting → AutoFormat → AutoFormat → AutoFormat Wizard. In the AutoFormat dialog box, choose the AutoFormat you want. Then, click Options to show three checkboxes at the bottom of the dialog box: Font, Color, and Border. Turn off the checkmark next to the types of formatting you *don't* want to apply, and then click OK.

- To revert to a plain report with no formatting, choose Report Layout Tools | Formatting → AutoFormat → AutoFormat → AutoFormat Wizard to show the AutoFormat dialog box. Then, choose None in the list of AutoFormats, and click OK.

- If you've applied some fancy formatting to your report, and you want to save it as your own custom AutoFormat, choose Report Layout Tools | Formatting → AutoFormat → AutoFormat → AutoFormat Wizard to show the AutoFormat dialog box. Then, click Customize, choose "Create a new AutoFormat," enter a name for your AutoFormat, and click OK. You'll see your AutoFormat appear in the AutoFormats list.

Formatting Columns and Column Headers

AutoFormats are a great way to get a bunch of formatting done in a hurry. However, sometimes you want to use more of a personal touch and format the different parts of your report by hand.

To apply more targeted formatting, you need to follow a two-step approach. First, select the portion of the report you want to format. Second, click a command in the Report Layout Tools | Formatting → Font section of the ribbon (Figure 32-15).

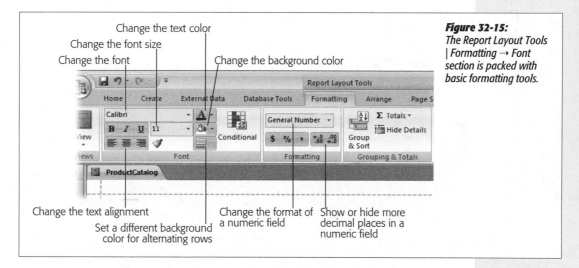

Figure 32-15:
The Report Layout Tools | Formatting → Font section is packed with basic formatting tools.

The Layout Tools | Formatting → Font section lets you adjust all the following details:

- The font and font size (11-point Calibri is the easy-on-the-eyes standard)

- The text alignment (left, right, or center)

- The text color and background color

Although you can format the title, date, or page number sections of the report, you'll spend most of your time formatting the column headers and the column values. To format a column header, click it. To format the column *values*, click any one of the values in the column. Figure 32-16 shows an example.

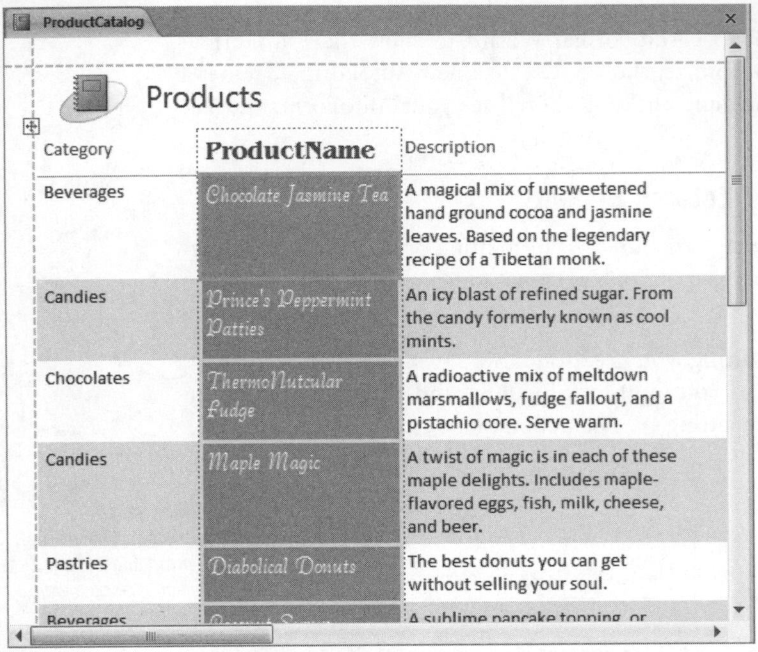

Figure 32-16:
Here, the ProductName column is singled out for special formatting. Although it looks like only a single value is selected, Access will apply formatting changes to the entire column.

You can't format the individual values in a column. That means that you can format the ProductName column to look different from the Price column, but you can't format Chocolate Jasmine Tea differently from Prince's Peppermint Patties. This limitation makes sense—after all, you could have thousands of records, and keeping track of the formatting of each one would be way too much work for Access.

Tip: One way around this shortcoming: Use conditional formatting to tell Access when it should kick in some extra formatting based on the value in a cell. See *Access 2007: The Missing Manual* for full details on this fancy maneuver.

Formatting numeric fields

You can use the Report Layout Tools | Formatting → Formatting section of the ribbon to adjust numeric fields (like the Price field in the ProductCatalog report). You'll find a drop-down list that lets you pick various options for formatting numbers:

- **General Number** gives a basic, no-frills number. Access gives each value the number of decimal digits it needs.

- **Currency** makes sure each number has two decimal points and gets the currency symbol that's configured for your computer (based on its geographic locale). Large numbers get thousands-separator commas to separate the digits, as in $1,111.99.

- **Euro** is similar to Currency, except it shows the currency symbol for the euro.

- **Fixed** gives each number the same number of decimal places. (Initially it's two, but you can use the Increase Decimals and Decrease Decimals buttons, shown in Figure 32-15, to change this.) Large numbers don't get commas.

- **Standard** is the same as fixed, except large numbers do get the thousands separator comma (as in 1,111.99).

- **Percent** assumes each number is a fractional value that represents a percentage, where 1.0 is 100 percent. So if you have the number 48, Access changes this to 4800.00 percent. (You can change the number of decimal places with the Increase Decimals and Decrease Decimals buttons.)

- **Scientific** displays each number using *scientific notation*, so 48 becomes 4. 80E+01 (which is a fancy way of saying 4.8 multiplied by 10^1 gives you the number that's stored in the field). Scientific notation is used to show numbers that have vastly different scales with a similar number of digits. You can change the number of decimal places using the Increase Decimals and Decrease Decimals buttons.

You can also change the number of digits that are displayed to the right of the decimal point by clicking the Increase Decimals and Decrease Decimals buttons in the Report Layout Tools | Formatting → Formatting section of the ribbon.

Alternating row formatting

Here's a simple but powerful formatting trick: Add a shaded background to every second row. Alternating row formatting gives a bit of polish to the plainest report, but it also serves a practical purpose. In dense reports, the shaded bands make it easier for readers to distinguish each row and follow a row from one column to the next.

To apply an alternating row format, you need to click immediately to the left of any row. At that point, the entire row becomes selected, and the Report Layout Tools | Formatting → Font → Alternate Fill button is turned on. (The Alternate Fill button looks like a mini-grid. It appears right under the Fill button.) You can click it, and then choose a color.

If you click one of the values in the row, the Alternate Fill button won't be turned on, and you won't be able to change the alternating fill color.

Gridlines

When you create a new report, your data is arranged in an invisible table. This table doesn't include any gridlines, so your printouts look sleek and lightweight. But if you're a closet gridline lover, you'll be happy to know you can add borders to the report table. It's up to you whether you want to add them everywhere to keep data carefully regimented in separate cells or just use them judiciously to highlight important columns.

Tip: Gridlines are useful with dense reports where the data may otherwise appear to run together into a jumbled mess. Access gurus know that less is more and using just a few gridlines is usually better than adding them between every column and row.

You can apply gridlines in two ways. The simplest and most common option is to apply them to the entire table. To do this, click anywhere inside the table of report data, and then choose one of the gridline options from the Report Layout Tools | Formatting → Gridlines → Gridlines list (Figure 32-17). Next, use the other buttons in the Report Layout Tools | Formatting → Gridlines section to change the thickness, color, and style (dashed, dotted, solid, and so on) of your gridlines.

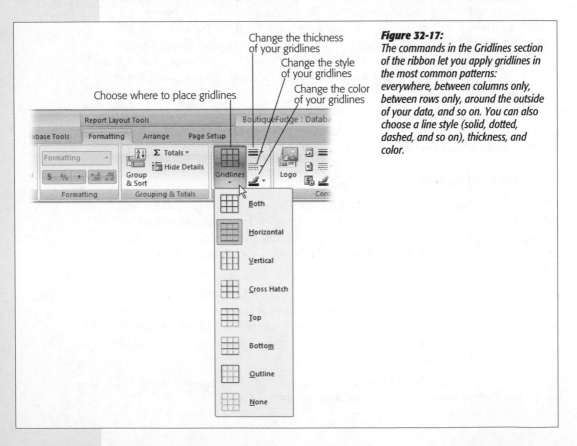

Change the thickness of your gridlines

Change the style of your gridlines

Change the color of your gridlines

Choose where to place gridlines

Figure 32-17:
The commands in the Gridlines section of the ribbon let you apply gridlines in the most common patterns: everywhere, between columns only, between rows only, around the outside of your data, and so on. You can also choose a line style (solid, dotted, dashed, and so on), thickness, and color.

Note: There's one trick to gridlines. You can apply gridlines to the column headings that are different from the ones you use for the rest of the table. To apply gridlines to the column-heading section, just click any column heading, and then choose your gridline options from the ribbon.

Borders

Along with report gridlines, you can also use a similar set of border options. The difference between gridlines and borders is that gridlines apply to the table of report data, while borders can be attached to any ingredient in your report.

You'll find the three border buttons (for choosing border thickness, color, and style) in the Report Layout Tools | Formatting → Controls section of the ribbon. The border options don't make much sense when you use them on column values, because you'll end up with a box around each value. Borders are more useful around other report elements, like the report title.

Filtering and Sorting a Report

Reports offer much the same filtering and sorting features that you learned to use with the datasheet in Chapter 28.

Filtering a Report

The ProductCatalog report presents all the records from the Products table. However, reports often need to filter out just an important subset of information. For example, you may want to analyze the sales of products in a specific category or the orders made by customers in a specific city. In the case of the ProductCatalog, it's logical to leave out discontinued items. After all, there's no reason for Boutique Fudge to advertise items it no longer sells.

You can pare down the results that are included in a report in two ways. You've already learned about one option: creating a query that extracts the results you want, and then using that query to build your report. This option is a good choice if you already have a query that fits the bill or you plan to use this subset of data for several purposes (reports, editing, other queries, and so on).

Another choice is to apply the filtering through report *settings*. The advantage of this technique is that you can change the filter settings quickly and repeatedly. If you plan to use the same report to print several different subsets of data, this approach is best. For example, you could filter out the products in one category, print them, and then adjust the filtering to select products in a different category, which you could also print.

Report filtering works the same way datasheet filtering does (discussed in detail on page 657). You have two options:

- If you want to quickly build a filter condition based on an existing value, right-click that value, as shown in Figure 32-18. For example, in the CategoryName field, you can right-click the value "Beverages." The menu that pops up includes several filtering options based on the current value. Depending on the option you choose, you can include records in the Beverages category, records in different categories, records that have a category name that includes Beverages (like "Alcoholic Beverages"), and so on.

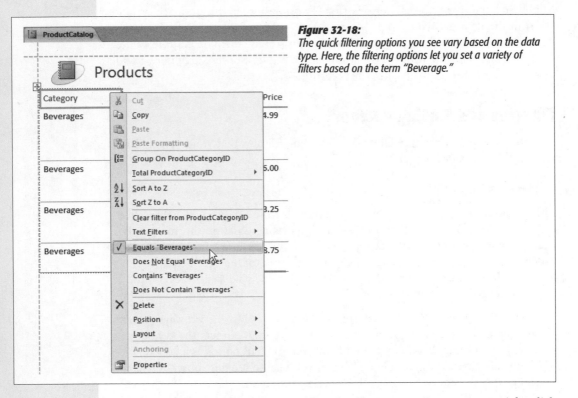

Figure 32-18:
The quick filtering options you see vary based on the data type. Here, the filtering options let you set a variety of filters based on the term "Beverage."

- If you need more flexibility to create the filter expression you want, right-click any value in a column, and then look for the filtering submenu. The exact name of the menu depends on the data type. For example, if you right-click the CategoryName field, you see a submenu named Text Filters. If you right-click the Price field, you see a submenu named Number Filters. These submenus include a range of filtering options that let you set specific ranges. For all the exquisite details and help creating a variety of filter expressions, refer to the instructions on page 657.

You can apply filters to multiple columns at once. To remove a filter, right-click the column, and then choose Clear Filter.

Sorting a Report

Ordinarily, a report has the same order as the underlying data source. If you've built your report on a query, the order is determined by the sort order you used in the query. If you've built your report on a table, the records have no particular order at all, although they'll typically appear in the order you added them.

Either way, you can apply formatting directly in your report, in much the same way that you can with the datasheet (page 648). Simply right-click the appropriate column header, and then look for the sorting options. The sort commands depend on the data type—for example, you can order text fields alphabetically, dates chronologically, and numeric fields in ascending or descending order.

Note: You can sort using only one field at a time. If you want to apply a more complex sort that uses more than one column (for example, a sort that separates products into alphabetical categories and then orders each category by price), you need to build a query for your report.

CHAPTER 33

Creating Simple Forms

So far, you've learned how to create tables that house your data, queries that search it, and reports that prepare it for printing. You've also learned about action queries that automate big updates. But your actual database users (whether that's you or someone else) will spend most of their time on an entirely different job: daily database upkeep.

Database upkeep includes reviewing, editing, and inserting information. Real databases go through this process continuously. In a typical day, the staff at Cacophoné Studios adds new students, the customer service department at Boutique Fudge places new orders, and the Gothic Wedding planners tweak the seating arrangements. Bobbleheads are bought, addresses are changed, purchases are logged, test scores are recorded, and your data grows and evolves.

You can perform your daily upkeep using the datasheet (Chapter 28), but that isn't the easiest approach. Although the datasheet packs a lot of information into a small space, it's often awkward to use, and it's intimidating to Access newcomers. The solution is *forms*: specialized database objects that make it easier for anyone to review and edit the information in a table.

Note: Remember, if you're using Access in a business environment, different people probably use your database. You may create it, but others need to be able to use it to perform a variety of tasks—usually data entry and searches. These other folks may not be as Access-savvy as you are.

Form Basics

Forms get their name from paper forms that people use to record information when a computer isn't handy. Depending on your situation, you may create an Access form that resembles a paper form that your company or organization uses. If you're working at a bank, you can create an Access form that lays out information in the same basic arrangement as a paper-based customer application form. This arrangement makes it easy to copy information from the paper into your database. However, most of the time the forms you design don't have a real-world equivalent. You'll create them from scratch, and use them to make data entry easier.

To understand why forms are an indispensable part of almost all databases, it helps to first consider the datasheet's shortcomings. Here are some areas where forms beat the datasheet:

- **Better arrangements.** In the datasheet, each field occupies a single column. This arrangement works well for tables with few fields, but leads to endless side-to-side scrolling in larger tables. In a form, you can make sure the data you need is always in sight. You can also use color, lines, and pictures to help separate different chunks of content.

- **Extra information.** You can pack a form with any text you want, which means you can add clues that help newbies understand the data they need to supply. You can also add calculated details—for example, you can calculate and display the total purchases made by a customer without forcing someone to fire up a separate query.

- **Table relationships.** Many tasks involve adding records to more than one related table. If a new customer places an order in the Boutique Fudge database, then you need to create a new record in the Customers and Orders tables, along with one or more records in the OrderDetails table. A form lets you do all this work in one place (rather than forcing you to open two or three datasheets).

- **Buttons and other widgets.** Forms support *controls*—buttons, links, lists, and other fancy pieces of user interface matter you can add to your form. The person using your database can then click a button to fire off a related task (like opening another form or printing a report).

Properly designed forms are what the geeks call a database's *front end*. In a database that uses forms, you can edit data, perform searches, and take care all of your day-to-day tasks without ever touching a datasheet.

Creating a Simple Form

As with reports, Access gives you an easy and a more advanced way to construct a form. The easy way creates a ready-made form based on a table or query. Keen eyes will notice that this process unfolds in more or less the same way as when you automatically generate a simple report (page 733).

Here's how it works:

1. **In the navigation pane, select the table or query you want to use to generate the form.**

   Try the Products table from the Boutique Fudge database.

Note: If you create a form for a parent table that's linked to other tables, then you wind up with a slightly different type of form. If you create a form for the Categories table (a parent of the Products table), then you end up with a two-part form that lets you view and modify the category record *and* the linked product records in each category.

---

2. **Choose Create → Forms → Form.**

   A new tab appears, with your form in Layout view. The simple form shows one record at a time, with each field on a separate line (Figure 33-1). If your table has lots of fields, then Access creates more than one column (Figure 33-2).

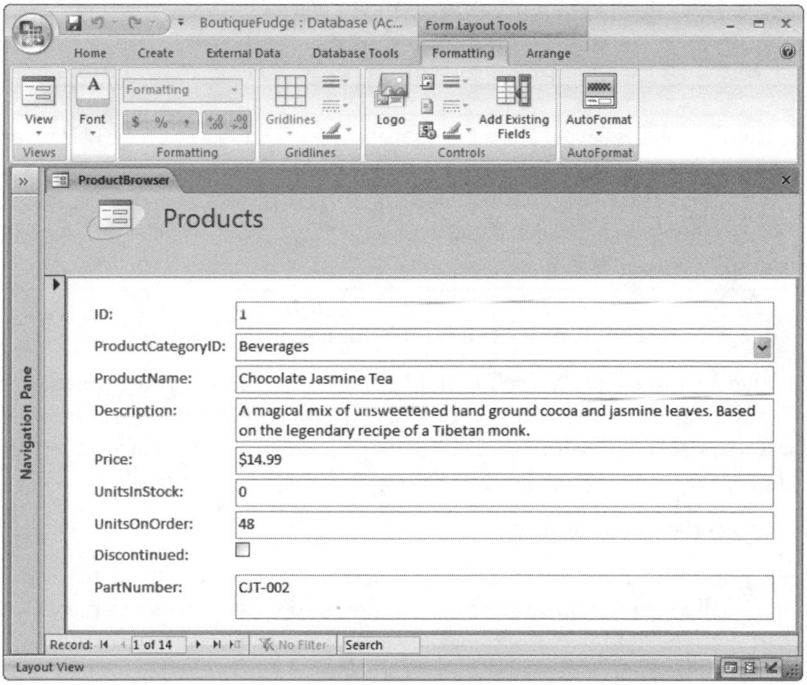

Figure 33-1:
This simple form for the Products table already shows a fair bit of intelligence. Access uses text boxes for all the text fields, a drop-down list box for fields that have a lookup (in this case, ProductCategoryID), and a checkbox for any Yes/No field (like Discontinued). It also makes some boxes (like Description) larger than others, because it notices that the underlying field has a larger maximum allowable length (page 622).

Tip: Good design practices pay off when you begin building forms. If your text fields store a far greater number of characters than they need (as controlled by the Field Size property described on page 622), then your form winds up with huge text boxes that waste valuable space. You need to resize them by hand.

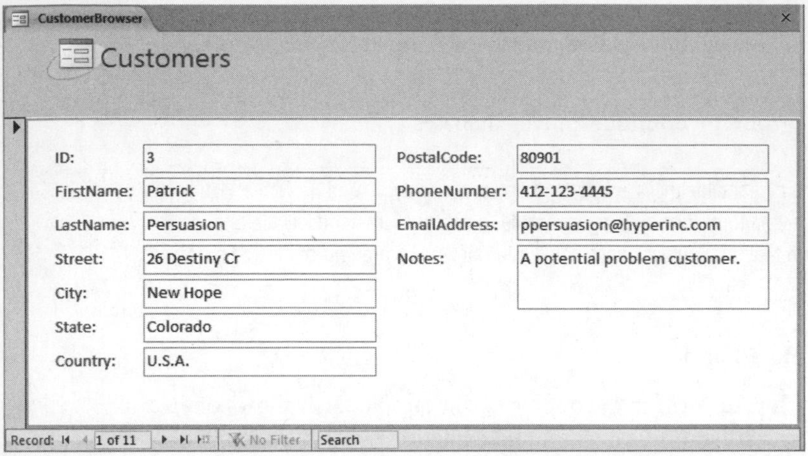

Figure 33-2:
In this form for the Customers table, Access can't fit all the fields using the ordinary one-field-per-line arrangement. Instead, it adds a second column.

When you first create a form, Access arranges the fields from top to bottom in the same order in which they're defined in the table. It doesn't make any difference if you've rearranged the columns in the datasheet. However, Access leaves any columns you've hidden in the datasheet (page 651) out of the form.

Tip: You can add or remove fields in a form in the same way you do with a report. If the Field List pane isn't open, then choose Form Layout Tools | Formatting → Controls → Add Existing Fields. Then, drag the field you want from the Field List pane onto the form. To remove a field, click to select it on the form, and then press Delete. However, keep in mind that people often use forms to add records, and if you want to preserve that ability, you need to make sure your form includes all the required fields for the table.

---

3. **Arrange the fields in the order you want by dragging them around.**

   Although a simple form doesn't look like the simple reports you learned about in Chapter 32, you can actually work with it in much the same way. One of the easiest ways to tailor your form is to drag fields from one place to another (Figure 33-3).

4. **Change your columns' widths.**

   When you create a new form in Layout view, Access makes all the fields quite wide. Usually, you'll want to shrink them down to make your form more compact. It's also hard to read long lines of text, so you can show large amounts of information better in a narrower, taller text box.

   To do so, just click to select the appropriate field; a yellow rectangle appears around it. Then, drag one of the edges. Figure 33-4 shows this process in action.

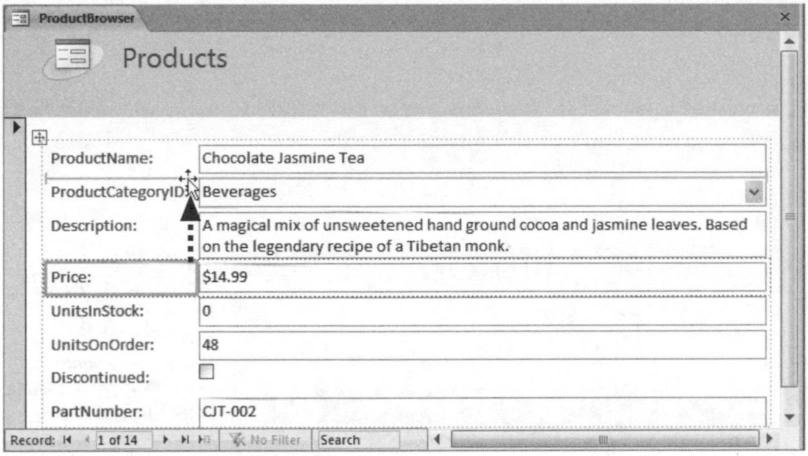

Figure 33-3:
To move a field, drag it to a new position. Access reshuffles all the other fields accordingly. In this example, the Price field's being relocated to the top of the form, just under the ProductName field. Access bumps all the other fields down the page to make room.

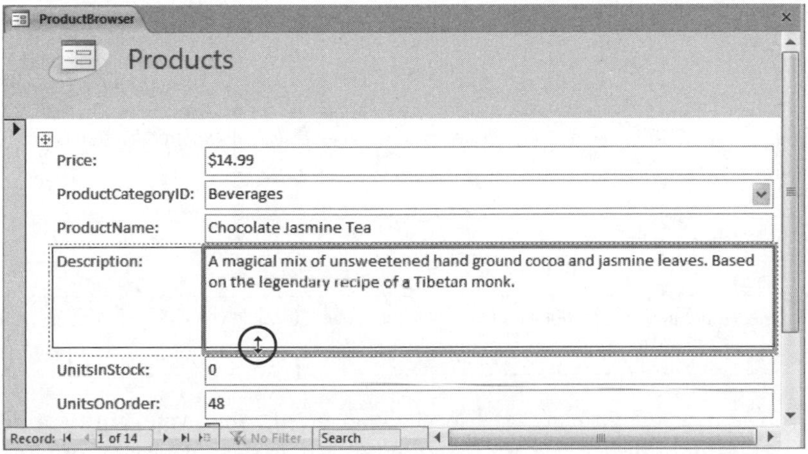

Figure 33-4:
Here, the Description field is being heightened to fit more lines of text at a time. You can also make a field wider or narrower, but there's a catch—when you do so, it affects the entire column. In this report for the Products table, every field always has the same width.

Note: You may like to make a number of changes that you can't accomplish just by dragging, such as adding a new column or giving each field a different width. To make changes like these, you need to understand layouts, which are covered in *Access 2007: The Missing Manual*.

5. **Optionally, you can click a field header to edit its text.**

   This option lets you change ProductCategoryID to just Category.

6. **Optionally, you can tweak the formatting to make the form more attractive, by changing fonts and colors.**

   You can most quickly change the formatting of your form by selecting the appropriate part (by clicking), and then using the buttons in the ribbon's Form Layout Tools | Formatting → Font section. You can also use the Form Layout

Tools | Formatting → Formatting section to adjust the way Access shows numeric values. You learned about all your formatting options on page 750 when you built basic reports.

Often, you'll want to format specific fields differently to make important information stand out. You can also format the title, header section, and form background. Figure 33-5 shows an example of judicious field formatting.

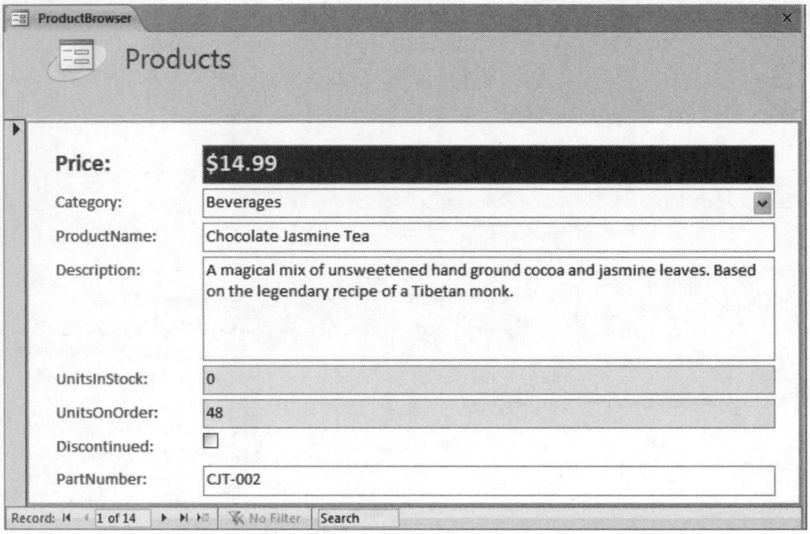

Figure 33-5:
You can select the field header (Price, for example) and the box with the field value separately, which means you can give these components different formatting. This form gives a shaded background fill to the Price, UnitsInStock, and UnitsOnOrder fields. It also gives a larger font size to the Price field and Price header, so this information stands out.

Tip: To select more than one part of a form at once, hold down Ctrl while you click. This trick allows you to apply the same formatting to several places at once.

If you're in a hurry (or just stylistically challenged), then you can use a nifty Access feature called AutoFormat to apply a whole slew of related formatting changes. Just make a choice from the Form Layout Tools | Formatting → Auto-Format section (which has the same AutoFormat choices you used with reports on page 748).

7. **Save your form.**

You can save your form at any time by choosing Office button → Save. Or, if you close the form without saving it, Access prompts you to save it at that time.

Using a Form

Now that you've created your first form, it's time to take it for a test spin. All forms have three different viewing modes:

- **Layout view.** This is the view you've been using so far. It lets you see what your form looks like (with live data), rearrange fields, and apply formatting.

AutoNumber Fields in Forms

The best way to uniquely identify each record is with an AutoNumber field (page 636). When you insert a record, Access fills in a value for the AutoNumber field. All the tables you'll see in this book include a field named ID that uses the AutoNumber data type.

Only Access can set an AutoNumber field. For that reason, you may not want to show it in your forms. (If you decide not to show it, just select it in Layout view and then press Delete.) However, there are some reasons that you might actually want to keep the AutoNumber field on display:

- **You use the AutoNumber field on some type of paperwork.** Cacophoné Studios puts each student's ID number on their registration papers. When

you need to look up the student record later on, it's easier to use the ID number than search by name.

- **You use the AutoNumber field as a tracking value or confirmation number.** After you enter a new order record in the Boutique Fudge database, you can record the order record's ID number. The next time you have a question about the order (has it shipped?), you can use the ID number to look it up.

Depending on how you use the ID number, you may choose to place it at the bottom of the form rather than in its usual position at the top. That approach avoids confusion. (It's less likely that people will try to type in their own ID numbers when they create new records.)

- **Design view.** While Layout view provides the simplest way to refine your form, Design view gives you complete power to fine-tune it. In Design view, you don't see the live data. Instead, you see a blueprint that tells Access how to construct your form.

- **Form view.** Both Layout view and Design view are there to help you create and refine your form. But once you've perfected it, it's time to stop designing your form and start *using* it to browse your table, review the information it contains, make changes, and add new records.

Note: When you open a form by double-clicking it in the navigation pane, it opens in Form view. If you don't want this view, then right-click your form in the navigation pane, and then choose Layout View or Design View to start out in a different view.

To try out the form you created, switch it to Form view if you're not already there. Just right-click the tab title, and choose Form View.

In Form view, you can perform all the same tasks you performed in the datasheet when you worked with a table. With a simple form, the key difference is that you see only one record at a time.

Most people find forms much more intuitive than the datasheet grid. The following sections give a quick overview of how you can use Form view to perform some common tasks.

Finding and editing a record

Rare is the record that never changes. Depending on the type of data you're storing, most of your work in Form view may consist of hunting down a specific record and making modifications. You may need to ratchet up the price of a product, change the address details of an itinerant customer, or reschedule a class.

Before you can make any of these changes, you need to find the right record. In Form view, you have four ways to get to the record you need. The first three of these methods use the navigation controls that appear at the bottom of the form window.

- **By navigating.** If your table's relatively small, then the fastest way to get going is to click the arrow buttons to move from one record to the next. Page 653 has a button-by-button breakdown.

- **By position.** If you know exactly where your record is, then you can type in the number that represents the position (for example, 100 for the one-hundredth record), and then hit Enter. If you don't get exactly where you want, then you can also use the navigation buttons to move to a nearby record.

- **By searching.** The quick search feature finds a record with a specific piece of text (or numeric value) in one of its fields. To use quick search, type the text you want to find in the search box, as shown in Figure 33-6. If you want a search that examines a specific field or gives you additional options, then use the Home → Find → Find command.

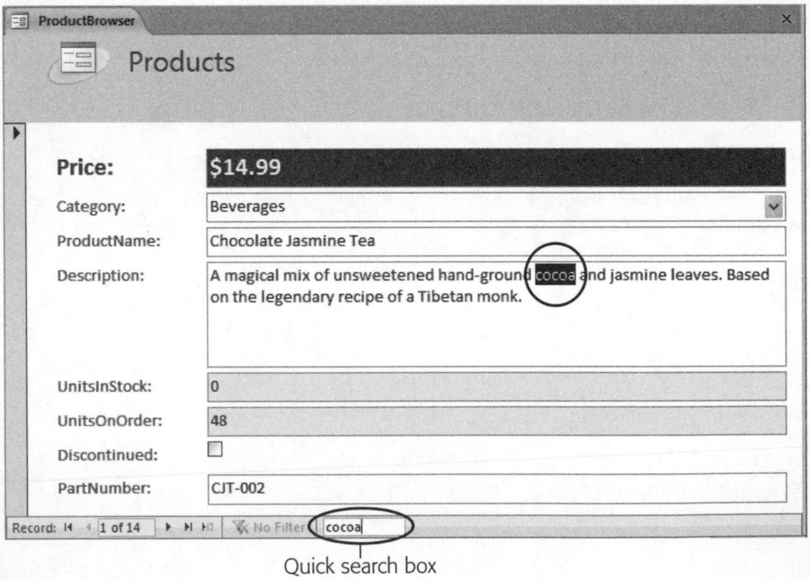

Figure 33-6:
When you use the quick search box, you don't need to hit Enter. Access finds the next match as you type.

Quick search box

- **By filtering.** Using filtering, you can narrow down the displayed records to a small set. Filtering's best-kept secret's that you can use a feature called *filter by form* to quickly hunt down a single record. You'll see how that works on page 769.

Once you've found the record you want to change, you can edit it in the same way you would in the datasheet. If you make a change that breaks a rule (like typing the text "*Exasperated Bananas*" in a date field), then you get the same familiar error messages.

Access commits any change you make as soon as you move to another record or field. To back out of a change, hit Esc before you move on. When you do, the original value reappears in the cell, and Access tosses out your changes. And if you do commit a change by accident, then you can use the Undo button in the Quick Access toolbar (above the ribbon), or hit Ctrl+Z, to reverse it.

Adding a record

As you already know, you add a new record in datasheet view by scrolling to the very bottom of the table, and typing just underneath the last row. In Form view, the concept's similar—scroll to the very end of your table, just past the last record.

You'll know you've reached the magic ready-to-add-a-record spot when all the fields in your form are blank (Figure 33-7). To save yourself the scrolling trip, use the New Record button at the bottom of the form (marked in Figure 33-7).

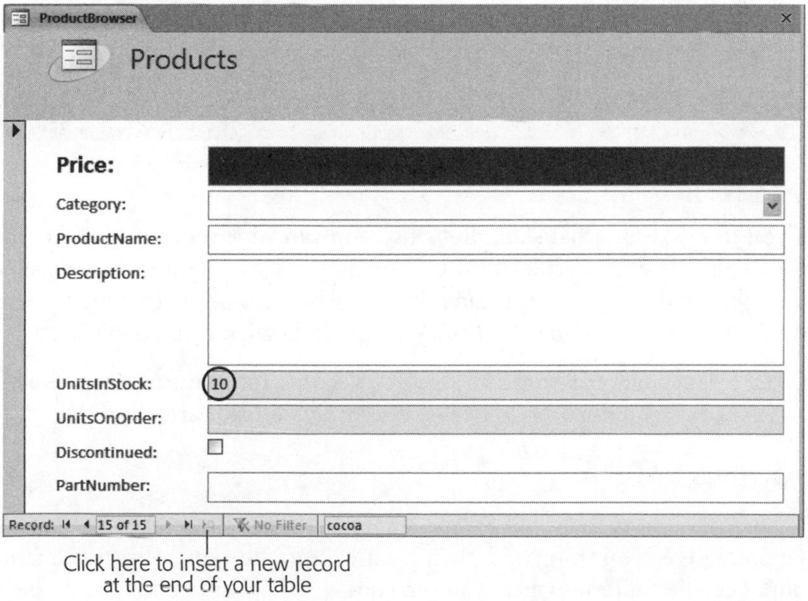

Figure 33-7:
When you create a new record, you start off with a clean slate that shows your form's formatting but no values. If you've set any default values for the table (page 670), then you see them appear instead of the blank values. In the Products table, the UnitsInStock field has a default value of 10.

Click here to insert a new record at the end of your table

If you've decided that you don't want to add a new record after all, then hit Esc twice. The first time you press Esc, Access wipes out the value in the current field. The second time, Access removes all the other values you entered. Now that your form's been restored to its original emptiness, you can safely scroll off to another record.

If you scroll away from your new record while there's still some data left in it, then Access creates the new record and adds it to the table. You can't reverse this action. If you want to get rid of a newly created record, then you need to delete it, as described in the next section.

GEM IN THE ROUGH

Showing Pictures from a Database

As you learned in Chapter 27, you can store a picture file as part of a record using the Attachment data type. Forms handle attachments gracefully using the *Attachment control*. The Attachment control has one truly useful perk—it shows picture content directly on your form.

Here's how it works. If your attachment field stores a picture, then that picture appears in the Attachment control box so you can admire it right on your form. This behavior's a great improvement over the datasheet, which forces you to open the picture file in another program to check it out. Even better, if the attachment field stores more than one picture, then you can use the arrows on the handy pop-up mini-toolbar to move from one image to the next, as shown in Figure 33-8.

As you know, attachment fields can store any type of file. If you're *not* storing a picture, then the Attachment control isn't nearly as useful. All you see's an icon for the program that owns that file type. If your attachment field contains a Word document, then you see a Word icon. If it contains a text document, then you see a Notepad icon, and so on. If your attachment fields don't include pictures, you may as well resize the box for the Attachment control so that it's just large enough to display the file type icon. There's no reason to make it any bigger, because the rest of the space will be wasted.

Deleting a record

When you find a record that shouldn't exist, you can wipe it out in seconds. The easiest way to delete the current record is to choose Home → Records → Delete. But you have another option. You can select the whole record by clicking the margin on the form window's left side. Then you can liquidate it by pressing Delete.

No matter what approach you use, Access asks you for confirmation before it removes a record. You can't recover deleted records, so tread carefully.

Printing records

Here's a little-known secret about forms: You can use them to create a quick printout. To do so, open your form, and then choose Office button → Print. The familiar Print dialog box appears, where you can choose your printer and the number of copies you want.

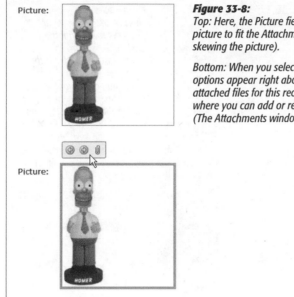

Figure 33-8:
Top: Here, the Picture field shows a bobblehead doll's picture. Access sizes the picture to fit the Attachment control box (without unnaturally stretching or skewing the picture).

Bottom: When you select the Picture field, you see a mini-toolbar with additional options appear right above the image. The arrows let you step through all the attached files for this record. The paper clip icon opens the Attachments window, where you can add or remove attachments, or open them in a different program. (The Attachments window is described on page 633.)

When you print a form, Access prints *all* the records, one after the other. If you want to print just the current record, then, in the Print dialog box, choose the Selected Records option before you click OK.

You can also use Office button → Print → Print Preview to check out the result before you send it to the printer (Figure 33-9). Click Print Preview → Close Preview → Close Print Preview to return to your form.

Although you might be tempted to use forms as a convenient way to create snazzy printouts, you'll always get more features and better control if you use reports.

Sorting and Filtering in a Form

Sorting and filtering are two indispensable features that Access gives you with Form view. Learning how to use them could hardly be easier—in fact, you already learned everything you need to know when you tackled the datasheet in Chapter 28. The creators of Access took great care to ensure that filtering and sorting work the same in forms as they do in the datasheet. You use the same commands, on the same part of the ribbon, to put them into action.

Sorting a Form

As you've probably realized by now, forms show your data in raw, unsorted order. So records appear in the order you created them. (The only exception is if you create a form that gets its data from a query, and that query uses sorting.)

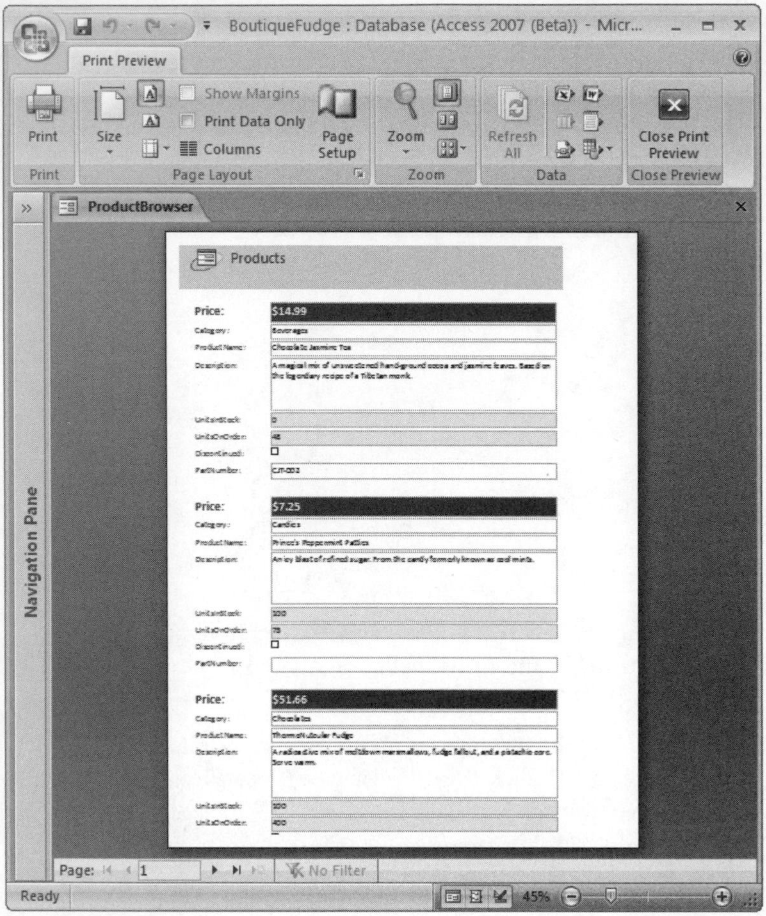

Figure 33-9:
This preview shows what you'll get if you print the CustomerList form. The printout closely matches the form, with the same formatting and layout. When Access first creates the form, it gives it the same width as an ordinary sheet of paper. When you print the form, Access crams as many records—three in this case—as it can fit on each page.

Fortunately, sorting's easy. In fact, you can sort the records that are shown in a form in exactly the same way you sort records in a datasheet. Choose the field you want to use for sorting, right-click it, and then choose one of the sorting options. In a text-based field, you'll see the sorting choices "Sort A to Z" (for an alphabetical sort) and "Sort Z to A" (for a reverse-alphabetical sort). You can also use the Ascending and Descending buttons on the ribbon's Home → Sort & Filter section.

For more information about your sorting options (including how to sort by multiple fields), see page 654.

Filtering a Form

Filtering's a feature that lets you cut down the total number of records so you see only those that interest you. Filtering can pick out active customers, in-stock products, expensive orders, and other groups of records based on specific criteria.

In a form, you have the following filtering choices:

- **Quick filter** shows you a list of all the values for a particular field and lets you choose which ones you want to hide. It's easy to use, but potentially time-consuming. If you want to hide numeric values that fall into a certain range, then you'll get the job done much faster with the "filter by condition" approach (as described later). To show the list of quick filter values, move to the field you want to filter, and then click Home → Sort & Filter → Filter. Page 657 has full details about quick filters.

- **Filter by selection** applies a filter based on an existing value. First, find the value in one of the records, right-click it, and then choose a filter option. You can right-click a price value of $25, and then choose "Greater Than or Equal to 25" to hide low-cost items. For more information, see page 658.

- **Filter by condition** lets you define the exact criteria you want to use to filter records. You don't need to base it on an existing value. To add this sort of filter, right-click the field and then look for a submenu with filtering options. This menu item's named according to the data, so text fields include a Text Filters option, number fields have a Number Filters option, and so on. You can learn more about this type of filter on page 659.

- **Advanced filters** are filters that you design using a window that looks just like the query designer. The advantage of advanced filters is that you can apply filters on more than one field in a single step. To create a set of advanced filters, choose Home → Sort & Filter → Advanced Filter Options → Advanced Filter/ Sort.

Note: If you insert a new record that doesn't match the currently active filter conditions, your new record disappears from sight as soon as you add it. To get it back, remove the filter settings using the ribbon: Select the Home tab, click the Advanced button in the Sort & Filter chunk, and then choose Clear All Filters. Or, use the Toggle Filter button to temporarily suspend your filter settings (and click Toggle Filter later to get them back).

Using the Filter by Form Feature

One other filtering technique works with forms: *filter by form*. Essentially, "filter by form" transforms your form into a full-fledged search form. Using this search form, you supply one or more criteria. Then you apply the filter to see the matching record (or records).

Although you can use "filter by form" with the datasheet, it really shines with forms. "Filter by forms" is particularly useful for searching out a single hard-to-find record. (If you want to use filtering to pull out a whole group of records, one of the other filtering options is generally easier.)

Here's how to use the "filter by form" feature:

1. **Choose Home → Sort & Filter → Advanced Filter Options → Filter By Form.**

   Access changes your form to search mode. In search mode, your form looks exactly the same, except all the fields are blank.

   If you've already used the "filter by form" feature and you're returning to change the filter settings, then you should start by clearing the previous set of filters. To do so, right-click a blank spot on the form surface, and then choose Clear Grid.

2. **Move to the field you want to use for filtering.**

   A drop-down arrow appears in the field.

3. **Click the drop-down arrow, and then choose the value you want to *include* in your results.**

   The drop-down list shows all the values from the different records in the table (Figure 33-10). When you choose one, it appears in the field box in quotation marks.

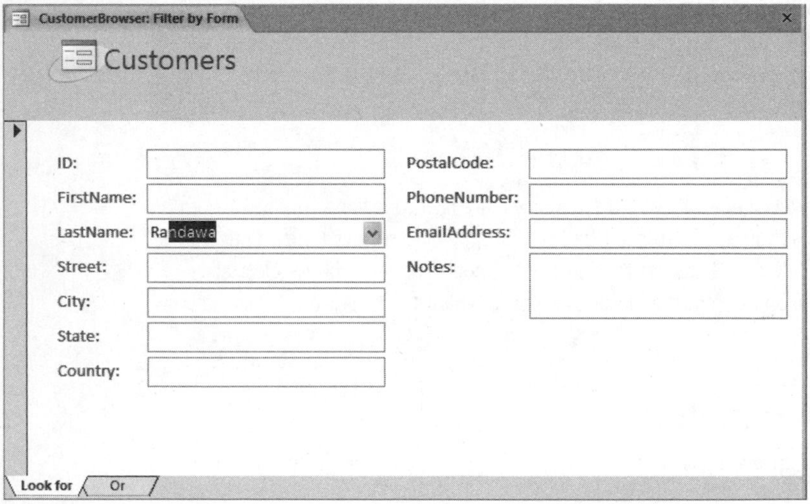

Figure 33-10:
Here's the Customers form in "filter-by-form" mode. Using the drop-down list, you can quickly find a customer by last name. Or you can find a name by typing the first few letters rather than scrolling through the list, as shown here. In this example, typing "Ra" brings up the first alphabetical match: the last name Randawa.

4. **If you want to apply a filter to more than one field, then return to step 2.**

   Use multiple filter conditions if a single filter condition may result in more matches than you want. If you don't remember a customer's last name, you could apply a FirstName filter. But if that customer has a common first name, then you may also want to apply a filter on another field, like City.

If you don't want to use exact matches, then you can write in more complex filters using an expression. Use *<10* to find numeric values under 10, and *Like Jon** to find text values like "Jones," "Jonathon," and "Jonson." This trick's particularly useful with date fields. Page 723 has the full scoop on filtering expressions.

5. **If you want to perform more than one filtering operation and *combine* the results, then click the Or tab and fill out more filter settings (Figure 33-11).**

   If you fill out your first search form so that it matches the LastName "Gorfinkel," and the second search form to match the FirstName "Jehosophat," your results will include all the records that have the last name Gorfinkel *and* all those that have the first name Jehosophat. However, if you put both those filter conditions on the same search form, your matches include only people named Jehosophat Gorfinkel.

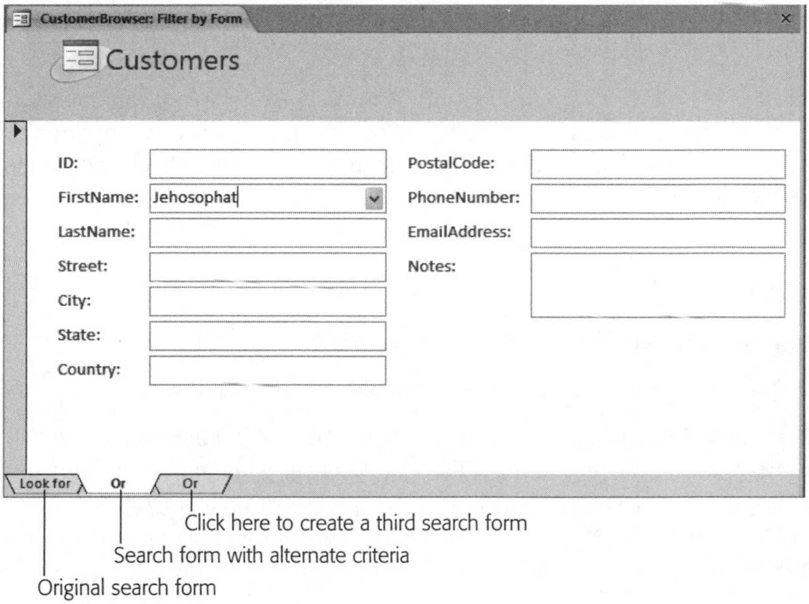

Figure 33-11:
The Or tab appears at the bottom of the form. When you click the Or tab, a second copy of your search form appears, where you can fill out additional filter conditions. Each time you click the Or tab, another Or tab appears. You can repeat this process to fill in a dozen search forms at once, but there's rarely any reason to go to such lengths.

Click here to create a third search form
Search form with alternate criteria
Original search form

6. **Right-click a blank spot on the form surface, and then choose Apply Filter/ Sort.**

   Access switches back to your normal form, and then applies the filter settings. At the bottom of the form, between the navigation buttons and the search box, you see the word "Filtered" appear to let you know that you aren't seeing all the records.

   If you decide not to apply the filter settings, just close the search form. Access switches back to your normal form but doesn't apply any filtering.

Tip: To remove your filter settings but keep them handy for later use, choose Home → Sort & Filter → Toggle Filter. To reapply the filter settings later on, click Toggle Filter a second time. Access stores the most recent filter settings with your form, so they're always available.

Saving Filters for the Future

One of form filtering's limitations is that Access remembers only your most recent set of filters. If you've perfected a complex filter expression that you want to reuse later, this quality's a problem. As soon as you apply a different filter, you'll lose all your hard work.

Fortunately, you have several solutions to this dilemma. One option's to create a whole new query that performs the filtering, and use that query in a whole new form. This choice is a good one if you want to use your filter criteria to perform a specific task, and you also want to customize the way the form works or the way it displays its data.

On the other hand, if you don't plan to use your filtering settings very often, but you just want to have them on hand for the next time you need them (or if you need to store dozens of different filter settings, and you don't want to be stuck with dozens of nearly identical forms), there's a better option. You can save your filter settings as a query in your database. Then, when you want them back, you can load them up and apply them to your form.

Here's how to pull this trick off:

1. **Apply your filters.**

   Use any of the techniques described on page 767.

2. **Choose Home → Sort & Filter → Advanced → Advanced Filter/Sort.**

   This action opens a query window. This query uses the same data source (table or query) as your form, and it applies your filtering using the Criteria box under the appropriate field (page 720). You don't need to make any changes in the query window because Access automatically fills in the Criteria box (or boxes) based on the current filter settings.

3. **Choose Home → Sort & Filter → Advanced → Save as Query. Supply a name for this query, and then click OK.**

   Although you can use this query like a normal query, you probably won't. So to prevent confusion, use a different type of name, like CustomerBrowser_Filter, that clearly indicates this query's designed for form filtering.

The next time you want to retrieve your filter settings and reapply them, open your form and follow these steps:

1. **Choose Home → Sort & Filter → Advanced → Advanced Filter/Sort.**

   This action shows the query window.

---

2. **Choose Home → Sort & Filter → Advanced → Load From Query.**

   Access shows all the queries that use the same table and don't involve joins (you can learn about joins in *Access 2007: The Missing Manual*).

3. **Pick the filter query you created earlier, and then click OK.**

   The filter settings for that query appear in the query window.

4. **Right-click anywhere on the blank space in the query window, and then choose Apply Filter/Sort to put your filter settings into effect.**

Tip: You can use this trick to apply the same filter expression to *different* forms, as long as these forms include the fields you want to filter. (You can use the filter settings that you created for the Customer-Browser form to filter another form that shows a list of customers, but not a form that shows products.)

The Access Form Family

Access forms manage to please just about everyone. If you're in a hurry, then you can create a ready-made form with a basic layout and a dash of formatting. Or, if you're feeling creative, you can pull your fields out of the standard layouts and place them absolutely anywhere. In other words, forms are flexible—time-pressed types get the convenience they need, while serious artists get the creative control they demand.

Here's a roundup of some of your form choices:

- **A simple form** shows one record at a time in a basic stacked layout. To create a simple form, choose Create → Forms → Form.

- **A layout-less form** lets you place controls anywhere you want on a form. It's up to you whether you want to show a single record at once, or several records at a time. When creating a layout-less form, you need to do all the work. You can get started by choosing Create → Forms → Form Design (to start in Design view) or Create → Forms → Blank Form (which starts you in Layout view).

- **A tabular form** shows records in a tabular layout. Usually, tabular forms show several records at once

(which gives the appearance of a table). To quickly create one of these babies, choose Create → Forms → Multiple Items.

- **A datasheet form** looks exactly like the Datasheet view you get with a table. This form's not as powerful as other form types, but it's still useful if you want a customized datasheet-like view of your data. You can create a datasheet form that shows fewer columns, uses filtering to hide certain records, prevents record insertions, uses different formatting, and so on. To create a datasheet form, choose Create → Forms → More Forms → Datasheet.

- **A split form** combines two types of form in one window. One portion of the window shows the current record in a simple form. The other portion of the window shows a datasheet with several records. To create a split form, choose Create → Forms → Split Form.

The advanced form types, pivot table and modal dialog, are covered in depth in *Access 2007: The Missing Manual*.

The Form Wizard

By now, you've learned how to create a number of common forms. Access gives you one other way to build a form: using the *Form wizard*. The Form wizard has an uncanny similarity to the report wizard you used in Chapter 32. It asks you a series of questions and then builds a form to match. However, the questions are fairly rudimentary, and the form it builds is little more than a good starting point for further customization.

Here's how to put the Form wizard through its paces:

1. **Choose Create → Forms → More Forms → Form Wizard.**

   The first step of the Form wizard appears.

2. **From the drop-down list, choose the table you want to use.**

   In the Available Fields list, the wizard shows all the fields that are in your table.

3. **Add the fields you want to include, as shown in Figure 33-12. When you're finished, click Next.**

   You can choose fields from more than one table, provided these tables are related.

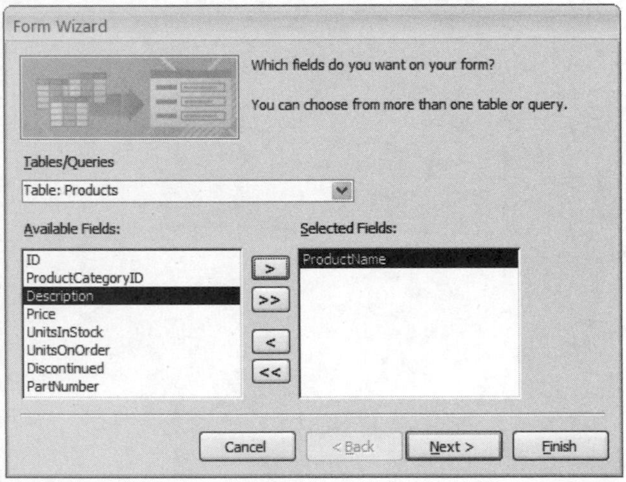

Figure 33-12:
To add a field, select it, and then click the > button to move it from the Available Fields list to the Selected Fields list. To add all the fields, click >>.

4. **Choose a layout option for your form.**

   Your layout options include:

   • **Columnar** creates a form with a stacked layout. It's similar to clicking Create → Forms → Form in the ribbon.

   • **Tabular** creates a form with a tabular layout. It's similar to clicking Create → Forms → Multiple Items in the ribbon.

- **Datasheet** creates a datasheet form. It's similar to selecting Create → Forms → More Forms → Datasheet in the ribbon.

- **Justified** creates a form that doesn't use any set layout. Instead, it packs controls closely together, combining several fields on a single line if they're small enough to fit. A justified form's the only kind of form you can't create directly from the ribbon using another command.

Note: Justified forms are difficult to modify later on. For example, if you need to add a field into the middle of a layout form, you're stuck with the painstaking task of moving many more fields out of the way to new positions. Often it's easier to recreate the form from scratch using the wizard.

---

5. **Choose one of the preset styles, and then click Next.**

   The styles determine the formatting that Access applies to your form. Unfortunately, it's difficult to get a feeling for what the final result will look like unless you actually try each option.

6. **Enter a name for your form.**

   When the Form wizard finishes, it immediately saves your form using this name.

7. **Choose "Open the form to view or edit information" if you want to start using your form to work with data, or "Modify the form's design" if you want to adjust it in Design view first. Then, click Finish.**

   Access saves your form and opens it in Form view or Design view, depending on your choice.

CHAPTER 34

Importing and Exporting Data

An Access database is like a carefully built fort. It takes strictly organized and error-tested information, and locks it up tight. Very few programs guard their data as protectively as database software does. Word processors and spreadsheet programs accept just about any content and let you build your document structure on the fly. Databases aren't nearly as freewheeling.

Most of the time, databases live in an independent world. But every once in a while, you need to bridge the gap in one of two ways:

- You want to take the information from another program and *import* it—basically, stuff it into your database.

- You want to take some of the information in an Access database and *export* it, so you can work with it in another program.

Access has several different options for transferring information. You can use the lowly clipboard, or sophisticated import and export features. In this chapter, you'll learn about all your options.

Note: The ever-popular XML standard is yet another option for importing and exporting, which is great for Access power users. You can learn more about Access and XML in *Access 2007: The Missing Manual*.

The Case for Importing and Exporting

If you haven't thought much about importing and exporting, it's probably because you don't need to use these features—yet. Many databases are completely happy living a quiet, solitary life. However, importing and exporting might come in handy for a few reasons. Sooner or later, one of these reasons will apply to you.

Understanding Exports

Exporting is the easier part of the equation. Exporting's simpler than importing, because it involves moving information from a stricter storage location (the database) to one with fewer rules (another type of document).

Note: Exporting is a way to transfer a copy of your information to another location. The original copy always remains in Access. There's no point in changing the exported copy. Instead, if you need changes, make them in the database, and then perform the export operation again.

Here are some of the most common reasons people decide to export information:

- **You want to email some information to a friend.** You don't want to send the Access database because your friend doesn't have a copy Access, or you want him to see only some—not all—of the data.

- **You're creating a presentation in PowerPoint.** The easiest way to dazzle and convince your peers is to show them some impressive information from your database.

- **You want to analyze the information in Excel.** Access is great for storing and managing your data, but it doesn't give you the tools to help you figure out what it all means. If you want to crunch the numbers with heavy duty formulas and slick charting features, it makes sense to move it to Excel.

Some programs are intelligent enough to pull the information out of an Access database all on their own. One example's Word, which provides a *mail merge* feature that lets you take a list of names and addresses from a database, and then use them to create mailing labels, personalized forms, or any other sort of batch paperwork. When using this feature, you don't need to perform any exporting—instead, you can just point Word to your Access database file. (For more information about Word's mail merge feature, see *Word 2007: The Missing Manual.*)

Understanding Imports

You need importing whenever there's information outside your database that belongs inside it. Suppose you create a state-of-the-art e-commerce database for your buffalo farm. However, some of your sales associates still fill out forms using an old Excel spreadsheet. Now, you need a way to get the information out of the Excel spreadsheet and into your database.

Tip: Your sales staff has let you down. They really shouldn't enter data into a document for another program. Instead, they should use a form that's designed for logging sales, as described in Chapter 33.

Import operations have two key challenges. The first is making sure the data fits the database's strict requirements. As you learned in Chapter 26, databases are rule-crazy, and they rudely toss out any information that doesn't fit (for example, text in a date field). The second challenge is dealing with information that doesn't quite line up—in other words, its representation in the database doesn't match its representation in the external document. This headache's more common that you may think.

In your database, you might use status codes (like 4302), while the spreadsheet you want to import uses status *names* (like High Priority). Or, you may need to break the information you're importing into more than one linked table, even though it's stored together in a single document. The customer order spreadsheet for your buffalo farm could include customer information (which corresponds to the Customers table) and order information (for the Orders table). Sadly, you don't have any easy way to solve these problems. If the external data doesn't match the representation in the database *exactly*, you'll need to change it by hand before or after the import operation.

Using the Clipboard

Anyone who's spent much time using a Windows computer is familiar with the clipboard—a behind-the-scenes container that temporarily stores information so you can transfer it from one program to another. Using the clipboard, you can copy a snippet of text in a Word document, and then paste it into a field in an Access table, or vice versa. That much is easy. But you probably don't realize that you can copy an entire *table* of information.

Tip: Almost all Windows programs respect the same shortcut keys for the clipboard. Use Ctrl+C to copy information, Ctrl+X to cut it (copy and delete it), and Ctrl+V to paste it.

Before you try this trick out, you need to understand two key facts about the clipboard:

- **The clipboard can store many different types of information.** Most of the time, you're using it to copy plain text. However, depending on the program you're using, you could also copy shapes, pictures, tables, and more.

- **Some types of information can convert themselves to other types.** If you copy a selection of cells in Excel, then you can paste it as a formatted table in a word processing program like Word or WordPerfect. Of, if you copy a diagram in Visio, then you can paste it as a picture in Paint. In both examples, you copy a specialized type of object (Excel cells or a Visio diagram) to the Windows clipboard. However, this object can *downgrade* itself when it needs to. You can paste a full-fledged copy of the object in the original program without losing anything, or you can paste and convert it to something simpler in a less powerful program.

This flexibility is the secret to transferring data to and from Access. The following sections explain how it works.

Note: The clipboard approach is simpler than the import and export features in Access. As a result, it's a faster choice (with fewer steps). Of course, it also gives you fewer choices and doesn't work with all programs.

Copying a Table from Access to Somewhere Else

Access lets you copy a selection of rows or an entire table to another program, without going through the hassle of the Export wizard. Access copies these rows to the clipboard as an intelligent object that can convert itself into a variety of software-friendly formats. You can paste them as Excel cells, HTML text (the formatting language of the Web), or RichText (a formatting standard created by Microsoft and supported by all major Word processors). Since HTML and Rich-Text are so widely supported, you'll almost never have a problem copying your rows into another program when you use this technique.

Here's how to try it out:

1. **If you want to copy an entire table, then, in the navigation pane, select the table. If you want to copy only a few rows, then select them in the Datasheet view, as shown in Figure 34-1.**

   You're not limited to copying tables. You can also copy a query's results. Just select the query in the navigation pane. You can't copy reports or forms, however.

   When you copy rows or an entire table, Access takes your column hiding settings (page 651) into account. If you've hidden a column so it doesn't appear in the datasheet (by selecting it, and then choosing Home → Records → More → Hide Columns), Access doesn't copy it to the clipboard. This technique helps you leave out information you don't want to copy.

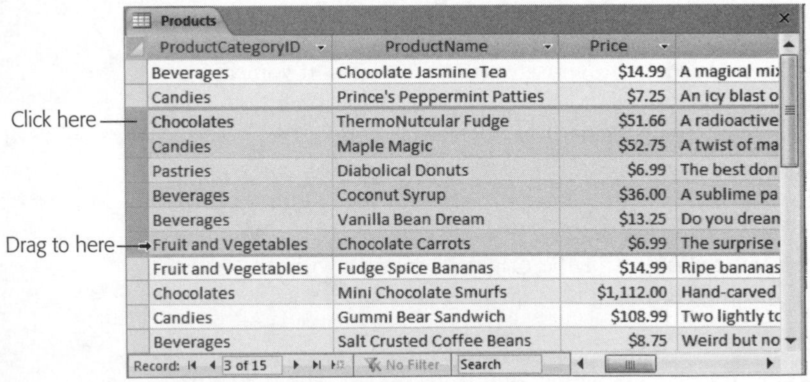

Figure 34-1:
When selecting rows in the datasheet, click the gray margin just to the left of the first row you want to select. Then, drag down to select as many rows as you want. If you don't want to take your hand off the mouse, then you can copy these rows by holding down the Ctrl key, and right-clicking one of them. Then, from the pop-up menu, choose Copy.

Note: You can copy only a contiguous selection of rows, which is a fancy way of saying you can copy only rows that are right next to each other. If you have 10 rows in a table, then you can copy rows three to six, but you can't copy just the first and last rows. (Of course, you can use several smaller copy operations to get the stragglers.)

2. **Hit Ctrl+C to copy your selection.**

   This action places the records on the Windows clipboard. You can now paste it inside Access or in another program.

3. **Switch to the program where you want to paste your information.**

   If you're just trying this feature out for the first time, then take a whirl with Excel or Word (shown in Figure 34-2).

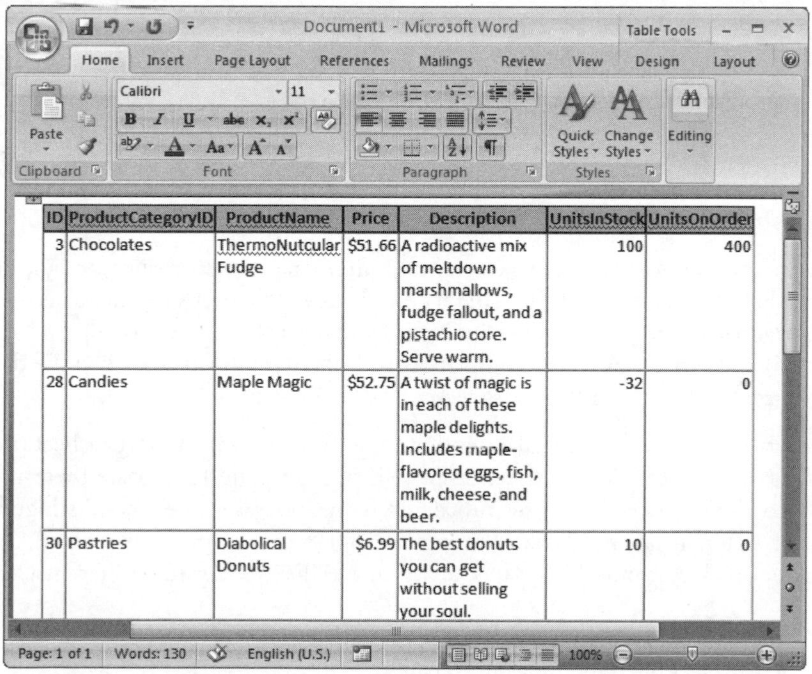

Figure 34-2:
Using cut and paste, you can transform a database table into a table in a Word document (shown here). Once you've pasted the content, you may need to fiddle with column widths to make sure it all looks right.

4. **Hit Ctrl+V to paste your selection (see Figure 34-2).**

   Access pastes the rows from your selection, complete with column headers. If you've applied formatting to the datasheet (page 648), then most of that formatting comes along.

   Depending on the program where you paste your records, you might see a smart tag icon appear at your newly pasted content's righthand corner. In Office applications, you can use this smart tag to change options about how the data's pasted (for example, with or without formatting).

Note: Copying text, numbers, and dates is easy. However, some data types don't make the transition as well. If you copy an attachment field, then the pasted content shows the number of attachment fields, but the files themselves are left out.

Copying from One Database to Another

You can also use the copying trick described on page 779 to copy data from one Access database to another Access database that's open in a separate window. However, it works only if you're copying a complete table (or other object), not a selection of rows.

To try it out, right-click the object you want in the navigation pane, and then choose Copy. Then, switch to the second Access database, right-click in the empty space in the navigation pane, and then choose Paste. Access asks you what you want to name the pasted table, and gives you three pasting options:

- **Structure** creates the table structure, but leaves it empty.

- **Structure and Data** creates an exact duplicate of the table, with all the data.

- **Append Data to Existing Table** doesn't create a new table—instead, it adds the data to the table that you specify. For this to work, the table must have the same structure as the one you've copied.

This trick also lets you create a duplicate copy of a table (or other object) in the *same* database.

Copying Cells from Excel into Access

You can copy information from Access into another program easily enough, but you probably don't expect to be able to do the reverse. After all, a database is a strict, rigorously structured collection of information. If you try to copy a table from a Word processing program, then you'll lack vital information, like the data types of each column. For that reason, Access doesn't allow it.

However, Access makes a special exception for everyone's favorite spreadsheet program, Excel. You can copy a selection of cells in Excel, and then paste them into Access to create a new table. This procedure works because Excel *does* distinguish between different types of data (although it isn't nearly as picky as Access). For example, Excel treats numbers, dates, text, and TRUE/FALSE values differently.

Here's how to use this feature:

1. **In Excel, select the cells you want to copy.**

   If your spreadsheet includes column titles, then include those headers in the selection. Access can use the titles as field names.

Note: It doesn't matter what version of Excel you have—this trick works with them all.

2. **Hit Ctrl+C to copy your selection.**

3. **Switch to Access.**

4. **Click anywhere in the navigation pane, and then press Ctrl+V.**

Access notices that you're trying to paste a group of Excel cells, and it tries to transform them into a table. First, it asks if the first row in your selection includes column titles.

5. **If you selected the column titles in step 1, then choose Yes. Otherwise, choose No.**

If you choose Yes, then Access doesn't need to create random field names—instead, it can use your headers.

Access creates a new table to deal with the new data. This table's named after the Excel sheet. If your sheet's named Sheet1 (as so many are in Excel), you now have a Sheet1 table.

Once Access finishes the paste, it shows a confirmation message to let you know everything's finished successfully.

6. **Click OK.**

Now you can refine your table to make sure the data types and field names are exactly what you want.

Import and Export Operations

Although the clipboard cut-and-paste approach is neat, it doesn't always work out. If you need to export data to a file and you don't have the corresponding program installed on your computer (or you just don't want to bother running it), then you need a different way to transfer your information. Similarly, if you're downloading data from the Web or fetching information from a program that doesn't support Windows cut-and-paste, you need the full-fledged Access import feature.

When Microsoft designed Access 2007, they spent a fair bit of time making the import and export features clearer and more straightforward. Nowadays, you can do all the importing and exporting you want from a single ribbon tab, which is named External Data (Figure 34-3).

Figure 34-3:
The External Data tab's Import section lets you pipe data into Access using a variety of formats. The Export section does the reverse—it takes your table, and exports it in a bunch of different flavors.

Note: The Import and Export sections have easy-to-access buttons for the most popular file formats. If you don't see what you want, then click the More button to see an expanded list of choices.

Whether you're importing or exporting data, the process is essentially the same. You answer a few questions about what file you want to use and how you want to make the conversion, and then Access does your bidding.

Once you finish performing an import or export operation, Access gives you the option of saving all your steps. If you do, you can reuse them later on. This method's a great way to save time if you need to perform the same export or import process again (like if you need to import some data every day, or export a summary at the end of every month).

Importable File Types

Most of the time, you'll import data that's in one of these five common formats:

- **Access.** When you use this option, you aren't performing a conversion. Instead, you're taking a database object from another Access database file, and copying it into the current database.

- **Excel.** Pulls the data from an Excel spreadsheet.

- **SharePoint List.** Pulls the data from a list that's hosted on a SharePoint server (which big companies use to help workers collaborate). You don't need to import SharePoint information in order to work with it. You can also edit SharePoint lists directly in Access. *Access 2007: The Missing Manual* has much more about getting Access and SharePoint to work together.

- **Text File.** Pulls the data out of a plain text file. Typically, plain text files use some sort of character (like a comma) to separate field values. This universally understood format's supported by many programs, including just about every piece of spreadsheet software ever written. When using this option, Access takes a look at the text file as it tries to figure out how it's organized. However, you get the chance to confirm or correct the hunch before you import any data, as described on page 789.

- **XML File.** Pulls the data out of a structured XML file. XML is a cross-platform format used to represent any type of information.

Using the More button, you'll find several other, more exotic import choices:

- **ODBC Database.** Grabs information from just about any database product, provided it has an ODBC driver. This option works particularly well if you need to get data out of a high-end server-side database like Oracle, SQL Server, or MySQL.

- **HTML Document.** Extracts information from a list or a table in an HTML Web page. Since HTML's a standard that's notoriously loose (and at times downright sloppy), you should try to avoid this option. You're likely to have importing problems.

- **Outlook Folder.** Pulls information out of a folder in Outlook or Outlook Express.

- **dBase File, Paradox File, and Lotus 1-2-3 File.** Pulls information out of a file created with one of these Paleolithic programs.

Importing Data

No matter what type of data you want to import, you'll go through the same basic steps. Here's an overview:

1. **In the ribbon's External Data → Import section, click the button that corresponds to the type of file you want to import.**

   When you choose a format, Access launches the Import wizard (Figure 34-4).

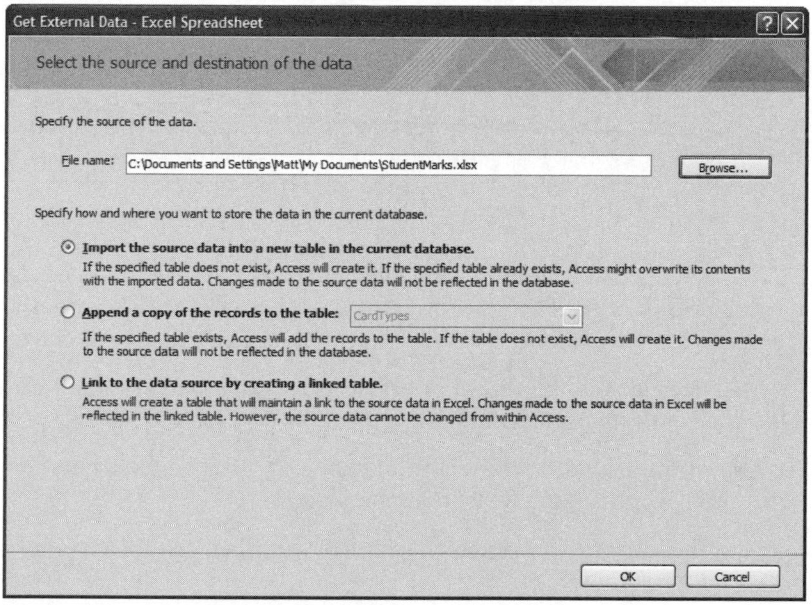

Figure 34-4:
No matter what format you choose, the Import wizard's more or less the same, although certain options may be restricted. In this first step, you choose the source file name, and the way Access inserts the information into your database.

2. **Enter the name of the file you want to import.**

   If you don't remember the file path (or you just don't want to type it in by hand), then click Browse, and then navigate to the right place in the File Open window. Once you find the file, double-click it.

3. **Choose where to place the imported content in your database.**

   You have three possible choices for placing your data. Depending on the file format you're using, all these may not be available.

   - **Create a new table.** This option creates a fresh new table for the data you're importing, which saves you the headache of worrying about conflicting records. However, if a table of the same name already exists in the Access database, then this option wipes it out.

- **Append to an existing table.** This option takes the rows you're importing and adds them to an existing table. In order for this option to work, the structure of the data you're importing must match the structure of the table you're using. For example, the field names much match exactly. However, the data you're importing can leave out fields that aren't required (page 668) or have default values (page 670).

- **Create a linked table.** If you use this approach, then Access doesn't actually transfer the information into your database. Instead, every time you view the linked table, Access checks the original file to get the most recent information. The neat thing here's that your linked table always shows the most recent information. With any other option, the imported table's left untouched if you change the original file. However, linked tables are also risky, because you don't have any guarantee that the file won't travel to another location on your hard drive (where Access can't find it).

Note: Linked tables are a good way to bridge the gap between different Access databases or other databases (like SQL Server). However, they don't work well with other more limited formats, like text files.

4. **Click OK.**

   A wizard launches that collects the remaining information that Access needs. If you're importing an Excel file, then Access asks you which worksheet to use. If you're importing a text file, then Access asks you how the fields are separated.

5. **Answer all questions in the wizard to tell Access what it needs to know about the structure of the data you're importing.**

   Once you're finished with this stage, Access asks you its final question— whether or not you want to save your import steps.

6. **If you want to perform this import again later on, then select "Save import steps". Then, click Close.**

Note: If Access finds any errors while importing your data, then it creates another table with the same name as the table you're importing to, with _ImportErrors_ tacked on the end. Access adds one record to that table for each problem. If you try to import a bunch of information into a table named SalesData, and Access can't convert the values to the data type you want (for example, there's text in a column that should only hold numbers), you get a table named SalesData_ImportErrors.

The following sections walk you through the specifics for two common data formats that need a few extra steps: Excel workbooks and text files.

Importing from an Excel File

In order to import from an Excel file, your data should be organized in a basic table. Ideally, you have column headings that match the fields in your database. You should trim out any data that you don't want to import (like other cells under the table that aren't a part of the table). You should also remove values calculated using Excel formulas. (As you learned on page 644, you shouldn't store calculated values in a table, because they introduce the risk of inconsistent data.)

Note: Earlier in this chapter, you learned how to take Excel data, and cut and paste your way to an Access table. However, when you perform a full-fledged import, you get the opportunity to change field names, fine-tune data types, and use indexing.

Once you have a cleaned-up table of data in an Excel file, you're ready to start the import process:

1. **Choose External Data → Import → Excel, choose your Excel file, and then specify how you want to add the imported information to your database. Then, click OK.**

   You learned how to make these decisions in steps 1 to 3 on page 785.

2. **Choose the worksheet that houses your data (Figure 34-5).**

   Excel files, or *workbooks*, begin with three worksheets. Most people plop their data on the first one, which is initially named Sheet1. If you're an Excel expert, then you might have designated a section of a more complex worksheet as a *named range*. If so, you can pick that named range from the list.

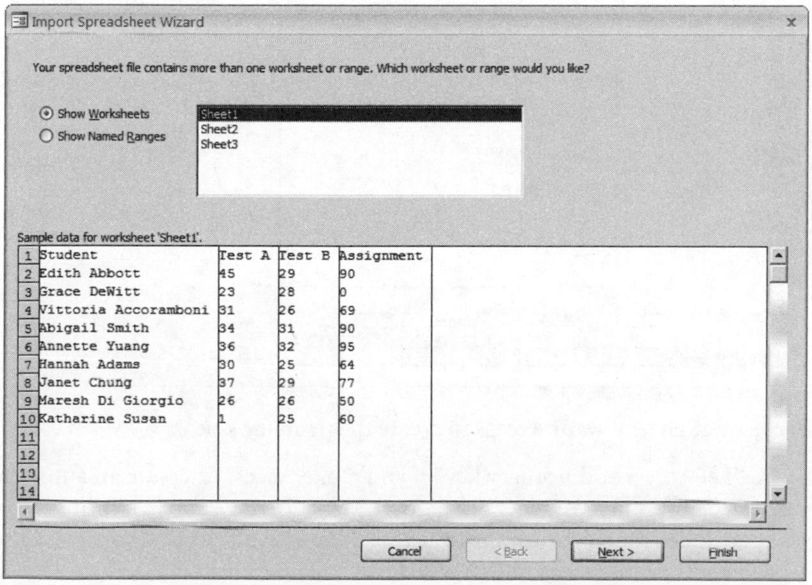

Figure 34-5:
This Excel workbook file has the standard three worksheets: Sheet1, Sheet2, and Sheet3. When you make a selection, you see a preview of the data.

3. Click Next.

4. **If your Excel data has a row with column headings, then choose First Row Contains Column Headings.**

   These headings become the starting point for your field names. If you don't choose First Row Contains Column Headings, then Excel treats the first row as an ordinary record.

5. **Click Next.**

   If you're creating a new table for your imported records, then Access asks you to configure the fields you're creating. If you're appending the records to an existing table, then skip ahead to step 7.

6. **For each field, you can choose a field name, the data type, and whether or not the field should be indexed (page 671). Then, click Next.**

   Access makes some intelligent guesses based on the data that's there, but it's up to you to fine-tune the details. For example, if you have a column with whole numbers, you may want to change the data type from Double (which supports fractional numbers) to Integer, as shown in Figure 34-6.

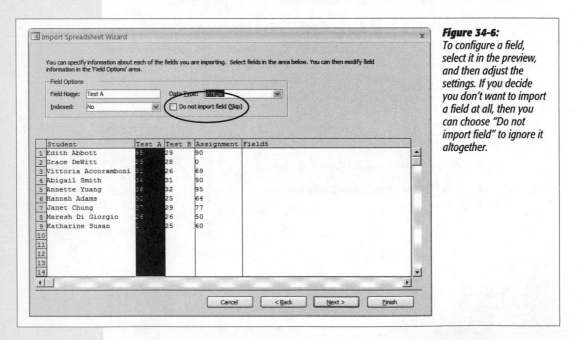

Figure 34-6:
To configure a field, select it in the preview, and then adjust the settings. If you decide you don't want to import a field at all, then you can choose "Do not import field" to ignore it altogether.

7. **Choose whether you want Access to create the primary key.**

   Choose "Let Access add primary key" if you'd like Access to create an autonumbered ID field (which is generally a good idea). If the data you're importing already includes a field you want to use as a key, then select "Choose my own primary key", and then pick the right field.

8. In the Import to Table text box, type the name of the table you want to create or add your records to.

9. Click Finish to finalize your choices.

Once the import's complete, you can choose whether or not to save your import steps for reuse.

You'll find some potential stumbling blocks when importing data from Excel. Blank values and fields, the commonest problems, occur when the Import wizard assumes there's data in a part of your worksheet that doesn't contain any information. (This could happen if there's a cell with just a space somewhere on your worksheet, or even if you have a cell that used to contain data but has since been deleted.) After you perform your import, you may need to clean up your table to fix problems like these by deleting empty fields and records.

Importing from a Text File

Text files are the lowest common denominator for data exchange. If you're using a program that creates files Access can't import, then plain text may be your only avenue.

Once again, you start by choosing your file, and then choosing how you want to add the information to your database. Then, the Import wizard takes you through a few more steps:

1. Specify the type of text file.

   Access can import from two types of text files:

   • **Delimited text files** use some sort of separator to indicate where each field ends. For example, *Joe,Piscapone,43* is a line of text you may find in a delimited text file—it's three field values separated by commas.

   • **Fixed-width text files** separates a record into separate fields by position. Each field has a certain number of characters allocated to it, and if you don't use them all up, then Access fills the remaining space (up until the next field) with space characters.

Note: Delimited text files are more common and more flexible than fixed-width text files (because they can accommodate data values of vastly different lengths).

---

2. Click Next.

   If you're importing delimited text, Access asks you what character's the *delimiter*—in other words, what character separates the fields (Figure 34-7). Commas and tabs are common delimiters.

   If you're importing fixed-width text, Access lets you set the field boundaries by dragging column lines to the right position in the preview window.

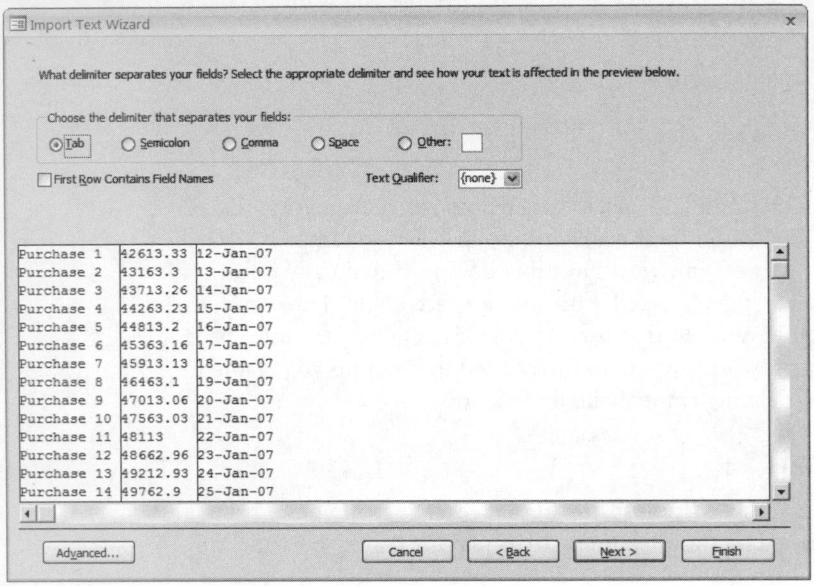

Figure 34-7:
In this example, fields are separated using tabs.

3. **Complete the wizard.**

The rest of the wizard unfolds in exactly the same way as it does for Excel data.

If you're creating a new table to hold your imported data, then the next step asks you to configure the fields you want to create by setting their names, data types, and indexing options (Figure 34-6). Once you've finished this part, you can choose whether or not you want Access to create an autonumbered ID field, and then use it as the primary key.

Finally, in the last step, you need to enter the name of the table you want to create or add to. You can then click Finish (and, optionally, choose to save your import steps for later reuse).

Exportable File Types

Just as you can import information from other files and pop it in your database, you can also take the existing information and ship it out to another format. You'll most often undertake this step to let some other person or program get their hands on your information without needing to go through Access.

When exporting your data, you can use all the same formats that you can use in an import operation, plus a few more. Here's a rundown of the most popular choices:

• **Access.** Transfers the Access table (or a different type of object) to another Access database file. This feature isn't as powerful as importing Access objects, because you're limited to one object at a time. For that reason, people don't use it as often.

- **Excel.** Puts the data into the cells of an Excel worksheet. Perfect if you want to use Excel's tools to analyze a sales trend or plot a profit chart.

- **Word.** Puts the data into a Word document, separating each column with tabs and each line with a hard return. This format leaves a lot to be desired, because it's difficult to rearrange the data after the fact in Word. (A nicer export feature would put the report data into a Word table, which would make it far easier to work with.)

- **PDF or XPS.** Creates a print-ready PDF file with the exact formatting and layout you'd see if you sent the table to your printer. Unlike Excel or Word documents, you can't edit a PDF file—you're limited to reviewing the report and printing it out.

Note: The PDF or XPS option appears only if you've installed a free add-in for Office. Page 746 describes how to get it.

- **HTML Document.** Creates a web-ready HTML Web page that you can post to a Web site or a company intranet. The HTML format that Access generates looks remarkably like your real, printed report.

- **Text File.** Dumps the data into a plain text file, with tabs and spaces used to arrange the data. You lose colors, fonts, borders, and other formatting details. This format isn't very useful—think of it as a last resort to transfer data to another program if none of the other export options work.

- **XML File.** Saves the data in a text .xml file, without any formatting. This option makes sense if you're using some sort of automated program that can read the exported XML file and process the data.

Exporting Data

To perform an export operation, follow these steps:

1. **In the navigation pane, select the table you want to export.**

   Unfortunately, you can't export more than one table at once. However, you can export just a *portion* of a table. One way to do this partial export is to open the table, and then select the rows you want to export. (Once you start the export process, you see an option that lets you export just the selected rows.) You can also create a query that gets just the rows you want. You can export the query results by selecting the query in the navigation pane instead of the underlying table.

2. **Click the button that corresponds to the type of file you want to export.**

   When you choose a format, Access launches the Export wizard (Figure 34-8).

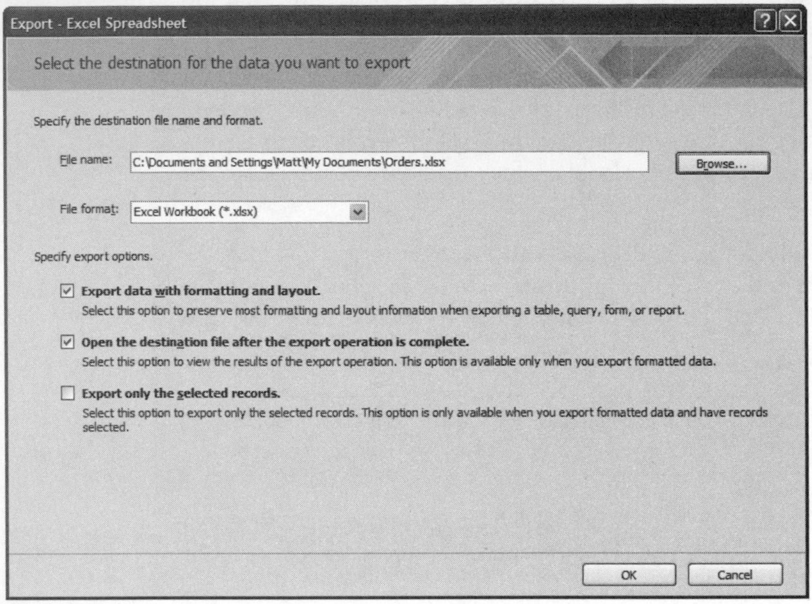

Figure 34-8:
The Export wizard varies depending on the export format you're using. But the first step's always to pick your file, and then set the export options shown here.

3. **Enter the name of the file you want to create.**

   Access creates this file during the export operation. In some cases, you may have a choice of file format. For example, if you're exporting to Excel you can use the newer XML-based spreadsheet format (the .xlsx standard), or the older .xls standard that supports older versions, like Excel 97.

4. **If you want to keep the formatting that's in your database, then choose "Export data with formatting and layout".**

   If you've tailored the datasheet with fancy fonts and colors (as described on page 648), Access preserves these details in the exported file. Obviously, this option doesn't work for all formats. For example, simple text files can't handle any formatting.

5. **If you want to double-check your exported document, then choose "Open the destination file after the export operation is complete".**

   It's always a good idea to make sure you got the data and the formatting you expect. If you use this option, then Access launches the exported file, opening it in the program that owns it (Excel for spreadsheets, Notepad for text files, and so on). Of course, this method works only if you have that application on your computer.

6. **If you've selected only a few records in a table, then choose "Export only the selected records".**

   This way, Access exports the current selection, not the entire table or query.

7. **Click OK to perform the export.**

   Access may ask you for additional details, if it needs any more information about how to create the exported file.

   Once you're finished this stage, Access asks you its final question—whether or not you want to save your export steps.

Part Five:
Appendixes

5

Customizing the Quick Access Toolbar

In previous versions of Office, you could move toolbars, rearrange buttons, and even scramble the order of items in the main menu. Reckless customizers could transform Office applications so completely that no one else would be able to use their computers, and the instructions in books like this one would be useless.

Office 2007 clamps down on customization. Unless you're willing to get your hands dirty with a serious programming language, the ribbon is off limits. Instead, Office lets you customize one tiny portion of screen real estate—the Quick Access toolbar. This appendix teaches you how to modify the Quick Access toolbar in all of the programs covered in this book: Word, Excel, PowerPoint, and Access.

This limitation might sound like a major one, but it's actually a reasonable compromise. People who love to tweak and refine their workplaces (you know who you are) get to add all the timesaving shortcuts they need. Everyone else can relax. No matter what computer you're working on, the ribbon is always there, with its comforting sameness and carefully organized tabs.

The Quick Access Toolbar

You've already seen the Quick Access toolbar (known to Office nerds as the QAT). It's the micro-size toolbar that sits above the ribbon. The Quick Access toolbar has only icons, but you can hover over a button to get the full command text.

When you first start out with Office, the Quick Access toolbar is a lonely place, with buttons for quickly saving your file and undoing or redoing the last action.

However, Microsoft gives you complete control over this space, including the ability to add new buttons. You can most quickly add stuff by clicking the down-pointing arrow at the far right side. Figure A-1 shows how it works.

Note: If you don't like Quick Access toolbar's placement, Office gives you one other option. Click the drop-down arrow, and then choose "Show Below the Ribbon" to move your toolbar under the ribbon so your mouse has less distance to travel.

You might add buttons to the Quick Access toolbar for two reasons:

- **To make it easier to get to a command you use frequently.** If it's in the Quick Access toolbar, you don't need to memorize a keyboard shortcut or change the current ribbon tab.

- **To get to a command that the ribbon doesn't provide.** Office has a small set of unpopular commands that it lets you use, but that it doesn't keep in the ribbon. Many of these commands are holdovers from previous versions of Office. If you have a long-lost favorite feature that's missing, it just might be available via the Quick Access toolbar's extra buttons.

Keyboard lovers can also trigger the commands in the Quick Access toolbar with lightning speed thanks to Office's keytips feature (page 6). When you press the Alt key, Office displays a number superimposed over every command in the Quick Access toolbar (starting at 1 and going up from there). You can then press the number to trigger the command. So in the Quick Access toolbar shown in Figure A-1, Alt+1 saves the workbook, Alt+2 opens the Undo list, and so on.

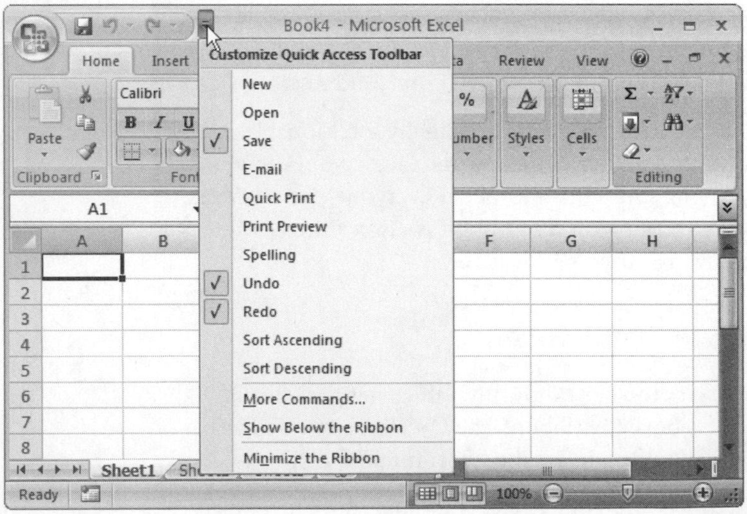

Figure A-1:
When you click the drop-down arrow on the Quick Access toolbar, Office shows a list of often-used commands that you can add just by clicking them, as you can see in this example from Excel. But to see all your possibilities, you need to choose More Commands.

Tip: If you want to add a command that duplicates something that's already in the ribbon, here's a shortcut. Find the command in the ribbon, right-click it, and then choose Add to Quick Access Toolbar.

Adding buttons

To add a button to the Quick Access toolbar, follow these steps:

1. **Click the drop-down arrow on the Quick Access toolbar, and then choose More Commands.**

    The [Word/Excel/PowerPoint/Access] Options dialog box opens, and positions you at the Customize section where you need to be (Figure A-2).

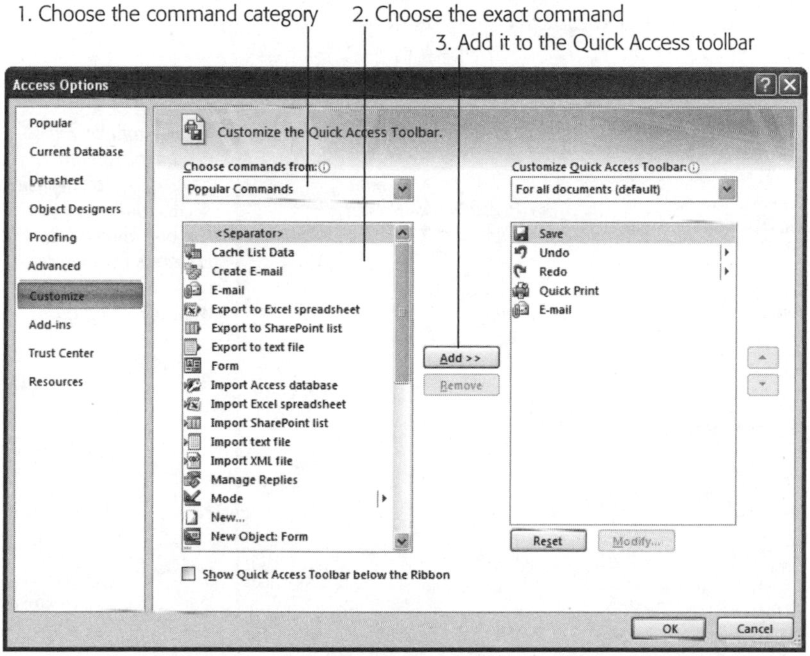

1. Choose the command category   2. Choose the exact command

3. Add it to the Quick Access toolbar

Figure A-2:
The Customize section of the Options window has two areas, as shown in this screenshot from Access. The list on the left lets you choose the command you want to add. The list on the right shows the commands that currently appear in the Quick Access toolbar.

2. **Choose a category from the "Choose commands from" list.**

    The library of commands that you can add to the Quick Access toolbar is enormous. To make it easier to find what you want, it makes sense to choose a specific category. Many of the categories overlap—Office simply provides them to make finding what you want easier. Here are the top choices:

    • **Popular Commands** gives you a short list of commands that Office jockeys love. If you're trying to get quick access to a commonly used feature, you just might find it here.

    • **Commands Not in the Ribbon** provides all the leftovers—commands that Microsoft didn't consider useful enough to include in the ribbon. This list holds some commands that are superseded or partially duplicated by other commands, commands that are included in other dialog boxes, and commands that were used in previous versions of Office and put out to pasture in this release.

- **All Commands** includes the full list of choices. As with the other categories, it's ordered alphabetically.

Under these categories are several additional categories that correspond to the Office menu and various tabs in the ribbon. For example, you can choose the Insert tab to see all the commands that appear in the ribbon's Insert tab.

3. **Once you've chosen the category you want, pick the command from the list below, and then click Add.**

The command moves from the list on the left to the list on the right, placing it on the Quick Access toolbar (Figure A-3).

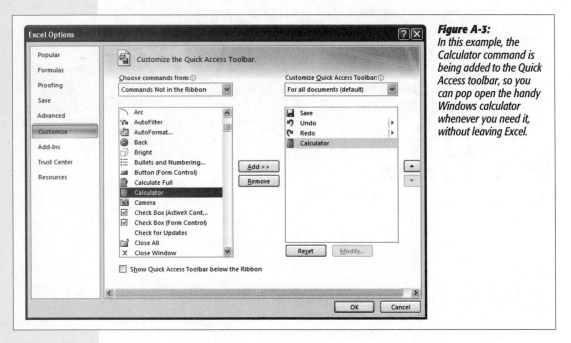

Figure A-3:
In this example, the Calculator command is being added to the Quick Access toolbar, so you can pop open the handy Windows calculator whenever you need it, without leaving Excel.

4. **You can repeat this process (starting at step 2) to add more commands.**

Optionally, you can rearrange the order of items in the Quick Access toolbar. Just pick a command, and then use the up and down arrow buttons to move it. The topmost commands in the list are displayed to the left on the Quick Access toolbar.

Tip: If you've customized the heck out of your Quick Access toolbar and want to go back to a simpler way of life, then click the Reset button.

---

5. **When you're finished, click OK to return to the program you're using so you can see the revamped Quick Access toolbar.**

Adding a Quick Access toolbar isn't a lifetime commitment. To get rid of a command you don't want anymore, right-click it, and then choose "Remove from Quick Access Toolbar".

Note: You might notice the tempting Modify button, which lets you change a command's name and picture. Unfortunately, it works only for macro commands (programmable shortcuts), which aren't covered in this book.

Customizing Specific Files

Do you have a button or two that you're using incessantly, but just for a specific file? For example, say you frequently print a particular Word document—like a fax cover letter—so you want the Quick Print button handy every time you open that document. In this situation, it may not make sense to customize the Quick Access toolbar in the normal way. If you do, you'll get your extra button in every Word document you use, including those in which the extra button isn't useful.

Office has a great feature to help you out in this situation. You can customize the Quick Access toolbar for an individual Word document, Excel workbook, PowerPoint presentation, or Access database. That way, whenever you open that particular file, the buttons you need appear in the Quick Access toolbar. When you close it (or open another file in a separate window), the buttons disappear.

Note: Customizing individual files has advantages and disadvantages. The disadvantage is that you need to perform this task separately for every file, which can take a lot of time. The advantage is that your customizations are recorded right in your file, so they stick around even if you open the file on someone else's computer.

To customize the toolbar for a single file, follow the same steps that you used in the previous section. Start by clicking the Quick Access toolbar's drop-down arrow, and then choosing More Commands. However, before you add any commands, change the selection in the "Customize Quick Access Toolbar" list, which appears just above the list of commands in the Quick Access toolbar. Instead of using "For all documents (default)", choose your files's name (as in "FaxCover Letter.docx"). This list starts off empty. Then, follow the normal steps to add buttons.

When Office displays the Quick Access toolbar, it combines the standard buttons (as configured in the previous section) with any buttons you've defined for the current file (Figure A-4).

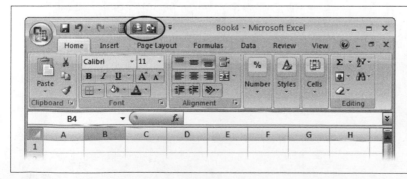

Figure A-4:
The file-specific buttons (circled) always appear after the standard buttons and have a slightly different appearance (a darker background), as shown in this Excel example. You can define the same button as a standard button and as a file-specific button, in which case it appears twice.

Getting Help

In a lot of ways, Office 2007 is easier to work with than its predecessors—after you get the hang of it. (And after you've had a chance to read this book, of course.) But sooner or later, you're going to run into a snag and need some help—and getting that help is what this appendix is all about.

Help with Office starts right there in the programs' windows and extends into the far reaches of the Internet. There are descriptive screen tips that pop up when you mouse over the item in question, help screens stored on your computer and on Microsoft's Web site, and a vast community of Office experts on message boards and Web sites. This appendix helps you explore all your help options.

NOSTALGIA CORNER

Goodbye, Clippy

And good riddance, some would add. Earlier versions of Microsoft Office programs included a contextual help system known as the *Office Assistant*, an animated character that lived in a small onscreen window, offering hints as you worked. You could also click it to type in the topic you needed help with.

No matter which incarnation you chose—Clippit the paper clip, Dot the bouncing ball, or any of the other cartoon choices—the Office Assistant always seemed to be watching what you were doing with a smug look on its face. And

before you could type in your search phrase, you had to wait while it furrowed its cartoon brows or wagged it cartoon tail (a delay that probably drew a chuckle the first time you saw it, but that made you want to commit cartoonicide by the thirty-fifth time.).

In Office 2007, Microsoft wisely pulled the Office Assistant for good. In its place, Microsoft designed a contextual help system in the form of expanded screen tips, which include direct links to each program's Help window

---

Using Office 2007's Built-in Help

When you're working in an Office 2007 application, help is never far away. The most convenient place to look for help is the built-in Help system. To access it, press the F1 key, or click the round blue button with the question mark in the upper-right corner of most Office windows to open Help (Figure B-1). The Help box conveniently opens in its own window (Figure B-2), so it's not hard to drag it out of the way when you want to look at your work.

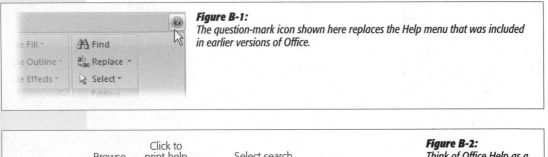

Figure B-1:
The question-mark icon shown here replaces the Help menu that was included in earlier versions of Office.

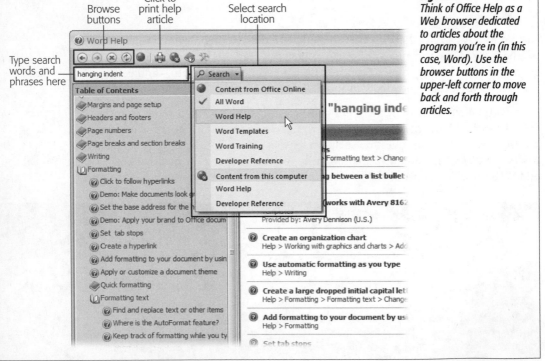

Figure B-2:
Think of Office Help as a Web browser dedicated to articles about the program you're in (in this case, Word). Use the browser buttons in the upper-left corner to move back and forth through articles.

If Help doesn't automatically open to a page that's useful to you, you'll have to do some searching. You can use two methods for finding the help you need: the Search tool in the upper-left corner, or the Table of Contents.

- **Search.** Using the Search text box, type in a word or phrase, like *margins* or *hanging indent*. If you press Enter, or click the Search button, then Office hunts for help. When it's finished, articles that match your search words appear in the right panel. Look through the headings, and then click the one that's most likely to be helpful. If you need to come back and try another topic, click the back button.

- **Table of Contents.** On the left side of the Help window, the Table of Contents works a lot like a Word outline. You can expand and contract the headings by clicking the little book icons to the left of the words. One click opens a heading and shows the contents. Another click closes the heading, hiding the subheads and articles inside. The icons with question marks are the actual help articles; click them to show the help articles in the pane on the right.

Tip: To get help while you're running a PowerPoint slideshow, right-click anywhere on the slide. When you do, a menu of options appears (unless the slideshow creator turned it off using kiosk mode, as described on page 536). In the PowerPoint Options dialog box (Figure A-2), many of the options include help icons.

Out of the box, Office assumes you want to see online help files, which are more numerous than the ones installed on your computer. You can tell Office whether you want it to search online help files or not (Figure B-3).

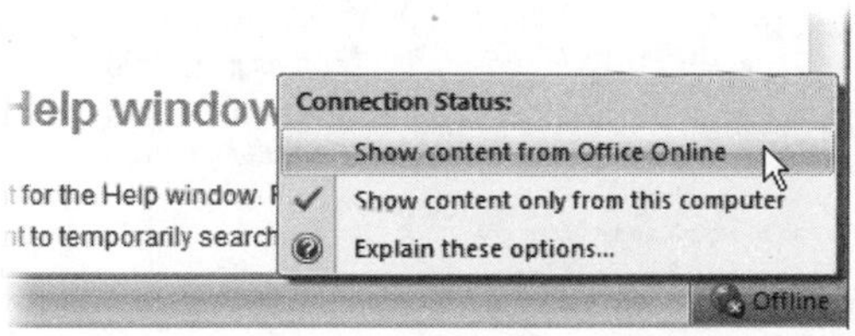

Figure B-3:
A button in the lower-right corner of the Help window shows whether you're online or not. Click the button, and a pop-up menu appears, as shown here.

Unless your Internet connection is down or is very, very slow, you want to search online. To do so:

- **To tell Office to access online help files:** At the bottom of the Help window, click the down-arrow next to Offline and, from the menu that appears, choose "Show content from the Internet." When you do, Offline changes to Connected, and Office attempts to access your Internet connection. If it can't get online, you'll get an error message.

- **To restrict Office to the help files stored on your computer:** Click the down-arrow next to Connected and choose "Only show content from this computer." When you do, Connected changes to Offline.

The help content that resides on your computer is pretty comprehensive. The help content that comes from Microsoft's Web site is kind of a mixed bag that includes all the articles stored on your computer as well as audiovisual demos, templates provided by third parties, clip art, and access to Microsoft's Knowledge Base of technical articles. One advantage of the online help content is that Microsoft continually updates and adds to it.

Using Help Articles

For the most part, Help works a lot like a Web browser. You can use the buttons in the upper-left corner to browse forward and backward through the articles that you've read. There's even a button to stop and refresh the page, just like on your Web browser. Click an article heading in the Help window to read the article. Some of the Help headings will open your browser and take you to Web pages where you can find resources like templates or view audiovisual demonstrations (Figure B-4).

Figure B-4:
Some help articles link to audiovisual demos on the Internet. When you click the Play Demo button, your browser opens to a page on the Microsoft Web site. The demo begins playing as soon as it starts to download to your computer.

If you want to print one of the help articles, click the little printer button at the top of the Help window. The Print box opens, and you can choose a printer and make other printing adjustments before you send the article to the printer. For example, if you've found a help article about Word margins, you may want to print a single page instead of all 10 pages.

Displaying Screen Tips

To get help on a specific button, menu, or dialog box option, first mouse over the option. A good-sized screen tip pops up with a description of the item, and advice on where to get further help (Figure B-5).

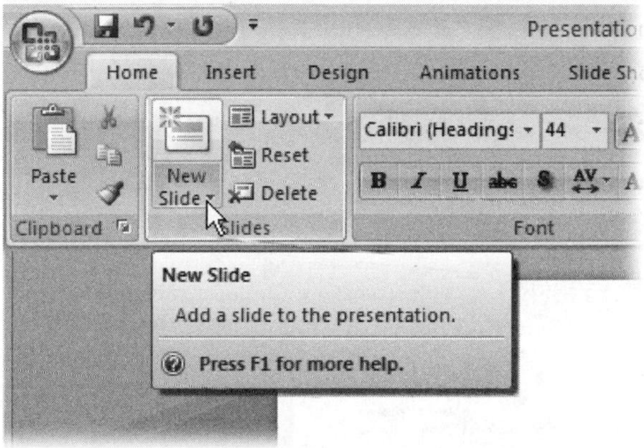

Figure B-5:
Not every screen tip you see contains a link you can click to get more help, but many do. New in Office 2007, this contextual help system was designed to whisk you directly to help articles describing the thing you're trying to do (instead of the old approach, which forced you to hunt for the right article yourself).

Using Microsoft's Office Web Site

You'll find the main Web site that supports Microsoft office products at *http://office. microsoft.com*. The home page is slick—and about as helpful as a magazine ad. You need to dig deeper to get to the helpful features. To zero in on some more useful articles and links, click the Products tab at the top of the page. Along the left side of the screen, you'll see links to specific Office products; click the one you're interested in.

Once you're on the Microsoft page dedicated to the application you need help with, you can focus in on just the 2007 version by selecting it from the list of versions displayed on the left-hand side of the screen under "Help and How-to." After you click on the 2007 version, you'll see a page with all kinds of information, where you can read an overview of changes to the program, watch a demo, and of course purchase the program, among other options. Figure B-6 shows the page dedicated to Word 2007.

Discussion Groups

Discussion groups are one of the great resources of the online world. You can post a question in a discussion group and come back in a couple hours or the next day and other people will be posting answers and debating the fine points of the issue. It's an excellent way to dig deep into a subject and make some online friends in the process. You can also search through discussion groups to see if someone else has asked the same question.

Tip: Before you post your question, it's good online etiquette to check the group to see if a FAQ (frequently asked questions) posting is available. Sometimes experts get annoyed when newbies ask the same question over and over.

Figure B-6:
The Microsoft Web page provides links to articles and other resources for Office. At the bottom of the left-hand column under Additional Resources, you find a link to discussion groups where you can ask questions and later come back and read the responses.

To get to the Office discussion groups, head to the application-specific Web page as described above. From there, at the bottom of the left-hand column under Additional Resources, you'll find a link to Discussion Groups where you can ask questions and then later come back and read the responses. Or, if you prefer, you can type *http://www.microsoft.com/office/community* into your Web browser. Either way, you'll be on the Office Discussion Groups home page (Figure B-7).

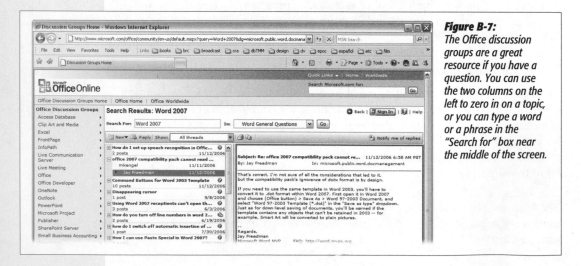

Figure B-7:
The Office discussion groups are a great resource if you have a question. You can use the two columns on the left to zero in on a topic, or you can type a word or a phrase in the "Search for" box near the middle of the screen.

To search for a specific topic, type a word or a phrase in the "Search for" box near the middle of the screen. After some churning, topics related to your search words appear in the center list. Click a + button to expand a topic, and then click a name to read the contents of a post.

The posts in a discussion are listed in chronological order, with the first message at the top. So, start at the top to read the question, and then work your way down the list to read the answers and other responses. Some questions will be answered quickly, with one or two on-target responses. A hot topic can result in a lengthy debate, with a dozen or so responses.

Some of the experts who participate in these discussion groups are Microsoft MVPs (see the box below). In general, you'll find the contributions from the Microsoft MVPs both accurate and concise.

UP TO SPEED

What's a Microsoft MVP?

About 11 years ago, Microsoft developed an MVP (Most Valuable Professional) program to recognize the folks who freely give their time to help others with Windows, Word, and other Microsoft programs. MVPs aren't Microsoft employees, but they're very good at what they do. You can find them offering free advice in computer forums, discussion groups, and newsgroups, or even publishing answers to frequently asked questions on their own Web sites.

Even better, these experts are often experts in other fields in addition to knowing the mysteries of Office. One expert may understand the financial world, while another may be knowledgeable about architecture and construction. Yet another may live in France and be able to answer Office questions particular to that language. This real-world experience along with a love of Microsoft makes MVPs a valuable resource when you have a specific or sticky question

---

Tutorials

The folks at Microsoft have created several dozen interactive tutorials on Office 2007. To see a list of these tutorials, head to Microsoft's Office training center—*http://office.microsoft.com/en-us/training*—and search for the program you want to learn about.

Online Articles, FAQs, and More

The Microsoft Technical Communities Web site (*www.microsoft.com/communities*) is the place to find user groups, technical chats, Web casts, an always-accessible knowledge base, and to find out about Office-related events and training.

You can also try Microsoft's Help and Support site, *http://support.microsoft.com*, which organizes questions (and answers) by topic and lists important security updates you can download to help keep your copy of Office (and your computer) healthy and virus-free.

Direct Person-to-Person Help

Sometimes, nothing will do but asking a real, live technical support person for help. The prices for contacting Microsoft start at $35 per email or phone call and go up from there—so you probably want to exhaust the other options described in this chapter before you begin the process. But if all else fails, go to *http://office.microsoft.com* and click Contact Us at the bottom of the screen.

Third-Party Web Sites

You're certainly not limited to Microsoft-sanctioned resources when it comes to getting help with Office 2007. Many Web sites are devoted to providing advice, services, and add-in software. The following sections list some of the best places on the Internet to find help with the applications covered in this book. These Web sites range from free to pricey, and everything in between. And if you can't find the information your looking for on these sites, you can always try your favorite search engine.

Note: Keep in mind that Office 2007 is still new, and not all of the sites listed here have updated their content just yet. Much of the information about earlier versions of Office still applies, but if you find instructions that are supposed to fix your problem and they just won't work, it could be because they're written for a previous version of Office.

Word Help Sites

If you type *Word help*, or *Word templates*, or *Word Add-in* into your favorite search engine, you'll see dozens of listings like the following:

- **The Word MVP site** (*http://word.mvps.org*): Run by a group of Microsoft MVPs, not Microsoft, this site sets out to tell the whole Word truth and nothing but the truth. As its home page declares: "Word rarely misses an opportunity to perplex." The site divides Word issues into a number of popular topics, and a handy search tool at the top of the home page makes it easy to quickly zero in on what you're looking for.

- **Woody's Office Portal** (*www.wopr.com*): For years, Woody Leonhard has provided the Word community with expert advice and his WOPR add-in. WOPR stands for Woody's Office Power Pack—a collection of Office-related add-ins. At the time of this writing, WOPR for Office 2007 was not yet on offer, but Woody's probably working on it. (There's been a WOPR for every version since Office 97.) The Web site is a little kitschy, but the information and tools are rock solid. Don't miss Woody's Lounge, an active online forum for Word and other Office programs. You can read the posts without becoming a member, but to leave a message, you need to sign up. Membership is free, and the sign-up process simply involves agreeing to the rules of the message board. You can sign up for a free email newsletter.

- **Wordsite Office Automation** (*www.wordsite.com*): Founded by Microsoft MVP Bill Coan, Wordsite provides products and services related to Word and Office automation. Not interested in creating your own templates and macros? You can hire the folks at Wordsite to do it for you. They offer a free analysis of your needs. Wordsite also offers training tailored to individual business needs. On the Wordsite Web site, you find products like DataPrompter 2007, an off-theshelf tool that enhances Word by automatically prompting people and updating documents. The site also offers free downloads with information about XML and utilities that are related to Word.

Excel Help Sites

If your Excel spreadsheet just won't do what you want, check out these sites for some helpful advice:

- **Tech on the Net** (*www.techonthenet.com/excel*): This site has Excel FAQs and—even more usefully—descriptions of most functions. And if you're on your way to becoming an Excel power user, check out the site's VBA reference for Excel programming.

- **MSDN Blogs** (*http://blogs.msdn.com/excel*): MSDN (which stands for "Microsoft Developer Network") has a blog covering just about every Microsoft product you can think of. In this blog, David Gainer, a Microsoft Excel Program Manager, occasionally posts entries about Excel-related news.

- **J-Walk** (*http://j-walk.com/ss/excel*): John Walkenbach (a.k.a. J-Walk) has written several books and articles about Excel. He's put together this helpful site which has Excel FAQs and lots of useful advice.

PowerPoint Help Sites

With an estimated 600 million folks just like you using PowerPoint to pound out everything from business presentations to school reports, sermons, prosecuting arguments, and who-knows-what-else, odds are good that whatever problem you've run into is one that someone else (or a whole lot of someone else's) has already run into and solved. Useful PowerPoint resources abound on the Web; here are a handful of the best:

- **The PowerPoint FAQ** (*www.rdpslides.com/pptfaq*): Created and maintained by PPTools (a company that also develops PowerPoint add-in programs), this site is so rich with practical advice, tips, and tricks that Microsoft's own PowerPoint site links to it.

- **MasterView International** (*www.masterviews.com/index.htm*): This site's articles, forums, links to blogs, and free online newsletter all focus on designing and managing effective PowerPoint presentations for international audiences. Michael Hyatt's Working Smart (*www.michaelhyatt.com/workingsmart/microsoft_powerpoint*) is an intelligent, well-written blog that address not just the technical aspects of PowerPoint, but the meatier issues of designing and delivering effective presentations.

Access Help Sites

If some aspect of Access is making you crazy, chances are someone else has run into the same problem. Here are some good places to seek help:

• **Tech On the Net** (*www.techonthenet.com/access*): This site has a few Access tutorials and handy function descriptions. The Question & Answer section (you might need to scroll down to spot it) is also really helpful.

• **MSDN Blogs** (*http://blogs.msdn.com/access*): This Microsoft Developer Network blog is written by a Microsoft Access Program Manager. His occasional posts will keep you up to date on the latest Access news.

Index: Word 2007

G

Gallery drop-down menu, 69
Genuine Advantage box (templates), 141
gift certificates (see marketing)
global templates
vs. document templates, 139
glossaries, indentation, 81
Go To tab, 57
Google (getting dictionaries), 154
grammar (see spelling and grammar)
graphical user interface (GUI), 59
graphics, 138
inline (spacing for), 81
Print drawings created in Word, 184
templates, 138
greeting cards (see stationery)
Gridlines box, 30
groups, 5

H

headers and footers, 112–118
Building Blocks, 114–116
custom, 117
margins, 108
removing, 118
small caps for headers, 77
tools, 112
headings, 189–192
controlling subheads during promotion/
demotion, 191
promoting and demoting, 189–192
subheads, 191
height of page, 105
help, 805–814
built-in, 806–809
Microsoft's Web site, 809–812
third-party sites, 812–814
HighBeam Research, 161
highlighting text
(see also selecting text)
hyphenation, 121–124
automatic, 122
guidelines, 122
justified text, 122
limit consecutive hyphens, 122
manual, 121, 123
proper names, 122
removing from document, 123
styles (3 to choose from), 121
zone, 122

I

ignore
punctuation in find and replace, 67
spell check, 150
white space characters in find and
replace, 67
indenting paragraphs, 79
hanging indent, 81
using Ruler, 94
using Tab key, 80
insert mode vs. overtype mode, 44
insertion point, 43, 45
installed templates, 142–143
Internet connection
research tools, 162
invitations (see stationery)
invoices (see business forms)

J

justification, 79

K

keyboard accelerators, 6
keyboard basics, selecting text, 49
keyboard shortcuts, 11, 24, 38, 59
Alt key, 38
Bold (Ctrl+B), 38
C key, 38
Copy (Ctrl+C), 59
Cut (Ctrl+X), 59
F key, 38
formatting, 74
new document (Ctrl+N), 38
old vs. new version of Word, 38
outlines, 190
Paste (Ctrl+V), 59
References tab (S key), 38
saving, 38
spell checking (F7), 38
Undo, 59
keystrokes
lessening, 67–69
Quick Parts, 67–69
keytips, 6

L

labels (see stationery)
launcher (Clipboard), 64
launching Word, 19–21
opening a Word document, 20
Quick Launch toolbar, 20
Start menu, 20
your name and initials, 20

Index: Excel 2007

OFFICE 2007: THE MISSING MANUAL

Index: PowerPoint 2007

Index: Access 2007

Symbols

A

OFFICE 2007: THE MISSING MANUAL

Colophon

Sanders Kleinfeld and Marlowe Shaeffer provided quality control for *Office 2007: The Missing Manual*. Michele Fishie wrote the index for the Word section. Lucie Haskins wrote the index for the Access section. Dawn Mann wrote the index for the Excel and PowerPoint sections.

The cover of this book is based on a series design originally created by David Freedman and modified by Mike Kohnke, Karen Montgomery, and Fitch (*www.fitch.com*). Back cover design, dog illustration, and color selection by Fitch.

David Futato designed the interior layout, based on a series design by Phil Simpson. This book was converted to FrameMaker 5.5.6 and prepared for layout by Abby Fox. The text font is Adobe Minion; the heading font is Adobe Formata Condensed; and the code font is LucasFont's TheSans Mono Condensed. The illustrations that appear in the book were produced by Robert Romano and Jessamyn Read using Macromedia FreeHand MX and Adobe Photoshop CS.

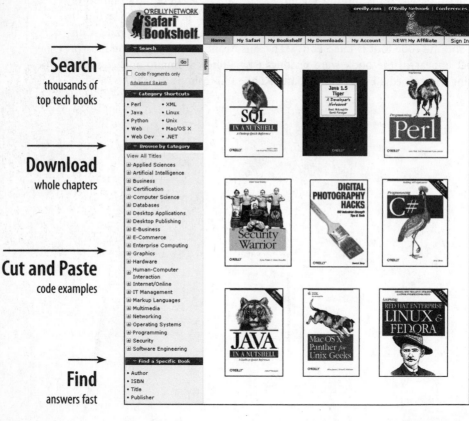